US TAX TREATIES

Edited by

Richard L. Doernberg
K.H. Gyr Professor of Law, Emory University

Kees van Raad
Professor of International Tax Law, University of Leiden,
of counsel to Loyens & Volkmaars

Kluwer Law and Taxation Publishers
Deventer-Boston

Kluwer Law and Taxation Publishers
P.O. Box 23 Tel.: +31 – 5700 – 47261
7400 GA Deventer Telex: 49295
The Netherlands Fax: +31 – 5700 – 22244

For customers in the USA and Canada:
Kluwer Law and Taxation Publishers
6 Bigelow Street Tel.: +1 (617) 354 – 0140
Cambridge, MA 02139 Fax: +1 (617) 354 – 8595
USA

Library of Congress Cataloging in Publication Data

United States.
[Treaties, etc.]
US tax treaties / edited by Richard L. Doernberg, Kees van Raad.
p. cm.
ISBN 9065445285
1. Taxation, Double — United States — Treaties. 2. Tax evation (International Law) I. Doernberg, Richard L. II. Raad, C. van (Cornelis), 1946—. III. Title: United States tax treaties.
K4473.2.U54 1991
341.4'844.—dc20

90–28871
CIP

Cover design: Eset
ISBN 90 6544 528 5

Foreword

The world grows smaller all the time. Technological advances in telecommunications and transportation have quickened the pace of international trade and investment. To participate in this burgeoning trade, nations must pay attention to the political, economic, and social environment of other nations. Domestic laws and policies must be coordinated with international laws and policies. In the tax area, the domestic tax laws of nations are coordinated through bilateral tax treaties which seek to prevent double taxation of income earned through international transactions.

It is our hope that this book will be useful to lawyers, those in business, and students. It brings together in a single volume a wealth of material that is not readily available in any other publication. For practicing lawyers and business people, the volume serves as a handy desk reference book that provides easy and quick access to the major United States tax treaties. For students, the volume offers the opportunity to compare several Model treaties with actual US treaties. A variety of charts is intended to enliven the material and to permit quick comparisons of treaty provisions.

This book contains an array of material relating to the United States tax treaty network. First and foremost are the following 20 United States income tax treaties: *Australia, Belgium, Canada, China, Egypt, France, Germany, India, Ireland, Italy, Japan, Korea, Luxembourg, the Netherlands, the Philippines, Spain, Sweden, Switzerland, USSR,* and *the United Kingdom*. Where a treaty provision has been supplemented by a protocol provision, we have added an asterisk (*) to the treaty provision so that the user will know when to refer to a treaty protocol which follows the treaty. Protocols and supplemental conventions which contain provisions that amend or supersede an existing treaty are integrated into the treaty and are not separately reproduced in this book.

These treaties are placed in context through the inclusion of four Model treaties – the 1981 US Model treaty, the 1963 and 1977 OECD Models, and the 1980 UN Model. We decided to include the 1963 OECD Model because it has not only served as a springboard for the other Model treaties but a number of the US treaties reflect its influence. We have also included most of the 1977 OECD Commentary which is helpful in interpreting the provisions that appear not only in the Model treaties but also in many US income tax treaties. Articles 31 through 33 of the 1969 Vienna Convention on the Law of Treaties are useful in understanding how treaties are to be interpreted.

To assist in the comprehension and use of US income tax treaties, we have included various charts. A chronological presentation of all US income tax treaties outlines the history of US income tax treaties, including those that have terminated and those that have been superseded by later treaties. To facilitate treaty comparison, we have included a table of correspondence that shows in which specific article(s) various treaty subjects are dealt with in each treaty. Among the most important treaty provisions are those that deal with the taxation of dividends, interest, and royalties. The book contains two unique charts that show the US income treaty tax rates for these income items. The charts also contain the tax rate applicable to these items under the domestic law of the United States and 20 of its treaty partners as well as the treaty rates in over 160 income tax treaties executed by the 20 US treaty partners with each other.

In addition to the income tax treaty material, the book includes two treaties which address the exchange of information between nations which is vital to the enforcement of domestic law. The Exchange of Tax Information Agreement with Mexico is a recent bilateral agreement to assist in mutual enforcement of domestic law. The Multilateral Convention on Mutual Administrative Assistance in Tax Matters represents an effort by nations in the Organization for Economic Cooperation and Development (OECD) and in the Council of Europe to counter international tax evasion through joint enforcement efforts. While income tax treaties form the backbone of the US tax treaty network, the United States also has concluded estate and gift tax treaties with a number of nations. The estate and gift tax treaty with Germany is included in the book as an example of these treaties.

The authors would like to thank Lael Bellamy, Robert Vernimmen and Jurgen Kuiper for their help in assembling the material used in this book. We hope we have chosen material wisely for inclusion, but we recognize that because of space constraints useful material has also been omitted. We welcome your suggestions concerning material to include or omit in subsequent editions.

Atlanta
August 1990

Richard L. Doernberg

The Hague
August 1990

Kees van Raad

Table of Contents

1981 US Model Provision	1. General Scope	2. Taxes Covered	3. General Definitions	4. Residence	5. Permanent Establishment	6. Income from Real Property (Immovable Property)	7. Business Profits
Australia	1	2	3	4	5	6	7
Belgium	1,28.2	2	3	4	5	6	7
Canada	I, XXIX.1-3	II	III	IV	V	VI	VII
China	1	2	3	4	5	6	7
Egypt	6	1	2	3	5	7	8,18
France	22	1	2	3	4	5	6
Germany	1,31	2	3	4	5	6	7
India	1	2	3	4	5	6	7
Ireland	–	I	II	II.*g,h*	II.1.*l*	IX	III
Italy		1,P3	2	3	4	5	67
Japan	4	1	2	3	9	15	8
Korea	4	1	2	3	9	15	8
Luxembourg	–	I	II	II.1*h*	II.1*f*	VI	III
Netherlands	–	I	II	–	II.1*i*	V,X	III
Philippines	6	1	2	3	5	7	8
Spain	1	2	3	4	5	6	7
Sweden	I,P7,9	I,P6	P1,2,4, 5,13,14	P3	P1	V,VI	II
Switzerland	XVIII.2,3	I	II	–	II.1*c*	IX	III
USSR	VII,VIII,IX	I	II	II.3,4	IV	–	III,IV
UK	1	2	3	4	5	6	7

US Treaty Table of Correspondence

8. Shipping and Air Transport	9. Associated Enterprises	10. Dividends	11. Interest	12. Royalties	13. Gains	14. Independent Personal Services	15. Dependent Personal Services
8	9	10	11	12	13	14,27.2	15,27.2
8	9	10	11	12	13	14	15
VIII	IX	X	XI	XII	XIII	XIV,XVII	XV
–	8	9	10	11	12	13	14
9	10	11	12	13	14	15	16
7	8	9	10	11	12	14,21	15,21
8	9	10,29	11,29	12,29	13	14	15
8	9	10	11	12	13	15	16
V	IV	VI,XV	VII,XV	VIII	XIV	XI	XI
8	9	10	11	12	13	14	15
10	11	12	13	14	16	17,22	18,22
10	11	12	13	14	16	18	19
V	IV	IX,XII,X	VIII,XII,X	VII	–	XII	XII
VI	IV	VII,XII	VIII,XII	IX	XI	XVI	XVI
9	10	11	12	13	14	15	16
8	9	10	11	12	13	15	16
IV	III	VII	VIII	VI	IX	XI	XI
V	IV	VI,XIV	VII,XIV	VIII	–	X	X
V	–	–	III.1*g*	III.1*a,b*	III.1*c*	VI.2	VI.2
8	9	10	11	12	13	14	15

1981 US Model Provision	16. Limitations on Benefits	17. Artistes and Athletes	18. Pensions, Annuities, Alimony, and Child Support	19. Governmental Service	20. Students and Teachers	21. Other Income	22. Capital
Australia	16	17,27.2	18	19,27.2	20	21	–
Belgium	12A	–	17,18	19	21	22	–
Canada	XXIX.6	XVI, XVII	XVIII, XXIX.5,7	XIX	XX	XXII	XXIII
China	P7*,P1-4**	16	17	18	20	21	–
Egypt	24	17	19,20	21	23	–	–
France	24A	15A,21	19,20	16,21	18	–	22A
Germany	28	17	18,19	19	20	21	22
India	24	18	20	19	21	23	–
Ireland	–	–	XII	X	XIX	–	–
Italy	P2	17	18	19	21	22	–
Japan	–	–	23	21,22	20,22	–	–
Korea	17	–	23,24,25	22	21	–	–
Luxembourg	XV	–	XI	XI	XIV	–	–
Netherlands	–	–	XV	XV	XVIII	–	–
Philippines	–	17	18,19	20	22	–	–
Spain	17	19	20	21	22	23	–
Sweden	–	–	X	X	XII	–	XIII
Switzerland	–	–	XI	XI	XIII	–	–
USSR	–	–	–	VI.1*a,b*	VI.1*d,e*	–	–
UK	16	17	18	19	21	22	–

23. Relief from Double Taxation	24. Non-Discrimination	25. Mutual Agreement Procedure	26. Exchange of Information and Administrative Assistance	27. Diplomatic Agents/ Consular Officers	28. Entry into Force	29. Termination	Other
22,27.1	23	24	25	26	28	29	–
23	24	25,28.3	26,27	28.1	30	31	16[2],20[3],29[4]
XXIV	XXV	XXVI	XXVII	XXVIII	XXX	XXXI	XXXI[5], XXIX.4[10]
22	23	24	25	26	27	28	15[2],19[3]
25	26	27	28,29	30	31	32	4[1],22[3]
23	24	25,25A	26,27,30	28	31	32	13[7],17[3],29[4]
23	24	25	26	30	32	33	16[2],20[3],27[5]
25	26	27	28	29	30	31	14[7],17[2],22[3]
XIII	XXI	–	XX	–	XXII	XXIII	XVI[8],XVII[6], XVIII[3]
23	24	25	26	27	28	29	16[2],20[3]
5	7	25	26,27	24	28	29	6[1],19[3]
5	7	27	28,30	26	31	32	6[1],20[3],29[4]
XIX,XVI	XX	XIX,XXI	XVIII	XX	XXII	XXII	XIII[3],XVII[1]
XIX	XXV	XXIV, XXVI	XXI, XXIII	–	XXVIII	XXVIII	XVII[3],XXVII[4], XIV[6],XX[6]
23	24	25	26,27	28	29	30	4[1],21[3]
24	25	26	27	28	29	30	14[7],18[2]
XIV,XX	P7	XVIII,XIX	XV,XVII	P8	XXII	XXII	XII[3]
XV	XVIII.3	XVII,XIX	XVI	XVIII.1	XX	XX	XII[3]
XI	X	XI	XII	–	XIII	XIV	VI.1c[3]
23	24	25	26	27	28	29	20[3],27A[9]

'P' refers to a Supplement Protocol

* 1984 Protocol
** 1986 Protocol

1. Source Rules
2. Director's Fees
3. Teachers
4. Extension to Territories
5. Exempt Organizations
6. Miscellaneous
7. Branch Profits Tax
8. Accumulated Profits
9. Offshore Drilling
10. Social Security Taxes

Chronological List
of US Income Tax Treaties

as of December 1, 1990

France	*1932, 1939, 1946*[1], *1956*[1], (1967)
Sweden	1939, 1963[1]
Canada	*1942, 1950*[1], *1956*[1], *1966*[1], (1980)
United Kingdom	*1945, 1954*[1], *1957*[1], *1966*[1], (1975)
Aden	*1945, 1958*[1], *1983*[2]
Antigua	*1945, 1958*[1], *1983*[2]
Barbados	*1945, 1958*[1], *1983*[2], (1984)
Belize	*1945, 1958*[1], *1983*[2]
Cyprus	*1945, 1958*[1], (1984)
Dominica	*1945, 1958*[1], *1983*[2]
Falkland Islands	*1945, 1958*[1], *1983*[2]
Gambia	*1945, 1958*[1], *1983*[2]
Grenada	*1945, 1958*[1], *1983*[2]
Jamaica	*1945, 1958*[1], (1980)
Malawi	*1945, 1958*[1], *1983*[2]
Montserrat	*1945, 1958*[1], *1983*[2]
St. Christopher, Nevis, and Anguilla	*1945, 1958*[1], *1983*[2]
St. Lucia	*1945, 1958*[1], *1983*[2]
St. Vincent	*1945, 1958*[1], *1983*[2]
Seychelles	*1945, 1958*[1], *1983*[2]
Sierra Leone	*1945, 1958*[1], *1983*[2]
Trinidad & Tobago	*1945, 1958*[1], *1966*, (1970)
British Virgin Islands	*1945, 1958*[1], (1981*)
Zambia	*1945, 1958*[1], *1983*[2]

Italics signify treaties which have been terminated.
Parentheses signify subsequent treaties.
[1] Protocol or Supplemental Convention. Protocols accompanying treaties are not separately listed.
[2] Termination agreement signed.
* Signed but not ratified.

Chronological List of US Income Tax Treaties

South Africa	*1946, 1950*[1], *1987*[2]
Belgium	*1948, 1952*[1], *1957*[1], *1965*[1], (1970)
Aruba	*1948, 1987*[2], (1986*)
Burundi	*1948, 1983*[2]
Denmark	1948, (1980*)
Netherlands	1948, 1965[1]
Netherlands Antilles	*1948, 1955*[1], *1963*[1], *1987*[2], (1986*)
New Zealand	*1948*, (1982)
Rwanda	*1948, 1983*[2]
Zaire	*1948, 1983*[2]
Ireland	1949
Norway	*1949, 1958*[1], (1971)
Greece	1950, 1953[1]
Switzerland	1951
Finland	*1952*, (1970)
Australia	*1953*, (1982)
Germany	1954, 1965[1], (1989*)
Japan	*1954, 1957*[1], *1960*[1], *1962*[1], (1971)
Italy	*1955*, (1984)
Austria	1956
Pakistan	1957
Luxembourg	1962
Thailand	1965*
Trinidad & Tobago	*1966, 1969*[2], (1970)
Brazil	1967*
France	1967, 1970[1], 1978[1], 1984[1], 1988[1]
Belgium	1970, 1987[1]
Finland	1970, (1989*)
Trinidad & Tobago	1970
Japan	1971
Norway	1971, 1980[1]
Romania	1973
USSR	1973
Poland	1974
Iceland	1975
Israel	1960*, 1965*, 1975*, 1980[1]*
United Kingdom	1975, 1976[1], 1977[1], 1979[1]
Korea	1976
Philippines	1976
Morocco	1977

Chronological List of US Income Tax Treaties

Hungary	1979
Bangladesh	1980*
Canada	1980, 1983[1], 1984[1]
Denmark	1980*, 1983[1]*
Egypt	1980
Jamaica	1980, 1981[1]
Malta	1980
Argentina	1981*
British Virgin Islands	1981*
Australia	1982
New Zealand	1982
Barbados	1984
China	1984, 1986[1]
Cyprus	1984
Italy	1984
Sri Lanka	1985*
Tunisia	1985*, 1989[1]*
Aruba	1986*
Netherlands Antilles	1986*
Indonesia	1988*
Germany	1989*
India	1989*
Spain	1990

Convention between the Government of the United States of America and the Government of Australia for the Avoidance of Double Taxation and the Prevention of Fiscal Evasion with Respect to Taxes on Income, concluded in Sydney on August 6, 1982.

The Government of the United States of America and the Government of Australia,

Desiring to conclude a Convention for the Avoidance of Double Taxation and the Prevention of Fiscal Evasion with Respect to Taxes on Income,

Have agreed as follows:

Article 1. Personal Scope

1. Except as otherwise provided in this Convention, this Convention shall apply to persons who are residents of one or both of the Contracting States.

2. This Convention shall not restrict in any manner any exclusion, exemption, deduction, rebate, credit or other allowance accorded from time to time:

a. by the Laws of either Contracting State; or

b. by any other agreement between the Contracting States.

3. Notwithstanding any provision of this Convention, except paragraph 4 of this Article, a Contracting State may tax its residents (as determined under Article 4 (Residence)) and individuals electing under its domestic Law to be taxed as residents of that State, and by reason of citizenship may tax its citizens, as if this Convention had not entered into force. For this purpose, the term 'citizen' shall, with respect to United States source income according to United States Law relating to United States tax, include a former citizen whose loss of citizenship had as one of its principal purposes the avoidance of tax, but only for a period of 10 years following such loss.

4. The provisions of paragraph 3 shall not affect:

a. the benefits conferred by a Contracting State under paragraph 2 of Article 9 (Associated Enterprises), paragraph 2 or 6 of Article 18 (Pensions, Annuities, Alimony and Child Support), Article 22 (Relief from Double Taxation), 23 (Non-Discrimination), 24 (Mutual Agreement Procedure) or paragraph 1 of Article 27 (Miscellaneous); or

b. the benefits conferred by a Contracting State under Article 19 (Governmental Remuneration), 20 (Students) or 26 (Diplomatic and Consular Privileges) upon individuals who are neither citizens of, nor have immigrant status in, that State (in the case of benefits conferred by the United States), or who are not ordinarily resident in that State (in the case of benefits conferred by Australia).

Article 2. Taxes Covered

1. The existing taxes to which this Convention shall apply are:

a. in the United States: the Federal income taxes imposed by the Internal Revenue Code, but excluding the accumulated earnings tax and the personal holding company tax; and

b. in Australia: the Australian income tax, including the additional tax upon the undistributed amount of the distributable income of a private company.

2. This Convention shall also apply to any identical or substantially similar taxes which are imposed by either Contracting State after the date of signature of this Convention in addition to, or in place of, the existing taxes. At the end of each calendar year, the competent authority of each Contracting State shall notify the competent authority of the other Contracting State of any substantial changes which have been made during that year in the laws of his State relating to the taxes to which this Convention applies or in the official interpretation of those laws or of this convention.

Article 3. General Definitions

1. For the purposes of this Convention, unless the context otherwise requires:

a. the term 'person' includes an individual, an estate of a deceased individual, a trust, a partnership, a company and any other body of persons;

b. the term 'company' means any body corporate or any entity which is treated as a company or body corporate for tax purposes;

c. the terms 'enterprise of one of the Contracting States' and 'enterprise of the other Contracting State' mean an enterprise carried on by a resident of Australia or an enterprise carried on by a resident of the United States, as the context requires;

d. the term 'international traffic' means any transport by a ship or aircraft, except where such transport is solely between places within a Contracting State;

e. the term 'competent authority' means:

(i) in the case of the United States: the Secretary of the Treasury or his delegate; and

(ii) in the case of Australia: the Commissioner of Taxation or his authorized representative;

f. the terms 'Contracting State', 'one of the Contracting States' and 'the other Contracting State' mean the United States or Australia, as the context requires;

g. (i) the term 'United States corporation' means a corporation which, under United States law relating to United States tax, is a domestic corporation or an unincorporated entity treated as a domestic corporation, and which is not, under the law of Australia relating to Australian tax, a resident of Australia; and

(ii) the term 'Australian corporation' means a company, as defined under the law of Australia relating to Australian tax, which, under that law, is a resident of Australia, and which is not, under United States law relating to United States tax, a domestic corporation or an unincorporated entity treated as a domestic corporation;

h. the term 'State' means any National State, whether or not one of the Contracting States;

i. the term 'United States tax' means tax imposed by the United States to which this Convention applies by virtue of Article 2 (Taxes Covered) and the term 'Australian tax' means tax imposed by Australia to which this Convention applies by virtue of Article 2 (Taxes Covered), but neither term includes any amount which represents a penalty or interest imposed under the law of either Contracting State relating to United States tax or Australian tax;

j. (i) the term 'United States' means the United States of America; and

(ii) when used in a geographical sense, the term 'United States' means the states thereof and the District of Columbia and also includes:

(A) the territorial waters thereof; and

(B) the seabed and subsoil of the submarine areas adjacent to the coast thereof, but beyond the territorial waters, over which the United States exercises rights, in accordance with international law, for the purposes of exploration for, or exploitation of, the natural resources of those areas;

k. (i) the term 'Australia' means the Commonwealth of Australia and, when used in a geographical sense, includes:

(ii) the Territory of Norfolk Island;

(iii) the Territory of Christmas Island;

(iv) the Territory of Cocos (Keeling) Islands;

(v) the Territory of Ashmore and Cartier Islands;

(vi) the Coral Sea Islands Territory; and

(vii) any area adjacent to the territorial limits of Australia or of the said Territories in respect of which there is for the time being in force, consistently with international law, a law of Australia or of a State or part of Australia or of a Territory aforesaid dealing with the exploitation of any of the natural resources of the seabed and subsoil of the continental shelf;

l. the terms 'resident of one of the Contracting States' and 'resident of the other Contracting State' mean a resident of Australia or a resident of the United States, as the context requires.

2. As regards the application of this Convention by one of the Contracting States, any term not defined herein shall, unless the context otherwise requires, have the meaning which it has under the laws of that State relating to the taxes to which this Convention applies.

Article 4. Residence

1. For the purposes of this Convention:

a. a person is a resident of Australia if the person is:

(i) an Australian corporation; or

(ii) any other person (except a company as defined under the law of Australia relating to Australian tax) who, under that law, is a resident of Australia, provided that, in relation to any income, a person who:

(iii) is subject to Australian tax on income which is from sources in Australia; or

(iv) is a partnership, an estate of a deceased individual or a trust (other than a trust that is a provident, benefit, superannuation or retirement fund, or that is established for public charitable purposes or for the purpose of enabling scientific research to be conducted by or in conjunction with a public university or public hospital, the income of which is exempt from tax under the law of Australia relating to Australian tax),

shall not be treated as a resident of Australia except to the extent that the income is subject to Australian tax as the income of a resident, either in the hands of that person or in the hands of a partner or beneficiary, or, if that income is exempt from Australian tax, is so exempt solely because it is subject to United States tax; and

b. a person is a resident of the United States if the person is:

(i) a United States corporation; or

(ii) any other person (except a corporation or unincorporated entity treated as a corporation for United States tax purposes) resident in the United States for purposes of its tax, provided that, in relation to any income derived by a partnership, an estate of a deceased individual or a trust, such person shall not be treated as a resident of the United States except to the extent that the income is subject to United States tax as the income of a resident, either in its hands or in the hands of a partner or beneficiary, or, if that income is exempt from United States tax, is exempt other than because such person, partner or beneficiary is not a United States person according to United States law relating to United States tax.

2. Where by application of paragraph 1 an individual is a resident of both Contracting States, he shall be deemed to be a resident of the State:

a. in which he maintains his permanent home;

b. if the provisions of sub-paragraph *a.* do not apply, in which he has an habitual abode if he has his permanent home in both Contracting States or in neither of the Contracting States; or

c. if the provisions of sub-paragraphs *a.* and *b.* do not apply, with which his personal and economic relations are closer if he has an habitual abode in both Contracting States or in neither of the Contracting States.

For the purposes of this paragraph, in determining an individual's permanent home, regard shall be given to the place where the individual dwells with his family, and in determining the Contracting State with which an individual's personal and economic relations are closer, regard shall be given to his citizenship (if he is a citizen of one of the Contracting States).

3. An individual who is deemed to be a resident of one of the Contracting States for any year of income, or taxable year, as the case may be by reason of the provisions of paragraph 2 shall, for all purposes

of this Convention, be deemed to be a resident only of that State for such year.

Article 5. Permanent Establishment

1. For the purposes of this Convention, the term 'permanent establishment' means a fixed place of business through which the business of an enterprise is wholly or partly carried on.

2. The term 'permanent establishment' shall include especially:

a. a place of management;

b. a branch;

c. an office;

d. a factory;

e. a workshop;

f. a mine, an oil or gas well, a quarry or any other place of extraction of natural resources;

g. an agricultural, pastoral or forestry property;

h. a building site or construction, assembly or installation project which exists for more than 9 months; and

i. an installation, drilling rig or ship that, for an aggregate period of at least 6 months in any 24 month period, is used by an enterprise of one of the Contracting States for dredging or for or in connection with the exploration or exploitation of natural resources of the seabed and subsoil.

3. Notwithstanding paragraphs 1 and 2, an enterprise of one of the Contracting States shall not be regarded as having a permanent establishment solely as a result of one or more of the following:

a. the use of facilities for the purpose of storage, display or delivery of goods or merchandise belonging to the enterprise;

b. the maintenance of a stock of goods or merchandise belonging to the enterprise for the purpose of storage, display or delivery;

c. the maintenance of a stock of goods or merchandise belonging to the enterprise for the purpose of processing by another enterprise;

d. the maintenance of a fixed place of business for the purpose of purchasing goods or merchandise, or for collecting information, for the enterprise;

e. the maintenance of a fixed place of business for the purpose of activities which have a preparatory or auxiliary character, such as advertising or scientific research, for the enterprise;

f. the maintenance of a building site or construction, assembly or installation project which does not exist for more than 9 months; or

g. the use by that enterprise in the other Contracting State, of an installation, drilling rig or ship for dredging, or for or in connection with the exploration or exploitation of natural resources of the seabed and subsoil, provided that such use is not for an aggregate period of at least 6 months in any 24 month period.

4. Notwithstanding paragraphs 1 and 2, an enterprise of one of the Contracting States shall be deemed to have a permanent establishment in the other Contracting State if:

a. it carries on business in that other State through a person, other than an agent of independent status to whom paragraph 5 applies, who has authority to conclude contracts on behalf of that enterprise and habitually exercises that authority in that other State, unless the activities of such person are limited to those mentioned in paragraph 3 which, if exercised through a fixed place of business, would not make that fixed place of business a permanent establishment under the provisions of that paragraph;

b. it maintains substantial equipment for rental or other purposes within that other State (excluding equipment let under a hire-purchase agreement) for a period of more than 12 months;

c. it engages in supervisory activities in that other State for more than 9 months in any 24 month period in connection with a building site or construction, assembly or installation project in that other State; or

d. it has goods or merchandise belonging to it that:

(i) were purchased by it in that other State, and not subjected to prior substantial processing outside that other State; or

(ii) were produced by it or on its behalf in that other State,

and are, after such purchase or production, subjected to substantial processing in that other State by an enterprise where either enterprise participates directly or indirectly in the management, control or capital of the other enterprise, or where the same persons participate directly or indirectly in the management, control or capital of both enterprises.

5. An enterprise of one of the Contracting States shall not be deemed to have a permanent establishment in the other Contracting State merely because that enterprise carries on business in that other State through a broker, general commission agent, or any other agent of independent status, where such broker or agent is acting in the ordinary course of business as a broker, general commission agent or other agent of independent status.

6. The fact that a company which is a resident of one of the Contracting States controls or is controlled by a company which is a resident of the other Contracting State, or which carries on business in that other State (whether through a permanent establishment or otherwise), shall not of itself constitute either company a permanent establishment of the other.

7. The principles set forth in the preceding paragraphs of this Article shall be applied in determining for purposes of this Convention whether there is a permanent establishment in a State other than one of the Contracting States and whether an enterprise other than an enterprise of one of the Contracting States has a permanent establishment in one of the Contracting States.

Article 6. Income from Real Property

1. Income from real property may be taxed by the Contracting State in which such real property is situated.

2. For the purposes of this Convention:

(i) a leasehold interest in land, whether or not improved, shall be regarded as real property situated where the land to which the interest relates is situated; and

(ii) rights to exploit or to explore for natural resources shall be regarded as real property situated where the natural resources are situated or sought.

Article 7. Business Profits

1. The business profits of an enterprise of one of the Contracting States shall be taxable only in that State unless the enterprise carries on business in the other Contracting State through a permanent establishment situated therein. If the enterprise carries on business as aforesaid, the business profits of the enterprise may be taxed in the other State but only so much of them as is attributable to that permanent establishment.

2. Subject to the provisions of paragraph 3, where an enterprise of one of the Contracting States carries on business in the other Contracting State through a permanent establishment situated therein, there shall in each Contracting State be attributed to that permanent establishment the business profits which it might be expected to make if it were a distinct and independent enterprise engaged in the same or similar activities under the same or similar conditions and dealing wholly independently with the enterprise of which it is a permanent establishment or with other enterprises with which it deals.

3. In the determination of the business profits of a permanent establishment, there shall be allowed as deductions expenses which are reasonably connected with the profits (including executive and general administrative expenses) and which would be deductible if the permanent establishment were an independent entity which paid those expenses, whether incurred in the Contracting State in which the permanent establishment is situated or elsewhere.

4. No business profits shall be attributed to a permanent establishment by reason of the mere purchase by that permanent establishment of goods or merchandise for the enterprise.

5. For the purposes of the preceding paragraphs of this Article, the business profits to be attributed to the permanent establishment shall be determined by the same method year by year unless there is good and sufficient reason to the contrary.

6. Where business profits include items of income which are dealt with separately in other Articles of this Convention, then the provisions of those Articles shall not be affected by the provisions of this Article.

7. Nothing in this Article shall affect the application of any law of a Contracting State relating to the determination of the tax liability of a person in cases where the information available to the competent authority of that State is inadequate to determine the profits to be attributed to a permanent establishment, provided that, on the basis of the available information, the determination of the profits of the permanent establishment is consistent with the principles stated in this Article.

8. Nothing in this Article shall in a Contracting State prevent the operation in that State of its law relating specifically to the taxation of any person who carries on the business of any form of insurance (as long as that law as in effect on the date of signature of this Convention is not varied otherwise than in minor respects so as not to affect its general character).

Article 8. Shipping and Air Transport

1. Profits derived by a resident of one of the Contracting States from the operation in international traffic of ships or aircraft shall be taxable only in that State. For the purpose of this Article, profits from the operation in international traffic of ships or aircraft include:

a. profits from the lease on a full basis of ships or aircraft operated in international traffic by the lessee, provided that the lessor either operates ships or aircraft otherwise than solely between places in the other Contracting State or regularly leases ships or aircraft on a full basis; and

b. profits from the lease of ships or aircraft on a bare boat basis or of containers and related equipment, provided that such lease is merely incidental to the operation in international traffic of ships or aircraft by the lessor and the leased ships or aircraft are operated in international traffic, or the containers and related equipment are used in international traffic, by the lessee.

2. The provisions of paragraph 1 shall apply to the share of the profits from the operation in international traffic of ships or aircraft derived by a resident of one of the Contracting States through participation in a pool service, in a joint transport operating organization or in an international operating agency.

3. For the purposes of this Article, profits derived from the carriage by ships or aircraft of passengers, livestock, mail, goods or merchandise shipped in a Contracting State for discharge at another place in that State shall not be treated as profits from the operation in international traffic of ships or aircraft and may be taxed in that State.

Article 9. Associated Enterprises

1. Where:

a. an enterprise of one of the Contracting States participates directly or indirectly in the management, control or capital of an enterprise of the other Contracting State; or

b. the same persons participate directly or indirectly in the management, control or capital of an enterprise of one of the Contracting States and an enterprise of the other Contracting State;

and in either case conditions operate between the two enterprises in their commercial or financial relations which differ from those which might be expected to operate between independent enterprises dealing wholly independently with one another, then any profits which, but for those conditions, might have been expected to accrue to one of the enterprises, but, by reason of those conditions, have not so accrued, may be included in the profits of that enterprise and taxed accordingly.

2. Where profits on which an enterprise of one of the Contracting States has been charged to tax in that State are also included, by virtue of paragraph 1, in the profits of an enterprise of the other Contracting State and taxed accordingly, and the profits so included are profits which might have been expected to have accrued to that enterprise of the other State if the conditions operative between the enterprises had been those which might have been expected to have operated between independent enterprises dealing wholly independently with one another, then the first-mentioned State shall make an appropriate adjustment to the amount of tax charged on those profits in the first-mentioned State. In determining such an adjustment, due regard shall be had to the other provisions of this Convention and the competent authorities of the Contracting States shall if necessary consult each other.

3. Nothing in this Article shall affect the application of any law of a Contracting State relating to the determination of the tax liability of a person, including determinations in cases where the information available to the competent authority of that State is inadequate to determine the income to be attributed to an enterprise, provided that, on the basis of the available information, the determination of that tax liability is consistent with the principles stated in this Article.

Article 10. Dividends

1. Dividends paid by a company which is a resident of one of the Contracting States for the purposes of its tax, being dividends to which a resident of the other Contracting State is beneficially entitled, may be taxed in that other State.

2. Such dividends may be taxed in the Contracting State of which the company paying the dividends is a resident for the purposes of its tax, and according to the law of that State, but the tax so charged shall not exceed 15 per cent of the gross amount of the dividends.

3. The term 'dividends' in this Article means income from shares and other income assimilated to income from shares by the taxation law of the Contracting State of which the company making the distribution is a resident for the purposes of its tax.

4. The provisions of paragraph 2 shall not apply if the person beneficially entitled to the dividends, being a resident of one of the Contracting States, carries on business in the other Contracting State, being the State of which the company paying the dividends is a resident, through a permanent establishment situated therein, or performs in that other State independent personal services from a fixed base situated therein, and the holding in respect of which the dividends are paid is effectively connected with such permanent establishment or fixed base. In such a case, the provisions of Article 7 (Business Profits) or Article 14 (Independent Personal Services), as the case may be, shall apply.

5. Where a company is a resident of one of the Contracting States, the other Contracting State may not impose any tax on dividends paid by the company, except insofar as:

a. a resident of that other State is beneficially entitled to the dividends;

b. the holding in respect of which the dividends are paid is effectively connected with a permanent establishment or a fixed base situated in that other State; or

c. that other State does not impose a tax of the kind described in paragraph 6 (excluding the accumulated earnings tax and the personal holding company tax imposed by the United States) and the dividends are paid out of profits attributable to one or more permanent establishments which such company had in that other State, provided that the gross income attributable to such permanent establishments constituted at least 50 per cent of such company's gross income from all sources. Where sub-paragraph *c.* applies and sub-paragraphs *a.* and *b.* do not apply, any such tax shall not exceed 15 per cent of the dividends.

6. Nothing in this Convention shall be construed as preventing a Contracting State from imposing on the income of a company which is a resident of the other Contracting State, tax in addition to the taxes referred to in Article 2 in relation to the first-mentioned Contracting State which are payable by a company which is a resident of the first-mentioned State, provided that any such additional tax shall not exceed 15 per cent of the amount by which the taxable income of the first-mentioned company of a year of income exceeds the tax payable on that taxable income to the first-mentioned State. Any tax payable to a Contracting State on the undistributed profits of a company which is a resident of the other Contracting State shall be calculated as if that company were not liable to the additional tax referred to in this paragraph and had paid dividends of such amount that tax equal to the amount of that additional tax would have been payable on the dividends in accordance with paragraph 2 of this Article.

Article 11. Interest

1. Interest from sources in one of the Contracting States, being interest to which a resident of the other Contracting State is beneficially entitled, may be taxed in that other State.

2. Such interest may be taxed in the Contracting State in which it has its source, and according to the law of that State, but the tax so charged shall not exceed 10 per cent of the gross amount of the interest.

3. Paragraph 2 shall not apply if the person beneficially entitled to the interest, being a resident of one of the Contracting States, has a permanent establishment in the other Contracting State or performs independent personal services in that other State from a fixed base situated therein and the indebtedness giving rise to the interest is effectively connected with such permanent establishment or fixed base. In such a case the provisions of Article 7 (Business Profits) or Article 14 (Independent Personal Services), as the case may be, shall apply.

4. Where, owing to a special relationship between the payer and the person beneficially entitled to the interest, or between both of them and some other person, the amount of the interest paid, having regard to the indebtedness for which it is paid, exceeds the amount which might have been expected to have been agreed upon by the payer and the

person so entitled in the absence of such relationship, the provisions of this Article shall apply only to the last-mentioned amount. In that case, the excess part of the interest paid shall remain taxable according to the law of each Contracting State, but subject to the other provisions of this Convention.

5. The term 'interest' as used in this Convention includes income which, under the taxation law of the Contracting State in which the income has its source, is assimilated to income from money lent.

6. A Contracting State may not impose any tax on interest paid by a resident of the other Contracting State, except insofar as:

a. such interest has its source in the first-mentioned State, or is interest to which a resident of that State is beneficially entitled; or

b. the indebtedness in respect of which the interest is paid is effectively connected with a permanent establishment or a fixed base of the beneficial owner of the interest situated in the first-mentioned State.

7. Interest shall be treated as income from sources in a Contracting State when the payer is that State itself or a political subdivision or local authority of that State or a person who is a resident of that State for the purposes of its tax. Where, however, the person paying the interest, whether he is a resident of one of the Contracting States or not, has in one of the Contracting States or outside both Contracting States a permanent establishment or fixed base in connection with which the indebtedness on which the interest is paid was incurred, and such interest is borne by such permanent establishment or fixed base, then such interest shall be deemed to have its source in the State in which the permanent establishment or fixed base is situated.

Article 12. Royalties

1. Royalties from sources in one of the Contracting States, being royalties to which a resident of the other Contracting State is beneficially entitled, may be taxed in that other State.

2. Such royalties may be taxed in the Contracting State in which they have their source, and according to the law of that State, but the tax so charged shall not exceed 10 per cent of the gross amount of the royalties.

3. Paragraph 2 shall not apply if the person beneficially entitled to the royalties, being a resident of one of the Contracting States, has a permanent establishment in the other Contracting State or performs independent personal services in that other State from a fixed base situated therein, and the property or rights giving rise to the royalties are effectively connected with such permanent establishment or fixed base. In such a case, the provisions of Article 7 (Business Profits) or Article 14 (Independent Personal Services), as the case may be, shall apply.

4. The term 'royalties' in this Article means:

a. payments or credits of any kind to the extent to which they are consideration for the use of or the right to use any:

(i) copyright, patent, design or model, plan, secret formula or process, trademark or other like property or right;

(ii) industrial, commercial or scientific equipment, other than equipment let under a hire purchase agreement;

(iii) motion picture films; or

(iv) films or video tapes for use in connection with television or tapes for use in connection with radio broadcasting;

b. payments or credits of any kind to the extent to which they are consideration for:

(i) the supply of scientific, technical, industrial or commercial knowledge or information owned by any person;

(ii) the supply of any assistance of an ancillary and subsidiary nature furnished as a means of enabling the application or enjoyment of knowledge or information referred to in sub-paragraph *b.*(i) or of any other property or right to which this Article applies; or

(iii) a total or partial forbearance in respect of the use or supply of any property or right described in this paragraph; or

c. income derived from the sale, exchange or other disposition of any property or right described in this paragraph to the extent to which the amounts realized on such sale, exchange or other disposition are contingent on the productivity, use or further disposition of such property or right.

5. Where, owing to a special relationship between the payer and the person beneficially entitled to the royalties or between both of them and some other person, the amount of the royalties paid or credited, having regard to what they are paid or credited for, exceeds the amount which might have been expected to have been agreed upon by the payer and the person so entitled in the absence of such relationship, the provisions of this Article shall apply only to the last-mentioned amount. In that case, the excess part of the amount of the royalties paid or credited shall remain taxable according to the law of each Contracting State, but subject to the other provisions of this Convention.

6. *a.* Royalties shall be treated as income from sources in a Contracting State when the payer is that State itself or a political subdivision or local authority of that State or a person who is a resident of that State for the purposes of its tax. Where, however, the person paying the royalties, whether he is a resident of one of the Contracting States or not, has in one of the Contracting States or outside both Contracting States a permanent establishment or fixed base in connection with which the liability to pay the royalties was incurred, and such royalties are borne by the permanent establishment or fixed base, then the royalties shall be deemed to have their source in the State in which the permanent establishment or fixed base is situated.

b. Where sub-paragraph *a.* does not operate to treat royalties as being from sources in one of the Contracting States, and the royalties relate to use or the right to use in one of the Contracting States of any property or right described in paragraph 4, the royalties shall be treated as income from sources in that State.

Article 13. Alienation of Property

1. Income or gains derived by a resident of one of the Contracting States from the alienation or disposition of real property situated in the other Contracting State may be taxed in that other State.

2. For the purposes of this Article:

a. the term 'real property situated in the other Contracting State', where the United States is that other Contracting State, includes a United States real property interest, and real property referred to in Article 6 which is situated in the United States; and

b. the term 'real property', in the case of Australia, shall have the meaning which it has under the Laws in force from time to time in Australia and, without limiting the foregoing, includes:

(i) real property referred to in Article 6;

(ii) shares or comparable interests in a company, the assets of which consist wholly or principally of real property situated in Australia; and

(iii) an interest in a partnership, trust or estate of a deceased individual, the assets of which consist wholly or principally of real property situated in Australia.

3. Income or gains derived by an enterprise of one of the Contracting States from the alienation of ships, aircraft or containers operated or used by it in international traffic shall, except to the extent to which that enterprise has been allowed depreciation in the other Contracting State in respect of those ships, aircraft or containers, be taxable only in that State, and income described in sub-paragraph 4*c.* of Article 12 (Royalties) shall be taxable only in accordance with the provisions of Article 12.

4. For the purposes of this Article, real property consisting of shares in a company referred to in sub-paragraph 2*b.*(ii), and interests in a partnership, trust or estate referred to in sub-paragraph 2*b.*(iii), shall be deemed to be situated in Australia.

Article 14. Independent Personal Services

Income derived by an individual who is a resident of one of the Contracting States from the performance of personal services in an independent capacity shall be taxable only in that State unless such services are performed in the other Contracting State and:

a. the individual is present in that other State for a period or periods aggregating more than 183 days in the taxable year or year of income of that other State; or

b. the individual has a fixed base regularly available to him in that other State for the purpose of performing his activities, in which case so much of the income as is attributable to that fixed base may be taxed in such other State.

Article 15. Dependent Personal Services

1. Subject to the provisions of Articles 18 (Pensions, Annuities, Alimony and Child Support) and 19 (Governmental Remuneration), salaries, wages and other similar remuneration derived by an individual

who is a resident of one of the Contracting States in respect of an employment or in respect of services performed as a director of a company shall be taxable only in that State unless the employment is exercised or the services performed in the other Contracting State. If the employment is so exercised or the services so performed, such remuneration as is derived from that exercise or performance may be taxed in that other State.

2. Notwithstanding the provisions of paragraph 1, remuneration derived by an individual who is a resident of one of the Contracting States in respect of an employment exercised in the other Contracting State or in respect of services performed in the other Contracting State as a director of a company shall be taxable only in the first-mentioned State if:

a. the recipient is present in that other State for a period or periods not exceeding in the aggregate 183 days in the taxable year or year of income of that other State;

b. the remuneration is paid by, or on behalf of, an employer or company who is not a resident of that other State; and

c. the remuneration is not deductible in determining taxable profits of a permanent establishment, a fixed base or a trade or business which the employer or company has in that other State.

3. Notwithstanding the preceding provisions of this Article, remuneration in respect of an employment exercised aboard a ship or aircraft operated in international traffic by a resident of one of the Contracting States may be taxed in that State.

Article 16. Limitation on Benefits

1. A person (other than an individual) which is a resident of one of the Contracting States shall not be entitled under this Convention to relief from taxation in the other Contracting State unless:

a. more than 75 per cent of the beneficial interest in such person (or in the case of a company, more than 75 per cent of the number of shares of each class of the company's shares) is owned, directly or indirectly, by any combination of one or more of:

(i) individuals who are residents of the United States;
(ii) citizens of the United States;
(iii) individuals who are residents of Australia;
(iv) companies as described in sub-paragraph *b.*; and
(v) the Contracting States;

b. it is a company in whose principal class of shares there is substantial and regular trading on a recognized stock exchange in one of the Contracting States; or

c. the establishment, acquisition and maintenance of such person and the conduct of its operations did not have as one of its principal purposes the purpose of obtaining benefits under the Convention.

2. For the purposes of sub-paragraph 1*b.*, the term 'a recognized stock exchange' includes, in relation to the United States, the NASDAQ System owned by the National Association of Securities Dealers, Inc.

3. Where:

a. income derived by a trustee is to be treated for the purposes of this Convention as income of a resident of one of the Contracting States; and

b. the trustee derived the income in connection with a scheme a principal purpose of which was to obtain a benefit under this Convention,

then, notwithstanding any other provision of this Convention, the Convention does not apply in relation to that income.

Article 17. Entertainers

1. Notwithstanding the provisions of Articles 14 (Independent Personal Services) and 15 (Dependent Personal Services), income derived by entertainers (such as theatrical, motion picture, radio or television artistes, musicians and athletes) from their personal activities as such may be taxed in the Contracting State in which these activities are exercised, except where the amount of the gross receipts derived by any such entertainer, including expenses reimbursed to him or borne on his behalf, from such activities does not exceed ten thousand United States dollars ($10,000) or its equivalent in Australian dollars for the taxable year or year of income concerned.

2. Where income in respect of activities exercised by an entertainer in his capacity as such accrues not to the entertainer, but to another person, that income may, notwithstanding the provisions of Articles 7 (Business Profits), 14 (Independent Personal Services) and 15 (Dependent Personal Services), be taxed in the Contracting State in which the activities of the entertainer are exercised, unless it is established that neither the entertainer nor any person related to him participates directly or indirectly in any profits of such other person in any manner, including the receipt of deferred remuneration, bonuses, fees, dividends, partnership distributions or other distributions.

Article 18. Pensions, Annuities, Alimony and Child Support

1. Subject to the provisions of Article 19 (Governmental Remuneration), pensions and other similar remuneration paid to an individual who is a resident of one of the Contracting States in consideration of past employment shall be taxable only in that State.

2. Social security payments and other public pensions paid by one of the Contracting States to an individual who is a resident of the other Contracting State or a citizen of the United States shall be taxable only in the first-mentioned State.

3. Annuities paid to an individual who is a resident of one of the Contracting States shall be taxable only in that State.

4. The term 'pensions and other similar remuneration', as used in this Article, means periodic payments made by reason of retirement or death, in consideration for services rendered, or by way of compensation paid after retirement for injuries received in connection with past employment.

5. The term 'annuities', as used in this Article, means stated sums paid periodically at stated times during life, or during a specified or ascertainable number of years, under an obligation to make the payments in return for adequate and full consideration (other than services rendered or to be rendered).

6. Any alimony or other maintenance payments, including payments for the support of a minor child, arising in one of the Contracting States and paid to a resident of the other Contracting State, shall be taxable only in the first-mentioned State.

Article 19. Government Remuneration

Wages, salaries, and similar remuneration, including pensions, paid from funds of one of the Contracting States, of a state or other political subdivision thereof or of an agency or authority of any of the foregoing for labor or personal services performed as an employee of any of the above in the discharge of governmental functions to a citizen of that State shall by exempt from tax by the other Contracting State.

Article 20. Students

Where a student, who is a resident of one of the Contracting States or who was a resident of that State immediately before visiting the other Contracting State and who is temporarily present in that other State for the purpose of his full-time education, receives payments from sources outside that other State for the purpose of his maintenance or education, those payments shall be exempt from tax in that other State.

Article 21. Income Not Expressly Mentioned

1. Items of income of a resident of one of the Contracting States which are not expressly mentioned in the foregoing Articles of this Convention shall be taxable only in that State.

2. However, if such income is derived by a resident of one of the Contracting States from sources in the other Contracting State, such income may also be taxed in the State in which it has its source.

3. The provisions of paragraph 1 shall not apply to income derived by a resident of one of the Contracting States which is effectively connected with a permanent establishment situated in the other Contracting State. In such a case, the provisions of Article 7 (Business Profits) shall apply.

Article 22. Relief from Double Taxation

1. Subject to paragraph 4 and in accordance with the provisions and subject to the limitations of the law of the United States (as it may be amended from time to time without changing the general principle hereof), in the case of the United States, double taxation shall be avoided as follows:

a. the United States shall allow to a resident or citizen of the United States as a credit against United States tax the appropriate amount of income tax paid to Australia; and

b. in the case of a United States corporation owning at least 10 per cent of the voting stock of a company which is a resident of Australia from which it receives dividends in any taxable year, the United States shall also allow as a credit against United States tax the appropriate amount of income tax paid to Australia by that company with respect to the profits out of which such dividends are paid.
Such appropriate amount shall be based upon the amount of income tax paid to Australia. For purposes of applying the United States credit in relation to income tax paid to Australia the taxes referred to in sub-paragraph 1*b.* and paragraph 2 of Article 2 (Taxes Covered) shall be considered to be income taxes. No provision of this Convention relating to source of income shall apply in determining credits against United States tax for foreign taxes other than those referred to in sub-paragraph 1*b.* and paragraph 2 of Article 2 (Taxes Covered).

2. Subject to paragraph 4, United States tax paid under the law of the United States and in accordance with this Convention, other than United States tax imposed in accordance with paragraph 3 of Article 1 (Personal Scope) solely by reason of citizenship or by reason of an election by an individual under United States domestic law to be taxed as a resident of the United States, in respect of income derived from sources in the United States by a person who, under Australian law relating to Australian tax, is a resident of Australia shall be allowed as a credit against Australian tax payable in respect of the income. The credit shall not exceed the amount of Australian tax payable on the income or any class thereof or on income from sources outside Australia. Subject to these general principles, the credit shall be in accordance with the provisions and subject to the limitations of the law of Australia as that law may be in force from time to time.

3. An Australian corporation that owns at least 10 per cent of the voting power in a United States corporation is, in accordance with the law of Australia as in force at the date of signature of this Convention, entitled to a rebate in its assessment, at the average rate of tax payable by it, in respect of dividends paid by the United States corporation that are included in the taxable income of the Australian corporation. However, should the law as so in force be amended so that the rebate in relation to the dividends ceases to be allowable under that law, Australia shall allow credit under paragraph 2 for the United States tax paid on the profits out of which the dividends are paid as well as for the United States tax paid on the dividends.

4. For the purposes of computing United States tax, where a United States citizen is a resident of Australia, the United States shall allow as a credit against United States tax the income tax paid to Australia after the credit referred to in paragraph 2. The credit so allowed against United States tax shall not reduce that portion of the United States tax that is creditable against Australian tax in accordance with paragraph 2.

Article 23. Non-Discrimination

1. Each Contracting State in enacting tax measures shall ensure that:

a. citizens of a Contracting State who are residents of the other Contracting State shall not be subjected in that other State to any taxation or any requirement connected therewith which is more burdensome than the taxation or connected requirements to which citizens of that other State who are residents of that other State in the same circumstances are or may be subjected;

b. except where the provisions of paragraph 1 of Article 9 (Associated Enterprises), paragraph 4 of Article 11 (Interest) or paragraph 5 of Article 12 (Royalties) apply, interest, royalties and other disbursements paid by a resident of a Contracting State to a resident of the other Contracting State shall, for the purpose of determining the taxable profits of the resident of the first-mentioned State, be deductible under the same conditions as if they had been paid to a resident of the first-mentioned State;

c. a corporation of a Contracting State, the capital of which is wholly or partly owned or controlled, directly or indirectly, by one or more residents of the other Contracting State, shall not be subjected in the first-mentioned State to any taxation or any requirement connected therewith which is more burdensome than the taxation or connected requirements to which other similar corporations of the first-mentioned State in the same circumstances are or may be subjected; and

d. the taxation on a permanent establishment which a resident of a Contracting State has in the other Contracting State shall not be less favorably levied in that other State than the taxation levied on residents of that other State that carry on the same activities in the same circumstances.

2. Nothing in this Article relates to any provision of the taxation laws of a Contracting State:

a. in force on the date of signature of this Convention;

b. adopted after the date of signature of this Convention but which is substantially similar in general purpose or intent to a provision covered by sub-paragraph *a.*; or

c. reasonably designed to prevent the avoidance or evasion of taxes; provided that, with respect to provisions covered by sub-paragraphs *b.* or *c.*, such provisions (other than provisions in international agreements) do not discriminate between citizens or residents of the other Contracting State and those of any third State.

3. Without limiting by implication the interpretation of this Article, it is hereby declared that, except to the extent expressly so provided, nothing in the Article prevents a Contracting State from distinguishing in its taxation laws between residents and non-residents solely on the ground of their residence.

4. Where one of the Contracting States considers that the taxation measures of the other Contracting State infringe the principles set forth in this Article the Contracting States shall consult together in an endeavour to resolve the matter.

Article 24. Mutual Agreement Procedure

1. *a.* Where a resident of one of the Contracting States considers that the action of one or both of the Contracting States results or will result for him in taxation not in accordance with this Convention, he may, notwithstanding the remedies provided by the domestic laws of those States, present his case to the competent authority of the Contracting State of which he is a resident or citizen. The case must be presented within three years from the first notification of that action.

b. Should the claim be considered to have merit by the competent authority of the Contracting State to which the claim is made, that competent authority shall seek to come to an agreement with the competent authority of the other Contracting State with a view to the avoidance of taxation contrary to the provisions of this Convention. Any agreement reached shall be implemented notwithstanding any time limits or other procedural limitations in the domestic law of the Contracting States.

2. The competent authorities of the Contracting States shall seek to resolve by agreement any difficulties or doubts arising as to the application or interpretation of this Convention. In particular the competent authorities of the Contracting States may agree:

a. to the same attribution of income, deductions, credits, or allowances of an enterprise of one of the Contracting States to its permanent establishment situated in the other Contracting State;

b. to the same allocation of income, deductions, credits, or allowances between persons;

c. to the same determination of the source of particular items of income;

d. to the same meaning of any term used in this Convention; or

e. to which of the Contracting States an individual described in subparagraph 2*c.* of Article 4 (Residence) has closer personal and economic relations.

3. The competent authorities of the Contracting States may communicate with each other directly for the purpose of reaching an agreement in the sense of this Article.

Article 25. Exchange of Information

1. The competent authorities shall exchange such information as is necessary for carrying out the provisions of this Convention or for the prevention of fraud or for the administration of statutory provisions concerning taxes to which this Convention applies provided the information is of a class that can be obtained under the laws and administrative practices of each Contracting State with respect to its own taxes.

2. Any information so exchanged shall be treated as secret and shall not be disclosed to any persons other than those (including a Court or administrative body) concerned with the assessment, collection, administration or enforcement of, or with litigation with respect to, the taxes to which this Convention applies.

3. No information shall be exchanged which would be contrary to public policy.

4. If specifically requested by the competent authority of one of the Contracting States, the competent authority of the other Contracting State shall provide information under this Article in the form of copies of unedited original documents (including books, papers, statements, records, accounts or writings) to the same extent such documents can be obtained under the laws and administrative practices of that other State with respect to its own taxes.

5. Each of the Contracting States shall endeavor to collect on behalf of the other Contracting State amounts equal to such taxes imposed by the other State as will ensure that any exemption or reduction in rate of tax granted under this Convention by that other State shall not be enjoyed by persons not entitled to such benefits.

Article 26. Diplomatic and Consular Privileges

Nothing in this Convention shall affect diplomatic and consular privileges under the general rules of international law or under the provisions of special agreements.

Article 27. Miscellaneous

1. *a.* Income derived by a resident of the United States which, under this Convention, may be taxed in Australia shall for the purposes of the income tax law of Australia and of this Convention be deemed to be income from sources in Australia.

b. Income derived by a resident of Australia which, under this Convention, may be taxed in the United States, other than income taxed by the United States in accordance with paragraph 3 of Article 1 (Personal Scope) solely by reason of citizenship or by reason of an election by an individual under United States domestic law to be taxed as a resident of the United States, shall for the purposes of paragraph 2 of Article 22 (Relief from Double Taxation) and of the income tax law of Australia be deemed to be income from sources in the United States.

c. Where paragraph 4 of Article 22 (Relief from Double Taxation) applies, income referred to in that paragraph shall be deemed to have its source in Australia to the extent necessary to give effect to the provisions of that paragraph.

2. Any exemption from tax by one of the Contracting States provided for in Article 14 (Independent Personal Services), 15 (Dependent Personal Services), 17 (Entertainers) or 19 (Governmental Remuneration) shall be inapplicable to the extent that the income to which the exemption relates is not or, upon the application of the relevant Article of this Convention (prior to application of this paragraph), will not be subject to tax by the other Contracting State.

Article 28. Entry into Force

1. This Convention shall be subject to ratification in accordance with the applicable procedures of each Contracting State, and instruments of ratification shall be exchanged at Washington, D.C., as soon as possible.

2. The Convention shall enter into force upon the exchange of instruments of ratification and its provisions shall have effect:

a. with respect to those dividends, interest and royalties to which Articles 10 (Dividends), 11 (Interest) and 12 (Royalties), respectively, apply and which are paid, credited or otherwise derived on or after the first day of the second month following the date on which the Convention enters into force; and

b. with respect to all other income of a taxpayer, for the taxpayer's years of income or taxable years, as the case may be, commencing on or after the first day of the second month following the date on which the Convention enters into force.

3. Subject to paragraph 4, the Convention between the Government of the United States of America and the Government of the Commonwealth of Australia for the Avoidance of Double Taxation and the Prevention of Fiscal Evasion with respect to Taxes on Income signed at Washington on May 14, 1953 (in this Article referred to as the 1953 Convention) shall cease to have effect with respect to taxes to which this Convention applies under paragraph 2.

4. The 1953 Convention shall terminate on the expiration of the last date on which it has effect in accordance with the foregoing provisions of this Article.

Article 29. Termination

1. This Convention shall remain in force until terminated by a Contracting State. Either Contracting State may terminate the Convention at any time after 5 years from the date on which the Convention enters into force, provided that at least 6 months prior notice of termination has been given through the diplomatic channel. In such event, the Convention shall cease to have effect:

a. with respect to those dividends, interest and royalties to which Articles 10 (Dividends), 11 (Interest) and 12 (Royalties) respectively apply, and which are paid, credited or otherwise derived on or after the first day of January following the expiration of the 6 month period; and

b. with respect to all other income of a taxpayer, for the taxpayer's years of income or taxable years, as the case may be, commencing on or after the first day of January following the expiration of the 6 month period.

2. Notwithstanding the provisions of paragraph 1, upon prior notice to be given through the diplomatic channel, the provisions of paragraph 2 of Article 18 (Pensions, Annuities, Alimony and Child Support) may be terminated by either Contracting State at any time after this Convention enters into force.

Done in duplicate at Sydney this sixth day of August 1982.

Convention between the United States of America and the Kingdom of Belgium for the avoidance of double taxation and the prevention of fiscal evasion with respect to taxes on income, concluded in Brussels on July 9, 1970, as amended by the Protocol of December 31, 1987.

The Government of the United States of America and the Government of the Kingdom of Belgium, Desiring to conclude a convention for the avoidance of double taxation and the prevention of fiscal evasion with respect to taxes on income,

Have agreed upon the following articles:

Article 1. Personal Scope

This Convention is generally applicable to persons who are residents of one or both of the Contracting States.

Article 2. Taxes Covered

1. The taxes which are the subject of this Convention are:

a. In case of the United States, the Federal income taxes imposed by the Internal Revenue Code, hereinafter referred to as the 'United States tax', and

b. In the case of Belgium:

(i) The individual income tax (*l'impôt des personnes physiques*);

(ii) The corporate income tax (*l'impôt des sociétés*);

(iii) The income tax on legal entities (*l'impôt des personnes morales*);

(iv) The income tax on nonresidents (*l'impôt des nonrésidents*);

(v) The prepayments and additional prepayments (*les précomptes et compléments de précomptes*); and

(vi) Surcharges (*centimes additionnels*) on any of the taxes referred to in (i) through (v), including the communal supplement to the individual income tax (*la taxe communale additionnelle à l'impôt des personnes physiques*),

hereinafter referred to as the 'Belgian tax'.

2. This Convention shall also apply to any identical or substantially similar taxes which are imposed after the date of signature of this Convention in addition to, or in place of, existing taxes.

3. The competent authorities of the Contracting States shall notify each other of any amendments of the laws imposing the taxes referred to in paragraph 1 and of the adoption of any taxes referred to in paragraph 2 by transmitting the texts of any amendments or new statutes at least once a year.

4. The competent authorities of the Contracting States shall notify each other of the publication by their respective Contracting States of

any material concerning the application of this Convention, whether in the form of regulations, rulings, or judicial decisions, by transmitting the texts of any such materials at least once a year.

Article 3. General Definitions

1. In this Convention, unless the context otherwise requires:

a. (i) the term 'United States' means the United States of America; and

(ii) When used in a geographical sense, the term 'United States' means the States thereof and the District of Columbia. Such a term also includes, (A) the territorial sea thereof (B) the seabed and subsoil of the adjacent submarine areas beyond the territorial sea, over which the United States exercises sovereign rights in accordance with international law for the purpose of exploration and exploitation of the natural resources of those areas, but only to the extent that the person, property, or activity to which this Convention is being applied is connected with such exploration or exploitation.

b. (i) The term 'Belgium' means the Kingdom of Belgium; and

(ii) When used in a geographical sense, the term 'Belgium' means the territory of Belgium. Such a term also includes (A) the territorial sea thereof, and (B) the seabed and subsoil of the adjacent submarine areas beyond the territorial sea over which Belgium exercises sovereign rights in accordance with international law, for the purpose of exploration and exploitation of the natural resources of those areas, but only to the extent that the person, property, or activity to which this Convention is being applied is connected with such exploration or exploitation.

c. The terms 'one of the Contracting States' or 'the other Contracting State' means the United States or Belgium, as the context requires.

d. The term 'person' includes an individual, a partnership, a corporation, a trust, or any body of persons.

e. (i) the term 'United States corporation' or 'corporation of the United States' means a corporation which is created or organized under the laws of the United States or any State thereof or the District of Columbia or any unincorporated entity treated as a United States corporation for United States tax purposes, provided that such corporation or entity is not a Belgian corporation for Belgian tax purposes; and

(ii) The term 'Belgian corporation' or 'corporation of Belgium' means any entity which under Belgian tax law (A) is either a body corporate or is treated as a body corporate and (B) is a resident of Belgium, provided that such entity is not a United States corporation for United States tax purposes.

f. The term 'competent authority' means:

(i) In the case of the United States, the Secretary of the Treasury or his delegate, and

(ii) In the case of Belgium, the competent authority according to Belgian legislation.

g. The term 'State' means any National State, whether or not one of the Contracting States.

2. Subject to paragraph *2d.* of Article 25 (Mutual Agreement Procedure), any other term used in this Convention and not defined in this Convention shall, unless the context otherwise requires, have the meaning which it has under the laws of the Contracting State whose tax is being determined.

Article 4. Fiscal Domicile

1. In this Convention:

a. The term 'resident of Belgium' means:

(i) A Belgian corporation, and

(ii) Any person (other than a corporation) who is a resident of Belgium for purposes of its tax.

b. The term 'resident of the United States' means:

(i) A United States corporation, and

(ii) Any person (except a corporation or any other entity treated as a corporation for United States tax purposes) resident in the United States for purposes of its tax, but in the case of a partnership, estate, or trust only to the extent that the income derived by such person is subject to United States tax as the income of a resident.

2. Where by reason of the provisions of paragraph 1 an individual is a resident of both Contracting States:

a. He shall be deemed to be a resident of that Contracting State in which he maintains his permanent home. If he has a permanent home in both Contracting States or in neither of the Contracting States, he shall be deemed a resident of that Contracting State with which his personal and economic relations are closest (center of vital interests);

b. If the Contracting State in which he has his center of vital interests cannot be determined, he shall be deemed a resident of that Contracting State in which he has a habitual abode;

c. If he has a habitual abode in both Contracting States or in neither of the Contracting States, he shall be deemed to be a resident of the Contracting State of which he is a citizen; and

d. If he is a citizen of both Contracting States or of neither Contracting State the competent authorities of the Contracting States shall settle the question by mutual agreement.

For purpose of this paragraph, a permanent home is the place where an individual dwells with his family.

Article 5. Permanent Establishment

1. For the purpose of this Convention, the term 'permanent establishment' means a fixed place of business through which a resident of one of the Contracting States engages in industrial or commercial activity.

2. The term 'fixed place of business' includes but is not limited to:

a. A place of management;

b. A branch;

c. An office;

d. A factory;

e. A workshop;

f. A warehouse;

g. A mine, quarry, or other place of extraction of natural resources; and

h. A building site or construction or installation project which exists for more than 12 months.

3. Notwithstanding paragraphs 1 and 2, a permanent establishment shall not include a fixed place of business used only for one or more of the following:

a. The use of facilities for the purpose of storage, display or delivery of goods or merchandise belonging to the resident;

b. The maintenance of a stock of goods or merchandise belonging to the resident for the purpose of storage, display or delivery;

c. The maintenance of a stock of goods or merchandise belonging to the resident for the purpose of processing by another person;

d. The maintenance of a fixed place of business for the purpose of purchasing goods or merchandise, or for collecting information, for the resident;

e. The maintenance of a fixed place of business for the purpose of advertising, for the supply of information, for scientific research, or for similar activities which have a preparatory or auxiliary character, for the resident; or

f. The maintenance of a building site or construction or installation project which does not exist for more than 12 months.

4. Notwithstanding subparagraph *a.*, *c.* and *d.* of paragraph 3, if a resident of one of the Contracting States has a fixed place of business in the other Contracting State and goods or merchandise are either:

a. Subjected to processing in the other Contracting State by another person (whether or not purchased in the other Contracting State); or

b. Purchased in the other Contracting State (and such goods or merchandise are not subjected to processing outside the other Contracting State)

such resident shall be considered to have a permanent establishment in that other Contracting State, if all or part of such goods or merchandise is sold by or on behalf of such resident for use, consumption, or disposition in that other Contracting State.

5. A person acting in one of the Contracting States on behalf of a resident of the other Contracting State, other than an agent of an independent status to whom paragraph 6 applies, shall be deemed to be a permanent establishment in the first-mentioned Contracting State if such person has, and habitually exercises in the first-mentioned Contracting State, an authority to conclude contracts in the name of that resident, unless the exercise of such authority is limited to the purchase of goods or merchandise for that resident.

6. A resident of one of the Contracting States shall not be deemed to have a permanent establishment in the other Contracting State merely because such resident engages in industrial or commercial activity in that other Contracting State through a broker, general commission agent, or any other agent of an independent status, where such broker or agent is acting in the ordinary course of his business. This paragraph

shall not apply if such broker or agent acting on behalf of an insurance company if such broker or agent has, and habitually exercises, an authority to conclude contracts in the name of that company.

7. The fact that a resident of one of the Contracting States is a related person with respect to a resident of the other Contracting State or with respect to a person who engages in industrial or commercial activity in that other Contracting State (whether through permanent establishment or otherwise) shall not be taken into account in determining whether that resident of the first-mentioned Contracting State has a permanent establishment in that other Contracting State.

8. The principles set forth in paragraphs 1 through 7 shall be applied in determining whether there is a permanent establishment in a State other than one of the Contracting States or whether a person other than a resident of one of the Contracting States has a permanent establishment in one of the Contracting States.

Article 6. Income from Real Property

1. Income from real property, including royalties in respect of the operation of mines, quarries, or other natural resources and gains derived from the sale, exchange, or other disposition of such property or of the right giving rise to such royalties, may be taxed by the Contracting State in which such real property, mines, quarries, or other natural resources are situated. For purposes of this Convention interest on indebtedness secured by real property or secured by a right giving rise to royalties in respect of the operation of mines, quarries, or other natural resources shall not be regarded as income from real property.

2. Paragraph 1 shall apply to income derived from the usufruct, direct use, letting, or use in any other form of real property.

Article 7. Business Profits

1. Industrial or commercial profits of a resident of one of the Contracting States shall be exempt from tax by the other Contracting State unless such resident is engaged in industrial or commercial activity in that other Contracting State through a permanent establishment situated therein. If such resident is so engaged, tax may be imposed by that other Contracting State on the industrial or commercial profits of such resident but only on so much of the profits as are attributable to the permanent establishment.

2. Where a resident of one of the Contracting States is engaged in industrial or commercial activity in the other Contracting State through a permanent establishment situated therein, there shall in each Contracting State be attributed to the permanent establishment the industrial or commercial profits which would be attributable to such permanent establishment if such permanent establishment were an independent entity engaged in the same or similar activities under the same or similar conditions and dealing wholly independently.

3. In the determination of the industrial or commercial profits of a permanent establishment, there shall be allowed as deductions expenses which are reasonably connected with such profits, including executive

and general administrative expenses, whether incurred in the Contracting State in which the permanent establishment is situated or elsewhere.

4. No profits shall be attributed to a permanent establishment of a resident of one of the Contracting States in the other Contracting State merely by reason of the purchase of goods or merchandise by the permanent establishment, or by the resident of which it is a permanent establishment, for the account of that resident.

5. For the purposes of this Convention the term 'industrial or commercial profits':

a. Does include rents or royalties derived from motion picture films or films or tapes used for radio or television broadcasting or from copyrights thereof and rents derived from the leasing of tangible personal property;

b. Does not include items of income specifically dealt with in other articles of this Convention, except as provided in such articles.

Subject to the provisions of this Convention, items of income excluded from industrial or commercial profits under subparagraph *b.* may be taxed separately or together with industrial or commercial profits in accordance with the laws of the Contracting State whose tax is being determined.

Article 8. Shipping and Transport

1. Notwithstanding Article 7 (Business Profits) and Article 13 (Capital Gains), income which a resident of one of the Contracting States derives from the operation in international traffic of ships registered in that Contracting State, and gains which a resident of one of the Contracting States derives from the sale, exchange, or other disposition of ships operated in international traffic by such resident and registered in that Contracting State, shall be exempt from tax by the other Contracting State.

2. Notwithstanding Article 7 (Business Profits) and Article 13 (Capital Gains), income which a resident of one of the Contracting States derives from the operation in international traffic of aircraft registered in either Contracting State or in a State with which the other Contracting State has an income tax convention exempting such income, and gains which a resident of one of the Contracting States derives from the sale, exchange, or other disposition of aircraft operated in international traffic by such resident and registered in either Contracting State or in a State with which the other Contracting State has an income tax convention exempting such income, shall be exempt from tax by the other Contracting State.

Article 9. Associated Enterprises

1. Where a resident of one of the Contracting States and a resident of the other Contracting State are related and where such related persons make arrangements or impose conditions between themselves which are different from those which would be made between independent persons, then any income which would, but for those arrangements or conditions, have accrued to the resident of the first-mentioned Con-

tracting State but, by reason of those arrangements or conditions, has not so accrued, may be included in the income of the resident of the first-mentioned Contracting State for purposes of this Convention and taxed accordingly.

2. A person is related to another person for purposes of this Convention if either person participates directly or indirectly in the management, control, or capital of the other, or if any third person or persons participate directly or indirectly in the management, control, or capital of both.

Article 10. Dividends

1. Dividends paid by a company which is a resident of a Contracting State to a resident of the other Contracting State may be taxed in that other State.

2. However, such dividends may also be taxed in the Contracting State of which the company paying the dividends is a resident, and according to the laws of that State, but if the beneficial owner of the dividends is a resident of the other Contracting State, the tax so charged shall not exceed:

a. 5 per cent of the gross amount of the dividends if the beneficial owner is a company which owns directly at least 10 per cent of the voting stock of the company paying the dividends;

b. 15 per cent of the gross amount of the dividends in all other cases.

This paragraph shall not affect the taxation of the company in respect of the profits out of which the dividends are paid.

3. The term 'dividends' as used in this Article means income from shares, 'jouissance' shares or 'jouissance' rights, mining shares, founders' shares or other rights, not being debt-claims, participating in profits, as well as income from other corporate rights which is subjected to the same taxation treatment as income from shares by the laws of the State of which the company making the distribution is a resident. The term also includes income – even if paid in the form of interest – which is taxable as income from capital invested by the members of a company, other than a company with share capital, which is a resident of Belgium.

4. The provisions of paragraph 1 and 2 shall not apply if the beneficial owner of the dividends, being a resident of a Contracting State, carries on business in the other Contracting State of which the company paying the dividends is a resident, through a permanent establishment situated therein, or performs in that other State independent personal services from a fixed base situated therein, and the holding in respect of which the dividends are paid forms part of the assets of such permanent establishment or fixed base. In such case, the provisions of Article 7 (Business Profits) or Article 14 (Independent Personal Services), as the case may be, shall apply.

5. Where a company which is a resident of a Contracting State pays dividends, the other Contracting State may not impose any tax on the dividends paid by that company to a resident of the first-mentioned

State, except insofar as the holding in respect of which the dividends are paid from part of the assets of a permanent establishment or a fixed base situated in that other State.

6. For the purpose of paragraph 4 and notwithstanding any other provision of the Convention, dividends paid by a company which is a resident of Belgium in respect of a holding which forms part of the assets of a permanent establishment situated in Belgium, may be taxed separately in accordance with Belgian law.

Article 11. Interest

1. Interest derived from sources within one of the Contracting States by a resident of the other Contracting State may be taxed by both Contracting States.

2. The rate of tax imposed by one of the Contracting States on interest derived from sources within that Contracting State by a resident of the other Contracting State shall not exceed 15 per cent.

3. Notwithstanding paragraph 1 and 2, interest derived by a resident of one of the Contracting States from sources in the other Contracting State shall be exempt from tax by the other Contracting State if it is:

a. Interest arising out of commercial credit – including credit which is represented by commercial paper – resulting from deferred payments for goods or merchandise or services supplied by a resident of one of the Contracting States to a resident of the other Contracting State.

b. Interest paid between banks, except on loans represented by bearer instruments, or

c. Interest arising from deposits, not represented by bearer instruments, made in banks or other financial institutions.

4. Notwithstanding paragraphs 1 and 2, interest beneficially derived by one of the Contracting States, or by an instrumentality of that Contracting State, not subject to tax by that Contracting State on its income, shall be exempt from tax by the other Contracting State.

5. The term 'interest' as used in this Convention means income from bonds, Government securities, notes or other evidences of indebtedness, whether or not secured and whether or not carrying a right to participate in profits, and debt-claims of every kind, as well as all other income assimilated to income from money lent by the taxation law of the Contracting State in which the income has its source, but not interest which is considered as dividends in accordance with the second sentence of paragraph 3 of Article 10 (Dividends); it includes, in the case of Belgium, prizes on lottery bonds.

6. Interest shall be treated as income from sources within a Contracting State only if paid by such Contracting State, a political subdivision or a local authority thereof, or by a resident of that Contracting State. Notwithstanding the preceding sentence:

a. If the person paying the interest (whether or not such person is a resident of one of the Contracting States) has a permanent establishment in one of the Contracting States in connection with which the indebtedness on which the interest is paid was incurred and such interest is borne by such permanent establishment, or *b.* If the person paying the interest is a resident of one of the Contracting States and has a permanent establishment in a State other than a Contracting State in connection with which the indebtedness on which the interest is paid was incurred and such interest is paid to a resident of the other Contracting State, and such interest is borne by such permanent establishment,

such interest shall be deemed to be from sources within the State in which the permanent establishment is situated.

7. Paragraphs 2, 3, and 4 shall not apply if the recipient of the interest, being a resident of one of the Contracting States, has a permanent establishment in the other Contracting State and the indebtedness giving rise to the interest is effectively connected with such permanent establishment. In such a case, the provisions of Article 7 (Business Profits) shall apply.

8. Where any interest paid by a person to any related person exceeds an amount which would have been paid to an unrelated person, the provisions of this article shall apply only to so much of the interest as would have been paid to an unrelated person. In such a case the excess payment may be taxed according to its own law by the Contracting State from which the interest is derived.

9. Interest paid by a resident of one of the Contracting States to a person other than a resident of the other Contracting State shall be exempt from tax by that other Contracting State. This paragraph shall not apply if:

a. Such interest is treated as income from sources within that other Contracting State under paragraph 6;

b. The recipient of the interest has a permanent establishment in that other Contracting State and the indebtedness giving rise to the interest is effectively connected with such permanent establishment, or

c. Such interest is from sources within the United States and is received within Belgium by a person who is not a citizen or resident of the United States.

Article 12. Royalties

1. Royalties from sources within one of the Contracting States by a resident of the other Contracting State shall be exempt from tax by the first-mentioned Contracting State.

2. The term 'royalties' as used in this article means:

a. Payment of any kind made as consideration for the use of, or the right to use, copyrights of literary, artistic or scientific works (but not including copyrights of motion picture films or films or tapes used for radio or television broadcasting), patents, designs, models, plans, secret processes or formulae, trademarks or other like property or rights, or knowledge, experience, or skill (know-how), and

b. Gains derived from the sale, exchange, or other disposition of any such right or property to the extent that the amounts realized on such sale, exchange, or other disposition for consideration are contingent on the productivity, use or disposition of such property or right.

3. Royalties shall be treated as income from sources within one of the Contracting States only if paid by such Contracting State, a political subdivision or a local authority thereof, or by a resident of that Contracting State. Notwithstanding the preceding sentence:

a. If the person paying the royalties (whether or not such a person is a resident of one of the Contracting States) has a permanent establishment in one of the Contracting States with which the right or property giving rise to the royalties is effectively connected and such royalties are borne by such permanent establishment, or

b. If the person paying the royalties is a resident of one of the Contracting States and has a permanent establishment in a State other than a Contracting State with which the right or property giving rise to the royalties is effectively connected and such royalties are borne by such permanent establishment,

such royalties shall be deemed to be from sources within the State in which the permanent establishment is situated.

4. Paragraph 1 shall not apply if the recipient of the royalty, being a resident of one of the Contracting States, has in the other Contracting State a permanent establishment and the right or property giving rise to the royalty is effectively connected with such permanent establishment. In such a case the provisions of Article 7 (Business Profits) shall apply.

5. Where any royalty paid by a person to any related person exceeds an amount which would have been paid to an unrelated person, the provisions of this article shall apply only to so much of the royalty as would have been paid to an unrelated person. In such a case the excess payment may be taxed according to its own law by the Contracting State from which the royalty is derived.

Article 12A. Limitation on Benefits

1. A person (other than an individual) which is a resident of a Contracting State and derives dividends, interest or royalties from the other Contracting State shall not be entitled under Articles 10 (Dividends), 11 (Interest) or 12 (Royalties) to relief from taxation in that other Contracting State unless:

a. both of the following conditions are satisfied:

(i) more than 50 per cent of the beneficial interest in such person (or in the case of a company, more than 50 per cent of the number of shares in each class of the company's shares) is owned, directly or indirectly, by one or more individual residents of one of the Contracting States, one of the Contracting States or its political subdivisions or local authorities, or citizens of the United States; and

(ii) more than 50 per cent of the gross income of such person is not used, directly or indirectly, to meet liabilities for interest or royalties to persons who are not residents of one of the Contracting States, one of the Contracting States or its political subdivisions or local authorities, or citizens of the United States; or

b. the dividends, interest or royalties derived from the other Contracting State are derived in connection with, or are incidental to, the active conduct by such person of a trade or business in the first-mentioned State (other than a business the principal activities of which are making or managing investments in the other Contracting State); or

c. the person deriving the dividends, interest or royalties is a resident of a Contracting State either in whose principal class of shares there is substantial and regular trading on a recognized securities exchange, or more than 50 per cent of whose shares of each class is owned by a resident of that Contracting State in whose principal class of shares there is such substantial and regular trading on a recognized securities exchange.

2. For purposes of subparagraph 1*a.*(ii), the term 'gross income' means:

a. in the case of the United States, gross income as defined under the Internal Revenue Code of 1986, as may be amended from time to time, without regard to the geographic source of the income.

b. in the case of Belgium, gross receipts, or where an enterprise is engaged in a business which includes the manufacture or production of goods, gross receipts reduced by the direct costs of labor and materials attributable to such manufacture or production and paid or payable out of such receipts.

3. For purposes of subparagraph 1*c.*, the term 'recognized securities exchange' means:

a. the NASDAQ System owned by the National Association of Securities Dealers, Inc. and any stock exchange registered with the Securities and Exchange Commission as a national securities exchange for purposes of the Securities Exchange Act of 1934;

b. the Belgian stock exchanges; and

c. any other securities exchanges agreed upon by the competent authorities of the Contracting States.

Article 13. Capital Gains

Gains derived by a resident of one of the Contracting States from the sale, exchange, or other disposition of capital assets shall be exempt from tax by the other Contracting State unless:

1. The gain is derived by a resident of the first-mentioned Contracting State from the sale, exchange, or other disposition of property described in Article 6 (Income from Real Property) situated within that other Contracting State.

2. The recipient of the gain, being a resident of the first-mentioned Contracting State, has a permanent establishment or maintains a fixed base in that other Contracting State and the property giving rise to the gain is effectively connected with such permanent establishment or such fixed base, or

3. The recipient of the gain, being an individual resident of the first-mentioned Contracting State, is present in that other Contracting State for a period or periods aggregating 183 days or more in the taxable year.

If under the provisions of paragraph 2 the property is effectively connected with a permanent establishment, the provisions of Article 7 (Business Profits) shall apply.

Article 14. Independent Personal Services

1. Income derived by an individual who is a resident of one of the Contracting States from the performance of personal services in an independent capacity, may be taxed by that Contracting State. Except as provided in paragraph 2, such income shall be exempt from tax by the other Contracting State.

2. Income derived by an individual who is a resident of one of the Contracting States from the performance of personal services in an independent capacity in the other Contracting State may be taxed by that other Contracting State, if:

a. The individual is present in that other Contracting State for a period or periods aggregating 183 days or more in the taxable year;

b. The individual maintains a fixed base in that other Contracting State for a period or periods aggregating 183 days or more in the taxable year, and the income is attributable to such fixed base; or

c. The individual derives the income from personal services as a public entertainer, such as a theatrical, motion picture, or television artist, a musician, or an athlete, unless such individual is present in that other Contracting State for a period or periods not exceeding a total of 90 days during the taxable year and such income does not exceed in the aggregate 3,000 United States dollars or its equivalent in Belgian francs during the taxable year.

Article 15. Dependent Personal Services

1. Wages, salaries, and similar remuneration derived by an individual who is a resident of one of the Contracting States from labor or personal services performed as an employee, including income from services performed by an officer of a company, may be taxed by that Contracting State. Except as provided by paragraph 2 and Article 20 (Teachers) and Article 21 (Students and Trainees) such remuneration derived from labor or personal services performed in the other Contracting State may also be taxed in that other Contracting State.

2. Remuneration described in paragraph 1 derived by an individual who is a resident of one of the Contracting States shall be exempt from tax by the other Contracting State if:

a. He is present in that other Contracting State for a period or periods aggregating less than 183 days in the taxable year;

b. He is an employee of a resident of the first-mentioned Contracting State or of a permanent establishment maintained in the first-mentioned Contracting State; and

c. The remuneration is not borne as such by a permanent establishment which the employer has in that other Contracting State.

3. Notwithstanding paragraphs 1 and 2, remuneration derived by an individual from labor or personal services performed as an employee aboard ships or aircraft registered in one of the Contracting States and

operated by a resident of that Contracting State in international traffic shall be exempt from tax by the other Contracting State if such individual is a member of the regular complement of the ship or aircraft.

Article 16. Directors' Fees

Notwithstanding Articles 14 (Independent Personal Services) and 15 (Dependent Personal Services), a director's fee derived by an individual who is a resident of one of the Contracting States in his capacity as a member of the board of directors of a corporation of the other Contracting State (but not including fixed or contingent payments derived in his capacity as an officer or employee), which cannot be taken as a deduction by the corporation but is treated in that other Contracting State as a distribution of profits, may be taxed by that other Contracting State.

Article 17. Social Security Payments

1. Social security payments and similar pensions paid by, or out of public funds created by, one of the Contracting States or a governmental instrumentality thereof to an individual who is a resident of the other Contracting State shall be taxable only in the first-mentioned Contracting State.

Article 18. Private Pensions and Annuities

1. Except as provided in Articles 17 (Social Security Payments) and 19 (Governmental Functions), pensions and other similar remuneration paid to an individual who is a resident of one of the Contracting States in consideration of past employment shall be taxable only in that Contracting State.

2. Alimony and annuities paid to an individual who is a resident of one of the Contracting States shall be taxable only in that Contracting State.

3. The term 'pensions and other similar remuneration', as used in this article, means periodic payments made after retirement or death in consideration for services rendered, or by way of compensation for injuries received in connection with past employment.

4. The term 'annuities', as used in this article, means a stated sum paid periodically at stated times during life, or during a specified number of years, under an obligation to make the payments in return for adequate and full consideration (other than for services rendered).

Article 19. Government Functions

1. Notwithstanding Articles 15 (Dependent Personal Services), 17 (Social Security Payments), and 18 (Private Pensions and Annuities), wages, salaries, and similar remuneration, including pensions or similar benefits, paid by or from public funds of one of the Contracting States, or a political subdivision or local authority thereof, for labor or personal services performed for that Contracting State, or for any of its political subdivisions or local authorities, in the discharge of governmental functions:

a. To a citizen of that Contracting State or

b. To a citizen of a State other than a Contracting State and who comes to the other Contracting State expressly for the purpose of being employed by the first-mentioned Contracting State, or a political subdivision or local authority thereof,

shall be exempt from tax by that other Contracting State.

2. The provisions of Articles 15 (Dependent Personal Services), 17 (Social Security Payments), and 18 (Private Pensions and Annuities) shall apply to wages, salaries, and pensions paid in respect of services rendered in connection with any trade or business carried on by the first-mentioned Contracting State, or a political subdivision or local authority thereof.

Article 20. Teachers

1. An individual who is a resident of one of the Contracting States at the time he becomes temporarily present in the other Contracting State and who, at the invitation of the Government of that other Contracting State or of a university or other recognized educational institution in that other Contracting State is temporarily present in that other Contracting State for the primary purpose of teaching or engaging in research, or both, at a university or other recognized educational institution shall be exempt from tax by that other Contracting State on his income from personal services for teaching or research at such university or educational institution, for a period not exceeding 2 years from the date of his arrival in that other Contracting State.

2. This article shall not apply to income from research if such research is undertaken not in the public interest but primarily for the private benefit of a specific person or persons.

Article 21. Students and Trainees

1. *a.* An individual who is a resident of one of the Contracting States at the time he becomes temporarily present in the other Contracting State and who is temporarily present in that other Contracting State for the primary purpose of:

(i) Studying at a university or other recognized educational institution in that other Contracting State, or

(ii) Securing training required to qualify him to practice a profession of professional specialty, or

(iii) Studying or doing research as a recipient of a grant, allowance, or award from a governmental, religious, charitable, scientific, literary, or educational organization,

shall be exempt from the tax by that other Contracting State with respect to amounts described in subparagraph *b.* for a period not exceeding 5 taxable years from the date of his arrival in that other Contracting State.

b. The amounts referred to in subparagraph *a.* are:

(i) Gifts from abroad for the purpose of his maintenance, education, study, research, or training;

(ii) The grant, allowance, or award; and

(iii) Income from personal services performed in that other Contracting State in an amount not in excess of 2,000 United States dollars or its equivalent in Belgian francs for any taxable year.

2. An individual who is a resident of one of the Contracting States at the time he becomes temporarily present in the other Contracting State as an employee of, or under contract with, a resident in the first-mentioned Contracting State, for the primary purpose of:

a. Acquiring technical, professional, or business experience from a person other than that resident of the first-mentioned Contracting State or other than a person related to such resident, or

b. Studying at a university or other recognized educational institution in that other Contracting State,

shall be exempt from tax by that other Contracting State for a period of 12 consecutive months with respect to his income from personal services in an aggregate amount not in excess of 5,000 United States dollars or its equivalent in Belgian francs.

3. An individual who is a resident of one of the Contracting States at the time he becomes temporarily present in the other Contracting State and who is temporarily present in that other Contracting State for a period not exceeding 1 year, as a participant in a program sponsored by the Government of that other Contracting State, for the primary purpose of training, research, or study, shall be exempt from tax by that other Contracting State with respect to his income from personal services in respect of such training, research, or study performed in that other Contracting State in an aggregate amount not in excess of 10,000 United States dollars or its equivalent in Belgian francs.

4. The benefits provided under Article 20 (Teachers) and paragraph 1 of this article shall extend only for such period of time as may reasonably or customarily be required to effectuate the purpose of the visit, but in no case shall any individual have the benefits provided therein for more than a total of 5 taxable years from the date of his arrival.

Article 22. Income Not Expressly Mentioned

Items of income of a resident of one of the Contracting States which are not expressly mentioned in the foregoing articles of this Convention shall be taxable only in that Contracting State except that if such income is derived from sources within the other Contracting State, that Contracting State may also tax such income.

Article 23. Relief from Double Taxation

1. Notwithstanding any other provision of this Convention, a Contracting State may tax its citizens and residents as determined under Article 4 (Fiscal Domicile) as if this Convention had not come into effect, provided however, that:

a. This provision shall not affect the benefits conferred by a Contracting State under this article and Articles 17 (Social Security Payments), 24 (Nondiscrimination), and 25 (Mutual Agreement Procedure).

b. This provision shall not affect the benefits conferred by a Contracting State under Articles 19 (Governmental Functions), 20 (Teachers), and 21 (Students and Trainees), upon individuals who are neither citizens of, nor have immigrant status in, that Contracting State.

2. Subject to the provisions of United States law as applicable for the taxable year, the United States shall allow to a citizen or resident of the United States as a credit against United States tax the appropriate amount of Belgian tax; such appropriate amount shall be based upon the amount of tax paid to Belgium but shall not exceed the amount of United States tax attributable to income from Belgian sources. Income which has been taxed by Belgium in accordance with Articles 6 through 21 shall, for the purpose of applying the United States credit in relation to Belgian tax, be treated as income from Belgian sources..

3. In the case of income derived from sources in the United States, relief from double taxation shall be granted in Belgium in the following manner:

a. Where a resident of Belgium derives income which is not subject to the provisions of subparagraph *b.* through *d.* below and which has been taxed by the United States in accordance with Article 6 through 21, Belgium shall exempt such income from tax but may, in calculating the amount of tax on the remainder of the income of that resident, apply the rate of tax which would have been applicable if such income had not been exempted.

b. Where a resident of Belgium receives dividends (which are not exempt under subparagraph *d.*) to which the provisions of paragraph 2 of Article 10 (Dividends) apply, interest to which the provisions of paragraph 2 or paragraph 8 of Article 11 (Interest) apply or royalties to which the provisions of paragraph 5 of Article 12 (Royalties) apply, Belgium shall reduce the Belgian tax imposed thereon by a credit in respect of the tax borne in the United States. The credit shall be allowed against the tax imposed on the net amount of the dividends from corporations of the United States, as well as of interest and royalties from sources in the United States which have been taxed there; the credit shall be the fixed amount in respect of the foreign tax for which provision is made in existing Belgian law, subject to any subsequent modification – which, however, shall not affect the principle hereof.

c. Where a resident of Belgium receives income to which the provisions of Article 22 (Income Not Expressly Mentioned) apply and which has been taxed by the United States, the amount of Belgian tax proportionately attributable to such income shall not exceed the amount which would be imposed in accordance with Belgian law, if such income were taxed as earned income derived from sources outside Belgium and subject to foreign tax.

d. Where a Belgian corporation owns shares in a United States corporation which is subject in the United States to tax on its profits, the dividends which are paid to it by the latter corporation and which may be taxed in the United States in accordance with the provisions of paragraph 2 of Article 10 (Dividends) shall be exempt from the corporate income tax in Belgium to the extent that exemption would have been accorded if the two corporations had been corporations of Belgium; this provision shall not prohibit the withholding from those dividends of the movable property prepayment (*précompte mobilier*) imposed by Belgian law.

e. A Belgian corporation which, during the whole of an accounting period of a United States corporation which is subject there to tax on its profits, has held the direct ownership of shares in the latter corporation, shall also be exempted from the movable property prepayment (*précompte mobilier*) imposed by Belgian law on the dividends derived from those shares, provided that it so requests in writing not later than the time limited for the submission of its annual return; on the redistribution to its own shareholders of the dividends so exempted those dividends may not be deducted from dividends distributed by that corporation which are subject to the movable property prepayment (*précompte mobilier*). This subparagraph shall not apply when the first-mentioned corporation has elected that its profits be charged to the individual income tax. However, the application of this subparagraph shall be limited to dividends paid by a United States corporation to a Belgian corporation which controls not less than 10 per cent of the voting power in the first-mentioned corporation where, for the application of the exemption referred to in subparagraph *d.*, a similar limitation would be imposed by Belgian legislation in respect of dividends paid by corporations of Belgium.

f. Where an individual who is a resident of Belgium and a citizen of the United States receives income from sources within the United States which is not exempt from Belgian tax under subparagraph *a.* nor covered by subparagraph *c.*, the amount of the Belgian individual income tax proportionately attributable to such income may not exceed:

(i) In the case of dividends, interest, and royalties, an amount which, after allowance of the fixed amount in respect of the foreign tax, where applicable, corresponds to 20 per cent of such income;

(ii) In the case of other income concerned, the amount which would be imposed in accordance with Belgian law, if such income were taxed as earned income derived from sources outside Belgium and subject to foreign tax.

g. When in accordance with Belgian law, losses incurred by a resident of Belgium in a permanent establishment situated in the United States have been effectively deducted from the profits of that resident for his taxation in Belgium, the exemption provided in subparagraph *a.* shall not apply in Belgium to the profits of other taxable periods attributable to that establishment to the extent that those profits have also been reduced for United States tax purposes by reason of compensation for the said losses.

4. In the case of a corporation which is treated as a United States corporation for United States tax purposes and as a Belgian corporation for Belgian tax purposes, relief from double taxation shall be granted in accordance with the principles of paragraphs 2 and 3.

Article 24. Nondiscrimination

1. A citizen of one of the Contracting States who is a resident of the other Contracting State shall not be subject in that other Contracting State to more burdensome taxes than a citizen of that other Contracting State who is a resident thereof.

2. A permanent establishment which a resident of one of the Contracting States has in the other Contracting State shall not be subject in that other Contracting State to more burdensome taxes than a resident of that other Contracting State carrying on the same activities. This paragraph shall not be construed as obliging a Contracting State to grant to individual residents of the other Contracting State any personal allowances, reliefs, or deductions for taxation purposes on account of civil status or family responsibilities which it grants to its own individual residents.

3. A corporation of one of the Contracting States, the capital of which is wholly or partly owned or controlled, directly or indirectly, by one or more residents of the other Contracting State, shall not be subjected in the first-mentioned Contracting State to any taxation or any requirement connected therewith which is other or more burdensome than the taxation or connected requirements to which a corporation of the first-mentioned Contracting State carrying on the same activities, the capital of which is wholly owned or controlled by one or more residents of the first-mentioned Contracting State, is or may be subjected.

4. The provisions of this article shall apply to taxes of every kind whether imposed at the National, State, or local level.

5. The provisions of paragraph 2 shall not be construed as preventing Belgium from taxing the total profits attributable to a permanent establishment which is maintained in Belgium by a United States corporation, or any unincorporated entity, which is a resident of the United States at a rate which – before the application of the surcharges specified in paragraph 1*b.*(vi) of Article 2 – is the highest rate at which the profits of a Belgian corporation may be taxed.

a. However, as long as Belgium imposes its tax on the distributed profits of a Belgian corporation at a rate which is lower than such highest rate then the Belgian tax on the portion of the profits of the permanent establishment which is deemed to be distributed shall be imposed at a rate which – before the application of the surcharges specified in paragraph 1*b.*(vi) of Article 2 – shall not exceed the highest rate at which such tax may be imposed on the distributed profits of a Belgian corporation.

b. For purposes of this paragraph, the permanent establishment which is maintained in Belgium shall be deemed to distribute the same percentage of its profits as such resident distributes from its total profits.

Article 25. Mutual Agreement Procedure

1. Where a resident of one of the Contracting States considers that the action of one or both of the Contracting States results or will result

for him in taxation not in accordance with this Convention, he may, notwithstanding the remedies provided by the national laws of the Contracting States, present his case to the competent authority of the Contracting State of which he is a resident within 2 years from the date of notification (or collection at source) of the tax which has been last asserted or collected. Should the resident's claim be considered to have merit by the competent authority of the Contracting State to which the claim is made, the competent authority shall endeavor to come to an agreement with the competent authority of the other Contracting State with a view to the avoidance of taxation contrary to the provisions of this Convention.

2. The competent authorities of the Contracting States shall endeavor to resolve by mutual agreement any difficulties or doubts arising as to the application of this Convention. In particular, the competent authorities of the Contracting States may agree:

a. To the same attribution of industrial or commercial profits to a resident of one of the Contracting States and its permanent establishment situated in the other Contracting State;

b. To the same allocation of income, deductions, credits, or allowances between a resident of one of the Contracting States and any related persons;

c. To the same determination of the source of particular items of income; or

d. To the same meaning of any term used in this Convention.

3. The competent authorities of the Contracting States may communicate with each other directly for the purpose of reaching an agreement in the sense of this article. When it seems advisable for the purpose of reaching an agreement, the competent authorities may meet together for an oral exchange of opinions.

4. In the event that the competent authorities reach such an agreement, taxes on such income shall be adjusted and refund or credit of taxes shall be allowed, by the Contracting States in accordance with such agreement.

Article 26. Exchange of Information

1. The competent authorities of the Contracting States shall exchange such information as is pertinent to carrying out the provisions of this Convention or preventing fraud or fiscal evasion in relation to the taxes which are the subject of this Convention. Any information so exchanged shall be treated as secret and shall not be disclosed to any persons other than those (including a court or administrative body) concerned with assessment, collection, enforcement, or prosecution in respect of the taxes which are the subject of this Convention.

2. In no case shall the provisions of paragraph 1 be construed so as to impose on one of the Contracting States the obligation:

a. To carry out administrative measures at variance with the laws or the administrative practice of that Contracting State or the other Contracting State;

b. To supply particulars which are not obtainable under the laws, or in the normal course of the administration, of that Contracting State or of the other Contracting State; or

c. To supply information which would disclose any trade, business, industrial, commercial, or professional secret or trade process or information, the disclosure of which would be contrary to public policy.

3. The exchange of information shall be either on a routine basis or on request with reference to particular cases. The competent authorities of the Contracting States may agree on the list of information which shall be furnished on a routine basis.

Article 27. Assistance in Collection

1. Each of the Contracting States shall endeavor to collect on behalf of the other Contracting State such taxes imposed by that other Contracting State as will ensure that any exemption or reduced rate of tax granted under this Convention by that other Contracting State shall not be enjoyed by persons not entitled to such benefits.

2. In no case shall this article be construed so as to impose upon a Contracting State the obligation to carry out administrative measures at variance with the regulations and practices of either Contracting State or which would be contrary to the first-mentioned Contracting State's sovereignty, security, or public policy.

Article 28. Miscellaneous

1. Nothing in this Convention shall affect the fiscal privileges of diplomatic and consular officials under the general rules of international law or under the provisions of special agreements.

2. The provisions of this Convention shall not be construed to restrict in any manner any exclusion, exemption, deduction, credit, or other allowance now or hereafter accorded:

a. By the laws of one of the Contracting States in the determination of the tax imposed by that Contracting State, or

b. By any other agreement between the Contracting States.

3. The competent authorities of the two Contracting States may communicate with each other directly for the purpose of carrying out the provisions of this Convention.

Article 29. Extension to Territories

1. The United States may, at any given time while this Convention continues in force, by a written notification given to Belgium through diplomatic channels, declare its desire that the operation of this Convention, either in whole or in part or with such modifications as may be found necessary for special application in a particular case, shall extend to all or any of the areas (to which this Convention is not otherwise applicable) for whose international relations it is responsible and which impose taxes substantially similar in character to those which are the subject of this Convention. When Belgium has, by a written communication through diplomatic channels, signified to the United States that such notification is accepted in respect of such area or areas,

and the notification and communication have been ratified and instruments of ratification exchanged, this Convention, in whole or in part, or with such modifications as may be found necessary for special application in a particular case, as specified in the notification, shall apply to the area or areas named in the notification and shall have effect on and after the date or dates specified therein.

2. At any time after the date of entry into force of an extension under paragraph 1, either of the Contracting States may, by 6 months' prior notice of termination given to the other Contracting State through diplomatic channels, terminate the application of this Convention to any area to which it has been extended under paragraph 1, and in such event this Convention shall cease to have effect, beginning on or after the first day of January next following the expiration of the 6-month period, in the area or areas named therein, but without affecting its continued application to the United States, Belgium, or any other area to which it has been extended under paragraph 1.

3. In the application of this Convention in relation to any area to which it is extended by notification by the United States, reference to the 'United States' shall be construed as referring to that area.

4. The termination in respect of the United States or Belgium of this Convention under Article 31 (Termination) shall, unless otherwise expressly agreed by both Contracting States, terminate the application of this Convention to any area to which the Convention has been extended under this article.

Article 30. Entry into Force

1. This Convention shall be ratified and instruments of ratification shall be exchanged at Washington as soon as possible. It shall enter into force 1 month after the date of exchange of the instruments of ratification. The provisions shall for the first time have effect with respect to income of calendar years or taxable years beginning (or, in the case of taxes payable at the source, payments made) on or after January 1, 1971.

2. As between the United States and Belgium, the Convention between Belgium and the United States for the Avoidance of Double Taxation and the Prevention of Fiscal Evasion with respect to Taxes on Income signed at Washington, D.C. on October 28, 1948; modified and supplemented by the Supplementary Conventions signed at Washington on September 9, 1952, and August 22, 1957, and by the Protocol signed at Brussels on May 21, 1965, shall terminate and cease to have effect in respect of income to which this Convention applies under paragraph 1 of this article.

Article 31. Termination

1. This Convention shall remain in force until terminated by one of the Contracting States. Either Contracting State may terminate the Convention at any time after 5 years from the date on which this Convention enters into force provided that at least 6 months' prior notice of termination has been given through diplomatic channels. In such event

the Convention shall cease to have effect as respects income of calendar years or taxable years beginning (or, in the case of taxes payable at the source, payments made) on or after January 1 next following the expiration of the 6-month period.

2. Notwithstanding the provision of paragraph 1, and upon prior notice to be given through diplomatic channels, the provisions of Article 17 (Social Security Payments) may be terminated by either Contracting State at any time after this Convention enters into force.

In witness whereof, the respective Plenipotentiaries have signed this Convention and have affixed their seals.

Done at Brussels, this 9th day of July, 1970, in duplicate, in the English, French, and Dutch languages, the three texts having equal authenticity.

Canada

Convention between the United States of America and Canada with Respect to Taxes on Income and on Capital, concluded in Washington on September 26, 1980, as amended by the Protocol of June 14, 1983 and March 28, 1984.

The United States of America and Canada, Desiring to conclude a Convention for the avoidance of double taxation and the prevention of fiscal evasion with respect to taxes on income and capital,

Have agreed as follows:

Article I. Personal Scope

This Convention is generally applicable to persons who are residents of one or both of the Contracting States.

Article II. Taxes Covered

1. This Convention shall apply to taxes on income and on capital imposed on behalf of each Contracting State, irrespective of the manner in which they are levied.

2. The existing taxes to which the Convention shall apply are:

a. In the case of Canada, the taxes imposed by the Government of Canada under Parts I, XIII and XIV of the Income Tax Act; and

b. In case of the United States, the Federal income taxes imposed by the Internal Revenue Code.

3. The Convention shall also apply to:

a. Any identical or substantially similar taxes on income; and

b. Taxes on capital which are imposed after the signature of the Convention in addition to, or in place of, the existing taxes.

4. Notwithstanding the provisions of paragraphs 2*b.* and 3, the Convention shall apply to:

a. The United States accumulated earnings tax and personal holding company tax, to the extent, and only to the extent, necessary to implement the provisions of paragraphs 5 and 8 of Article X (Dividends);

b. The United States excise taxes imposed with respect to private foundations, to the extent, and only to the extent, necessary to implement the provisions of paragraph 4 of Article XXI (Exempt Organizations); and

c. The United States social security taxes, to the extent, and only to the extent, necessary to implement the provisions of paragraph 4 of Article XXIX (Miscellaneous Rules).

Article III. General Definitions

1. For the purposes of this Convention, unless the context otherwise requires:

a. When used in a geographical sense, the term 'Canada' means the territory of Canada, including any area beyond the territorial seas of Canada which, in accordance with international law and the laws of Canada, is an area within which Canada may exercise rights with respect to the seabed and subsoil and their natural resources;

b. the term 'United States' means:

(i) The United States of America, but does not include Puerto Rico, the Virgin Islands, Guam or any other United States possession or territory; and

(ii) When used in a geographical sense, such term also includes any area beyond the territorial seas of the United States which, in accordance with international law and the laws of the United States, is an area within which the United States may exercise rights with respect to the seabed and subsoil and their natural resources;

c. The term 'Canadian tax' means the Canadian taxes referred to in paragraphs 2*a.* and 3*a.* of Article II (Taxes Covered);

d. The term 'United States tax' means the United States taxes referred to in paragraphs 2*b.* and 3*a.* of Article II (Taxes Covered);

e. The term 'person' includes an individual, an estate, a trust, a company and any other body of persons;

f. The term 'company' means any body corporate or any entity which is treated as a body corporate for tax purposes;

g. The term 'competent authority' means:

(i) In the case of Canada, the Minister of National Revenue or his authorized representative;

(ii) In the case of the United States, the Secretary of the Treasury or his delegate;

h. The term 'international traffic' with reference to a resident of a Contracting State means any voyage of a ship or aircraft to transport passengers or property (whether or not operated or used by that resident) except where the principal purpose of the voyage is to transport passengers or property between places within the other Contracting State;

i. The term 'State' means any National State, whether or not a Contracting State; and

j. The term 'the 1942 Convention' means the Convention and Protocol between the United States of America and Canada for the Avoidance of Double Taxation and the Prevention of Fiscal Evasion in the case of Income Taxes signed at Washington on March 4, 1942, as amended by the Convention signed at Ottawa on June 12, 1950, by the Convention signed at Ottawa on August 8, 1956 and by the Supplementary Convention signed at Washington on October 25, 1966.

2. As regards the application of the Convention by a Contracting State any term not defined therein shall, unless the context otherwise requires and subject to the provisions of Article XXVI (Mutual Agreement Procedure), have the meaning which it has under the law of that State concerning the taxes to which the Convention applies.

Article IV. Residence

1. For the purposes of this Convention, the term 'resident of a Contracting State' means any person who, under the laws of that State, is liable to tax therein by reason of his domicile, residence, place of management, place of incorporation or any other criterion of a similar nature, but in the case of an estate or trust, only to the extent that the income derived by such estate or trust is liable to tax in that State, either in its hands or in the hands of its beneficiaries.

2. Where by reason of the provisions of paragraph 1 an individual is a resident of both Contracting States, then his status shall be determined as follows:

a. He shall be deemed to be a resident of the Contracting State in which he has a permanent home available to him; if he has a permanent home available to him in both States or in neither State, he shall be deemed to be a resident of the Contracting State with which his personal and economic relations are closer (centre of vital interests);

b. If the Contracting State in which he has his centre of vital interests cannot be determined, he shall be deemed to be a resident of the Contracting State in which he has an habitual abode;

c. If he has an habitual abode in both States or in neither State, he shall be deemed to be a resident of the Contracting State of which he is a citizen; and

d. If he is a citizen of both States or of neither of them, the competent authorities of the Contracting States shall settle the question by mutual agreement.

3. Where by reason of the provisions of paragraph 1 a company is a resident of both Contracting States, then if it was created under the laws in force in a Contracting State, it shall be deemed to be a resident of that State.

4. Where by reason of the provisions of paragraph 1 an estate, trust or other person (other than an individual or a company) is a resident of both Contracting States, the competent authorities of the States shall by mutual agreement endeavor to settle the question and to determine the mode of application of the Convention to such person.

5. Notwithstanding the provisions of the preceding paragraphs, an individual shall be deemed to be a resident of a Contracting State if:

a. The individual is an employee of that State or of a political subdivision, local authority or instrumentality thereof rendering services in the discharge of functions of a governmental nature in the other Contracting State or in a third State; and

b. The individual is subjected in the first-mentioned State to similar obligations in respect of taxes on income as are residents of the first-mentioned State.

The spouse and dependent children residing with such an individual and meeting the requirements of subparagraph *b.* above shall also be deemed to be residents of the first-mentioned State.

Article V. Permanent Establishment

1. For the purposes of this Convention, the term 'permanent establishment' means a fixed place of business through which the business of a resident of a Contracting State is wholly or partly carried on.

2. The term 'permanent establishment' shall include especially:

a. A place of management;

b. A branch;

c. An office;

d. A factory;

e. A workshop; and

f. A mine, an oil or gas well, quarry or any other place of extraction of natural resources.

3. A building site or construction or installation project constitutes a permanent establishment if, but only if, it lasts more than 12 months.

4. The use of an installation of drilling rig or ship in a Contracting State to explore for or exploit natural resources constitutes a permanent establishment if, but only if, such use is for more than three months in any twelve-month period.

5. A person acting in a Contracting State on behalf of a resident of the other Contracting State – other than an agent of an independent status to whom paragraph 7 applies – shall be deemed to be a permanent establishment in the first-mentioned State if such person has, and habitually exercises in that State, an authority to conclude contracts in the name of the resident.

6. Notwithstanding the provisions of paragraphs 1, 2 and 5, the term 'permanent establishment' shall be deemed not to include a fixed place of business used solely for, or a person referred to in paragraph 5 engaged solely in, one or more of the following activities:

a. The use of facilities for the purpose of storage, display or delivery of goods or merchandise belonging to the resident;

b. The maintenance of a stock of goods or merchandise belonging to the resident for the purpose of storage, display or delivery;

c. The maintenance of a stock of goods or merchandise belonging to the resident for the purpose of processing by another person;

d. The purchase of goods or merchandise, or the collection of information, for the resident; and

e. Advertising, the supply of information, scientific research or similar activities which have a preparatory or auxiliary character, for the resident.

7. An resident of a Contracting State shall not be deemed to have a permanent establishment in the other Contracting State merely because such resident carries on business in that other State through a broker, general commission agent or any other agent of an independent status, provided that such persons are acting in the ordinary course of their business.

8. The fact that a company which is a resident of a Contracting State controls or is controlled by a company which is a resident of the other Contracting State, or which carries on business in that other State

(whether through permanent establishment or otherwise), shall not constitute either company a permanent establishment of the other.

9. For the purposes of the Convention, the provisions of this Article shall be applied in determining whether any person has a permanent establishment in any State.

Article VI. Income from Real Property

1. Income derived by a resident of a Contracting State from real property (including income from agriculture, forestry or other natural resources) situated in the other Contracting State may be taxed in that other State.

2. For the purposes of this Convention, the term 'real property' shall have the meaning which it has under the taxation laws of the Contracting State in which the property in question is situated and shall include any option or similar right in respect thereof. The term shall in any case include usufruct of real property, rights to explore for or to exploit mineral deposits, sources and other natural resources and rights to amounts computed by reference to the amount or value of production from such resources; ships and aircraft shall not be regarded as real property.

3. The provisions of paragraph 1 shall apply to income derived from the direct use, letting or use in any other form of real property and to income from the alienation of such property.

Article VII. Business Profits

1. The business profits of a resident of a Contracting State shall be taxable only in that State unless the resident carries on business in the other Contracting State through a permanent establishment situated therein. If the resident carries on, or has carried on, business as aforesaid, the business profits of the resident may be taxed in the other State but only so much of them as is attributable to that permanent establishment.

2. Subject to the provisions of paragraph 3, where a resident of a Contracting State carries on business in the other Contracting State through a permanent establishment situated therein, there shall in each Contracting State be attributed to that permanent establishment the business profits which it might be expected to make if it were a distinct and separate person engaged in the same or similar activities under the same or similar conditions and dealing wholly independently with the resident and with any other person related to the resident (within the meaning of paragraph 2 of Article IX (Related Persons).

3. In determining the business profits of a permanent establishment, there shall be allowed as deductions expenses which are incurred for the purposes of the permanent establishment, including executive and general administrative expenses so incurred, whether in the State in which the permanent establishment is situated or elsewhere. Nothing in this paragraph shall require a Contracting State to allow the deduction of any expenditure which, by reason of its nature, is not generally allowed as a deduction under the taxation laws of that State.

4. No business profits shall be attributed to a permanent establishment of a resident of a Contracting State by reason of the use thereof for either the mere purchase of goods or merchandise or the mere provision of executive, managerial or administrative facilities for such resident.

5. For the purposes of the preceding paragraphs, the business profits to be attributed to a permanent establishment shall be determined by the same method year by year unless there is good and sufficient reason to the contrary.

6. Where business profits include items of income which are dealt with separately in other Articles of this Convention, then the provisions of those Articles shall not be affected by the provisions of this Article.

7. For the purposes of the Convention, the business profits attributable to a permanent establishment shall include only those profits derived from the assets or activities of the permanent establishment.

Article VIII. Transportation

1. Notwithstanding the provisions of Article VII (Business Profits), XII (Royalties) and XIII (Gains), profits derived by a resident of a Contracting State from the operation of ships or aircraft in international traffic, and gains derived by a resident of a Contracting State from the alienation of ships, aircraft or containers (including trailers and related equipment for the transport of containers) used principally in international traffic, shall be exempt from tax in the other Contracting State.

2. For the purposes of this Convention, profits derived by a resident of a Contracting State from the operation of ships or aircraft in international traffic include profits from:

a. The rental of ships or aircraft operated in international traffic;

b. The use, maintenance or rental of containers (including trailers and related equipment for the transport of containers) used in international traffic; and

c. The rental of ships, aircraft or containers (including trailers and related equipment for the transport of containers) provided that such profits are incidental to profits referred to in paragraph 1, 2*a.* or 2*b.*.

3. Notwithstanding the provisions of Article VII (Business Profits), profits derived by a resident of a Contracting State from a voyage of a ship where the principal purpose of the voyage is to transport passengers or property between places in the other Contracting State may be taxed in that other State.

4. Notwithstanding the provisions of Articles VII (Business Profits) and XII (Royalties), profits of a resident of a Contracting State engaged in the operation of motor vehicles or a railway as a common carrier or a contract carrier derived from:

a. The transportation of passengers or property between a point outside the other Contracting State and any other point; or

b. The rental of motor vehicles (including trailers) or railway rolling stock, or the use, maintenance or rental of containers (including trailers and related equipment for the transport of containers) used to transport passengers or property between a point outside the other Contracting State and any other point

shall be exempt from tax in that other Contracting State.

5. The provisions of paragraphs 1, 3 and 4 shall also apply to profits or gains referred to in those paragraphs derived by a resident of a Contracting State from the participation in a pool, a joint business or an international operating agency.

6. Notwithstanding the provisions of Article XII (Royalties), profits derived by a resident of a Contracting State from the use, maintenance or rental of railway rolling stock, motor vehicles, trailers or containers (including trailers and related equipment for the transport of containers) used in the other Contracting State for a period or periods not expected to exceed in the aggregate 183 days in any twelve-month period shall be exempt from tax in the other Contracting State except to the extent that such profits are attributable to a permanent establishment in the other State and liable to tax in the other State by reason of Article VII (Business Profits).

Article IX. Related Persons

1. Where a person in a Contracting State and a person in the other Contracting State are related and where the arrangements between them differ from those which would be made between unrelated persons, each State may adjust the amount of the income, loss or tax payable to reflect the income, deductions, credits or allowances which would, but for those arrangements, have been taken into account in computing such income, loss or tax.

2. For the purposes of this Article, a person shall be deemed to be related to another person if either person participates directly or indirectly in the management or control of the other, or if any third person or persons participate directly or indirectly in the management or control of both.

3. Where an adjustment is made or to be made by a Contracting State in accordance with paragraph 1, the other Contracting State shall (notwithstanding any time or procedural limitations in the domestic law of that other State) make a corresponding adjustment to the income, loss or tax of the related person in that other State if:

a. It agrees with the first-mentioned adjustment; and

b. Within six years from the end of the taxable year to which the first-mentioned adjustment relates, the competent authority of the other State has been notified of the first-mentioned adjustment.

4. In the event that the notification referred to in paragraph 3 is not given within the time period referred to therein, and if the person to whom the first-mentioned adjustment relates has not received, as least six months prior to the expiration of such time period, notification of such adjustment from the Contracting State which has made or is to make such adjustment that State shall, notwithstanding the provisions of paragraph 1, not make the first-mentioned adjustment to the extent that such adjustment would give rise to double taxation.

5. The provisions of paragraphs 3 and 4 shall not apply in the case of fraud, wilful default or neglect or gross negligence.

Article X. Dividends

1. Dividends paid by a company which is a resident of a Contracting State to a resident of the other Contracting State may be taxed in that other State.

2. However, such dividends may also be taxed in the Contracting State of which the company paying the dividends is a resident and according to the laws of that State; but if a resident of the other Contracting State is the beneficial owner of such dividends, the tax so charged shall not exceed:

a. 10 per cent of the gross amount of the dividends if the beneficial owner is a company which owns at least 10 per cent of the voting stock of the company paying the dividends;

b. 15 per cent of the gross amount of the dividends in all other cases.

This paragraph shall not affect the taxation of the company in respect of the profits out of which the dividends are paid.

3. The term 'dividends' as used in this Article means income from shares and other rights, not being debt-claims, participating in profits, as well as income subjected to the same taxation treatment as income from shares by the taxation laws of the State of which the company making the distribution is a resident.

4. The provisions of paragraph 2 shall not apply if the beneficial owner of the dividends, being a resident of a Contracting State, carries on business in the other Contracting State of which the company paying the dividends is a resident, through a permanent establishment situated therein, or performs in that other State independent personal services from a fixed base situated therein, and the holding in respect of which the dividends are paid is effectively connected with such permanent establishment or fixed base. In such case, the provisions of Article VII (Business Profits) or Article XIV (Independent Personal Services), as the case may be, shall apply.

5. Where a company is a resident of one of the Contracting States, the other Contracting State may not impose any tax on dividends paid by the company, except insofar as such dividends are paid to a resident of that other State or insofar as the holding in respect of which the dividends are paid is effectively connected with a permanent establishment or a fixed base situated in that other State, nor subject the company's undistributed profits to a tax, even if the dividends paid or the undistributed profits consist wholly or partly of profits or income arising in such other State.

6. Nothing in this Convention shall be construed as preventing a Contracting State from imposing a tax on the earnings of a company attributable to permanent establishments in that State, in addition to the tax which would be chargeable on the earnings of a company which is a resident of that State, provided that any additional tax so imposed shall not exceed 10 per cent of the amount of such earnings which

have not been subjected to such additional tax in previous taxation years. For the purposes of this paragraph, the term 'earnings' means the amount by which the business profits attributable to permanent establishments in a Contracting State (including gains from the alienation of property forming part of the business property of such permanent establishments) in a year and previous years exceeds the sum of:

a. Business losses attributable to such permanent establishments (including losses from the alienation of property forming part of the business property of such permanent establishments) in such year and previous years;

b. All taxes, other than the additional tax referred to in this paragraph, imposed on such profits in that State;

c. The profits reinvested in that State, provided that where that State is Canada, such amount shall be determined in accordance with the existing provisions of the law of Canada regarding the computation of the allowance in respect of investment in property in Canada, and any subsequent modification of those provisions which shall not affect the general principle hereof; and

d. Five hundred thousand Canadian dollars ($500,000) or its equivalent in United States currency, less any amounts deducted by the company, or by an associated company with respect to the same or a similar business, under this subparagraph *d.*; for the purposes of this subparagraph *d.* a company is associated with another company if one company directly or indirectly controls the other, or both companies are directly or indirectly controlled by the same person or persons, or if the two companies deal with each other not at arm's length.

7. Notwithstanding the provisions of paragraph 5, a Contracting State, other than a Contracting State that imposes the additional tax on earnings referred to in paragraph 6, may tax a dividend paid by a company to the extent that the dividend is attributable to profits earned in taxable years beginning after the date of signature of the Convention if, for the three-year period ending with the close of the company's taxable period preceding the declaration of the dividend (or for such part of that three-year period as the company has been in existence, or for the first taxable year if the dividend was declared in that taxable year), at least 50 per cent of such company's gross income from all sources was included in the computation of the business profits attributable to a permanent establishment which such company had in that State; provided that where a resident of the other Contracting State is the beneficial owner of such dividend any tax so imposed on the dividend shall be subject to the limitations of paragraph 2 or the rules of paragraph 4, as the case may be.

8. Notwithstanding the provisions of paragraph 5, a company which is a resident of Canada and which has income subject to tax in the United States (without regard to the provisions of the Convention) may be liable to the United States accumulated earnings tax and personal holding company tax but only if 50 per cent or more in value of the outstanding voting shares of the company is owned, directly or indirectly, throughout the last half of its taxable year by citizens or residents

of the United States (other than citizens of Canada who do not have immigrant status in the United States or who have not been residents in the United States for more than three taxable years) or by residents of a third state.

Article XI. Interest

1. Interest arising in a Contracting State and paid to a resident of the other Contracting State may be taxed in that other State.

2. However, such interest may also be taxed in the Contracting State in which it arises, and according to the laws of that State; but if a resident of the other Contracting State is the beneficial owner of such interest, the tax so charged shall not exceed 15 per cent of the gross amount of the interest.

3. Notwithstanding the provisions of paragraph 2, interest arising in a Contracting State shall be exempt from tax in that State if:

a. The interest is beneficially owned by a resident of the other Contracting State, a political subdivision or local authority thereof or an instrumentality of such other State, subdivision or authority, and is not subject to tax by that other State;

b. The interest is beneficially owned by a resident of the other Contracting State and is paid with respect to debt obligations issued at arm's length and guaranteed or insured by that other State or a political subdivision thereof or an instrumentality of such other State or subdivision which is not subject to tax by that other State;

c. The interest is beneficially owned by a resident of the other Contracting State and is paid by the first-mentioned State, a political subdivision or local authority thereof or an instrumentality of such first-mentioned State, subdivision or authority which is not subject to tax by that first-mentioned State;

d. The interest is beneficially owned by a seller who is a resident of the other Contracting State and is paid by a purchaser in connection with the sale on credit of any equipment, merchandise or services, except where the sale is made between persons dealing with each other not at arm's length; or

e. The interest is paid by a company created under the laws in force in the other Contracting State with respect to an obligation entered into before the date of signature of this Convention, provided that such interest would have been exempt from tax in the first-mentioned State under Article XII of the 1942 Convention.

4. The term 'interest' as used in this Article means income from debt-claims of every kind, whether or not secured by mortgage, and whether or not carrying a right to participate in the debtor's profits, and in particular, income from government securities and income from bonds or debentures, including premiums and prizes attaching to such securities, bonds or debentures, as well as income assimilated to income from money lent by the taxation laws of the Contracting State in which the income arises. However, the term 'interest' does not include income dealt with in Article X (Dividends).

5. The provisions of paragraphs 2 and 3 shall not apply if the beneficial owner of the interest, being a resident of a Contracting State, carries on business in the other Contracting State in which the interest arises, through a permanent establishment situated therein, or performs in that other State independent personal services from a fixed base situated therein, and the debt-claim in respect of which the interest is paid is effectively connected with such permanent establishment or fixed base. In such case, the provisions of Article VII (Business Profits) or Article XIV (Independent Personal Services), as the case may be, shall apply.

6. For the purposes of this Article, interest shall be deemed to arise in a Contracting State when the payer is that State itself, or a political subdivision, local authority or resident of that State. Where, however, the person paying the interest, whether he is a resident of a Contracting State or not, has in a State other than that of which he is a resident a permanent establishment or a fixed base in connection with which the indebtedness on which the interest is paid was incurred, and such interest is borne by such permanent establishment or fixed base, then such interest shall be deemed to arise in the State in which the permanent establishment or fixed base is situated and not in the State of which the payer is a resident.

7. Where, by reason of a special relationship between the payer and the beneficial owner or between both of them and some other person, the amount of the interest, having regard to the debt-claim for which it is paid, exceeds an amount which would have been agreed upon by the payer and the beneficial owner in the absence of such relationship, the provisions of this Article shall apply only to the last-mentioned amount. In such case, the excess part of the payments shall remain taxable according to the laws of each Contracting State, due regard being had to the other provisions of the Convention.

8. Where a resident of a Contracting State pays interest to a person other than a resident of the other Contracting State, that other State may not impose any tax on such interest except insofar as it arises in that other State or insofar as the debt-claim in respect of which the interest is paid is effectively connected with a permanent establishment or a fixed base situated in that other State.

Article XII. Royalties

1. Royalties arising in a Contracting State and paid to a resident of the other Contracting State may be taxed in that other State.

2. However, such royalties may also be taxed in the Contracting State in which they arise, and according to the laws of that State; but if a resident of the other Contracting State is the beneficial owner of such royalties, the tax so charged shall not exceed 10 per cent of the gross amount of the royalties.

3. Notwithstanding the provisions of paragraph 2, copyright royalties and other like payments in respect of the production or reproduction of any literary, dramatic, musical or artistic work (but not including royalties in respect of motion pictures and works on film, videotape

or other means of reproduction for use in connection with television) arising in a Contracting State and beneficially owned by a resident of the other Contracting State shall be taxable only in that other State.

4. The term 'royalties' as used in this Article means payments of any kind received as a consideration for the use of, or the right to use, any copyright of literary, artistic or scientific work (including motion pictures and works on film, videotape or other means of reproduction for use in connection with television), any patent, trade mark, design or model, plan, secret formula or process, or for the use of, or the right to use, tangible personal property or for information concerning industrial, commercial or scientific experience, and, notwithstanding the provisions of Article XIII (Gains), includes gains from the alienation of any intangible property or rights described in this paragraph to the extent that such gains are contingent on the productivity, use or subsequent disposition of such property or rights.

5. The provisions of paragraphs 2 and 3 shall not apply if the beneficial owner of the royalties, being a resident of a Contracting State, carries on business in the other Contracting State in which the royalties arise, through a permanent establishment situated therein, or performs in that other State independent personal services from a fixed base situated therein, and the right or property in respect of which the royalties are paid is effectively connected with such permanent establishment or fixed base. In such case the provisions of Article VII (Business Profits) or Article XIV (Independent Personal Services), as the case may be, shall apply.

6. For the purposes of this Article, royalties shall be deemed to arise in a Contracting State when the payer is that State itself, or a political subdivision, local authority or resident of that State. However:

a. Except as provided in subparagraph *b.*, where the person paying the royalties, whether he is a resident of a Contracting State or not, has in a State other than that of which he is a resident a permanent establishment or a fixed base in connection with which the obligation to pay the royalties was incurred, and such royalties are borne by such permanent establishment or fixed base, then such royalties shall be deemed to arise in the State in which the permanent establishment or fixed base is situated and not in the State of which the payer is a resident; and

b. Where the royalties are for the use of, or the right to use, intangible property or tangible personal property in a Contracting State, then such royalties shall be deemed to arise in that State and not in the State of which the payer is a resident.

7. Where, by reason of a special relationship between the payer and the beneficial owner or between both of them and some other person, the amount of the royalties, having regard to the use, right or information for which they are paid, exceeds the amount which would have been agreed upon by the payer and the beneficial owner in the absence of such relationship, the provisions of this Article shall apply only to the last-mentioned amount. In such case, the excess part of the payments shall remain taxable according to the laws of each Contracting State, due regard being had to the other provisions of the Convention.

8. Where a resident of a Contracting State pays royalties to a person other than a resident of the other Contracting State, that other State may not impose any tax on such royalties except insofar as they arise in that other State or insofar as the right or property in respect of which the royalties are paid is effectively connected with a permanent establishment or a fixed base situated in that other State.

Article XIII. Gains

1. Gains derived by a resident of a Contracting State from the alienation of real property in the other Contracting State may be taxed in that other State.

2. Gains from the alienation of personal property forming part of the business property of a permanent establishment which a resident of a Contracting State has or had (within the twelve-month period preceding the date of alienation) in the other Contracting State or of personal property pertaining to a fixed base which is or was available (within the twelve-month period preceding the date of alienation) to a resident of a Contracting State in the other Contracting State for the purpose of performing independent personal services, including such gains from the alienation of such a permanent establishment or of such a fixed base, may be taxed in that other State.

3. For the purposes of this Article the term 'real property situated in the other Contracting State'

a. In the case of real property situated in the United States, means a United States real property interest and real property referred to in Article VI (Income from Real Property) situated in the United States; and

b. In the case of real property situated in Canada means:

(i) Real property referred to in Article VI (Income from Real Property) situated in Canada;

(ii) A share of the capital stock of a company, the value of whose shares is derived principally from real property situated in Canada; and

(iii) An interest in a partnership, trust or estate, the value of which is derived principally from real property situated in Canada.

4. Gains from the alienation of any property other than that referred to in paragraphs 1, 2 and 3 shall be taxable only in the Contracting State of which the alienator is a resident.

5. The provisions of paragraph 4 shall not affect the right of a Contracting State to levy tax on gains from the alienation of property derived by an individual who is a resident of the other Contracting State if such individual:

a. Was a resident of the first-mentioned State for 120 months during any period of 20 consecutive years preceding the alienation of the property; and

b. Was a resident of the first-mentioned State at any time during the ten years immediately preceding the alienation of the property;

and if such property (or property for which such property was substituted in an alienation the gain on which was not recognized for the purposes of taxation in the first-mentioned State) was owned by the individual at the time he ceases to be a resident of the first-mentioned State.

6. Where an individual (other than a citizen of the United States) who was a resident of Canada became a resident of the United States, in determining his liability to United States taxation in respect of any gain from the alienation of a principal residence in Canada owned by him at the time he ceased to be a resident of Canada, the adjusted basis of such property shall be no less than its fair market value at that time.

7. Where at any time an individual is treated for the purposes of taxation by a Contracting State as having alienated a property and is taxed in that State by reason thereof and the domestic law of the other Contracting State at such time defers (but does not forgive) taxation, that individual may elect in his annual return of income for the year of such alienation to be liable to tax in the other Contracting State in that year as if he had, immediately before that time, sold and repurchased such property for an amount equal to its fair market value at that time.

8. Where a resident of a Contracting State alienates property in the course of a corporate organization, reorganization, amalgamation, division or similar transaction and profit, gain or income with respect to such alienation is not recognized for the purpose of taxation in that State, if requested to do so by the person who acquires the property, the competent authority of the other Contracting State may agree, in order to avoid double taxation and subject to terms and conditions satisfactory to such competent authority, to defer the recognition of the profit, gain or income with respect to such property for the purpose of taxation in that other State until such time and in such manner as may be stipulated in the agreement.

9. Where a person who is a resident of a Contracting State alienates a capital asset which may in accordance with this Article be taxed in the other Contracting State and

a. That person owned the asset on September 26, 1980 and was resident in the first-mentioned State on that date; or

b. The asset was acquired by that person in an alienation of property which qualified as a non-recognition transaction for the purposes of taxation in that other State;

the amount of the gain which is liable to tax in that other State in accordance with this Article shall be reduced by the proportion of the gain attributable on a monthly basis to the period ending on December 31 of the year in which the Convention enters into force, or such greater portion of the gain as is shown to the satisfaction of the competent authority of the other State to be reasonably attributable to that period. For the purposes of this paragraph the term 'non-recognition transaction' includes a transaction to which paragraph 8 applies and, in the case of taxation in the United States, a transaction that would have been a non-recognition transaction but for Sections 897(d) and 897(e) of the Internal Revenue Code. The provisions of this paragraph shall not apply to

c. An asset that on September 26, 1980 formed part of the business property of a permanent establishment or pertained to a fixed base of a resident of a Contracting State situated in the other Contracting State;

d. An alienation by a resident of a Contracting State of an asset that was owned at any time after September 26, 1980 and before such alienation by a person who was not at all times after that date while the asset was owned by such person a resident of that State; or

e. An alienation of an asset that was acquired by a person at any time after September 26, 1980 and before such alienation in a transaction other than a non-recognition transaction.

Article XIV. Independent Personal Services

Income derived by an individual who is a resident of a Contracting State in respect of independent personal services may be taxed in that State. Such income may also be taxed in the other Contracting State if the individual has or had a fixed base regularly available to him in that other State but only to the extent that the income is attributable to the fixed base.

Article XV. Dependent Personal Services

1. Subject to the provisions of Article XVIII (Pensions and Annuities) and XIX (Government Service), salaries, wages and other similar remuneration derived by a resident of a Contracting State in respect of an employment shall be taxable only in that State unless the employment is exercised in the other Contracting State. If the employment is so exercised, such remuneration as is derived therefrom may be taxed in that other State.

2. Notwithstanding the provisions of paragraph 1, remuneration derived by a resident of a Contracting State in respect of an employment exercised in a calendar year in the other Contracting State shall be taxable only in the first-mentioned State if:

a. Such remuneration does not exceed ten thousand dollars ($10,000) in the currency of that other State; or

b. The recipient is present in the other Contracting State for a period or periods not exceeding in the aggregate 183 days in that year and the remuneration is not borne by an employer who is a resident of that other State or by a permanent establishment or a fixed base which the employer has in that other State.

3. Notwithstanding the provisions of paragraphs 1 and 2, remuneration derived by a resident of a Contracting State in respect of an employment regularly exercised in more than one State on a ship, aircraft, motor vehicle or train operated by a resident of that Contracting State shall be taxable only in that State.

Article XVI. Artistes and Athletes

1. Notwithstanding the provisions of Articles XIV (Independent Personal Services) and XV (Dependent Personal Services), income derived by a resident of a Contracting State as an entertainer, such as a theatre, motion picture, radio or television artiste, or a musician, or

as an athlete, from his personal activities as such exercised in the other Contracting State, may be taxed in that other State, except where the amount of the gross receipts derived by such entertainer or athlete, including expenses reimbursed to him or borne on his behalf, from such activities do not exceed fifteen thousand dollars ($15,000) in the currency of that other State for the calendar year concerned.

2. Where income in respect of personal activities exercised by an entertainer or an athlete in his capacity as such accrues not to the entertainer or athlete but to another person, that income may, notwithstanding the provisions of Article VII (Business Profits), XIV (Independent Personal Services) and XV (Dependent Personal Services), be taxed in the Contracting State in which the activities of the entertainer or athlete are exercised. For the purposes of the preceding sentence, income of an entertainer or athlete shall be deemed not to accrue to another person if it is established that neither the entertainer or athlete, nor persons related thereto, participate directly or indirectly in the profits of such other person in any manner, including the receipt of deferred remuneration, bonuses, fees, dividends, partnership distributions or other distributions.

3. The provisions of paragraphs 1 and 2 shall not apply to the income of:

a. An athlete in respect of his activities as an employee of a team which participates in a league with regularly scheduled games in both Contracting States; or

b. A team described in subparagraph *a.*

4. Notwithstanding the provisions of Articles XIV (Independent Personal Services) and XV (Dependent Personal Services) an amount paid by a resident of a Contracting State to a resident of the other Contracting State as an inducement to sign an agreement relating to the performance of the services of an athlete (other than an amount referred to in paragraph 1 of Article XV (Dependent Personal Services)) may be taxed in the first-mentioned State, but the tax so charged shall not exceed 15 per cent of the gross amount of such payment.

Article XVII. Withholding of Taxes in Respect of Personal Services

1. Deduction and withholding of tax on account of the tax liability for a taxable year on remuneration paid to an individual who is a resident of a Contracting State (including an entertainer or athlete) in respect of the performance of independent personal services in the other Contracting State may be required by that other State, but with respect to the first five thousand dollars ($5,000) in the currency of that other State, paid as remuneration in that taxable year by each payer, such deduction and withholding shall not exceed 10 per cent of the payment.

2. Where the competent authority of a Contracting State considers that an amount that would otherwise be deducted or withheld from any amount paid or credited to an individual who is a resident of the other Contracting State in respect of the performance of personal services

in the first-mentioned State is excessive in relation to the estimated tax liability for the taxable year of that individual in the first-mentioned State, it may determine that a lesser amount will be deducted or withheld.

3. The provisions of this Article shall not affect the liability of a resident of a Contracting State referred to in paragraph 1 or 2 for tax imposed by the other Contracting State.

Article XVIII. Pensions and Annuities

1. Pensions and annuities arising in a Contracting State and paid to a resident of the other Contracting State may be taxed in that other State, but the amount of any such pension that would be excluded from taxable income in the first-mentioned State if the recipient were a resident thereof shall be exempt from taxation in that other State.

2. However:

a. Pensions may also be taxed in the Contracting State in which they arise and according to the laws of that State; but if a resident of the other Contracting State is the beneficial owner of a periodic pension payment, the tax so charged shall not exceed 15 per cent of the gross amount of such payment; and

b. Annuities may also be taxed in the Contracting State in which they arise and according to the laws of that State; but if a resident of the other Contracting State is the beneficial owner of an annuity payment, the tax so charged shall not exceed 15 per cent of the portion of such payment that would not be excluded from taxable income in the first-mentioned State if the beneficial owner were a resident thereof.

3. For the purposes of this Convention, the term 'pensions' includes any payment under a superannuation, pension or retirement plan, Armed Forces retirement pay, war veterans pensions and allowances and amounts paid under a sickness, accident or disability plan, but does not include payments under an income-averaging annuity contract of any benefit referred to in paragraph 5.

4. For the purposes of the Convention, the term 'annuities' means a stated sum paid periodically at stated times during life or during a specified number of years, under an obligation to make the payments in return for adequate and full consideration (other than services rendered), but does not include a payment that is not a periodic payment or any annuity the cost of which was deductible for the purposes of taxation in the Contracting State in which it was acquired.

5. Benefits under the social security legislation in a Contracting State paid to a resident of the other Contracting State shall be taxable as follows:

a. Such benefits shall be taxable only in that other State;

b. Notwithstanding the provisions of subparagraph *a.*, one-half of the total amount of any such benefit paid in a taxable year shall be exempt from taxation in that other State.

6. Alimony and other similar amounts (including child support payments) arising in a Contracting State and paid to a resident of the other Contracting State shall be taxable as follows:

a. Such amounts shall be taxable only in that other State;

b. Notwithstanding the provisions of subparagraph *a.*, the amount that would be excluded from taxable income in the first-mentioned State if the recipient were a resident thereof shall be exempt from taxation in that other State.

Article XIX. Government Service

Remuneration, other than a pension, paid by a Contracting State or a political subdivision or local authority thereof to a citizen of that State in respect of services rendered in the discharge of functions of a governmental nature shall be taxable only in that State. However, the provisions of Articles XIV (Independent Personal Services), XV (Dependent Personal Services) or XVI (Artistes and Athletes), as the case may be, shall apply, and the preceding sentence shall not apply, to remuneration paid in respect of services rendered in connection with a trade or business carried on by a Contracting State or a political subdivision or local authority thereof.

Article XX. Students

Payments which a student, apprentice or business trainee, who is or was immediately before visiting a Contracting State a resident of the other Contracting State, and who is present in the first-mentioned State for the purpose of his full-time education or training, receives for the purpose of his maintenance, education or training shall not be taxed in that State provided that such payments are made to him from outside that State.

Article XXI. Exempt Organizations

1. Subject to the provisions of paragraph 3, income derived by a religious, scientific, literary, educational or charitable organization shall be exempt from tax in a Contracting State if it is resident in the other Contracting State but only to the extent that such income is exempt from tax in that other State.

2. Subject to the provisions of paragraph 3, income referred to in Articles X (Dividends) and XI (Interest) derived by:

a. A trust, company or other organization which is resident in a Contracting State, generally exempt from tax in a taxable year in that State and constituted and operated exclusively to administer or provide benefits under one or more funds or plans established to provide pension, retirement or other employee benefits; or

b. A trust, company or other organization which is resident in a Contracting State, not taxed in a taxable year in that State and constituted and operated exclusively to earn income for the benefit of an organization referred to in subparagraph *a.*;

shall be exempt from tax in that taxable year in the other Contracting State.

3. The provisions of paragraphs 1 and 2 shall not apply with respect to the income of a trust, company or other organization from carrying

on a trade or business or from a related person other than a person referred to in paragraph 1 or 2.

4. A religious, scientific, literary, educational or charitable organization which is resident in Canada and which has received substantially all of its support from persons other than citizens or residents of the United States shall be exempt in the United States from the United States excise taxes imposed with respect to private foundations.

5. For the purposes of United States taxation, contributions by a citizen or resident of the United States to an organization which is resident in Canada, which is generally exempt from Canadian tax and which could qualify in the United States to receive deductible contributions if it were resident in the United States shall be treated as charitable contributions; however, such contributions (other than such contributions to a college or university at which the citizen or resident or a member of his family is or was enrolled) shall not be deductible in any taxable year to the extent that they exceed an amount determined by applying the percentage limitations of the laws of the United States in respect of the deductibility of charitable contributions to the income of such citizen or resident arising in Canada. The preceding sentence shall not be interpreted to allow in any taxable year deductions for charitable contributions in excess of the amount allowed under the percentage limitations of the laws of the United States in respect of the deductibility of charitable contributions.

6. For the purposes of Canadian taxation, gifts by a resident of Canada to an organization which is resident in the United States, which is generally exempt from United States tax and which could qualify in Canada to receive deductible gifts if it were created or established and resident in Canada shall be treated as gifts to a registered charity; however, such gifts (other than such gifts to a college or university at which the resident or member of his family is or was enrolled) shall not be deductible in any taxable year to the extent that they exceed an amount determined by applying the percentage limitations of the laws of Canada in respect of the deductibility of gifts to registered charities to the income of such resident arising in the United States. The preceding sentence shall not be interpreted to allow in any taxable year deductions for gifts to registered charities in excess of the amount allowed under the percentage limitations of the laws of Canada in respect of the deductibility of gifts to registered charities.

Article XXII. Other Income

1. Items of income of a resident of a Contracting State, wherever arising, not dealt with in the foregoing Articles of this Convention shall be taxable only in that State, except that if such income arises in the other Contracting State it may also be taxed in that other State.

2. To the extent that income distributed by an estate or trust is subject to the provisions of paragraph 1, then, notwithstanding such provisions, income distributed by an estate or trust which is a resident of a Contracting State to a resident of the other Contracting State who is a beneficiary of the estate or trust may be taxed in the first-mentioned

State and according to the laws of that State, but the tax so charged shall not exceed 15 per cent of the gross amount of the income; provided, however, that such income shall be exempt from tax in the first-mentioned State to the extent of any amount distributed out of income outside that State.

Article XXIII. Capital

1. Capital represented by real property, owned by a resident of a Contracting State and situated in the other Contracting State, may be taxed in that other State.

2. Capital represented by personal property forming part of the business property of a permanent establishment which a resident of a Contracting State has in the other Contracting State, or by personal property pertaining to a fixed base available to a resident of a Contracting State in the other Contracting State for the purpose of performing independent personal services, may be taxed in that other State.

3. Capital represented by ships and aircraft operated by a resident of a Contracting State in international traffic, and by personal property pertaining to the operation of such ships and aircraft, shall be taxable only in that State.

4. All other elements of capital of a resident of a Contracting State shall be taxable only in that State.

Article XXIV. Elimination of Double Taxation

1. In the case of the United States, subject to the provisions of paragraphs 4, 5 and 6, double taxation shall be avoided as follows: In accordance with the provisions and subject to the limitations of the law of the United States (as it may be amended from time to time without changing the general principle hereof), the United States shall allow to a citizen or resident of the United States, or to a company electing to be treated as a domestic corporation, as a credit against the United States tax on income the appropriate amount of income tax paid or accrued to Canada; and, in the case of a company which is a resident of the United States owning at least 10 per cent of the voting stock of a company which is a resident of Canada from which it receives dividends in any taxable year, the United States shall allow as a credit against the United States tax on income the appropriate amount of income tax paid or accrued to Canada by that company with respect to the profits out of which such dividends are paid.

2. In the case of Canada, subject to the provisions of paragraphs 4, 5 and 6, double taxation shall be avoided as follows:

a. Subject to the provisions of the law of Canada regarding the deduction from tax payable in Canada of tax paid in a territory outside Canada and to any subsequent modifications of those provisions (which shall not affect the general principle hereof), and unless a greater deduction or relief is provided under the law of Canada, income tax paid or accrued to the United States on profits, income or gains arising in the United States shall be deducted from any Canadian tax payable in respect of such profits, income or gains;

b. Subject to the provisions of the law of Canada regarding the determination of the exempt surplus of a foreign affiliate and to any subsequent modification of those provisions (which shall not affect the general principle hereof), for the purposes of computing Canadian tax, a company which is a resident of Canada shall be allowed to deduct in computing its taxable income any dividend received by it out of the exempt surplus of a foreign affiliate which is a resident of the United States; and

c. Notwithstanding the provisions of subparagraph *a.*, where Canada imposes a tax on gains from the alienation of property that, but for the provisions of paragraph 5 of Article XIII (Gains), would not be taxable in Canada, income tax paid or accrued to the United States on such gains shall be deducted from any Canadian tax payable in respect of such gains.

3. For the purposes of this Article:

a. Profits, income or gains (other than gains to which paragraph 5 of Article XIII (Gains) applies) of a resident of a Contracting State which may be taxed in the other Contracting State in accordance with the Convention (without regard to paragraph 2 of Article XXIX (Miscellaneous Rules)) shall be deemed to arise in that other State; and

b. Profits, income or gains of a resident of a Contracting State which may not be taxed in the other Contracting State in accordance with the Convention (without regard to paragraph 2 of Article XXIX (Miscellaneous Rules)) or to which paragraph 5 of Article XIII (Gains) applies shall be deemed to arise in the first-mentioned State.

4. Where a United States citizen is a resident of Canada, the following rules shall apply:

a. Canada shall allow a deduction from the Canadian tax in respect of income tax paid or accrued to the United States in respect of profits, income or gains which arise (within the meaning of paragraph 3) in the United States, except that such deduction need not exceed the amount of the tax that would be paid to the United States if the resident were not a United States citizen; and

b. For the purposes of computing the United States tax, the United States shall allow as a credit against United States tax the income tax paid or accrued to Canada after the deduction referred to in subparagraph *a.* The credit so allowed shall not reduce that portion of the United States tax that is deductible from Canadian tax in accordance with subparagraph *a.*

5. Notwithstanding the provisions of paragraph 4, where a United States citizen is a resident of Canada, the following rules shall apply in respect of the items of income referred to in Article X (Dividends), XI (Interest) or XII (Royalties) which arise (within the meaning of paragraph 3) in the United States, as long as the law in force in Canada allows a deduction in computing income for the portion of any foreign tax paid in respect of such items which exceeds 15 per cent of the amount thereof:

a. The deduction so allowed in Canada shall not be reduced by any credit or deduction for income tax paid or accrued to Canada allowed in computing the United States tax on such items;

b. Canada shall allow a deduction from the Canadian tax in respect of the income tax paid or accrued to the United States on such items, except that such deduction need not exceed 15 per cent of the gross amount of such items that has been included in computing the income of the citizen for Canadian tax purposes; and

c. For the purposes of computing the United States tax on such items, the United States shall allow as a credit against United States tax the income tax paid or accrued to Canada after the deduction referred to in subparagraph *b.* The credit so allowed shall reduce only that portion of the United States tax on such items which exceeds 15 per cent of the amount thereof included in computing United States taxable income.

6. Where a United States citizen is a resident of Canada, items of income referred to in paragraph 4 or 5 shall, notwithstanding the provisions of paragraph 3, be deemed to arise in Canada to the extent necessary to avoid the double taxation of such income under paragraph 4*b.* or paragraph 5*c.*

7. For the purposes of this Article, any reference to 'income tax paid or accrued' to a Contracting State shall include Canadian tax and United States tax, as the case may be, and taxes of general application which are paid or accrued to a political subdivision or local authority of that State, which are not imposed by that political subdivision or local authority in a manner inconsistent with the provisions of the Convention and which are substantially similar to the taxes of that State referred to in paragraphs 2 and 3*a.* of Article II (Taxes Covered).

8. When a resident of a Contracting State owns capital which, in accordance with the provisions of the Convention, may be taxed in the other Contracting State, the first-mentioned State shall allow as a deduction from the tax on the capital of that resident an amount equal to the capital tax paid in that other State. The deduction shall not, however, exceed that part of the capital tax, as computed before the deduction is given, which is attributable to the capital which may be taxed in that other State.

9. The provisions of this Article relating to the source of profits, income or gains shall not apply for the purpose of determining a credit against United States tax for any foreign taxes other than income taxes paid or accrued to Canada.

Article XXV. Non-discrimination

1. Citizens of a Contracting State, who are residents of the other Contracting State, shall not be subjected in that other State to any taxation or any requirement connected therewith which is other or more burdensome than the taxation and connected requirements to which citizens of that other State in the same circumstances are or may be subjected.

2. Citizens of a Contracting State, who are not residents of the other Contracting State, shall not be subjected in that other State to any taxation or any requirement connected therewith which is other or more burdensome than the taxation and connected requirements to which citizens of any third State in the same circumstances (including State of residence) are or may be subjected.

3. In determining the taxable income of an individual who is a resident of a Contracting State there shall be allowed as a deduction in respect of any other person who is a resident of the other Contracting State and who is dependent on the individual for support the amount that would be so allowed if that other person were a resident of the first-mentioned State.

4. Where a married individual who is a resident of Canada and not a citizen of the United States has income that is taxable in the United States pursuant to Article XV (Dependent Personal Services), the United States tax with respect to such income shall not exceed such proportion of the total United States tax that would be payable for the taxable year if both the individual and his spouse were United States citizens as the individual's taxable income determined without regard to this paragraph bears to the amount that would be the total taxable income of the individual and his spouse. For the purposes of this paragraph,

a. The 'total United States tax' shall be determined as if all the income of the individual and his spouse arose in the United States; and

b. A deficit of the spouse shall not be taken into account in determining taxable income.

5. Any company which is a resident of a Contracting State, the capital of which is wholly or partly owned or controlled, directly or indirectly, by one or more residents of the other Contracting State, shall not be subjected in the first-mentioned State to any taxation or any requirement connected therewith which is other or more burdensome than the taxation or connected requirements to which other similar companies of the first-mentioned State, the capital of which is wholly or partly owned or controlled, directly or indirectly, by one or more residents of a third State, are or may be subjected.

6. Notwithstanding the provisions of Article XXIV (Elimination of Double Taxation), the taxation on a permanent establishment which a resident of a Contracting State has in the other Contracting State shall not be less favorably levied in the other State than the taxation levied on residents of the other State carrying on the same activities. This paragraph shall not be construed as obliging a Contracting State:

a. To grant to a resident of the other Contracting State any personal allowances, reliefs and reductions for taxation purposes on account of civil status or family responsibilities which it grants to its own residents; or

b. To grant to a company which is a resident of the other Contracting State the same tax relief that it provides to a company which is a resident of the first-mentioned State with respect to dividends received by it from a company.

7. Except where the provisions of paragraph 1 of Article IX (Related Persons), paragraph 7 of Article XI (Interest) or paragraph 7 of Article XII (Royalties) apply, interest, royalties and other disbursements paid by a resident of a Contracting State to a resident of the other Contracting State shall, for the purposes of determining the taxable profits of the first-mentioned resident, be deductible under the same conditions as if they had been paid to a resident of the first-mentioned State. Similarly, any debt of a resident of a Contracting State to a resident of the other Contracting State shall, for the purpose of determining the taxable capital of the first-mentioned resident, be deductible under the same conditions as if they had been contracted to a resident of the first-mentioned State.

8. The provisions of paragraph 7 shall not affect the operation of any provision of the taxation laws of a Contracting State:

a. Relating to the deductibility of interest and which is in force on the date of signature of this Convention (including any subsequent modification of such provisions that does not change the general nature thereof); or

b. Adopted after such date by a Contracting State and which is designed to ensure that a person who is not a resident of that State does not enjoy, under the laws of that State, a tax treatment that is more favorable than that enjoyed by residents of that State.

9. Expenses incurred by a citizen or resident of a Contracting State with respect to any convention (including any seminar, meeting, congress or other function of a similar nature) held in the other Contracting State shall, for the purposes of taxation in the first-mentioned State, be deductible to the same extent that such expenses would be deductible if the convention were held in the first-mentioned State.

10. Notwithstanding the provisions of Article II (Taxes Covered), this Article shall apply:

a. In the case of Canada, to all taxes imposed under the Income Tax Act; and

b. In the case of the United States, to all taxes imposed under the Internal Revenue Code.

Article XXVI. Mutual Agreement Procedure

1. Where a person considers that the actions of one or both of the Contracting States result or will result for him in taxation not in accordance with the provisions of this Convention, he may, irrespective of the remedies provided by the domestic law of those States, present his case in writing to the competent authority of the Contracting State of which he is a resident or, if he is a resident of neither Contracting State, of which he is a national.

2. The competent authority of the Contracting State to which the case has been presented shall endeavor, if the objection appears to it to be justified and if it is not itself able to arrive at a satisfactory solution, to resolve the case by mutual agreement with the competent authority of the other Contracting State, with a view to the avoidance of taxation which is not in accordance with the Convention. Except

where the provisions of Article IX (Related Persons) apply, any agreement reached shall be implemented notwithstanding any time or procedural limitations in the domestic law of the Contracting States, provided that the competent authority of the other Contracting State has received notification that such a case exists within six years from the end of the taxable year to which the case relates.

3. The competent authorities of the Contracting States shall endeavor to resolve by mutual agreement any difficulties or doubts arising as to the interpretation or application of the Convention. In particular, the competent authorities of the Contracting States may agree:

a. To the same attribution of profits to a resident of a Contracting State and its permanent establishment situated in the other Contracting State;

b. To the same allocation of income, deductions, credits, or allowances between persons;

c. To the same determination of the source, and the same characterization, of particular items of income;

d. To a common meaning of any term used in the Convention;

e. To the elimination of double taxation with respect to income distributed by an estate or trust;

f. To the elimination of double taxation with respect to a partnership; or

g. To increases in any dollar amounts referred to in the Convention to reflect monetary or economic developments.

They may also consult together for the elimination of double taxation in cases not provided for in the Convention.

4. Each of the Contracting States will endeavor to collect on behalf of the other Contracting State such amounts as may be necessary to ensure that relief granted by the Convention from taxation imposed by that other State does not enure to the benefit of persons not entitled thereto. However, nothing in this paragraph shall be construed as imposing on either of the Contracting States the obligation to carry out administrative measures of a different nature from those used in the collection of its own tax or which would be contrary to its public policy (*ordre public*).

5. The competent authorities of the Contracting States may communicate with each other directly for the purpose of reaching an agreement in the sense of the preceding paragraphs.

Article XXVII. Exchange of Information

1. The competent authorities of the Contracting States shall exchange such information as is necessary for carrying out the provisions of this Convention or of the domestic laws of the Contracting States concerning taxes covered by the Convention insofar as the taxation thereunder is not contrary to the Convention. The exchange of information is not restricted by Article I (Personal Scope). Any information received by a Contracting State shall be treated as secret in the same manner as information obtained under the taxation laws of that State and shall be disclosed only to persons or authorities (including

courts and administrative bodies) involved in the assessment or collection of, the administration and enforcement in respect of, or the determination of appeals in relation to, the taxes covered by the Convention. Such persons or authorities shall use the information only for such purposes. They may disclose the information in public court proceedings or in judicial decisions.

2. If information is requested by a Contracting State in accordance with this Article, the other Contracting State shall endeavor to obtain the information to which the request relates in the same way as if its own taxation was involved notwithstanding the fact that the other State does not, at that time, need such information. If specifically requested by the competent authority of a Contracting State, the competent authority of the other Contracting State shall endeavor to provide information under this Article in the form requested, such as depositions of witnesses and copies of unedited original documents (including books, papers, statements, records, accounts or writings), to the same extent such depositions and documents can be obtained under the laws and administrative practices of that other State with respect to its own taxes.

3. In no case shall the provisions of paragraphs 1 and 2 be construed so as to impose on a Contracting State the obligation:

a. To carry out administrative measures at variance with the laws and administrative practice of that or the other Contracting State;

b. To supply information which is not obtainable under the laws or in the normal course of the administration of that or of the other Contracting State; or

c. To supply information which would disclose any trade, business, industrial, commercial, or professional secret or trade process, or information the disclosure of which would be contrary to public policy (*ordre public*).

4. Notwithstanding the provisions of Article II (Taxes Covered), for the purposes of this Article the Convention shall apply:

a. In the case of Canada, to all taxes imposed by the Government of Canada on estates and gifts and under the Income Tax Act; and

b. In the case of the United States, to all taxes imposed under the Internal Revenue Code.

Article XXVIII. Diplomatic Agents and Consular Officers

Nothing in this Convention shall affect the fiscal privileges of diplomatic agents or consular officers under the general rules of international law or under the provisions of special agreements.

Article XXIX. Miscellaneous Rules

1. The provisions of this Convention shall not restrict in any manner any exclusion, exemption, deduction, credit or other allowance now or hereafter accorded by the laws of a Contracting State in the determination of the tax imposed by that State.

2. Except as provided in paragraph 3, nothing in the Convention shall be construed as preventing a Contracting State from taxing its

residents (as determined under Article IV (Residence)) and, in the case of the United States, its citizens (including a former citizen whose loss of citizenship had as one of its principal purposes the avoidance of tax, but only for a period of ten years following such loss) and companies electing to be treated as domestic corporations, as if there were no convention between the United States and Canada with respect to taxes on income and on capital.

3. The provisions of paragraph 2 shall not affect the obligations undertaken by a Contracting State:

a. Under paragraphs 3 and 4 of Article IX (Related Persons), paragraphs 6 and 7 of Article XIII (Gains), paragraphs 1, 3, 4, 5*b.* and 6*b.* of Article XVIII (Pensions and Annuities), paragraphs 5 and 7 of Article XXIX (Miscellaneous Rules), paragraphs 3 and 5 of Article XXX (Entry into Force), and Articles XIX (Government Service), XXI (Exempt Organizations), XXIV (Elimination of Double Taxation), XXV (Non-Discrimination) and XXVI (Mutual Agreement Procedure); and

b. Under Article XX (Students), toward individuals who are neither citizens of, nor have immigrant status in, that State.

4. With respect to taxable years not barred by the statute of limitations ending on or before December 31 of the year before the year in which the Social Security Agreement between Canada and the United States (signed in Ottawa on March 11, 1981) enters into force, income from personal services not subject to tax by the United States under this Convention or the 1942 Convention shall not be considered wages or net earnings from self-employment for purposes of social security imposed under the Internal Revenue Code.

5. A beneficiary of a Canadian registered retirement savings plan may elect, under rules established by the competent authority of the United States, to defer United States taxation with respect to any income accrued in the plan but not distributed by the plan, until such time as a distribution is made from such plan, or any plan substituted therefor. The provisions of the preceding sentence shall not apply to income which is reasonably attributable to contributions made to the plan by the beneficiary while he was not a resident of Canada.

6. Notwithstanding any other provision of the Convention,

a. Where profits, income or gains derived by a trust is to be treated for the purposes of the Convention as income of a resident of a Contracting State, and a principal purpose for the establishment, acquisition or maintenance of the trust was to obtain a benefit under the Convention or the 1942 Convention for persons who are not residents of that State, Articles VI (Income from Real Property) through XXIV (Elimination of Double Taxation) shall not apply in relation to the profits, income or gains of the trust; and

b. Articles VI (Income from Real Property) through XXIV (Elimination of Double Taxation) shall not apply to non-resident-owned investment corporations as defined under section 133 of the Income Tax Act of Canada, or under any similar provision enacted by Canada after the date of signature of the Protocol.

7. One-half of the total amount of benefits under the social security legislation in Canada paid in a taxable year to a resident of Canada who is a citizen of the United States shall be exempt from taxation in the United States.

Article XXX. Entry into Force

1. This Convention shall be subject to ratification in accordance with the applicable procedure of each Contracting State and instruments of ratification shall be exchanged at ...... as soon as possible.

2. The Convention shall enter into force upon the exchange of instruments of ratification and, subject to the provisions of paragraph 3, its provisions shall have effect:

a. For tax withheld at the source on income referred to in Articles X (Dividends), XI (Interest), XII (Royalties) and XVIII (Pensions and Annuities), with respect to amounts paid or credited on or after the first day of the second month next following the date on which the Convention enters into force;

b. For other taxes, with respect to taxable years beginning on or after the first day of January next following the date on which the Convention enters into force;

c. Notwithstanding the provisions of subparagraph *b.*, for the taxes covered by paragraph 4 of Article XXIX (Miscellaneous Rules) with respect to all taxable years referred to in that paragraph.

3. For the purposes of applying the United States foreign tax credit in relation to taxes paid or accrued to Canada:

a. Notwithstanding the provisions of paragraph 2*a.* of Article II (Taxes Covered), the tax on 1971 undistributed income on hand imposed by Part IX of the Income Tax Act of Canada shall be considered to be an income tax for distributions made on or after the first day of January 1972 and before the first day of January 1979 and shall be considered to be imposed upon the recipient of a distribution, in the proportion that the distribution out of undistributed income with respect to which the tax has been paid bears to 85 per cent of such undistributed income;

b. The principles of paragraph 6 of Article XXIV (Elimination of Double Taxation) shall have effect for taxable years beginning on or after the first day of January 1976; and

c. The provisions of paragraph 1 of Article XXIV shall have effect for taxable years beginning on or after the first day of January 1981. Any claim for refund based on the provisions of this paragraph may be filed on or before June 30 of the calendar year following that in which the Convention enters into force, notwithstanding any rule of domestic law to the contrary.

4. Subject to the provisions of paragraph 5, the 1942 Convention shall cease to have effect for taxes for which this Convention has effect in accordance with the provisions of paragraph 2.

5. Where any greater relief from tax would have been afforded by any provision of the 1942 Convention than under this Convention, any such provision shall continue to have effect for the first taxable year

with respect to which the provisions of this Convention have effect under paragraph 2*b*.

6. The 1942 Convention shall terminate on the last date on which it has effect in accordance with the preceding provisions of this Article.

7. The Exchange of Notes between the United States and Canada dated August 2 and September 17, 1928, providing for relief from double income taxation on shipping profits, is terminated. Its provisions shall cease to have effect with respect to taxable years beginning on or after the first day of January next following the date on which this Convention enters into force.

8. The provisions of the Convention between the Government of Canada and the Government of the United States of America for the Avoidance of Double Taxation and the Prevention of Fiscal Evasion with Respect to Taxes on the Estates of Deceased Persons signed at Washington on February 17, 1961 shall continue to have effect with respect to estates of persons deceased prior to the first day of January next following the date on which this Convention enters into force but shall cease to have effect with respect to estates of persons deceased on or after that date. Such Convention shall terminate on the last date on which it has effect in accordance with the preceding sentence.

Article XXXI. Termination

1. This Convention shall remain in force until terminated by a Contracting State.

2. Either Contracting State may terminate the Convention at any time after 5 years from the date on which the Convention enters into force provided that at least 6 months' prior notice of termination has been given through diplomatic channels.

3. Where a Contracting State considers that a significant change introduced into the taxation laws of the other Contracting State should be accommodated by a modification of the Convention, the Contracting States shall consult together with a view to resolving the matter; if the matter cannot be satisfactorily resolved, the first-mentioned State may terminate the Convention in accordance with the procedures set forth in paragraph 2, but without regard to the 5 year limitation provided therein.

4. In the event the Convention is terminated, the Convention shall cease to have effect:

a. For tax withheld at the source on income referred to in Articles X (Dividends), XI (Interest), XII (Royalties) and XVIII (Pensions and Annuities) and paragraph 2 of Article XXII (Other Income), with respect to amounts paid or credited on or after the first day of January next following the expiration of the 6 month's period referred to in paragraph 2; and

b. For other taxes, with respect to taxable years beginning on or after the first day of January next following the expiration of the 6 month's period referred to in paragraph 2.

Canada

In witness whereof, the undersigned, being duly authorized thereto by their respective Governments, have signed this Convention.

Done in two copies at Washington this twenty-sixth day of September, 1980, in the English and French languages, each text being equally authentic.

Agreement between the Government of the United States of America and the Government of the People's Republic of China for the Avoidance of Double Taxation and the Prevention of Tax Evasion with Respect to Taxes on Income, concluded in Beijing on April 30, 1984, as amended by the Protocol of May 10, 1986.

The Government of the United States of America and the Government of the People's Republic of China,

Desiring to conclude an Agreement for the avoidance of double taxation and the prevention of tax evasion with respect to taxes on income,

Have agreed as follows:

Article 1

1. This Agreement shall apply to persons who are residents of one or both of the Contracting States.

Article 2

1. The taxes to which this Agreement applies are

a. in the People's Republic of China:

(i) the individual income tax;

(ii) the income tax concerning joint ventures with Chinese and foreign investment;

(iii) the income concerning foreign enterprises;

(iv) the local income tax

(hereinafter referred to as 'Chinese tax').

b. in the United States of America: the Federal income taxes imposed by the Internal Revenue Code

(hereinafter referred to as 'United States tax').

2. The Agreement shall apply also to any identical or substantially similar taxes which are imposed after the date of signature of the Agreement in addition to, or in place of, those referred to in paragraph 1. Within an appropriate time period, the competent authority of the Contracting States shall notify each other of any substantial changes which have been made in their respective taxation laws.

Article 3*

1. In this Agreement, unless the context otherwise requires:

a. the term 'the People's Republic of China', when used in a geographical sense, means all the territory of the People's Republic of China, including its territorial sea, in which the laws relating to Chinese tax are in force and all the area beyond its territorial sea, including the seabed and subsoil thereof, over which the People's Republic of China has jurisdiction in accordance with international law and in which the laws relating to Chinese tax are in force;

b. the term 'United States of America', when used in a geographical sense, means all the territory of the United States of America, including its territorial sea, in which the laws relating to United States tax are in force and all the area beyond its territorial sea, including the seabed and subsoil thereof, over which the United States of America has jurisdiction in accordance with international law and in which the laws relating to United States tax are in force;

c. the terms 'a Contracting State' and 'the other Contracting State' mean the People's Republic of China or the United States, as the context requires;

d. the term 'tax' means Chinese tax of United States tax, as the context requires;

e. the term 'person' includes an individual, a company, a partnership and any other body of persons;

f. the term 'company' means any body corporate or any entity which is treated as a body corporate for tax purposes;

g. the terms 'enterprise of a Contracting State' and 'enterprise of the other Contracting State' mean respectively an enterprise carried on by a resident of a Contracting State and an enterprise carried on by a resident of the other Contracting State;

h. the term 'nationals' means all individuals having the nationality of a Contracting State and all legal persons, partnerships and other bodies of persons deriving their status as such from the law in force in a Contracting State;

i. the term 'competent authority' means:

(i) in the People's Republic of China, the Ministry of Finance or its authorized representative; and

(ii) in the United States, the Secretary of the Treasury or his authorized representative.

2. As regards the application of the Agreement by a Contracting State any term not defined therein shall, unless the context otherwise requires, have the meaning which it has under the laws of that Contracting State concerning the taxes to which the Agreement applies.

Article 4*

1. For the purposes of this Agreement, the term 'resident of a Contracting State' means any person who, under the laws of that Contracting State, is liable to tax therein by reason of his domicile, residence, place of head office, place of incorporation or any other criterion of a similar nature.

2. Where by reason of the provisions of paragraph 1 an individual is a resident of both Contracting States, then the competent authorities shall determine through consultations the Contracting State of which that individual shall be deemed to be a resident for the purposes of this Agreement.

3. Where by reason of the provisions of paragraph 1 a company is a resident of both Contracting States, then the competent authorities

shall determine through consultations the Contracting State of which the company shall be deemed to be a resident for the purposes of this Agreement, and, if they are unable to so determine, the company shall not be considered to be a resident of either Contracting State for purposes of enjoying benefits under this Agreement.

4. Where by reason of the provisions of paragraph 1 a company is a resident of the United States of America, and, under a tax agreement between the People's Republic of China and a third country is also a resident of that third country, the company shall not be considered to be a resident of the United States of America for purposes of enjoying benefits under this Agreement.

Article 5

1. For the purposes of this Agreement, the term 'permanent establishment' means a fixed place of business through which the business of an enterprise is wholly or partly carried on.

2. The term 'permanent establishment' includes especially:

a. a place of management;

b. a branch;

c. an office;

d. a factory;

e. a workshop; and

f. a mine, an oil or gas well, a quarry or any other place of extraction of natural resources.

3. The term 'permanent establishment' also includes:

a. a building site, a construction, assembly or installation project, or supervisory activities in connection therewith, but only where such site, project or activities continue for a period of more than six months;

b. an installation, drilling rig or ship used for the exploration or exploitation of natural resources, but only if so used for a period of more than three months; and

c. the furnishing of services, including consultancy services, by an enterprise through employees or other personnel engaged by the enterprise for such purpose, but only where such activities continue (for the same or a connected project) within the country for a period or periods aggregating more than six months within any twelve month period.

4. Notwithstanding the provisions of paragraphs 1 through 3, the term 'permanent establishment; shall be deemed not to include:

a. the use of facilities solely for the purpose of storage, display or delivery of goods or merchandise belonging to the enterprise;

b. the maintenance of a stock of goods or merchandise belonging to the enterprise solely for the purpose of storage, display or delivery;

c. the maintenance of a stock of goods or merchandise belonging to the enterprise solely for the purpose of processing by another enterprise;

d. the maintenance of a fixed place of business solely for the purpose of purchasing goods or merchandise, or of collecting information, for the enterprise;

e. the maintenance of a fixed place of business solely for the purpose of carrying on, for the enterprise, any other activity of a preparatory or auxiliary character;

f. the maintenance of a fixed place of business solely for any combination of the activities mentioned in subparagraphs *a.* through *e.*, provided that the overall activity of the fixed place of business resulting from this combination is of a preparatory or auxiliary character.

5. Notwithstanding the provisions of paragraphs 1 and 2, where a person, other than an agent of an independent status to whom paragraph 6 applies, is acting on behalf of an enterprise and has and habitually exercises in a Contracting State an authority to conclude contracts in the name of the enterprise, that enterprise shall be deemed to have a permanent establishment in that Contracting State in respect of any activities which that person undertakes for the enterprise, unless the activities of such person are limited to those mentioned in paragraph 4 which, if exercised through a fixed place of business, would not make this fixed place of business a permanent establishment under the provisions of that paragraph.

6. An enterprise of a Contracting State shall not be deemed to have a permanent establishment in the other Contracting State merely because it carries on business in that other Contracting State through a broker, general commission agent or any other agent of an independent status, provided that such persons are acting in the ordinary course of their business. However, when the activities of such an agent are devoted wholly or almost wholly on behalf of that enterprise, he will not be considered an agent of an independent status within the meaning of this paragraph if it is shown that the transactions between the agent and the enterprise were not made under arm's-length conditions.

7. The fact that a company which is a resident of a Contracting State controls or is controlled by a company which is a resident of the other Contracting State, or which carries on business in that other Contracting State (whether through a permanent establishment or otherwise), shall not of itself constitute either company a permanent establishment of the other.

Article 6

1. Income derived by a resident of a Contracting State from real property situated in the other Contracting State may be taxed in that other Contracting State.

2. The term 'real property' shall have the meaning which it has under the laws of the Contracting State in which the property in question is situated. The term shall in any case include property accessory to real property, livestock and equipment used in agriculture and forestry, rights to which the provisions of general law respecting landed property apply, usufruct of real property and rights to variable or fixed payments as consideration for the working of, or the right to work, mineral deposits, sources and other natural resources; ships and aircraft shall not be regarded as real property.

3. The provisions of paragraph 1 shall apply to income derived from the direct use, letting or use in any other form of real property.

4. The provisions of paragraphs 1 and 3 shall also apply to the income from real property of an enterprise and to income from real property used for the performance of independent personal services.

Article 7

1. The profits of an enterprise of a Contracting State shall be taxable only in that Contracting State unless the enterprise carries on business in the other Contracting State through a permanent establishment situated therein. If the enterprise carries on business as aforesaid, the profits of the enterprise may be taxed in the other Contracting State but only so much of them as is attributable to that permanent establishment.

2. Subject to the provisions of paragraph 3, where an enterprise of a Contracting State carries on business in the other Contracting State through a permanent establishment situated therein, there shall in each Contracting State be attributed to that permanent establishment the profits which it might be expected to make if it were a distinct and separate enterprise engaged in the same or similar activities under the same or similar conditions and dealing wholly independently with the enterprise of which it is a permanent establishment.

3. In the determination of the profits of a permanent establishment, there shall be allowed as deductions expenses which are incurred for the purposes of the permanent establishment, including executive and general administrative expenses so incurred, whether in the State where the permanent establishment is situated or elsewhere. However, no such deduction shall be allowed in respect of amounts, if any, paid (otherwise than towards reimbursement of actual expenses) by the permanent establishment to the head office of the enterprise or any of its other offices, by way of royalties or other similar payments or by way of interest on money lent to the permanent establishment. Likewise, no account shall be taken, in the determination of the profits of a permanent establishment,for amounts charged (otherwise than towards reimbursement of actual expenses) by the permanent establishment to the head office of the enterprise or any of its other offices, by way of royalties or other similar payments or by way of interest on money lent to the head office of the enterprise or any of its other offices.

4. Insofar as the tax law of a Contracting State provides with respect to a specific industry that the profits to be attributed to a permanent establishment are to be determined on the bases of a deemed profit, nothing in paragraph 2 shall preclude that Contracting State from applying those provisions of its law, provided that the result is in accordance with the principles contained in this Article.

5. No profits shall be attributed to a permanent establishment by reason of the mere purchase by that permanent establishment of goods or merchandise for the enterprise.

6. For the purposes of paragraphs 1 through 5, the profits to be attributed to the permanent establishment shall be determined by the

same method year by year unless there is good and sufficient reason to the contrary.

7. Where profits include items of income which are dealt with separately in other Articles of this Agreement, then the provisions of those Articles shall not be affected by the provisions of this Article.

Article 8

1. Where:

a. an enterprise of a Contracting State participates directly or indirectly in the management, control or capital of an enterprise of the other Contracting State; or

b. the same persons participate directly or indirectly in the management, control or capital of an enterprise of a Contracting State and an enterprise of the other Contracting State;

and in either case the relationship between the two enterprises in their commercial or financial relations differs from that which would exist between independent enterprises, then any profits which, but for those conditions would have accrued to one of the enterprises, but by reason of those conditions have not so accrued, may be included in the profits of that enterprise and taxed accordingly.

2. Where a Contracting State includes in the profits of an enterprise of that Contracting State – and taxes accordingly – profits on which an enterprise of the other Contracting State has been charged to tax in that other Contracting State, and the profits so included are profits which would have accrued to the enterprise of the first-mentioned State if the conditions made between the two enterprises had been those which would have been made between independent enterprises, then that other Contracting State shall make an appropriate adjustment to the amount of tax charged therein on those profits. In determining such adjustment, due regard shall be paid to the other provisions of this Agreement and the competent authorities of the Contracting States shall if necessary consult each other.

Article 9*

1. Dividends paid by a company which is a resident of a Contracting State to a resident of the other Contracting State may be taxed in that other Contracting State.

2. However, such dividends may also be taxed in the Contracting State of which the company paying the dividends is a resident, and according to the laws of that Contracting State, but if the recipient is the beneficial owner of the dividends the tax so charged shall not exceed 10 per cent of the gross amount of the dividends.

This paragraph shall affect the taxation of the company in respect of the profits out of which the dividends are paid.

3. The term 'dividends' as used in this Article means income from shares or other rights, not being debt-claims, participating in profits, as well as income from other corporate rights which is subjected to the same taxation treatment as income from shares by the taxation laws

of the Contracting State of which the company making the distribution is a resident.

4. The provisions of paragraphs 1 and 2 shall not apply if the beneficial owner of the dividends, being a resident of a Contracting State, carries on business in the other Contracting State, of which the company paying the dividends is a resident, through a permanent establishment situated therein, or performs in that other Contracting State independent personal services from a fixed base situated therein, and the holding or other corporate rights in respect of which the dividends are paid is effectively connected with such permanent establishment or fixed base. In such case the provisions of Article 7 or 13, as the case may be, shall apply.

5. Where a company which is a resident of a Contracting State derives profits or income from the other Contracting State, that other Contracting State may not impose any tax on the dividends paid by the company, except insofar as such dividends are paid to a resident of that other Contracting State or insofar as the holding or other corporate rights in respect of which the dividends are paid is effectively connected with a permanent establishment or a fixed base situated in that other Contracting State, nor subject the company's undistributed profits to a tax on the company's undistributed profits, even if the dividends paid or the undistributed profits consist wholly or partly of profits or income arising in that other Contracting State.

Article 10*

1. Interest arising in a Contracting State and paid to a resident of the other Contracting State may be taxed in that other Contracting State.

2. However, such interest may also be taxed in the Contracting State in which it arises and according to the laws of that Contracting State, but if the recipient is the beneficial owner of the interest, the tax so charged shall not exceed 10 per cent of the gross amount of the interest.

3. Notwithstanding the provisions of paragraph 2, interest arising in a Contracting State and derived by the government of the other Contracting State, a political subdivision or local authority thereof, the Central Bank of that other Contracting State or any financial institution wholly owned by that government, or by any resident of the other Contracting State with respect to debt-claims indirectly financed by the government of that other Contracting State, a political subdivision or local authority thereof, the Central Bank of that other Contracting State or any financial institution wholly owned by that government, shall be exempt from tax in the first-mentioned Contracting State.

4. The term 'interest' as used in this Article means income from debt-claims of every kind, whether or not secured by mortgage, and whether or not carrying a right to participate in the debtor's profits, and in particular, income from government securities, and income from bonds or debentures, including premiums and prizes attaching to such securities, bonds or debentures.

5. The provisions of paragraphs 1, 2 and 3 shall not apply if the beneficial owner of the interest, being a resident of a Contracting State, carries on business in the other Contracting State in which the interest arises, through a permanent establishment situated therein, or performs in that other Contracting State independent personal services from a fixed base situated therein, and the debt-claim in respect of which the interest is paid is effectively connected with such permanent establishment or fixed base. In such case the provisions of Article 7 or 13, as the case may be, shall apply.

6. Interest shall be deemed to arise in a Contracting State when the payer is the government of that Contracting State itself, a political subdivision, a local authority or a resident of that Contracting State. Where, however, the person paying the interest, whether he is a resident of a Contracting State or not, has in a Contracting State a permanent establishment or a fixed base in connection with which the indebtedness on which the interest is paid was incurred, and such interest is borne by such permanent establishment or fixed base, then such interest shall be deemed to arise in the Contracting State in which the permanent establishment or fixed base is situated.

7. Where, by reason of a special relationship between the payer and the beneficial owner or between both of them and some other person, the amount of the interest, having regard to the debt-claim for which it is paid, exceeds the amount which would have been agreed upon by the payer and the beneficial owner in the absence of such relationship, the provisions of this Article shall apply only to the last-mentioned amount. In such case the excess part of the payments shall remain taxable according to the laws of each Contracting State, due regard being had to the other provisions of this Agreement.

Article 11*

1. Royalties arising in a Contracting State and paid to a resident of the other Contracting State may be taxed in that other Contracting State.

2. However, such royalties may also be taxed in the Contracting State in which they arise, and according to the laws of that Contracting State, but if the recipient is the beneficial owner of the royalties, the tax so charged shall not exceed 10 per cent of the gross amount of the royalties.

3. The term 'royalties' as used in this Article means payments of any kind received as a consideration for the use of, or the right to use, any copyright of literary, artistic or scientific work, including cinematographic films or films or tapes used for radio or television broadcasting, any patent, technical know-how, trademark, design or model, plan, secret formula or process, or for the use of, or the right to use, industrial, commercial or scientific equipment, or for information concerning industrial, commercial or scientific experience.

4. The provisions of paragraphs 1 and 2 shall not apply if the beneficial owner of the royalties, being a resident of a Contracting State, carries on business in the other Contracting State in which the royalties

arise, through a permanent establishment situated therein; or performs in that other Contracting State independent personal services from a fixed base situated therein, and the right or property in respect of which the royalties are paid is effectively connected with such permanent establishment or fixed base. In such case the provisions of Article 7 or 13, as the case may be, shall apply.

5. *a.* Royalties will be deemed to arise in a Contracting State when the payer is the government of that Contracting State itself, a political subdivision, a local authority or a resident of that Contracting State. Where, however, the person paying the royalties, whether he is a resident of a Contracting State or not, has in a Contracting State a permanent establishment or a fixed base in connection with which the liability to pay the royalties was incurred, and such royalties are borne by such permanent establishment or fixed base, then such royalties shall be deemed to arise in the Contracting State in which the permanent establishment or fixed base is situated.

b. Where under subparagraph *a.* royalties do not arise in one of the Contracting States, and the royalties relate to the use of, or the right to use, the right or property in one of the Contracting States, the royalties shall be deemed to arise in that Contracting State.

6. Where, by reason of a special relationship between the payer and the beneficial owner or between both of them and some other person, the amount of the royalties, having regard to the use, right, or information for which they are paid, exceeds the amount which would have been agreed upon by the payer and the beneficial owner in the absence of such relationship, the provisions of this Article shall apply only to the last-mentioned amount. In such case the excess part of the payments shall remain taxable according to the laws of each Contracting State, due regard being had to the other provisions of this Agreement.

Article 12

1. Gains derived by a resident of a Contracting State from the alienation of real property referred to in Article 6 and situated in the other Contracting State may be taxed in that other Contracting State.

2. Gains from the alienation of movable (personal) property forming part of the business assets of a permanent establishment which an enterprise of a Contracting State has in the other Contracting State, or of movable (personal) property pertaining to a fixed base available to a resident of a Contracting State in the other Contracting State for the purpose of performing independent personal services, including such gains from the alienation of such a permanent establishment (alone or together with the whole enterprise) or such a fixed base, may be taxed in that other Contracting State.

3. Gains derived by a resident of a Contracting State from the alienation of ships or aircraft operated in international traffic and of movable (personal) property pertaining to the operation of such ships or aircraft shall be taxable only in that Contracting State.

4. Gains from the alienation of shares of the capital stock of a company the property of which consists directly or indirectly principally

of real property situated in a Contracting State may be taxed in that Contracting State.

5. Gains from the alienation of shares other than those mentioned in paragraph 4 representing a participation of 25 per cent in a company which is resident of a Contracting State may be taxed in that Contracting State.

6. Gains derived by a resident of a Contracting State from the alienation of any property other than that referred to in paragraphs 1 through 5 and arising in the other Contracting State may be taxed in that other Contracting State.

Article 13

1. Income derived by an individual who is a resident of a Contracting State in respect of professional services or other activities of an independent character shall be taxable only in that Contracting State, unless he has a fixed base regularly available to him in the other Contracting State for the purpose of performing his activities or he is present in that other Contracting State for a period or periods exceeding in the aggregate 183 days in the calendar year concerned. If he has such a fixed base or remains in that other Contracting State for the aforesaid period or periods, the income may be taxed in that other Contracting State, but only so much of it as is attributable to that fixed base or is derived in that other Contracting State during the aforesaid period or periods.

2. The term 'professional services' includes, especially, independent scientific, literary, educational or teaching activities as well as the independent activities of physicians, lawyers, engineers, architects, dentists and accountants.

Article 14

1. Subject to the provisions of Articles 15, 17, 18, 19 and 20, salaries, wages and other similar remuneration derived by a resident of a Contracting State in respect of an employment shall be taxable only in that Contracting State unless the employment is exercised in the other Contracting State. If the employment is so exercised, such remuneration as is derived therefrom may be taxed in that other Contracting State.

2. Notwithstanding the provisions of paragraph 1, remuneration derived by a resident of a Contracting State in respect of an employment exercised in the other Contracting State shall be taxable only in the first-mentioned State if:

a. the recipient is present in the other Contracting State for a period or periods not exceeding in the aggregate 183 days in the calendar year concerned;

b. the remuneration is paid by, or on behalf of, an employer who is not a resident of the other Contracting State; and

c. the remuneration is not borne by a permanent establishment or a fixed base which the employer has in the other Contracting State.

Article 15

Director's fees and other similar payments derived by a resident of a Contracting State in his capacity as a member of the board of directors of a company which is a resident of the other Contracting State may be taxed in that other Contracting State.

Article 16

1. Notwithstanding the provisions of Articles 13 and 14, income derived by a resident of a Contracting State as an entertainer, such as a theatre, motion picture, radio or television artiste, or a musician, or as an athlete, from his personal activities as such exercised in the other Contracting State, may be taxed in that other Contracting State.

However, income derived by a resident of a Contracting State as an entertainer or athlete from activities exercised in accordance with a special program for cultural exchange agreed upon by the governments of both Contracting States shall be exempt from tax by the other Contracting State.

2. Where income in respect of personal activities exercised by an entertainer or an athlete in his capacity as such accrues not to the entertainer or athlete himself but to another person, that income may, notwithstanding the provisions of Articles 7, 13 and 14, be taxed in the Contracting State in which the activities of the entertainer or athlete are exercised.

However, if those activities are exercised in accordance with a special program for cultural exchange agreed upon by the governments of both Contracting States, the income so derived shall be exempt from tax by that Contracting State.

Article 17

1. Subject to the provisions of paragraph 2 of Article 18, pensions and other similar remuneration paid to a resident of a Contracting State in consideration of past employment shall be taxable only in that Contracting State.

2. Notwithstanding the provisions of paragraph 1, pensions and other payments made by the government, a political subdivision or a local authority of a Contracting State under its social security system or public welfare plan shall be taxable only in that Contracting State.

Article 18

1. *a.* Remuneration, other than a pension, paid by the government or a political subdivision or a local authority of a Contracting State to an individual in respect of services rendered to that government or subdivision or authority shall be taxable only in that Contracting State.

b. However, such remuneration shall be taxable only in the other Contracting State if the services are rendered in that other Contracting State and the individual is a resident of that other Contracting State who:

(i) is a national of that other Contracting State; or

(ii) did not become a resident of that other Contracting State solely for the purpose of rendering the services.

2. *a.* Any pension paid by, or out of funds created by, the government or a political subdivision or a local authority of a Contracting State to an individual in respect of services rendered to that government or subdivision or authority shall be taxable only in that Contracting State.

b. However, such pension shall be taxable only in the other Contracting State if the individual is a resident of, and a national of, that other Contracting State.

3. The permanent establishments of Articles 14, 15, 16 and 17 shall apply to remuneration and pensions in respect of services rendered in connection with a business carried on by the government or a political subdivision or a local authority of a Contracting State.

Article 19

1. An individual who is, or immediately before visiting a Contracting State was, a resident of the other Contracting State and is temporarily present in the first-mentioned Contracting State for the primary purpose of teaching, giving lectures or conducting research at a university, college, school or other accredited educational institution or scientific research institution in the first-mentioned Contracting State shall be exempt from tax in the first-mentioned Contracting State for a period not exceeding three years in the aggregate in respect of remuneration for such teaching, lectures or research.

Article 20

A student, business apprentice or trainee who is, or was immediately before visiting a Contracting State, a resident of the other Contracting State and who is present in the first-mentioned Contracting State solely for the purpose of his education, training or obtaining special technical experience shall be exempt from tax in that Contracting State with respect to:

a. payments received from abroad for the purpose of his maintenance, education, study, research or training;

b. grants or awards from a government, scientific, educational or other tax-exempt organization; and

c. income from personal services performed in that Contracting State in an amount not in excess of 5,000 United States dollars or its equivalent in Chinese yuan for any taxable year.

The benefits provided under this Article shall extend only for such period of time as is reasonably necessary to complete the education or training.

Article 21

1. Items of income of a resident of a Contracting State, wherever arising, not dealt with in the foregoing Articles of this Agreement shall be taxable only in that Contracting State.

2. The provisions of paragraph 1 shall not apply to income other than that from real property as defined in paragraph 2 of Article 6 if the recipient of such income, being a resident of a Contracting State, carries on business in the other Contracting State through a permanent establishment situated therein, or performs in that other Contracting State independent personal services from a fixed base situated therein, and the right or property in respect of which the income is paid is effectively connected with such permanent establishment or fixed base. In such case the provisions of Article 7 or 13, as the case may be, shall apply.

3. Notwithstanding the provisions of paragraphs 1 and 2, items of income of a resident of a Contracting State not dealt with in the foregoing Articles of this Agreement and arising in the other Contracting State may also be taxed in that other Contracting State.

Article 22

1. In the People's Republic of China, double taxation shall be eliminated as follows:

a. Where a resident of China derives income from the United States, the amount of the United States income tax payable in respect of that income in accordance with the provisions of this Agreement shall be allowed as a credit against the Chinese tax imposed on that resident. The amount of credit, however, shall not exceed the amount of the Chinese tax computed with respect to that income in accordance with the taxation laws and regulations of China.

b. Where the income derived from the United States is a dividend paid by a company which is a resident of the United States to a company which is a resident of China and which owns not less than 10 per cent of the shares of the company paying the dividend, the credit shall take into account the United States income tax payable by the company paying the dividend in respect of the profits out of which the dividends are paid.

2. In the United States of America, in accordance with the provisions of the law of the United States, the United States shall allow to a resident or citizen of the United States as a credit against the United States tax on income:

a. the income tax paid to China by or on behalf of such resident or citizen; and

b. in the case of a United States company owning at least 10 per cent of the voting rights in a company which is a resident of China and from which the United States company receives dividends, the income tax paid to China by or on behalf of the distributing company with respect to the profits out of which the dividends are paid.

For the purposes of this paragraph of this Agreement, the taxes referred to in paragraph 1*a.* and 2 of Article 2 shall be considered income taxes.

3. Income derived by a resident of a Contracting State which may be taxed in the other Contracting State in accordance with this Agreement shall be deemed to arise in that other Contracting State.

Article 23

1. Nationals of a Contracting State shall not be subjected in the other Contracting State to any taxation or any requirement connected therewith which is other or more burdensome than the taxation and connected requirements to which nationals of that other Contracting State in the same circumstances are or may be subjected. This provision shall, notwithstanding the provisions of Article 1, apply to persons who are not residents of one or both of the Contracting States.

2. The taxation on a permanent establishment which an enterprise of a Contracting State has in the other Contracting State shall not be less favorably levied in that other Contracting State than the taxation levied on enterprises of that other Contracting State carrying on the same activities. This provision shall not be construed as obliging a Contracting State to grant to residents of the other Contracting State any personal allowances, reliefs and reductions for taxation purposes on account of civil status or family responsibilities which it grants to its own residents.

3. Except where the provisions of Article 8, paragraph 7 of Article 10 or paragraph 6 of Article 11 apply, interest, royalties and other disbursements paid by a resident of a Contracting State to a resident of the other Contracting State shall, for the purposes of determining the taxable profits of the first-mentioned resident, be deductible under the same conditions as if they had been paid to a resident of the first-mentioned Contracting State.

4. Enterprises of a Contracting State, the capital of which is wholly or partly owned or controlled, directly or indirectly, by one or more residents of the other Contracting State, shall not be subjected in the first-mentioned Contracting State to any taxation or any requirement connected therewith which is other or more burdensome than the taxation and connected requirements to which other similar enterprises of the first-mentioned Contracting State are or may be subjected.

Article 24

1. Where a person considers that the actions of one or both of the Contracting States result or will result for him in taxation not in accordance with the provisions of this Agreement, he may, irrespective of the remedies provided by the domestic laws of those Contracting States, present his case to the competent authority of the Contracting State of which he is a resident or, if his case comes under paragraph 1 of Article 23, to that of the Contracting State of which he is a national. The case must be presented within three years from the first notification of the action resulting in taxation not in accordance with the provisions of this Agreement.

2. The competent authority shall endeavor, if the objection appears to it to be justified and if it is not itself able to arrive at a satisfactory solution, to resolve the case through consultation with the competent authority of the other Contracting State, with a view to the avoidance of taxation which is not in accordance with the Agreement. Any agree-

ment reached shall be implemented notwithstanding any time limits in the domestic law of the Contracting States.

3. The competent authorities of the Contracting States shall endeavor to resolve by mutual agreement any difficulties or doubts arising as to the interpretation or application of this Agreement. They may also consult together for the elimination of double taxation in cases not provided for in this Agreement.

4. The competent authorities of the Contracting States may communicate with each other directly for the purpose of reaching an agreement in the sense of paragraphs 2 and 3. To facilitate reaching a mutual agreement, the competent authorities of both Contracting States may meet for an oral exchange of opinions.

Article 25

1. The competent authorities of the Contracting States shall exchange such information as is necessary for carrying out the provisions of this Agreement or of the domestic laws of the Contracting States concerning taxes covered by this Agreement insofar as the taxation thereunder is not contrary to this Agreement, in particular for the prevention of fraud or evasion of such taxes. The exchange of information is not restricted by Article 1. Any information received by a Contracting State shall be treated as secret and shall be disclosed only to persons or authorities (including courts and administrative bodies) involved in the assessment, collection, or administration of, the enforcement or prosecution in respect of, or the determination of appeals in relation to, the taxes covered by this Agreement. Such persons or Authorities shall use the information only for such purposes. They may disclose the information in public court proceedings or in judicial decisions.

2. In no case shall the provisions of paragraph 1 be construed so as to impose on a Contracting State the obligation:

a. to carry out administrative measures at variance with the laws and administrative practice of that or of the other Contracting State;

b. to supply information which is not obtainable under the laws or in the normal course of the administration of that or of the other Contracting State; or

c. to supply information which would disclose any trade, business, industrial, commercial, or professional secret or trade process, or information the disclosure of which would be contrary to public policy.

Article 26

Nothing in this Agreement shall affect the fiscal privileges of diplomatic agents or consular officers under the general rules of international law or under the provisions of special agreements.

Article 27

Each of the Contracting States shall notify the other Contracting State in writing, through diplomatic channels, upon the completion of their respective legal procedures to bring this Agreement into force.

The Agreement shall enter into force on the thirtieth day after the date of the latter of such notifications and shall take effect as respects income derived during taxable years beginning on or after the first day of January next following the date on which this Agreement enters into force.

Article 28

This Agreement shall remain in force indefinitely, but either Contracting State may terminate the Agreement by giving notice to the other Contracting State in writing through diplomatic channels on or before June 30 in any calendar year after five years from the date on which this Agreement enters into force. In such event, the Agreement shall cease to have effect with respect to income derived during taxable years beginning on or after the first day of January of the year following that in which the notice of termination is given.

Done at Beijing on the 30th day of April, 1984, in duplicate, in the Chinese and English languages, the two texts having equal authenticity.

Protocol I

At the signing of the Agreement between the Government of the United States of America and the Government of the People's Republic of China for the Avoidance of Double Taxation and the Prevention of Tax Evasion with Respect to Taxes on Income (hereinafter referred to as 'the Agreement'), both sides have agreed upon the following provisions which form an integral part of the Agreement:

1. This Agreement shall not restrict in any manner tax benefit which is or may hereafter be accorded in a Contracting State by the laws of that Contracting State or by any agreement between the governments of the Contracting States.

2. Notwithstanding any provision of the Agreement, the United States may tax its citizens. Except as provided in paragraph 2 of Article 8, paragraph 2 of Article 17, and Articles 18, 19, 20, 22, 23, 24 and 26 of this Agreement, the United States may tax its residents (as determined under Article 4).

3. The United States may impose its social security tax, its personal holding company tax and its accumulated earnings tax notwithstanding any provision of this Agreement. However, a Chinese company shall be exempt from the personal holding company tax or the accumulated earnings tax in the United States during a taxable year if during that taxable year the company is wholly-owned, directly or indirectly, either by one or more individuals who are residents of China (and who are not citizens of the United States) or by the Government of China or any wholly-owned agency thereof.

4. The term 'person' as defined in Article 3 of the Agreement shall include an estate or a trust.

5. In applying paragraph 2 of Article 4 of this Agreement, the competent authorities of both Contracting States shall be guided by the rules contained in paragraph 2 of Article 4 of the United Nations Model Double Taxation Convention between Developed and Developing Countries.

6. For purposes of paragraph 3 of Article 11 of this Agreement, it is agreed by both sides that, in the case of royalties paid for the rental of industrial, commercial or scientific equipment, the tax shall be imposed on 70 per cent of the gross amount of such royalties.

7. It is agreed by both sides that the competent authorities of the Contracting States may through consultation deny the benefits of Articles 9, 10 and 11 to a company of a third country if the company becomes a resident of a Contracting State for the principal purpose of enjoying benefits under this Agreement.

8. This Agreement shall not affect the application of the agreement between the two governments with respect to mutual exemption from taxation of transportation income of shipping and air transport enterprises, signed at Beijing on March 5, 1982.

Done at Beijing on the 30th day of April, 1984, in duplicate, in the Chinese and English languages, the two texts having equal authenticity.

Protocol II

The Government of the People's Republic of China and the Government of the United States of America, desiring to conclude a Protocol in addition to the Agreement between them for the avoidance of double taxation and the prevention of tax evasion, and the supplementary Protocol attached thereto, have agreed as follows:

Both sides have agreed, with respect to the interpretation of Paragraph 7 of the Protocol to the Agreement, that their understanding is as follows:

1. A person (other than an individual) which is a resident of a Contracting State shall not be entitled under this Agreement to relief from taxation in the other Contracting State unless:

a. (i) more than 50 per cent of the beneficial interest in such person (or in the case of a company more than 50 per cent of the number of shares of each class of the company's shares) is owned, directly or indirectly, by any combination of one or more of:

(A) individuals who are residents of one of the Contracting States;

(B) citizens of the United States;

(C) companies as described in subparagraph 1*b*. of this protocol; and

(D) one of the Contracting States, its political subdivisions or local authorities; and

(ii) in the case of relief from taxation under Articles 9 (Dividends), 10 (Interest), and 11 (Royalties), not more than 50 per cent of the gross income of such person is used to make payments of interest to persons who are other than persons described in clauses (A) through (D) of subparagraph *a.*(i), whether directly or indirectly; or

b. it is a company which is a resident of a Contracting State and in whose principal class of shares there is substantial and regular trading on a recognized stock exchange.

2. Paragraph 1 shall not apply if the establishment, acquisition and maintenance of such person and the conduct of its operations did not have as a principal purpose the purpose of obtaining benefits under the Agreement.

3. For the purposes of paragraph 1*b.*, the term 'a recognized stock exchange' means:

a. the NASDAQ System owned by the National Association of Securities Dealers, Inc. and any stock exchange registered with the Securities and Exchange Commission as a national securities exchange for the purposes of the Securities Exchange Act of 1934; and

b. any national securities exchange approved to be established by the Government of the People's Republic of China or its authorized institution; and

c. any other stock exchange agreed upon by the competent authorities of the Contracting State.

4. Before a resident of a Contracting State is denied relief from taxation in the other Contracting State by reason of paragraph 1, 2 and/or 3, the competent authorities of the Contracting States shall consult each other.

This Protocol is certified for addition to the Agreement and its supplemental Protocol by the undersigned.

Done at Beijing on the 10th day of May, 1986, in duplicate, in the English and Chinese languages, the two texts having equal authenticity.

Convention between the Government of the United States of America and the Government of the Arab Republic of Egypt for the Avoidance of Double Taxation and the Prevention of Fiscal Evasion with Respect to Taxes on Income, concluded in Cairo on August 24, 1980.

The Government of the United States of America and the Government of the Arab Republic of Egypt, desiring to conclude a convention for the avoidance of double taxation of income, the prevention of fiscal evasion with respect to taxes on income, and the elimination of obstacles to international trade and investment;

Have agreed as follows:

Article 1. Taxes Covered

1. The taxes which are the subject of this Convention are:

a. In the case of the United States, the Federal income taxes imposed by the Internal Revenue Code but excluding the accumulated earnings tax and the personal holding company tax, and

b. In the case of Egypt:

(i) Tax on income derived from immovable property (including the land tax, the building tax, and the ghaffir tax);

(ii) Tax on income from movable capital;

(iii) Tax on commercial and industrial profits;

(iv) Tax on wages, salaries, indemnities, and pensions;

(v) Tax on profits from liberal professions and all other non-commercial professions;

(vi) General income tax;

(vii) Defense tax;

(viii) National security tax;

(ix) War tax; and

(x) Supplementary taxes imposed as a percentage of taxes mentioned above.

2. This Convention shall also apply to taxes substantially similar to those covered by paragraph 1 which are imposed in addition to, or in place of, existing taxes after the date of signature of this Convention.

3. For the purpose of Article 26 (Non-Discrimination), this Convention shall also apply to taxes of every kind imposed at the national, or local level. For the purpose of Article 28 (Exchange of Information), this Convention shall also apply to taxes of every kind imposed at the national level.

4. The competent authorities of the Contracting States shall notify each other promptly of any amendments of the tax laws referred to in paragraph 1 and of the adoption of any taxes referred to in paragraph 2 by transmitting the texts of any amendments or new statutes.

5. The competent authorities of the Contracting States shall notify each other promptly of the publication by their respective Contracting States of any material concerning the application of this Convention, whether in the form of regulations, rulings, or judicial decisions, by transmitting the texts of any such materials.

Article 2. General Definitions

1. In this Convention, unless the context otherwise requires:

a. (i) The term 'United States' means the United States of America; and

(ii) When used in a geographical sense, the term 'United States' means the states thereof and the District of Columbia. Such term also includes,

(A) The territorial sea thereof, and

(B) The seabed and subsoil of the submarine areas adjacent to the coast thereof, but beyond the territorial sea, over which the United States exercises sovereign rights, in accordance with international law, for the purpose of exploration for and exploitation of the natural resources of such areas, but only to the extent that the person, property, or activity to which the Convention is being applied is connected with such exploration or exploitation.

b. (i) The term 'Egypt' means the Arab Republic of Egypt; and

(ii) When used in a geographical sense, the term 'Egypt' includes:

(A) The territorial sea thereof, and

(B) The seabed and subsoil of the submarine areas adjacent to the coast thereof, but beyond the territorial sea, over which Egypt exercises sovereign rights, in accordance with international law, for the purpose of exploration for and exploitation of the natural resources of such area, but only to the extent that the person, property, or activity to which this Convention is being applied is connected with such exploration or exploitation.

c. The term 'Contracting State' means the United States or Egypt, as the context requires.

d. The term 'State' means any national State, whether or not one of the Contracting States.

e. The term 'person' includes an individual, a partnership, a corporation, an estate, or a trust.

f. (i) The term 'United States corporation' means a corporation (or any unincorporated entity treated as a corporation for United States tax purposes) which is created or organized under the laws of the United States or any state thereof or the District of Columbia; and

(ii) The term 'Egyptian corporation' means a corporation or any unincorporated entity treated as a corporation for Egyptian tax purposes which is created or organized under the laws of Egypt.

g. The term 'competent authority' means:

(i) In the case of the United States, the Secretary of the Treasury or his delegate, and

(ii) In the case of Egypt, the Minister of Finance or his delegate.

h. The term 'tax' means tax imposed by the United States or Egypt whichever is applicable, to which this Convention applies by virtue of Article 1 (Taxes Covered).

i. The term 'international traffic' means any voyage of a ship or aircraft operated by a resident of one of the Contracting States except where such voyage is confined solely to places within a Contracting State.

2. Any other term used in this Convention and not defined in this Convention shall, unless the context otherwise requires, have the meaning which it has under the laws of the Contracting State whose tax is being determined. Notwithstanding the preceding sentence, if the meaning of such a term under the laws of one of the Contracting States is different from the meaning of the term under the laws of the other Contracting State, or if the meaning of such a term is not readily determinable under the laws of one of the Contracting States, the competent authorities of the Contracting States may, in order to prevent double taxation or to further any other purpose of this Convention, establish a common meaning of the term for the purposes of this Convention.

Article 3. Fiscal Residence

1. In this Convention:

a. The term 'resident of Egypt' means:

(i) A Egyptian corporation, and

(ii) Any other person (except a corporation or an entity treated under Egyptian law as a corporation) resident in Egypt for purposes of Egyptian tax, but in the case of a partnership, estate, or trust only to the extent that the income derived by such partnership, estate, or trust is subject to Egyptian tax as the income of a resident either in the hands of the respective entity or of its partners or beneficiaries.

b. The term 'resident of the United States' means:

(i) A United States corporation, and

(ii) Any other person (except a corporation or any entity treated as a corporation for United States tax purposes) resident in the United States for purposes of United States tax, but in the case of a partnership, estate, or trust only to the extent that the income derived by such partnership, estate, or trust is subject to United States tax as the income of a resident either in the hands of the respective entity or of its partners or beneficiaries.

2. Where by reason of the provisions of paragraph 1 an individual is a resident of both Contracting States, then his residence shall be determined in accordance with the following rules:

a. He shall be deemed to be a resident of that Contracting State in which he maintains his permanent home. If he has a permanent home in both Contracting States or in neither of the Contracting States, he shall be deemed to be a resident of that Contracting State with which his personal and economic relations are closest (center of vital interests);

b. If the Contracting State in which he has his center of vital interests cannot be determined, he shall be deemed to be a resident of that Contracting State in which he has an habitual abode;

c. If he has an habitual abode in both Contracting States or in neither of the Contracting States, he shall be deemed to be a resident of the Contracting State of which he is a citizen; and

d. If he is a citizen of both Contracting States or of neither Contracting State, the competent authorities of the Contracting States shall settle the question by mutual agreement.

Article 4. Source of Income

For purposes of this Convention:

1. Dividends shall be treated as income from sources within a Contracting State only if paid by a corporation of that Contracting State. Notwithstanding the preceding sentence, a dividend shall be treated as from sources within—

a. Egypt if paid by a United States corporation whose activities lie solely or mainly in Egypt and to which paragraph 5 of Article 11 (Dividends) applies.

b. The United States if paid by a corporation other than a United States corporation if, for the 3-year period ending with the close of such corporation's taxable year preceding the declaration of the dividend (or for such part of that period as such corporation has been in existence), at least 50 per cent of such corporation's gross income from all sources was industrial or commercial profits attributable to a permanent establishment which such corporation had in the United States.

2. Interest shall be treated as income from sources within a Contracting State only if paid by such Contracting State, a political subdivision or a local authority thereof, or by a resident of that Contracting State. Notwithstanding the preceding sentence, if such interest is paid on an indebtedness incurred in connection with a permanent establishment which bears such interest, then such interest shall be deemed to be from sources within the State (whether or not a Contracting State) in which the permanent establishment is situated.

3. Royalties described in paragraph 2 of Article 13 (Royalties) for the use of, or the right to use, property or rights described in such paragraph shall be treated as income from sources within a Contracting State only to the extent that such royalties are for the use of, or the right to use, such property or rights within that Contracting State.

4. Income from real property (including royalties) described in Article 7 (Income from Real Property) shall be treated as income from sources within a Contracting State only if such property is situated in that Contracting State.

5. Income from the rental of tangible personal (movable) property shall be treated as income from sources within a Contracting State only if such property is situated in that Contracting State.

6. Income from the purchase and sale or exchange of intangible or tangible personal property (other than gains defined as royalties by paragraph 2 of Article 13 (Royalties) shall be treated as income from

sources within a Contracting State only if such sale or exchange is within that Contracting State.

7. Income received by an individual for his performance of labor or personal services whether as an employee or in an independent capacity, shall be treated as income from sources within a Contracting State only to the extent that such services are performed in that Contracting State. Income from personal services performed aboard ships or aircraft operated by a resident of one of the Contracting States in international traffic shall be treated as income from sources within that Contracting State if rendered by a member of the regular complement of the ship or aircraft. Notwithstanding the preceding provisions of this paragraph, remuneration described in Article 21 (Governmental Functions) and payments described in Article 20 (Social Security Payments) paid from the public funds of a Contracting State or a political subdivision or local authority thereof shall be treated as income from sources within that Contracting State only.

8. Notwithstanding paragraphs 1 through 6, industrial or commercial profits which are attributable to a permanent establishment which the recipient, a resident of one of the Contracting States, has in the other Contracting State shall be treated as income from sources within that other Contracting State. Industrial or commercial profits attributable to such permanent establishment include any item of income described in paragraphs 1 through 6 to the extent provided in paragraph 6 of Article 8 (Business Profits).

9. The source of any item of income to which paragraphs 1 through 8 are not applicable shall be determined by each of the Contracting States in accordance with its own law. Notwithstanding the preceding sentence, if the source of any item of income under the laws of one Contracting State is different from the source of such item of income under the laws of the other Contracting State or if the source of such income is not readily determinable under the laws of one of the Contracting States, the competent authorities of the Contracting States may, in order to prevent double taxation or further any other purpose of this Convention, establish a common source of the item of income for purposes of this Convention.

Article 5. Permanent Establishment

1. For the purpose of this Convention, the term 'permanent establishment' means a fixed place of business through which a resident of one of the Contracting States engages in industrial or commercial activity.

2. The term 'permanent establishment' includes but is not limited to:

a. A seat of management;
b. A branch;
c. An office;
d. A factory;
e. A workshop;

f. A mine, quarry, or other place of extraction of natural resources; and

g. The maintenance of a building site or construction or installation project which exists for more than 6 months.

3. Notwithstanding paragraphs 1 and 2, a permanent establishment shall not include a fixed place of business used only for one or more of the following:

a. The use of facilities for the purpose of storage, display or delivery of goods or merchandise belonging to the resident;

b. The maintenance of a stock of goods or merchandise belonging to the resident for the purpose of storage, display or delivery;

c. The maintenance of a stock of goods or merchandise belonging to the resident for the purpose of processing by another person;

d. The maintenance of a fixed place of business for the purpose of purchasing goods or merchandise, or for collecting information, for the resident;

e. The maintenance of a fixed place of business for the purpose of advertising, for the supply of information, for scientific research, or for similar activities which have a preparatory or auxiliary character, for the resident; and

f. The maintenance of a building site or construction or installation project which does not exist for more than 6 months.

4. A person acting in one of the Contracting States on behalf of a resident of the other Contracting State, other than an agent of an independent status to whom paragraph 5 applies, shall be deemed to give rise to a permanent establishment in the first-mentioned Contracting State if such person has, and habitually exercises in the first-mentioned Contracting State, an authority to conclude contracts in the name of that resident, unless the exercise of such authority is limited to the purchase of goods or merchandise for that resident.

5. An resident of one of the Contracting States shall not be deemed to have a permanent establishment in the other Contracting State merely because such resident engages in industrial or commercial activity in that other Contracting State through a broker, general commission agent, or any other agent of an independent status, where such broker or agent is acting in the ordinary course of his business.

6. A resident of one of the Contracting States shall not be deemed to have a permanent establishment in the other Contracting State merely because such resident sells at the termination of a trade fair or convention in such other Contracting State goods or merchandise which such resident displayed at such trade fair or convention.

7. In determining whether a resident of one Contracting State has a permanent establishment in the other Contracting State there shall not be taken into account the fact that such resident may be related to either a resident of the other Contracting State or to any other person who engages in business in that other Contracting State.

8. The principles set forth in paragraphs 1 through 7 shall be applied in determining for purposes of this Convention whether there is a permanent establishment in a State other than one of the Contracting

States or whether a person other than a resident of one of the Contracting States has a permanent establishment in one of the Contracting States.

Article 6. General Rules of Taxation

1. A resident of one of the Contracting States may be taxed by the other Contracting State on any income from sources within that other Contracting State and only on such income, subject to any limitations set forth in this Convention. For this purpose, the rules set forth in Article 4 (Source of Income) shall be applied to determine the source of income.

2. The provisions of this Convention shall not be construed to restrict in any manner any exclusion, exemption, deduction, credit, or other allowance now or hereafter accorded—

a. By the laws of one of the Contracting States in determination of the tax imposed by that Contracting State, or

b. By any other agreement between the Contracting States.

3. Notwithstanding any provisions of this Convention except paragraph 4, a Contracting State may tax its residents (as determined under Article 3 (Fiscal Residence)) and its citizens as if this Convention had not come into effect.

4. The provisions of paragraph 3 shall not affect:

a. The benefits conferred by a Contracting State under paragraph 3 of Article 19 (Private Pensions and Annuities) and under Articles 20 (Social Security Payments), 25 (Relief from Double Taxation), 26 (Non-Discrimination), and 27 (Mutual Agreement Procedure); and

b. The benefits conferred by a Contracting State under Articles 21 (Governmental Functions), 22 (Teachers), 23 (Students and Trainees), and 30 (Diplomatic and Consular Officers) upon individuals who are neither citizens of, nor have immigrant status in, that Contracting State.

5. The competent authorities of the two Contracting States may each prescribe regulations necessary to carry out the provisions of this Convention.

Article 7. Income from Real Property

1. Income from real property, including royalties and other payments in respect of the exploitation of natural resources and gains derived from the sale, exchange, or other disposition of such property or of the right giving rise to such royalties or other payments, may be taxed by the Contracting State in which such real property or natural resources are situated. For purposes of this Convention interest on indebtedness secured by real property or secured by a right giving rise to royalties or other payments in respect of the exploitation of natural resources shall be regarded as income from real property.

2. Paragraph 1 shall apply to income derived from the usufruct, direct use, letting, or use in any other form of real property.

3. For purposes of paragraph 1 of this Article and paragraph 4 of Article 4 (Source of Income), gains from the alienation of shares in a corporation or of an interest in a partnership, estate, or trust, the prop-

erty of which consists, directly or indirectly, principally of real property situated in a Contracting State, shall be regarded as income from real property.

4. Income or gain referred to in this Article derived from sources in a Contracting State by a resident of the other Contracting State may be taxed by both Contracting States.

Article 8. Business Profits

1. Industrial or commercial profits of a resident of one of the Contracting States shall be exempt from tax by the other Contracting State unless the resident has a permanent establishment in that other Contracting State. If the resident has a permanent establishment in that other Contracting State, tax may be imposed by that other Contracting State on the industrial or commercial profits of the resident but only on so much of them as are attributable to the permanent establishment.

2. Where a resident of one of the Contracting States has a permanent establishment in the other Contracting State, there shall in each Contracting State be attributed to the permanent establishment the industrial or commercial profits which would reasonably be expected to have been derived by it if it were an independent entity engaged in the same or similar activities under the same or similar conditions and dealing wholly independently with the resident of which it is a permanent establishment.

3. In the determination of the industrial or commercial profits of a permanent establishment, there shall be allowed as deductions expenses which are reasonably connected with such profits, including executive and general administrative expenses, whether incurred in the Contracting State in which the permanent establishment is situated or elsewhere.

4. No profits shall be attributed to a permanent establishment of a resident of one of the Contracting States in the other Contracting State merely by reason of the purchase of goods or merchandise by that permanent establishment, or by the resident of which it is a permanent establishment, for the account of that resident.

5. The term 'industrial or commercial profits' includes, but is not limited to, income derived from manufacturing, mercantile, banking, insurance, agricultural, fishing or mining activities, the operation of ships or aircraft, the furnishing of services, the rental of tangible personal (movable) property, and the rental or licensing of motion picture films or films or tapes used for radio or television broadcasting. Such term does not include the performance of personal services by an individual either as an employee or in an independent capacity.

6. For purposes of paragraph 1, industrial or commercial profits which are attributable to a permanent establishment include income from dividends, interest, royalties (as defined in paragraph 2 of Article 13 (Royalties)), and capital gains and income derived from property and natural resources, but only if such income is effectively connected with the permanent establishment. To determine whether income is effectively connected with a permanent establishment, the factors taken into account shall include whether the rights or property giving rise to

such income are used in or held for use in carrying on an activity giving rise to industrial or commercial profits through such permanent establishment and whether the activities carried on through such permanent establishment were a material factor in the realization of such income. For this purpose, due regard shall be given to whether or not such property or rights or such income were accounted for through such permanent establishment.

7. Where industrial or commercial profits include items of income which are dealt with separately in other articles of this Convention, the provisions of those articles shall, except as otherwise provided therein, supersede the provisions of this Article.

Article 9. Shipping and Air Transport

1. Notwithstanding Article 8 (Business Profits): Profits derived by a resident of a Contracting State from the operation of ships or aircraft in international traffic shall taxable only in that Contracting State.

2. For purposes of this Article, income derived from the operation in international traffic of ships or aircraft does not include dividends received by a person by virtue of an ownership interest in a corporation engaged in the operation of ships or aircraft in international traffic, and includes:

a. Income derived from the rental of ships or aircraft operated in international traffic if such rental income is incidental to other income described in paragraph 1; and

b. Income derived from the use, maintenance, and lease of:

(i) Containers,

(ii) Trailers for the inland transport of containers, and

(iii) Other related equipment,

in connection with the operation by the resident in international traffic of ships or aircraft described in paragraph 1.

3. The existing exemption of United States air transport enterprises afforded by Decree of the Egyptian Council of Ministers shall cease to have effect upon the entry into force of this Convention.

Article 10. Related Persons

1. Where a person subject to the taxing jurisdiction of one of the Contracting States and any other person are related and where such related persons make arrangements or impose conditions between themselves which are different from those which would be made between independent persons, any income, deductions, credits, or allowances which would, but for those arrangements or conditions, have been taken into account in computing the income (or loss) of, or the tax payable by, one of such persons, may be taken into account in computing the amount of the income subject to tax and the taxes payable by such person.

2. Where a redetermination has been made by one Contracting State of the income of one of its residents in accordance with paragraph 1 then the other Contracting State shall, if it agrees with such redetermination and if necessary to prevent double taxation, make a

corresponding adjustment to the income of a person in such other Contracting State related to such resident. In the event the other Contracting State disagrees with such redetermination, the two Contracting States shall endeavor to reach agreement in accordance with the mutual agreement procedure in paragraph 2 of Article 27 (Mutual Agreement Procedure).

3. For purposes of this Convention, a person is related to another person if either person owns or controls directly or indirectly the other, or if any third person or persons own or control directly or indirectly both. For this purpose, the term 'control' includes any kind of control, whether or not legally enforceable, and however exercised or exercisable.

Article 11. Dividends

1. Dividends derived from sources within one of the Contracting States by a resident of the other Contracting State may be taxed by both Contracting States.

2. The rate of tax imposed by the United States on dividends paid by a United States corporation to a resident of Egypt shall not exceed:

a. 15 per cent of the gross amount of the dividend; or

b. When the recipient is a corporation, 5 per cent of the gross amount of the dividend if:

(i) During the part of the paying corporation's taxable year which precedes the date of payment of the dividend and during the whole of its prior taxable year (if any), at least 10 per cent of the outstanding shares of the voting stock of the paying corporation was owned by the recipient corporation, and

(ii) Not more than 25 per cent of the gross income of the paying corporation for such prior taxable year (if any) consists of interest or dividends (other than interest derived from the conduct of a banking, insurance, or financing business and dividends or interest received from subsidiary corporations, 50 per cent or more of the outstanding shares of the voting stock of which is owned by the paying corporation at the time such dividends or interest is received).

3. Dividends paid by an Egyptian corporation to a resident of the United States shall in Egypt be subject (a) to the tax on income derived from movable capital, the defense tax, national security tax, war tax, the supplementary taxes on the foregoing, and substantially similar taxes enacted after the date of signature of this Convention (which taxes shall be deducted at source), provided that such dividends, if distributed out of the taxable profits of the same taxable year and not out of accumulated reserves or assets, shall be allowed as a deduction from the amount of the company's taxable income or profits subject to tax as industrial or commercial profits, and (b) when paid to a natural person, to the general income tax levied on net total income. However, the general income tax thus imposed shall in no case exceed an average of 20 per cent of the net dividends payable to such natural person. The dividends payable to a United States corporation shall not be subject to any taxes other than those described in subparagraph (a).

4. Paragraphs 2 and 3 shall not apply if such dividends are treated, under paragraph 6 of Article 8 (Business Profits), as industrial or commercial profits attributable to a permanent establishment which the recipient, a resident of one Contracting State, has in the other Contracting State. In such case the provisions of Article 8 shall apply.

5. Dividends paid by a United States corporation whose activities lie solely or mainly in Egypt shall in Egypt be treated in the manner provided by paragraph 3.

6. Dividends deemed to be paid, according to the provisions of Egyptian taxation law, out of yearly profits by a permanent establishment maintained in Egypt by a United States corporation whose activities extend to countries other than Egypt shall in Egypt be treated in the manner provided by paragraph 3.

7. The term 'dividends' as used in this Article means income from shares, 'jouissance' shares or 'jouissance' rights, mining shares, founders' shares or other rights, not being debt-claims, participating in profits, as well as income from other corporate rights which is subjected to the same taxation treatment as income from shares by the laws of the State of which the corporation making the distribution is a resident.

Article 12. Interest

1. Interest derived by a resident of one of the Contracting States from sources within the other Contracting State may be taxed by both Contracting States.

2. Interest derived by a resident of one of the Contracting States from sources within the other Contracting State shall not be taxed by the other Contracting State at a rate in excess of 15 per cent of the gross amount of such interest.

3. Notwithstanding paragraphs 1 and 2, interest beneficially derived by (a) one of the Contracting States, or by an instrumentality of that Contracting State, not subject to tax by that Contracting State on its income, or (b) a resident of such Contracting State with respect to loans made, guaranteed, or insured by that Contracting State or an instrumentality thereof, shall be exempt from tax by the other Contracting State.

4. Interest paid by a resident of one of the Contracting States to a person other than a resident of the other Contracting State (and in the case of interest paid by a resident of Egypt to a person other than a citizen of the United States) shall be exempt from tax by the other Contracting State unless such interest is treated as income from sources within the other Contracting State under paragraph 2 of Article 4 (Source of Income).

5. Paragraphs 2, 3, and 4 shall not apply if the interest is treated, under paragraph 6 of Article 8 (Business Profits) as industrial or commercial profits attributable to a permanent establishment which the recipient, a resident of one Contracting State, has in the other Contracting State. In such a case, the provisions of Article 8 shall apply.

6. Where an amount is paid to a related person and would be treated as interest but for the fact that it exceeds an amount which would have been paid to an unrelated person, the provisions of this Article shall apply only to so much of the amount as would have been paid to an unrelated person. In such a case the excess amount may be taxed by each Contracting State according to its own law, including the provisions of this Convention where applicable.

7. The term 'interest' as used in this Convention means income from money lent and other income which under the taxation law of the Contracting State in which the income has its source is assimilated to income from money lent, but does not include interest on indebtedness secured by mortgages on real estate or other amounts considered income from real property under Article 7 (Income from Real Property).

Article 13. Royalties

1. Royalties derived by a resident of one of the Contracting States from sources within the other Contracting State may be taxed by both Contracting States. However, royalties shall not be taxed by the other Contracting State at a rate in excess of 15 per cent of the gross amount of such royalty.

2. For purposes of this Article the term 'royalties' means:

a. Payments of any kind made as consideration for the use of, or the right to use, copyrights of literary, artistic or scientific works, but not including copyrights of motion picture films or films or tapes used for radio or television broadcasting which are industrial and commercial profits within the meaning of paragraph 5 of Article 8 (Business Profits), and patents, designs, models, plans, secret processes or formulae, trademarks or other like property or rights; and

b. Gains derived from the sale, exchange, or other disposition of any such property or rights to the extent that the amounts realized on such sale, exchange, or other disposition for consideration are contingent on the productivity, use or disposition of such property or rights.

3. Paragraph 1 shall not apply if the recipient of the royalty, being a resident of one of the Contracting States, has in the other Contracting State a permanent establishment and the property or rights giving rise to the royalty is effectively connected with such permanent establishment. In such a case, the provisions of Article 8 (Business Profits) shall apply.

4. The provisions of this Article shall not apply to dividends on founders' shares issued in Egypt as consideration for the rights mentioned in paragraph 2 of this Article and which are taxed in accordance with the provisions of Article 1 of Law No. 14 of 1939. In such a case, the provisions of Article 11 (Dividends) shall apply.

5. Where an amount is paid to a related person and would be treated as a royalty but for the fact that it exceeds an amount which would have been paid to an unrelated person, the provisions of this Article shall apply only to so much of the amount as would have been paid

to an unrelated person. In such a case, the excess amount may be taxed by each Contracting State according to its own law, including the provisions of this Convention where applicable.

Article 14. Capital Gains

1. A resident of one of the Contracting States shall be exempt from tax by the other Contracting State on gains from the sale, exchange, or other disposition of capital assets unless:

a. The gain is derived by a resident of one of the Contracting States from the sale, exchange, or other disposition of property described in Article 7 (Income from Real Property) situated within the other Contracting State;

b. The gain arises out of a sale, exchange of other disposition described in paragraph 2 of Article 13 (Royalties);

c. The gain is treated, under paragraph 6 of Article 8 (Business Profits), as industrial or commercial profits attributable to a permanent establishment which the recipient has in such other Contracting State; or

d. The recipient of the gain, being an individual who is a resident of one of the Contracting States is present in the other Contracting State for a period or periods aggregating 183 days or more during the taxable year.

2. In the case of gains described in paragraph 1*a.*, the provisions of Article 7 (Income from Real Property) shall apply. In the case of gains described in paragraph 1*b.*, the provisions of Article 13 (Royalties) shall apply. In the case of gains described in paragraph 1*c.*, the provisions of Article 8 (Business Profits) shall apply.

Article 15. Independent Personal Services

1. Income derived by an individual who is a resident of one of the Contracting States from the performance of personal services in an independent capacity may be taxed by that Contracting State. Except as provided in paragraph 2, such income shall be exempt from tax by the other Contracting State.

2. Income derived by an individual who is a resident of one of the Contracting States from the performance of personal services in an independent capacity in the other Contracting State may be taxed by that other Contracting State, if the individual is present in that other Contracting State for a period or periods aggregating 90 days or more in the taxable year.

3. The term 'personal services in an independent capacity' includes, but is not limited to, scientific, literary, artistic, educational or teaching activities, as well as independent activities of physicians, lawyers, engineers, architects, dentists, and accountants.

Article 16. Dependent Personal Services

1. Except as provided in Articles 21 (Governmental Functions), 22 (Teachers), and 23 (Students and Trainees), wages, salaries, and similar remuneration derived by an individual who is a resident of one of the

Contracting States from labor or personal services performed as an employee, including income from services performed by an officer of a corporation or company, may be taxed by that Contracting State. Except as provided by paragraph 2 and in Articles 19 (Private Pensions and Annuities), 21 (Governmental Functions), 22 (Teachers), and 23 (Students and Trainees), such remuneration derived from sources within the other Contracting State may also be taxed by that other Contracting State.

2. Remuneration described in paragraph 1 derived by an individual who is a resident of one of the Contracting States shall be exempt from tax by the other Contracting State if:

a. He is present in that other Contracting State for a period or periods aggregating less than 90 days in the taxable year;

b. He is an employee of a resident of, or of a permanent establishment maintained in, the first-mentioned Contracting State;

c. The remuneration is not borne as such by a permanent establishment which the employer has in that other Contracting State; and

d. The remuneration is subject to tax in the first-mentioned Contracting State.

3. Notwithstanding paragraphs 1 and 2, remuneration derived by an employee of a resident of one of the Contracting States for labor or personal services performed as a member of the regular complement of a ship or aircraft operated in international traffic by a resident of that Contracting State may be taxed by that Contracting State.

Article 17. Public Entertainers

Notwithstanding Articles 15 (Independent Personal Services) and 16 (Dependent Personal Services), the income derived by an individual who is a resident of one Contracting State from his performance of personal services in the other Contracting State as a public entertainer, such as a theater, motion picture, radio or television artist, a musician, or an athlete, may be taxed by the other Contracting State, but only if the gross amount of such income exceeds 400 United States dollars or its equivalent in Egyptian pounds for each day such person is present in the other Contracting State for the purpose of performing such services therein.

Article 18. Amounts Received for Furnishing Personal Services of Others

1. Notwithstanding the provisions of Article 8 (Business Profits), amounts received by a resident of one of the Contracting States in consideration of furnishing in the other Contracting State the personal services of one or more other persons shall be subject to tax under the taxation laws of each Contracting State to the extent that:

a. (i) The person for whom the services were furnished designated the person or persons who would render the services, whether or not he had the legal right to do so and whether or not the designation had been made formally;

(ii) The person for whom the services were furnished had the right to designate the person or persons who would render the services; or

(iii) By reason of the facts and circumstances the arrangement for personal services had the effect of designating the person or persons who would render the services; and

b. The resident of the first-mentioned Contracting State directly or indirectly pays compensation for such services to any person, other than another resident of the first-mentioned Contracting State or of that other Contracting State who is subject to tax on such compensation.

2. Paragraph 1 shall not apply to any amount received if it is established to the satisfaction of the competent authority of that other Contracting State, with respect to such amount, that neither the creation or organization of the resident of the first-mentioned Contracting State (where such resident is a corporation or other entity), nor the furnishing of the services through such resident has the effect of a substantial reduction of income, war profits, excess profits, or similar taxes.

Article 19. Private Pensions and Annuities

1. Except as provided in Articles 21 (Governmental Functions), pensions and other similar remuneration paid to an individual in consideration of past employment shall be taxable only in the Contracting State of which he is a resident.

2. Alimony and annuities paid to an individual who is a resident of one of the Contracting States shall be taxable only in that Contracting State.

3. Child support payments made by an individual who is a resident of one of the Contracting States to an individual who is a resident of the other Contracting State shall be exempt from tax in that other Contracting State.

4. The term 'pensions and other similar remuneration', as used in this Article, means periodic payments other than social security payments covered in Article 20 (Social Security Payments) made (a) by reason of retirement or death and in consideration for services rendered or (b) by way of compensation for injuries or sickness received in connection with past employment.

5. The term 'annuities', as used in this Article, means a stated sum paid periodically at stated times during life, or during a specified number of years, under an obligation to make the payments in return for adequate and full consideration (other than for services rendered).

6. The term 'alimony', as used in this Article, means periodic payments made pursuant to a written separation agreement or a decree of divorce, separate maintenance, or compulsory support which payments are taxable to the recipient under the internal laws of the Contracting State of which he is a resident.

7. The term 'child support payments', as used in this Article, means periodic payments for the support of a minor child made pursuant to written separation agreement or a decree of divorce, separate maintenance, or compulsory support.

Article 20. Social Security Payments

Social security payments and similar amounts paid by one of the Contracting States to an individual who is a resident of the other Contracting State shall be taxable only in the other Contracting State. This Article shall not apply to payments described in Article 21 (Governmental Functions).

Article 21. Governmental Functions

1. Wages, salaries, or similar remuneration, including pensions, annuities, or similar benefits, paid from public funds of one of the Contracting States:

a. To a citizen of that Contracting State, or

b. To a citizen of a State other than a Contracting State who comes to the other Contracting State expressly for the purpose of being employed by the first-mentioned Contracting State

for labor or personal services performed as an employee of the national Government of that Contracting State, or any agency thereof, in the discharge of functions of a governmental nature shall be exempt from tax by the other Contracting State.

2. The provisions of Articles 16 (Dependent Personal Services) and 19 (Private Pensions and Annuities) shall apply to remuneration or pensions paid in respect of services rendered in connection with any trade or business carried on by one of the Contracting States or any agency thereof.

Article 22. Teachers

1. Where a resident of one of the Contracting States is invited by the Government of the other Contracting State, a political subdivision, or a local authority thereof, or by a university or other recognized educational institution in that other Contracting State to come to that other Contracting State for a period not expected to exceed 2 years for the purpose of teaching or engaging in research, or both, at a university or other recognized educational institution and such resident comes to that other Contracting State primarily for such purpose, his income from personal services for teaching or research at such university or educational institution shall be exempt from tax by that other Contracting State for a period not exceeding 2 years from the date of his arrival in that other Contracting State.

2. This article shall not apply to income from research if such research is undertaken not in the public interest but primarily for the private benefit of a specific person or persons.

Article 23. Students and Trainees

1. *a.* An individual who is a resident of one of the Contracting States at the time he becomes temporarily present in the other Contracting State and who is temporarily present in that other Contracting State for the primary purpose of:

(i) Studying at a university or other recognized educational institution in that other Contracting State, or

(ii) Securing training required to qualify him to practice a profession of professional specialty, or

(iii) Studying or doing research as a recipient of a grant, allowance, or award from a governmental, religious, charitable, scientific, literary, or educational organization,

shall be exempt from tax by that other Contracting State with respect to amounts described in subparagraph *b.* for a period not exceeding 5 taxable years from the date of his arrival in that other Contracting State, and for such additional period of time as is necessary to complete, as a full-time student, educational requirements as a candidate for a postgraduate or professional degree from a recognized educational institution.

b. The amounts referred to in subparagraph *a.* are:

(i) Gifts from abroad for the purpose of his maintenance, education, study, research, or training;

(ii) The grant, allowance, or award; and

(iii) Income from personal services performed in that other Contracting State in an amount not in excess of 3,000 United States dollars or its equivalent in Egyptian pounds for any taxable year.

2. An individual who is a resident of one of the Contracting States at the time he becomes temporarily present in the other Contracting State and who is temporarily present in that other Contracting State as an employee of, or under contract with, a resident of the first-mentioned Contracting State, for the primary purpose of:

a. Acquiring technical, professional, or business experience from a person other than that resident of the first-mentioned Contracting State or other than a person related to such resident, or

b. Studying at a university or other recognized educational institution in that other Contracting State,

shall be exempt from tax by that other Contracting State for a period not exceeding 12 consecutive months with respect to his income from personal services in an aggregate amount not in excess of 7,500 United States dollars or its equivalent in Egyptian pounds.

3. An individual who is a resident of one of the Contracting States at the time he becomes temporarily present in the other Contracting State and who is temporarily present in that other Contracting State for a period not exceeding 1 year, as a participant in a program sponsored by the Government of that other Contracting State, for the primary purpose of training, research, or study shall be exempt from tax by that other Contracting State with respect to his income from personal services in respect of such training, research, or study performed in that other Contracting State in an aggregate amount not in excess of 10,000 United States dollars or its equivalent in Egyptian pounds.

4. The benefits provided under Article 22 (Teachers) and paragraph 1 of this Article shall, when taken together, extend only for such period of time, not to exceed 5 taxable years from the date of arrival of the individual claiming such benefits, as may reasonably or customarily be required to effectuate the purpose of the visit, and for such additional period of time as is necessary to complete, as a full-time student,

educational requirements as a candidate for a postgraduate or professional degree from a recognized educational institution. The benefits provided under Article 22 (Teachers) shall not be available to an individual if, during the immediately preceding period, such individual enjoyed the benefits of paragraph 1 of this Article.

Article 24. Investment or Holding Companies

A corporation of one of the Contracting States deriving dividends, interest, royalties, or capital gains from sources within the other Contracting State shall not be entitled to the benefits of Articles 11 (Dividends), 12 (Interest), 13 (Royalties), or 14 (Capital Gains) if:

a. By reason of special measures the tax imposed on such corporation by the first-mentioned Contracting State with respect to such dividends, interest, royalties, or capital gains is substantially less than the tax generally imposed by such Contracting State on corporate profits, and

b. 25 per cent or more of the capital of such corporation is held of record or is otherwise determined, after consultation between the competent authorities of the Contracting States, to be owned, directly or indirectly by one or more persons who are not individual residents of the first-mentioned Contracting State (or, in the case of an Egyptian corporation, who are citizens of the United States).

Article 25. Relief from Double Taxation

Double taxation of income shall be avoided in the following manner:

1. In accordance with the provisions and subject to the limitations of the law of the United States (as it may be amended from time to time without changing the general principle hereof), the United States shall allow to a citizen or resident of the United States as a credit against the United States tax the appropriate amount of taxes paid or accrued to Egypt and, in the case of a United States corporation owning at least 10 per cent of the voting stock of an Egyptian corporation from which it receives dividends in any taxable year, shall allow credit for the appropriate amount of taxes paid or accrued to Egypt by the Egyptian corporation paying such dividends with respect to the profits out of which such dividends are paid. Such appropriate amount shall be based upon the amount of tax paid or accrued to Egypt, but the credit shall not exceed the limitations (for the purpose of limiting the credit to the United States tax on income from sources within Egypt or on income from sources outside the United States) provided by United States law for the taxable year. For purpose of applying the United States credit in relation to taxes paid or accrued to Egypt, the rules set forth in Article 4 (Source of Income) shall be applied to determine the source of income. For purposes of applying the United States credit in relation to taxes paid or accrued to Egypt, the taxes referred to in paragraphs 1*b.* and 2 of Article 1 (Taxes Covered) shall be considered to be income taxes.

2. Egypt shall allow to a citizen or resident of Egypt as a credit against Egyptian tax the appropriate amount of income taxes paid or

accrued to the United States and, in the case of an Egyptian corporation owning at least 10 per cent of the voting stock of a United States corporation from which it receives dividends in any taxable year, shall allow credit for the appropriate amount of taxes paid or accrued to the United States by the United States corporation paying such dividends with respect to the profits out of which such dividends are paid. Such appropriate amount shall be based upon the amount of tax paid or accrued to the United States but shall not exceed that portion of Egyptian tax which such citizen's or resident's net income from sources within the United States bears to his entire net income for the same taxable year. For the purpose of applying the Egyptian credit in relation to taxes paid or accrued to the United States, the rules set forth in Article 4 (Source of Income) shall be applied to determine the source of income.

Article 26. Non-Discrimination

1. A citizen of one of the Contracting States who is a resident of the other Contracting State shall not be subject in that other Contracting State to more burdensome taxes than a citizen of that other Contracting State who is a resident thereof.

2. A permanent establishment which a resident of one of the Contracting States has in the other Contracting State shall not be subject in that other Contracting State to more burdensome taxes than a resident of that other Contracting State carrying on the same activities. This paragraph shall not be construed as:

a. Obliging a Contracting State to grant to individual residents of the other Contracting State any personal allowances, reliefs, or deductions for taxation purposes on account of civil status or family responsibilities which it grants to its own individual residents;

b. Obliging Egypt to grant United States corporations the exemptions granted to Egyptian corporations by Articles 5 and 6 of Law 14 of 1939; or

c. Affecting the application in Egypt of the first and second paragraphs of Article 11 and Article 11 bis of Law 14 of 1939.

3. A corporation of one of the Contracting States, the capital of which is wholly or partly owned or controlled, directly or indirectly, by one or more residents of the other Contracting State, shall not be subjected in the first-mentioned Contracting State to any taxation or any requirement connected with taxation which is other or more burdensome than the taxation and requirements to which a corporation of the first-mentioned Contracting State carrying on the same activities, the capital of which is wholly owned or controlled by one or more residents of the first-mentioned Contracting State, is or may be subjected.

Article 27. Mutual Agreement Procedure

1. Where a resident or citizen of one of the Contracting States considers that the action of one or both of the Contracting States results or will result for him in taxation not in accordance with this Conven-

tion, he may, notwithstanding the remedies provided by the national laws of the Contracting States, present his case to the competent authority of the Contracting State of which he is a resident or citizen. Should the resident's or citizen's claim be considered to have merit by the competent authority of the Contracting State to which the claim is made, it shall endeavor to come to an agreement with the competent authority of the other Contracting State with a view to the avoidance of taxation not in accordance with the provisions of this Convention.

2. The competent authorities of the Contracting States shall endeavor to resolve by mutual agreement any difficulties or doubts arising as to the application of this Convention. In particular, the competent authorities of the Contracting States may agree:

a. To the same attribution of industrial or commercial profits to a resident of one of the Contracting States and its permanent establishment situated in the other Contracting State;

b. To the same allocation of income, deductions, credits, or allowances between a resident of one of the Contracting States and any related persons and to the readjustment of taxes imposed by each Contracting State to reflect such allocation;

c. To the same determination of the source of particular items of income; or

d. To the same characterization of particular items of income.

3. The competent authorities of the Contracting States may communicate with each other directly for the purpose of reaching an agreement in the sense of this Article. When it seems advisable for the purpose of reaching an agreement, the competent authorities may meet together for an oral exchange of opinions.

4. In the event that the competent authorities reach such an agreement, taxes shall be imposed on such income, and refund or credit of taxes shall be allowed, by the Contracting States in accordance with such agreement, notwithstanding any procedural rule (including statutes of limitations) applicable under the law of either Contracting State.

Article 28. Exchange of Information

1. The competent authorities shall exchange such information as is necessary for carrying out the provisions of this Convention or for the prevention of fraud or for the administration of statutory provisions concerning taxes to which this Convention applies provided the information is of a class that can be obtained under the laws and administrative practices of each Contracting State with respect to its own taxes.

2. Any information so exchanged shall be treated as secret, except that such information may be:

a. Disclosed to any person concerned with, or

b. Made part of a public record with respect to,

the assessment, collection, or enforcement of, or litigation with respect to, the taxes to which this Convention applies.

3. No information shall be exchanged which would be contrary to public policy.

4. If specifically requested by the competent authority of a Contracting State, the competent authority of the other Contracting State shall provide information under this Article in the form of depositions of witnesses and copies of unedited original documents (including books, papers, statements, records, accounts, or writings) to the same extent such depositions and documents can be obtained under the laws and administrative practices of each Contracting State with respect to its own taxes.

5. Depositions and evidence which may be furnished in accordance with this Article shall not be withheld by reason of any doctrine of law under which international judicial assistance is not accorded in tax matters.

6. The exchange of information shall be carried out promptly either on a routine basis or on request with reference to particular cases. The competent authorities of the Contracting State may agree on the list of information which shall be furnished on a routine basis.

Article 29. Assistance in Collection

1. Each of the Contracting States shall endeavor to collect on behalf of the other Contracting State such taxes imposed by that other Contracting State as will ensure that any exemption or reduced rate of tax granted under this Convention by that other Contracting State shall not be enjoyed by persons not entitled to such benefits.

2. In no case shall this Article be construed so as to impose upon a Contracting State the obligation to carry out measures at variance with the laws or administrative practices of either Contracting State with respect to the collection of its own taxes.

Article 30. Diplomatic and Consular Officers

Nothing in this Convention shall affect the fiscal privileges of diplomatic and consular officials under the general rules of international law or under the provisions of special agreements.

Article 31. Entry into Force

This Convention shall be subject to ratification in accordance with the constitutional procedures of each Contracting State and instruments of ratification shall be exchanged at ...... as soon as possible. It shall enter into force 30 days after the date of exchange of instruments of ratification and shall then have effect for the first time:

a. As respects the rate of withholding tax, to amounts paid on or after the first day of the second month following the date on which this Convention enters into force.

b. As respects other taxes, to taxable years beginning on or after January 1 of the year following the date on which this Convention enters into force.

Article 32. Termination

1. This Convention shall remain in force until terminated by one of the Contracting States. Either Contracting State may terminate the Con-

vention at any time after 5 years from the date on which this Convention enters into force provided that at least 6 months' prior notice of termination has been given through diplomatic channels. In such event, the Convention shall cease to have force and effect as respects income of calendar years or taxable years beginning (or, in the case of taxes payable at the source, payments made) on or after January 1 next following the expiration of the 6-month period.

2. Notwithstanding the provisions of paragraph 1, and upon prior notice to be given through diplomatic channels, the provisions of this Convention exempting social security payments from taxation in the Contracting State which makes the payments may be terminated by either Contracting State at any time after this Convention enters into force.

In witness whereof, the undersigned, duly authorized thereto, have signed this Convention.

Convention between the United States of America and the French Republic with Respect to Taxes on Income and Property, concluded in Paris on July 28, 1967, as amended by the Protocols of October 12, 1970, November 24, 1978, January 17, 1984, and June 16, 1988.

The President of the French Republic and the President of the United States of America, desiring to conclude a convention for the avoidance of double taxation of income and capital and the prevention of fiscal evasion, have appointed for that purpose as their respective Plenipotentiaries:

The President of the United States of America: The Honorable Charles E. Bohlen, Ambassador of the United States of America in Paris, and

The President of the French Republic: Mr. Hervé Alphand, Ambassador of France, Secretary General of the Ministry of Foreign Affairs,

who, having communicated to each other their full powers, found in good and due form, have agreed upon the following Articles:

Article 1. Taxes Covered

1. The taxes which are the subject of the present Convention are:

a. In the case of the United States, the Federal income taxes imposed by the Internal Revenue Code of 1986 and the excise tax on insurance premiums paid to foreign insurers. The excise tax on insurance premiums paid to foreign insurers, however, is covered only to the extent that the foreign insurer does not reinsure such risks with a person not entitled to exemption from such tax under this or another convention.

b. In the case of France:

(i) the income tax, the corporation tax, including any withholding tax, prepayment (*précompte*) or advance payment with respect to the aforesaid taxes; and

(ii) the tax on Stock Exchange transactions.

(iii) the wealth tax (*l'impôt sur les Grandes Fortunes*).

2. The Convention shall also apply to any documentary taxes on sales or transfers of shares or certificates of stock or bonds which are subsequently imposed.

3. The Convention shall also apply to any identical or substantially similar taxes which are subsequently imposed in addition to, or in place of, the existing taxes.

4. For the purpose of Article 24 (Non-Discrimination), this Convention shall also apply to taxes of every kind and to those imposed at the national, State, and local level.

Article 2. General Definitions

1. In this Convention, unless the context otherwise requires:

a. (i) The term 'United States' means the United States of America and, when used in a geographical sense, includes the States thereof and the District of Columbia. Such term also includes any area outside the States and the District of Columbia which is, in accordance with international law, an area within which the United States may exercise rights with respect to the natural resources of the seabed and sub-soil.

(ii) The term 'France' means the French Republic and, when used in a geographical sense, means the European and Overseas departments of the French Republic. Such term also includes any area outside those departments which is, in accordance with international law, an area within which France may exercise rights with respect to the natural resources of the seabed and sub-soil.

b. The terms 'a Contracting State' and 'the other Contracting State' mean the United States or France, as the context requires.

c. The term 'person' comprises an individual or a corporation, or any other body of individuals or persons.

d. (i) The term 'United States corporation' or 'corporation of the United States' means a corporation, or any entity treated as a corporation for United States tax purposes, which is created or organized under the laws of the United States or any State thereof or the District of Columbia; and

(ii) The term 'French corporation' or 'corporation of France' means any body corporate, or any entity which is treated as a body corporate under French tax law, which is resident within France for French tax purposes.

e. The term 'international traffic' means any transport by a ship or aircraft, except where such transport is solely between places in the other Contracting State.

f. The term 'competent authority' means:

(i) In the case of the United States, the Secretary of the Treasury or his delegate, and

(ii) In the case of France, the Minister of Economy and Finance or his delegate.

2. As regards the application of the Convention by a Contracting State any term not otherwise defined shall, unless the context otherwise requires, have the meaning which it has under the laws of that Contracting State relating to the taxes which are the subject of the Convention.

Article 3. Fiscal Domicile

1. The term 'resident of France' means:

a. A French corporation,

b. Any person (other than a body corporate or any entity which under French law is treated as a body corporate) who is resident in France for purposes of its tax, and

c. France or any of its local authorities.

2. The term 'resident of the United States' means:

a. A United States corporation,

b. Any person (except a corporation or an entity treated under United States law as a corporation) who is resident in the United States for purposes of its tax, but in the case of a person acting as a partner or fiduciary only to the extent that the income derived by such person in that capacity is taxed as the income of a resident, and

c. The United States or any of its political subdivisions or local authorities.

3. An individual who is a resident in both Contracting States shall be deemed a resident of that Contracting State in which he maintains his permanent home. If he has a permanent home in both Contracting States or in neither of the Contracting States, he shall be deemed a resident of that Contracting State with which his personal and economic relations are closest (center of vital interests). If the Contracting State in which he has his center of vital interests cannot be determined, he shall be deemed a resident of that Contracting State in which he has an habitual abode. If he has an habitual abode in both Contracting States or in neither of the Contracting States, the competent authorities of the Contracting States shall settle the question by mutual agreement. For purposes of this Article, a permanent home is the place in which an individual dwells with his family. An individual who is deemed to be a resident of one Contracting State and not a resident of the other Contracting State by reason of the provisions of this paragraph shall be deemed a resident only of the former State for all purposes of this Convention (including Article 22).

Article 4. Permanent Establishment

1. For the purpose of this Convention, the term 'permanent establishment' means a fixed place of business through which a resident of one of the Contracting States engages in industrial or commercial activity.

2. The term 'permanent establishment' shall include especially:

a. A seat of management;

b. A branch;

c. An office;

d. A factory;

e. A workshop;

f. A warehouse;

g. A mine, quarry, or other place of extraction of natural resources;

h. A building site or construction or assembly project which exists for more than 12 months.

3. Notwithstanding paragraph 1 of this Article, a permanent establishment shall not include a fixed place of business used only for one or more of the following activities:

a. The use of facilities for the purpose of storage, display, or delivery of goods or merchandise belonging to the resident;

b. The maintenance of a stock of goods or merchandise belonging to the resident for the purpose of storage, display, or delivery;

c. The maintenance of a stock of goods or merchandise belonging to the resident for the purpose of processing by another person;

d. The maintenance of a fixed place of business for the purpose of purchasing goods or merchandise, or for collecting information, for the resident;

e. The maintenance of a fixed place of business for the purpose of advertising, for the supply of information, for scientific research, or for similar activities which have a preparatory or auxiliary character, for the resident.

4. A person acting in a Contracting State on behalf of a resident of the other Contracting State – other than an agent of an independent status to whom paragraph 5 applies – shall be deemed to be a permanent establishment in the first-mentioned State if such person:

a. Has, and habitually exercises in that State, an authority to conclude contracts in the name of that resident, unless the exercise of such authority is limited to the purchase of goods or merchandise for that resident, or

b. Maintains substantial equipment or machinery within the first-mentioned State for a period of twelve months or more.

5. An resident of a Contracting State shall not be deemed to have a permanent establishment in the other Contracting State merely because such resident carries on business in that other Contracting State through a broker, general commission agent, or any other agent of an independent status, where such persons are acting in the ordinary course of their business.

6. The fact that a resident of one of the Contracting States is a related person, as defined in Article 8 of this Convention, with respect to a resident of the other Contracting State or with respect to a person who engages in industrial or commercial activity in that other Contracting State (whether through permanent establishment or otherwise) shall not be taken into account in determining whether that resident of the first Contracting State has a permanent establishment in the other Contracting State.

7. An insurance company of one of the Contracting States shall be considered as having a permanent establishment in the other Contracting State if through a representative other than one described in paragraph 5, such company receives premiums from or insures risks in the territory of that other Contracting State.

Article 5. Income from Real Property

1. Income from real property and royalties in respect of the operations of mines, quarries, or other natural resources (not including interest on debts secured by mortgages or other encumbrances on such real property or royalty interest but including gains derived from the sale or exchange of such property or the right giving rise to such royalties) shall be taxable by the Contracting State in which such real property, mines, quarries, or other natural resources are situated.

2. The provisions of paragraph 1 shall apply to income derived from the usufruct, direct use, letting, or use in any other form of real property.

Article 6. Business Profits

1. Industrial or commercial profits of a resident of one of the Contracting States shall taxable only in that State unless such resident is engaged in industrial or commercial activity in the other Contracting State through a permanent establishment situated therein. If such resident is so engaged, tax may be imposed by such other State on the industrial or commercial profits of such residents but only on so much of them as are attributable to the permanent establishment.

2. Where a resident of a Contracting State carries on business in the other Contracting State through a permanent establishment situated therein, there shall in each Contracting State be attributed to that permanent establishment the industrial or commercial profits which would be attributable to such permanent establishment if such permanent establishment were an independent entity engaged in the same or similar activities under the same or similar conditions and dealing at arm's length with the resident of which it is a permanent establishment.

3. For the implementation of paragraphs 1 and 2, any income or gain attributable to a permanent establishment during its existence is taxable in the Contracting State where such permanent establishment is situated even if the payments are deferred until such permanent establishment has ceased to exist.

4. In the determination of the profits of a permanent establishment, there shall be allowed as deductions expenses which are reasonably connected with such profits including executive and general administrative expenses, whether incurred in the State in which the permanent establishment is situated or elsewhere.

5. A partner shall be considered to have realized income or incurred deductions to the extent of his ratable share of the profits or losses of the partnership. For this purpose, the character of any item of income or deduction accruing to the partner shall be determined as if it were realized or incurred from the same source and in the same manner as realized or incurred by the partnership. A partner will be considered to have realized or incurred a proportionate share of each item of income and deduction of the partnership, except to the extent that his share of the profits depends on the source of the income.

6. No profits shall be attributed to a permanent establishment merely by reason of the purchase of goods or merchandise by that permanent establishment, or by the resident of which it is a permanent establishment, for the account of that resident.

7. When an insurance company of one of the Contracting States has a permanent establishment in the other Contracting State, the reinsurance premiums received shall be taken into account for the determination of taxable profits only in the Contracting State of which the company is a resident.

8. The term 'industrial or commercial profits of a resident' includes income derived from manufacturing, mercantile, agricultural, fishing or mining activities, from the operation of ships or aircraft, from the furnishing of personal services, from the rental of tangible personal property, and from insurance activities and rents or royalties derived from motion picture films, films or tapes of radio or television broadcasting. It also includes income derived from real property and natural resources and dividends, interest, royalties (as defined in paragraphs 3 and 4 of Article 11), and capital gains but only if the right or property giving rise to such income, dividends, interest, royalties, or capital gains is effectively connected with a permanent establishment which the recipient, being a resident of one Contracting State, has in the other Contracting State. It does not include income received by an individual as compensation for personal services either as an employee or in an independent capacity.

Article 7. Shipping and Air Transport

1. Notwithstanding Articles 6 and 12:

a. Where a resident of the United States derives income from the operation in international traffic of ships or aircraft, or gains from the sale, exchange or other disposition of ships or aircraft used in international traffic by such resident, such income or gain shall be taxable only in the United States.

b. Where a resident of France derives income from the operation in international traffic of ships or aircraft, or gains from the sale, exchange or other disposition of ships or aircraft used in international traffic by such resident, such income or gain shall be taxable only in France.

2. The provisions of this Article shall also apply to the proportionate share of income derived by a resident of a Contracting State from participation in a pool, a joint business or an international operating agency. The proportionate share shall be treated as derived directly from the operation in international traffic of ships or aircraft.

3. In the case of a corporation, the provisions of paragraphs 1 and 2 shall apply only if more than 50 per cent of the capital of such corporation is owned, directly or indirectly:

a. by individuals who are residents of the Contracting State in which such corporation is resident or of a State with which the other Contracting State has a convention which exempts such income; or

b. by such Contracting State.

However, if more than 50 per cent in value of the shares of a corporation or of its parent are listed on one or more recognized securities exchanges in a Contracting State, and there is substantial trading activity in those shares on such exchange or exchanges, then the provisions of paragraphs 1 and 2 shall apply if it can be shown that 20 per cent or more of the capital of such corporation is owned, directly or indirectly, by individuals and the Contracting States specified in this paragraph.

4. For purposes of this Article, income derived from the operation in international traffic of ships or aircraft includes:

a. profits derived from the rental on a full or bareboat basis of ships or aircraft if operated in international traffic by the lessee or if such rental profits are incidental to other profits described in paragraph 1, or

b. profits of a resident of a Contracting State from the use or maintenance of containers (including trailers, barges and related equipment for the transport of containers) used for the transport in international traffic of goods or merchandise if such income is incidental to other profits described in paragraph 1.

Article 8. Related Persons

1. Where a resident of a Contracting State and a resident of the other Contracting State are related and where such related persons make arrangements or impose conditions between themselves which are different from those which would be made between independent persons, then any income which would, but for those arrangements or conditions, have accrued to the resident of the first Contracting State but, by reason of those arrangements or conditions, has not so accrued, may be included in the income of the resident of the first Contracting State for purposes of the present Convention and taxed accordingly.

2. *a.* A person other than a corporation is related to a corporation if such person participates directly or indirectly in the management, control or capital of the corporation.

b. A corporation is related to another corporation if either participates directly or indirectly in the management, control, or capital of the other, or if any person or persons participate directly or indirectly in the management, control, or capital of both corporations.

Article 9. Dividends

1. Dividends derived from sources within a Contracting State by a resident of the other Contracting State may be taxed in that other State.

2. Dividends derived from sources within a Contracting State by a resident of the other Contracting State may also be taxed by the former Contracting State but the tax imposed on such dividends shall not exceed:

a. 15 per cent of the amount actually distributed; or

b. When the recipient is a corporation, 5 per cent of the amount actually distributed if:

(i) During the part of the paying corporation's taxable year which precedes the date of payment of the dividend and during the whole of its prior taxable year (if any), at least ten per cent of the outstanding shares of the voting stock of the paying corporation was owned by the recipient corporation, and

(ii) Not more than 25 per cent of the gross income of the paying corporation for such prior taxable year (if any) consisted of interest and dividends (other than interest derived in the conduct of a banking, insurance, or financing business and dividends or interest received from subsidiary corporations, 50 per cent or more of the outstanding shares of the voting stock of which was owned by the paying corporation at the time such dividends or interest were received).

3. Paragraphs 2 and 6 of this Article and, in the case of dividends derived by a resident of France, paragraph 1 of this Article, shall not apply if the recipient of the dividends has a permanent establishment in the other Contracting State and the shares with respect to which the dividends are paid are effectively connected with the permanent establishment. In such a case, the provisions of Article 6 shall apply.

4. Dividends paid by a corporation of one of the Contracting States shall be treated as income from sources within that Contracting State, and dividends paid by any other corporation shall be treated as income from sources outside that Contracting State.

5. When the prepayment (*précompte*) is levied on dividends paid by a French corporation to a resident of the United States, who is not entitled to payment described in paragraph 6 with respect to dividends, such resident shall be entitled to the refund of that prepayment, subject to deduction of the withholding tax with respect to the refunded amount in accordance with paragraph 2 of this Article.

6. *a.* A resident of the United States who receives a dividend from a French corporation which, if received by a resident of France would entitle such resident to a tax credit (*avoir fiscal*), shall be entitled to a payment from the French Treasury equal to such credit (*avoir fiscal*), subject to the deduction from such payment of withholding tax in the amount provided for in paragraph 2*a.* of this Article.

b. The provisions of subparagraph *a.* shall be applicable to the following residents of the United States:

(i) An individual or other person (other than a corporation or an entity treated under United States law as a corporation) who is a resident of the United States;

(ii) A corporation which is not a regulated investment company and which, within the meaning of the provisions of the United States Internal Revenue Code providing a credit for taxes paid by a foreign corporation, owns less than 10 per cent of the voting stock of the French corporation referred to in subparagraph *a.*; or

(iii) A corporation which is a regulated investment company owning less than 10 per cent of the voting stock of the French corporation referred to in subparagraph *a.* and which has less than 20 per cent of its shares owned by persons who are neither citizens nor residents of the United States.

c. The payment provided for under subparagraph *a.* shall be deemed to be a distribution by the French corporation.

d. The competent authorities may prescribe regulations to implement the provisions of this paragraph and further define and determine the terms and conditions under which any payment provided for in subparagraph *a.* may be made.

7. The term 'dividends' as used in this Article means income from shares, 'jouissance' shares or 'jouissance' rights, mining shares, founders shares or other rights, not being debt-claims, participating in

profits, as well as income treated as a distribution by the taxation laws of the Contracting State of which the company making the distribution is a resident.

Article 10. Interest

1. Interest derived and beneficially owned by a resident of a Contracting State shall be taxable only in that State.

2. Notwithstanding that under Article 3 of the Convention a permanent establishment in one of the Contracting States of an enterprise of the other Contracting State is not a resident of the first-mentioned State, a permanent establishment in the United States of a French bank or financial or credit institution shall be treated by France solely for purposes of paragraph 1 of this Article for purposes of French taxes as if it were a resident of the United States, provided that the indebtedness in respect of which the interest is paid is effectively connected with such permanent establishment in the ordinary course of its business.

3. The term 'interest' as used in this Convention means income from indebtedness of every kind, whether or not secured by mortgage, and whether or not carrying a right to participate in the debtor's profits, and in particular, income from government securities, and income from bonds or debentures, including premiums or prizes attaching to such securities, bonds or debentures. Penalty charges for late payment shall not be regarded as interest for the purposes of the Convention.

4. The provisions of paragraph 1 shall not apply if the beneficial owner of the interest, being a resident of a Contracting State, carries on business in the other Contracting State, in which the interest arises, through a permanent establishment established therein, or performs in that other State independent personal services from a fixed base situated therein, and the interest is attributable to such permanent establishment or fixed base. In such case the provisions of Article 6 or Article 14, as the case may be, shall apply.

5. Interest shall be deemed to arise in a Contracting State when the payor is that State itself or a political subdivision, local authority, or resident of that State. Where, however, the person paying the interest, whether he is a resident of a Contracting State or not, has in a Contracting State a permanent establishment or a fixed base in connection with which the indebtedness in respect of which the interest is paid was incurred, and such interest is borne by such permanent establishment or fixed base, then such interest shall be deemed to arise in the State in which the permanent establishment or fixed base is situated. In that case the interest shall be deemed to be paid by the permanent establishment or fixed base to the beneficial owner at the latest when it is taken into account as an expense of that permanent establishment or fixed base.

6. Where, by reason of a special relationship between the payer and the beneficial owner or between both of them and some other person, the amount of the interest, having regard to the debt-claim for which it is paid, exceeds the amount which would have been agreed upon by

the payer and the beneficial owner in the absence of such relationship, the provisions of this Article shall apply only to the last-mentioned amount. In such case the excess part of the payments shall remain taxable according to the laws of each Contracting State, due regard being had to the other provisions of the Convention.

7. A Contracting State may not impose any tax on interest paid by a resident of the other Contracting State, except insofar as:

a. the interest is paid to a resident of the first-mentioned State;

b. the interest is attributable to a permanent establishment or fixed base of the beneficial owner of the interest situated in the first-mentioned State; or

c. the interest arises in the first-mentioned State and is not paid to a resident of the other State.

Article 11. Royalties

1. Royalties derived from sources within one Contracting State by a resident of the other Contracting State may be taxed in that other State.

2. Except as provided in paragraph 3, royalties may also be taxed in the Contracting State in which they arise, and according to the laws of that State, but if the beneficial owner of the royalties is a resident of the other Contracting State, the tax imposed on such royalties shall not exceed 5 per cent of the gross amount paid.

3. Royalties derived from copyrights of literary, artistic, or scientific works (including gain from the sale or exchange of property giving rise to such royalties) and beneficially owned by a resident of one Contracting State shall be taxable only in that Contracting State.

4. The term 'royalties' as used in paragraph 1 of this Article means:

a. Any royalties, rentals, or other amounts paid as consideration for the use of, or the right to use, patents, designs or models, plans, secret processes or formulae, trademarks, or other like property or rights, or for knowledge, experience, or skill (know-how), and

b. Gains derived from the sale or exchange of any such right or property, if payment of the amounts realized on such sale or exchange is contingent, in whole or in part, on the productivity, use or disposition of such right or property. If the amounts derived from the sale or exchange of any such right or property are not so contingent, the provisions of Article 12 shall apply.

5. Paragraphs 2 and 3 of this Article, and, in the case of royalties derived by a resident of France, paragraph 1 of this Article, shall not apply if the recipient of the royalty, being a resident of one of the Contracting States, has in the other Contracting State a permanent establishment and the right or property giving rise to the royalties is effectively connected with such permanent establishment. In such a case, the provisions of Article 6 shall apply.

6. *a.* Royalties shall be deemed to arise in a Contracting State when the payer is that State itself, a local authority, a statutory body or a resident of that State.

b. Where, however, the person paying the royalties, whether he is a resident of a Contracting State or not, has in a Contracting State a permanent establishment or a fixed base in connection with which the liability to pay the royalties was incurred, and such royalties are borne by such permanent establishment or fixed base, then such royalties shall be deemed to arise in the Contracting State in which the permanent establishment or fixed base is situated.

c. Notwithstanding subparagraphs *a.* and *b.*, royalties paid for the use of or the right to use property in the United States shall be deemed to arise therein.

7. Where, owing to a special relationship between the payer and the recipient, or between both of them and some other person, the amount of the royalties paid exceeds the amount which would have been agreed upon by the payer and the recipient in the absence of such relationship, the provisions of this Article shall apply only to the last-mentioned amount. In that case, the excess part of the payments shall remain taxable according to the laws of each Contracting State, due regard being had to the other provisions of this Convention.

8. For purposes of this Article, royalties shall be deemed to be paid to the beneficial owner at the latest when they are taken into account as expenses.

Article 12. Capital Gains

1. A resident of one of the Contracting States shall not be taxable only in that State on gains from the sale or exchange of capital assets.

2. Paragraph 1 of this Article shall apply if:

a. The gain is received by a resident of one of the Contracting States and arises out of the sale or exchange of property described in Article 5 (income from real property) located within the other Contracting State or of the sale or exchange of shares or comparable interests in a real property co-operative or of a corporation whose assets consist principally of such property,

b. The recipient of the gain, being a resident of one of the Contracting States, has a permanent establishment in the other Contracting State and the property giving rise to the gain is effectively connected with such permanent establishment, or

c. The recipient of the gain, being an individual resident of one of the Contracting States:

(i) Maintains a fixed base in the other Contracting State and the property giving rise to such gain is effectively connected to such fixed base, or

(ii) Is present in the other Contracting State for a period or periods exceeding in the aggregate 183 days during the taxable year.

3. In the case of gains described in paragraph 2*b.*, the provisions of Article 6 shall apply.

Paragraph 1 of this Article shall not apply in the case of gains described in paragraph 3 of Article 6.

Article 13. Branch Profits

1. *a.* A French corporation shall be exempt from the United States personal holding company tax in any taxable year if all of its stock is owned by one or more individual residents of France in their individual capacities for that entire year.

b. A French corporation shall be exempt from the United States accumulated earnings tax in any taxable year if it is a corporation described in paragraph 1*a.* of Article 24A.

2. *a.* A corporation which is a resident of a Contracting State and which has a permanent establishment in the other Contracting State may be subject in that other Contracting State to a tax in addition to the tax allowable under the other provisions of this Contracting State. Such tax, however, may be imposed only on:

(i) in the case of the United States, that portion of the business profits of the corporation attributable to the permanent establishment which represents the 'dividend equivalent amount' of those profits, in accordance with the provisions of the Internal Revenue Code; and

(ii) in the case of France, that portion of the business profits of the corporation attributable to the permanent establishment and which is included in the base of the French withholding tax in accordance with the provisions of French internal law.

b. The taxes referred to in subparagraph *a.* shall apply to the portion of the business profits attributable to a trade or business conducted in one Contracting State through a partnership by a corporation resident of the other Contracting State which is a member of such partnership.

c. The taxes referred to in subparagraphs *a.* and *b.* shall not be imposed at a rate exceeding the rate specified in paragraph 2*b.* of Article 9 (Dividends).

3. Profits realized by a French permanent establishment of a United States corporation and incorporated in its capital shall not be subject in France to the *'droit d'apport majoré'*.

Article 14. Independent Personal Services

1. Income derived by a resident of a Contracting State in respect of independent activities shall be taxable only in that State unless such activities were performed in the other Contracting State. Income in respect of independent activities performed within such other State may be taxed by such other State.

2. Notwithstanding the provisions of paragraph 1, income derived by a resident of a Contracting State in respect of independent activities performed in the other Contracting State shall not be taxable in such other State if:

a. The recipient is present in the other State for a period or periods not exceeding in the aggregate 183 days in the fiscal year concerned, and

b. The recipient does not maintain a fixed base in the other State for a period or periods exceeding in the aggregate 183 days in such year.

3. The term 'independent activities' means all activities – other than commercial, industrial, or agricultural activities – carried on on his own account independently by a person who receives the proceeds or bears the losses arising from these activities.

4. Article 6, paragraph 4, shall apply by analogy. In no event, however, shall that provision result in France exempting under Article 23 more than 50 per cent of the earned income from a partnership accruing to a resident of France. The amount of such a partner's income which is not exempt under Article 23 solely by reason of the preceding sentence shall reduce the amount of partnership earned income from sources within France on which France can tax partners who are not residents of France.

Article 15. Dependent Personal Services

1. Salaries, wages, and other similar remuneration paid to a resident of a Contracting State for labor or personal services shall be taxable only in that State unless such labor or personal services were performed in the other Contracting State. Remuneration received for labor or personal services performed within such other State may be taxed by such other State.

2. Notwithstanding the provisions of paragraph 1, remuneration derived by a resident of a Contracting State in respect of an employment exercised in the other Contracting State shall not be taxable in such other State if:

a. The recipient is present in the other State for a period or periods not exceeding in the aggregate 183 days in the fiscal year concerned,

b. The remuneration is paid by, or on behalf of, an employer who is not a resident of the other State, and

c. The remuneration is not borne by a permanent establishment which the employer has in the other State.

3. Notwithstanding the preceding provisions of this Article, remuneration derived by a resident of a Contracting State in respect of employment as a member of the regular complement of a ship or aircraft operated in international traffic may be taxed only in that State.

Article 15A. Artistes and Athletes

1. Notwithstanding the provisions of Articles 14 and 15, income derived by a resident of a Contracting State as an entertainer, such as a theatre, motion picture, radio or television artiste, or a musician, or as an athlete, from his personal activities as such exercised in the other Contracting State, may be taxed in that other State, except where the amount of the gross receipts derived by such entertainer or athlete, including expenses reimbursed to him or borne on his behalf, from such activities does not exceed ten thousand United States dollars ($10,000) or its equivalent in French francs for the taxable year concerned.

2. Where income in respect of activities exercised by an entertainer or an athlete in his capacity as such accrues not to the entertainer or athlete but to another person, that income of that other person may,

notwithstanding the provisions of Articles 6 and 14, be taxed in the Contracting State in which the activities of the entertainer or athlete are exercised, unless it is established that neither the entertainer or athlete nor persons related thereto participate directly or indirectly in any profits of that other person in any manner, including the receipt of deferred remuneration, bonuses, fees, dividends, partnership distributions, or other distributions.

Article 16. Governmental Functions

1. Remuneration, including pensions, paid by, or out of funds created by, a Contracting State or a political subdivision or local authority thereof to any individual who is a national of that State in respect of services rendered to that State or a subdivision or local authority thereof in the discharge of functions of a governmental nature shall be taxable only in that Contracting State.

2. The provisions of Articles 15, 19, and 20 shall apply to remuneration or pensions in respect of services rendered in connection with any industrial or commercial activity carried on by one of the Contracting States or a political subdivision or a local authority thereof.

3. In the case of an individual who is a national of both Contracting States, the provisions of Article 22, paragraph 4, shall apply to remuneration described in paragraph 1 but such remuneration shall be treated as income from sources within the Contracting State from which such individual receives such remuneration.

Article 17. Teachers

1. An individual who is a resident of one of the Contracting States at the beginning of his visit to the other Contracting State and who, at the invitation of the Government of the other Contracting State or of a university or other accredited educational or research institution situated in the other Contracting State, visits the latter Contracting State for the primary purpose of teaching or engaging in research, or both, at a university or other accredited institution shall be exempt from tax by the latter Contracting State on his income from personal services for teaching or research at such educational or research institution, or at other such institutions, for a period not exceeding 2 years from the date of his arrival in the latter Contracting State.

2. This Article shall not apply to income from research if such research is undertaken not in the public interest but primarily for the private benefit of a specific person or persons.

Article 18. Students and Trainees

1. *a.* An individual who is a resident of one of the Contracting States at the beginning of his visit to the other Contracting State and who is temporarily present in the other Contracting State for the primary purpose of:

(i) Studying at a university or other accredited educational institution in that other Contracting State, or

(ii) Securing training required to qualify him to practice a profession of professional specialty, or

(iii) Studying or doing research as a recipient of a grant, allowance, or award from a governmental, religious, charitable, scientific, literary, or educational organization,

shall be exempt from tax by that other Contracting State with respect to amounts described in subparagraph *b*.

b. The amounts referred to in subparagraph *a*. include:

(i) Gifts from abroad for the purpose of his maintenance, education, study, research, or training;

(ii) The grant, allowance, or award; and

(iii) Income from personal services performed in the other Contracting State in an amount not in excess of $2,000 or its equivalent in francs for any taxable year.

c. The benefits under this paragraph shall only extend for such period of time as may be reasonably or customarily required to effectuate the purpose of the visit, but in no event shall any individual have the benefits of this Article and Article 17 for more than a total of five taxable years.

2. A resident of one of the Contracting States who is present in the other Contracting State as an employee of, or under contract with, a resident of the former State, for the primary purpose of:

a. Acquiring technical, professional, or business experience from a person other than that resident of the former State or a corporation 50 per cent or more of the voting stock of which is owned by that resident of the former State, or

b. Studying at a university or other accredited educational institution in that other Contracting State,

shall be exempt from tax by that other Contracting State for one taxable year with respect to his income from personal services in an amount not in excess of $5,000 or its equivalent in francs.

Article 19. Private Pensions and Annuities

1. Except as provided in Article 16, pensions and other similar remuneration paid to a resident of a Contracting State in consideration of past employment shall be taxable only in that Contracting State.

2. Alimony and annuities paid to a resident of a Contracting State shall be taxable only in that Contracting State.

3. The term 'annuities,' as used in this Article, means a stated sum paid periodically at stated times during life, or during a specified number of years, under an obligation to make the payments in return for adequate and full consideration (other than services rendered).

4. The term 'pensions,' as used in this Article, means periodic payments made after retirement in consideration for, or by way of compensation for injuries received in connection with, past employment.

5. *a.* Contributions paid by, or on behalf of, an individual resident of a Contracting State, who is not a citizen of that State, to pension, profit-sharing, and other retirement plans that are recognized for tax purposes in the other Contracting State will be treated in the same way

for tax purposes in the first-mentioned State as contributions paid to pension, profit-sharing, and other retirement plans that are recognized for tax purposes in that first-mentioned State, provided that the competent authority of the first-mentioned State agrees that the plans correspond to pension, profit-sharing, or other retirement plans recognized for tax purposes by that State.

b. Payments received by the beneficiary in respect of the plans referred to in *a.* will be included in income for tax purposes of the State of residence, to the extent that they are not exempt under Article 23, when and to the extent that such payments are considered gross income by the other 'Contracting State.'

Article 20. Social Security Payments

Social security payments (whether representing employee or employer contributions or accretions thereto) paid by one of the Contracting States to an individual who is a resident of the other Contracting State or a citizen of the United States shall be taxable only in the former Contracting State.

Article 21. Rules Applicable to Personal Income Articles

1. Articles 14 through 18 shall apply to reimbursed travel expenses, but such expenses shall not be taken into account in computing the maximum amount of exemptions specified in Article 18.

2. An individual who qualifies for benefits under more than one of the provisions of Articles 14 through 18 may apply that provision most favorable to him, but shall not be entitled to the benefits of more than one provision in any taxable year.

Article 22. General Rules of Taxation

1. Items of income of a resident of a Contracting State, wherever arising, not dealt with in the foregoing Articles of this Convention shall be taxable only in that State.

2. A resident of one of the Contracting States shall be taxed by the other Contracting State only on:

a. Commercial or industrial profits attributable to a permanent establishment located in that other Contracting State, and

b. Income from sources within that other Contracting State, in accordance with the limitations set forth in the present Convention.

3. The provisions of the present Convention shall not be construed to restrict in any manner any exclusion, exemption, deduction, credit, or other allowance now or hereafter accorded:

a. By the laws of one of the Contracting States in the determination of the tax imposed by that State, or

b. By any other agreement between the Contracting States.

4. *a.* The United States may tax its citizens and residents as if the present Convention had not come into effect. For this purpose the term 'citizen' shall include a former citizen whose loss of citizenship had as one of its principal purposes the avoidance of income tax, but only for a period of 10 years following such loss.

(i) This provision shall not affect the rules laid down in Article 20 (Social Security Payment), Article 23 (Relief from Double Taxation), and Article 24 (Non-Discrimination).

(ii) This provision shall not affect the rules laid down in Article 17, 18, and 21 (Students, Teachers, Rules applicable thereto) when applicable to individuals who are not citizens of the United States and who do not have immigrant status in the United States.

(iii) This provision shall not affect the rules laid down in Articles 16 and 21 (Governmental Functions, Rules applicable thereto) when they apply to:

an individual who is not a citizen of the United States and who does not have immigrant status in the United States;

an individual who, having immigrant status in the United States, has elected to claim the benefits of these articles; in that case, such person must agree that any calendar year or portion of a calendar year for which Articles 16 and 21 apply shall not be counted as a period during which he has resided or has been physically present in the United States in the calculation of periods of residence or presence in the United States required for naturalization pursuant to the immigration and nationality laws of the United States.

5. Any transactions in which an order for the purchase, sale or exchange of stocks, securities or commodities originates in one of the Contracting States and is executed through a stock or commodities exchange in the other State shall be exempt by the former State from stamp or like tax otherwise arising with respect to such transaction.

Article 22A. Capital

1. Capital represented by real property or interests in real property or by shares or rights in a corporation or a body corporate the assets of which consist principally of real property or interests in real property may be taxed in the Contracting State where such real property is situated. For the purposes of this provision, real property pertaining to the industrial, commercial or agricultural operation of such corporation or body corporate or to the performance of independent personal services shall not be taken into account.

2. Capital represented by furniture and fixtures may be taxed in the Contracting State in which they are situated.

3. Capital represented by movable property forming part of the assets of a permanent establishment of a business or pertaining to a fixed base used for the performance of independent personal services may be taxed in the Contracting State where the permanent establishment or the fixed base is situated.

4. Capital of a resident of a Contracting State represented by ships and aircraft operated in international traffic and movable property pertaining to the operation of such ships and aircraft shall be taxable only in that State.

5. Capital represented by shares or rights forming part of a substantial interest in the capital of a corporation which is a resident of a Contracting State may be taxed in that State. A person is considered

to have a substantial interest if he or she owns, alone or with related persons, directly or indirectly, shares or rights the total of which gives right to at least 25 per cent of the corporate earnings.

6. All other elements of capital of a resident of a Contracting State are taxable only in that State.

7. Notwithstanding the provisions of the preceding paragraphs of this Article, for the purposes of taxation with respect to the wealth tax referred to in subparagraph 1*b*.(iii) of Article 1 of an individual resident of France who is a citizen of the United States and not a French national, the assets situated outside of France that such a person owns on the first of January of each of the five years following the calendar year in which he becomes a resident of France shall be excluded from the base of assessment of the taxes referred to in subparagraph 1*b*.(iii) of Article 1 relating to each of those five years. If such an individual loses the status of resident of France for a duration of at least three years and then again becomes a resident of France, the assets situated outside of France that such a person owns on the first of January of each of the five years following the calendar year in which he again becomes a resident of France shall be excluded from the base of assessment of the taxes referred to in subparagraph 1*b*.(iii) of Article 1 relating to each of those five years.

Article 23. Relief from Double Taxation

1. In accordance with the provisions and subject to the limitations of the law of the United States (as it may be amended from time to time without changing the general principle hereof), the United States shall allow to a citizen or resident of the United States as a credit against the United States income tax:

a. the income tax paid to France by or on behalf of such citizen or resident; and

b. in the case of a United States corporation owning at least 10 per cent of the voting stock of a corporation which is a resident of France and from which the United States corporation receives dividends, the income tax paid to France by or on behalf of the distributing corporation with respect to the profits out of which the dividends are paid.

For the purposes of this paragraph, the taxes referred to in subparagraph 1*b*.(i) and paragraph 3 of Article 1 shall be considered income taxes.

2. In the case of France:

a. income referred to below derived by a resident of France shall be exempt from the French taxes mentioned in subparagraph 1*b*.(i) of Article 1:

(i) income (other than income referred to in paragraph 2*b*. of this Article) which is taxable in the United States under this Convention other than by reason of the citizenship of the taxpayer; and

(ii) in the case of an individual who is a citizen of the United States:

(a) income which would be exempt from United States tax under Articles 17 or 18 if the recipient were not an individual who is a citizen of the United States,

(b) income dealt with in paragraph 1 of Article 19 to the extent attributable to services performed while his principal place of employment was in the United States, and alimony and annuities dealt with in paragraph 2 of Article 19,

(c) income consisting of dividends derived from sources within the United States (as described in paragraph 4 of Article 9), interest arising in the United States (as described in paragraph 5 of Article 10), or royalties derived from sources within the United States (as described in paragraph 6 of Article 11) which is beneficially owned by a resident of France and which is:

(A) paid by the United States, any political subdivision or any authority thereof; or

(B) paid by a United States legal entity the principal class of shares of or interests in which are substantially and regularly traded on a recognized stock exchange as defined in paragraph 3 of Article 24A; or

(C) paid by a United States corporation other than one 10 per cent or more of the outstanding shares of the voting stock of which the resident of France owned (either directly or indirectly) at all times during the part of such corporation's taxable year preceding the date of payment of the income to the owner of the income and during the prior taxable year (if any) of such corporation, provided that less than 50 per cent of such stock is owned by residents of France during the same period; or

(D) paid by a resident of the United States not more than 25 per cent of the gross income of which for the prior taxable year (if any) consisted directly or indirectly of income derived from sources outside the United States,

(d) capital gains derived from the sale or exchange of capital assets generating income as defined in subparagraph (c). However such sale or exchange shall remain taken into account for the determination of the threshold of taxation applicable in France to capital gains on movable property, and

(e) profits or gains derived from transactions on a public United States options or futures market.

b. As regards income or profits taxable in the United States under Articles 9, 11, 13 or 15A, France shall allow to a resident of France a tax credit corresponding to the amount of tax levied by the United States under this Convention other than by reason of citizenship. Such tax credit, not to exceed the amount of French tax levied on such income, shall be allowed against taxes mentioned in subparagraph 1*b*.(i) and paragraph 3 of Article 1 of the Convention in the bases of which such income is included.

c. Notwithstanding the provisions of subparagraphs *a*. and *b*., French tax may be computed on income chargeable in France by virtue of this

Convention at the rate appropriate to the total of the income chargeable in accordance with French law.

d. As regards capital taxable in the United States under Article 22A that is also taxable in France, France shall allow to a resident of France a tax credit corresponding to the amount of tax levied by the United States on such capital. Such tax credit, not to exceed the amount of French tax levied on such capital, shall be allowed against the wealth tax referred to in subparagraph 1*b*.(iii) of Article 1 of the Convention in the bases of assessment of which such capital is included.

e. The exemption provided by paragraph 2*a*.(ii) shall be granted:

(i) only if the citizens of the United States who are residents of France demonstrate that they have complied with their United States income tax obligations, and

(ii) upon receipt by the competent authority of France of such certification as may be prescribed by such authority or upon request to such authority for refund of tax withheld together with the presentation of any required certification.

3. In the case of an individual who is both a resident of France and a citizen of the United States:

a. The amount of the tax credit referred to in subparagraph *b.* of paragraph 2 shall be equal to the amount of tax which the United States would be entitled to levy in respect of the item of income if the individual deriving the income were not a citizen of the United States, but shall not exceed the amount of French tax levied on such item of income;

b. The United States shall allow as a credit against United States tax the income tax paid to France after the credit referred to in paragraph 2*b*. However, the credit so allowed against United States tax shall not reduce that portion of the United States tax that is creditable against French tax in accordance with paragraph 2*b*.

c. Income referred to in paragraph 2 and income that, but for the citizenship of the taxpayer, is exempt from United States tax under the Convention, shall be considered income from sources within France to the extent necessary to give effect to the provisions of paragraph 3*b*. This provision shall apply only to the extent that an item of income is included in gross income for purposes of determining French tax. No provision of this paragraph 3*c*. relating to source of income shall apply in determining credits against United States tax for foreign taxes other than those referred to in subparagraph 1*b*.(i) and paragraph 3 of Article 1.

4. If, for any taxable year a partnership of which an individual member is a resident of France so elects, for United States tax purposes,

a. any income which solely by reason of paragraph 4 of Article 14 is not exempt from French tax under this Article shall be considered income from sources within France; and

b. the amount of income to which subparagraph *a.* applies shall reduce (but not below zero) the amount of partnership earned income from sources outside the United States which would otherwise be allocated to partners who are not residents of France. For this purpose the reduction shall apply first to income from sources within France and then to other income from sources outside the United States.

If the individual member of the partnership is both a resident of France and a citizen of the United States, this provision shall not result in a reduction of United States tax below that which the taxpayer would have incurred without the benefit of deductions or exclusions available solely by reason of his presence or residence outside the United States.

5. A resident of a Contracting State who maintains one or several abodes in the territory of the other Contracting State shall not be subject in that other State to an income tax according to an 'imputed' income based on the rental of that or those abodes.

Article 24. Non-Discrimination

1. A citizen of one of the Contracting States who is a resident of the other Contracting State shall not be subjected in that other Contracting State to more burdensome taxes than a citizen of that other Contracting State who is a resident thereof.

2. The taxation on a permanent establishment which a resident of a Contracting State has in the other Contracting State shall not be less favorably levied in that other State than the taxation levied on a resident of that other Contracting State carrying on the same activities. This provision shall not be construed as obliging a Contracting State to grant to residents of the other Contracting State any personal allowances, reliefs, and deductions for taxation purposes on account of civil status or family responsibilities which it grants to its own individual residents. The provisions of this paragraph shall not be construed to prevent the application by either Contracting State of its tax on branch profits described in paragraph 2 of Article 13 (Branch Profits) of the Convention.

3. A corporation of a Contracting State, the capital of which is wholly or partly owned or controlled, directly or indirectly, by one or more residents of the other Contracting State, shall not be subjected in the first-mentioned Contracting State to any taxation or any requirement connected therewith which is other or more burdensome than the taxation and connected requirements to which a corporation of that first-mentioned Contracting State carrying on the same activities, the capital of which is wholly owned by one or more residents of that first-mentioned Contracting State, is or may be subjected.

Article 24A. Limitation on Benefits

1. A person (other than an individual) which is a resident of a Contracting State and derives income from the other Contracting State shall not be entitled under this Convention to relief from taxation in that other Contracting State, nor to relief from double taxation in the first-mentioned Contracting State, unless:

a. more than 50 per cent of the beneficial interest in such person (or, in the case of a corporation, more than 50 per cent of the number of shares in each class of the corporation's shares) is owned, directly or indirectly, by any combination of one or more of:

(i) individuals who are residents of the United States;
(ii) citizens of the United States;
(iii) individuals who are residents of France;
(iv) corporations in whose principal class of shares there is substantial and regular trading on a recognized stock exchange as defined in paragraph 3; and
(v) the Contracting States, their local authorities, or political subdivisions of the United States; and

b. not more than 50 per cent of the gross income of such person is used, directly or indirectly, to meet liabilities (including liabilities for interest or royalties) to persons who are not residents of the Contracting States, one of the Contracting States or its local authorities, or political subdivisions of the United States or citizens of the United States.

2. The provisions of paragraph 1 shall not apply if the establishment, acquisition and maintenance of such person and the conduct of its operations did not have as one of its principal purposes the purpose of obtaining benefits under the Convention.

3. The provisions of paragraph 1 shall not apply if the person deriving the income is a corporation which is a resident of a Contracting State in whose principal class of shares there is substantial and regular trading on a recognized stock exchange. For purposes of the preceding sentence, the term 'recognized stock exchange' means:

a. the NASDAQ System owned by the National Association of Securities Dealers, Inc. and any stock exchange registered with the Securities and Exchange Commission as a national securities exchange for purposes of the Securities Exchange Act of 1934;

b. the French stock exchanges (*Bourses de Valeurs*); and

c. any other stock exchange agreed upon by the competent authorities of the Contracting States.

Article 25. Mutual Agreement Procedure

1. Where a resident of a Contracting State considers that the actions of one or both of the Contracting States results or will result for him in taxation not in accordance with this Convention, he may, notwithstanding the remedies provided by the national laws of those States, present his case to the competent authority of the Contracting State of which he is a resident.

2. The competent authorities of the Contracting States shall endeavor to resolve by mutual agreement any difficulties or doubts arising as to the application of the Convention. In particular, the competent authorities of the Contracting States may consult together to endeavor to agree:

a. To the same attribution of industrial or commercial profits to a resident of one of the Contracting States and its permanent establishment situated in the other Contracting State;

b. To the same allocation of income between a resident of one of the Contracting States and any related person, provided for in Article 8; or *c.* To the same determination of the source of particular items of income.

3. The competent authorities of the Contracting States may communicate with each other directly for the purpose of reaching an agreement in the sense of the preceding paragraphs. When it seems advisable for the purpose of reaching agreement, the competent authorities may meet together for an oral exchange of opinions.

4. In the event that the competent authorities reach such an agreement, taxes shall be imposed on such income, and refund or credit of taxes shall be allowed, by the Contracting States in accordance with such agreement. Any agreement reached shall be implemented notwithstanding any time limits or other procedural limitations in the domestic law of the Contracting States.

Article 25A. Provisions for Implementation

The competent authorities of the Contracting States may prescribe rules and procedures jointly or separately, to determine the mode of application of the provisions of this Convention.

Article 26. Exchange of Information

1. The competent authorities of the Contracting States shall exchange such information as is pertinent to carrying out the provisions of this Convention or preventing fraud or fiscal evasion in relation to the taxes which are the subject of this Convention. Any information so exchanged shall be treated as secret and shall not be disclosed to any persons other than those (including a court or administrative body) concerned with the assessment, collection, or administration of, or the enforcement or prosecution in respect of, or the determination of appeals in relation to, the taxes which are the subject of the Convention.

2. In no case shall the provisions of paragraph 1 be construed so as to impose on one of the Contracting States the obligation:

a. To carry out administrative measures at variance with the laws or the administrative practice of that or the other Contracting State;

b. To supply particulars which are not obtainable under the laws or in the normal course of the administration of that or of the other Contracting State;

c. To supply information which would disclose any trade, business, industrial, commercial, or professional secret or trade process, or information, the disclosure of which would be contrary to public policy (*ordre public*).

3. The exchange of information shall be either on a routine basis or on request with reference to particular cases. The competent authorities of the Contracting States shall agree on the list of information which shall be furnished on a routine basis.

Article 27. Assistance in Collection

1. The two Contracting States undertake to lend assistance and support to each other in the collection of the taxes to which the present

Convention relates, together with interest, costs, and additions to the taxes and fines not being of a penal character according to the laws of the State requested, in the cases where the taxes are definitively due according to the laws of the State making the application.

2. In the case of an application for enforcement of taxes, revenue claims of each of the Contracting States which have been finally determined will be accepted for enforcement by the State to which application is made and collected in that State in accordance with the laws applicable to the enforcement and collection of its own taxes.

3. The application will be accompanied by such documents as are required by the laws of the State making the application to establish that the taxes have been finally determined.

4. If the revenue claim has not been finally determined, the State to which application is made will take such measures of conservancy (including measures with respect to transfer of property of nonresident aliens) as are authorized by its laws for the enforcement of its own taxes.

5. The assistance provided for in this Article shall not be accorded with respect to citizens, corporations, or other entities of the State to which application is made.

Article 28. Diplomatic and Consular Officers

Nothing in the present Convention shall affect the fiscal privileges of diplomatic or consular officials under the general rules of international law or under the provisions of special agreements.

Article 29. Territorial Extension

1. This Convention may be extended, either in its entirety or with any necessary modifications, to the Overseas Territories of the French Republic which impose taxes substantially similar in character to those to which the Convention applies. Any such extension shall take effect from such date and subject to such modifications and conditions, as may be specified and agreed between the Contracting States in notes to be exchanged through diplomatic channels or in any other manner in accordance with their constitutional procedure.

2. At any time after the expiration of a period of 1 year from the effective date of an extension made by virtue of paragraph 1 either of the Contracting States may by a written notice of termination given to the other Contracting State through diplomatic channels, terminate the application of the provisions in respect to any territory to which such application has been extended, in which case the provisions shall cease to be applicable to such territory on and after the first day of January following the date of such notice; provided, however, that this shall not affect the continued application of such provisions to the United States, to France, or to any other territory to which such provisions apply and which is not named in the notice of termination.

3. Unless otherwise agreed by both Contracting States, the termination of the Convention by one of the Contracting States under

Article 32 shall also terminate the application of the Convention to any territory to which it has been extended under this Article.

Article 30. Exchange of Official Information

1. The competent authorities of the Contracting States shall notify each other of any amendments of the tax laws referred to in Article 1.1 and of the adoption of any taxes referred to in Article 1.2 by transmitting the texts of any amendments or new statutes at least once a year.

2. The competent authorities of the Contracting States shall exchange the texts of all published material interpreting the present Convention under their respective laws, whether in the form of regulations, rulings, or judicial decisions.

3. Where, by reason of any change made in the taxation laws of one of the Contracting States, it seems advisable to adjust some provisions of this Convention without affecting its general principles, the necessary adjustments may be agreed between the Contracting States by notes to be exchanged through diplomatic channels or in any other manner in accordance with their respective constitutional procedure.

Article 31. Entry into Force

1. This Convention shall be ratified and instruments of ratification shall be exchanged at Washington. It shall enter into force one month after the date of exchange of the instruments of ratification. Its provisions shall for the first time have effect:

a. In the case of France:

(i) As respects withholding taxes, to any proceeds payable and transactions completed on or after the date on which this Convention enters into force;

(ii) As respects other income taxes, to taxes which are levied for the assessment year 1967; and

(iii) As respects the tax on stock exchange transactions, the date on which this Convention enters into force.

b. In the case of the United States:

(i) As respects the rate of withholding tax, to amounts received on or after the date on which this Convention enters into force;

(ii) As respects other income taxes, to taxable years beginning on or after January 1, 1967.

2. Upon the coming into effect of this Convention, three shall terminate:

a. The Convention of July 25, 1939, relating to income and other taxes,

b. The Convention of October 18, 1946, the supplementary Protocol of May 17, 1948, and the Convention of June 22, 1956, insofar as they concern taxes on income, on capital and tax on stock exchange transactions.

The provisions of those Conventions and of that Protocol will cease to have effect from the date on which the corresponding provisions of the present Convention shall for the first time have effect according to the subparagraph 1 above-mentioned.

Article 32. Termination

This Convention shall remain in force until denounced by one of the Contracting States. Either Contracting State may denounce the Convention, through diplomatic channels, by giving notice of termination at least 6 months before the end of any calendar year after the year 1969. In such event, the Convention shall cease to have effect:

1. In the case of France:

a. As respects withholding taxes, on January 1 of the year following the year in which notice is given.

b. As respects other income taxes, for any year of assessment beginning on or after January 1 of the year next following the year in which notice is given; and

c. As respects the tax on stock exchange transactions, for any transactions occurring on or after January 1 of the year following the year in which notice is given;

d. As regards the wealth tax, to capital owned on the first of January of the calendar year following the year in which notice is given.

2. In the case of the United States:

a. As respects withholding taxes, on January 1 of the year following the year in which notice is given.

b. As respects other income taxes, for any taxable year beginning on or after January 1 of the year following the year in which notice is given; and

c. As respects taxes referred to in paragraph 2 of Article 1, for any transactions occurring on or after January 1 of the year following the year in which notice is given.

In witness whereof, the respective plenipotentiaries have signed the present Convention.

Done at Paris in duplicate, in the English and French languages, each text being equally authentic, this 28th day of July, 1967.

Convention between the United States of America and the Federal Republic of Germany for the Avoidance of Double Taxation and the Prevention of Fiscal Evasion with Respect to Taxes on Income and Capital and to Certain Other Taxes, concluded in Bonn on August 29, 1989.

The United States of America and the Federal Republic of Germany, desiring to conclude a new Convention for the avoidance of double taxation and the prevention of fiscal evasion with respect to taxes on income and capital and certain other taxes, have agreed as follows:

Article 1. Personal Scope

This Convention shall apply to persons who are residents of one or both of the Contracting States, except as otherwise provided in this Convention.

Article 2. Taxes Covered

1. The existing taxes to which this Convention shall apply are:

a. In the United States:

(aa) the federal income taxes imposed by the Internal Revenue Code (but excluding the accumulated earnings tax, the personal holding company tax, and social security taxes); and

(bb) the excise tax imposed on insurance premiums paid to foreign insurers (hereinafter referred to as 'United States tax').

This Convention shall, however, apply to the excise tax imposed on insurance premiums paid to foreign insurers only to the extent that the risks covered by such premiums are not reinsured with a person not entitled to the benefits of this or any other convention that provides exemption from such tax.

b. In the Federal Republic of Germany:

(aa) the income tax (*Einkommensteuer*);

(bb) the corporation tax (*Körperschaftsteuer*);

(cc) the trade tax (*Gewerbesteuer*); and

(dd) the capital tax (*Vermögensteuer*) (hereinafter referred to as 'German tax').

2. This Convention shall apply also to any identical or substantially similar taxes that are imposed after the date of signature of this Convention in addition to, or in place of, the existing taxes. The competent authorities of the Contracting States shall notify each other of any significant changes that have been made in their taxation laws.

Article 3. General Definitions

1. For the purposes of this Convention, unless the context otherwise requires:

a. the terms 'a Contracting State' and 'the other Contracting State' mean the United States or the Federal Republic of Germany as the context requires;

b. the term 'United States', when used in a geographical sense, means the United States of America, but does not include Puerto Rico, the Virgin Islands, Guam, or any other possession or territory of the United States of America;

c. the term 'Federal Republic of Germany', when used in a geographical sense, means the area in which the tax law of the Federal Republic of Germany is in force;

d. the term 'person' includes but is not limited to an individual and a company;

e. the term 'company' means any body corporate or any entity that is treated as a body corporate for tax purposes;

f. the terms 'enterprise of a Contracting State' and 'enterprise of the other Contracting State' mean respectively an enterprise carried on by a resident of a Contracting State and an enterprise carried on by a resident of the other Contracting State;

g. the term 'international traffic' means any transport by a ship or aircraft, except when the ship or aircraft is operated solely between places in one of the Contracting States;

h. the term 'national' means:

(aa) in respect of the United States, United States citizens and any legal person, partnership, or association deriving its status as such from the law in force in the United States; and

(bb) in respect of the Federal Republic of Germany, any German within the meaning of paragraph 1 of Article 116 of the Basic Law of the Federal Republic of Germany and any legal person, partnership, or association deriving its status as such from the law in force in the Federal Republic of Germany; and

i. The term 'competent authority' means:

(aa) in the United States, the Secretary of the Treasury or his delegate; and

(bb) in the Federal Republic of Germany, the Federal Minister of Finance or his delegate.

2. As regards the application of this Convention by a Contracting State any term not defined therein shall, unless the context otherwise requires or the competent authorities agree to a common meaning pursuant to the provisions of Article 25 (Mutual Agreement Procedure), have the meaning which it has under the laws of that State concerning the taxes to which this Convention applies.

Article 4.* Residence

1. For the purposes of this Convention, the term 'resident of a Contracting State' means any person who, under the laws of that State, is liable to tax therein by reason of his domicile, residence, place of management, place of incorporation or any other criterion of a similar nature, provided, however, that

a. this term does not include any person who is liable to tax in that State in respect only of income from sources in that State or capital situated therein; and

b. in the case of income derived or paid by a partnership, estate, or trust, this term applies only to the extent that the income derived by such partnership, estate, or trust is subject to tax in that State as the income of a resident, either in its hands or in the hands of its partners or beneficiaries.

2. Where by reason of the provisions of paragraph 1 an individual is a resident of both Contracting States, then his status shall be determined as follows:

a. he shall be deemed to be a resident of the State in which he has a permanent home available to him; if he has a permanent home available to him in both States, he shall be deemed to be a resident of the State with which his personal and economic relations are closer (center of vital interests);

b. if the State in which he has his center of vital interests cannot be determined, or if he has not a permanent home available to him in either State, he shall be deemed to be a resident of the State in which he has an habitual abode;

c. if he has an habitual abode in both States or in neither of them, he shall be deemed to be a resident of the State of which he is a national; and

d. If he is a national of both States or of neither of them, the competent authorities of the Contracting States shall settle the question by mutual agreement.

3. Where by reason of the provisions of paragraph 1 a person other than an individual is a resident of both Contracting States, then the competent authorities of the Contracting States shall seek to determine through consultation the Contracting State of which the person shall be deemed to be a resident for the purposes of this Convention, and, if they are unable so to determine, such person shall not be considered to be a resident of either Contracting State for purposes of enjoying benefits under this Convention.

Article 5.* Permanent Establishment

1. For the purposes of this Convention, the term 'permanent establishment' means a fixed place of business through which the business of an enterprise is wholly or partly carried on.

2. The term 'permanent establishment' includes especially:

a. a place of management;

b. a branch;

c. an office;

d. a factory;

e. a workshop; and

f. a mine, an oil or gas well, a quarry, or any other place of extraction of natural resources.

3. A building site or a construction, assembly or installation project constitutes a permanent establishment only if it lasts more than twelve months.

4. Notwithstanding the foregoing provisions of this Article, the term 'permanent establishment' shall be deemed not to include:

a. the use of facilities for the purpose of storage, display or delivery of goods or merchandise belonging to the enterprise;

b. the maintenance of a stock of goods or merchandise belonging to the enterprise solely for the purpose of storage, display or delivery;

c. the maintenance of a stock of goods or merchandise belonging to the enterprise solely for the purpose of processing by another enterprise;

d. the maintenance of a fixed place of business solely for the purpose of purchasing goods or merchandise, or of collecting information, for the enterprise;

e. the maintenance of a fixed place of business solely for the purpose of advertising, of the supply of information, of scientific activities, or of similar activities that have a preparatory or auxiliary character for the enterprise; or

f. the maintenance of a fixed place of business solely for any combination of activities mentioned in subparagraphs *a.* to *e.*, provided that the overall activity of the fixed place of business resulting from this combination is of a preparatory or auxiliary character.

5. Notwithstanding the provisions of paragraphs 1 and 2, where a person (other than an agent of an independent status to whom paragraph 6 applies) is acting on behalf of an enterprise and has, and habitually exercises, in a Contracting State an authority to conclude contracts in the name of the enterprise, that enterprise shall be deemed to have a permanent establishment in that State in respect of any activities which that person undertakes for the enterprise, unless the activities of such person are limited to those mentioned in paragraph 4 that, if exercised through a fixed place of business, would not make this fixed place of business a permanent establishment under the provisions of that paragraph.

6. An enterprise shall not be deemed to have a permanent establishment in a Contracting State merely because it carries on business in that State through a broker, general commission agent, or any other agent of an independent status, provided that such persons are acting in the ordinary course of their business.

7. The fact that a company that is a resident of a Contracting State controls or is controlled by a company that is a resident of the other Contracting State, or that carries on business in that other State (whether through a permanent establishment or otherwise), shall not of itself constitute either company a permanent establishment of the other.

Article 6. Income from Immovable (Real) Property

1. Income derived by a resident of a Contracting State from immovable (real) property (including income from agriculture or forestry) situated in the other Contracting State may be taxed in that other State.

2. The term 'immovable property' shall have the meaning that it has under the law of the Contracting State in which the property in question is situated. The term shall in any case include property accessory to immovable property; livestock and equipment used in agriculture and forestry; rights to which the provisions of general law respecting landed property apply; usufruct of immovable property; and rights to variable or fixed payments as consideration for the working of, or the right to work, mineral deposits, sources, and other natural resources. Ships and aircraft shall not be regarded as immovable property.

3. The provisions of paragraph 1 shall apply to income derived from the direct use, letting or use in any other form of immovable property.

4. The provisions of paragraphs 1 and 3 shall also apply to the income from immovable property of an enterprise and to income from immovable property used for the performance of independent personal services.

Article 7.* Business Profits

1. The business profits of an enterprise of a Contracting State shall be taxable only in that State unless the enterprise carries on business in the other Contracting State through a permanent establishment situated therein. If the enterprise carries on business as aforesaid, the business profits of the enterprise may be taxed in the other State but only so much of them as is attributable to that permanent establishment.

2. Subject to the provisions of paragraph 3, where an enterprise of a Contracting State carries on business in the other Contracting State through a permanent establishment situated therein, there shall in each Contracting State be attributed to that permanent establishment the business profits that it might be expected to make if it were a distinct and independent enterprise engaged in the same or similar activities under the same or similar conditions.

3. In determining the business profits of a permanent establishment, there shall be allowed as deductions expenses that are incurred for the purposes of the permanent establishment, including research and development expenses, interest, and other similar expenses and a reasonable amount of executive and general administrative expenses, whether incurred in the State in which the permanent establishment is situated or elsewhere.

4. No business profits shall be attributed to a permanent establishment by reason of the mere purchase by that permanent establishment of goods or merchandise for the enterprise.

5. For the purposes of this Convention, the business profits to be attributed to the permanent establishment shall include only the profits derived from the assets or activities of the permanent establishment.

6. Where business profits include items of income that are dealt with separately in other Articles of this Convention, then the provisions of those Articles shall not be affected by the provisions of this Article.

7. For the purposes of this Convention the term 'business profits' includes income derived from the rental of tangible personal property and the rental or licensing of cinematographic films or works on film, tape, or other means of reproduction for use in radio and television broadcasting.

Article 8. Shipping and Air Transport

1. Profits of an enterprise of a Contracting State from the operation of ships or aircraft in international traffic shall be taxable only in that State.

2. Profits of an enterprise of a Contracting State from the use or rental of containers (including trailers, barges, and related equipment for the transport of containers) used in international traffic shall be taxable only in that State.

3. The provisions of paragraphs 1 and 2 shall also apply to profits from the participation in a pool, a joint business, or an international operating agency.

Article 9.* Associated Enterprises

1. Where:

a. an enterprise of a Contracting State participates directly or indirectly in the management, control, or capital of an enterprise of the other Contracting State, or

b. the same persons participate directly or indirectly in the management, control, or capital of an enterprise of a Contracting State and an enterprise of the other Contracting State,

and in either case conditions are made or imposed between the two enterprises in their commercial or financial relations that differ from those that would be made between independent enterprises, then any profits which would, but for those conditions, have accrued to one of the enterprises, but, by reason of those conditions, have not so accrued, may be included in the profits of that enterprise and taxed accordingly.

2. Where a Contracting State includes in the profits of an enterprise of that State, and taxes accordingly, profits on which an enterprise of the other Contracting State has been charged to tax in that other State, and that other Contracting State agrees that profits so included are profits that would have accrued to the enterprise of the first-mentioned State if the conditions made between the two enterprises had been those that would have been made between independent enterprises, then that other State shall make an appropriate adjustment to the amount of tax charged therein on those profits. In determining such adjustment, due regard shall be paid to the other provisions of this Convention and the competent authorities of the Contracting States shall if necessary consult each other.

Article 10.* Dividends

1. Dividends paid by a company that is a resident of a Contracting State to a resident of the other Contracting State may be taxed in that other State.

2. However, such dividends may also be taxed in the Contracting State of which the company paying the dividends is a resident and according to the laws of that State, but if the beneficial owner of the dividends is a resident of the other Contracting State the tax so charged shall not exceed:

a. 5 per cent of the gross amount of the dividends if the beneficial owner is a company that holds directly at least 10 per cent of the voting stock of the company paying the dividends;

b. 15 per cent of the gross amount of the dividends in all other cases.

Subparagraph *b.* and not subparagraph *a.* shall apply in the case of dividends paid by a United States person that is a Regulated Investment Company or of distributions on certificates of a German investment trust (*Kapitalanlagegesellschaft*). Subparagraph *a.* shall not apply to dividends paid by a United States person that is a Real Estate Investment Trust, and subparagraph *b.* shall apply only if the dividend is beneficially owned by an individual holding a less than 10 per cent interest in the Real Estate Investment Trust. This paragraph shall not affect the taxation of the company in respect of the profits out of which the dividends are paid.

3. As long as a natural person resident in the Federal Republic of Germany is entitled under German law to a tax credit (*Anrechnung der Körperschaftsteuer*) in respect of dividends paid by a company that is a resident of the Federal Republic of Germany, the following rules shall apply to dividends paid by such company:

a. the beneficial owner of dividends subject to paragraph 2*b.* shall be entitled to a further relief of tax of 5 per cent of the gross amount of the dividends; and

b. for United States income tax purposes (including for the purposes of credit for foreign taxes paid) the benefit resulting from the application of subparagraph *a.* shall be treated as a dividend paid to a beneficial owner resident in the United States.

The provisions of this paragraph shall not apply to distributions on certificates of an investment trust.

4. The term 'dividends' as used in this Article means income from shares, 'jouissance' shares or 'jouissance' rights, mining shares, founders' shares, or other rights (not being debt-claims) participating in profits, as well as other income derived from other rights that is subjected to the same taxation treatment as income from shares by the laws of the Contracting State of which the company making the distribution is a resident. The term 'dividends' also includes in the Federal Republic of Germany income under a sleeping partnership (*Stille Gesellschaft*), '*partiarisches Darlehen*', or '*Gewinnobligation*' as well as distributions on certificates of an investment trust.

5. Notwithstanding the first sentence of paragraph 2 of this Article and paragraph 1 of Article 11 (Interest), income from arrangements, including debt obligations, carrying the right to participate in profits (including in the Federal Republic of Germany income under a sleeping partnership (*Stille Gesellschaft*), '*partiarisches Darlehen*', '*Gewinnobligation*', or 'jouissance' shares or 'jouissance' rights) that is deductible in determining the profits of the payer may be taxed in the Contracting State in which it arises according to the laws of that State.

6. The provisions of paragraphs 1 and 2 shall not apply if the beneficial owner of the dividends, being a resident of a Contracting State, carries on business in the other Contracting State of which the company paying the dividends is a resident through a permanent establishment situated therein, or performs in that other State independent personal services from a fixed base situated therein, and the holding in respect of which the dividends are paid forms part of the business property of such permanent establishment or fixed base. In such a case the provisions of Article 7 (Business Profits) or Article 14 (Independent Personal Services), as the case may be, shall apply.

7. Where a company that is a resident of a Contracting State derives profits or income from the other Contracting State, that other State may not impose any tax on the dividends paid by the company, except insofar as such dividends are paid to a resident of that other State or insofar as the holding in respect of which the dividends are paid forms part of the business property of a permanent establishment or a fixed base situated in that other State, even if the dividends paid consist wholly or partly of profits or income arising in such other State.

8. A company that is a resident of a Contracting State and that has a permanent establishment in the other Contracting State, or that is subject to tax on a net basis in that other Contracting State on items of income that may be taxed in that other State under Article 6 (Income from Immovable (Real) Property) or under paragraph 1 of Article 13 (Gains), may be subject in that other Contracting State to a tax in addition to the tax allowable under the other provisions of this Convention. Such a tax, however, may

a. in the case of the United States be imposed only on

(aa) the portion of the business profits of the company attributable to the permanent establishment, and

(bb) the portion of the income referred to in the preceding sentence that is subject to tax under Article 6 or paragraph 1 of Article 13,

that represents the 'dividend equivalent amount' of those profits and income; the term 'dividend equivalent amount' shall, for the purposes of this subparagraph, have the meaning that it has under the law of the United States as it may be amended from time to time without changing the general principle thereof; and

b. in the case of the Federal Republic of Germany be imposed only on that portion of the income described in subparagraph *a.* that is comparable to the amount that would be distributed as a dividend by a locally incorporated subsidiary.

9. The tax referred to in paragraph 8*a*. shall not be imposed at a rate exceeding the rate specified in paragraph 2*a*.

10. The tax described in paragraph 8*b*. may be imposed only if, under German law, a company that is not a resident of the Federal Republic of Germany is subject to corporation tax on items of income mentioned in paragraph 8*a*. at a rate that does not exceed the rate of corporation tax applicable to the distributed profits of a German company by 5 percentage points or more. The maximum rate at which the tax described in paragraph 8*b*. may be applied may not, when added to the excess of the corporation tax rate on a permanent establishment over the rate of corporation tax on the distributed profits of a German company, exceed 5 per cent.

Article 11. Interest

1. Interest derived and beneficially owned by a resident of a Contracting State shall be taxable only in that State.

2. The term 'interest' as used in this Article means income from debt-claims of every kind, whether or not secured by mortgage, and, in particular, income from government securities and income from bonds or debentures, including premiums and prizes attaching to such securities, bonds or debentures, as well as all other income that is treated as income from money lent by the taxation law of the Contracting State in which the income arises. Penalty charges for late payment shall not be regarded as interest for the purposes of this Convention. However, the term 'interest' does not include income dealt with in Article 10 (Dividends).

3. The provisions of paragraph 1 shall not apply if the beneficial owner of the interest, being a resident of a Contracting State, carries on business in the other Contracting State through a permanent establishment situated therein, or performs in that other State independent personal services from a fixed base situated therein, and the debt-claim in respect of which the interest is paid forms part of the business property of such permanent establishment or fixed base. In such a case the provisions of Article 7 (Business Profits) or Article 14 (Independent Personal Services), as the case may be, shall apply.

4. Where, by reason of a special relationship between the payer and the beneficial owner or between both of them and some other person, the amount of the interest, having regard to the debt-claim for which it is paid, exceeds the amount that would have been agreed upon by the payer and the beneficial owner in the absence of such relationship, the provisions of this Article shall apply only to the last-mentioned amount. In such a case the excess part of the payments shall remain taxable according to the laws of each Contracting State, due regard being had to the other provisions of this Convention.

5. Where a company that is a resident of a Contracting State derives profits or income from the other Contracting State, then that other State may not impose any tax on interest paid by the company except insofar as such interest is paid by a permanent establishment of such company located in that other State, or out of income described in paragraph

8*a*.(bb) of Article 10 (Dividends), or insofar as such interest is paid to a resident of that other State, or insofar as the debt-claim underlying such interest payment forms part of the business property of a permanent establishment or a fixed base situated in that other State.

Article 12.* Royalties

1. Royalties derived and beneficially owned by a resident of a Contracting State shall be taxable only in that State.

2. The term 'royalties' as used in this Article means payments of any kind received as a consideration for the use of, or the right to use, any copyright of a literary, artistic or scientific work (but not including cinematographic films, or works on film, tape, or other means of reproduction for use in radio and television broadcasting); for the use of, or the right to use, any patent, trademark, design or model, plan, secret formula or process, or other like right or property; or for information concerning industrial, commercial or scientific experience. The term 'royalties' also includes gains derived from the alienation of any such right or property that are contingent on the productivity, use, or further alienation thereof.

3. The provisions of paragraph 1 shall not apply if the beneficial owner of the royalties, being a resident of a Contracting State, carries on business in the other Contracting State through a permanent establishment situated therein, or performs in that other State independent personal services from a fixed base situated therein, and the right or property in respect of which the royalties are paid forms part of the business property of such permanent establishment or fixed base. In such a case the provisions of Article 7 (Business Profits) or Article 14 (Independent Personal Services), as the case may be, shall apply.

4. Where, by reason of a special relationship between the payer and the beneficial owner or between both of them and some other person, the amount of the royalties, having regard to the use, right or information for which they are paid, exceeds the amount that would have been agreed upon by the payer and the beneficial owner in the absence of such relationship, the provisions of this Article shall apply only to the last-mentioned amount. In such a case the excess part of the payments shall remain taxable according to the laws of each Contracting State, due regard being had to the other provisions of this Convention.

Article 13.* Gains

1. Gains derived by a resident of a Contracting State from the alienation of immovable property referred to in Article 6 (Income from Immovable (Real) Property) and situated in the other Contracting State may be taxed in that other State.

2. For the purposes of this Article the term 'immovable property situated in the other Contracting State' shall include

a. immovable property referred to in Article 6 (Income from Immovable (Real) Property); and

b. shares or comparable interests in a company that is, or is treated as, a resident of that other Contracting State, the assets of which company consist or consisted wholly or principally of immovable property situated in the other Contracting State, and an interest in a partnership, trust, or estate, to the extent that its assets consist of immovable property situated in that other Contracting State.

3. Gains from the alienation of movable property forming part of the business property of a permanent establishment that an enterprise of a Contracting State has in the other Contracting State or of movable property pertaining to a fixed base available to a resident of a Contracting State in the other Contracting State for the purpose of performing independent personal services, including such gains from the alienation of such a permanent establishment (alone or with the whole enterprise) or of such fixed base, may be taxed in that other State.

4. Gains from the alienation of ships, aircraft, or containers operated in international traffic or movable property pertaining to the operation of such ships, aircraft, or containers shall be taxable only in the Contracting State in which the profits of the enterprise deriving such income are taxable according to Article 8 (Shipping and Air Transport).

5. Gains from the alienation of any property other than that referred to in the preceding paragraphs shall be taxable only in the Contracting State of which the alienator is a resident.

6. In the case of an individual who was a resident of a Contracting State and who, after giving up residence in that State, has become a resident of the other Contracting State under the rules of Article 4 (Residence), paragraph 5 shall not affect the right of the first-mentioned State under its national laws to tax the individual in respect of a capital gain from the alienation of shares of any kind forming part of an interest of at least 25 per cent in a company that is a resident of the first-mentioned State, provided such alienation occurs within 10 years of the date on which he gave up residence in the first-mentioned State. Gains subject to tax pursuant to the preceding sentence shall be limited to gains accrued during the period the individual was resident in the first-mentioned State. The other Contracting State shall calculate the gain in the case of a subsequent alienation on the basis of the value of such shares on the date on which the individual has ceased to be a resident of the first-mentioned State but shall not be prevented from including in income any gain accrued up to this date which has not been subject to tax in that first-mentioned State.

Article 14.* Independent Personal Services

1. Income derived by an individual who is a resident of a Contracting State from the performance of personal services in an independent capacity shall be taxable only in that State, unless such services are performed in the other Contracting State and the income is attributable to a fixed base regularly available to the individual in that other State for the purpose of performing his activities.

2. The term 'personal services in an independent capacity' includes but is not limited to independent scientific, literary, artistic, educational, or teaching activities as well as the independent activities of physicians, lawyers, engineers, economists, architects, dentists, and accountants.

Article 15. Dependent Personal Services

1. Subject to the provisions of Article 16 (Directors' Fees), 17 (Artistes and Athletes), 18 (Pensions, Annuities, Alimony, and Child Support), 19 (Government Service; Social Security), and 20 (Visiting Professors and Teachers; Students and Trainees), salaries, wages and other similar remuneration derived by a resident of a Contracting State in respect of an employment shall be taxable only in that State, unless the employment is exercised in the other Contracting State. If the employment is so exercised, such remuneration as is derived therefrom may be taxed in that other State.

2. Notwithstanding the provisions of paragraph 1, remuneration derived by a resident of a Contracting State in respect of an employment exercised in the other Contracting State shall be taxable only in the first-mentioned State if:

a. the recipient is present in the other State for a period or periods not exceeding in the aggregate 183 days in the calendar year concerned; and

b. the remuneration is paid by, or on behalf of, an employer who is not a resident of the other State; and

c. the remuneration is not borne by a permanent establishment of a fixed base that the employer has in the other State.

3. Notwithstanding the foregoing provisions of this Article, remuneration derived by a resident of a Contracting State in respect of an employment as a member of the regular complement of a ship or aircraft operated in international traffic may be taxed only in that State.

Article 16. Directors' Fees

Directors' fees and other similar payments derived by a resident of a Contracting State for services rendered in the other Contracting State in his capacity as a member of the board of directors of a company that is a resident of the other Contracting State may be taxed in that other Contracting State.

Article 17.* Artistes and Athletes

1. Notwithstanding the provisions of Articles 7 (Business Profits), 14 (Independent Personal Services), and 15 (Dependent Personal Services), income derived by a resident of a Contracting State as an entertainer (such as a theater, motion picture, radio or television artiste, or a musician), or as an athlete, from his personal activities as such exercised in the other Contracting State may be taxed in that other State, except where the amount of the gross receipts derived by such entertainer or athlete, including expenses reimbursed to him or borne on his behalf, from such activities does not exceed $20,000 (twenty thousand United States dollars) or its equivalent in Deutsche Mark for the calendar year concerned.

2. Where income in respect of activities exercised by an entertainer or an athlete in his capacity as such accrues not to the entertainer or athlete but to another person, that income of that other person may, notwithstanding the provisions of Article 7 (Business Profits) and 14

(Independent Personal Services), be taxed in the Contracting State in which the activities of the entertainer or athlete are exercised, unless it is established that neither the entertainer or athlete nor persons related thereto participate directly or indirectly in the profits of that other person, including the accrual or receipt of deferred remuneration, bonuses, fees, dividends, partnership income, or other income or distributions.

3. The provisions of paragraphs 1 and 2 shall not apply to income derived from activities performed in a Contracting State by entertainers or athletes if the visit to that State is substantially supported, directly or indirectly, by public funds of the other Contracting State or a political subdivision or a local authority thereof. In such a case the income shall be taxable only in the Contracting State of which the entertainer or athlete is a resident.

Article 18.* Pensions, Annuities, Alimony, and Child Support

1. Subject to the provisions of Article 19 (Government Service; Social Security), pensions and other similar remuneration derived and beneficially owned by a resident of a Contracting State in consideration of past employment shall be taxable only in that State.

2. Subject to the provisions of Article 19 (Government Service; Social Security), annuities derived and beneficially owned by a resident of a Contracting State shall be taxable only in that State. The term 'annuities' as used in this paragraph means a stated sum paid periodically at stated times during a specified number of years, under an obligation to make the payments in return for adequate and full consideration (other than services rendered).

3. Alimony paid by a resident of a Contracting State and deductible therein to a resident of the other Contracting State shall be taxable only in that other State. The term 'alimony' as used in this Article means periodic payments (made pursuant to a written separation agreement or a decree of divorce, separate maintenance, or compulsory support) that are taxable to the recipient under the laws of the State of which he is a resident.

4. Nondeductible alimony, and periodic payments for the support of a minor child (made pursuant to a written separation agreement or a decree of divorce, separate maintenance, or compulsory support), paid by a resident of a Contracting State to a resident of the other Contracting State shall be taxable only in the first-mentioned State.

Article 19. Government Service; Social Security

1. *a.* Wages, salaries, and similar compensation and pensions paid by the United States or by its states or political subdivisions to a natural person, other than a German national, shall be exempt from tax by the Federal Republic of Germany.

b. Wages, salaries, and similar compensation and pensions paid by the Federal Republic of Germany or by its *Länder* or by municipalities, or pensions paid by a public pension fund thereof to a natural person, other than a citizen of the United States and other than an individual who has been admitted to the United States for permanent residence therein, shall be exempt from tax by the United States.

c. Pensions, annuities, and other amounts paid by one of the Contracting States or by a juridical person organized under the public laws of that State as compensation for an injury or damage sustained as a result of hostilities or political persecution shall be exempt from tax by the other State.

d. For the purpose of this paragraph the term 'pensions' includes annuities paid to a retired civilian government employee.

2. Social security benefits paid under the social security legislation of a Contracting State and other public pensions (not dealt with in paragraph 1) paid by a Contracting State to a resident of the other Contracting State shall be taxable only in that other Contracting State. In applying the preceding sentence, that other Contracting State shall treat such benefit or pension as though it were a social security benefit paid under the social security legislation of that other Contracting State.

Article 20.* Visiting Professors and Teachers; Students and Trainees

1. Remuneration that a professor or teacher who is a resident of a Contracting State and who is present in the other Contracting State for a period not exceeding two years for the purpose of carrying out advanced study or research or for teaching at an accredited university, college, school, or other educational institution, or a public research institution or other institution engaged in research for the public benefit, receives for such work shall be taxable only in the first-mentioned State. This Article shall not apply to income from research if such research is undertaken not in the public interest but primarily for the private benefit of a specific person or persons. The benefits provided in this paragraph shall not be granted to an individual who, during the immediately preceding period, enjoyed the benefits of paragraph 2, 3, or 4.

2. Payments other than compensation for personal services that a student or business apprentice (including *Volontäre* and *Praktikanten* in the Federal Republic of Germany) who is or was immediately before visiting a Contracting State a resident of the other Contracting State and who is present in the first-mentioned State for the purpose of his full-time education or training receives for the purpose of his maintenance, education, or training shall not be taxed in that State, provided that such payments arise from sources, or are remitted from, outside that State.

3. Payments other than compensation for personal services that a person who is or was immediately before visiting a Contracting State a resident of the other Contracting State receives as a grant, allowance, or award from a non-profit religious, charitable, scientific, literary, or educational private organization or a comparable public institution shall not be taxed in the first-mentioned State.

4. A student or business apprentice within the meaning of paragraph 2, or a recipient of a grant, allowance, or award within the meaning

of paragraph 3, who is present in a Contracting State for a period not exceeding four years shall not be taxed in that State on any income from dependent personal services that is not in excess of $5,000 (five thousand United States dollars) or its equivalent in Deutsche Mark per taxable year, provided that such services are performed for the purpose of supplementing funds available otherwise for maintenance, education, or training.

5. A resident of one of the Contracting States who is an employee of an enterprise of such State or of an organization or institution described in paragraph 3, and who is temporarily present in the other Contracting State for a period not exceeding one year solely to acquire technical, professional, or business experience from any person other than such enterprise, organization, or institution, shall be exempt from tax by that other State on compensation remitted from outside that other State for services wherever performed paid by such enterprise, organization, or institution if such compensation does not exceed $10,000 (ten thousand United States dollars) or its equivalent in Deutsche Mark.

Article 21.* Other Income

1. Items of income of a resident of a Contracting State, wherever arising, not dealt with in the foregoing Articles of this Convention shall be taxable only in that State.

2. The provisions of paragraph 1 shall not apply to income, other than income from immovable property as defined in paragraph 2 of Article 6 (Income from Immovable (Real) Property), if the recipient of such income, being a resident of a Contracting State, carries on business in the other Contracting State through a permanent establishment situated therein, and the right or property in respect of which the income is paid forms part of the business property of the permanent establishment; or the recipient performs in that other State independent personal services from a fixed base situated therein, and the income is attributable to the fixed base.

Article 22. Capital

1. Capital represented by immovable property referred to in Article 6 (Income from Immovable (Real) Property), owned by a resident of a Contracting State, and situated in the other Contracting State may be taxed in that other State.

2. Capital represented by movable property forming part of the business property of a permanent establishment that an enterprise of a Contracting State has in the other Contracting State, or by movable property pertaining to a fixed base available to a resident of a Contracting State in the other Contracting State for the purpose of performing independent personal services, may be taxed in that other State.

3. Capital represented by ships, aircraft, or containers operated in international traffic and by movable property pertaining to the operation of such ships, aircraft, or containers shall be taxable only in the Con-

tracting State in which the profits of the enterprise owning such capital are taxable according to Article 8 (Shipping and Air Transport).

4. All other elements of capital of a resident of a Contracting State shall be taxable only in that State.

Article 23.* Relief from Double Taxation

1. Tax shall be determined in the case of a resident of the United States or citizen thereof as follows: In accordance with the provisions and subject to the limitations of the law of the United States (as it may be amended from time to time without changing the general principle hereof), the United States shall allow to a resident or citizen of the United States as a credit against the United States tax on income

a. the income tax paid to the Federal Republic of Germany by or on behalf of such citizen or resident; and

b. in the case of a United States company owning at least 10 per cent of the voting shares of a company that is a resident of the Federal Republic of Germany and from which the United States company receives dividends, the income tax paid to the Federal Republic of Germany by or on behalf of the distributing company with respect to the profits out of which the dividends are paid.

For the purposes of this paragraph, the taxes referred to in paragraphs 1*b.* and 2 of Article 2 (Taxes Covered), other than the capital tax (*Vermögensteuer*) and that portion of the trade tax (*Gewerbesteuer*) computed on a basis other than profits, shall be considered income taxes paid to the Federal Republic of Germany. Credits allowed solely by reason of this Article, when added to otherwise allowable credits for taxes referred to in paragraphs 1*b.* and 2 of Article 2, shall not in any taxable year exceed that proportion of the United States tax on income that taxable income arising in the Federal Republic of Germany bears to total taxable income.

2. Tax shall be determined in the case of a resident of the Federal Republic of Germany as follows:

a. Except as provided in subparagraph *b.*, there shall be excluded from the basis upon which German tax is imposed any item of income from sources within the United States and any item of capital situated within the United States that, according to this Convention, may be taxed in the United States. The Federal Republic of Germany, however, retains the right to take into account in the determination of its rate of tax the items of income and capital so excluded. In the case of income from dividends the foregoing provisions shall apply only to such income from distributions of profits on corporate rights subject to tax under United States law as are paid to a company (not including partnerships) being a resident of the Federal Republic of Germany by a company being a resident of the United States at least 10 per cent of the voting shares of which is owned directly by the German company. The preceding sentence shall not apply to dividends paid by a Regulated Investment Company and distributions of amounts that have been deducted when calculating for United States tax purposes the profits of the company distributing them. For the purposes of taxes on capital there shall also be excluded from the basis upon which German tax is imposed any shareholding the dividends of which, if paid, would be excluded, according to the two immediately foregoing sentences, from the basis upon which German tax is imposed.

b. There shall be allowed as a credit against German tax on income, subject to the provisions of German tax law regarding credit for foreign tax, the United States tax paid in accordance with the law of the United States and with the provisions of this Convention on the following items of income:

(aa) income from dividends within the meaning of Article 10 (Dividends) to which subparagraph *a.* does not apply;

(bb) gains to which Article 13 (Gains) applies provided such gains are taxable in the United States by reason only of paragraph 2*b.* of Article 13;

(cc) income to which Article 16 (Directors' Fees) applies;

(dd) income to which Article 17 (Artistes and Athletes) applies;

(ee) income within the meaning of paragraph 1*a.* of Article 19 (Government Service; Social Security) paid to a German national;

(ff) income which would, but for Article 28 (Limitation on Benefits), remain exempt from United States tax under this Convention; and

(gg) income to which Paragraph 21 of the Protocol applies.

For the purposes of this paragraph, profits, income, or gains of a resident of the Federal Republic of Germany shall be deemed to arise from sources in the United States if they are taxed in the United States in accordance with this Convention.

3. Where a United States citizen is a resident of the Federal Republic of Germany:

a. with respect to items of income not excluded from the basis of German tax under paragraph 2 that are exempt from United States tax or that are subject to a reduced rate of United States tax when derived by a resident of the Federal Republic of Germany who is not a United States citizen, the Federal Republic of Germany shall allow as a credit against German tax, subject to the provisions of German tax law regarding credit for foreign tax, only the tax paid, if any, that the United States may impose under the provisions of this Convention, other than taxes that may be imposed solely by reason of citizenship under Paragraph 1 of the Protocol;

b. for purposes of computing United States tax, the United States shall allow as a credit against United States tax the income tax paid to the Federal Republic of Germany after the credit referred to in subparagraph *a.*; the credit so allowed shall not reduce that portion of the United States tax that is creditable against the German tax in accordance with subparagraph *a.*; and

c. for the exclusive purpose of relieving double taxation in the United States under subparagraph *b.*, items of income referred to in subparagraph *a.* shall be deemed to arise in the Federal Republic of Germany to the extent necessary to avoid double taxation of such income under subparagraph *b.*

4. Where a company that is a resident of the Federal Republic of Germany distributes income derived from sources within the United States, this Article shall not preclude the compensatory imposition of corporation tax on such distributions in accordance with the provisions of the tax law of the Federal Republic of Germany.

Article 24.* Non-Discrimination

1. Nationals of a Contracting State shall not be subjected in the other Contracting State to any taxation or any requirement connected therewith that is other or more burdensome than the taxation and connected requirements to which nationals of that other State in the same circumstances are or may be subjected. Notwithstanding the provisions of Article 1, this provision shall also apply to persons who are not residents of one or both of the Contracting States.

2. The taxation on a permanent establishment that an enterprise of a Contracting State has in the other Contracting State shall not be less favorably levied in that other State than the taxation levied on enterprises of that other State carrying on the same activities. This provision shall not be construed as obliging a Contracting State to grant to residents of the other Contracting State any personal allowances, reliefs, and reductions for taxation purposes on account of civil status or family responsibilities that it grants to its own residents.

3. Except where the provisions of paragraph 1 of Article 9 (Associated Enterprises), paragraph 4 of Article 11 (Interest), or paragraph 4 of Article 12 (Royalties) apply, interest, royalties, and other disbursements paid by an enterprise of a Contracting State to a resident of the other Contracting State shall, for purposes of determining the taxable profits of such enterprise, be deductible under the same conditions as if they had been paid to a resident of the first-mentioned State. Similarly, any debts of an enterprise of a Contracting State to a resident of the other Contracting State shall, for purposes of determining the taxable capital of such enterprise, be deductible under the same conditions as if they had been contracted to a resident of the first-mentioned State.

4. Enterprises of a Contracting State, the capital of which is wholly or partly owned or controlled, directly or indirectly, by one or more residents of the other Contracting State, shall not be subjected in the first-mentioned State to any taxation or any requirement connected therewith that is other or more burdensome than the taxation and connected requirements to which other similar enterprises of the first-mentioned State are or may be subjected.

5. Nothing in this Article shall prevent a Contracting State from imposing the tax described in paragraph 8 of Article 10 (Dividends).

6. The provisions of this Article shall, notwithstanding the provisions of Article 2 (Taxes Covered), apply to taxes of every kind and description imposed by a Contracting State or a political subdivision or local authority thereof.

Article 25.* Mutual Agreement Procedure

1. Where a person considers that the actions of one or both of the Contracting States result or will result for him in taxation not in accordance with the provisions of this Convention, he may, irrespective of the remedies provided by the domestic laws of those States, present his case to the competent authority of the Contracting State of which he is a resident or, if his case comes under paragraph 1 of Article 24 (Non-Discrimination), to that of the Contracting State of which he is a national. The case must be presented within four years from the notification of the assessment giving rise to double taxation or to taxation not in accordance with the provisions of this Convention.

2. The competent authority shall endeavor, if the objection appears to it to be justified and if it is not itself able to arrive at a satisfactory solution, to resolve the case by mutual agreement with the competent authority of the other Contracting State, with a view to the avoidance of taxation which is not in accordance with the Convention. Any agreement reached shall be implemented notwithstanding any time limits or other procedural limitations in the domestic law of the Contracting States.

3. The competent authorities of the Contracting States shall endeavor to resolve by mutual agreement any difficulties or doubts arising as to the interpretation or application of this Convention. In particular the competent authorities of the Contracting States may agree

a. to the same attribution of income, deductions, credits, or allowances of an enterprise of a Contracting State to its permanent establishment situated in the other Contracting State;

b. to the same allocation of income, deductions, credits, or allowances between associated enterprises and other persons in accordance with the principles of Article 9 (Associated Enterprises);

c. to the settlement of conflicting application of this Convention, including conflicts regarding

(aa) the characterization of particular items of income;

(bb) the characterization of persons;

(cc) the application of source rules with respect to particular items of income, and

(dd) to the treatment of income that is assimilated to income from shares by the taxation law of the State of source and that is treated as a different class of income in the other State;

d. to a common meaning of a term;

e. to the application of the procedural provisions of domestic law including those regarding penalties, fines, and interest, in a manner consistent with the purposes of this Convention; and

f. to increase the amounts referred to in Articles 17 (Artistes and Athletes) and 20 (Visiting Professors and Teachers; Students and Trainees) to reflect economic or monetary developments.

They may also consult together for the elimination of double taxation in cases not provided for in this Convention.

4. The competent authorities of the Contracting States may communicate with each other directly for purposes of reaching an agree-

ment in the sense of the preceding paragraphs. Where the procedure relates to a particular case, the persons concerned shall be permitted to present their views to the competent authority of either or both of the Contracting States. When it seems advisable in order to reach agreement to have an oral exchange of opinions, such exchange may take place through a Commission consisting of representatives of the competent authorities of the Contracting States.

5. Disagreements between the Contracting States regarding the interpretation or application of this Convention shall, as far as possible, be settled by the competent authorities. If a disagreement cannot be resolved by the competent authorities it may, if both competent authorities agree, be submitted for arbitration. The procedures shall be agreed upon and shall be established between the Contracting States by notes to be exchanged through diplomatic channels.

Article 26.* Exchange of Information and Administrative Assistance

1. The competent authorities of the Contracting States shall exchange such information as is necessary for carrying out the provisions of this Convention and of the domestic law of the Contracting States concerning taxes covered by this Convention insofar as the taxation thereunder is not contrary to this Convention. The exchange of information is not restricted by Article 1 (Personal Scope). Any information received by a Contracting State shall be treated as secret in the same manner as information obtained under the domestic laws of that State and shall be disclosed only to persons or authorities (including courts and administrative bodies) involved in the assessment, collection, or administration of, the enforcement or prosecution in respect of, or the determination of appeals in relation to the taxes covered by this Convention. Such persons or authorities shall use the information only for such purposes. They may disclose the information in public court proceedings or in judicial decisions, unless the competent authority of the Contracting State supplying the information raises an objection.

2. In no case shall the provisions of paragraph 1 be construed to impose on a Contracting State the obligation:

a. to carry out administrative measures at variance with the laws and administrative practice of that or of the other Contracting State;

b. to supply information that is not obtainable under the laws or in the normal course of the administration of that or of the other Contracting State;

c. to supply information that would disclose any trade, business, industrial, commercial, or professional secret or trade process, or information, the disclosure of which would be contrary to public policy.

3. If information is requested by a Contracting State in accordance with this Article, the other Contracting State shall obtain the information to which the request relates in the same manner and to the same extent as if the tax of the first-mentioned State were the tax of that other State and were being imposed by that other State. If specifically

requested by the competent authority of a Contracting State, the competent authority of the other Contracting State shall, if possible, provide information under this Article in the form of depositions of witnesses and authenticated copies of unedited original documents (including books, papers, statements, records, accounts, and writings) to the same extent such depositions and documents can be obtained under the laws and administrative practices of that other State with respect to its own taxes.

4. Each of the Contracting States shall endeavor to collect on behalf of the other Contracting State such amounts of tax as may be necessary to ensure that relief granted by this Convention from taxation imposed by that other State does not inure to the benefit of persons not entitled thereto.

5. Paragraph 4 shall not impose upon either of the Contracting States the obligation to carry out administrative measures that are of a different nature from those used in the collection of its own taxes, or that would be contrary to its sovereignty, security, or public policy.

6. The Contracting States may, through diplomatic channels, exchange notes under which they may, subject to the provisions of this Article, exchange information for the purposes of taxes imposed by a Contracting State not referred to in Article 2 (Taxes Covered).

Article 27.* Exempt Organizations

1. Notwithstanding the provisions of Article 28 (Limitation on Benefits), a German company or organization operated exclusively for religious, charitable, scientific, educational, or public purposes shall be exempt from tax by the United States in respect of items of income, if and to the extent that

a. such company or organization is exempt from tax in the Federal Republic of Germany; and

b. such company or organization would be exempt from tax in the United States in respect of such items of income if it were organized, and carried on all its activities, in the United States.

2. Notwithstanding the provisions of Article 28 (Limitation on Benefits), a United States company or organization operated exclusively for religious, charitable, scientific, educational, or public purposes shall be exempt from tax by the Federal Republic of Germany in respect of items of income, if and to the extent that

a. such company or organization is exempt from tax in the United States; and

b. such company or organization would be exempt from tax in the Federal Republic of Germany in respect of such items of income if it were a German company or organization and carried on all its activities in the Federal Republic of Germany.

Article 28.* Limitation on Benefits

1. A person that is a resident of a Contracting State and derives income from the other Contracting State shall be entitled, in that other

Contracting State, to all the benefits of this Convention only if such person is:

a. an individual;

b. a Contracting State, or a political subdivision or local authority thereof;

c. engaged in the active conduct of a trade or business in the first-mentioned Contracting State (other than the business of making or managing investments, unless these activities are banking or insurance activities carried on by a bank or insurance company), and the income derived from the other Contracting State is derived in connection with, or is incidental to, that trade or business;

d. a company in whose principal class of shares there is substantial and regular trading on a recognized stock exchange:

e. (aa) a person, more than 50 per cent of the beneficial interest in which (or in the case of a company, more than 50 per cent of the number of shares of each class of whose shares) is owned, directly or indirectly, by persons entitled to benefits of this Convention under subparagraphs *a., b., d.*, or *f.* or who are citizens of the United States; and

(bb) a person, more than 50 per cent of the gross income of which is not used, directly or indirectly, to meet liabilities (including liabilities for interest or royalties) to persons not entitled to benefits of this Convention under subparagraphs *a., b., d.*, or *f.* or who are not citizens of the United States; or

f. a not-for-profit organization that, by virtue of that status, is generally exempt from income taxation in its Contracting State of residence, provided that more than half of the beneficiaries, members, or participants, if any, in such organizations are persons that are entitled, under this Article, to the benefits of this Convention.

2. A person that is not entitled to the benefits of this Convention pursuant to the provisions of paragraph 1 may, nevertheless, be granted the benefits of the Convention if the competent authority of the State in which the income in question arises so determines.

3. For the purposes of paragraph 1, the term 'recognized stock exchange' means:

a. the NASDAQ System owned by the National Association of Securities Dealers, Inc. and any stock exchange registered with the Securities and Exchange Commission as a national securities exchange for purposes of the Securities Exchange Act of 1934;

b. any German stock exchange on which registered dealings in shares take place;

c. any other stock exchange agreed upon by the competent authorities of the Contracting States.

4. The competent authorities of the Contracting States shall consult together with a view to developing a commonly agreed application of the provisions of this Article. The competent authorities shall, in accordance with the provisions of Article 26 (Exchange of Information and Administrative Assistance), exchange such information as is

necessary for carrying out the provisions of this Article and safeguarding, in cases envisioned therein, the application of their domestic law.

Article 29. Refund of Withholding Tax

1. If in one of the Contracting States the taxes on dividends, interest, royalties, or other items of income are levied by withholding at source, then the right to apply the withholding of tax at the rate provided for under the domestic law of that State is not affected by the provisions of this Convention.

2. The tax so withheld at source shall be refunded on application to the extent that its levying is limited by this Convention.

3. The period for application for a refund is four years from the end of the calendar year in which the dividends, interest, royalties, or other items of income have been received.

4. The Contracting State in which the income arises may require an administrative certification by the Contracting State of which the taxpayer is a resident, with respect to the fulfilment of the conditions for the unlimited tax liability in that State.

5. The competent authorities of the Contracting States shall implement the foregoing provisions by mutual agreement pursuant to Article 25 (Mutual Agreement Procedure).

6. The competent authorities of the Contracting States may establish by mutual agreement other procedures for the implementation of tax reductions provided under this Convention.

Article 30. Members of Diplomatic Missions and Consular Posts

1. Nothing in this Convention shall affect the fiscal privileges of diplomatic or consular officers under the general rules of international law or under the provisions of special agreements.

2. To the extent that, due to such privileges, income or capital is not taxed in the receiving State, the sending State shall have the right to tax such income or capital.

3. Notwithstanding the provisions of Article 4 (Residence), an individual who is a member of a diplomatic mission or a consular post of a Contracting State that is situated in the other Contracting State or in a third State shall be deemed for the purposes of this Convention to be a resident of the sending State if:

a. in accordance with international law he is not liable to tax in the receiving State in respect of income from sources outside that State or on capital situated outside that State, and

b. he is liable in the sending State to the same obligations in relation to tax on his total income or on capital as are residents of that State.

4. This Convention shall not apply to international organizations, to organs or officials thereof, or to persons who are members of a diplomatic mission, consular post, or permanent mission of a third State, being present in a Contracting State and not liable in either Contracting State to the same obligations in respect of taxes on income or on capital as are residents.

Article 31. Berlin Clause

This Convention shall also apply to Land Berlin, provided that the Government of the Federal Republic of Germany does not make a contrary declaration to the Government of the United States of America within three months of the date of entry into force of this Convention.

Article 32. Entry into Force

1. This Convention shall be ratified and the instruments of ratification shall be exchanged at Washington as soon as possible.

2. This Convention shall enter into force on the date on which the instruments of ratification are exchanged and shall have effect in both Contracting States

a. in respect of taxes withheld at source as well as excise taxes imposed on insurance premiums for amounts paid or credited on or after 1 January, 1990;

b. in respect of other taxes on income for any taxable year (*Steuerjahr*) or assessment period (*Veranlagungszeitraum*), as the case may be, beginning on or after 1 January, 1990, but excluding any fiscal year (*Wirtschaftsjahr*) commencing before such date; and

c. in respect of taxes on capital for the taxes levied on items of capital owned on or after 1 January, 1990.

3. Where any greater relief from tax would have been afforded to a person entitled to the benefits of the Convention between the United States of America and the Federal Republic of Germany for the Avoidance of Double Taxation with Respect to Taxes on Income and to certain other Taxes, signed on 22 July, 1954, as amended by the Protocol signed on 17 September, 1965 ('the 1954 Convention'), under that Convention than under this Convention, the 1954 Convention shall, at the election of such person, continue to have effect in its entirety for the first assessment period, or taxable year, with respect to which the provisions of this Convention would otherwise have effect under paragraph 2*b*.

4. Notwithstanding the foregoing provisions of this Article, the tax charged pursuant to paragraph 2*a*. of Article 10 (Dividends) on dividends (within the meaning of paragraph 4 of that Article) paid or credited before 1 January, 1992, may exceed 5 per cent of the gross amount of the dividends, but shall not exceed 10 per cent thereof.

5. Notwithstanding the foregoing provisions of this Article,

a. the provisions of paragraph 8 of Article 10 (Dividends) shall have effect in respect of taxes levied on the dividend equivalent amount for assessment periods or taxable years beginning on or after 1 January, 1991, but excluding fiscal years commencing before such date; for purposes of the preceding sentence the dividend equivalent amount shall be treated as paid on the last day of the company's fiscal year;

b. the provisions of the fourth sentence of paragraph 2*a*. of Article 23 (Relief from Double Taxation) shall not have effect on dividends paid by a Regulated Investment Company prior to 1 January, 1991, provided that such Regulated Investment Company was in existence on 1 October, 1988.

6. Notwithstanding the foregoing provisions of this Article, the following shall apply with respect to items of income described in Article 11 (Interest) and in paragraphs 4 and 5 of Article 10 (Dividends):

a. the 1954 Convention, and not this Convention, shall apply to interest as that term is used in the 1954 Convention, including interest derived from a *'partiarisches Darlehen'* or a *'Gewinnobligation'*, paid or credited before 1 January, 1991;

b. income from debt obligations to which paragraph 4 of Article 10 (Dividends) applies, and income derived from a *'partiarisches Darlehen'* or a *'Gewinnobligation'* to which paragraph 5 of Article 10 (Dividends) does not apply, and that is paid or credited on or after 1 January, 1991, shall be taxable in the Contracting State in which it arises at the rates provided for in paragraphs 2 and 3 of Article 10;

c. income derived under a *'Stille Gesellschaft'*, and income derived from 'jouissance' shares or 'jouissance' rights, to which paragraph 5 of Article 10 (Dividends) applies and that is paid or credited before 1 January, 1991, shall be taxable in the Contracting State in which it arises at a rate not exceeding 15 per cent of the gross amount;

d. income derived under a *'Stille Gesellschaft'*, and income derived from 'jouissance' shares or 'jouissance' rights, to which paragraph 5 of Article 10 (Dividends) does not apply, shall be taxable in the Contracting State in which it arises at the rates provided for in paragraphs 2 and 3 of Article 10 if such income is paid or credited on or after 1 January, 1990; and

e. the foregoing provisions of this paragraph shall not apply to income described in paragraph 6 of Article 10 (Dividends) or in paragraph 3 of Article 11 (Interest).

7. The 1954 Convention shall cease to have effect when the provisions of this Convention take effect in accordance with this Article.

Article 33. Termination

This Convention shall continue in effect indefinitely but either of the Contracting States may, on or before the thirtieth day of June in any calendar year beginning after the expiration of a period of five years from the date of its entry into force, give to the other Contracting State, through diplomatic channels, written notice of termination and, in such event, this Convention shall cease to have effect

a. in respect of taxes withheld at source as well as excise taxes imposed on insurance premiums for amounts paid or credited on or after 1 January of the calendar year following the year in which the notice of termination is given;

b. in respect of other taxes on income for taxes levied for taxable years or assessment periods beginning on or after 1 January of the calendar year following the year in which the notice of termination is given (but excluding any fiscal year commencing before such date); and *c.* in respect of taxes on capital for taxes levied on items of capital existing on or after 1 January of the calendar year following the year in which the notice of termination is given.

Done in duplicate at Bonn this in the English and German languages, both texts being equally authentic.

Protocol

At the signing today of the Convention between the United States of America and the Federal Republic of Germany for the Avoidance of Double Taxation and the Prevention of Fiscal Evasion with respect to Taxes on Income and Capital and to Certain Other Taxes, the undersigned have agreed upon the following provisions, which shall form an integral part of the Convention:

1. With reference to the general effects of the Convention

a. Notwithstanding any provision of the Convention or this Protocol except subparagraph *b.*, the United States may tax its residents (as determined under Article 4 (Residence) and its citizens as if the Convention had not come into effect. For this purpose, the term 'citizen' shall include a former citizen whose loss of citizenship had as one of its principal purposes the avoidance of income tax, but only for a period of 10 years following such loss.

b. The provisions of subparagraph *a.* shall not affect the benefits conferred by the United States

(aa) under paragraph 2 of Article 9 (Associated Enterprises), paragraph 6 of Article 13 (Gains), paragraphs 3 and 4 of Article 18 (Pensions, Annuities, Alimony, and Child Support) and paragraphs 1*c.* and 2 of Article 19 (Government Service; Social Security), and under Articles 23 (Relief from Double Taxation), 24 (Nondiscrimination), and 25 (Mutual Agreement Procedure); and

(bb) under paragraph 1*b.* of Article 19 (Government Service; Social Security), and under Articles 20 (Visiting Professors and Teachers; Students and Trainees) and 30 (Members of Diplomatic Missions and Consular Posts), upon individuals who are neither citizens of, nor have immigrant status in, the United States.

c. The Convention shall not restrict in any manner any exclusion, exemption, deduction, credit, or other allowance now or hereafter accorded

(aa) by the laws of either Contracting State; or

(bb) by any other agreement between the Contracting States.

d. Nothing in the Convention shall be construed to prevent the Federal Republic of Germany from imposing its taxes on amounts included in the income of a resident of the Federal Republic of Germany according to part 4 of the German '*Außensteuergesetz*'. Where such imposition of tax gives rise to a double taxation, the competent authorities shall consult for the elimination of such double taxation according to paragraph 3 of Article 25 (Mutual Agreement Procedure).

2. *With reference to paragraph 1 of Article 4 (Residence)*

The Federal Republic of Germany shall treat a United States citizen or an alien lawfully admitted for permanent residence (a 'green card' holder) as a resident of the United States only if such person has a substantial presence, permanent home, or habitual abode in the United States.

3. *With reference to Article 5 (Permanent Establishment) and Article 14 (Independent Personal Services)*

A resident of a Contracting State that performs in the other Contracting State concerts, theatrical or artistic performances, or similar shows and revues and that may not be taxed in that other State under the provisions of Article 17 (Artistes and Athletes) shall not be deemed to have a permanent establishment or fixed base in that State if its presence does not exceed in the aggregate 183 days in the calendar year concerned.

4. *With reference to paragraphs 1 and 2 of Article 7 (Business Profits) and paragraph 3 of Article 13 (Gains)*

For the implementation of paragraphs 1 and 2 of Article 7 and paragraph 3 of Article 13 any income, gain, or expense attributable to a permanent establishment or a fixed base during its existence is taxable or deductible in the Contracting State where such permanent establishment or fixed base is situated even if the payments are deferred until such permanent establishment or fixed base has ceased to exist. Nothing in the preceding sentence shall affect the application to such deferred payments of rules regarding the accrual of income and expenses according to the domestic law of a Contracting State.

5. *With reference to Article 7 (Business Profits) and Article 13 (Gains)*

Gains from the alienation of movable property that at any time formed part of the business property of a permanent establishment or fixed base that a resident of one Contracting State has or had in the other Contracting State may be taxed by that other State only to the extent of the gain that accrued during that time. Notwithstanding any provision of Article 7 or Article 13, such tax may be imposed on such gains at the time when realized and recognized under the laws of that other State, if its is within ten years of the date on which the property ceases to be part of the business property of the permanent establishment or fixed base (or such shorter period provided by the laws of either Contracting State).

6. With reference to paragraph 3 of Article 7 (Business Profits)

The competent authorities may mutually agree to common procedures different from those under national law for the allocation to a permanent establishment of expenses mentioned in paragraph 3 of Article 7.

7. With reference to Article 9 (Associated Enterprises)

Either State may apply the rules of its national law that permit the distribution, apportionment, or allocation of income, deductions, credits, or allowances between related persons with a view to apportioning or allocating such deductions, credits, or allowances in accordance with the general principles of paragraph 1 of Article 9. Article 9 shall not be construed to limit either Contracting State in allocating income between persons that are related other than by direct or indirect participation within the meaning of paragraph 1, such as by commercial or contractual relationships resulting in controlling influence, so long as such allocation is otherwise in accordance with the general principles of paragraph 1 of Article 9.

8. With reference to paragraph 3 of Article 10 (Dividends)

For United States income tax purposes, the United States shareholder shall be treated as if it had received as a dividend a refund of German tax equal to 5.88 per cent of the dividend actually paid, determined before the German withholding tax on such dividend. The sum of this refund and such actual dividend shall be deemed to have been subject to German withholding tax at the rate prescribed in paragraph 2*b*. of Article 10.

9. With reference to paragraph 8 of Article 10 (Dividends)

The general principle of the 'dividend equivalent amount', as used in the United States law, is to approximate that portion of the income mentioned in paragraph 8*a*. that is comparable to the amount that would be distributed as a dividend if such income were earned by a locally incorporated subsidiary.

10. With reference to Articles 10 (Dividends), 11 (Interest), and 12 (Royalties)

A Contracting State shall deem the recipient of dividends, interest, or royalties who is a resident of the other Contracting State to be the beneficial owner for the purposes of Articles 10, 11, and 12 if the recipient is the person to which the income is attributable for tax purposes under the laws of the first-mentioned State.

11. With reference to Article 11 (Interest)

The excess of the amount of interest deductible by a United States permanent establishment of a German company since the interest actually paid by such permanent establishment shall be treated as interest derived and beneficially owned by a resident of the Federal Republic of Germany.

12. With reference to Article 12 (Royalties)

Where an artiste resident in one Contracting State records a performance in the other Contracting State, has a copyrightable interest in the recording, and receives consideration for the right to use the recording based on the sale or public playing of such recording, then such consideration shall be governed by this Article.

13. With reference to paragraph 2 of Article 13 (Gains)

The term 'immovable property situated in the other Contracting State' as described in this paragraph, when the United States is that other Contracting State includes a United States real property interest.

14. With reference to paragraph 3 of Article 13 (Gains)

Nothing in this Article shall prevent gains from the alienation by a resident of a Contracting State of an interest in a partnership, trust, or estate that has a permanent establishment situated in the other Contracting State from being treated as gain under paragraph 3.

15. With reference to paragraph 1 of Article 17 (Artistes and Athletes)

If an artiste or athlete is not subject to tax in the Federal Republic of Germany under the provisions of paragraph 1 of Article 17, tax may be withheld at source in the Federal Republic of Germany, and shall be refunded to the taxpayer only upon application at the end of the calendar year concerned. Paragraph 6 of Article 29 (Refund of Withholding Tax) shall remain unaffected.

16. With reference to paragraph 3 of Article 18 (Pensions, Annuities, Alimony, and Child Support)

In determining the taxable income of an individual who is a resident of the Federal Republic of Germany there shall be allowed as a deduction in respect of alimony or similar allowances paid to an individual who is a resident of the United States the amount that would he allowed as a deduction if that last-mentioned individual were subject to unlimited tax liability in the Federal Republic of Germany.

17. With reference to paragraph 2 of Article 20 (Visiting Professors and Teachers; Students and Trainees)

Payments that are made out of public funds of a Contracting State or by a scholarship organization endowed with such funds shall be considered to arise in full from sources outside the other State. The preceding sentence shall also apply when such payments are made under programs funded jointly by organizations of both Contracting States if more than 50 per cent of these funds are provided out of public funds of the first-mentioned State or by a scholarship organization endowed with such funds. The competent authorities shall consult with each other to identify those scholarship programs whose payments shall be treated as arising from sources outside a Contracting State under the foregoing rules.

18. With reference to paragraphs 1, 4, and 5 of Article 20 (Visiting Professors and Teachers; Students and Trainees)

If a resident of a Contracting State remains in the other Contracting State for a period of time exceeding that prescribed, that other State may tax the individual under its national law for the entire period of the visit, unless in a particular case the competent authorities of the Contracting States agree otherwise.

19. With reference to paragraph 2 of Article 21 (Other Income)

Where the recipient and the payor of a dividend are both residents of the Federal Republic of Germany and the dividend is attributed to a permanent establishment or fixed base that the recipient of the dividend has in the United States, the Federal Republic of Germany may tax such a dividend at the rates provided for in paragraphs 2 and 3 of Article 10 (Dividends). The United States shall give a credit for such tax according to the provisions of Article 23 (Relief from Double Taxation).

20. With reference to paragraph 1 of Article 23 (Relief from Double Taxation)

In cases where the Convention gives to the Federal Republic of Germany the right to tax income and such income is regarded as United States source income under United States law the United States shall grant the credit provided for in paragraph 1 of Article 23, subject to any law of the United States limiting the foreign tax credit in a way that prevents the crediting of a foreign tax against United States source income, and the credit provided for in paragraph 2 of Article 22. See preamble of paragraph 1 of Article 23, the 'general principle hereof' means the avoidance of double taxation by allowing a credit for taxes imposed on items of income arising in Germany, as determined under applicable United States source rules, as modified by the Convention.

While the details and limitations of the credit pursuant to this paragraph may change as provisions of United States law change, any such changes must preserve a credit for German taxes paid or accrued with respect to items of German source income.

21. With reference to Article 23 (Relief from Double Taxation) and Article 25 (Mutual Agreement Procedure)

The Federal Republic of Germany shall avoid double taxation by a tax credit as provided for in paragraph 2*b*. of Article 23, and not by a tax exemption under paragraph 2*a*. of Article 23,

a. if in the Contracting States income or capital is placed under differing provisions of the Convention or attributed to different persons (other than under Article 9 (Associated Enterprises)) and this conflict cannot be settled by a procedure pursuant to Article 25 and

(aa) if as a result of such placement or attribution the relevant income or capital would be subject to double taxation; or

(bb) if as a result of such placement or attribution the relevant income or capital would remain untaxed or be subject only to inappropriately reduced taxation in the United States and would (but for the application of this Paragraph) remain exempt from tax in the Federal Republic of Germany; or

b. if the Federal Republic of Germany has, after due consultation and subject to the limitations of its internal law, notified the United States through diplomatic channels of other items of income to which it intends to apply this Paragraph in order to prevent the exemption of income from taxation in both Contracting States or other arrangements for the improper use of the Convention.

In the case of a notification under subparagraph *b*., the United States may, subject to notification through diplomatic channels, characterize such income under the Convention consistently with the characterization of that income by the Federal Republic of Germany. A notification made under this Paragraph shall have effect only from the first day of the calendar year following the year in which it was transmitted and any legal prerequisites under the domestic law of the notifying State for giving it effect have been fulfilled.

22. With reference to paragraph 1 of Article 24 (Non-Discrimination)

Paragraph 1 of Article 24 does not obligate the United States to subject an individual who is a German national not resident in the United States to the same taxing regime as that applied to a citizen of the United States not resident in the United States.

23. With reference to Article 25 (Mutual Agreement Procedure)

Nothing in this Article shall be construed to obligate a Contracting State to disregard a person's waiver of rights under this Article.

24. *With reference to paragraph 5 of Article 25 (Mutual Agreement Procedure)*

The decision of the arbitration board in a particular case shall be binding on both Contracting States with respect to that case.

25. *With reference to paragraph 5 of Article 25 (Mutual Agreement Procedure) and Article 26 (Exchange of Information and Administrative Assistance)*

The Contracting States may release to the arbitration board such information as is necessary for carrying out the arbitration procedure, provided that the members of the arbitration board shall be subject to the limitations on disclosure described in Article 26.

26. *With reference to Article 26 (Exchange of Information and Administrative Assistance)*

The Federal Republic of Germany shall under this Article exchange information with or without request to the extent provided for in the law of December 19, 1985 (*EG-Amtshilfegesetz*) as amended from time to time without changing the general principles thereof.

27. *With reference to Article 27 (Exempt Organizations)*

The competent authorities of the Contracting States shall develop procedures for implementing this Article.

28. *With reference to paragraph 1*f *of Article 28 (Limitation on Benefits)*

The not-for-profit organizations described in paragraph 1 of Article 28 include, but are not limited to, pension funds, pension trusts, private foundations, trade unions, trade associations, and similar organizations. In all events, a pension fund, pension trust, or similar entity organized for purposes of providing retirement, disability, or other employment benefits that is organized under the laws of a Contracting State shall be entitled to the benefits of the Convention if the organization sponsoring such fund, trust, or entity is entitled to the benefits of the Convention under Article 28.

Done in duplicate at Bonn this in the English and German languages, both texts being equally authentic.

Understandings regarding the Scope of the Limitation on Benefits Article in the Convention between the Federal Republic of Germany and the United States of America

A. Business Connection

Paragraph 1*c.* of Article 28 (Limitation on Benefits) of the Convention provides that benefits will be granted with respect to income derived in connection with or incidental to an active trade or business in the State in which the income recipient resides. This provision is self-executing; unlike the provisions of paragraph 2, discussed in section B, below, it does not require advance competent authority ruling or approval.

The following examples illustrate the intention of the negotiators with respect to the interpretation of the provisions of paragraph 1*c.* The examples are not intended to be exhaustive of the kinds of cases which would fall within the scope of the paragraph.

For purposes of exposition, the examples are structured in terms of a German entity claiming U.S. treaty benefits; they are intended to be understood reciprocally. Paragraph 1*c.* is relevant only in cases in which the entity claiming treaty benefits is not entitled to benefits under either the ownership and base erosion tests of paragraph 1*e.* or the public trading test of paragraph 1*d.*

Example I

Facts: A German resident company is owned by three persons, each resident in a different third country. The company is engaged in an active manufacturing business in the Federal Republic of Germany (Germany). It has a wholly-owned subsidiary in the United States which has been capitalized with debt and equity. The subsidiary is engaged in selling the output of the German parent. The active manufacturing business in Germany is substantial in relation to the activities of the U.S. subsidiary. Are the subsidiary's interest and dividend payments to its German parent eligible for treaty benefits in the United States?

Analysis: Treaty benefits would be allowed because the treaty requirement that the U.S. income 'is derived in connection with or is incidental to' the German active business is satisfied. This conclusion is based on two elements in the fact pattern presented: (1) the income is connected with the active German business – in this example in the form of a 'downstream' connection; and (2) the active German business is substantial in relation to the business of the U.S. subsidiary.

Example II

Facts: The facts are the same as in Example I except that while the income is derived by the German parent of the U.S. subsidiary, the relevant business activity in Germany is carried on by a German subsidiary company. The German subsidiary's activities meet the business relationship and substantiality tests of the business connection provision as described in the preceding example. Are the U.S. subsidiary's dividends and interest payments to the German parent eligible for U.S. treaty benefits?

Analysis: Benefits are allowed because the two German entities (i.e., the one deriving the income and the one carrying on the substantial active business in Germany) are related. Benefits are not denied merely because the income is earned by a German holding company and the relevant activity is carried on in Germany by a German subsidiary. The existence of a similar holding company structure in the United States would not affect the right of the German parent to treaty benefits. Thus, if the German parent owns a subsidiary in the United States which is, itself, a holding company for the group's U.S. activities, which are related to the business activity in Germany, dividends paid by the U.S. holding company to the German parent holding company would be tested for eligibility for benefits in the same way as described above, ignoring the fact that the activities are carried on by one entity and the income in respect of which benefits are claimed is paid by another, related, entity.

Example III

Facts: A German resident company is owned by three persons, each resident in a different third country. The company is the worldwide headquarters and parent of an integrated international business carried on through subsidiaries in many countries. The company's wholly-owned U.S. and German subsidiaries manufacture, in their countries of residence, products which are part of the group's product line. The United States subsidiary has been capitalized with debt and equity. The active manufacturing business of the German subsidiary is substantial in relation to the activities of the U.S. subsidiary. The German parent manages the worldwide group and also performs research and development to improve the manufacture of the group's product line. Are the U.S. subsidiary's dividend and interest payments to its German parent eligible for treaty benefits in the United States?

Analysis: Treaty benefits would be allowed because the treaty requirement that the United States income 'is derived in connection with or is incidental to' the German active business is satisfied. This conclusion is based on two elements in the fact pattern presented: (1) the income is connected with the German active business because the United States subsidiary and the German subsidiary manufacture products which are part of the group's product line, the German parent manages the worldwide group, and the parent performs research and development that benefits both subsidiaries; and (2) the active German business is substantial in relation to the business of the U.S. subsidiary.

Example IV

Facts: A third-country resident establishes a German company for the purpose of acquiring a large U.S. manufacturing company. The sole business activity of the German company (other than holding the stock of the U.S. company) is the operation of a small retailing outlet which sells products manufactured by the U.S. company. Is the German company entitled to treaty benefits under paragraph 1*c.* with respect to dividends it receives from the U.S. manufacturer?

Analysis: The dividends would not be entitled to benefits. Although there is, arguably, a business connection between the U.S. and the German businesses, the 'substantiality' test described in the preceding examples is not met.

Example V

Facts: German, French and Belgian companies create a joint venture in the form of a partnership organized in Germany to manufacture a product in a developing country. The joint venture owns a U.S. sales company, which pays dividends to the joint venture. Are these dividends eligible for benefits of the Convention?

Analysis: Under Article 4, only the German parent is a resident of Germany for purposes of the Convention. The question arises under this Convention, therefore, only with respect to the German partner's share of the dividends. If the German partner meets the ownership and base erosion tests, or the public trading test of paragraph 1*d.* or *e.*, it is entitled to benefits without reference to paragraph 1*c.* If not, the analysis of the previous examples would be applied to determine eligibility for benefits under 1*c.* The determination of treaty benefits available to the French and Belgian partners will be made under the United States Conventions with France and Belgium.

Example VI

Facts: A German company, a French company and a Belgian company create a joint venture in the form of a German resident company in which they take equal shareholdings. The joint venture company engages in an active manufacturing business in Germany. Income derived from that business that is retained as working capital is invested in U.S. Government securities and other U.S. debt instruments until needed for use in the business. Is interest paid on these instruments eligible for benefits of the Convention?

Analysis: The interest would be eligible for treaty benefits. Interest income earned from short-term investment of working capital is incidental to the business in Germany of the German joint venture company.

B. Competent Authority Discretion under Paragraph 2

As indicated above, treaty benefits may be claimed by the taxpayer under the provisions of paragraph 1 (ownership, base erosion, public trading, or business connection) without reference to competent authority. It is anticipated that in the vast majority of cases, eligibility for treaty benefits will be determinable without resort to competent authorities. The tax authorities of the Contracting States may, of course, in reviewing a case determine that the taxpayer has improperly interpreted the provisions of paragraph 1, and that benefits should not have been granted. Furthermore, under paragraph 2 the competent authority of the source State may determine that, notwithstanding failure to qualify for benefits under paragraph 1, benefits should be granted.

It is assumed that, for purposes of implementing paragraph 2, taxpayers will be permitted to present their cases of the competent authority for an advance determination based on the facts, and will not be required to wait until the tax authorities of one of the Contracting States have determined that benefits are denied. In these circumstances, it is also expected that if the competent authority determines that benefits are to be allowed, they will be allowed retroactively to the time of entry into force of the relevant treaty provision or the establishment of the structure in question, whichever is later.

In making determinations under paragraph 2, it is understood that the competent authorities will take into account all relevant facts and circumstances. The factual criteria which the competent authorities are expected to take into account include the existence of a clear business purpose for the structure and location of the income earning entity in question; the conduct of an active trade or business (as opposed to a mere investment activity) by such entity; and a valid business nexus between that entity and the activity giving rise to the income. The competent authorities will, furthermore, consider, for example, whether and to what extent a substantial headquarters operation conducted in a Contracting State by employees of a resident of that State contribute to such valid business nexus, and should not, therefore, be treated merely as the 'making or managing [of] investments' within the meaning of paragraph 1*c*. of Article 28.

The discretionary authority granted to the competent authorities in paragraph 2 is particularly important in view of, and should be exercised with particular cognizance of, the developments in, and objectives of, international economic integration, such as that between the member countries of the European Communities and between the United States and Canada.

The following example illustrates the application of the principles described in Section B, above.

Example VII

Facts: German, French and Belgian companies, each of which is engaged directly or through its affiliates in substantial active business operations in its country of residence, decide to cooperate in the development, production, and marketing of an advanced passenger aircraft through a corporate joint venture with its statutory seat in Germany. The development, production and marketing aspects of the project are carried out by the individual joint venturers. The joint venture company, which is staffed with a significant number of managerial and financial personnel seconded by the joint venturers, acts as the general headquarters for the joint venture, responsible for the overall management of the project including coordination of the functions separately performed by the individual joint venturers on behalf of the joint venture company, the investment of working capital contributed by the joint venturers and the financing of the project's additional capital requirements through public and private borrowings. The joint venture company derives portfolio investment income from U.S. sources. Is this income eligible for benefits of the Convention?

Analysis: If the joint venture company's activities constitute an active business and the income is connected to that business, benefits would be allowed under paragraph 1*c*. If not, it is expected that the U.S. competent authority would determine that treaty benefits should be allowed in accordance with paragraph 2 under the facts presented, particularly in view of (1) the clear business purpose for the formation and location of the joint venture company; (2) the significant headquarters functions performed by that company in addition to financial functions; and (3) the fact that all of the joint venturers are companies resident in EC member countries in which they are engaged directly or through their affiliates in substantial active business operations.

The competent authorities will consult further on these issues, and may also take into account the views of the tax authorities of other States, including, in particular, member States of the European Communities.

Embassy of the
United States of America

Bonn, August 29, 1989

Excellency,

I have the honor to confirm receipt of your Note of today's date which reads as follows:

'I have the honor to refer to the Convention signed today between the Federal Republic of Germany and the United States of America for the Avoidance of Double Taxation and the Prevention of Fiscal Evasion with respect to Taxes on Income and Capital and to certain other Taxes and to inform you on behalf of the Government of the Federal Republic of Germany of the following:

In the course of the negotiations leading to the conclusion of the Convention signed today, the negotiators developed and agreed upon a memorandum of understanding intended to give guidance both to the taxpayers and the tax authorities of our two countries in interpreting Article 28 (Limitation on Benefits). This memorandum of understanding, attached to this Note, represents the current views of the Government of the Federal Republic of Germany with respect to Article 28. It is my Government's view that as we both gain experience in administering the Convention, and particularly Article 28, the competent authorities may develop and publish amendments and further understandings and interpretations.

If this position meets with the approval of the Government of the United States of America, this Note and your Note in reply thereto will indicate that our Governments share a common understanding of the role of the memorandum of understanding relating to Article 28 of the Convention.'

I have the honor to inform you, that my Government agrees to the above.

Accept, Excellency, the expression of my highest consideration.

Vernon A. Walters

His Excellency
Dr. Hans Werner Lautenschlager
State Secretary
of the Foreign Office

Bonn

Convention between the Government of the United States of America and the Government of the Republic of India for the Avoidance of Double Taxation and the Prevention of Fiscal Evasion with Respect to Taxes on Income, concluded in New Delhi on September 12, 1989.

The Government of the United States of America and the Government of the Republic of India, desiring to conclude a Convention for the avoidance of double taxation and the prevention of fiscal evasion with respect to taxes on income, have agreed as follows:

Article 1. General Scope

1. This Convention shall apply to persons who are residents of one or both of the Contracting States, except as otherwise provided in the Convention.

2. The Convention shall not restrict in any manner any exclusion, exemption, deduction, credit, or other allowance now or hereafter accorded:

a. by the laws of either Contracting State; or

b. by any other agreement between the Contracting States.

3. Notwithstanding any provision of the Convention except paragraph 4, a Contracting State may tax its residents (as determined under Article 4 (Residence)), and by reason of citizenship may tax its citizens, as if the Convention had not come into effect. For this purpose, the term 'citizen' shall include a former citizen whose loss of citizenship had as one of its principal purposes the avoidance of tax, but only for a period of 10 years following such loss.

4. The provisions of paragraph 3 shall not affect

a. the benefits conferred by a Contracting State under paragraph 2 of Article 9 (Associated Enterprises), under paragraphs 2 and 6 of Article 20 (Private Pensions, Annuities, Alimony, and Child Support), and under Articles 25 (Relief from Double Taxation), 26 (Non-Discrimination), and 27 (Mutual Agreement Procedure); and

b. the benefits conferred by a Contracting State under Articles 19 (Remuneration and Pensions in Respect of Government Service), 21 (Payments Received by Students and Apprentices), 22 (Payments Received by Professors, Teachers and Research Scholars) and 29 (Diplomatic Agents and Consular Officers), upon individuals who are neither citizens of, nor have immigrant status in, that State.

Article 2. Taxes Covered

1. The existing taxes to which this Convention shall apply are:

a. in the United States, the Federal income taxes imposed by the Internal Revenue Code (but excluding the accumulated earnings tax, the personal holding company tax, and social security taxes), and the excise taxes imposed on insurance premiums paid to foreign insurers and with respect to private foundations (hereinafter referred to as 'United States tax'); provided, however, the Convention shall apply to the excise taxes imposed on insurance premiums paid to foreign insurers only to the extent that the risks covered by such premiums are not reinsured with a person not entitled to exemption from such taxes under this or any other Convention which applies to these taxes; and

b. in India:

(i) the income tax including any surcharge thereon, but excluding income tax on undistributed income of companies, imposed under the Income-tax Act; and

(ii) the surtax (hereinafter referred to as 'Indian tax').

Taxes referred to in *a.* and *b.* above shall not include any amount payable in respect of any default or omission in relation to the above taxes or which represent a penalty imposed relating to those taxes.

2. The Convention shall apply also to any identical or substantially similar taxes which are imposed after the date of signature of the Convention in addition to, or in place of, the existing taxes. The competent authorities of the Contracting States shall notify each other of any significant changes which have been made in their respective taxation laws and of any official published material concerning the application of the Convention.

Article 3. General Definitions

1. In this Convention, unless the context otherwise requires:

a. the term 'India' means the territory of India and includes the territorial sea and airspace above it, as well as any other maritime zone in which India has sovereign rights, other rights and jurisdictions, according to the Indian law and in accordance with international law;

b. the term 'United States', when used in a geographical sense means all the territory of the United States of America, including its territorial sea, in which the laws relating to United States tax are in force, and all the area beyond its territorial sea, including the seabed and subsoil thereof, over which the United States has jurisdiction in accordance with international law and in which the laws relating to United States tax are in force;

c. the terms 'a Contracting State' and 'the other Contracting State' mean India or the United States as the context requires;

d. the term 'tax' means Indian tax or United States tax, as the context requires;

e. the term 'person' includes an individual, an estate, a trust, a partnership, a company, any other body of persons, or other taxable entity;

f. the term 'company' means any body corporate or any entity which is treated as a company or body corporate for tax purposes;

g. the terms 'enterprise of a Contracting State' and 'enterprise of the other Contracting State' mean respectively an enterprise carried on by a resident of a Contracting State and an enterprise carried on by a resident of the other Contracting State;

h. the term 'competent authority' means, in the case of India, the Central Government in the Ministry of Finance (Department of Revenue) or their authorized representative, and in the case of the United States, the Secretary of the Treasury or his delegate;

i. the term 'national' means any individual possessing the nationality or citizenship of a Contracting State;

j. the term 'international traffic' means any transport by a ship or aircraft operated by an enterprise of a Contracting State, except when the ship or aircraft is operated solely between places within the other Contracting State;

k. the term 'taxable year' in relation to Indian tax means 'previous year' as defined in the Income-tax Act, 1961.

2. As regards the application of this Convention by a Contracting State any term not defined therein shall, unless the context otherwise requires or the competent authorities agree to a common meaning pursuant to the provisions of Article 27 (Mutual Agreement Procedure), have the meaning which it has under the laws of that State concerning the taxes to which this Convention applies.

Article 4. Residence

1. For the purposes of this Convention, the term 'resident of a Contracting State' means any person who, under the laws of that State, is liable to tax therein by reason of his domicile, residence, citizenship, place of management, place of incorporation or any other criterion of a similar nature, provided, however, that

a. this term does not include any person who is liable to tax in that State in respect only of income from sources in that State; and

b. in the case of income derived or paid by a partnership, estate, or trust, this term applies only to the extent that the income derived by such partnership, estate, or trust is subject to tax in that State as the income of a resident, either in its hands or in the hands of its partners or beneficiaries.

2. Where by reason of the provisions of paragraph 1, an individual is a resident of both Contracting States, then his status shall be determined as follows:

a. he shall be deemed to be a resident of the State in which he has a permanent home available to him; if he has a permanent home available to him in both States, he shall be deemed to be a resident of the State with which his personal and economic relations are closer (centre of vital interests);

b. if the State in which he has his centre of vital interests cannot be determined, or if he does not have a permanent home available to him in either State, he shall be deemed to be a resident of the State in which he has an habitual abode;

c. if he has an habitual abode in both States or in neither of them, he shall be deemed to be a resident of the State of which he is a national;

d. If he is a national of both States or of neither of them, the competent authorities of the Contracting States shall settle the question by mutual agreement.

3. Where, by reason of the provisions of paragraph 1, a company is a resident of both Contracting States, such company shall be considered to be outside the scope of this Convention except for purposes of paragraph 2 of Article 10 (Dividends), Article 26 (Non-Discrimination), Article 27 (Mutual Agreement Procedure), Article 28 (Exchange of Information and Administrative Assistance) and Article 30 (Entry Into Force).

4. Where, by reason of the provisions of paragraph 1, a person other than an individual or a company is a resident of both Contracting States, the competent authorities of the Contracting States shall settle the question by mutual agreement and determine the mode of application of the Convention to such person.

Article 5.* Permanent Establishment

1. For purposes of this Convention, the term 'permanent establishment' means a fixed place of business through which the business of an enterprise is wholly or partly carried on.

2. The term 'permanent establishment' includes especially:

a. a place of management;

b. a branch;

c. an office;

d. a factory;

e. a workshop;

f. a mine, an oil or gas well, a quarry, or any other place of extraction of natural resources;

g. a warehouse, in relation to a person providing storage facilities for others;

h. a farm, plantation or other place where agriculture, forestry, plantation or related activities are carried on;

i. a store or premises used as a sales outlet;

j. an installation or structure used for the exploration or exploitation of natural resources, but only if so used for a period of more than 120 days in any twelve month period;

k. a building site or construction, installation or assembly project or supervisory activities in connection therewith, where such site, project or activities (together with such sites, projects or activities, if any) continue for a period of more than 120 days in any twelve month period;

l. the furnishing of services, other than included services as defined in Article 12 (Royalties and Fees for Included Services), within a Contracting State by an enterprise through employees or other personnel, but only if:

(i) activities of that nature continue within that state for a period or periods aggregating more than 90 days within any twelve-month period; or

(ii) the services are performed within that State for a related enterprise (within the meaning of paragraph 1 of Article 9 (Associated Enterprises)).

3. Notwithstanding the preceding provisions of this Article, the term 'permanent establishment' shall be deemed not to include any or more of the following:

a. the use of facilities solely for the purpose of storage, display, or occasional delivery of goods or merchandise belonging to the enterprise;

b. the maintenance of a stock of goods or merchandise belonging to the enterprise solely for the purpose of storage, display, or occasional delivery;

c. the maintenance of a stock of goods or merchandise belonging to the enterprise solely for the purpose of processing by another enterprise;

d. the maintenance of a fixed place of business solely for the purpose of purchasing goods or merchandise, or of collecting information, for the enterprise;

e. the maintenance of a fixed place of business solely for the purpose of advertising, for the supply of information, for scientific research or for other activities which have a preparatory or auxiliary character for the enterprise.

4. Notwithstanding the provisions of paragraphs 1 and 2, where a person – other than an agent of an independent status to whom paragraph 5 applies – is acting in a Contracting State on behalf of an enterprise of the other Contracting State, that enterprise shall be deemed to have a permanent establishment in the first-mentioned State if:

a. he has and habitually exercises in the first-mentioned State an authority to conclude contracts on behalf of the enterprise, unless his activities are limited to those mentioned in paragraph 3 which, if exercised through a fixed place of business, would not make that fixed place of business a permanent establishment under the provisions of that paragraph;

b. he has no such authority but habitually maintains in the first-mentioned State a stock of goods or merchandise from which he regularly delivers goods or merchandise on behalf of the enterprise, and some additional activities conducted in that State on behalf of the enterprise have contributed to the sale of the goods or merchandise; or

c. he habitually secures orders in the first-mentioned State, wholly or almost wholly for the enterprise.

5. An enterprise of a Contracting State shall not be deemed to have a permanent establishment in the other Contracting State merely because it carries on business in that other State through a broker, general commission agent, or any other agent of an independent status, provided that such persons are acting in the ordinary course of their business. However, when the activities of such an agent are devoted wholly or almost wholly on behalf of that enterprise and the transactions between the agent and the enterprise are not made under arm's-

length conditions, he shall not be considered an agent of independent status within the meaning of this paragraph.

6. The fact that a company which is a resident of a Contracting State controls or is controlled by a company which is a resident of the other Contracting State, or which carries on business in that other State (whether through a permanent establishment or otherwise), shall not of itself constitute either company a permanent establishment of the other.

Article 6. Income from Immovable Property (Real Property)

1. Income derived by a resident of a Contracting State from immovable property (real property), including income from agriculture or forestry, situated in the other Contracting State may be taxed in that other State.

2. The term 'immovable property' shall have the meaning which it has under the law of the Contracting State in which the property in question is situated.

3. The provisions of paragraph 1 shall also apply to income derived from the direct use, letting, or use in any other form of immovable property.

4. The provisions of paragraphs 1 and 3 shall also apply to the income from immovable property of an enterprise and to income from immovable property used for the performance of independent personal services.

Article 7.* Business Profits

1. The profits of an enterprise of a Contracting State shall be taxable only in that State unless the enterprise carries on business in the other Contracting State through a permanent establishment situated therein. If the enterprise carries on business as aforesaid, the profits of the enterprise may be taxed in the other State but only so much of them as is attributable to *a.* that permanent establishment; *b.* sales in the other State of goods or merchandise of the same or similar kind as those sold through that permanent establishment; or *c.* other business activities carried on in the other State of the same or similar kind as those effected through that permanent establishment.

2. Subject to the provisions of paragraph 3, where an enterprise of a Contracting State carries on business in the other Contracting State through a permanent establishment situated therein, there shall in each Contracting State be attributable to that permanent establishment the profits which it might be expected to make if it were a distinct and independent enterprise engaged in the same or similar activities under the same or similar conditions and dealing wholly at arm's-length with the enterprise of which it is a permanent establishment and other enterprises controlling, controlled by or subject to the same common control as that enterprise. In any case where the correct amount of profits attributable to a permanent establishment is incapable of determination or the determination thereof presents exceptional difficulties, the profits attributable to the permanent establishment may be estimated on a

reasonable basis. The estimate adopted shall, however, be such that the result shall be in accordance with the principles contained in this Article.

3. In the determination of the profits of a permanent establishment, there shall be allowed as deductions expenses which are incurred for the purposes of the business of the permanent establishment, including a reasonable allocation of executive and general administrative expenses, research and development expenses, interest, and other expenses incurred for the purposes of the enterprise as a whole (or the part thereof which includes the permanent establishment), whether incurred in the State in which the permanent establishment is situated or elsewhere, in accordance with the provisions of and subject to the limitations of the taxation laws of that State. However, no such deduction shall be allowed in respect of amounts, if any, paid (otherwise than toward reimbursement of actual expenses) by the permanent establishment to the head office of the enterprise or any of its other offices, by way of royalties, fees or other similar payments in return for the use of patents, know-how or other rights, or by way of commission or other charges for specific services performed or for management, or, except in the case of banking enterprises, by way of interest on moneys lent to the permanent establishment. Likewise, no account shall be taken, in the determination of the profits of a permanent establishment, for amounts charged (otherwise than toward reimbursement of actual expenses), by the permanent establishment to the head office of the enterprise or any of its other offices, by way of royalties, fees or other similar payments in return for the use of patents, know-how or other rights, or by way of commission or other charges for specific services performed or for management, or, except in the case of banking enterprises, by way of interest on moneys lent to the head office of the enterprise or any of its other offices.

4. No profits shall be attributed to a permanent establishment by reason of the mere purchase by that permanent establishment of goods or merchandise for the enterprise.

5. For the purposes of this Convention, the profits to be attributed to the permanent establishment as provided in paragraph 1*a*. of this Article shall include only the profits derived from the assets and activities of the permanent establishment and shall be determined by the same method year by year unless there is good and sufficient reason to the contrary.

6. Where profits include items of income which are dealt with separately in other Articles of the Convention, then the provisions of those Articles shall not be affected by the provisions of this Article.

7. For the purposes of the Convention, the term 'business profits' means income derived from any trade or business including income from the furnishing of services as defined in Article 12 (Royalties and Fees for Included Services) and including income from the rental of tangible personal property other than property described in paragraph 3*b*. of Article 12 (Royalties and Fees for Included Services).

Article 8. Shipping and Air Transport

1. Profits derived by an enterprise of a Contracting State from the operation by that enterprise of ships or aircraft in international traffic shall be taxable only in that State.

2. For the purposes of this Article, profits from the operation of ships or aircraft in international traffic mean profits derived by an enterprise described in paragraph 1 from the transportation by sea or air respectively of passengers, mail, livestock or goods carried on by the owners or lessees or charterers of ships or aircraft including:

a. the sale of tickets for such transportation on behalf of other enterprises;

b. other activity directly connected with such transportation; and

c. the rental of ships or aircraft incidental to any activity directly connected with such transportation.

3. Profits of an enterprise of a Contracting State described in paragraph 1 from the use, maintenance, or rental of containers (including trailers, barges, and related equipment) used in connection with the operation of ships or aircraft in international traffic shall be taxable only in that State.

4. The provisions of paragraphs 1 and 3 shall also apply to profits from participation in a pool, a joint business, or an international operating agency.

5. For the purposes of this Article, interest on funds connected with the operation of ships or aircraft in international traffic shall be regarded as profits derived from the operation of such ships or aircraft, and the provisions of Article 11 (Interest) shall not apply in relation to such interest.

6. Gains derived by an enterprise of a Contracting State described in paragraph 1 from the alienation of ships, aircraft or containers owned and operated by the enterprise, the income from which is taxable only in that State, shall be taxed only in that State.

Article 9. Associated Enterprises

1. Where:

a. an enterprise of a Contracting State participates directly or indirectly in the management, control, or capital of an enterprise of the other Contracting State, or

b. the same persons participate directly or indirectly in the management, control, or capital of an enterprise of a Contracting State and an enterprise of the other Contracting State,

and in either case conditions are made or imposed between the two enterprises in their commercial or financial relations which differ from those which would be made between independent enterprises, then any profits which, but for those conditions would have accrued to one of the enterprises, but by reason of those conditions have not so accrued, may be included in the profits of that enterprise and taxed accordingly.

2. Where a Contracting State includes in the profits of an enterprise of that State, and taxes accordingly, profits on which an enterprise of the other Contracting State has been charged to tax in that other State,

and the profits so included are profits which would have accrued to the enterprise of the first-mentioned State if the conditions made between the two enterprises had been those which would have been made between independent enterprises, then that other State shall make an appropriate adjustment to the amount of tax charged therein on those profits. In determining such adjustment, due regard shall be had to the other provisions of this Convention and the competent authorities of the Contracting States shall if necessary consult each other.

Article 10.* Dividends

1. Dividends paid by a company which is a resident of a Contracting State to a resident of the other Contracting State may be taxed in that other State.

2. However, such dividends may also be taxed in the Contracting State of which the company paying the dividends is a resident, and according to the laws of that State, but if the beneficial owner of the dividends is a resident of the other Contracting State, the tax so charged shall not exceed:

a. 15 per cent of the gross amount of the dividends if the beneficial owner is a company which owns at least 10 per cent of the voting stock of the company paying the dividends;

b. 25 per cent of the gross amount of the dividends in all other cases.

Subparagraph *b.* and not subparagraph *a.* shall apply in the case of dividends paid by the United States person which is a Regulated Investment Company. Subparagraph *a.* shall not apply to dividends paid by a United States person which is a Real Estate Investment Trust, and subparagraph *b.* shall only apply if the dividend is beneficially owned by an individual holding a less than 10 per cent interest in the Real Estate Investment Trust. This paragraph shall not affect the taxation of the company in respect of the profits out of which the dividends are paid.

3. The term 'dividends' as used in this Article means income from shares or other rights, not being debt-claims, participating in profits, income from other corporate rights which are subjected to the same taxation treatment as income from shares by the taxation laws of the State of which the company making the distribution is a resident; and income from arrangements, including debt-obligations, carrying the right to participate in profits, to the extent so characterized under the laws of the Contracting State in which the income arises.

4. The provisions of paragraphs 1 and 2 shall not apply if the beneficial owner of the dividends, being a resident of a Contracting State, carries on business in the other Contracting State, of which the company paying the dividends is a resident, through a permanent establishment situated therein, or performs in that other State independent personal services from a fixed base situated therein, and dividends are attributable to such permanent establishment or fixed base. In such case the provisions of Article 7 (Business Profits) or Article 15 (Independent Personal Services), as the case may be, shall apply.

5. Where a company which is a resident of a Contracting State derives profits or income from the other Contracting State, that other State may not impose any tax on the dividends paid by the company except insofar as such dividends are paid to a resident of that other State or insofar as the holding in respect of which the dividends are paid is effectively connected with a permanent establishment or a fixed base situated in that other State, nor subject the company's undistributed profits to a tax on the company's undistributed profits, even if the dividends paid or the undistributed profits consist wholly or partly of profits or income arising in such other State.

Article 11.* Interest

1. Interest arising in a Contracting State and paid to a resident of the other Contracting State may be taxed in that other State.

2. However, such interest may also be taxed in the Contracting State in which it arises and according to the laws of that State, but if the beneficial owner of the interest is a resident of the other Contracting State, the tax so charged shall not exceed:

a. 10 per cent of the gross amount of the interest if such interest is paid on a loan granted by a bank carrying on a bona fide banking business or by a similar financial institution (including an insurance company); and

b. 15 per cent of the gross amount of the interest in all other cases.

3. Notwithstanding the provisions of paragraph 2 of this Article, interest arising in a Contracting State:

a. and derived and beneficially owned by the Government of the other Contracting State, a political subdivision or local authority thereof, the Reserve Bank of India, or the Federal Reserve Banks of the United States, as the case may be, and such other institutions of either Contracting State as the competent authorities may agree pursuant to Article 27 (Mutual Agreement Procedure);

b. with respect to loans or credits extended or endorsed

(i) by the Export Import Bank of the United States, when India is the first-mentioned Contracting State; and

(ii) by the EXIM bank of India, when the United States is the first-mentioned Contracting State; and

c. to the extent approved by the Government of that State, and derived and beneficially owned by any person, other than a person referred to in subparagraphs *a.* and *b.*, who is a resident of the other Contracting State, provided that the transaction giving rise to the debt-claim has been approved in this behalf by the Government of the first-mentioned Contracting State;

shall be exempt from tax in the first-mentioned Contracting State.

4. The term 'interest' as used in this Convention means income from debt-claims of every kind, whether or not secured by mortgage, and whether or not carrying a right to participate in the debtor's profits, and in particular, income from government securities, and income from bonds or debentures, including premiums or prizes attaching to such securities, bonds, or debentures. Penalty charges for late payment shall

not be regarded as interest for the purposes of the Convention. However, the term 'interest' does not include income dealt with in Article 10 (Dividends).

5. The provisions of paragraphs 2 and 3 shall not apply if the beneficial owner of the interest, being a resident of a Contracting State, carries on business in the other Contracting State in which the interest arises, through a permanent establishment situated therein, or performs in that other State independent personal services from a fixed base situated therein, and the interest is attributable to such permanent establishment or fixed base. In such case the provisions of Article 7 (Business Profits) or Article 15 (Independent Personal Services), as the case may be, shall apply.

6. Interest shall be deemed to arise in a Contracting State when the payer is that State itself or a political subdivision, local authority, or resident of that State. Where, however, the person paying the interest, whether he is a resident of a Contracting State or not, has in a Contracting State a permanent establishment or a fixed base, and such interest is borne by such permanent establishment or fixed base, then such interest shall be deemed to arise in the Contracting State in which the permanent establishment or fixed base is situated.

7. Where, by reason of a special relationship between the payer and the beneficial owner or between both of them and some other person, the amount of the interest, having regard to the debt-claim for which it is paid, exceeds the amount which would have been agreed upon by the payer and the beneficial owner in the absence of such relationship, the provisions of this Article shall apply only to the last-mentioned amount. In such case the excess part of the payments shall remain taxable according to the laws of each Contracting State, due regard being had to the other provisions of the Convention.

Article 12.* Royalties and Fees for Included Services

1. Royalties and fees for included services arising in a Contracting State and paid to a resident of the other Contracting State may be taxed in that other State.

2. However, such royalties and fees for included services may also be taxed in the Contracting State in which they arise and according to the laws of that State; but if the beneficial owner of the royalties or fees for included services is a resident of the other Contracting State, the tax so charged shall not exceed:

a. in the case of royalties referred to in sub-paragraph *a.* of paragraph 3 and fees for included services as defined in this Article (other than services described in sub-paragraph *b.* of this paragraph):

(i) during the first five taxable years for which this Convention has effect,

(A) 15 per cent of the gross amount of the royalties or fees for included services as defined in this Article, where the payer of the royalties or fees is the Government of that Contracting State, a political subdivision or a public sector company; and

(B) 20 per cent of the gross amount of the royalties or fees for included services in all other cases; and

(ii) during the subsequent years, 15 per cent of the gross amount of royalties or fees for included services; and

b. in the case of royalties referred to in sub-paragraph *b.* of paragraph 3 and fees for included services as defined in this Article that are ancillary and subsidiary to the enjoyment of the property for which payment is received under paragraph 3*b.* of this Article, 10 per cent of the gross amount of the royalties or fees for included services.

3. The term 'royalties' as used in this Article means:

a. payments of any kind received as a consideration for the use of, or the right to use, any copyright of a literary, artistic or scientific work, including cinematographic films or work on film, tape or other means of reproduction for use in connection with radio or television broadcasting, any patent, trademark, design or model, plan, secret formula or process, or for information concerning industrial, commercial or scientific experience, including gains derived from the alienation of any such right or property which are contingent on the productivity, use, or disposition thereof; and

b. payments of any kind received as consideration for the use of, or the right to use, any industrial, commercial, or scientific equipment, other than payments derived by an enterprise described in paragraph 1 of Article 8 (Shipping and Air Transport) from activities described in paragraph 2*c.* or 3 of Article 8.

4. For purposes of this Article, 'fees for included services' means payments of any kind to any person in consideration for the rendering of any technical or consultancy services (including through the provision of services of technical or other personnel) if such services:

a. are ancillary and subsidiary to the application or enjoyment of the right, property or information for which a payment described in paragraph 3 is received; or

b. make available technical knowledge, experience, skill, know-how, or processes, or consist of the development and transfer of a technical plan or technical design.

5. Not withstanding paragraph 4, 'fees for included services' does not include amounts paid:

a. for services that are ancillary and subsidiary, as well as inextricably and essentially linked, to the sale of property other than a sale described in paragraph 3*a.*;

b. for services that are ancillary and subsidiary to the rental of ships, aircraft, containers or other equipment used in connection with the operation of ships or aircraft in international traffic;

c. for teaching in or by educational institutions;

d. for services for the personal use of the individual or individuals making the payment; or

e. to an employee of the person making the payments or to any individual or firm of individuals (other than a company) for professional services as defined in Article 15 (Independent Personal Services).

6. The provisions of paragraphs 1 and 2 shall not apply if the beneficial owner of the royalties or fees for included services, being a resident of a Contracting State, carries on business in the other Contracting State, in which the royalties or fees for included services arise, through a permanent establishment situated therein, or performs in that other State independent personal services from a fixed base situated therein, and the royalties or fees for included services are attributable to such permanent establishment or fixed base. In such case the provisions of Article 7 (Business Profits) or Article 15 (Independent Personal Services), as the case may be, shall apply.

7. *a.* Royalties and fees for included services shall be deemed to arise in a Contracting State when the payer is that State itself, a political subdivision, a local authority, or a resident of that State. Where, however, the person paying the royalties or fees for included services, whether he is a resident of a Contracting State or not, has in a Contracting State a permanent establishment or a fixed base in connection with which the liability to pay the royalties or fees for included services was incurred, and such royalties or fees for included services are borne by such permanent establishment or fixed base, then such royalties or fees for included services shall be deemed to arise in the Contracting State in which the permanent establishment or fixed base is situated.

b. Where under subparagraph *a.* royalties or fees for included services do not arise in one of the Contracting States, and the royalties relate to the use of, or the right to use, the right or property, or the fees for included services relate to services performed, in one of the Contracting States, the royalties or fees for included services shall be deemed to arise in that Contracting State.

8. Where, by reason of a special relationship between the payer and the beneficial owner or between both of them and some other person, the amount of the royalties or fees for included services paid exceeds the amount which would have been paid in the absence of such relationship, the provisions of this Article shall apply only to the last-mentioned amount. In such case, the excess part of the payments shall remain taxable according to the laws of each Contracting State, due regard being had to the other provisions of the Convention.

Article 13. Gains

Except as provided in Article 8 (Shipping and Air Transport) of this Convention, each Contracting State may tax capital gains in accordance with the provisions of its domestic law.

Article 14.* Permanent Establishment Tax

1. A company which is a resident of India may be subject in the United States to a tax in addition to the tax allowable under the other provisions of this Convention.

a. Such tax, however, may be imposed only on:

(i) the portion of the business profits of the company subject to tax in the United States which represents the dividend equivalent amount; and

(ii) the excess, if any, of interest deductible in the United States in computing the profits of the company that are subject to tax in the United States and either attributable to a permanent establishment in the United States or subject to tax in the United States under Article 6 (Income from Immovable Property (Real Property)), Article 12 (Royalties and Fees for Included Services) as fees for included services, or Article 13 (Gains) of this Convention over the interest paid by or from the permanent establishment or trade or business in the United States.

b. For purposes of this article, business profits means profits that are effectively connected (or treated as effectively connected) with the conduct of a trade or business within the United States and are either attributable to a permanent establishment in the United States or subject to tax in the United States under Article 6 (Income from Immovable Property (Real Property)), Article 12 (Royalties and Fees for Included Services) as fees for included services or Article 13 (Gains) of this Convention.

c. The tax referred to in subparagraph *a.* shall not be imposed at a rate exceeding:

(i) the rate specified in paragraph 2*a.* of Article 10 (Dividends) for the tax described in subparagraph *a.*(i); and

(ii) the rate specified in paragraph 2*a.* or *b.* (whichever is appropriate) of Article 11 (Interest) for the tax described in subparagraph *a.*(ii)

2. A company which is a resident of the United States may be subject to tax in India at a rate higher than that applicable to the domestic companies. The difference in the tax rate shall not, however, exceed the existing difference of 15 percentage points.

3. In the case of a banking company which is a resident of the United States, the interest paid by the permanent establishment of such a company in India to the head office may be subject in India to a tax in addition to the tax imposable under the other provisions of this Convention at a rate which shall not exceed the rate specified in paragraph 2*a.* of Article 11 (Interest).

Article 15.* Independent Personal Services

1. Income derived by a person who is an individual or firm of individuals (other than a company) who is a resident of a Contracting State from the performance in the other Contracting State of professional services or other independent activities of a similar character shall be taxable only in the first-mentioned State except in the following circumstances when such income may also be taxed in the other Contracting State:

a. if such person has a fixed base regularly available to him in the other Contracting State for the purpose of performing his activities; in that case, only so much of the income as is attributable to that fixed base may be taxed in that other State; or

b. if the person's stay in the other Contracting State is for a period or periods exceeding in the aggregate 90 days in the relevant taxable year.

2. The term 'professional services' includes independent scientific, literary, artistic, educational or teaching activities as well as the independent activities of physicians, surgeons, lawyers, engineers, architects, dentists and accountants.

Article 16. Dependent Personal Services

1. Subject to the provisions of Articles 17 (Directors' Fees), 18 (Income Earned by Entertainers and Athletes), 19 (Remuneration and Pensions in Respect of Government Service), 20 (Private Pensions, Annuities, Alimony, and Child Support), 21 (Payments Received by Students and Apprentices) and 22 (Payments Received by Professors, Teachers and Research Scholars), salaries, wages and other similar remuneration derived by a resident of a Contracting State in respect of an employment shall be taxable only in that State unless the employment is exercised in the other Contracting State. If the employment is so exercised, such remuneration as is derived therefrom may be taxed in that other State.

2. Notwithstanding the provisions of paragraph 1, remuneration derived by a resident of a Contracting State in respect of an employment exercised in the other Contracting State shall be taxable only in the first-mentioned State if:

a. the recipient is present in the other State for a period or periods not exceeding in the aggregate 183 days in the relevant taxable year;

b. the remuneration is paid by, or on behalf of, an employer who is not a resident of the other State; and

c. the remuneration is not borne by a permanent establishment or a fixed base or a trade or business which the employer has in the other State.

3. Notwithstanding the preceding provisions of this Article, remuneration derived in respect of an employment exercised aboard a ship or aircraft operated in international traffic by an enterprise of a Contracting State may be taxed in that State.

Article 17. Directors' Fees

Directors' fees and similar payments derived by a resident of a Contracting State in his capacity as a member of the board of directors of a company which is a resident of the other Contracting State may be taxed in that other Contracting State.

Article 18. Income Earned by Entertainers and Athletes

1. Notwithstanding the provisions of Articles 15 (Independent Personal Services) and 16 (Dependent Personal Services), income derived by a resident of a Contracting State as an entertainer, such as a theatre, motion picture, radio or television artiste, or a musician, or as an ath-

lete, from his personal activities as such exercised in the other Contracting State, may be taxed in that other State, except where the amount of the net income derived by such entertainer or athlete from such activities (after deduction of all expense incurred by him in connection with his visit and performance) does not exceed one thousand five hundred United States dollars ($1,500) or its equivalent in Indian rupees for the taxable year concerned.

2. Where income in respect of activities exercised by an entertainer or an athlete in his capacity as such accrues not to the entertainer or athlete but to another person, that income of that other person may, notwithstanding the provisions of Article 7 (Business Profits), 15 (Independent Personal Services), and 16 (Dependent Personal Services), be taxed in the Contracting State in which the activities of the entertainer or athlete are exercised unless the entertainer, athlete, or other person establishes that neither the entertainer or athlete nor persons related thereto participate directly or indirectly in the profits of that other person in any manner, including the receipt of deferred remuneration, bonuses, fees, dividends, partnership distributions, or other distributions.

3. Income referred to in the preceding paragraphs of this Article derived by a resident of a Contracting State in respect of activities exercised in the other Contracting State shall not be taxed in that other State if the visit of the entertainers or athletes to that other State is supported wholly or substantially from the public funds of the Government of the first-mentioned Contracting State, or of a political subdivision or local authority thereof.

4. The competent authorities of the Contracting State may, by mutual agreement, increase the dollar amounts referred to in paragraph 1 to reflect economic or monetary developments.

Article 19. Remuneration and Pensions in Respect of Government Service

1. *a.* Remuneration, other than a pension, paid by a Contracting State or a political subdivision or local authority thereof to an individual in respect of services rendered to that State or subdivision or authority shall be taxable only in that State.

b. However, such remuneration shall be taxable only in the other Contracting State if the services are rendered in that other State and the individual is a resident of that State who:

(i) is a national of that State; or

(ii) did not become a resident of that State solely for the purpose of rendering the services.

2. *a.* Any pension paid by, or out of funds created by, a Contracting State or a political subdivision or local authority thereof to an individual in respect of services rendered to that State or subdivision or authority shall be taxable only in that State.

b. However, such pension shall be taxable only in the other Contracting State if the individual is a resident of, and a national of, that State.

3. The provisions of Articles 16 (Dependent Personal Services), 17 (Directors' Fees), 18 (Income Earned by Entertainers and Athletes) and 20 (Private Pensions, Annuities, Alimony and Child Support) shall apply to remuneration and pensions in respect of services rendered in connection with a business carried on by a Contracting State or a political subdivision or local authority thereof.

Article 20. Private Pensions, Annuities, Alimony and Child Support

1. Any pension, other than a pension referred to in Article 19 (Remuneration and Pensions in Respect of Government Service), or any annuity derived by a resident of a Contracting State from sources within the other Contracting State may be taxed only in the first-mentioned Contracting State.

2. Notwithstanding paragraph 1, and subject to the provisions of Article 19 (Remuneration and Pensions in Respect of Government Service), social security benefits and other public pensions paid by a Contracting State to a resident of the other Contracting State or a citizen of the United States shall be taxable only in the first-mentioned State.

3. The term 'pension' means a periodic payment made in consideration of past services or by way of compensation for injuries received in the course of the performance of services.

4. The term 'annuity' means stated sums payable periodically at stated times during life or during a specified or ascertainable number of years, under an obligation to make the payments in return for adequate and full consideration in money or money's worth (but not for services rendered).

5. Alimony paid to a resident of a Contracting State shall be taxable only in that State. The term 'alimony' as used in this paragraph means periodic payments made pursuant to a written separation agreement or a decree of divorce, separate maintenance, or compulsory support, which payments are taxable to the recipient under the laws of the State of which he is a resident.

6. Periodic payments for the support of a minor child made pursuant to a written separation agreement or a decree of divorce, separate maintenance or compulsory support, paid by a resident of a Contracting State to a resident of the other Contracting State, shall be taxable only in the first-mentioned State.

Article 21. Payments Received by Students and Apprentices

1. A student or business apprentice who is or was a resident of one of the Contracting States immediately before visiting the other Contracting State and who is present in that other State principally for the purpose of his education or training shall be exempt from tax in that other State, on payments which arise outside that other State for the purpose of his maintenance, education or training.

2. In respect of grants, scholarships and remuneration from employment not covered by paragraph 1, a student or business

apprentice described in paragraph 1 shall, in addition, be entitled during such education or training to the same exemptions, reliefs or reductions in respect of taxes available to residents of the State which he is visiting.

3. The benefits of this Article shall extend only for such period of time as may be reasonable or customarily required to complete the education or training undertaken.

4. For the purpose of this Article, an individual shall be deemed to be a resident of a Contracting State if he is a resident in that Contracting State in the taxable year in which he visits the other Contracting State or in the immediately preceding taxable year.

Article 22. Payments Received by Professors, Teachers and Research Scholars

1. An individual who visits a Contracting State for a period not exceeding two years for the purpose of teaching or engaging in research at a university, college or other recognized educational institution in that State, and who was immediately before that visit a resident of the other Contracting State, shall be exempted from tax by the first-mentioned Contracting State on any remuneration for such teaching or research for a period not exceeding two years from the date he first visits that State for such purpose.

2. This Article shall apply to income from research only if such research is undertaken by the individual in the public interest and not primarily for the benefit of some other private person or persons.

Article 23.* Other Income

1. Subject to the provisions of paragraph 2, items of income of a resident of a Contracting State, wherever arising, which are not expressly dealt with in the foregoing Articles of this Convention shall be taxable only in that Contracting State.

2. The provisions of paragraph 1 shall not apply to income, other than income from immovable property as defined in paragraph 2 of Article 6 (Income from Immovable Property (Real Property)), if the beneficial owner of the income, being a resident of a Contracting State, carries on business in the other Contracting State through a permanent establishment situated therein, or performs in that other State independent personal services from a fixed base situated therein, and the income is attributable to such permanent establishment or fixed base. In such case the provisions of Article 7 (Business Profits) or Article 15 (Independent Personal Services), as the case may be, shall apply.

3. Notwithstanding the provisions of paragraphs 1 and 2, items of income of a resident of a Contracting State not dealt with in the foregoing articles of this Convention and arising in the other Contracting State may also be taxed in that other State.

Article 24. Limitation on Benefits

1. A person (other than an individual) which is a resident of a Contracting State and derives income from the other Contracting State shall

be entitled under this Convention to relief from taxation in that other Contracting State only if:

a. more than 50 per cent of the beneficial interest in such person (or in the case of a company, more than 50 per cent of the number of shares of each class of the company's shares) is owned, directly or indirectly, by one or more individual residents of one of the Contracting States, one of the Contracting States or its political subdivisions or local authorities, or other individuals subject to tax in either Contracting State on their worldwide incomes, or citizens of the United States; and

b. the income of such person if not used in substantial part, directly or indirectly, to meet liabilities (including liabilities for interest or royalties) to persons who are not residents of one of the Contracting States, one of the Contracting States or its political subdivisions or local authorities, or citizens of the United States.

2. The provisions of paragraph 1 shall not apply if the income derived from the other Contracting State is derived in connection with, or is incidental to, the active conduct by such person of a trade or business in the first-mentioned State (other than the business of making or managing investments, unless these activities are banking or insurance activities carried on by a bank or insurance company).

3. The provisions of paragraph 1 shall not apply if the person deriving the income is a company which is a resident of a Contracting State in whose principal class of shares there is substantial and regular trading on a recognized stock exchange. For purposes of the preceding sentence, the term 'recognized stock exchange' means:

a. in the case of the United States, the NASDAQ System owned by the National Association of Securities Dealers, Inc. and any stock exchange registered with the Securities and Exchange Commission as a national securities exchange for purposes of the Securities Exchange Act of 1934;

b. in the case of India, any stock exchange which is recognized by the Central Government under the Securities Contracts Regulation Act, 1956; and

c. any other stock exchange agreed upon by the competent authorities of the Contracting States.

4. A person that is not entitled to the benefits of this Convention pursuant to the provisions of the preceding paragraphs of this Article may, nevertheless, be granted the benefits of the Convention if the competent authority of the State in which the income in question arises so determines.

Article 25. Relief from Double Taxation

1. In accordance with the provisions and subject to the limitations of the law of the United States (as it may be amended from time to time without changing the general principle hereof), the United States shall allow to a resident or citizen of the United States as a credit against the United States tax on income

a. the income tax paid to India by or on behalf of such citizen or resident; and

b. in the case of a United States company owning at least 10 per cent of the voting stock of a company which is a resident of India and from which the United States company receives dividends, the income tax paid to India by or on behalf of the distributing company with respect to the profits out of which the dividends are paid.

For the purposes of this paragraph, the taxes referred to in paragraphs 1*b.* and 2 of Article 2 (Taxes Covered) shall be considered income taxes.

2. *a.* Where a resident of India derives income which, in accordance with the provisions of this Convention, may be taxed in the United States, India shall allow as a deduction from the tax on the income of that resident an amount equal to the income tax paid in the United States, whether directly or by deduction. Such deduction shall not, however, exceed that part of the income tax (as computed before the deduction is given) which is attributable to the income which may be taxed in the United States.

b. Further, where such resident is a company by which a surtax is payable in India, the deduction in respect of income tax paid in the United States shall be allowed in the first instance from income tax payable by the company in India and as to the balance, if any, from surtax payable by it in India.

3. For the purposes of allowing relief from double taxation pursuant to this Article, income shall be deemed to arise as follows:

a. income derived by a resident of a Contracting State which may be taxed in the other Contracting State in accordance with this Convention (other than solely by reason of citizenship in accordance with paragraph 3 of Article 1 (General Scope) shall be deemed to arise in that other State;

b. income derived by a resident of a Contracting State which may not be taxed in the other Contracting State in accordance with the Convention shall be deemed to arise in the first-mentioned State.

Notwithstanding the preceding sentence, the determination of the source of income for purposes of this Article shall be subject to such source rules in the domestic laws of the Contracting States as apply for the purpose of limiting the foreign tax credit. The preceding shall not apply with respect to income dealt with in Article 12 (Royalties and Fees for Included Services). The rules of this paragraph shall not apply in determining credits against United States tax for foreign taxes other than the taxes referred to in paragraphs 1*b.* and 2 of Article 2 (Taxes Covered).

Article 26. Non-Discrimination

1. Nationals of a Contracting State shall not be subjected in the other Contracting State to any taxation or any requirement connected therewith which is other or more burdensome than the taxation and connected requirements to which nationals of that other State in the

same circumstances are or may be subjected. This provision shall apply to persons who are not residents of one or both of the Contracting States.

2. Except where the provisions of paragraph 3 of Article 7 (Business Profits) apply, the taxation on a permanent establishment which an enterprise of a Contracting State has in the other Contracting State shall not be less favorably levied in that other State than the taxation levied on enterprises of that other State carrying on the same activities. This provision shall not be construed as obliging a Contracting State to grant to residents of the other Contracting State any personal allowances, reliefs, and reductions for taxation purposes on account of civil status or family responsibilities which it grants to its own residents.

3. Except where the provisions of paragraph 1 of Article 9 (Associated Enterprises), paragraph 7 of Article 11 (Interest), or paragraph 8 of Article 12 (Royalties and Fees for Included Services) apply, interest, royalties, and other disbursements paid by a resident of a Contracting State to a resident of the other Contracting State shall, for the purposes of determining the taxable profits of the first-mentioned resident, be deductible under the same conditions as if they had been paid to a resident of the first-mentioned Contracting State.

4. Enterprises of a Contracting State, the capital of which is wholly or partly owned or controlled, directly or indirectly, by one or more residents of the other Contracting State, shall not be subjected in the first-mentioned State to any taxation or any requirement connected therewith which is other or more burdensome than the taxation and connected requirements to which other similar enterprises of the first-mentioned State are or may be subjected.

5. Nothing in this article shall be construed as preventing either Contracting State from imposing the taxes described in Article 14 (Permanent Establishment Tax) or the limitations described in paragraph 3 of Article 7 (Business Profits).

Article 27. Mutual Agreement Procedure

1. Where a person considers that the actions of one or both of the Contracting States result or will result for him in taxation not in accordance with the provisions of this Convention, he may, irrespective of the remedies provided by the domestic law of those Contracting States, present his case to the competent authority of the Contracting State of which he is a resident or national. The case must be presented within three years of the date of receipt of notice of the action which gives rise to taxation not in accordance with the Convention.

2. The competent authority shall endeavor, if the objection appears to it to be justified and if it is not itself able to arrive at a satisfactory solution, to resolve the case by mutual agreement with the competent authority of the other Contracting State, with a view to the avoidance of taxation which is not in accordance with the Convention. Any agreement reached shall be implemented notwithstanding any time limits or other procedural limitations in the domestic law of the Contracting States.

3. The competent authorities of the Contracting States shall endeavor to resolve by mutual agreement any difficulties or doubts arising as to the interpretation or application of the Convention. They may also consult together for the elimination of double taxation in cases not provided for in the Convention.

4. The competent authorities of the Contracting States may communicate with each other directly for the purpose of reaching an agreement in the sense of the preceding paragraphs. The competent authorities, through consultations, shall develop appropriate bilateral procedures, conditions, methods and techniques for the implementation of the mutual agreement procedure provided for in this Article. In addition, a competent authority may devise appropriate unilateral procedures, conditions, methods and techniques to facilitate the above-mentioned bilateral actions and the implementation of the mutual agreement procedure.

Article 28. Exchange of Information and Administrative Assistance

1. The competent authorities of the Contracting States shall exchange such information (including documents) as is necessary for carrying out the provisions of this Convention or of the domestic laws of the Contracting States concerning taxes covered by the Convention insofar as the taxation thereunder is not contrary to the Convention, in particular, for the prevention of fraud or evasion of taxes. The exchange of information is not restricted by Article 1 (General Scope). Any information received by a Contracting State shall be treated as secret in the same manner as information obtained under the domestic laws of that State. However, if the information is originally regarded as secret in the transmitting State, it shall be disclosed only to persons or authorities (including courts and administrative bodies) involved in the assessment, collection, or administration of, the enforcement or prosecution in respect of, or the determination of appeals in relation to, the taxes which are the subject of the Convention. Such persons or authorities shall use the information only for such purposes, but may disclose the information in public court proceedings or in judicial decisions. The competent authorities shall, through consultation, develop appropriate conditions, methods and techniques concerning the matters in respect of which such exchange of information shall be made, including, where appropriate, exchange of information regarding tax avoidance.

2. The exchange of information or documents shall be either on a routine basis or on request with reference to particular cases, or otherwise. The competent authorities of the Contracting States shall agree from time to time on the list of information or documents which shall be furnished on a routine basis.

3. In no case shall the provisions of paragraph 1 be construed so as to impose on a Contracting State the obligation:

a. to carry out administrative measures at variance with the laws and administrative practice of that or of the other Contracting State;

b. to supply information which is not obtainable under the laws or in the normal course of the administration of that or of the other Contracting State; or

c. to supply information which would disclose any trade, business, industrial, commercial, or professional secret or trade process, or information the disclosure of which would be contrary to public policy (*ordre public*).

4. If information is requested by a Contracting State in accordance with this Article, the other Contracting State shall obtain the information to which the request relates in the same manner and in the same form as if the tax of the first-mentioned State were the tax of that other State and were being imposed by that other State. If specifically requested by the competent authority of a Contracting State, the competent authority of the other Contracting State shall provide information under this Article in the form of depositions of witnesses and authenticated copies of unedited original documents (including books, papers, statements, records, accounts, and writings), to the same extent such depositions and documents can be obtained under the laws and administrative practices of that other State with respect to its own taxes.

5. For the purposes of this Article, the Convention shall apply, notwithstanding the provisions of Article 2 (Taxes Covered):

a. in the United States, to all taxes imposed under Title 26 of the United States Code; and

b. in India, to the income tax, the wealth tax and the gift tax.

Article 29. Diplomatic Agents and Consular Officers

Nothing in this Convention shall affect the fiscal privileges of diplomatic agents or consular officers under the general rules of international law or under the provisions of special agreements.

Article 30. Entry Into Force

1. Each of the Contracting States shall notify the other Contracting State in writing, through diplomatic channels, upon the completion of their respective legal procedures to bring this Convention into force.

2. The Convention shall enter into force on the date of the latter of such notification and its provisions shall have effect:

a. in the United States

(i) in respect of taxes withheld at source, for amounts paid or credited after the first day of January next following the date on which the Convention enters into force;

(ii) in respect of other taxes, for taxable periods beginning on or after the first day of January next following the date on which the Convention enters into force; and

b. in India, in respect of income arising in any taxable year beginning on or after the first day of April next following the calendar year in which the Convention enters into force.

Article 31. Termination

This Convention shall remain in force indefinitely, but either of the Contracting States may, on or before the thirtieth day of June in any calendar year beginning after the expiration of a period of five years from the date of entry into force of the Convention, give the other Contracting State through diplomatic channels, written notice of termination and, in such event, the Convention shall cease to have effect:

a. in the United States

(i) in respect of taxes withheld at source, for amounts paid or credited on or after the first day of January next following the calendar year in which notice of termination is given;

(ii) in respect of other taxes, for taxable periods beginning on or after the first day of January next following the calendar year in which the notice of termination is given; and

b. in India, in respect of income arising in any taxable year beginning on or after the first day of April next following the calendar year in which the notice of termination is given;

In witness whereof, the undersigned, being duly authorized by their respective Governments, have signed this Convention.

Done at New Delhi in duplicate, this 12th day of September, 1989, in the English and Hindi languages, both texts being equally authentic. In case of divergence between the two texts, the English text shall be the operative one.

Protocol

At the signing today of the Convention between the United States of America and the Republic of India for the Avoidance of Double Taxation and the Prevention of Fiscal Evasion with respect to Taxes on Income, the undersigned have agreed upon the following provisions, which shall form an integral part of the Convention.

I. Ad Article 5

It is understood that where an enterprise of a Contracting State has a permanent establishment in the other Contracting State in accordance with the provisions of paragraphs 2*j*., 2*k*. or 2*l*. of Article 5 (Permanent Establishment), and the time period referred to in that paragraph extends over two taxable years, a permanent establishment shall not be deemed to exist in a year, if any, in which the use, project or activity, as the case may be, continues for a period or periods aggregating less than 30 days in that taxable year. A permanent establishment will exist in the other taxable year, and the enterprise will be subject to tax in that other Contracting State in accordance with the provisions of Article 7 (Business Profits), but only on income arising during that other taxable year.

II. Ad Article 7

Where the law of a Contracting State in which a permanent establishment is situated imposes, in accordance with the provisions of paragraph 3 of Article 7 (Business Profits), a restriction on the amount of executive and general administrative expenses which may be allowed as a deduction in determining the profits of such permanent establishment, it is understood that in making such a determination of profits the deduction in respect of such executive and general administrative expenses in no case shall be less than that allowable under the Indian Income-tax Act as on the date of signature of this Convention.

III. Ad Articles 7, 10, 11, 12, 15, and 23

It is understood that for the implementation of paragraphs 1 and 2 of Article 7 (Business Profits), paragraph 4 of Article 10 (Dividends), paragraph 5 of Article 11 (Interest), paragraph 6 of Article 12 (Royalties and Fees for Included Services), paragraph 1 of Article 15 (Independent Personal Services), and paragraph 2 of Article 23 (Other Income), any income attributable to a permanent establishment or fixed base during its existence is taxable in the Contracting State in which such permanent establishment or fixed base is situated even if the payments are deferred until such permanent establishment or fixed base has ceased to exist.

IV. Ad Article 12

It is understood that fees for included services, as defined in paragraph 4 of Article 12 (Royalties and Fees for Included Services), will, in accordance with United States law, be subject to income tax in the United States based on net income and, when earned by a company, will also be subject to the taxes described in paragraph 1 of Article 14 (Permanent Establishment Tax). The total of these taxes which may be imposed on such fees, however, may not exceed the amount computed by multiplying the gross fee by the appropriate tax rate specified in subparagraph *a.* or *b.*, whichever is applicable, of paragraph 2 of Article 12.

V. Ad Article 14

It is understood that references in paragraph 1 of Article 14 (Permanent Establishment Tax) to profits that are subject to tax in the United States under Article 6 (Income from Immovable Property (Real Property)), under Article 12 (Royalties and Fees for Included Services), as fees for included services as defined in that Article, or under Article 13 (Gains) of this Convention, are intended to refer only to cases in which the profits in question are subject to United States tax based on net income (*i.e.*, by virtue of being effectively connected, or being treated as effectively connected, with the conduct of a trade or business in the United States). Any income which is subject to tax under those Articles based on gross income is not subject to tax under Article 14.

In witness whereof, the undersigned, being duly authorized by their respective Governments, have signed this Protocol.

Done at New Delhi in duplicate, this 12th day of September, 1989, in the English and Hindi languages, both texts being equally authentic. In case of divergence between the two texts, the English text shall be the operative one.

Convention between the Government of United States of America and the Government of Ireland for the Avoidance of Double Taxation and the Prevention of Fiscal Evasion with Respect to Taxes on Income, concluded in Dublin on September 13, 1949.

The Government of the United States of America and the Government of Ireland,

Desiring to conclude a Convention for the avoidance of double taxation and the prevention of fiscal evasion with respect to taxes on income,

Have appointed for that purpose as their Plenipotentiaries:

The Government of the United States of America:

George A. Garret, Envoy Extraordinary and Minister Plenipotentiary of the United States of America at Dublin;

The Government of Ireland:

Patrick McGilligan, Minister for Finance; Seán MacBride, Minister for External Affairs;

Who, having exhibited their respective full powers, found in good and due form, have agreed as follows:

Article I

1. The taxes which are the subject of the present Convention are:

a. In the United States of America: The Federal income taxes, including surtaxes (hereinafter referred to as United States tax).

b. In Ireland: The income tax (including surtax) and the corporation profits tax (hereinafter referred to as Irish tax).

2. The present Convention shall also apply to any other taxes of a substantially similar character imposed by either Contracting Party subsequently to the date of signature of the present Convention.

Article II

1. In the present Convention, unless the context otherwise requires:

a. The term 'United States' means the United States of America, and when used in a geographical sense means the United States, the Territories of Alaska and of Hawaii, and the District of Columbia.

b. The term 'Ireland' means the Republic of Ireland and the term 'Irish' has a corresponding meaning.

c. The terms 'territory of one of the Contracting Parties' and 'territory of the other Contracting Party' means the United States of America or Ireland as the context requires.

d. The term 'United States corporation' means a corporation, association or other like entity created or organised in or under the laws of the United States.

e. The term 'Irish corporation' means any kind of juridical person created under the laws of Ireland.

f. The terms 'corporation of one Contracting Party' and 'corporation of the other Contracting Party' mean a United States corporation or an Irish corporation as the context requires.

g. The term 'resident of Ireland' means any person (other than a citizen of the United States or a United States corporation) who is resident in Ireland for the purposes of Irish tax and not resident in the United States for the purposes of United States tax. A corporation is to be regarded as resident in Ireland if its business is managed and controlled in Ireland.

h. The term 'resident of the United States' means any individual who is resident in the United States for the purposes of United States tax and not resident in Ireland for the purposes of Irish tax, and any United States corporation and any partnership created or organised in or under the laws of the United States, being a corporation or partnership which is not resident in Ireland for the purposes of Irish tax.

i. The term 'Irish enterprise' means an industrial or commercial enterprise or undertaking carried on by a resident of Ireland.

j. The term 'United States enterprise' means an industrial or commercial enterprise or undertaking carried on by a resident of the United States.

k. The terms 'enterprise of one of the Contracting Parties' and 'enterprise of the other Contracting Party' mean a United States enterprise or an Irish enterprise, as the context requires.

l. The term 'permanent establishment' when used with respect to an enterprise of one of the Contracting Parties means a branch, management, factory or other fixed place of business, but does not include an agency unless the agent has, and habitually exercises, a general authority to negotiate and conclude contracts on behalf of such enterprise or has a stock of merchandise from which he regularly fills orders on its behalf. An enterprise of one of the Contracting Parties shall not be deemed to have a permanent establishment in the territory of the other Contracting Party merely because it carries on business dealings in the territory of such other Contracting Party through a bona fide commission agent or broker acting in the ordinary course of his business as such. The fact that a corporation of one of the Contracting Parties maintains in the territory of the other Contracting Party a fixed place of business exclusively for the purchase of goods or merchandise shall not of itself constitute such fixed place of business a permanent establishment of such enterprise. The fact that an enterprise of one of the Contracting Parties has a subsidiary corporation which is a corporation of the other Contracting Party or which is engaged in trade or business in the territory of such other Contracting Party (whether through a permanent establishment or otherwise) shall not of itself constitute such subsidiary corporation a permanent establishment of its parent corporation.

2. For the purposes of Article VI, VII, VIII, IX and XIV a resident of Ireland shall not be deemed to be engaged in trade or business in

the United States in any taxable year unless such resident has a permanent establishment situated therein in such taxable year. The same principle shall be applied, *mutatis mutandis*, by Ireland in the case of a resident of the United States.

3. In the application of the provisions of the present Convention by one of the Contracting Parties any term not otherwise defined shall, unless the context otherwise requires, have the meaning which it has under the laws of that Contracting Party relating to the taxes which are the subject of the present Convention.

Article III

1. An Irish enterprise shall not be subject to United States tax in respect of its industrial or commercial profits unless it is engaged in trade or business in the United States through a permanent establishment situated therein. If it is so engaged, United States tax may be imposed upon the entire income of such enterprise from all sources within the United States.

2. A United States enterprise shall not be subject to Irish tax in respect of its industrial or commercial profits unless it is engaged in trade or business in Ireland through a permanent establishment situated therein. If it is so engaged, Irish tax may be imposed upon the entire income of such enterprise from all sources within Ireland.

3. Where an enterprise of one of the Contracting Parties is engaged in trade or business in the territory of the other Contracting Party through a permanent establishment situated therein, there shall be attributed to such permanent establishment the industrial or commercial profits which it might be expected to derive if it were an independent enterprise engaged in the same or similar activities under the same or similar conditions and dealing at arm's length with the enterprise of which it is a permanent establishment, and the profits so attributed shall, subject to the law of such other Contracting Party, be deemed to be income from sources within the territory of such other Contracting Party.

4. In determining the industrial or commercial profits from sources within the territory of one of the Contracting Parties of a enterprise of the other Contracting Party, no profits shall be deemed to arise from the mere purchase of goods or merchandise within the territory of the former Contracting Party by such enterprise.

Article IV

Where an enterprise of one of the Contracting Parties, by reason of its participation in the management, control or capital of an enterprise of the other Contracting Party, makes with or imposes on the latter, in their commercial and financial relations, conditions different from those which would be made with an independent enterprise, any profits which would normally have accrued to one of the enterprises but by reason of those conditions have not so accrued, may be included in the profits of that enterprise and taxed accordingly.

Article V

1. Notwithstanding the provisions of Articles III and IV of the present Convention, profits which an individual resident of Ireland or an Irish corporation derives from operating ships documented or aircraft registered under the laws of Ireland, shall be exempt from United States tax.

2. Notwithstanding the provisions of Articles III and IV of the present Convention, profits which a citizen of the United States not resident in Ireland or a United States corporation derives from operating ships documented or aircraft registered under the laws of the United States, shall be exempt from Irish tax.

3. This Article shall not be deemed to affect the arrangement between Ireland and the United States, providing for reciprocal exemption of shipping profits from income tax, effected between the Government of the United States and the Government of Ireland by exchange of Notes dated August 24, 1933, and January 8, 1934.

Article VI

1. The rate of United States tax on dividends derived from a United States corporation by a resident of Ireland who is subject to Irish tax on such dividends and not engaged in trade or business in the United States shall not exceed 15 per cent; provided that such rate of tax shall not exceed five per cent if such resident is a corporation controlling, directly or indirectly, at least 95 per cent of the entire voting power in the corporation paying the dividend, and not more than 25 per cent of the gross income of such paying corporation is derived from interest and dividends, other than interest and dividends received from its own subsidiary corporations. Such reduction of the rate to five per cent shall not apply if the relationship of the two corporations has been arranged or is maintained primarily with the intention of securing such reduced rate.

2. Dividends derived from sources within Ireland by an individual who is (a) a resident of the United States, (b) subject to United States tax with respect to such dividends, and (c) not engaged in trade or business in Ireland, shall be exempt from Irish surtax.

3. Either of the Contracting Parties may terminate this Article by giving written notice of termination to the other Contracting Party, through diplomatic channels, on or before the thirtieth day of June in any calendar year after the calendar year in which the exchange of the instruments of ratification takes place and in such event paragraph 1 hereof shall cease to be effective as to United States tax on and after the first day of January, and paragraph 2 hereof shall cease to be effective as to Irish tax on and after the 6th day of April, in the calendar year next following that in which such notice is given.

Article VII

1. Interest (on bonds, securities, notes, debentures, or on any other form of indebtedness) derived from sources within the United States by a resident of Ireland who is subject to Irish tax on such interest and

not engaged in trade or business in the United States, shall be exempt from United States tax; but such exemption shall not apply to such interest paid by a United States corporation to a corporation resident in Ireland controlling, directly or indirectly, more than 50 per cent of the entire voting power in the paying corporation.

2. Interest (on bonds, securities, notes, debentures, or on any other form of indebtedness) derived from sources within Ireland by a resident of the United States who is subject to United States tax on such interest and not engaged in trade or business in Ireland, shall be exempt from Irish tax; but such exemption shall not apply to such interest paid by a corporation resident in Ireland to a United States corporation controlling, directly or indirectly, more than 50 per cent of the entire voting power in the paying corporation.

Article VIII

1. Royalties and other amounts paid as consideration for the use of, or for the privilege of using, copyrights, patents, designs, secret processes and formulae, trade-marks, and other like property, and derived from sources within the United States by a resident of Ireland who is subject to Irish tax on such royalties or other amounts and not engaged in trade or business in the United States, shall be exempt from United States tax.

2. Royalties and other amounts paid as consideration for the use of, or for the privilege of using, copyrights, patents, designs, secret processes and formulae, trade-marks, and other like property, and derived from sources within Ireland by a resident of the United States who is subject to United States tax on such royalties or other amounts and not engaged in trade or business in Ireland shall be exempt from Irish tax.

3. For the purposes of this Article, the term 'royalties' shall be deemed to include rentals in respect of motion picture films.

Article IX

1. The rate of United States tax on royalties in respect of the operation of mines or quarries or of other extraction of natural resources, and on rentals from real property or from an interest in such property, derived from sources within the United States by a resident of Ireland who is subject to Irish tax with respect to such royalties or rentals and not engaged in trade or business in the United States, shall not exceed 15 per cent; provided that any such resident may elect for any taxable year to be subject to United States tax as if such resident were engaged in trade or business in the United States.

2. Royalties in respect of the operation of mines or quarries or of other extraction of natural resources, and rentals from real property or from an interest in such property, derived from sources within Ireland by an individual who is (a) a resident of the United States, (b) subject to United States tax with respect to such royalties and rentals, and (c) not engaged in trade or business in Ireland, shall be exempt from Irish surtax.

Article X

1. Any salary, wage, similar remuneration, or pension, paid by the Government of the United States to an individual (other than a citizen of Ireland who is not also a citizen of the United States) in respect of services rendered to the United States in the discharge of governmental functions, shall be exempt from Irish tax.

2. Any salary, wage, similar remuneration, or pension, paid by the Government of Ireland to an individual (other than a citizen of the United States who is not also a citizen of Ireland) in respect of services rendered to Ireland in the discharge of governmental functions, shall be exempt from United States tax.

3. The provisions of this Article shall not apply to payments in respect of services rendered in connection with any trade or business carried on by either of the Contracting Parties for purposes or profit.

Article XI

1. An individual who is a resident of Ireland shall be exempt from United States tax upon compensation for personal (including professional) services performed during the taxable year within the United States if (a) he is present within the United States for a period or periods not exceeding in the aggregate 183 days during such taxable year; and (b) such services are performed on behalf of a person resident in Ireland.

2. An individual who is a resident of the United States shall be exempt from Irish tax upon profits, emoluments, or other remuneration in respect of personal (including professional) services performed within Ireland in any year of assessment if (a) he is present within Ireland for a period or periods not exceeding in the aggregate 183 days during that year; and (b) such services are performed on behalf of a person resident in the United States.

Article XII

1. Any pension (other than a pension to which Article X applies) and any life annuity, derived from sources within the United States by an individual who is a resident of Ireland shall be exempt from United States tax.

2. Any pension (other than a pension to which Article X applies) and any life annuity, derived from sources within Ireland by an individual who is a resident of the United States shall be exempt from Irish tax.

3. The term 'life annuity' means a stated sum payable periodically at stated times, during life or during a specified or ascertainable period of time, under an obligation to make the payments in consideration of money paid.

Article XIII

1. Subject to section 131 of the United States Internal Revenue Code as in effect on the day on which this Convention shall come into effect, Irish tax shall be allowed as a credit against United States tax. For this

purpose, the recipient of a dividend paid by a corporation which is a resident of Ireland shall be deemed to have paid the Irish income tax appropriate to such dividend if such recipient elects to include in his gross income for the purposes of United States tax the amount of such Irish income tax. For the purposes only of this Article, income derived from sources in the United Kingdom by an individual who is resident in Ireland shall be deemed to be income from sources in Ireland if such income is not subject to United Kingdom income tax.

2. Subject to such provisions (which shall not affect the general principle hereof) as may be enacted in Ireland, United States tax payable in respect of income from sources within the United States shall be allowed as a credit against any Irish tax payable in respect of that income. Where such income is an ordinary dividend paid by a United States corporation, such credit shall take into account (in addition to any United States income tax deducted from or imposed on such dividend) the United States income tax imposed on such corporation in respect of its profits, and where it is a dividend paid on participating preference shares and representing both a dividend at the fixed rate to which the shares are entitled and an additional participation in profits, such tax on profits shall likewise be taken into account in so far as the dividend exceeds such fixed rate.

3. For the purposes of this Article, compensation, profits, emoluments and other remuneration for personal (including professional) services shall be deemed to be income from sources within the territory of the Contracting Party where such services are performed.

Article XIV[1]

A resident of Ireland not engaged in trade or business in the United States shall be exempt from United States tax on gains from the sale or exchange of capital assets.

Article XV

1. Dividends and interest paid, on or after the first day of January in the calendar year in which the exchange of instruments of ratification takes place, by an Irish corporation shall be exempt from United States tax except where the recipient is a citizen of or a resident in the United States or a United States corporation.

2. Dividends and interest paid, on or after the 6th day of April of the first year of assessment specified in Article XXII.2*b*.(i) of this Convention, by a United States corporation shall be exempt from Irish tax except where the recipient is a resident of Ireland.

1. Convention ratified by US with a reservation rejecting Art. XIV.

Article XVI[1]

An Irish corporation shall be exempt from United States tax on its accumulated or undistributed earnings, profits, income or surplus, if individuals who are residents of Ireland control, directly or indirectly, throughout the latter half of the taxable year, more than 50 per cent of the entire voting power in such corporation.

Article XVII

1. The United States income tax liability for any taxable year beginning prior to January 1, 1936, of any individual (other than a citizen of the United States) resident in Ireland, or of any Irish corporation, remaining unpaid on the date of signature of the present Convention, may be adjusted on a basis satisfactory to the United States Commissioner of Internal Revenue: provided that the amount to be paid in settlement of such liability shall not exceed the amount of the liability which would have been determined if:

a. the United States Revenue Act of 1936 (except in the case of an Irish corporation in which more than 50 per cent of the entire voting power was controlled, directly or indirectly, throughout the latter half of the taxable year, by citizens or residents of the United States), and

b. Articles XV and XVI of the present Convention, had been in effect for such year. If the taxpayer was not, within the meaning of such Revenue Act, engaged in trade or business in the United States and had no office or place of business therein during the taxable year, the amount of interest and penalties shall not exceed 50 per cent of the amount of the tax with respect to which such interest and penalties have been computed.

2. The United States income tax unpaid on the date of signature of the present Convention for any taxable year beginning after the thirty-first day of December, 1935, and prior to the first day of January in the calendar year in which the exchange of instruments of ratification takes place in the case of an individual resident of Ireland, or in the case of any Irish corporation shall be determined as if the provisions of Articles XV and XVI of the present Convention had been in effect for such taxable year.

3. The provisions of paragraph 1 of this Article shall not apply:

a. unless the taxpayer files with the Commissioner of Internal Revenue on or before the thirty-first day of December of the second calendar year following the calendar year in which the exchange of the instruments of ratification takes place a request that such tax liability be so adjusted and furnishes such information as the Commissioner may require; or

b. in any case in which the Commissioner is satisfied that any deficiency in tax is due to fraud with intent to evade the tax.

---

1. Convention ratified by US with a reservation rejecting Art. XVI.

Article XVIII

A professor or teacher from the territory of one of the Contracting Parties who visits the territory of the other Contracting Party for the purpose of teaching, for a period not exceeding two years, at a university, college, school or other educational institution in the territory of such other Contracting Party shall be exempted by such other Contracting Party from tax on his remuneration for such teaching for such period.

Article XIX

A student or business apprentice from the territory of one of the Contracting Parties who is receiving full-time education or training in the territory of the other Contracting Party shall be exempted by such other Contracting Party from tax on payments made to him by persons within the territory of the former Contracting Party for the purposes of his maintenance, education or training.

Article XX

1. The taxation authorities of the Contracting Parties shall exchange such information (being information available under the respective taxation laws of the Contracting Parties) as is necessary for carrying out the provisions of the present Convention or for the prevention of fraud or the administration of statutory provisions against legal avoidance in relation to the taxes which are the subject of the present Convention. Any information so exchanged shall be treated as secret and shall not be disclosed to any person other than those concerned with the assessment and collection of the taxes which are the subject of the present Convention. No information shall be exchanged which would disclose any trade secret or trade process.

2. As used in this Article, the term 'taxation authorities' means, in the case of the United States, the Commissioner of Internal Revenue or his authorised representative and, in the case of Ireland, the Revenue Commissioners or their authorised representative.

Article XXI

1. The nationals of one of the Contracting Parties shall not, while resident in the territory of the other Contracting Party, be subjected therein to other or more burdensome taxes than are the nationals of such other Contracting Party resident in its territory.

2. The term 'nationals' as used in this Article means:

a. in relation to Ireland, all citizens of Ireland; and

b. in relation to the United States, United States citizens;

and includes all legal persons, partnerships, and associations deriving their status as such from, or created or organized under, the laws in force in any territory of the Contracting Parties to which the present Convention applies.

Article XXII

1. The present Convention shall be ratified and the instruments of ratification shall be exchanged at Washington, District of Columbia, as soon as possible.

2. Upon exchange of ratifications, the present Convention shall have effect

a. as respects United States tax, for the taxable years beginning on or after the first day of January in the calendar year in which the exchange of instruments of ratification takes place;

b. (i) as respects Irish income tax, for the year of assessment beginning on the 6th day of April in the calendar year in which the exchange of instruments of ratification takes place and subsequent years; (ii) as respects Irish surtax, for the year of assessment beginning on the 6th day of April immediately preceding the calendar year in which the exchange of instruments of ratification takes place, and subsequent years; and (iii) as respects Irish corporation profits tax, for any chargeable accounting period beginning on or after the first day of April in the calendar year in which the exchange of instruments of ratification takes place, and for the unexpired portion of any chargeable accounting period current at that date.

Article XXIII

1. The present Convention shall continue in effect indefinitely but either of the Contracting Parties may, on or before the 30th day of June in any calendar year following the calendar year in which the exchange of instruments of ratification takes place, give to the other Contracting Party, through diplomatic channels, notice of termination and, in such event, the present Convention shall cease to be effective

a. as respects United States tax, for the taxable years beginning on or after the first day of January in the calendar year next following that in which such notice is given;

b. (i) as respects Irish income tax, for any year of assessment beginning on or after the 6th day of April in the calendar year next following that in which such notice is given; (ii) as respects Irish surtax, for any year of assessment beginning on or after the 6th day of April in the calendar year in which such notice is given; and (iii) as respects Irish corporation tax, for any chargeable accounting period beginning on or after the first day of April in the calendar year next following that in which such notice is given and for the unexpired portion of any chargeable accounting period current at that date.

2. The termination of the present Convention or of any Article thereof shall not have the effect of reviving any treaty or arrangement abrogated by the present Convention or by treaties previously concluded between the Contracting Parties.

In witness whereof the above-named Plenipotentiaries have signed the present Convention and have affixed thereto their seals.

Done in Dublin, in duplicate, this 13th day of September, 1949.

Convention between the Government of the United States of America and the Government of the Republic of Italy for the Avoidance of Double Taxation with Respect to Taxes on Income and the Prevention of Fraud or Fiscal Evasion, concluded in Rome on April 17, 1984.

The Government of the United States of America and the Government of the Republic of Italy, desiring to conclude a convention for the avoidance of double taxation with respect to taxes on income and the prevention of fraud or fiscal evasion, have agreed as follows:

Article 1.* Personal Scope

1. Except as otherwise provided in this Convention, this Convention shall apply to persons who are residents of one or both of the Contracting States.

2. Notwithstanding any provision of this Convention except paragraph 3 of this Article, a Contracting State may tax:

a. its residents (as determined under Article 4 (Residence)); and

b. its citizens by reason of citizenship as if there were no convention between the Government of the United States of America and the Government of Italy for the avoidance of double taxation with respect to taxes on income and the prevention of fraud or fiscal evasion.

3. The provisions of paragraph 2 shall not affect:

a. the benefits conferred by a Contracting State under paragraph 3 of Article 18 (Pensions, etc.), and under Articles 23 (Relief from Double Taxation), 24 (Non-Discrimination), and 25 (Mutual Agreement Procedure); and

b. the benefits conferred by a Contracting State under Articles 19 (Government Service), 20 (Professors and Teachers), 21 (Students and Trainees), and 27 (Diplomatic Agents and Consular Officials), upon individuals who are neither citizens of, nor have immigrant status in, that State.

Article 2.* Taxes Covered

1. This Convention shall apply to taxes on income imposed on behalf of a Contracting State.

2. The existing taxes to which this Convention shall apply are:

a. in the case of the United States: the Federal income taxes imposed by the Internal Revenue Code and the excise taxes imposed on insurance premiums paid to foreign insurers and with respect to private foundations, but excluding (notwithstanding paragraph 5 of Article 10 (Dividends)) the accumulated earnings tax and the personal holding company tax, (hereinafter referred to as 'United States tax');

b. in the case of Italy:

(i) the individual income tax (*l'imposta sul reddito delle persone fisiche*);
(ii) the corporation income tax (*l'imposta sul reddito delle persone giuridiche*); and
(iii) the local income tax (*l'imposta locale sui redditi*) except to the extent imposed on cadastral income;
even if they are collected by withholding taxes at the source (hereinafter referred to as 'Italian tax').

3. This Convention shall apply also to any identical or substantially similar taxes which are imposed after the date of signature of this Convention in addition to, or in place of, the existing taxes. The competent authorities of the Contracting States shall notify each other of any significant changes which have been made in their respective taxation laws and shall transmit to each other any significant official published material concerning the application of this Convention, including explanations, regulations, rulings, or judicial decisions.

Article 3. General Definitions

1. For the purpose of this Convention, unless the context otherwise requires:

a. the term 'person' includes an individual, a company, an estate, a trust, and any body of persons;

b. the term 'company' means any body corporate or any entity which is treated as a body corporate for tax purposes;

c. the terms 'enterprise of a Contracting State' and 'enterprise of the other Contracting State' mean respectively an enterprise carried on by a resident of a Contracting State and an enterprise carried on by a resident of the other Contracting State;

d. the term 'international traffic' means any transport by a ship or aircraft, except where such transport is solely between places in the other Contracting State;

e. The term 'competent authority' means:
(i) in the United States: the Secretary of the Treasury or his delegate; and
(ii) in Italy: the Ministry of Finance;

f. the term 'United States' means the United States of America but does not include Puerto Rico, the Virgin Islands, Guam, or any other United States possession or territory. When used in a geographical sense, the term 'United States' includes any area beyond the territorial waters of the United States which, in accordance with customary international law and the laws of the United States concerning the exploration and exploitation of natural resources, may be designated as an area within which the United States may exercise rights with respect to the seabed and subsoil and natural resources;

g. the term 'Italy' means the Republic of Italy and includes any area beyond the territorial waters of Italy which, in accordance with customary international law and the laws of Italy concerning the exploration and exploitation of natural resources, may be designated as an area within which Italy may exercise rights with respect to the seabed and subsoil and natural resources.

h. the term 'nationals' means:

(i) all individuals possessing the citizenship of a Contracting State; and

(ii) all legal persons, partnerships, and associations deriving their status as such from the law in force in a Contracting State.

2. As regards the application of this Convention by a Contracting State any term not defined therein shall, unless the context otherwise requires, have the meaning which it has under the laws of that State concerning the taxes to which this Convention applies.

Article 4. Resident

1. For purposes of this Convention, the term 'resident of a Contracting State' means any person who, under the laws of that State, is liable to tax therein by reason of his domicile, residence, place of management, place of incorporation, or any other criterion of a similar nature, provided, however, that

a. this term does not include any person who is liable to tax in that State in respect only of income from sources in that State;

b. in the case of income derived or paid by a partnership, estate, or trust, this term applies only to the extent that the income derived by such partnership, estate, or trust is subject to tax in that State, either in its hands or in the hands of its partners or beneficiaries.

2. Where by reason of the provisions of paragraph 1 an individual is a resident of both Contracting States, then his status shall be determined as follows:

a. he shall be deemed to be a resident of the State in which he has a permanent home available to him; if he has a permanent home available to him in both States, he shall be deemed to be a resident of the State with which his personal and economic relations are closer (center of vital interests);

b. if the State in which he has his center of vital interests cannot be determined, or if he has not a permanent home available to him in either State, he shall be deemed to be a resident of the State in which he has an habitual abode;

c. if he has an habitual abode in both States or in neither of them, he shall be deemed to be a resident of the State of which he is a national;

d. If he is a national of both States or of neither of them, the competent authorities of the Contracting States shall settle the question by mutual agreement.

3. Where by reason of the provisions of paragraph 1 a person other than an individual or a company is a resident of both Contracting States, the competent authorities of the Contracting States shall by mutual agreement endeavor to settle the question and to determine the mode of application of the Convention to such person.

Article 5.* Permanent Establishment

1. For the purposes of this Convention, the term 'permanent establishment' means a fixed place of business in which the business of the enterprise is wholly or partly carried on.

2. The term 'permanent establishment' shall include especially:

a. a place of management;

b. a branch;

c. an office;

d. a factory;

e. a workshop;

f. a mine, quarry, or other place of extraction of natural resources; and

g. a building site or construction or assembly project which exists for more than twelve months.

3. The term 'permanent establishment' shall be deemed not to include:

a. the use of facilities solely for the purpose of storage, display, or delivery of goods or merchandise belonging to the enterprise;

b. the maintenance of a stock of goods or merchandise belonging to the enterprise solely for the purpose of storage, display or delivery;

c. the maintenance of a stock of goods or merchandise belonging to the enterprise solely for the purpose of processing by another enterprise;

d. the maintenance of a fixed place of business solely for the purpose of purchasing goods or merchandise, or of collecting information, for the enterprise;

e. the maintenance of a fixed place of business solely for the purpose of advertising, for the supply of information, for scientific research, or for similar activities which have a preparatory or auxiliary character, for the enterprise.

4. A person acting in a Contracting State on behalf of an enterprise of the other Contracting State – other than an agent of an independent status to whom paragraph 5 applies – shall be deemed to be a permanent establishment in the first-mentioned State if he has, and habitually exercises, an authority to conclude contracts in the name of the enterprise, unless his activities are limited to the purchase of goods or merchandise for the enterprise.

5. An enterprise of a Contracting State shall not be deemed to have a permanent establishment in a Contracting State merely because it carries on business in that other State through a broker, general commission agent, or any other agent of an independent status, where such persons are acting in the ordinary course of their business.

6. The fact that a company which is a resident of a Contracting State controls or is controlled by a company which is a resident of the other Contracting State, or which carries on business in that other State (whether through a permanent establishment or otherwise), shall not of itself constitute either company a permanent establishment of the other.

Article 6. Income from Immovable Property

1. Income derived by a resident of a Contracting State from immovable property (including income from agriculture or forestry) situated in the other Contracting State may be taxed in that other State.

2. The term 'immovable property' ('real property') shall have the meaning which it has under the law of the Contracting State in which the property in question is situated. The term shall in any case include property accessory to immovable property, livestock and equipment used in agriculture and forestry, and rights to which the provisions of general law respecting landed property apply. Usufruct of immovable property and rights to variable or fixed payments as consideration for the working of, or the right to work, mineral deposits, sources, and other natural resources shall also be considered immovable property; ships, boats, and aircraft shall not be regarded as immovable property.

3. The provisions of paragraph 1 shall apply to income derived from the direct use, letting, or use in any other form of immovable property.

4. The provisions of paragraphs 1 and 3 shall also apply to the income from immovable property of an enterprise and to income from immovable property used for the performance of independent personal services.

Article 7. Business Profits

1. The profits of an enterprise of a Contracting State shall be taxable only in that State unless the enterprise carries on business in the other Contracting State through a permanent establishment situated therein. If the enterprise carries on business as aforesaid, the profits of the enterprise may be taxed in the other State but only so much of them as is attributable to that permanent establishment.

2. Subject to the provisions of paragraph 3, where an enterprise of a Contracting State carries on business in the other Contracting State through a permanent establishment situated therein, there shall in each Contracting State be attributed to that permanent establishment the profits which it might be expected to make if it were a distinct and separate enterprise engaged in the same or similar activities under the same or similar conditions and dealing wholly independently with the enterprise of which it is a permanent establishment and other associated enterprises.

3. In determining the profits of a permanent establishment, there shall be allowed as deductions expenses that are attributable to the activities of the permanent establishment, including a reasonable allocation of executive and general administrative expenses, whether incurred in the State in which the permanent establishment is situated or elsewhere.

4. No profits shall be attributable to a permanent establishment by reason of the mere purchase by that permanent establishment of goods or merchandise for the enterprise.

5. For the purposes of the preceding paragraphs, the profits to be attributed to the permanent establishment shall be determined by the

same method year by year unless there is good and sufficient reason to the contrary.

6. Where profits include items of income which are dealt with separately in other Articles of this Convention, then the provisions of those Articles shall not be affected by the provisions of this Article.

Article 8.* Shipping and Air Transport

1. Profits of an enterprise of a Contracting State from the operation in international traffic of ships or aircraft shall be taxable only in that State.

2. The provisions of paragraph 1 shall also apply to profits derived from the participation in a pool, a joint business, or an international operating agency.

Article 9.* Associated Enterprises

Where:

a. an enterprise of a Contracting State participates directly or indirectly in the management, control, or capital of an enterprise of the other Contracting State; or

b. the same persons participate directly or indirectly in the management, control, or capital of an enterprise of a Contracting State and an enterprise of the other Contracting State,

and in either case conditions are made or imposed between the two enterprises in their commercial or financial relations which differ from those which would be made between independent enterprises, then any profits which would, but for those conditions, have accrued to one of the enterprises, but, by reason of those conditions, have not so accrued, may be included in the profits of that enterprise and taxed accordingly.

Article 10.* Dividends

1. Dividends paid by a company which is a resident of a Contracting State to a resident of the other Contracting State may be taxed in that other State.

2. However, such dividends may also be taxed in the Contracting State of which the company paying the dividends is a resident and according to the laws of that State, but if the beneficial owner of the dividends is a resident of the other Contracting State, the tax so charged shall not exceed:

a. (i) 5 per cent of the gross amount of the dividends if the beneficial owner is a company which has owned more than 50 per cent of the voting stock of the company paying the dividends for a 12 month period ending on the date the dividend is declared; and

(ii) 10 per cent of the gross amount of the dividends if the beneficial owner is a company which is not entitled to the benefits of clause (i) but which has owned 10 per cent or more of the voting stock of the company paying the dividends for a 12-month period ending on the date the dividend is declared,

provided that not more than 25 per cent of the gross income of the company paying the dividends is derived from interest and dividends (other than interest derived in the conduct of a banking or financing business and interest or dividends received from subsidiary companies); and

b. 15 per cent of the gross amount of the dividends in all other cases.

This paragraph shall not affect the taxation of the company in respect of the profits out of which the dividends are paid.

3. The term 'dividends' as used in this Article means income from shares, 'jouissance' shares or 'jouissance' rights, mining shares, founders' shares, or other rights, not being debt-claims, participating in profits, as well as income derived from other corporate rights which is subjected to the same taxation treatment as income from shares by the laws of the State of which the company making the distribution is a resident.

4. The provisions of paragraph 1 and 2 shall not apply if the beneficial owner of the dividends, being a resident of a Contracting State, carries on business in the other Contracting State of which the company paying the dividends is a resident, through a permanent establishment situated therein, or performs in that other State independent personal services from a fixed base situated therein, and the holding in respect of which the dividends are paid is effectively connected with such permanent establishment or fixed base. In such case the dividends are taxable in that other Contracting State according to its own laws.

5. Where a company which is a resident of a Contracting State and not a resident of the other Contracting State derives profits or income from the other Contracting State, that other State may not impose any tax on the dividends paid by the company, except insofar as such dividends are paid to a resident of that other State or insofar as the holding in respect of which the dividends are paid is effectively connected with a permanent establishment or a fixed base situated in that other State, nor subject the company's undistributed profits to a tax on the company's undistributed profits, even if the dividends paid or the undistributed profits consist wholly or partly of profits or income arising in such other State.

Article 11. Interest

1. Interest arising in a Contracting State and paid to a resident of the other Contracting State may be taxed in that other State.

2. However, such interest may also be taxed in the Contracting State in which it arises and according to the laws of that State, but if the beneficial owner of the interest is a resident of the other Contracting State, the tax so charged shall not exceed 15 per cent of the gross amount of the interest.

3. Notwithstanding paragraph 2, interest beneficially derived by

a. a Contracting State or an instrumentality wholly owned by that State; or

b. a resident of a Contracting State with respect to debt obligations guaranteed or insured by that Contracting State or by an instrumentality wholly owned by that State shall be exempt from tax by the other Contracting State.

4. The term 'interest' as used in this Article means income from Government securities, bonds, or debenture, whether or not secured by mortgage and whether or not carrying a right to participate in profits, and debt-claims of every kind as well as all other income assimilated to income from money lent by the taxation law of the State in which the income arises.

5. The provisions of paragraphs 1, 2, and 3 shall not apply if the beneficial owner of the interest, being a resident of a Contracting State, carries on business in the other Contracting State in which the interest arises, through a permanent establishment situated therein, or performs in that other State independent personal services from a fixed base situated therein, and the debt-claim in respect of which the interest is paid is effectively connected with such permanent establishment or fixed base. In such case, the interest is taxable in that other Contracting State according to its own laws.

6. Interest shall be deemed to arise in a Contracting State when the payer is that State itself, a political or administrative subdivision, a local authority, or a resident of that State. Where, however, the person paying the interest, whether he is a resident of a Contracting State or not, has in a Contracting State a permanent establishment or a fixed base in connection with which the indebtedness on which the interest is paid was incurred, and such interest is borne by such permanent establishment or fixed base, then such interest shall be deemed to arise in the State in which the permanent establishment or fixed base is situated.

7. Where, by reason of a special relationship between the payer and the beneficial owner or between both of them and some other person, the amount of the interest, having regard to the debt-claim for which it is paid, exceeds the amount which would have been agreed upon by the payer and the beneficial owner in the absence of such relationship, the provisions of this Article shall apply only to the last-mentioned amount. In such case, the excess part of the payments is taxable according to the laws of each Contracting State, due regard being had to the other provisions of this Convention.

Article 12.* Royalties

1. Royalties arising in a Contracting State and paid to a resident of the other Contracting State may be taxed in that other State.

2. However, such royalties may also be taxed in the Contracting State in which they arise and according to the laws of that State, but if the beneficial owner of the royalties is a resident of the other Contracting State, the tax so charged shall not exceed:

a. 5 per cent of the gross amount of the royalties in respect of payments of any kind received as a consideration for the use of, or the right to use, any copyright of literary, artistic, or scientific work;

b. 8 per cent of the gross amount of the royalties in respect of payments of any kind received as a consideration for the use of, or the right to use, motion pictures and films, tapes or other means of reproduction used for radio or television broadcasting;

c. 10 per cent of the gross amount of the royalties in all other cases.

3. The term 'royalties' as used in this Article means payments of any kind received as a consideration for the use of, or the right to use, any copyright of literary, artistic or scientific work including motion pictures, films, tapes or other means of reproduction used for radio or television broadcasting, any patent, trademark, design or model, plan, secret formula or process, or other like right or property, or for the use of, or the right to use, industrial, commercial, or scientific equipment, or for information concerning industrial, commercial, or scientific experience.

4. The provisions of paragraphs 1 and 2 shall not apply if the beneficial owner of the royalties, being a resident of a Contracting State, carries on business in the other Contracting State in which the royalties arise, through a permanent establishment situated therein, or performs in that other State independent personal services from a fixed base situated therein, and the right or property in respect of which the royalties are paid is effectively connected with such permanent establishment or fixed base. In such case, the royalties are taxable in that other Contracting State according to its own laws.

5. Royalties shall be deemed to arise in a Contracting State when the payer is that State itself, a political or administrative subdivision, a local authority, or a resident of that State. Where, however, the person paying the royalties, whether he is a resident of a Contracting State or not, has in a Contracting State a permanent establishment or a fixed base in connection with which the obligation to pay the royalties was incurred, and such royalties are borne by such permanent establishment or fixed base, then such royalties shall be deemed to arise in the State in which the permanent establishment or fixed base is situated. Notwithstanding the preceding provisions of this paragraph, royalties with respect to the use of, or the right to use, rights or property within a Contracting State may be deemed to arise within that State.

6. Where, by reason of a special relationship between the payer and the beneficial owner or between both of them and some other person, the amount of the royalties, having regard to the use, right or information for which they are paid, exceeds the amount which would have been agreed upon by the payer and the beneficial owner in the absence of such relationship, the provisions of this Article shall apply only to the last-mentioned amount. In such case, the excess part of the payments is taxable according to the laws of each Contracting State, due regard being had to the other provisions of this Convention.

Article 13.* Capital Gains

1. Gains derived by a resident of a Contracting State from the alienation of immovable property referred to in Article 6 (Income from Immovable Property) and situated in the other Contracting State may be taxed in that other State.

2. Gains from the alienation of movable property forming part of the business property of a permanent establishment which an enterprise of a Contracting State has in the other Contracting State or of movable property pertaining to a fixed base available to a resident of a Contracting State in the other Contracting State for the purpose of performing independent personal services, including such gains from the alienation of such permanent establishment (alone or with the whole enterprise) or of such fixed base, may be taxed in that other State.

3. Gains derived by an enterprise of a Contracting State from the alienation of ships or aircraft operated by such enterprise in international traffic or of movable property pertaining to the operation of such ships or aircraft shall be taxable only in that State.

4. Gains from the alienation of any property other than that referred to in paragraphs 1, 2, and 3 shall be taxable only in the Contracting State of which the alienator is a resident.

Article 14. Independent Personal Services

1. Income derived by an individual who is a resident of a Contracting State from the performance of personal services in an independent capacity shall be taxable only in that State unless such services are performed in the other Contracting State and

a. the individual has a fixed base regularly available to him in that other State for the purpose of performing his activities, but only so much of the income as is attributable to that fixed base may be taxed in that other State; or

b. the individual is present in that other State for a period or periods aggregating more than 183 days in the fiscal year concerned.

2. The term 'personal services in an independent capacity' includes, but is not limited to, scientific, literary, artistic, educational, and teaching activities as well as independent activities of physicians, lawyers, engineers, architects, dentists, and accountants.

Article 15. Dependent Personal Services

1. Subject to the provisions of Article 16 (Directors' Fees), 18 (Pensions, etc.), and 19 (Government Service), salaries, wages, and other similar remuneration derived by a resident of a Contracting State in respect of an employment shall be taxable only in that State unless the employment is exercised in the other Contracting State. If the employment is so exercised, such remuneration as is derived therefrom may be taxed in that other State.

2. Notwithstanding the provisions of paragraph 1, remuneration derived by a resident of a Contracting State in respect of an employment exercised in the other Contracting State shall be taxable only in the first-mentioned State if:

a. the recipient is present in the other State for a period or periods not exceeding in the aggregate 183 days in the fiscal year concerned;

b. the remuneration is paid by, or on behalf of, an employer who is not a resident of the other State; and *c.* the remuneration is not borne by a permanent establishment or a fixed base that the employer has in the other State.

3. Notwithstanding the preceding provisions of this Article, remuneration derived in respect of an employment regularly exercised aboard a ship or aircraft operated by an enterprise of a Contracting State in international traffic shall be taxable only in that Contracting State.

Article 16.* Directors' Fees

Directors' fees and other similar payments derived by a resident of a Contracting State in his capacity as a member of the board of directors of a company which is a resident of the other Contracting State may be taxed in that other State.

Article 17. Artistes and Athletes

1. Notwithstanding the provisions of Articles 14 (Independent Personal Services), and 15 (Dependent Personal Services), income derived by a resident of a Contracting State as an entertainer, such as a theatre, motion picture, radio, or television artiste, or a musician, or as an athlete, from his personal activities as such exercised in the other Contracting State, may be taxed in that other State, if:

a. the amount of the gross receipts derived by such entertainer or athlete, including expenses reimbursed to him or borne on his behalf, from such activities exceeds twelve thousand United States dollars ($12,000) or its equivalent in Italian Lire for the fiscal year concerned; or

b. such entertainer or athlete is present in that other State for a period or periods aggregating more than 90 days in the fiscal year concerned.

2. Where income in respect of activities exercised by an entertainer or an athlete in his capacity as such accrues not to him but to another person, that income may, notwithstanding the provisions of Articles 7 (Business Profits), 14 (Independent Personal Services), and 15 (Dependent Personal Services), be taxed in the Contracting State in which the activities of the entertainer or athlete are exercised. For purposes of the preceding sentence, income of an entertainer or athlete shall be deemed not to accrue to another person if it is proved by the entertainer or athlete that neither he nor persons related to him participate directly or indirectly in the profits of such other person in any manner, including the receipt of deferred remuneration, bonuses, fees, dividends, partnership distributions, or other distributions.

Article 18.* Pensions, etc.

1. Subject to the provisions of paragraph 2 of Article 19 (Government Service), pensions and other similar remuneration beneficially derived by a resident of a Contracting State in consideration of past employment shall be taxable only in that State.

2. Annuities beneficially derived by a resident of a Contracting State shall be taxable only in that State. The term 'annuities' as used in this paragraph means a stated sum paid periodically at stated times during

a life or during a specified number of years, under an obligation to make the payments in return for adequate and full consideration (in money or money's worth).

3. Alimony and child support payments paid to a resident of a Contracting State by a resident of the other Contracting State shall be taxable only in the first-mentioned State. However, such payments shall not be taxable in either State if the person making such payments is not entitled to a deduction for such payments in the State of which he is a resident. The term 'alimony' as used in this paragraph means periodic payments made pursuant to a written separation agreement or a decree of divorce, separate maintenance, or compulsory support, which payments are taxable to the recipient under the laws of the State of which he is a resident. The term 'child support' as used in this paragraph means periodic payments for the support of a minor child made pursuant to a written separation agreement or a decree of divorce, separate maintenance, or compulsory support.

Article 19. Government Service

1. *a.* Remuneration, other than a pension, paid by a Contracting State or a political or administrative subdivision or local authority thereof to an individual in respect of services rendered to that State or subdivision or authority shall be taxable only in that State.

b. However, such remuneration shall be taxable only in the other Contracting State if the services are rendered in that State and the individual is a resident of that State who:

(i) is a national of that State; or

(ii) did not become a resident of that State solely for the purpose of rendering the services;

provided that the provisions of clause (ii) shall not apply to the spouse or dependent children of an individual who is receiving remuneration to which the provisions of subparagraph *a.* apply and who does not come within the terms of clause (i) or (ii).

2. *a.* Any pension paid by, or out of funds created by, a Contracting State or a political or administrative subdivision or local authority thereof to an individual in respect of services rendered to that State or subdivision or authority shall be taxable only in that State.

b. However, such pension shall be taxable only in the other Contracting State if the individual is a resident and a national of that State.

3. The provisions of Article 14 (Independent Personal Services), 15 (Dependent Personal Services), 16 (Directors' Fees), 17 Artistes and Athletes), or 18 (Pensions, etc.), as the case may be, shall apply to remuneration and pensions in respect of services rendered in connection with a business carried on by a Contracting State or a political or administrative subdivision or a local authority thereof.

Article 20. Professors and Teachers

1. A professor or teacher who makes a temporary visit to a Contracting State for the purpose of teaching or conducting research at a university, college, school, or other educational institution, or at a

medical faculty primarily funded from governmental sources, and who is, or immediately before such visit was, a resident of the other Contracting State shall, for a period not exceeding two years, be exempt from tax in the first-mentioned Contracting State in respect of remuneration from such teaching or research.

2. This Article shall not apply to income from research if such research is undertaken not in the public interest but primarily for the private benefit of a specific person or persons.

Article 21. Students and Trainees

Payments which a student or business apprentice (trainee) who is, or immediately before visiting a Contracting State was, a resident of the other Contracting State and who is present in the first-mentioned State exclusively for the purpose of his education or training receives for the purpose of his maintenance, education, or training shall not be taxed in that State provided that such payments arise outside that State.

Article 22. Other Income

1. Items of income of a resident of a Contracting State, wherever arising, not dealt with in the foregoing Articles of this Convention shall be taxable only in that State.

2. The provisions of paragraph 1 shall not apply to income, other than income from immovable property as defined in paragraph 2 of Article 6 (Income from Immovable Property), if the person deriving the income, being a resident of a Contracting State, carries on business in the other Contracting State through a permanent establishment situated therein, or performs in that other State independent personal services from a fixed base situated therein, and the right or property in respect of which the income is paid is effectively connected with such permanent establishment or fixed base. In such case the items of income are taxable in the other Contracting State according to its own law.

Article 23. Relief from Double Taxation

1. It is agreed that double taxation shall be avoided in accordance with the following paragraphs of this Article.

2. In accordance with the provisions and subject to the limitations of the law of the United States (as it may be amended from time to time without changing the general principle hereof), the United States shall allow to a resident or citizen of the United States as a credit against the United States tax on income the appropriate amount of income tax paid to Italy; and in the case of a United States company owning at least ten per cent of the voting stock of a company which is a resident of Italy from which receives dividends in any taxable year, the United States shall allow as a credit against the United States tax on income the appropriate amount of income tax paid to Italy by that company with respect to the profits out of which such dividends are paid. Such appropriate amount shall be based upon the amount of tax paid to Italy, but shall not exceed the limitations of the law of the

United States (for the purpose of limiting the credit to the United States tax on income from sources without the United States). For purposes of applying the United States credit in relation to tax paid to Italy, the taxes referred to in paragraphs 2*b*. and 3 of Article 2 (Taxes covered) shall be considered to be income taxes.

3. If a resident of Italy derives items of income which are taxable in the United States under the Convention (without regard to paragraph 2*b*. of Article 1 (Personal Scope), Italy may, in determining its income taxes specified in Article 2 of this Convention, include in the basis upon which such taxes are imposed the said items of income (unless specified provisions of this Convention otherwise provide). In such case, Italy shall deduct from the taxes so calculated the tax on income paid to the United States, but in an amount not exceeding the tax that would be due to the United States if the resident of Italy were not a citizen of the United States, and not exceeding that proportion of the aforesaid Italian tax which such items of income bear to the entire income. However, no deduction will be granted if the item of income is subjected in Italy to a final withholding tax by request of the recipient of the said income in accordance with Italian law. For purposes of applying the Italian credit in relation to tax paid to the United States the taxes referred to in paragraphs 2*a*. and 3 of Article 2 (Taxes Covered) shall be considered to be income taxes.

4. For purposes of the United States obligation to avoid double taxation with respect to Italian tax under the preceding paragraphs of this Article:

a. subject to the provisions of subparagraph *b*., except for income or profits taxed by the United States solely by reason of citizenship in accordance with paragraph 2*b*. of Article 1 (Personal Scope), income or profits derived by a resident of a Contracting State (who is not a resident of the other Contracting State) which may be taxed in the other Contracting State in accordance with this Convention shall be deemed to arise in that other Contracting State; and

b. in the case of an individual who is a resident of Italy, income or profits which may be taxed by the United States by reason of citizenship in accordance with paragraph 2*b*. of Article 1 (Personal Scope) shall be deemed to arise in Italy to the extent necessary to avoid double taxation, provided that in no event the tax paid to the United States will be less than the tax that would be paid if the individual were not a citizen of the United States. The rules of this subparagraph with respect to the source of income shall not apply in determining credits against US tax for foreign taxes other than the taxes referred to in paragraphs 2*b*. and 3 of Article 2 (Taxes Covered).

Article 24. Non-Discrimination

1. Nationals of a Contracting State shall not be subjected in the other State to any taxation or any requirement connected therewith, which is other or more burdensome than the taxation and connected requirements to which nationals of that other State in the same circumstances are or may be subjected. This provision shall, notwithstanding

the provisions of Article 1 (Personal Scope), also apply to persons who are not residents of one or both of the Contracting States. However, for purposes of United States taxation, United States citizens who are subject to tax on a worldwide basis are not in the same circumstances as Italian nationals who are not residents of the United States.

2. The taxation on a permanent establishment which an enterprise of a Contracting State has in the other Contracting State shall not be less favorably levied in that other State than the taxation levied on enterprises of that other State carrying on the same activities. This provision shall not be construed as obliging a Contracting State to grant to residents of the other State any personal allowances, reliefs, and reductions for taxation purposes on account of civil status or family responsibilities which it grants to its own residents.

3. Except where the provisions of Article 9 (Associated Enterprises), paragraph 7 of Article 11 (Interest), or paragraph 6 of Article 12 (Royalties) apply, interest, royalties, and all other disbursements paid by an enterprise of a Contracting State to a resident of the other Contracting State shall, for the purpose of determining the taxable profits of such enterprise, be deductible under the same conditions as if they had been paid to a resident of the first-mentioned State.

4. Enterprises of a Contracting State, the capital of which is wholly or partly owned or controlled, directly or indirectly, by one or more residents of the other Contracting State shall not be subjected in the first-mentioned State to any taxation or any requirement connected therewith which is other or more burdensome than the taxation and connected requirements to which other similar enterprises of the first-mentioned State are or may be subjected.

5. For purposes of this Article, this Convention shall apply to taxes of every kind and description imposed by a Contracting State or a political or administrative subdivision or local authority thereof.

Article 25.* Mutual Agreement Procedure

1. Where a person considers that the actions of one or both of the Contracting States result or will result for him in taxation not in accordance with the provisions of this Convention, he may, irrespective of the remedies provided by the domestic law of those States, present his case to the competent authority of the Contracting State of which he is a resident or, if his case comes under Article 23 (Relief from Double Taxation) or paragraph 1 of Article 24 (Non-Discrimination), to the competent authority of the Contracting State of which he is a national.

2. The competent authority shall endeavour, if the objection appears to it to be justified and if it is not itself able to arrive at a satisfactory solution, to resolve the case by mutual agreement with the competent authority of the other Contracting State, with a view to the avoidance of taxation which is not in accordance with the Convention.

3. The competent authorities of the Contracting States shall endeavour to resolve by mutual agreement any difficulties or doubts arising as to the interpretation or application of this Convention.

4. The competent authorities of the Contracting States may communicate with each other directly for the purpose of reaching an agreement in the sense of the preceding paragraphs.

Article 26.* Exchange of Information

1. The competent authorities of the Contracting States shall exchange such information as is necessary for carrying out the provisions of this Convention or of the domestic laws of the Contracting States concerning taxes covered by the Convention insofar as the taxation thereunder is not contrary to the Convention. The exchange of information is not restricted by Article 1 (Personal Scope). Any information received by a Contracting State shall be treated as secret in the same manner as information obtained under the domestic laws of that State and shall be disclosed only to persons or authorities (including courts and administrative bodies) involved in the assessment or collection of, the enforcement or prosecution in respect of, or the determination of appeals in relation to, the taxes covered by the Convention. Such persons or authorities shall use the information only for such purposes. They may disclose the information in public court proceedings or in judicial decisions.

2. In no case shall the provisions of paragraph 1 be construed so as to impose on a Contracting State the obligation:

a. to carry out administrative measures at variance with the laws and administrative practice of that or of the other Contracting State;

b. to supply information which is not obtainable under the laws or in the normal course of the administration of that or of the other Contracting State;

c. to supply information which would disclose any trade, business, industrial, commercial, or professional secret or trade process, or information, the disclosure of which would be contrary to public policy (*ordre public*).

Article 27. Diplomatic Agents and Consular Officials

Nothing in this Convention shall affect the fiscal privileges of diplomatic agents or consular officials under the general rules of international law or under the provisions of special agreements.

Article 28. Entry into Force

1. This Convention shall be subject to ratification in accordance with the applicable procedures of each Contracting State and instruments of ratification shall be exchanged at Washington as soon as possible.

2. The Convention shall enter into force upon the exchange of instruments of ratification and its provisions shall have effect:

a. in respect of tax withheld at the source, for amounts paid or credited on or after the first day of the second month following the date on which this Convention enters into force;

b. in respect of other taxes, for taxable periods beginning on or after January 1 of the year in which this Convention enters into force.

3. Subject to the provisions of paragraph 4, the Convention for the Avoidance of Double Taxation and the Prevention of Fiscal Evasion with Respect to Taxes on Income, signed at Washington March 30, 1955, and the exchange of letters concerning the application of the Convention of March 30, 1955, for the Avoidance of Double Taxation and the Prevention of Fiscal Evasion with Respect to Taxes on Income, exchanged at Rome December 13, 1974, are terminated. Their provisions shall cease to have effect for taxes for which the provisions of this Convention have effect in accordance with paragraph 2.

4. Where any greater relief from tax would have been afforded by any provision of the 1955 Convention than under this Convention, any such provision shall continue to have effect for the first taxable period with respect to which the provisions of this Convention have effect under paragraph 2.

5. The arrangement between the United States and Italy providing for relief from double income taxation on shipping profits elected by exchange of notes dated March 10, 1926, and May 5, 1926, is terminated.

Article 29. Termination

This Convention shall remain in force until terminated by one of the Contracting States. Either Contracting State may terminate the Convention at any time after 5 years from the date on which this Convention enters into force provided that at least 6 months' prior notice of termination has been given through diplomatic channels. In such event, the Convention shall cease to have effect:

a. in respect of tax withheld at the source, for amounts paid or credited on or after the first day of January next following the expiration of the 6 months' period;

b. in respect of other taxes, for taxable periods beginning on or after the first day of January next following the expiration of the 6 months' period.

Done at Rome in duplicate, in the English and Italian languages, the two texts having equal authenticity, this 17th day of April, 1984.

Protocol

The Government of the United States of America and the Government of the Republic of Italy, desiring to conclude a Protocol clarifying and supplementing the Convention for the avoidance of double taxation with respect to taxes on income and the prevention of fraud or fiscal evasion to be signed simultaneously with the signing of this Protocol, have agreed upon the following provisions.

Article 1

1. For purposes of paragraph 2*b*. of Article 1 (Personal Scope) of the Convention, the term 'citizen' as applied to the United States shall include a former citizen whose loss of citizenship had as one of its principal purposes the avoidance of tax, but only for a period of 10 years following such loss.

2. The provisions of paragraph 2 of Article 1 (Personal Scope) of the Convention shall not affect:

a. the benefits conferred by a Contracting State under paragraph 14 of Article 1 of this Protocol to residents of the other Contracting State who are nationals of that other State, even if they are also nationals of the first-mentioned State;

b. the benefits conferred by a Contracting State under Article 4 of this Protocol.

3. For purposes of paragraph 2*a*. of Article 2 (Taxes Covered) of the Convention, the Convention shall apply to the excise tax imposed by the United States on insurance premiums paid to foreign insurers only to the extent that the foreign insurer does not reinsure such risks with a person not entitled to exemption from such tax under this or any other Convention.

4. For purposes of paragraph 2 of Article 5 (Permanent Establishment) of the Convention, a drilling rig or ship used for the exploration or development of natural resources constitutes a permanent establishment in a Contracting State only if it remains in that State for more than 180 days in a twelve month period.

5. For purposes of paragraph 1 of Article 8 (Shipping and Air Transport) of the Convention, profits from the operation in international traffic of ships or aircraft include:

a. profits from the use, maintenance, or rental of containers (including trailers, barges, and related equipment for the transport of containers) used for the transport in international traffic of goods or merchandise; and

b. profits derived from the rental on a full basis of ships or aircraft and profits derived from the rental on a bareboat basis of ships or aircraft, provided in the latter case that such rental profits are incidental to other profits from the operation of ships or aircraft in international traffic.

6. For purposes of Article 8 (Shipping and Air Transport) of the Convention, and notwithstanding any other provision of the Convention, profits which a national of the United States not resident in Italy or a United States corporation derives from operating ships documented or aircraft registered under the laws of the United States shall be exempt from tax in Italy.

7. If, in accordance with Article 9 (Associated Enterprises) of the Convention, a redetermination has been made by one Contracting State with respect to a person, the other Contracting State shall, to the extent it agrees that such redetermination reflects arrangements or conditions which would be made between two independent persons, make the

corresponding adjustments with respect to persons who are related to such person and are subject to the taxing jurisdiction of that other State. Any such adjustment shall be made only in accordance with the mutual agreement procedure in Article 25 (Mutual Agreement Procedure) of the Convention and with paragraph 15 of Article 1 of this Protocol.

8. The provisions of Article 9 (Associated Enterprises) of the Convention shall not limit any provisions of the law of either Contracting State which permit the distribution, apportionment, or allocation of income, deductions, credits, or allowances between persons owned or controlled directly or indirectly by the same interests when necessary in order to prevent evasion of taxes or clearly to reflect the income of any of such persons.

9. For purposes of paragraph 2*a*. of Article 10 (Dividends), the term 'subsidiary company' means a corporation in which the company paying the dividends owns more than 50 per cent of the voting stock.

10. Notwithstanding paragraph 2 of Article 12 (Royalties) of the Convention, in the Convention, in the case of royalties derived with respect to tangible personal (movable) property, the tax imposed by the Contracting State in which such royalties arise may not exceed 7 per cent of the gross amount of such royalties.

11. For purposes of paragraph 1 of Article 13 (Capital Gains) of the Convention:

a. the term 'immovable property', in the case of the United States, includes a United States real property interest; and

b. the term 'immovable property' in the case of Italy includes:

(i) immovable property referred to in Article 6;

(ii) shares or comparable interests in a company or other body of persons, the assets of which consist wholly or principally of real property situated in Italy; and

(iii) an interest in an estate of a deceased individual, the assets of which consist wholly or principally of real property situated in Italy.

c. property described in subparagraph *a.* of this paragraph shall be deemed to be situated in the United States and property described in subparagraph *b.* of this paragraph shall be deemed to be situated in Italy.

12. For purposes of paragraph 3 of Article 13 (Capital Gains) of the Convention, gains derived by an enterprise of a Contracting State from the alienation of ships or aircraft operated by such enterprise in international traffic include:

a. gains from the alienation of containers (including trailers, barges, and related equipment for the transport of containers) used for the transport in international traffic of goods or merchandise; and

b. gains from the alienation of ships or aircraft rented on a full basis or gains from the alienation of ships or aircraft on a bareboat basis if, in the latter case, rental profits were incidental to other profits from the operation of ships or aircraft in international traffic.

13. Directors' fees and other similar payments derived by a resident of a Contracting State which are described in Article 16 (Directors'

Fees) of the Convention may be taxed in the other Contracting State only to the extent that the fees and other payments are attributable to services performed in such other State.

14. With respect to Article 18 (Pensions, etc.) of the Convention, it is agreed that social security payments and similar public pensions not covered by Article 19 (Government Service) of the Convention are covered by paragraph 1 of said Article 18 (Pensions, etc.).

15. With respect to Article 25 (Mutual Agreement Procedure) of the Convention, it is understood that an adjustment of taxes pursuant to that Article may be made only prior to the final determination of such taxes. It is further understood that, in the case of Italy, the preceding sentence means that invoking the mutual agreement procedure does not relieve a taxpayer of the obligation to initiate the procedures of domestic law for resolving tax disputes.

16. For purposes of Article 26 (Exchange of Information) of the Convention, the Convention shall apply to taxes of every kind imposed by a Contracting State, but only insofar as the information is relevant to the assessment of taxes covered by Article 2 (Taxes Covered) of the Convention. It is understood that appropriate United States Congressional Committees and the General Accounting Office shall be afforded access to the information exchanged under the Convention where such access is necessary to carry out their oversight responsibilities, subject only to the limitations and procedures of the Internal Revenue Code.

Article 2

1. A person (other than an individual) which is a resident of a Contracting State shall not be entitled under this Convention to benefits provided in Articles 7 (Business Profits), 10 (Dividends), 11 (Interest), 12 (Royalties), 13 (Capital Gains) or 22 (Other Income) unless:

a. more than 50 per cent of the beneficial ownership of such person (or in the case of a company, more than 50 per cent of the number of shares of each class of the company's shares) is owned, directly or indirectly, by any combination of one or more of:

(i) individuals who are residents of the United States;
(ii) citizens of the United States;
(iii) individuals who are residents of Italy;
(iv) companies as described in subparagraph *b.*; or
(v) the Contracting States; or

b. it is a company in whose principal class of shares there is substantial and regular trading on a recognized stock exchange.

2. Paragraph 1 shall not apply unless the competent authority of the other Contracting State determines that either the establishment, acquisition or maintenance of such person or the conduct of its operations had as a principal purpose obtaining benefits under the Convention.

3. For the purpose of subparagraph 1*b.*, the term 'a recognized stock exchange' means:

a. the NASDAQ System owned by the National Association of Securities Dealers, Inc. and any stock exchange registered with the

Securities and Exchange Commission as a national securities exchange for the purposes of the Securities Exchange Act of 1934;

b. any stock exchange constituted and organized according to Italian laws; and

c. any other stock exchange agreed upon by the competent authorities of the Contracting States.

Article 3

The Convention shall not restrict in any manner any exclusion, exemption, deduction, credit, or other allowance now or hereafter accorded:

a. by the laws of either Contracting State, or

b. by any other agreement between the Contracting States.

Article 4

It is agreed that a United States citizen resident in Italy who is a partner of a partnership that is a national of the United States shall be entitled to a refundable credit against that partner's individual income tax (*l'imposta sul reddito delle persone fisiche*) imposed by Italy for the taxable period equal to the portion of the corporation income tax (*l'imposta sul reddito delle persone giuridiche*) imposed by Italy for the same period on the partnership that is attributable to that partner's share of the partnership income.

Article 5

Taxes withheld at the source in a Contracting State at the rates provided by domestic law will be refunded by request of the taxpayer if the right to collect the said taxes is limited by the provisions of the Convention. Claims for refund, which shall be made within the time limit fixed by the law of the Contracting State which is obliged to make the refund, shall be accompanied by an official certificate of the Contracting State of which the taxpayer is a resident certifying the existence of the conditions required for being entitled to the benefits provided for by the Convention. This provision shall not be construed to prevent the competent authority of each Contracting State from establishing other modes of application of the benefits provided for by the Convention.

Article 6

Each of the Contracting States may collect on behalf of the other Contracting State such amounts as may be necessary to ensure that relief granted by the Convention from taxation imposed by such other State does not enure to the benefit of persons not entitled thereto. The preceding sentence shall not, however, impose upon either of the Contracting States the obligation to carry out administrative measures which are of a different nature from those used in the collection of its own tax, or which would be contrary to its sovereignty, security, or public policy.

Article 7

1. This Protocol shall be subject to ratification in accordance with the applicable procedures of each Contracting State, and instruments of ratification shall be exchanged at Washington.

2. The Protocol shall enter into force upon the exchange of instruments of ratification and shall thereafter have effect in accordance with Article 28 of the Convention.

Article 8

This Protocol shall remain in force as long as the Convention between the United States of America and Italy for the avoidance of double taxation with respect to taxes on income and the prevention of fraud or fiscal evasion of this date shall remain in force.

Done at Rome, in duplicate, in the English and Italian languages, the two texts having equal authenticity, this 17th day of April, 1984.

Convention between the United States of America and Japan for the Avoidance of Double Taxation and the Prevention of Fiscal Evasion with Respect to Taxes on Income, concluded in Tokyo on March 8, 1971.

The United States of America and Japan,

Desiring to conclude a new convention for the avoidance of double taxation and the prevention of fiscal evasion with respect to taxes on income,

Have agreed upon the following articles:

Article 1

1. The taxes which are the subject of this Convention are:

a. In the case of the United States, the Federal income taxes imposed by the Internal Revenue Code, hereinafter referred to as 'United States tax'; and

b. In the case of Japan, the income tax and the corporation tax, hereinafter referred to as 'Japanese tax'.

2. This Convention shall also apply to taxes substantially similar to those covered by paragraph 1 of this article which are imposed in addition to, or in place of, existing taxes after the date of signature of this Convention.

3. For the purpose of Article 7, this Convention shall also apply to taxes of every kind imposed by a Contracting State or a political subdivision or local authority thereof. For the purpose of Article 26, this Convention shall also apply to taxes of every kind imposed by a Contracting State.

Article 2

1. In this Convention, unless the context otherwise requires:

a. The term 'United States' means the United States of America and, when used in a geographical sense, means the states thereof and the District of Columbia.

b. The term 'Japan', when used in a geographical sense, means all the territory in which the laws relating to Japanese tax are in force.

c. The term 'a Contracting State' or 'the other Contracting State' means the United States or Japan, as the context requires.

d. The term 'person' means an individual, a corporation, or any other body of persons.

e. (i) The term 'United States corporation' means a corporation which is created or organized under the laws of the United States or any state thereof or the District of Columbia, or any unincorporated entity treated as a United States corporation for purposes of United States tax; and

(ii) The term 'Japanese corporation' means a juridical person which has its head or main office in Japan or any organization without juridical personality treated for purposes of Japanese tax as a Japanese juridical person.

f. The term 'competent authority' means:

(i) In the case of the United States, the Secretary of the Treasury or his delegate, and

(ii) In the case of Japan, the Minister of Finance or his authorized representative.

g. The term 'citizen' means:

(i) In the case of the United States, a citizen of the United States, and

(ii) In the case of Japan, a national of Japan.

2. As regards the application of this Convention by a Contracting State, any term used in this Convention and not otherwise defined shall, unless the context otherwise requires, have the meaning which it has under the laws of that Contracting State relating to the taxes which are the subject of this Convention.

Article 3

In this Convention:

1. The term 'resident of Japan' means:

a. A Japanese corporation, or

b. Any other person resident in Japan for purposes of Japanese tax.

2. The term 'resident of the United States' means:

a. A United States corporation, or

b. Any other person (except a corporation or an entity treated under United States law as a corporation) resident in the United States for purposes of United States tax, but in the case of an estate or trust only to the extent that the income derived by such person is subject to United States tax as the income of a resident.

3. An individual who is a resident of both Contracting States shall be deemed to be a resident of that Contracting State in which he maintains his permanent home. If he has a permanent home in both Contracting States or in neither Contracting State, he shall be deemed to be a resident of that Contracting State with which his personal and economic relations are closest (center of vital interests). If the Contracting State in which he has his center of vital interests cannot be determined, he shall be deemed to be a resident of that Contracting State in which he has a habitual abode. If he has a habitual abode in both Contracting States or in neither Contracting State, he shall be deemed to be a resident of that Contracting State of which he is a citizen. If he is a citizen of both Contracting States or of neither Contracting State, the competent authorities of the Contracting States shall settle the question by mutual agreement. An individual who is deemed to be a resident of a Contracting State and not a resident of the other Contracting State by reason of the provision of this paragraph shall be deemed to be a resident only of the first-mentioned Contracting State for all purposes of this Convention, including Article 4.

Article 4

1. A resident of a Contracting State may be taxed by the other Contracting State on any income from sources within that other Contracting State and only on such income, subject to any limitations set forth in this Convention. For this purpose, the rules set forth in Article 6 shall be applied to determine the source of income.

2. The provisions of this Convention shall not be construed to restrict in any manner any exclusion, exemption, deduction, credit, or other allowance now or hereafter accorded:

a. By the laws of a Contracting State in the determination of the tax imposed by that Contracting State, or

b. By any other agreement between the Contracting States.

3. Except to the extent provided in paragraph 4 of this article, this Convention shall not affect the taxation by a Contracting State of its residents (and, in the case of the United States, its citizens).

4. The provisions of paragraph 3 of this article shall not affect:

a. The benefits provided under Articles 5, 7, 21, and 25; and

b. The benefits provided under Articles 19, 20, and 22, but in the case of benefits conferred by the United States only if the person claiming the benefits neither is a citizen of, nor has immigrant status in, the United States.

5. There shall be allowed, for purposes of United States tax, in the case of a resident of Japan who is not a resident of the United States (other than an officer or employee of the Government of Japan or local authority thereof), in addition to the deduction for one personal exemption provided in section 873 of the United States Internal Revenue Code as in effect on the first day of December 1968, a deduction for personal exemptions, subject to the conditions prescribed in sections 151 through 154 of the Internal Revenue Code as in effect on the said date, for the spouse of the taxpayer and for each child of the taxpayer present in the United States and residing with him in the United States at any time during the taxable year, but such additional deduction shall not exceed that proportion thereof which the taxpayer's gross income from sources within the United States which is treated as effectively connected with the conduct of a trade or business within the United States within the meaning of section 864(c) of the Internal Revenue Code for the taxpayer's taxable year bears to his entire income from all sources for such taxable year.

6. The United States may impose its personal holding company tax and its accumulated earnings tax notwithstanding any provision of this Convention. However, a Japanese corporation shall be exempt from the United States personal holding company tax in any taxable year if all of its stock is owned, directly or indirectly, by one or more individuals who are residents of Japan (and not citizens of the United States) for that entire year. A Japanese corporation shall be exempt from the United States accumulated earnings tax in any taxable year unless such corporation is engaged in trade or business in the United States through a permanent establishment at any time during such year.

7. Where, pursuant to any provision of this Convention, a Contracting State reduces the rate of tax on, or exempts from tax, income of a resident of the other Contracting State and under the law in force in that other Contracting State the resident is subject to tax by that other Contracting State only on that part of such income which is remitted to or received in that other Contracting State, then the reduction or exemption shall apply only to so much of such income as is remitted to or received in that other Contracting State.

Article 5

1. Double taxation of income shall be avoided in the following manner:

a. In accordance with the provisions of the law of the United States, as in force from time to time, regarding the allowance of a credit against United States tax of tax payable in any country other than the United States, the United States shall allow to a citizen or resident of the United States as a credit against United States tax the appropriate amount of Japanese tax and, in the case of a United States corporation owning at least 10 per cent of the voting power of a Japanese corporation from which it receives dividends, shall allow credit for the appropriate amount of Japanese tax paid by the Japanese corporation paying such dividends with respect to the profits out of which such dividends are paid. For the purpose of applying the United States credit in relation to taxes paid to Japan, the rules set forth in Article 6 shall be applied to determine the source of income.

b. In accordance with the provisions of the laws of Japan, as in force from time to time, regarding the allowance of a credit against Japanese tax of tax payable in any country other than Japan, Japan shall allow to a resident of Japan as a credit against Japanese tax the appropriate amount of United States tax and, in the case of a Japanese corporation owning at least 10 per cent of the voting shares of a United States corporation from which it receives dividends, shall allow credit for the appropriate amount of United States tax paid by the United States corporation paying such dividends with respect to the profits out of which such dividends are paid. For the purpose of applying the Japanese credit in relation to taxes paid to the United States, the rules set forth in Article 6 shall be applied to determine the source of income.

2. The tax of a Contracting State which shall be credited by the other Contracting State in accordance with this article shall include any tax on income or profits imposed by any political subdivision or any local authority of the first-mentioned Contracting State.

Article 6

For purposes of this Convention:

1. Dividends shall be treated as income from sources within a Contracting State only if paid by a corporation of that Contracting State.

2. Interest shall be treated as income from sources within a Contracting State only if paid by that Contracting State, a political subdivision or local authority thereof, or by a resident of that Contracting State. Notwithstanding the preceding sentence, if the person paying the interest (other than interest paid on indebtedness incurred in connection with the purchase of ships or aircraft):

a. Whether or not such person is a resident of a Contracting State, has a permanent establishment in a Contracting State in connection with which the indebtedness on which the interest is paid was incurred and such interest is borne by such permanent establishment; or

b. Is a resident of a Contracting State and has a permanent establishment in a State other than the Contracting States in connection with which the indebtedness on which the interest is paid was incurred and such interest is borne by such permanent establishment,

such interest shall be deemed to be from sources within the State in which the permanent establishment is located.

3. Royalties for the use of, or the right to use, property (other than ships or aircraft) or rights described in paragraph 3*a*. of Article 14, and gains to the extent that they are contingent on the productivity, use, or disposition of such property or rights described in paragraph 3*b*. of Article 14, shall be treated as income from sources within a Contracting State only if the royalties, or the amount realized on the sale, exchange, or other disposition from which the gain is derived is paid for the use of, or the right to use, such property or rights within that Contracting State.

4. Income from real property including royalties in respect of the operation of mines or quarries, or the exploitation of any natural resources and gains derived from the sale, exchange, or other disposition of such property or of the right giving rise to such royalties, shall be treated as income from sources within a Contracting State only if such property is situated in that Contracting State.

5. Income from the rental of tangible personal property (other than the rental of ships or aircraft) shall be treated as income from sources within a Contracting State only if such property is situated in that Contracting State. Income from the rental of ships or aircraft derived by a person not engaged in the operation of ships or aircraft in international traffic shall be treated as income from sources within a Contracting State only if the lessee is a resident of that Contracting State.

6. Income (other than directors' fees described in paragraph 5 of Article 18) received by an individual for his performance of labor or personal services whether as an employee or in an independent capacity shall be treated as income from sources within a Contracting State only if such services are performed in that Contracting State. Income from labor or personal services performed aboard ships or aircraft operated by a resident of a Contracting State in international traffic shall be treated as income from sources within that Contracting State, if rendered by a member of the regular complement of the ship or aircraft. For the purposes of this paragraph, income from labor or personal services includes pensions (as defined in paragraph 2 of Article 23)

paid in respect of such services. Notwithstanding the preceding provisions of this paragraph, remuneration described in Article 21 shall be treated as income from sources within a Contracting State only if paid by, or out of the funds to which contributions are made by, that Contracting State or a political subdivision or local authority thereof. Directors' fees described in paragraph 5 of Article 18 shall be treated as income from sources within a Contracting State only if the corporation of which the individual is a director is a corporation of that Contracting State.

7. Income from the purchase and sale of personal property (other than gains defined as royalties in paragraph 3*b*. of Article 14) shall be treated as income from sources within a Contracting State only if such property is sold in that Contracting State.

8. Notwithstanding paragraphs 1 through 7 of this article, industrial or commercial profits which are attributable to a permanent establishment which the recipient, being a resident of a Contracting State, has in the other Contracting State, including income derived from real property and natural resources and dividends, interest, royalties (as defined in paragraph 3 of Article 14), and capital gains, but only if the property or rights giving rise to such income, dividends, interest, royalties, or capital gains are effectively connected with such permanent establishment, shall be treated as income from sources within that other Contracting State. To determine whether property or rights are effectively connected with a permanent establishment, the factors taken into account shall include whether the property or rights are used in or held for use in carrying on industrial or commercial activity through such permanent establishment, and whether the activities carried on through such permanent establishment were a material factor in the realization of the income derived from such property or rights. For this purpose, due regard shall be given to whether or not such property or rights or such income were accounted for through such permanent establishment.

9. The source of any item of income to which paragraphs 1 through 8 of this article are not applicable shall be determined by each of the Contracting States in accordance with its own law.

Article 7

1. A citizen of a Contracting State who is a resident of the other Contracting State shall not be subjected in that other Contracting State to more burdensome taxes than a citizen of that other Contracting State who is a resident thereof.

2. A permanent establishment which a resident of a Contracting State has in the other Contracting State shall not be subjected in that other Contracting State to more burdensome taxes than a resident of that other Contracting State carrying on the same activities. This paragraph shall not be construed as obliging a Contracting State to grant to individual residents of the other Contracting State any personal allowances, reliefs, and deductions for taxation purposes on account of civil status or family responsibilities which it grants to its own individual residents.

3. A corporation of a Contracting State, the capital of which is wholly or partly owned or controlled, directly or indirectly, by one or more residents of the other Contracting State, shall not be subjected in the first-mentioned Contracting State to any taxation or any requirement connected therewith which is other or more burdensome than the taxation and connected requirements to which a corporation of the first-mentioned Contracting State carrying on the same activities, the capital of which is wholly owned or controlled by one or more residents of the first-mentioned Contracting State, is or may be subjected.

Article 8

1. Industrial or commercial profits of a resident of a Contracting State shall be exempt from tax by the other Contracting State unless such resident is engaged in industrial or commercial activity in that other Contracting State through a permanent establishment situated therein. If such resident is so engaged, tax may be imposed by that other Contracting State on the industrial and commercial profits of such resident but only on so much of the profits as are attributable to the permanent establishment.

2. Where a resident of one of the Contracting States is engaged in industrial or commercial activity in the other Contracting State through a permanent establishment situated therein, there shall in each Contracting State be attributed to the permanent establishment the industrial or commercial profits which would be attributable to such permanent establishment if such permanent establishment were an independent entity engaged in the same or similar activities under the same or similar conditions and dealing wholly independently with the resident of which it is a permanent establishment.

3. In the determination of the industrial or commercial profits of a permanent establishment, there shall be allowed as deductions expenses which are reasonably connected with such profits, including executive and general administrative expenses, whether incurred in the Contracting State in which the permanent establishment is situated or elsewhere.

4. No profits shall be attributed to a permanent establishment of a resident of a Contracting State in the other Contracting State merely by reason of the purchase of goods or merchandise by that permanent establishment, or by the resident of which it is a permanent establishment, for the account of that resident.

5. The term 'industrial or commercial profits' includes income derived from manufacturing, mercantile, insurance, agricultural, fishing, or mining activities, from the operation of ships or aircraft, from the furnishing of personal services, and from the rental of tangible personal property (other than ships or aircraft). Such term also includes income derived from real property and natural resources; dividends, interest, royalties (as defined in paragraph 3 of Article 14); and capital gains but only if the right or property giving rise to such income, dividends, interest, royalties, or capital gains is effectively connected with a permanent establishment which the recipient, being a resident of a Con-

tracting State, has in the other Contracting State. Such term does not include:

a. Income received by an individual as compensation for his personal services either as an employee or in an independent capacity, or

b. Income derived by a corporation or other entity of a Contracting State from sources within the other Contracting State from furnishing personal services of an individual who does not or would not qualify for exemption under paragraph 2 of Article 18 by reason of paragraph 3 thereof.

Article 9

1. For the purpose of this Convention, the term 'permanent establishment' means a fixed place of business through which a resident of a Contracting State engages in industrial or commercial activity.

2. The term 'fixed place of business' includes but is not limited to:

a. A branch;

b. An office;

c. A factory;

d. A workshop;

e. A mine, quarry, or other place of extraction of natural resources; and

f. A building site or construction or installation project which exists for more than 24 months.

3. Notwithstanding paragraphs 1 and 2 of this article, a permanent establishment shall not include a fixed place of business used only for one or more of the following:

a. The use of facilities for the purpose of storage, display, or delivery of goods or merchandise belonging to the resident;

b. The maintenance of a stock of goods or merchandise belonging to the resident for the purpose of storage, display or delivery;

c. The maintenance of a stock of goods or merchandise belonging to the resident for the purpose of processing by another person;

d. The purchase of goods or merchandise, or the collection of information, for the resident; or

e. Advertising, the supply of information, the conduct of scientific research, or similar activities which have a preparatory or auxiliary character, for the resident.

4. A person acting in a Contracting State on behalf of a resident of the other Contracting State, other than an agent of an independent status to whom paragraph 5 of this article applies, shall be deemed to be a permanent establishment in the first-mentioned Contracting State if such person has, and habitually exercises in the first-mentioned Contracting State, an authority to conclude contracts in the name of that resident, unless the exercise of such authority is limited to the purchase of goods or merchandise for that resident.

5. An resident of a Contracting State shall not be deemed to have a permanent establishment in the other Contracting State merely because such resident engages in industrial or commercial activity in

that other Contracting State through a broker, general commission agent, or any other agent of an independent status, where such broker or agent is acting in the ordinary course of his business.

6. The fact that a resident of a Contracting State is a related person with respect to a resident of the other Contracting State or with respect to a person who engages in industrial or commercial activity in that other Contracting State (whether through a permanent establishment or otherwise) shall not be taken into account in determining whether that resident of the first-mentioned Contracting State has a permanent establishment in that other Contracting State.

Article 10

1. Notwithstanding Article 8 and Article 16, income which a resident of the United States derives from operation in international traffic of ships or aircraft registered in the United States and gains which a resident of the United States derives from the sale, exchange, or other disposition of ships or aircraft operated in international traffic by such resident and registered in the United States shall be exempt from Japanese tax.

2. Notwithstanding Article 8 and Article 16, income which a resident of Japan derives from the operation in international traffic of ships or aircraft which are either registered in Japan or leased by such resident and gains which a resident of Japan derives from the sale, exchange, or other disposition of ships or aircraft operated in international traffic by such resident and registered in Japan shall be exempt from United States tax.

Article 11

1. Where a resident of a Contracting State and any other person are related and where such related persons make arrangements or impose conditions between themselves which are different from those which would be made between independent persons, then any income, deductions, credits, or allowances, which would, but for those arrangements or conditions, have been taken into account in computing the income (or loss) of, or the tax payable by, one of such persons, may be allocated and utilised in computing the amount of the income subject to tax and the taxes payable by such resident of that Contracting State.

2. A person is related to another person if either person owns or controls directly or indirectly the other, or if any third person or persons own or control directly or indirectly both. For this purpose, the term 'control' includes any kind of control, whether or not legally enforceable, and however exercised or exercisable.

Article 12

1. Dividends derived from sources within a Contracting State by a resident of the other Contracting State may be taxed by both Contracting States.

2. The rate of tax imposed by a Contracting State on dividends derived from sources within that Contracting State by a resident of the other Contracting State shall not exceed:

a. 15 per cent of the gross amount actually distributed; or

b. When the recipient is a corporation, 10 per cent of the gross amount actually distributed if:

(i) During the part of the paying corporation's taxable year which precedes the date of payment of the dividend and during the whole of its prior taxable year (if any), at least 10 per cent of the voting shares of the paying corporation was owned by the recipient corporation, and

(ii) Not more than 25 per cent of the gross income of the paying corporation for such prior taxable year (if any) consists of interest or dividends (other than interest derived from the conduct of a banking, insurance, or financing business and dividends or interest received from subsidiary corporations, 50 per cent or more of the outstanding shares of the voting stock of which is owned by the paying corporation at the time such dividends or interest is received).

3. Paragraph 2 of this article shall not apply if the recipient of the dividends, being a resident of a Contracting State, has a permanent establishment in the other Contracting State and the shares with respect to which the dividends are paid are effectively connected with such permanent establishment.

Article 13

1. Interest derived from sources within a Contracting State by a resident of the other Contracting State may be taxed by both Contracting States.

2. Notwithstanding paragraph 1 of this article, interest derived from sources within the United States by the Bank of Japan or by the Export-Import Bank of Japan, or by any resident of Japan with respect to debt obligations guaranteed or indirectly financed by either of such banks or with respect to debt obligations insured by the Government of Japan pursuant to the Law concerning Export Insurance of March 31, 1950 (Law No. 67), shall be exempt from United States tax.

3. Notwithstanding paragraph 1 of this article, interest derived from sources within Japan by any Federal Reserve Bank in the United States or by the Export-Import Bank of the United States, or by any resident of the United States with respect to debt obligations guaranteed or insured or indirectly financed by any of such banks, shall be exempt from Japanese tax.

4. The rate of tax imposed by a Contracting State on interest derived from sources within that Contracting State by a resident of the other Contracting State shall not exceed 10 per cent.

5. Paragraphs 2, 3, and 4 of this article shall not apply if the recipient of the interest, being a resident of a Contracting State, has a permanent establishment in the other Contracting State and the indebtedness giving rise to the interest is effectively connected with such permanent establishment.

6. Where any interest paid by a person to any related person exceeds an amount which would have been paid to an unrelated person, the provisions of this article shall apply only to so much of the interest as would have been paid to an unrelated person. In such a case, the excess payment may be taxed by each Contracting State according to its own law, including the provisions of this Convention where applicable.

7. The term 'interest', as used in this Convention, includes income from bonds, debenture, Government securities, notes, or other evidences of indebtedness, whether or not secured, and whether or not carrying a right to participate in profits, and debt-claims of every kind, as well as all other income assimilated to income from money lent by the taxation law of the Contracting State in which the income has its source.

Article 14

1. Royalties derived from sources within a Contracting State by a resident of the other Contracting State may be taxed by both Contracting States.

2. The rate of tax imposed by a Contracting State on royalties derived from sources within that Contracting State by a resident of the other Contracting State shall not exceed 10 per cent.

3. The term 'royalties', as used in this article, means:

a. Payment of any kind made as consideration for the use of, or the right to use, copyrights of literary, artistic, scientific works, or motion picture films or films or tapes used for radio or television broadcasting, patents, designs or models, plans, secret processes or formulae, trademarks, or other like property or rights, or know-how, or ships or aircraft (but only if the lessor is a person not engaged in the operation in international traffic of ships or aircraft), and

b. Gains derived from the sale, exchange, or other disposition of any property or rights referred to in subparagraph *a.* of this paragraph (other than ships or aircraft) to the extent that the amounts realized on such sale, exchange, or other disposition for consideration are contingent on the productivity, use or disposition of such property or rights.

4. Paragraph 2 of this Article shall not apply if the recipient of the royalty, being a resident of a Contracting State, has in the other Contracting State a permanent establishment and the property or rights giving rise to the royalty are effectively connected with such permanent establishment.

5. Where any royalty paid by a person to any related person exceeds an amount which would have been paid to an unrelated person, the provisions of this article shall apply only to so much of the royalty as would have been paid to an unrelated person. In such a case, the excess payment may be taxed by each Contracting State according to its own law, including the provisions of this Convention where applicable.

Article 15

1. Income from real property, including royalties in respect of the operation of mines or quarries, or the exploitation of any natural

resources and gains derived from the sale, exchange, or other disposition of such property or of the right giving rise to such royalties, may be taxed by the Contracting State in which such real property, mines, quarries, or natural resources are situated. For purposes of this Convention, interest on indebtedness secured by real property or secured by a right giving rise to royalties in respect of the operation of mines or quarries, or the exploitation of any natural resources shall be regarded as income from real property.

2. Paragraph 1 of this article shall apply to income derived from the usufruct, direct use, letting, or use in any other form of real property.

Article 16

Gains from the sale, exchange, or other disposition of capital assets derived by a resident of a Contracting State shall be exempt from tax by the other Contracting State unless:

1. The gain is derived by a resident of a Contracting State from the sale, exchange, or other disposition of property described in Article 15 situated within the other Contracting State,

2. The gain arises out of the sale, exchange, or other disposition described in paragraph 3*b*. of Article 14,

3. The recipient of the gain, being a resident of a Contracting State, has a permanent establishment in the other Contracting State and the property giving rise to the gain is effectively connected with such permanent establishment, or

4. The recipient of the gain, being an individual who is a resident of a Contracting State:

a. Maintains a fixed base in the other Contracting State for a period or periods aggregating more than 183 days during the taxable year and the property giving rise to such gains is effectively connected with such fixed base, or

b. Is present in the other Contracting State for a period or periods aggregating more than 183 days during the taxable year.

Article 17

1. Income derived by an individual who is a resident of a Contracting State from the performance of personal services in an independent capacity may be taxed by that Contracting State. Except as provided in paragraph 2 of this article, such income shall be exempt from tax by the other Contracting State.

2. Income derived by an individual who is a resident of a Contracting State from the performance of personal services in an independent capacity in the other Contracting State may be taxed by that other Contracting State, if:

a. The individual is present in that other Contracting State for a period or periods aggregating more than 183 days in the taxable year, or

b. The individual maintains a fixed base in that other Contracting State for a period or periods aggregating more than 183 days in the taxable year, but only so much of it as is attributable to such fixed base, or

c. The individual is a public entertainer, such as a theater, motion picture or television artist, musician, or athlete, and the income is derived from his personal services as such public entertainer, unless such individual is present in that other Contracting State for a period or periods not exceeding a total of 90 days during the taxable year and such income does not exceed 3,000 United States dollars in the aggregate or its equivalent in Japanese yen in the aggregate during the taxable year.

Article 18

1. Wages, salaries, and similar remuneration derived by an individual who is a resident of a Contracting State from labor or personal services performed as an employee, including remuneration derived by an officer or a member of the board of directors of a corporation, may be taxed by that Contracting State. Except as provided in paragraph 2 of this article, such remuneration derived from sources within the other Contracting State may also be taxed by that other Contracting State.

2. Remuneration of the type described in paragraph 1 of this article derived by an individual who is a resident of a Contracting State shall be exempt from tax by the other Contracting State if:

a. He is present in that other Contracting State for a period or periods not exceeding in the aggregate 183 days in the taxable year;

b. He is an employee of a resident of the first-mentioned Contracting State or of a permanent establishment of a resident of a State other than the first-mentioned Contracting State if such permanent establishment is situated in the first-mentioned Contracting State (such resident, including a corporation or other entity to which the permanent establishment belongs, is referred to in this article as 'the employer'); and

c. The remuneration is not borne as such by a permanent establishment which the employer has in that other Contracting State.

3. Paragraph 2 of this article shall not apply to remuneration of the type described in paragraph 1 of this article if the individual receiving such remuneration is a substantial owner of the employer and 50 per cent or more of the income of the employer for the taxable year from sources within that other Contracting State is derived from furnishing the labor or personal services of one or more individuals (computed without deductions for compensation paid to such individuals) each of whom is a substantial owner of the employer. For purposes of the preceding sentence, an individual shall be treated as the substantial owner of the employer if the employer is a corporation or other entity and such individual:

a. Owns directly or indirectly 25 per cent or more of the total voting power of all classes of stock entitled to vote, or of the total value of all classes of stock, of such corporation or other entity, or

b. Has directly or indirectly an interest of 25 per cent or more in the assets, or has a right to 25 per cent or more of the profits of such other entity.
In computing the ownership of an individual, he shall be deemed to own the stock, assets, or rights owned directly or indirectly by his brother, sister, spouse, ancestor, or descendant.

4. Notwithstanding paragraph 2 of this article, remuneration derived by an individual from the performance of labor or personal services as an employee aboard ships or aircraft operated by a resident of a Contracting State in international traffic shall be exempt from tax by the other Contracting State if such individual is a member of the regular complement of the ship or aircraft.

5. Notwithstanding paragraph 2 of this article and Article 17, a director's fee derived by an individual resident of a Contracting State in his capacity as a member of the board of directors of a corporation of the other Contracting State, which cannot be taken as a deduction by the corporation but is treated as being a distribution of profits in that other Contracting State, may be taxed by that other Contracting State.

Article 19

1. An individual:

a. Who is a resident of a Contracting State at the beginning of his visit to the other Contracting State, or

b. Who was, immediately before receiving the invitation referred to below, exempt from tax in that other Contracting State under paragraph 1*a*. of Article 20,

and who, at the invitation of the Government of that other Contracting State or of a university or other accredited educational institution situated in that other Contracting State, is temporarily present in that other Contracting State for the primary purpose of teaching or engaging in research, or both, at a university or other accredited educational institution shall be exempt from tax by that other Contracting State on his income from personal services for teaching or research at such university or educational institution, for a period not exceeding 2 years from the date of his arrival or the date he completed the study, training, or research in that other Contracting State with respect to which the exemption in paragraph 1*a*. of Article 20 applied.

2. This article shall not apply to income from research if such research is undertaken not in the public interest but primarily for the private benefit of a specific person or persons.

Article 20

1. *a.* An individual who is a resident of a Contracting State at the beginning of his visit to the other Contracting State and who is temporarily present in that other Contracting State for the primary purpose of:

(i) Studying at a university or other accredited educational institution in that other Contracting State, or

(ii) Securing training required to qualify him to practice a profession or professional specialty, or

(iii) Studying or doing research as a recipient of a grant, allowance, or award from a governmental, religious, charitable, scientific, literary, or educational organization,

shall be exempt from tax by that other Contracting State with respect to amounts described in subparagraph *b.* of this paragraph for a period not exceeding five taxable years from the date of his arrival in that other Contracting State.

b. The amounts referred to in subparagraph *a.* are:

(i) Gifts from abroad for the purpose of his maintenance, education, study, research, or training;

(ii) The grant, allowance, or award; and

(iii) Income from personal services performed in that other Contracting State in an aggregate amount not in excess of 2,000 United States dollars or its equivalent in Japanese yen for any taxable year.

2. An individual who is a resident of a Contracting State at the beginning of his visit to the other Contracting State and who is temporarily present in that other Contracting State as an employee of, or under contract with, a resident of the first-mentioned Contracting State, for the primary purpose of:

a. Acquiring technical, professional, or business experience from a person other than that resident of the first-mentioned Contracting State, or

b. Studying at a university or other accredited educational institution in that other Contracting State,

shall be exempt from tax by that other Contracting State for a period of 12 consecutive months with respect to his income from personal services in an aggregate amount not in excess of 5,000 United States dollars or its equivalent in Japanese yen.

3. An individual who is a resident of a Contracting State at the beginning of his visit to the other Contracting State and who is temporarily present in that other Contracting State for a period not exceeding one year, as a participant in a program sponsored by the Government of that other Contracting State, for the primary purpose of training, research, or study, shall be exempt from tax by that other Contracting State with respect to his income from personal services in respect of such training, research, or study, performed in that other Contracting State in an aggregate amount not in excess of 10,000 United States dollars or its equivalent in Japanese yen.

Article 21

1. Wages, salaries, and similar remuneration, including pensions or similar benefits, paid by, or from public funds of, the United States, or political subdivision or local authority thereof to a citizen of the United States for labor or personal services performed for the United States or for any of its political subdivisions or local authorities in the discharge of governmental functions shall not be subject to Japanese

tax, if such individual is not a national of Japan and has not been admitted to Japan for permanent residence.

2. Wages, salaries, and similar remuneration, including pensions or similar benefits, paid by, or out of funds to which contributions are made by, Japan, or a local authority thereof to an individual who is a national of Japan for labor or personal services performed for Japan or for any of its local authorities in the discharge of governmental functions shall not be subject to United States tax, if such individual is not a citizen of the United States and does not have immigrant status in the United States.

Article 22

1. Reimbursed travel expenses shall be subject to Articles 17 through 21, but such expenses shall not be taken into account in computing the maximum amount of exemptions specified in paragraph 2 of Article 17 and in Article 20.

2. If an individual qualifies for benefits under more than one of the provisions of Articles 17 through 21, he may apply those provisions which are most favorable to him. He may not claim benefits under more than one of the provisions of such articles with respect to the same income.

3. The benefits provided under Article 19 and paragraph 1 of Article 20 shall extend only for such period of time as may be reasonably or customarily required to effectuate the purpose of the visit, but in no case shall any individual have the benefits provided therein for more than a total of five taxable years from the date of his arrival.

Article 23

1. Except as provided in Article 21, pensions and annuities paid to an individual who is a resident of a Contracting State shall be taxable only in that Contracting State.

2. The term 'pensions', as used in this article, includes periodic payments made after retirement or death in consideration for services rendered, or by way of compensation for injuries received, in connection with past employment, including United States and Japanese social security payments.

3. The term 'annuities', as used in this article, includes a stated sum paid periodically at stated times during life, or during a specified number of years, under an obligation to make the payments in return for adequate and full consideration (other than for services rendered).

Article 24

Nothing in this Convention shall affect the fiscal privileges of diplomatic and consular officials under the general rules of international law or under the provisions of special agreements.

Article 25

1. Where a resident of a Contracting State considers that the action of one or both of the Contracting States results or will result for him

in taxation not in accordance with this Convention, he may, notwithstanding the remedies provided by the national laws of the Contracting States, present his case to the competent authority of the Contracting State of which he is a resident. Should the resident's claim be considered to have merit by the competent authority of the Contracting State to which the claim is made, it shall endeavor to come to an agreement with the competent authority of the other Contracting State with a view to the avoidance of taxation contrary to the provisions of this Convention.

2. The competent authorities of the Contracting States shall endeavor to resolve by mutual agreement any difficulties or doubts arising as to the interpretation or application of this Convention. In particular, the competent authorities of the Contracting States may consult together to endeavor to agree:

a. To the same attribution of industrial or commercial profits to a resident of a Contracting State and its permanent establishment situated in the other Contracting State;

b. To the same allocation of income, deductions, credits, or allowances between a resident of a Contracting State and any related persons;

c. To the same determination of the source of particular items of income; or

d. To the same meaning of any term used in this Convention.

3. The competent authorities of the Contracting States may communicate with each other directly for the purpose of reaching an agreement in the sense of this article. When it seems advisable for the purpose of reaching agreement, the competent authorities may meet together for an oral exchange of opinions.

4. In the event that the competent authorities reach such an agreement, taxes shall be imposed, and refund or credit of taxes shall be allowed, by the Contracting States in accordance with such agreement.

Article 26

1. The competent authorities of the Contracting States shall exchange such information as is pertinent to carrying out the provisions of this Convention or for preventing fraud or fiscal evasion in relation to the taxes which are the subject of this Convention. Any information so exchanged shall be treated as secret and shall not be disclosed to any persons other than those (including a court or administrative body) concerned with assessment, collection, enforcement, or prosecution in respect of the taxes which are the subject of this Convention.

2. In no case shall the provisions of paragraph 1 of this article be construed so as to impose on one of the Contracting States the obligation:

a. To carry out administrative measures at variance with the laws or the administrative practice of that Contracting State or the other Contracting State;

b. To supply particulars which are not obtainable under the laws or in the normal course of the administration of that Contracting State or of the other Contracting State; or

c. To supply information which would disclose any trade, business, industrial, commercial, or professional secret or trade process, or information, the disclosure of which would be contrary to public policy.

3. The exchange of information shall be either on a routine basis or on request with reference to particular cases. The competent authorities of the Contracting States shall agree on the list of information which shall be furnished on a routine basis.

4. The competent authorities of the Contracting States shall notify each other of any amendments of the laws relating to the taxes referred to in paragraph 1 of Article 1 and of the adoption of any taxes referred to in paragraph 2 of Article 1 by transmitting the texts of any amendments or new statutes at least once a year.

5. The competent authorities of the Contracting States shall exchange the texts of all published material interpreting this Convention under their respective laws, whether in the form of regulations, rulings, or judicial decisions.

Article 27

1. Subject to the provisions of paragraph 2 of this article, each of the Contracting States shall endeavor to collect such taxes imposed by the other Contracting State as will ensure that any exemption or reduced rate of tax granted under this Convention by that other Contracting State shall not be enjoyed by persons not entitled to such benefits. The Contracting State making such collections shall be responsible to the other Contracting State for the sums thus collected. The competent authorities of the Contracting States may consult together for the purpose of giving effect to this article.

2. In no case shall this article be construed so as to impose upon a Contracting State the obligation to carry out administrative measures at variance with the regulations and practices of either Contracting State or which would be contrary to the first-mentioned Contracting State's sovereignty, security, or public policy.

Article 28

1. This Convention shall be ratified and instruments of ratification shall be exchanged at Washington as soon as possible. It shall enter into force on the thirtieth day after the day of the exchange of instruments of ratification. Its provisions shall for the first time have effect:

a. In the case of Japan: for income derived during any taxable year beginning on or after January 1 of the year next following the year in which this Convention enters into force; and

b. In the case of the United States:

(i) As respects taxes withheld at source on dividends, interest, royalties, and similar payments, to any obligation to pay such taxes arising on or after January 1 next following the year in which this Convention enters into force; and

(ii) As respects other taxes on income, to taxable years beginning on or after January 1 of the year next following the year in which this Convention enters into force.

2. The Convention between the United States of America and Japan for the Avoidance of Double Taxation and the Prevention of Fiscal Evasion with respect to Taxes on Income signed at Washington, D.C. on April 16, 1954, modified and supplemented by the Protocols signed at Tokyo on May 7, 1960, and August 14, 1962, shall terminate and cease to have effect in respect of income to which this Convention applies under paragraph 1 of this article.

Article 29

This Convention shall remain in force until terminated by a Contracting State. Either Contracting State may terminate the Convention at any time after five years from the date on which this Convention enters into force by giving to the other Contracting State notice of termination at least six months before the end of any calendar year through diplomatic channels. In such event, this Convention shall cease to have effect:

1. In the case of Japan: for income derived during any taxable year beginning on or after January 1 of the year next following the year in which the notice of termination is given;

2. In the case of the United States:

a. As respects taxes withheld at source on dividends, interest, royalties, and similar payments, on January 1 of the year next following the year in which the notice of termination is given; and

b. As respects other taxes on income, for any taxable year beginning on or after January 1 of the year next following the year in which the notice of termination is given.

In witness whereof, the undersigned, duly authorized thereto, have signed this Convention.

Done at Tokyo, in duplicate, in the English and Japanese languages, the two texts having equal authenticity, this eighth day of March, 1971.

Convention Between the United States of America and the Republic of Korea for the Avoidance of Double Taxation and the Prevention of Fiscal Evasion with Respect to Taxes on Income and the Encouragement of International Trade and Investment, concluded in Seoul on June 4, 1976.

The Government of the United States of America and the Government of the Republic of Korea, desiring to conclude a convention for the avoidance of double taxation of income and the prevention of fiscal evasion and the encouragement of international trade and investment have appointed for that purpose as their respective Plenipotentiaries:

The Government of the United States of America: His Excellency Richard L. Schneider, Ambassador Extraordinary and Plenipotentiary of the United States of America to the Republic of Korea;

The Government of the Republic of Korea: His Excellency Park Tong-jin, Minister of Foreign Affairs of the Republic of Korea;

Who, having communicated to each other their full powers, found in good and due form, have agreed upon the following articles.

Article 1. Taxes Covered

1. The taxes which are the subject of this Convention are:

a. In the case of the United States, the Federal income taxes imposed by the Internal Revenue Code (the United States tax), and

b. In the case of Korea, the income tax and the corporation tax (the Korean tax).

2. This Convention shall also apply to taxes substantially similar to those covered by paragraph 1 which are imposed in addition to, or in place of, existing taxes after the date of signature of this Convention.

3. For the purpose of Article 7 (Non-Discrimination), this Convention shall also apply to taxes of every kind imposed at the national, state, or local level. For the purpose of Article 28 (Exchange of Information), this Convention shall also apply to taxes of every kind imposed at the National level.

Article 2. General Definitions

1. In this Convention, unless the context otherwise requires:

a. (i) The term 'United States' means the United States of America; and

(ii) When used in a geographical sense, the term 'United States' means the states thereof and the District of Columbia. Such term also includes:

(A) The territorial sea thereof, and

(B) The seabed and subsoil of the submarine areas adjacent to the coast thereof, but beyond the territorial sea, over which the United

States exercises sovereign rights, in accordance with international law, for the purpose of exploration and exploitation of the natural resources of such areas, but only to the extent that the person, property, or activity to which this Convention is being applied is connected with such exploration or exploitation.

b. (i) The term 'Korea' means the Republic of Korea; and

(ii) When used in a geographical sense, the term 'Korea' means all the territory to which the laws relating to Korean tax are in force. The term also includes:

(A) The territorial sea thereof, and

(B) The seabed and subsoil of the submarine areas adjacent to the coast thereof, but beyond the territorial sea, over which Korea exercises sovereign rights, in accordance with international law, for the purpose of exploration and exploitation of the natural resources of such areas, but only to the extent that the person, property, or activity to which this Convention is being applied is connected with such exploration or exploitation.

c. The term 'Contracting State' means the United States or Korea, as the context requires.

d. The term 'person' includes an individual, a partnership, a corporation, an estate, a trust, or any body of persons.

e. (i) The term 'United States corporation' or 'corporation of the United States' means a corporation which is created or organized under the laws of the United States or of any state thereof or the District of Columbia, or any unincorporated entity treated as a United States corporation for United States tax purposes; and

(ii) The term 'Korean corporation' or 'corporation of Korea' means a corporation (other than a United States corporation) which has its head or main office in Korea, or any entity treated as a Korean corporation for Korean tax purposes.

f. The term 'competent authority' means:

(i) In the case of the United States, the Secretary of the Treasury or his delegate, and

(ii) In the case of Korea, the Minister of Finance or his delegate.

g. The term 'State' means any National State, whether or not one of the Contracting States.

h. The term 'citizen' means:

(i) In the case of the United States, a citizen of the United States, and

(ii) In the case of Korea, a national of Korea.

2. Any other term used in this Convention and not defined in this Convention shall, unless the context otherwise requires, have the meaning which it has under the laws of the Contracting State whose tax is being determined. Notwithstanding the preceding sentence, if the meaning of such a term under the laws of one Contracting State is different from the meaning of the term under the laws of the other Contracting State, or if the meaning of such a term is not readily determinable under the laws of one of the Contracting States, the competent authorities of the Contracting States may, in order to prevent double taxation

or to further any other purpose of this Convention, establish a common meaning of the term for the purposes of this Convention.

Article 3. Fiscal Domicile

1. In this Convention:

a. The term 'resident of the United States' means:

(i) A United States corporation, and

(ii) Any other person (except a corporation or an entity treated under United States law as a corporation) resident in the United States for purposes of its tax, but in the case of a person acting as a partner or fiduciary only to the extent that the income derived by such person is subject to United States tax as the income of a resident.

b. The term 'resident of Korea' means:

(i) A Korean corporation, and

(ii) Any other person (except a corporation or an entity treated under Korean law as a corporation) resident in Korea for purposes of its tax, but in the case of a person acting as a partner or fiduciary only to the extent that the income derived by such person is subject to Korean tax as the income of a resident.

c. In determining the residence of a partnership which makes a payment, a partnership shall be considered a resident of the State under the laws of which it was created or organized.

2. Where by reason of the provisions of paragraph 1 an individual is a resident of both Contracting States:

a. He shall be deemed to be a resident of that Contracting State in which he maintains his permanent home;

b. If he has a permanent home in both Contracting States or in neither of the Contracting States, he shall be deemed a resident of that Contracting State with which his personal and economic relations are closest (center of vital interests);

c. If his center of vital interests is in neither of the Contracting State or cannot be determined, he shall be deemed to be a resident of that Contracting State in which he has an habitual abode;

d. If he has an habitual abode in both Contracting States or in neither of the Contracting States, he shall be deemed to be a resident of the Contracting State of which he is a citizen; and

e. If he is a citizen of both Contracting States or of neither Contracting State the competent authorities of the Contracting States shall settle the question by mutual agreement.

For the purpose of this paragraph, a permanent home is the place where an individual dwells with his family.

3. An individual who is deemed to be a resident of one of the Contracting States and not a resident of the other Contracting State by reason of the provisions of paragraph 2 shall be deemed to be a resident only of the first-mentioned Contracting State for all purposes of this Convention, including Article 4 (General Rules of Taxation).

Article 4. General Rules of Taxation

1. A resident of one of the Contracting States may be taxed by the other Contracting State on any income from sources within that other Contracting State and only on such income, subject to any limitations set forth in this Convention. For this purpose, the rules set forth in Article 6 (Source of Income) shall be applied to determine the source of income.

2. The provisions of this Convention shall not be construed to restrict in any manner any exclusion, exemption, deduction, credit, or other allowance now or hereafter accorded:

a. By the laws of one of the Contracting States in determination of the tax imposed by that Contracting State, or

b. By any other agreement between the Contracting States.

3. The provisions of this Convention shall not affect Korean law so as to deny benefits accorded residents of the United States under the provisions of the Korean Foreign Capital Inducement Law Number 2598 of March 12, 1973 as amended or any similar law to encourage investment in Korea.

4. Notwithstanding any provisions of this Convention except paragraph 5, a Contracting State may tax a citizen or resident of that Contracting State as if this Convention had not come into effect.

5. The provisions of paragraph 4 shall not affect:

a. The benefits conferred by a Contracting State under Articles 5 (Relief from Double Taxation), 7 (Non-Discrimination), 24 (Social Security Payments), and 27 (Mutual Agreement Procedure); and

b. The benefits conferred by a Contracting State under Articles 20 (Teachers), 21 (Students and Trainees), and 22 (Government Functions) upon individuals who are neither citizens of, nor have immigrant status in, that Contracting State.

6. The competent authorities of the two Contracting States may prescribe regulations necessary to carry out the provisions of this Convention.

7. There shall be allowed, for purposes of United States tax, in the case of a resident of Korea who is not a resident of the United States (other than an officer or employee of the Government of Korea or local authority thereof), as long as the United States Internal Revenue Code provides only one personal exemption, a deduction for personal exemptions, subject to the conditions prescribed in sections 151 through 154 of the Internal Revenue Code as in effect on the date of the signature of this Convention, for the spouse of the taxpayer and for each child of the taxpayer present in the United States and residing with him in the United States at any time during the taxable year, but such additional deduction shall not exceed that proportion thereof which the taxpayer's gross income from sources within the United States which is treated as effectively connected with the conduct of a trade or business within the United States within the meaning of section 864(c) of the Internal Revenue Code for the taxpayer's taxable year bears to his entire income from all sources for such taxable year.

8. The United States may impose its personal holding company tax and its accumulated earnings tax notwithstanding any provision of this Convention. However, a Korean corporation shall be exempt from the United States personal holding company tax in any taxable year if all of its stock is owned, directly or indirectly, by one or more individuals who are residents of Korea (and not citizens of the United States) for that entire year. A Korean corporation shall be exempt from the United States accumulated earnings tax in any taxable year unless such corporation is engaged in trade or business in the United States through a permanent establishment at any time during such year.

Article 5. Relief from Double Taxation

Double taxation of income shall be avoided in the following manner:

1. In accordance with the provisions and subject to the limitations of the law of the United States (as it may be amended from time to time without changing the principles hereof), the United States shall allow to a citizen or resident of the United States as a credit against the United States tax the appropriate amount of Korean taxes and, in the case of a United States corporation owning at least 10 per cent of the voting power of a Korean corporation from which it receives dividends in any taxable year, shall allow credit for the appropriate amount of taxes paid to Korea by the Korean corporation paying such dividends with respect to the profits out of which such dividends are paid. Such appropriate amount shall be based upon the amount of tax paid to Korea but the credit shall not exceed the limitations (for the purpose of limiting the credit to the United States tax on income from sources within Korea or on income from sources outside the United States) provided by United States law for the taxable year. For the purpose of applying the United States credit in relation to taxes paid to Korea, the rules set forth in Article 6 (Source of Income) shall be applied to determine the source of income.

2. In accordance with the provisions and subject to the limitations of the law of Korea (as it may be amended from time to time without changing the principles hereof), Korea shall allow to a citizen or resident of Korea as a credit against Korean tax the appropriate amount of income taxes paid to the United States and, in the case of a Korean corporation owning at least 10 per cent of the voting power of a United States corporation from which it receives dividends in any taxable year, shall allow credit for the appropriate amount of taxes paid to the United States by the United States corporation paying such dividends with respect to the profits out of which such dividends are paid. Such appropriate amount shall be based upon the amount of tax paid to the United States but shall not exceed that portion of Korean tax which such citizen's or resident's net income from sources within the United States bears to his entire net income for the same taxable year. For the purpose of applying the Korean credit in relation to taxes paid to the United States, the rules set forth in Article 6 (Source of Income) shall be applied to determine the source of income.

Article 6. Source of Income

For the purposes of this Convention:

1. Dividends shall be treated as income from sources within a Contracting State only if paid by a corporation of that Contracting State.

2. Interest shall be treated as income from sources within one of the Contracting States only if paid by that Contracting State, a political subdivision or a local authority thereof, or by a resident of that Contracting State. Notwithstanding the preceding sentence:

a. If the person paying the interest (whether or not he is a resident of one of the Contracting States) has a permanent establishment in one of the Contracting States in connection with which the indebtedness on which the interest is paid was incurred and such interest is borne by such permanent establishment, or

b. If the person paying the interest is a resident in one of the Contracting States and has a permanent establishment in a State other than a Contracting State in connection with which the indebtedness on which the interest is paid was incurred and such interest is paid to a resident of the other Contracting State, and such interest is borne by such permanent establishment, such interest shall be deemed to be from sources within the State in which the permanent establishment is situated.

3. Royalties described in paragraph 4 of Article 14 (Royalties) for the use of, or the right to use, property (other than as provided in paragraph 5 with respect to ships or aircraft) described in such paragraph shall be treated as income from sources within one of the Contracting States only if paid for the use of, or the right to such, such property within that Contracting State.

4. Income from real property and royalties from the operation of mines, quarries, or other natural resources (including gains derived from the sale of such property or the right giving rise to such royalties) shall be treated as income from sources within one of the Contracting State only if such property is located in that Contracting State.

5. Income from the rental of tangible property (movable property) shall be treated as income from sources within one of the Contracting States only if such property is located in that Contracting State. Income from the rental of ships or aircraft derived by a person not engaged in the operation of ships or aircraft in international traffic shall be treated as income from sources within a Contracting State only if the lessee is a resident of that Contracting State.

6. Income received by an individual for his performance of labor or personal services, whether as an employee or in an independent capacity, or for furnishing the personal services of another person and income received by a corporation for furnishing the personal services of its employees or others, shall be treated as income from sources within one of the Contracting States only to the extent that such services are performed in that Contracting State. Income from personal services performed aboard ships or aircraft operated by a resident of one of the Contracting States in international traffic shall be treated as income from sources within that Contracting State if rendered by a

member of the regular complement of the ship or aircraft. For purposes of this paragraph, income from labor or personal services includes pensions (as defined in paragraph 13) of Article 23 (Private Pensions and Annuities)) paid in respect of such services. Notwithstanding the preceding provisions of this paragraph, remuneration described in Article 22 (Governmental Functions) and payments described in Article 24 (Social Security Payments) shall be treated as income from sources within one of the Contracting States only if paid by or from the public funds of that Contracting State or local authority thereof.

7. Income from the purchase and sale of intangible or tangible personal (including movable) property (other than gains defined as royalties by paragraph 4*b.* of Article 14 (Royalties) shall be treated as income from sources within one of the Contracting States only if such property is sold in that Contracting State.

8. Notwithstanding paragraphs 1 through 7, industrial or commercial profits which are attributable to a permanent establishment which the recipient, a resident of one of the Contracting States, has in the other Contracting State, including income from real property and natural resources and dividends, interest, royalties (as defined in paragraph 4 of Article 14 (Royalties)), and capital gains, but only if the rights or property giving rise to such income, dividends, interest, royalties, or capital gains are effectively connected with such permanent establishment, shall be treated as income from sources within that other Contracting State.

9. The source of any item of income to which paragraphs 1 through 8 of this article are not applicable shall be determined by each of the Contracting States in accordance with its own law. Notwithstanding the preceding sentence, if the source of any item of income under the laws of one Contracting State is different from the source of such item of income under the laws of the other Contracting State or if the source of such income is not readily determinable under the laws of one of the Contracting States, the competent authorities of the Contracting States may, in order to prevent double taxation or further any other purpose of this Convention, establish a common source of the item of income for purposes of this Convention.

Article 7. Non-Discrimination

1. A citizen of one of the Contracting States who is a resident of the other Contracting State shall not be subjected in that other Contracting State to more burdensome taxes than a citizen of that other Contracting State who is a resident thereof.

2. A permanent establishment which a resident of one of the Contracting States has in the other Contracting State shall not be subject in that other Contracting State to more burdensome taxes than a resident of that other Contracting State carrying on the same activities. This paragraph shall not be construed as obliging one of the Contracting States to grant to individual residents of the other Contracting State any personal allowances, reliefs, or deductions for taxation purposes

on account of civil status or family responsibilities which the first-mentioned Contracting State grants to its own individual residents.

3. A corporation of one of the Contracting States, the capital of which is wholly or partly owned or controlled, directly or indirectly, by one or more residents of the other Contracting State, shall not be subjected in the first-mentioned Contracting State to any taxation or any requirement connected therewith which is other or more burdensome than the taxation and connected requirements to which a corporation of the first-mentioned Contracting State carrying on the same activities, the capital of which is wholly owned or controlled by one or more residents of the first-mentioned Contracting State, is or may be subjected.

Article 8. Business Profits

1. Industrial or commercial profits of a resident of one of the Contracting States shall be exempt from tax by the other Contracting State unless such resident is engaged in industrial or commercial activity in that other Contracting State through a permanent establishment situated therein. If such resident is so engaged, tax may be imposed by that other Contracting State on the industrial or commercial profits of such resident but only on so much of such profits as are attributable to the permanent establishment.

2. Where a resident of one of the Contracting States is engaged in industrial or commercial activity in the other Contracting State through a permanent establishment situated therein, there shall in each Contracting State be attributed to the permanent establishment the industrial or commercial profits which would be attributable to such permanent establishment if such permanent establishment were an independent entity engaged in the same or similar activities under the same or similar conditions and dealing wholly independently with the resident of which it is a permanent establishment.

3. In the determination of the industrial or commercial profits of a permanent establishment, there shall be allowed as deductions expenses which are reasonably connected with such profits, including executive and general administrative expenses, whether incurred in the Contracting State in which the permanent establishment is situated or elsewhere.

4. No profits shall be attributed to a permanent establishment of a resident of one of the Contracting States in the other Contracting State merely by reason of the purchase of goods or merchandise by that permanent establishment, or by the resident of which it is a permanent establishment, for the account of that resident.

5. The term 'industrial or commercial activity' means the active conduct of a trade or business. In includes the conduct of manufacturing, mercantile, insurance, banking, financing, agricultural, fishing, or mining activities, the operation of ships or aircraft, the furnishing of services and the rental of tangible personal property (including ships or aircraft). Such term does not include the performance of personal services by an individual either as an employee or in an independent capacity.

6. *a.* The term 'industrial or commercial profits' means income derived from industrial or commercial activity, and income derived from real property and natural resources and dividends, interest, royalties (as defined in paragraph 4 of Article 14 (Royalties)), and capital gains but only if the property or rights giving rise to such income, dividends, interest, royalties, or capital gains are effectively connected with a permanent establishment which the recipient, being a resident of one of the Contracting States, has in the other Contracting State, whether or not such income is derived from industrial or commercial activity.

b. To determine whether property or rights are effectively connected with a permanent establishment, the factors taken into account shall include whether the rights or property are used in or held for use in carrying on industrial or commercial activity through such permanent establishment and whether the activities carried on through such permanent establishment were a material factor in the realization of the income from such property or rights. For this purpose, due regard shall be given to whether or not such property or rights or such income were accounted for through such permanent establishment.

7. Where industrial or commercial profits include items of income which are dealt with separately in other articles of this Convention, the provisions of those articles shall, except as otherwise provided therein, supersede the provisions of this Article.

Article 9. Permanent Establishment

1. For the purpose of this Convention, the term 'permanent establishment' means a fixed place of business through which a resident of one of the Contracting States engages in industrial or commercial activity.

2. The term 'fixed place of business' includes but is not limited to:

a. A branch;

b. An office;

c. A factory;

d. A workshop;

e. A warehouse;

f. A shop or other sales outlet;

g. A mine, quarry, or other place of extraction of natural resources; and

h. A building site or construction or installation project which exists for more than 6 months.

3. Notwithstanding paragraphs 1 and 2, a permanent establishment shall not include a fixed place of business used only for one or more of the following:

a. The use of facilities for the purpose of storage, display, or delivery of goods or merchandise belonging to the resident;

b. The maintenance of a stock of goods or merchandise belonging to the resident for the purpose of storage, display, or delivery;

c. The maintenance of a stock of goods or merchandise belonging to the resident for the purpose of processing by another person;

d. The maintenance of a fixed place of business for the purpose of purchasing goods or merchandise, or for collecting information, for the resident;

e. The maintenance of a fixed place of business for the purpose of advertising, for the supply of information, for scientific research, or for similar activities which have a preparatory or auxiliary character, for the resident; or

f. The maintenance of a building site or construction or installation project which does not exist for more than 6 months.

4. Even if a resident of one of the Contracting States does not have a permanent establishment in the other Contracting State under paragraphs 1 through 3 of this Article, nevertheless he shall be deemed to have a permanent establishment in that other Contracting State if he engages in trade or business in that other Contracting State through an agent who:

a. Has an authority to conclude contracts in the name of that resident and regularly exercises that authority in that other Contracting State, unless the exercise of the authority is limited to the purchase of goods or merchandise for the account of the resident; or

b. Maintains in that other Contracting State a stock of goods or merchandise belonging to that resident from which he regularly fills orders or makes deliveries.

5. Notwithstanding subparagraphs *a., c.* and *d.* of paragraph 3, if a resident of one of the Contracting States has a fixed place of business in the other Contracting State and goods or merchandise are either:

a. Subject to processing in that other Contracting State by another person (whether or not purchased in that Contracting State); or

b. Purchased in that other Contracting State (and such goods or merchandise are not subjected to processing outside that other Contracting State);

such resident shall be considered to have a permanent establishment in that other Contracting State, if all or part of such goods or merchandise is sold by or on behalf of such resident for use, consumption, or disposition in that other Contracting State.

6. Notwithstanding the provisions of paragraphs 4 and 5, a resident of one of the Contracting States shall not be deemed to have a permanent establishment in the other Contracting State merely because such resident engages in industrial or commercial activity in that other Contracting State through a broker, general commission agent or any other agent of an independent status, where such broker or agent is acting in the ordinary course of his business.

7. The fact that a resident of one of the Contracting States is a related person (as defined under Article 11 (Related Persons)) with respect to a resident of the other Contracting State or with respect to a person who engages in industrial or commercial activity in that other Contracting State (whether through a permanent establishment or otherwise) shall not be taken into account in determining whether that resident of the first-mentioned Contracting State has a permanent establishment in that other Contracting State.

8. The principles set forth in paragraphs 1 through 7 shall be applied in determining for the purpose of this Convention whether there is a permanent establishment in a State other than one of the Contracting States or whether a person other than a resident of one of the Contracting States has a permanent establishment in one of the Contracting States.

Article 10. Shipping and Air Transport

Notwithstanding Article 8 (Business Profits), income which a resident of one of the Contracting States derives from the operation in international traffic of ships or aircraft shall be exempt from tax by the other Contracting State. For purposes of this Article, income derived from the operation in international traffic of ships or aircraft includes income incidental to such operation, such as income derived from the use or lease of containers, trailers for the inland transportation of containers and other related equipment, but does not include other income from the inland transportation of containers.

Article 11. Related Persons

1. Where a person subject to the taxing jurisdiction of one of the Contracting States and any other person are related and where such related persons make arrangements or impose conditions between themselves which are different from those which would be made between independent persons, any income, deductions, credits, or allowances which would, but for those arrangements or conditions, have been taken into account in computing the income (or loss) of, or the tax payable by, one of such persons, may be taken into account in computing the amount of the income subject to tax and the taxes payable by such person.

2. For purposes of this Convention, a person is related to another person if either person owns or controls directly or indirectly the other, or if any third person or persons owns or controls directly or indirectly the other. For this purpose, the term 'control' includes any kind of control, whether or not legally enforceable, and however exercised or exercisable.

Article 12. Dividends

1. Dividends derived from sources within one of the Contracting States by a resident of the other Contracting State may be taxed by both Contracting States.

2. The rate of tax imposed by one of the Contracting States on dividends derived from sources within that Contracting State by a resident of the other Contracting State shall not exceed:

a. 15 per cent of the gross amount of the dividend; or

b. When the recipient is a corporation, 10 per cent of the gross amount of the dividend if:

(i) During the part of the paying corporation's taxable year which precedes the date of payment of the dividend and during the whole of its prior taxable year (if any), at least 10 per cent of the outstanding shares of the voting stock of the paying corporation was owned by the recipient corporation, and

(ii) Not more than 25 per cent of the gross income of the paying corporation for such prior taxable year (if any) consists of interest or dividends (other than interest derived from the conduct of a banking, insurance, or financing business and dividends or interest received from subsidiary corporations, 50 per cent or more of the outstanding shares of the voting stock of which is owned by the paying corporation at the time such dividends or interest is received).

3. Paragraph 2 shall not apply if the recipient of the dividends, being a resident of one of the Contracting States, has a permanent establishment in the other Contracting State and the shares with respect to which the dividends are paid are effectively connected with such permanent establishment. In such a case, paragraph *6a.* of Article 8 (Business Profits) shall apply.

Article 13. Interest

1. Interest from sources within one of the Contracting States by a resident of the other Contracting State may be taxed by both Contracting States.

2. The rate of tax imposed by one of the Contracting States on interest derived from sources within that Contracting State by a resident of the other Contracting State shall not exceed 12 per cent of the gross amount thereof.

3. Notwithstanding paragraphs 1 and 2, interest derived from sources within one of the Contracting States shall be exempt from tax by that Contracting State if it is beneficially derived by the Government of the other Contracting State, by any local authority thereof, the central bank of that other Contracting State, or any instrumentality wholly owned by that Government or that central bank or both, not subject to tax by that other Contracting State on its income.

4. Paragraph 2 shall not apply if the recipient of the interest, being a resident of one of the Contracting States, has a permanent establishment in the other Contracting State and the indebtedness giving rise to the interest is effectively connected with such permanent establishment. In such case, paragraph *6a.* of Article 8 (Business Profits) shall apply.

5. Where any amount designated as interest paid to any related person exceeds an amount which would have been paid to an unrelated person, the provisions of this Article shall apply only to so much of the interest as would have been paid to an unrelated person. In such a case the excess payment may be taxed by each Contracting State according to its own law, including the provisions of this Convention where applicable.

6. The term 'interest' as used in this Convention means income from debentures, Government securities, notes, or other evidences of indebtedness, whether or not secured and whether or not carrying a right to participate in profits, and debt-claims of every kind as well as all other

income which, under the taxation law of the Contracting State in which the income has its source, is assimilated to income from money lent.

Article 14. Royalties

1. The tax imposed by one of the Contracting States on royalties derived from sources within that Contracting State by a resident of the other Contracting State shall not exceed 15 per cent of the gross amount thereof, except as provided in paragraphs 2 and 3.

2. Royalties derived from copyrights, or rights to produce or reproduce any literary, dramatic, musical, or artistic work, by a resident of one Contracting State, as well as royalties received as consideration for the use of, or the right to use, motion picture films including films and tapes used for radio or television broadcasting, may not be taxed by the other Contracting State at a rate of tax which exceeds 10 per cent of the gross amount of such royalties.

3. Paragraphs 1 and 2 shall not apply if the recipient of the royalty, being a resident of one of the Contracting States, has in the other Contracting State a permanent establishment and the right or property giving rise to the royalties is effectively connected with such permanent establishment. In such a case, paragraph *6a.* of Article 18 (Business Profits) shall apply.

4. The term 'royalties' as used in this article means:

a. Payments of any kind made as consideration for the use of, or the right to use, copyrights of literary, artistic, or scientific works, copyrights of motion picture films or films or tapes used for radio or television broadcasting, patents, designs, models, plans, secret processes or formulae, trademarks, or other like property or rights, or knowledge, experience, or skill (know-how), or ships or aircraft (but only if the lessor is a person not engaged in the operation in international traffic of ships or aircraft), and

b. Gains derived from the sale, exchange, or other disposition of any such property or rights (other than ships or aircraft) to the extent that the amounts realized on such sale, exchange, or other disposition for consideration are contingent on the productivity, use or disposition of such property or rights.

The term does not include any royalties, rentals or other amounts paid in respect of the operation of mines, quarries, or other natural resources.

5. Where an amount is paid to a related person which would be treated as royalty but for the fact that it exceeds an amount which would have been paid to an unrelated person, the provisions of this Article shall apply only to so much of the royalty as would have been paid to an unrelated person. In such a case, the excess payment may be taxed by each Contracting State according to its own law, including the provisions of this Convention where applicable.

Article 15. Income from Real Property

1. Income from real property, including royalties and other payments in respect of the exploitation of natural resources and gains derived

from the sale, exchange, or other disposition of such property or of the right giving rise to such royalties or other payments, may be taxed by the Contracting State in which such real property or natural resources are situated. For purposes of this Convention, interest on indebtedness secured by real property or secured by a right giving rise to royalties or other payments in respect of the exploitation of natural resources shall be regarded as income from real property.

2. Paragraph 1 shall apply to income derived from the usufruct, direct use, letting, or use in any other form of real property.

Article 16. Capital Gains

1. A resident of one of the Contracting States shall be exempt from tax by the other Contracting State on gains from the sale, exchange, or other disposition of capital assets unless:

a. The gain is derived by a resident of one of the Contracting States from the sale, exchange, or other disposition of property described in Article 15 (Income from Real Property) situated within the other Contracting State,

b. The recipient of the gain, being a resident of one of the Contracting States, has a permanent establishment in the other Contracting State and the property giving rise to the gain is effectively connected with such permanent establishment, or

c. The recipient of the gain, being an individual who is a resident of one of the Contracting States:

(i) Maintains a fixed base in the other Contracting State for a period or periods aggregating 183 days or more during the taxable year and the property giving rise to such gains is effectively connected with such fixed base, or

(ii) Is present in the other Contracting State for a period or periods aggregating 183 days or more during the taxable year.

2. In the case of gains described in paragraph 1*a.*, the provisions of Article 15 (Income from Real Property) shall apply. In the case of gains described in paragraph 1*b.*, the provisions of Article 8 (Business Profits) shall apply.

Article 17. Investment or Holding Companies

A corporation of one of the Contracting States deriving dividends, interest, royalties, or capital gains from sources within the other Contracting State shall not be entitled to the benefits of Articles 12 (Dividends), 13 (Interest), 14 (Royalties), or 16 (Capital Gains) if:

a. By reason of special measures the tax imposed on such corporation by the first-mentioned Contracting State with respect to such dividends, interest, royalties, or capital gains is substantially less than the tax generally imposed by such Contracting State on corporate profits, and

b. 25 per cent or more of the capital of such corporation is held of record or is otherwise determined, after consultation between the competent authorities of the Contracting States, to be owned directly or indirectly, by one or more persons who are not individual residents of the first-mentioned Contracting State (or, in the case of an Korean corporation, who are citizens of the United States).

Article 18. Independent Personal Services

1. Income derived by an individual who is a resident of one of the Contracting States from the performance of personal services in an independent capacity, may be taxed by that Contracting State. Except as provided in paragraph 2, such income shall be exempt from tax by the other Contracting State.

2. Income derived by an individual who is a resident of one of the Contracting States from the performance of personal services in an independent capacity in the other Contracting State may be taxed by that other Contracting State, if:

a. The individual is present in that other Contracting State for a period or periods aggregating 183 days or more in the taxable year;

b. Such income exceeds 3,000 United States dollars or its equivalent in Korean won in a taxable year; or

c. The individual maintains a fixed base in that other Contracting State for a period or periods aggregating 183 days or more in the taxable year, but only so much of his income as is attributable to such fixed base.

Article 19. Dependent Personal Services

1. Wages, salaries, and similar remuneration derived by an individual who is a resident of one of the Contracting States from labor or personal services performed as an employee, including remuneration from services performed by an officer of a corporation, may be taxed by that Contracting State. Except as provided by paragraph 2, such remuneration derived from sources within the other Contracting State may also be taxed by that other Contracting State.

2. Remuneration described in paragraph 1 derived by an individual who is a resident of one of the Contracting States shall be exempt from tax by the other Contracting State if:

a. He is present in that other Contracting State for a period or periods aggregating less than 183 days in the taxable year;

b. He is an employee of a resident of the first-mentioned Contracting State or of a permanent establishment maintained in, the first-mentioned Contracting State;

c. The remuneration is not borne as such by a permanent establishment which the employer has in that other Contracting State; and

d. Such income does not exceed 3,000 United States dollars or its equivalent in Korean won.

3. Notwithstanding paragraph 2, remuneration derived by an individual from the performance of labor or personal services as an employee aboard ships or aircraft operated by a resident of one of the Contracting States in international traffic shall be exempt from tax by the other Contracting State if such individual is a member of the regular complement of the ship or aircraft.

Article 20. Teachers

1. Where a resident of one of the Contracting States is invited by the Government of the other Contracting State, a political subdivision, or a local authority thereof, or by a university or other recognized educational institution in that other Contracting State to come to that other Contracting State for a period not expected to exceed 2 years for the purpose of teaching or engaging in research, or both, at a university or other recognized educational institution and such resident comes to that other Contracting State primarily for such purpose, his income from personal services for teaching or research at such university or educational institution shall be exempt from tax by that other Contracting State for a period not exceeding 2 years from the date of his arrival in that other Contracting State.

2. This Article shall not apply to income from research if such research is undertaken not in the public interest but primarily for the private benefit of a specific person or persons.

Article 21. Students and Trainees

1. *a.* An individual who is a resident of one of the Contracting States at the time he becomes temporarily present in the other Contracting State and who is temporarily present in that other Contracting State for the primary purpose of:

(i) Studying at a university or other recognized educational institution in that other Contracting State, or

(ii) Securing training required to qualify him to practice a profession or professional specialty, or

(iii) Studying or doing research as a recipient of a grant, allowance, or award from a governmental, religious, charitable, scientific, literary, or educational organization,

shall be exempt from tax by that other Contracting State with respect to amounts described in subparagraph *b.* for a period not exceeding 5 taxable years from the date of his arrival in that other Contracting State.

b. The amounts referred to in subparagraph *a.* are:

(i) Remittances from abroad for the purpose of his maintenance, education, study, research, or training;

(ii) The grant, allowance, or award; and

(iii) Income from personal services performed in that other Contracting State in an amount not in excess of 2,000 United States dollars or its equivalent in Korean won for any taxable year.

2. An individual who is a resident of one of the Contracting States at the time he becomes temporarily present in the other Contracting State and who is temporarily present in that other Contracting State as an employee of, or under contract with, a resident of the first-mentioned Contracting State, for the primary purpose of:

a. Acquiring technical, professional, or business experience from a person other than that resident of the first-mentioned Contracting State or other than a person related to such resident, or *b.* Studying at a university or other recognized educational institution in that other Contracting State,

shall be exempt from tax by that other Contracting State for a period not exceeding 1 year with respect to his income from personal services in an aggregate amount not in excess of 5,000 United States dollars or its equivalent in Korean won.

3. An individual who is a resident of one of the Contracting States at the time he becomes temporarily present in the other Contracting State and who is temporarily present in that other Contracting State for a period not exceeding 1 year, as a participant in a program sponsored by the Government of that other Contracting State, for the primary purpose of training, research, or study, shall be exempt from tax by that other Contracting State with respect to his income from personal services in respect of such training, research, or study performed in that other Contracting State in an aggregate amount not in excess of 10,000 United States dollars or its equivalent in Korean won.

4. The benefits provided under Article 20 (Teachers) and paragraph 1 of this Article shall, when taken together, extend only for such period of time, not to exceed 5 taxable years from the date of arrival of the individual claiming such benefits, as may reasonably or customarily be required to effectuate the purpose of the visit.

Article 22. Governmental Functions

Wages, salaries, or similar remuneration including pensions, annuities, or similar benefits, paid from public funds of one of the Contracting States to a citizen of that Contracting State for labor or personal services performed as an employee of that Contracting State or an instrumentality thereof in the discharge of governmental functions shall be exempt from tax by the other Contracting State.

Article 23. Private Pensions and Annuities

1. Except as provided in Article 22 (Governmental Functions), pensions and other similar remuneration paid to an individual who is a resident of one of the Contracting States in consideration of past employment shall be taxable only in that Contracting State.

2. Alimony and annuities paid to an individual who is a resident of one of the Contracting States shall be taxable only in that Contracting State.

3. The term 'pensions and other similar remuneration', as used in this Article, means periodic payments made *a.* by reason of retirement or death in consideration for services rendered or *b.* by way of compensation for injuries received in connection with past employment.

4. The term 'annuities', as used in this Article, means a stated sum paid periodically at stated times during life, or during a specified number of years, under an obligation to make the payments in return for adequate and full consideration (other than services rendered).

5. The term 'alimony', as used in this Article, means periodic payments made pursuant to a decree of divorce, separate maintenance agreement, or support or separation agreement which is taxable to the

recipient under the internal laws of the Contracting State of which he is a resident.

Article 24. Social Security Payments

Social security payments and other public pensions paid by one of the Contracting States to an individual who is a resident of the other Contracting State (or in the case of such payments by Korea, to an individual who is a citizen of the United States) shall be taxable only in the first-mentioned Contracting State. This Article shall not apply to payments described in Article 22 (Governmental Functions).

Article 25. Exemption from Social Security Taxes

1. The taxes imposed by Chapter 21 of the Internal Revenue Code shall not apply with respect to wages paid for services performed in Guam by a resident of Korea while in Guam on a temporary basis as a non-immigrant alien admitted to Guam pursuant to section 101(a)(15)(H)(ii) of the United States Immigration and Nationality Act (8 USC 1101(a)(15)(H)(ii).

2. The exemption provided in paragraph 1 shall continue only so long as the similar exemption provided by section 3121(b)(18) of the Internal Revenue Code.

Article 26. Diplomatic and Consular Officers

Nothing in this Convention shall affect the fiscal privileges of diplomatic and consular officials under the general rules of international law or under the provisions of special agreements.

Article 27. Mutual Agreement Procedure

1. Where a resident of one of the Contracting States considers that the action of one or both of the Contracting States results or will result for him in taxation not in accordance with this Convention, he may, notwithstanding the remedies provided by the national laws of the Contracting States, present his case to the competent authority of the Contracting State of which he is a resident. Should the resident's claim be considered to have merit by the competent authority of the Contracting State to which the claim is made, it shall endeavor to come to an agreement with the competent authority of the other Contracting State with a view to the avoiding of taxation contrary to the provisions of this Convention.

2. The competent authorities of the Contracting States shall endeavor to resolve by mutual agreement any difficulties or doubts arising as to the application of this Convention. In particular, the competent authorities of the Contracting States may agree:

a. To the same attribution of industrial or commercial profits to a resident of one of the Contracting States and its permanent establishment situated in the other Contracting State;

b. To the same allocation of income, deductions, credits, or allowances between a person subject to the taxing jurisdiction of one of the Contracting States and any related person;

c. To the same determination of the source of particular items of income;

d. To the uniform accounting for income and deductions; or

e. To the same meaning of any term used in this Convention.

3. The competent authorities of the Contracting States may communicate with each other directly for the purpose of reaching an agreement in the sense of this Article. When it seems advisable for the purpose of reaching an agreement, the competent authorities may meet together for an oral exchange of opinions.

4. In the event that the competent authorities reach such an agreement, taxes shall be imposed on such income, and refund or credit of taxes shall be allowed, by the Contracting States in accordance with such agreement.

Article 28. Exchange of Information

1. The competent authorities shall exchange such information as is necessary for carrying out the provisions of this Convention or for the prevention of fraud or for the administration of statutory provisions concerning taxes to which this Convention applies provided the information is of a class that can be obtained under the laws and administrative practices of each Contracting State with respect to its own taxes.

2. Any information so exchanged shall be treated as secret, except that such information may be:

a. Disclosed to any person concerned with, or

b. Made part of a public record with respect to,

the assessment, collection, or enforcement of, or litigation with respect to, the taxes to which this Convention applies.

3. No information shall be exchanged which would be contrary to public policy.

4. If specifically requested by the competent authority of one of the Contracting States, the competent authority of the other Contracting State shall provide information under this Article in the form of depositions of witnesses and copies of unedited original documents (including books, papers, statements, records, accounts, or writings), to the same extent such depositions and documents can be obtained under the laws and administrative practices of each Contracting State with respect to its own taxes.

5. The exchange of information shall be either on a routine basis or on request with reference to particular cases. The competent authorities of the Contracting States may agree on the list of information which shall be furnished on a routine basis.

6. The competent authorities of the Contracting States shall notify each other of any amendments of the tax laws referred to in paragraph 1 of Article 1 (Taxes Covered) and of the adoption of any taxes referred to in paragraph 2 of Article 1 (Taxes Covered) by transmitting the texts of any amendments or new statutes at least once a year.

7. The competent authorities of the Contracting States shall notify each other of the publication by their respective Contracting States of any material concerning the application of this Convention, whether

in the form of regulations, rulings, or judicial decisions by transmitting the texts of any such materials at least once a year.

Article 29. Extension to Territories

1. Either one of the Contracting States may, at any time while this Convention continues in force, by a written notification given to the other Contracting State through diplomatic channels, declare its desire that the operation of this Convention, either in whole or in part or with such modifications as may be found necessary for special application in a particular case, shall extend to all or any of the areas (to which this Convention is not otherwise applicable) for whose international relations it is responsible and which impose taxes substantially similar in character to those which are the subject of this Convention. When the other Contracting State has, by a written communication through diplomatic channels, signified to the first-mentioned Contracting State that such notification is accepted in respect of such area or areas, and the notification and communication have been ratified and instruments of ratification exchanged, this Convention, in whole or in part, or with such modifications as may be found necessary for special application in a particular case, as specified in the notification, shall apply to the area or areas named in the notification and shall enter into force and effect on and after the date or dates specified therein. None of the provisions of this Convention shall apply to any such area in the absence of such acceptance and exchange of instruments of ratification in respect of that area.

2. At any time after the date of entry into force of an extension under paragraph 1, either of the Contracting States may, by 6 months' prior notice of termination given to the other Contracting State through diplomatic channels, terminate the application of this Convention to any area to which it has been extended under paragraph 1, and in such event this Convention shall cease to apply and have force and effect, beginning on or after the first day of January next following the expiration of the 6-month period, to the area or areas named therein, but without affecting its continued application to the United States, Korea, or any other area to which it has been extended under paragraph 1.

3. In the application of this Convention in relation to any area to which it is extended by notification by the United States or Korea, reference to the 'United States' or 'Korea', as the case may be, shall be construed as referring to that area.

4. The termination in respect of the United States or Korea of this Convention under Article 32 (Termination) shall, unless otherwise expressly agreed by both Contracting States, terminate the application of this Convention to any area to which the Convention has been extended under this Article by the United States or Korea.

Article 30. Assistance in Collection

1. Each of the Contracting States shall endeavor to collect on behalf of the other Contracting State such taxes imposed by that other Contracting State as will ensure that any exemption or reduced rate of tax

granted under this Convention by that other Contracting State shall not be enjoyed by persons not entitled to such benefits.

2. In no case shall this Article be construed so as to impose upon one of the Contracting States the obligation to carry out measures at variance with the laws, or administrative practices, or public policy of either Contracting State with respect to the collection of its own taxes.

Article 31. Entry into Force

This Convention shall be ratified and instruments of ratification shall be exchanged at Washington as soon as possible. It shall enter into force on the thirtieth day following the exchange of instruments of ratification and shall then have effect for the first time:

a. As respects the rate of withholding taxes and Article 25 (Exemption from Social Security Taxes), to amounts paid on or after the first day of the second month following the date on which this Convention enters into force;

b. As respects other taxes, to taxable years beginning on or after January 1 of the year following the date on which this Convention enters into force.

Article 32. Termination

This Convention shall remain in force until terminated by one of the Contracting States. Either Contracting State may terminate the Convention at any time after 5 years from the date on which this Convention enters into force provided that at least 6 months' prior notice of termination has been given through diplomatic channels. In such event, the Convention shall cease to have force and effect as respects income of taxable years beginning (or, in the case of withholding taxes and social security taxes, payments made) on or after January 1 next following the expiration of the 6-month period.

Done at Seoul in duplicate in the English and Korean languages this 4th day of June 1976.

Convention between the United States of America and the Grand Duchy of Luxembourg with Respect to Taxes on Income and Property, concluded in Washington on December 18, 1962.

The President of the United States of America and Her Royal Highness the Grand Duchess of Luxembourg, desiring to conclude a convention for the avoidance of double taxation of income, the prevention of fiscal evasion, and the promotion of trade and investment, have appointed for that purpose as their respective Plenipotentiaries:

The President of the United States of America: Dean Rusk, Secretary of State of the United States of America, and

Her Royal Highness the Grand Duchess of Luxembourg: Georges Heisbourg, Ambassador Extraordinary and Plenipotentiary of the Grand Duchy of Luxembourg at Washington

who, having communicated to each other their full powers, found in good and due form, have agreed upon the following Articles:

Article I

1. The taxes which are the subject of the present Convention are:

a. In case of the United States:
the Federal income tax, including surtax.

b. In the case of Luxembourg:

(i) The income taxes on individuals and corporations, the tax on fees of directors of corporations, and the communal tax on commercial profits, and

(ii) The wealth tax and the communal taxes on invested capital and land.

2. The present Convention shall also apply to substantially similar taxes which are subsequently imposed in addition to, or in place of, the existing taxes.

3. The competent authorities of the Contracting States shall notify each other of the adoption of new taxes or of substantial changes, or the abolition of, existing taxes covered by the present Convention.

Article II

1. In the present Convention, unless the context otherwise requires:

a. The term 'United States' means the United States of America, and when used in a geographical sense means the States thereof and the District of Columbia;

b. The term 'Luxembourg' when used in a geographical sense means only the Grand Duchy of Luxembourg;

c. The term 'enterprise of one of the Contracting States' means, as the case may be, 'United States enterprise' or 'Luxembourg enterprise';

d. The term 'United States enterprise' means an industrial or commercial enterprise or undertaking carried on by a citizen or resident (including an individual in his individual or fiduciary capacity or as a member of a partnership) of the United States or by a United States corporation; the term 'United States corporation' means a corporation or other entity created or organized under the laws of the United States or of any State or Territory of the United States;

e. The term 'Luxembourg enterprise' means an industrial or commercial enterprise or undertaking carried on by a resident of Luxembourg (including an individual in his individual capacity or as a member of a partnership) or by a Luxembourg corporation; the term 'Luxembourg corporation' means a juridical person or an entity treated as a juridical person for tax purposes under the laws of Luxembourg if such person or entity has its business management or seat in Luxembourg but does not include a United States corporation;

f. (i) The term 'permanent establishment' means a fixed place of business in which the business of an enterprise is wholly or partly carried on;

(ii) A permanent establishment shall include especially:

(A) a place of management;

(B) a branch;

(C) an office;

(D) a factory;

(E) a workshop;

(F) a mine, quarry, or other place of extraction of natural resources; and

(G) a building site, or construction or assembly project, which exists for more than six months;

(iii) The term 'permanent establishment' shall be deemed not to include:

(A) the use of facilities solely for the purpose of storage, display or delivery of goods or merchandise belonging to the enterprise;

(B) the maintenance of a stock of goods or merchandise belonging to the enterprise solely for the purpose of storage, display or delivery;

(C) the maintenance of a stock of goods or merchandise belonging to the enterprise solely for the purpose of processing by another enterprise;

(D) the maintenance of a fixed place of business solely for the purpose of purchasing goods or merchandise, or for collecting information, for the enterprise;

(E) the maintenance of a fixed place of business solely for the purpose of advertising, for the supply of information, for scientific research, or for similar activities, which have a preparatory or auxiliary character for the enterprise;

(iv) A person acting in one of the Contracting States on behalf of an enterprise of the other Contracting State, other than an agent of an independent status to whom subdivision (v) applies, shall be deemed to be a permanent establishment in the first-mentioned State if he has, and habitually exercises in that State, an authority to conclude contracts in the name of the enterprise, unless his activities are limited to the purchase of goods or merchandise for the enterprise;

(v) An enterprise of one of the Contracting States shall not be deemed to have a permanent establishment in the other State merely because it carries on business in that other State through a broker, general commission agent, or any other agent of an independent status, where such persons are acting in the ordinary course of their business;

(vi) The fact that a corporation of one of the Contracting States controls or is controlled by (A) a corporation of the other State, or (B) a corporation which carries on business in that other State (whether through a permanent establishment or otherwise), shall not of itself constitute either corporation a permanent establishment of the other;

g. The term 'competent authority' or 'competent authorities' means, in the case of the United States, the Secretary of the Treasury or his delegate and, in the case of Luxembourg, the Minister of Finance or his delegate; and

h. The terms 'resident of one of the Contracting States' and 'resident of the other Contracting State' mean a resident of the United States or a resident of Luxembourg, as the context requires. An individual shall be considered to be a resident of Luxembourg if under its law his income from sources within and from sources without Luxembourg is subject to income tax. An individual present in one of the Contracting States solely for one of the purposes specified in Articles XIII and XIV of the present Convention shall not be considered a resident of that State merely because of his presence there for that purpose.

2. In the application of the provisions of the present Convention by either of the Contracting States, any term which is not defined in the present Convention shall, unless the context otherwise requires, have the meaning which that term has under the laws of such State relating to the taxes which are the subject of the present Convention.

3. A resident of corporation of one of the Contracting States, or an enterprise of such State, shall be considered to have a permanent establishment in the other State for purposes of Articles III, VII, VIII, and IX if such person has a permanent establishment in that State at any time during the taxable year in which the income is received.

Article III

1. The industrial or commercial profits of an enterprise of one of the Contracting States shall be taxable only by that State unless the enterprise carries on business in the other Contracting State through a permanent establishment situated therein. If the enterprise carries on business as aforesaid, tax may be imposed by the other State on the industrial or commercial profits of the enterprise but only on so much of them as is attributable to that permanent establishment. In applying the preceding sentence for purposes of the United States tax, all industrial or commercial profits of the enterprise from sources within the United States shall be deemed to be attributable to the permanent establishment.

2. Where an enterprise of one of the Contracting States carries on business in the other Contracting State through a permanent establishment situated therein, there shall in each State be attributed to such permanent establishment the industrial or commercial profits which it might be expected to make if it were a distinct and separate enterprise engaged in the same or similar activities under the same or similar conditions and dealing independently with the enterprise of which it is a permanent establishment.

3. In the determination of the industrial or commercial profits of a permanent establishment, there shall be allowed as deductions expenses which are incurred for the purpose of the permanent establishment, including executive and general administrative expenses so incurred, whether in the State in which the permanent establishment is situated or elsewhere.

4. No profits shall be attributed to a permanent establishment by reason of the mere purchase by that permanent establishment of goods or merchandise for the enterprise.

Article IV

Where:

a. an enterprise of one of the Contracting States participates directly or indirectly in the management, control, or capital of an enterprise of the other Contracting State, or

b. the same persons participate directly or indirectly in the management, control, or capital of an enterprise of one of the Contracting States and an enterprise of the other Contracting State,

and in either case conditions are made or imposed between the two enterprises in their commercial or financial relations which differ from those which would be made between independent enterprises, then any profits which would, but for those conditions, have accrued to one of the enterprises may be included in the profits of that enterprise and taxed accordingly.

Article V

Income which an enterprise of one of the Contracting States derives from the operation of ships or aircraft registered in that State shall be exempt from taxation by the other Contracting State.

Article VI

Income from real property, including gains derived from the sale or exchange of such property and interest on debts (other than bonds) secured by mortgages on real property, and royalties in respect of the operation of mines, quarries, or other natural resources shall be taxable, except as otherwise provided in Article XVI, only by the Contracting State in which such property, mines, quarries, or other natural resources are situated; provided that a resident or corporation of one of the Contracting States deriving any such income from sources within the other Contracting State may elect for any taxable year to be subject to such other State's tax on such income on a net income basis.

Article VII

1. Royalties, rentals, and similar payments derived as consideration for the use of, or the privilege of using,

a. copyrights, artistic or scientific works, patents, designs, plans, secret processes or formulae, trademarks, motion picture films, films or tapes for radio or television broadcasting, or other like property or rights, or

b. industrial, commercial or scientific equipment, knowledge, experience, or skill, or know-how

and received by a resident or corporation of one of the Contracting States not having a permanent establishment in the other Contracting State shall be exempt from tax by such other State.

Article VIII

Interest on bonds, notes, debentures, securities, or any other form of indebtedness (exclusive of interest on debts, other than bonds, secured by mortgages on real property) received by a resident or corporation of one of the Contracting States not having a permanent establishment in the other Contracting State shall be exempt from tax by such other State.

Article IX

1. Dividends received from sources within one of the Contracting States by a resident or corporation of the other Contracting State not having a permanent establishment in the former State shall be subject to tax by the former State:

a. at a rate which is equal to 50 per cent per cent of the statutory rate of tax otherwise imposed on such dividends by the former State, or

b. when the recipient is a corporation, at the rate of 5 per cent if

(i) during the part of the payer corporation's taxable year which precedes the date of payment of the dividend and during the whole of its prior taxable year, at least 50 per cent of the voting stock of the payer corporation was owned by the recipient corporation either alone or in association with not more than three other corporations of the other State and at least ten per cent of the voting stock of the payer corporation was owned by each such corporation of the other State; and

(ii) not more than 25 per cent of the gross income of the payer corporation (other than a corporation the principal business of which is the making of loans) for such prior taxable year was derived from interest and dividends received from its subsidiary corporations.

2. The term 'statutory rate', as used in this Article, means, in the case of United States tax, the rate of tax imposed by section 871(a) or section 881(a) Internal Revenue Code of 1954, as in effect on January 1 of the year in which the instruments of ratification are exchanged, and, in the case of Luxembourg tax, the rate of tax imposed by Article 4 of Decree Law of August 7, 1945, as amended by Article 1 of the Law of November 27, 1952.

3. The term 'subsidiary corporation', as used in this Article, means any corporation of which at least 50 per cent of the total voting power of all classes of stock entitled to vote, or of the total value of all classes of stock, is owned by the payer corporation.

Article X

1. Dividends and interest paid by a Luxembourg corporation to a person other than a citizen, resident, or corporation of the United States shall be exempt from tax by the United States.

2. Dividends and interest paid by a United States corporation to a person other than *(a)* a resident of Luxembourg or *(b)* a corporation having its business management or seat in Luxembourg shall be exempt from tax by Luxembourg.

Article XI

1. *a.* Wages, salaries and similar compensation, and pensions, annuities, or similar benefits paid by Luxembourg, its political subdivisions, or its compulsory social security funds to an individual (other than an individual who is a citizen of the United States or has been admitted to the United States for permanent residence therein) for services rendered to Luxembourg or to any of its political subdivisions in the discharge of governmental functions shall be exempt from tax by the United States.

b. Wages, salaries and similar compensation, and pensions, annuities, or similar benefits paid by, or from public funds of, the United States or the political subdivisions thereof to an individual (other than a citizen of Luxembourg) for services rendered to the United States or to any political subdivisions in the discharge of governmental functions shall be exempt from tax by Luxembourg.

2. Private pensions and life annuities which are from sources within one of the Contracting States and are paid to individuals who are residents of the other Contracting State shall be exempt from tax by the former State.

3. The term 'life annuities' as used in paragraph 2, means a stated sum payable periodically at stated times during life, or during a specified number of years, under an obligation to make the payments in return for adequate and full consideration.

Article XII

1. Compensation for labor or personal services (other than fees of directors of corporations) performed in the United States during the taxable year by a resident of Luxembourg shall be exempt from tax by the United States if he is temporarily present in the United States for a period or periods not exceeding a total of 180 days during the taxable year and the compensation:

a. is received for labor or personal services performed as an employee of a resident or corporation of Luxembourg, or of a permanent establishment within Luxembourg of a United States enterprise, and the burden of such compensation is borne by such resident, corporation, or establishment; or

b. does not exceed $3,000.

2. The exemption of paragraph 1 shall apply, *mutatis mutandis*, to tax by Luxembourg upon the compensation for labor or personal services performed in Luxembourg during the taxable year by a resident of the United States.

3. Compensation for labor or personal services (other than fees of directors of corporations) performed in the United States (whether or not put to use in Luxembourg) by a resident of the United States shall be exempt from tax by Luxembourg.

4. The exemption of paragraph 3 shall apply, *mutatis mutandis*, to tax by the United States upon compensation for labor or personal services performed in Luxembourg.

Article XIII

1. A resident of one of the Contracting States who, at the invitation of a university, college, school, or other recognized educational institution situated in the other Contracting State, is temporarily present in the other State solely for the purpose of teaching, or engaging in research, or both, at that educational institution shall, for a period not exceeding two years from the date of his arrival in the other State, be exempt from tax by the other State on his remuneration for such teaching or research.

2. No exemption shall be granted under this Article with respect to any remuneration for research carried on for the benefit of any person other than the educational institution which extended the invitation referred to in paragraph 1.

Article XIV

1. A resident of one of the Contracting States who is temporarily present in the other Contracting State solely:

a. as a student at a university, college, school, or other recognized educational institution situated in the other State, or

b. as a business apprentice for a period not exceeding one year, or

c. as the recipient of a grant, allowance, or award which is for the primary purpose of study or research from a religious, charitable, scientific, literary, or educational organization,

shall be exempt from tax by the other State with respect to his remuneration from abroad for employment or remittances from abroad for the purposes of his maintenance, education, or training.

2. A resident of one of the Contracting States who is temporarily present in the other Contracting State for a period not exceeding one year, as an employee of, or under contract with, an enterprise of the former State or an organization of the former State referred to in paragraph 1*c.*, solely to acquire technical, professional, or business experience from a person other than that enterprise or organization shall be exempt from tax by the other State with respect to his remuneration from abroad for that period (including remuneration, if any, from an

employer abroad), in an amount not in excess of $5,000 or its equivalent in Luxembourg currency.

3. A resident of one of the Contracting States who is temporarily present in the other Contracting State for a period not exceeding one year solely for the purpose of training, research, or study, under arrangements with the Government of the other State, shall be exempt from tax by the other State with respect to his remuneration for services directly related to such training, research, or study (including any remuneration from his employer abroad) in an amount not in excess of $10,000 or its equivalent in Luxembourg currency.

4. An individual who qualifies for exemption under more than one provision of the preceding paragraphs of this Article, or under one of the preceding paragraphs and Article XII or Article XIII, shall be entitled to claim the exemption most favorable to him.

Article XV

The present Convention shall not apply to the income of any holding company entitled to any special tax benefit under Luxembourg Law of July 31, 1929, and Decree Law of December 27, 1937, or under any similar law subsequently enacted, or to any income derived from such companies by any shareholder thereof. In the event that substantially similar benefits are granted to other corporations under any law enacted by Luxembourg after the date of signature of the present Convention, the provisions of the present Convention shall not apply to the income of any such corporation or to any income derived from such corporation by any shareholder thereof. The expression 'substantially similar benefits' shall be deemed not to include tax reduction or exemption granted to any corporation in respect of dividends derived from another corporation, 25 per cent or more of the stock of which is owned by the recipient corporation.

Article XVI

1. It is agreed that double taxation of income shall be avoided in the following manner:

a. The United States, in determining the income tax of individuals who are citizens or residents of the United States or of its corporations may, regardless of any other provision of the present Convention, include in the basis upon which such tax is imposed all items of income taxable under the revenue laws of the United States as if the present Convention had not come into effect. The United States shall, however, deduct from its tax so calculated the amount of the Luxembourg income taxes specified in paragraph 1*b*.(i) of Article I. Except as otherwise provided in the present Convention, the amount of Luxembourg tax thus to be deducted shall be determined in accordance with the revenue laws of the United States. It is agreed that by virtue of the provisions of subparagraph *b*. of this paragraph Luxembourg satisfies the similar credit requirement prescribed by section 901(b)(3), Internal Revenue Code of 1954.

b. Luxembourg, in determining the income taxes and the tax on fees of directors of corporations in the case of its residents or of corporations having their business management or seat in Luxembourg, may, regardless of any other provision of the present Convention, include in the basis upon which such taxes are imposed all items of income taxable under the tax laws of Luxembourg as if the present Convention had not come into effect. Luxembourg shall, however, deduct from its taxes so calculated the amount of the income tax of the United States upon income from sources therein, but the amount so to be deducted shall not exceed that proportion of such taxes of Luxembourg which the income from sources within the United States and taxable by Luxembourg bears to the entire income subject to the taxes of Luxembourg.

c. This paragraph shall not be construed to deny the benefits conferred by Articles XI.1 and XX.3 of the present Convention.

2. Luxembourg, in determining the following taxes of its residents or of corporations having their business management or seat in Luxembourg, shall exclude from the basis upon which such taxes are imposed:

a. in the case of the communal land tax, any real property situated in the United States;

b. in the case of the communal tax on commercial profits and invested capital, the profits and capital of a permanent establishment situated in the United States; and

c. in the case of the wealth tax,

(i) any real property situated in the United States and all accessories appertaining thereto,

(ii) all debts (other than bonds) secured by real property situated in the United States,

(iii) the invested capital of a permanent establishment situated in the United States and not appertaining to a maritime shipping or air transport undertaking, and

(iv) the invested capital of a maritime shipping or air transport undertaking, but only in that proportion which the income of such undertaking from sources within the United States bears to its entire income,

provided, however, that Luxembourg reserves the right, in the determination of the rate of its wealth tax, to take into account all items excluded from the tax base pursuant to this subparagraph.

3. Luxembourg, in determining the wealth tax and the communal taxes on invested capital and lands of citizens, residents, or corporations of the United States, shall not tax the property of such persons consisting of:

a. real property and all accessories appertaining thereto,

b. debts secured by mortgages on real property, and

c. any property used by commercial or industrial enterprises, including maritime shipping or air transport enterprises,

unless it is entitled under other provisions of the present Convention to tax the income derived from such property.

Article XVII

For the purposes of the present Convention:

a. Industrial or commercial profits attributable to a permanent establishment which an enterprise of one of the Contracting States has in the other Contracting State shall be treated as income from sources within such other State.

b. Gains, profits, and income (other than profits described in subparagraph *a.*) from the purchase and sale of personal property shall be treated as income from sources within the Contracting State in which the property is sold.

c. Gains, profits, and income derived by a taxpayer from the sale in one of the Contracting States of goods produced in the other Contracting State by such taxpayer shall, to the extent not otherwise allocable under other provisions of the present Convention, be treated as derived in part from the State in which produced and in part from the State in which sold.

d. Income which is exempt from tax by one of the Contracting States pursuant to Article V of the present Convention shall be treated as income from sources within the other Contracting State.

e. Income from real property, including gains derived from the sale or exchange of such property and interest on debts (other than bonds) secured by mortgages on real property, and royalties in respect of the operation of mines, quarries, or other natural resources shall be treated as income from sources within the Contracting State in which such real property, mines, quarries, or other natural resources are situated.

f. Royalties, rentals, and similar payments for the use of, or for the privilege of using, in one of the Contracting State of copyrights, artistic or scientific works, patents, designs, plans, secret processes or formulae, trademarks, motion picture films, films or tapes for radio or television broadcasting, or other like property or rights, or industrial, commercial, or scientific equipment, knowledge, experience, skill, or know-how shall be treated as income from sources within that State.

g. Interest (exclusive of interest on debts, other than bonds, secured by mortgages on real property) paid by one of the Contracting States, including any political subdivision thereof, or by a resident, corporation, or enterprise of one of the Contracting States shall be treated as income from sources within that State.

h. Dividends paid by a corporation of one of the Contracting States shall be treated as income from sources within that State.

i. Compensation for labor or personal services, including compensation or remuneration from the practice of the liberal professions or from public entertainment but not including fees described in subparagraph *j.*, shall be treated as income from sources within the Contracting State where the labor or personal services are performed.

j. Directors' fees paid by a corporation of one of the Contracting States shall be treated as income from sources within that State.

Article XVIII

1. The competent authorities of the Contracting States shall exchange such information, being information available under the respective taxation laws of the Contracting States, as is necessary for carrying out the provisions of the present Convention or for the prevention of fraud or the like in relation to the taxes which are the subject of the present Convention. Any information so exchanged shall be treated as secret and shall not be disclosed to any persons other than those concerned with the assessment or collection of the taxes which are the subject of the present Convention. No information shall be exchanged which would disclose any trade, business, industrial, or professional secret, or any trade process.

2. Each of the Contracting States may collect such taxes imposed by the other Contracting State as though such taxes were the taxes of the former State as will ensure that any exemption or reduced rate of tax granted under the present Convention by the other State shall not be enjoyed by persons not entitled to such benefits.

3. In no case shall the provisions of this Article be construed so as to imposed upon either of the Conventions the obligation to carry out administrative measures at variance with the regulations and practice of either Contracting State or which would be contrary to its sovereignty, security, or public policy or to supply particulars which are not procurable under its own legislation or that of the State making application.

Article XIX

1. Where a taxpayer shows proof that the action of the tax authorities of the Contracting States has resulted, or will result, in double taxation contrary to the provisions of the present Convention, he shall be entitled to present his case to the State of which he is a citizen or resident, or, if the taxpayer is a corporation of one of the Contracting States, to that State. Should the taxpayer's claim be deemed worthy of consideration, the competent authority of the State to which the claim is made shall endeavour to come to an agreement with the competent authority of the other State with a view to avoidance of the double taxation.

2. For the settlement of difficulties or doubts in the interpretation or application of the present Convention or in respect of its relation to Conventions of the Contracting States with third States the competent authorities of the Contracting States shall endeavor to reach a mutual agreement as quickly as possible.

Article XX

1. The provisions of the present Convention shall not be construed to restrict in any manner the right of diplomatic or consular officers to additional exemptions now enjoyed or which may hereafter be granted to such officers.

2. The provisions of the present Convention shall not be construed to restrict in any manner any exclusion, exemption, deduction, credit

or other allowance now or hereafter accorded *(a)* by the laws of one of the Contracting States in the determination of tax imposed by that State or *(b)* by any other agreement between the Contracting States.

3. The citizens of one of the Contracting States shall not, while residents of the other Contracting State, be subject therein to other or more burdensome taxes than are the citizens of such other State who are residents of its territory. The term 'citizens', as used in this Article, includes all juridical persons, partnerships, and associations created or organized under the laws in force in the respective Contracting States. In this Article the word 'taxes' means taxes of every kind or description, whether national, State, communal, or municipal.

4. The provisions of the law of Luxembourg granting a carry-over of losses to taxpayers domiciled therein shall apply with respect to the taxation of a permanent establishment, which is maintained in Luxembourg by a resident or corporation of the United States, under the same conditions and in the same manner as in the case of taxpayers who are domiciled in Luxembourg.

Article XXI

1. The competent authorities of the two Contracting States may prescribe regulations necessary to carry into effect the present Convention within the respective States.

2. The competent authorities of the two Contracting States may communicate with each other directly for the purpose of giving effect to the provisions of the present Convention.

Article XXII

1. The present Convention shall be ratified and the instruments of ratification shall be exchanged at Luxembourg as soon as possible. It shall have effect for taxable years beginning on or after the first day of January of the calendar year in which such exchange takes place.

2. The present Convention shall continue effective for a period of five years, beginning with the calendar year in which the exchange of the instruments of ratification takes place and indefinitely after that period, but may be terminated by either of the Contracting States at the end of the five-year period or any time thereafter, provided that at least six months' prior notice of termination has been given; and, in such event, the present Convention shall cease to be effective for taxable years beginning on or after the first day of January next following the expiration of the six-month period.

Done in duplicate, in the English and French languages, at Washington, the two texts having equal authenticity, this 18th day of December, 1962.

Convention between the United States of America and the Kingdom of the Netherlands with respect to taxes on income and certain other taxes, concluded in Washington on April 29, 1948, as amended by the Protocol of December 30, 1965.

The Government of the United States of America and the Government of the Kingdom of the Netherlands, desiring to conclude a convention for the avoidance of double taxation and the prevention of fiscal evasion with respect to taxes on income and certain other taxes, have appointed for that purpose as their respective Plenipotentiaries:

The Government of the United States of America: Mr. George C. Marshall, Secretary of State, and

The Government of the Kingdom of the Netherlands: Mr. E.N. van Kleffens, Ambassador Extraordinary and Plenipotentiary of the Kingdom of the Netherlands,

who, having communicated to each other their full powers, found in good and due form, have agreed upon the following Articles:

Article I

1. The taxes which are the subject of the present Convention are:

a. In case of the United States, the Federal income taxes.

b. In the case of the Netherlands:

(i) for the application of the provisions of the Convention other than Article XX, the income tax and the Netherlands taxes credited against it, the corporation tax and the Netherlands taxes credited against it, the property tax, and the tax on fees of directors and managers of corporations; and

(ii) for the application of Articles XX to XXVIII inclusive (except Articles XXIV and XXVII), the capital accretions tax and the extraordinary capital tax.

2. The present Convention shall also apply to any other taxes of a substantially similar character imposed by either Contracting State subsequently to the date of signature of the present Convention, or, by the government of any overseas part of the Kingdom (in the case of the Netherlands) or overseas territory (in the case of the United States) to which the present Convention is extended under Article XXVII, subsequently to the date of the notification of extension.

3. In the event of appreciable changes in the fiscal laws of either of the Contracting States the competent authorities of the Contracting State will consult together.

Article II

1. In the present Convention, unless the context otherwise requires:

a. The term 'United States' means the United States of America, and when used in a geographical sense means the States thereof and the District of Columbia.

b. The term 'Netherlands' means only the Kingdom of the Netherlands in Europe.

c. The term 'United States corporation' means a corporation, association or other organization or juridical entity created in the United States or under the laws of the United States or of any State or territory of the United States.

d. The term 'Netherlands corporation' means a corporation, association or other organization or juridical entity created in the Netherlands or under the laws of the Netherlands.

e. The terms 'corporation of one Contracting State' and 'corporation of the other Contracting State' means a United States corporation or a Netherlands corporation, as the context requires.

f. The term 'United States enterprise' means an industrial or commercial enterprise or undertaking carried on in the United States by a citizen or resident of the United States or by a United States corporation.

g. The term 'Netherlands enterprise' means an industrial or commercial enterprise or undertaking carried on in the Netherlands by a citizen or resident of the Netherlands or by a Netherlands corporation.

h. The terms 'enterprise of one of the Contracting States' and 'enterprise of the other Contracting State' means a United States enterprise or a Netherlands enterprise, as the context requires.

i. (A) The term 'permanent establishment' means a fixed place of business in which the business of an enterprise of one of the Contracting States is wholly or partly carried on.

(B) A permanent establishment shall include especially:

(i) a branch;

(ii) an office;

(iii) a factory;

(iv) a workshop;

(v) a mine, quarry, or other place of extraction of natural resources;

(vi) a building site or construction or assembly project which exists for more than twelve months.

(C) Notwithstanding sub-paragraph (i)(A) of this paragraph a permanent establishment shall not be deemed to include one or more of the following activities:

(i) the use of facilities for the purpose of storage, display or delivery of goods or merchandise belonging to the enterprise;

(ii) the maintenance of a stock of goods or merchandise belonging to the enterprise for the purpose of storage, display or delivery;

(iii) the maintenance of a stock of goods or merchandise belonging to the enterprise for the purpose of processing by another enterprise;

(iv) the maintenance of a fixed place of business for the purpose of purchasing goods or merchandise, or for collecting information, for the enterprise;

(v) the maintenance of a fixed place of business for the purpose of advertising, for the supply of information, for scientific research or for similar activities, if they have a preparatory or auxiliary character for the enterprise.

(D) Even if an enterprise of one of the Contracting States does not have a permanent establishment in the other State under sub-paragraph (i)(A) to (C) of this paragraph, nevertheless it shall be deemed to have a permanent establishment in the latter State if it is engaged in trade or business in that State through an agent who has an authority to conclude contracts in the name of the enterprise and regularly exercises that authority in that State, unless the exercise of authority is limited to the purchase of goods or merchandise for the account of the enterprise.

(E) An enterprise of one of the Contracting States shall not be deemed to have a permanent establishment in the other State merely because it is engaged in trade or business in that other State through a broker, general commission agent, or any other agent of an independent status, where such persons are acting in the ordinary course of their business.

(F) The fact that a resident or a corporation of one of the Contracting States controls, is controlled by, or is under common control with:

(i) a corporation of the other State;

(ii) a corporation which engages in trade or business in that other State (whether through a permanent establishment or otherwise)

shall not be taken into account in determining whether such resident or corporation has a permanent establishment in the other State.

2. In the application of the provisions of the present Convention by either of the Contracting States, any term which is not defined in the present Convention shall, unless the context otherwise requires, have the meaning which that term has under the laws of such Contracting States relating to the taxes which are the subject of the present Convention.

Article III

1. Industrial or commercial profits of an enterprise of one of the Contracting States shall be exempt from tax by the other State unless the enterprise has a permanent establishment in such other State. If the enterprise has such a permanent establishment, tax may be imposed by such other State on the industrial or commercial profits of the enterprise, but only on so much of them as are attributable to the permanent establishment or are derived within such other State from the sale of goods or merchandise of the same kind as those sold, or from other business transactions of the same kind as those effected, through the permanent establishment.

2. Where an enterprise of one of the Contracting States has a permanent establishment in the other State, there shall in each Contracting State be attributed to such permanent establishment the industrial or commercial profits which it might be expected to derive if it were an independent enterprise engaged in the same or similar activities under the same or similar conditions and dealing at arm's length with the enterprise of which it is a permanent establishment. Where the enterprise, in addition to the profits derived through the permanent establishment, derives other profits of the kind referred to in paragraph 1, such other profits shall be treated as if they were derived through the permanent establishment.

3. In determining the industrial or commercial profits of an enterprise of one of the Contracting States which are taxable in the other State in accordance with paragraphs 1 and 2, there shall be allowed as deductions all expenses, wherever incurred, which are reasonably connected with the profits so taxable, including executive and general administrative expenses.

4. No profits shall be attributed to a permanent establishment merely by reason of the purchase by that permanent establishment or by the enterprise itself, of goods or merchandise for the account of the enterprise.

5. The term 'industrial or commercial profits' means income derived from the active conduct of a trade or business, but does not include income dealt with in Article VII (dividends), Article VIII (interest), Article IX (royalties), Articles V and X (income from real property and natural resources), Article XI (capital gains) and Article XVI (personal services), other than income described in Articles VII, paragraph 3, VIII, paragraph 2, IX, paragraph 3 and XI, paragraph 2. The term 'industrial or commercial profits' includes profits derived by an enterprise from the furnishing of services of employees or other personnel.

Article IV

1. Where a resident or corporation of a Contracting State and any other person are related and where such related persons make arrangements or impose conditions between themselves which are different from those which would be made between independent persons, then any income which, but for those arrangements or conditions, would have accrued to such resident of corporation, may be included in the income of such resident or corporation for purposes of the present Convention and taxed accordingly.

2. *a.* A person other than a corporation is related to a corporation if such person participates directly or indirectly in the management, control, or capital of the corporation.

b. A corporation is related to another corporation if either participates directly or indirectly in the management, control, or capital of the other, or if any person or persons participate directly or indirectly in the management, control, or capital of both corporations.

Article V

Income from real property (including gains derived from the sale of such property, but not including interest from mortgages or bonds secured by real property) and royalties from the operation of mines, quarries, or other natural resources may be taxed in the Contracting State in which such real property is situated.

Article VI

1. Income which an enterprise of one of the Contracting States derives from the operation of ships or aircraft registered in that State shall be taxable only in the State in which such ships or aircraft are registered. Income derived by such an enterprise from the operation of ships or aircraft not so registered shall be subject to the provisions of Article III.

2. The present Convention shall be deemed to suspend, for the duration of the Convention as between the parties to which this Article applies, the provisions of the arrangement effected by exchange of notes between the United States and the Netherlands, dated September 13, October 19, and November 27, 1926, providing for relief from double income taxation on shipping profits.

3. In the event that the application of this Article is extended to the Netherlands Indies in accordance with Article XXVII, the exchange of notes between the United States and the Netherlands, dated March 8, May 23, and November 8, 1939, relating to the applications to the Netherlands Indies of the arrangement referred to in paragraph 2 of this Article, shall be deemed to be suspended for so long as this Article continues to be applicable with respect to the Netherlands Indies.

Article VII

1. Dividends paid by a corporation of one of the Contracting States to a resident or corporation of the other Contracting State shall be taxed as follows in the former State:

a. at a rate not exceeding 15 per cent of the gross amount actually distributed; or

b. at a rate not exceeding 5 per cent of the gross amount actually distributed, if during the part of the paying corporation's taxable year which precedes the date of payment of the dividend and the whole of its prior taxable year (if any), the recipient is a corporation owning at least 25 per cent of the voting stock of the paying corporation, either alone or in combination with another corporation of such other State, provided each recipient corporation owned at least 10 per cent of such voting stock.

2. The rules of subparagraph *b.* shall not apply if more than 25 per cent of the gross income of the paying corporation for such prior taxable year (if any) consisted of interest and dividends (other than interest derived in the conduct of a banking, insurance or financing business and dividends or interest received from subsidiary corporations, 50 per cent or more of the voting stock of which was owned by the paying corporation at the time such dividends or interest were received).

3. Paragraph 1 of this Article shall not apply if the recipient of the dividends has a permanent establishment in the former Contracting State and the shares with respect to which the dividends are paid are effectively connected with the permanent establishment. In such a case, the provisions of Article III shall apply.

Article VIII

1. Interest on bonds, notes, debentures, securities, deposits or any other form of indebtedness (including interest from mortgages or bonds secured by real property) paid to a resident or corporation of one of the Contracting States shall be exempt from tax by the other Contracting State.

2. Paragraph 1 of this Article shall not apply if the recipient of the interest has a permanent establishment in the other Contracting State and the indebtedness giving rise to the interest is effectively connected with the permanent establishment. In such a case, the provisions of Article III shall apply.

3. Where any interest paid by a person to a related person, as defined in Article IV, exceeds a fair and reasonable consideration in respect of the indebtedness for which it is paid, paragraph 1 of this Article shall apply only to so much of the interest as represents such fair and reasonable consideration; the excess payment shall be characterized and taxed according to the laws of each Contracting State, including the provisions of this Convention where applicable.

Article IX

1. Royalties paid to a resident or corporation of one of the Contracting States shall be exempt from tax by the other Contracting State.

2. For the purposes of this Article, the term 'royalties' means any royalties, rentals or other amounts paid as consideration for the use of, or the right to use:

a. copyrights, artistic or scientific works, patents, designs, plans, secret processes or formulae, trademarks, motion picture films, films or tapes for radio or television broadcasting, or other like property or rights, or

b. information concerning industrial, commercial or scientific knowledge, experience, or skill.

3. Paragraph 1 of this Article shall not apply if the recipient of the royalties has a permanent establishment in the other Contracting State and the right or property giving rise to the royalties is effectively connected with the permanent establishment. In such a case, the provisions of Article III shall apply.

4. Where any royalty paid by a person to a related person, as defined in Article IV, exceeds a fair and reasonable consideration in respect of the rights for which it is paid, paragraph 1 of this Article shall apply only to so much of the royalty as represents such fair and reasonable consideration; the excess payment shall be characterized and taxed according to the laws of each Contracting State, including the provisions of this Convention where applicable.

Article X

A resident or corporation of one of the Contracting States, deriving from sources within the other Contracting State royalties in respect of the operation of mines, quarries, or natural resources, or rentals from real property, may elect for any taxable year to be subject to the tax of such other Contracting State, on a net basis, as if such resident or corporation were engaged in trade or business within such other Contracting State through a permanent establishment therein during such taxable year.

Article XI

1. Gains derived by a resident or corporation of one of the Contracting States from the alienation of a capital asset (other than gain from the alienation of real property to which Article V applies) shall be exempt from tax by the other Contracting State.

2. If such resident or corporation has a permanent establishment in the other Contracting State, paragraph 1 of this Article shall not apply to gains derived by such resident or corporation from the alienation of a capital asset which is effectively connected with the permanent establishment. In such a case, the provisions of Article III shall apply.

3. Paragraph 1 of this Article shall not apply if:

a. the person deriving the gain is an individual who is a resident of the Netherlands and who is present in the United States for a period of 183 days or more during the taxable year, and

b. the asset alienated was held by such person for six months or less.

4. Paragraph 1 of this Article does not affect the right of the Netherlands to levy, according to its own law, a tax on the gains derived from the alienation of shares, or 'jouissance' shares, in a Netherlands joint stock corporation, by an individual who is a resident of the United States and who at the time of alienation:

a. is a Netherlands citizen,

b. has, at any time during the five-year period preceding such alienation, been a resident of the Netherlands, and

c. owns, either alone or together with his close relatives, at least 25 per cent of the voting stock of such corporation.

Article XII

Dividends and interest paid by a Netherlands corporation shall be exempt from United States tax except where the recipient is a citizen, resident, or corporation of the United States.

Article XIII[1]

A Netherlands corporation shall be exempt from United States tax on its accumulated or undistributed earnings, profits, income or surplus if it can prove to the satisfaction of the competent authorities of the United States that individuals who are residents of the Netherlands (other than citizens of the United States) control, directly or indirectly, throughout the last half of the taxable year, more than 50 per cent of the entire voting power in such corporation.

Article XIV

1. The United States income tax liability for any taxable year beginning prior to January 1, 1936, of any individual (other than a citizen of the United States) resident in the Netherlands, or of any Netherlands corporation, remaining unpaid on the effective date of the present Convention, may be adjusted on a basis satisfactory to the United States Commissioner of Internal Revenue: Provided that the amount to be paid in settlement of such liability shall not exceed the amount of the liability which would have been determined if

a. the United States Revenue Act of 1936 (except in the case of a Netherlands corporation in which more than 50 per cent of the entire voting power was controlled, directly or indirectly, throughout the latter half of the taxable year, by citizens or residents of the United States), and

b. Articles XII and XIII of the present Convention, had been in effect for such year. If the taxpayer was not, within the meaning of such Revenue Act, engaged in trade or business in the United States and had no office or place of business therein during the taxable year, the amount of interest and penalties shall not exceed 50 per cent of the amount of the tax with respect to which such interest and penalties have been computed.

2. The United States income tax unpaid on the effective date of the present Convention for any taxable year beginning after December 31, 1935, and prior to the effective date of the present Convention in the case of an individual (other than a citizen of the United States) resident of the Netherlands, or in the case of any Netherlands corporation, shall be determined as if the provisions of Articles XII and XIII of the present Convention had been in effect for such taxable year.

3. The provisions of paragraph 1 of this Article shall not apply

a. unless the taxpayer files with the Commissioner of Internal Revenue within a period of two years following the effective date of

---

1. The US ratified the convention with a reservation rejecting Articles XI and XIII and modifying Article XIV to eliminate any reference to Article XIII and other language that might preclude US taxation of capital gains. In the supplementary convention signed December 30, 1965, the US ratified Article XI, as reproduced above, without reservation.

the present Convention a request that such tax liability be so adjusted and furnishes such information as the Commissioner may require; or

b. in any case in which the Commissioner is satisfied that any deficiency in tax is due to fraud with intent to evade the tax.

Article XV

1. Wages, salaries and similar compensation and pensions, annuities or similar benefits paid by, or out of funds created by, of one of the Contracting States or the political subdivisions thereof to an individual who is a citizen of that Contracting State for services rendered to that Contracting State or to any of its political subdivisions in the discharge of governmental functions shall be exempt from tax by the other Contracting State.

2. Private pensions and life annuities derived from within one of the Contracting States and paid to individuals in the other Contracting State shall be exempt from taxation in the former State.

3. The term 'pensions' as used in this Article means periodic payments made in consideration for services rendered or by way of compensation for injuries received.

4. The term 'life annuities' as used in this Article means a stated sum payable periodically at stated times during life, or during a specified number of years, under an obligation to make the payments in return for adequate and full consideration in money or money's worth.

Article XVI

1. An individual who is a resident of one of the Contracting States shall be exempt from tax by the other Contracting State with respect to income from personal services if:

a. he is present within the latter Contracting State for a period or periods not exceeding in the aggregate 183 days during the taxable year, and

b. in the case of employment income:

(i) such individual is an employee of a resident or corporation of a State other than the latter Contracting State or of a permanent establishment of a resident of corporation of the latter Contracting State located outside the latter Contracting State, and

(ii) such income is not deducted as such in computing the profits of a permanent establishment in the latter Contracting State.

2. For purposes of paragraph 1, the term 'income from personal services' includes employment income and income earned by an individual from the performance of personal services in an independent capacity. The term 'employment income' includes income from services performed by officers and directors of corporations, but does not include income from personal services performed by partners.

Article XVII

1. An individual who is a resident of one of the Contracting States at the beginning of his visit to the other Contracting State and who, at the invitation of the Government of the other Contracting State or of

a university or other accredited educational institution situated in the other Contracting State, visits the other Contracting State for the primary purpose of teaching or engaging in research, or both, at a university or other accredited educational institution shall be exempt from tax by the other Contracting State on his income from personal services for teaching or research at such educational institution, or at other such institutions, for a period not exceeding two years from the date of his arrival in the other Contracting State.

2. This Article shall not apply to income from research if such research is undertaken not in the public interest but primarily for the private benefit of a specific person or persons.

Article XVIII

1. *a.* An individual who is a resident of one of the Contracting States at the beginning of his visit to the other Contracting State and who is temporarily present in the other Contracting State for the primary purpose of:

(i) studying at a university or other accredited educational institution in that other Contracting State or otherwise engaging in research of an educational nature, or

(ii) securing training required to qualify him to practice a profession or professional specialty,

shall be exempt from tax by that other Contracting State with respect to:

(A) gifts from abroad for the purpose of his maintenance, education, study, research, or training;

(B) a grant, allowance, or award by a government, educational institution, or nonprofit organization; and

(C) income from personal services performed in the other Contracting State in an amount not in excess of $2,000 (in the case of services performed in the United States) or 3,600 guilders (in the case of services performed in the Netherlands) for any taxable year.

b. The benefits under this paragraph shall only extend for such period of time as may be reasonably or customarily required to effectuate the purpose of the visit, but in no event shall any individual have the benefits of this paragraph for more than five taxable years.

2. A resident of one of the Contracting States who is present in the other Contracting State as an employee of, or under contract with, a resident or corporation of the former State, for the primary purpose of:

(i) acquiring technical, professional, or business experience from a person other than that resident or corporation of the former State or a corporation 50 per cent or more of the voting stock of which is owned by such corporation of the former State, or

a. studying at a university or other accredited educational institution in that other Contracting State,

shall be exempt from tax by that other Contracting State for one taxable year with respect to his income from personal services in an amount not in excess of $5,000 (in the case of services performed in the United States) or 18,000 guilders (in the case of services performed in the Netherlands).

Article XIX

1. Notwithstanding any provisions of the present Convention (other than paragraph 1 of Article XV when applicable in the case of an individual who is deemed by each Contracting State to be a citizen thereof), each of the two Contracting States, in determining the taxes, including all surtaxes, of its citizens or corporations, may include in the basis upon which such taxes are imposed all items of income taxable under its own revenue laws as though this Convention had not come into effect.

2. The United States shall allow to a citizen, resident or corporation of the United States as a credit against its tax specified in subparagraph 1*a*. of Article I the appropriate amount of taxes paid to the Netherlands. Such appropriate amount shall be based upon the amount of tax paid to the Netherlands on income from sources within the Netherlands but shall not exceed that proportion of the United States tax which taxable income from sources within the Netherlands bears to the entire taxable income. For purposes of this paragraph, taxable income shall be computed without any deduction for personal exemptions. It is agreed that, by virtue of the provisions of paragraph 3 of this Article, the Netherlands has satisfied the similar credit requirement of the Internal Revenue Code with respect to taxed paid to the Netherlands.

3. As far as may be in accordance with the provisions of Netherlands law, the Netherlands agrees to allow a deduction from Netherlands tax with respect to income from sources within the United States, in order to take into account the Federal income taxes paid to the United States, whether paid directly by the taxpayer or by withholding at the source. In addition, the Netherlands shall allow a deduction from the Netherlands tax, determined in conformity with paragraph 1, with respect to dividends received from a United States corporation by a resident or corporation of the Netherlands. The amount of this deduction shall be the lesser of the following:

a. an amount equal to 15 per cent of the dividends; or

b. an amount that is the same proportion of the Netherlands tax, determined in conformity with paragraph 1 of this Article, as the amount of the dividends bears to the income which forms the basis for the determination of the Netherlands tax.

Article XX

1. All persons who left the Netherlands between April 30, 1939 and December 31, 1945, inclusive (other than persons who were citizens of the United States at the time of leaving the Netherlands or Netherlands subjects who by reason of their function as governmental officials in established service reside abroad and the members of their family living with them), and who are deemed to be taxpayers under the provisions of Netherlands law relating to the capital accretions tax or the extraordinary capital tax, and who became residents of the United

States (according to the income tax law of the United States) during that period, and who did not return to the Netherlands on or before December 31, 1945 to resume residence in the Netherlands (according to the income tax law of the Netherlands), shall be taxable by the Netherlands:

a. under the law relating to the capital accretions tax, only in respect of accretions arising from their property situated in the Netherlands (as defined in that law in the case of non-residents) and from their activities in the Netherlands;

b. under the law relating to the extraordinary capital tax, only in respect of their property situated in the Netherlands (as defined in that law in the case of non-residents).

2. All persons who left the Netherlands between April 30, 1939 and December 31, 1945, inclusive, and who were citizens of the United States at the time of leaving the Netherlands, and who are deemed to be taxpayers under the provisions of Netherlands law relating to the capital accretions tax or the extraordinary capital tax, and who became residents of the United States (according to the income tax law of the United States) on or before December 31, 1945, shall be taxable by the Netherlands:

a. under the law relating to the capital accretions tax, only in respect of accretions arising from their property situated in the Netherlands (as defined in that law in the case of non-residents) and from their activities in the Netherlands;

b. under the law relating to the extraordinary capital tax, only in respect of their property situated in the Netherlands (as defined in that law in the case of non-residents).

3. The provisions of this Article shall be deemed to be effective as though the present Convention had entered into force on the effective date of the Netherlands law relating to the capital accretions tax or the extraordinary capital tax as the case may be.

Article XXI

The competent authorities of the Contracting States shall exchange such information (being information which such authorities have in proper order at their disposal) as is necessary for carrying out the provisions of the present Convention or for the prevention of fraud or the administration of statutory provisions against legal avoidance in relation to the taxes which are the subject of the present Convention. Any information so exchanged shall be treated as secret and shall not be disclosed to any person other than those concerned with the assessment and collection of the taxes which are the subject of the present Convention. No information as aforesaid shall be exchanged which would disclose any trade, business, industrial, or professional secret or trade process.

Article XXII

1. The Contracting States undertake to lend assistance and support to each other in the collection of the taxes which are the subject of the

present Convention, together with interest, costs, and additionals to the taxes and fines not being of a penal character.

2. In the case of applications for enforcement of taxes, revenue claims of each of the Contracting States which have been finally determined may be accepted for enforcement by the other Contracting State and collected in that State in accordance with the laws applicable to the enforcement and collection of its own taxes. The State to which application is made shall not be required to enforce executory measures for which there is no provision in the law of the State making the application.

3. Any application shall be accompanied by documents establishing that under the laws of the State making the application the taxes have been finally determined.

4. The assistance provided for in this Article shall not be accorded with respect to the citizens, corporations, or other entities of the State to which the application is made, except as is necessary to insure that the exemption or reduced rate of tax granted under the convention to such citizens, corporations or other entities shall not be enjoyed by persons not entitled to such benefits.

Article XXIII

1. In no case shall the provisions of Articles XXI and XXII be construed so as to impose upon either of the Contracting States the obligation

a. to carry out administrative measures at variance with the regulations and practices of either Contracting State, or

b. to supply particulars which are not procurable under its own legislation or that of the State making application.

2. The State to which application is made for information or assistance shall comply as soon as possible with the request addressed to it. Nevertheless, such State may refuse to comply with the request for reasons of public policy or if compliance would involve violation of a trade, business, industrial or professional secret or trade process. In such case it shall inform, as soon as possible, the State making the application.

Article XXIV

1. Where a taxpayer shows proof that the action of the tax authorities of the Contracting States has resulted or will result in taxation not in accordance with the provisions of the present Convention, he shall be entitled to present his case to the State of which he is a citizen or resident, or, if the taxpayer is a corporation of one of the Contracting States, to that State.

2. Should the taxpayer's claim be deemed worthy of consideration, the competent authority of the State to which the claim is made shall endeavour to come to an agreement with the competent authority of the other State with a view to avoidance of taxation not in accordance with the provisions of the present Convention. In particular, the com-

petent authorities of the Contracting States may consult together to endeavour to agree:

a. to the same attribution of industrial or commercial profits to a permanent establishment situated in one of the States of an enterprise of the other State, or

b. to the same allocation of profits between related enterprises as provided for in Article VI.

In the event that the competent authorities reach such an agreement taxes shall be imposed, and refund or credit of taxes shall be allowed, by the Contracting States on such income in accordance with such agreement. If the taxpayer does not accept such agreement, the preceding sentence shall not be construed to deny a taxpayer the right to appeal to the courts the decision reached in such agreement.

3. The competent authorities of the Contracting States may communicate with each other directly to implement the provisions of the present Convention. Should any difficulty or doubt arise as to the interpretation or application of the present Convention, the competent authorities shall endeavour to settle the question as quickly as possible by mutual agreement.

Article XXV

1. The provisions of the present Convention shall not be construed to restrict in any manner any exemption, deduction, credit or other allowance accorded by the laws of one of the Contracting States in the determination of the tax imposed by such State.

2. A citizen of one of the Contracting States who is a resident of the other Contracting State shall not be subjected in that other Contracting State to more burdensome taxes than is a citizen of that other Contracting State who is a resident thereof.

3. A permanent establishment which a citizen or corporation of one of the Contracting States has in the other Contracting State shall not be subjected in that other Contracting State to more burdensome taxes than is a citizen or corporation of that other Contracting State carrying on the same activities. This paragraph shall not be construed as obliging either Contracting State to grant to citizens of the other Contracting State who are not residents of the former Contracting State any personal allowances or deductions which are by its law available only to residents of that former Contracting State.

4. A corporation of one of the Contracting States, the capital of which is wholly or partly owned by one or more citizens or corporations of the other Contracting State, shall not be subjected in the former Contracting State to more burdensome taxes than is a corporation of the former Contracting State, the capital of which is wholly owned by one or more citizens or corporations of that former Contracting State.

5. As used in paragraphs 2, 3 and 4 of this Article the term 'taxes' means taxes of every kind whether imposed at the national, state or local level.

Article XXVI

1. The authorities of each of the Contracting States, in accordance with the practices of that State, may prescribe regulations necessary to carry out the provisions of the present Convention.

2. With respect to the provisions of the present Convention relating to exchange of information and mutual assistance in the collection of taxes, the competent authorities may, by common agreement, prescribe rules concerning matters of procedure, forms of application and replies thereto, conversion of currency, disposition of amounts collected, minimum amounts subject to collection, and related matters.

Article XXVII

1. Either of the Contracting States may, at the time of exchange of instruments of ratification or thereafter while the present Convention continues in force, by a written notification of extension given to the other Contracting State through diplomatic channels, declare the desire of the government of any overseas part of the Kingdom (in the case of the Netherlands) or overseas territory (in the case of the United States), which imposes taxes substantially similar in character to those which are the subject of the present Convention, that the operation of the present Convention, either in whole or as to such provisions thereof as may be deemed to have special application, shall extend to such part or territory.

2. In the event that a notification is given by one of the Contracting States in accordance with paragraph 1 of this Article, the present Convention, or such provisions thereof as may be specified in the notification, shall apply to any part or territory named in such notification on and after the first day of January following the date of a written communication through diplomatic channels addressed to such Contracting State by the other Contracting State, after such action by the latter State as may be necessary in accordance with its own procedures, stating that such notification is accepted in respect of such part or territory. In the absence of such acceptance, none of the provisions of the present Convention shall apply to such part or territory.

3. At any time after the expiration of one year from the effective date of an extension made by virtue of paragraphs 1 and 2 of this Article, either of the Contracting States may, by a written notice of termination given to the other Contracting State through diplomatic channels, terminate the application of the present Convention to any part or territory to which the Convention, or any of its provisions, has been extended. In that case, the present Convention, or the provisions thereof specified in the notice of termination, shall cease to be applicable to the part or territory named in such notice of termination on and after the first day of January following the expiration of a period of six months after the date of such notice; provided, however, that this shall not affect the continued application of the Convention, or any of the provisions thereof, to the United States, to the Netherlands, or to any part or territory (not named in the notice of termination) to which the Convention, or such provision thereof, applies.

4. For the application of the present Convention in relation to any part or territory to which it is extended by notification given by the United States or the Netherlands, references to 'the United States' or to 'the Netherlands' or to one or the other Contracting State, as the case may be, shall be construed to refer to such part or territory.

Article XXVIII

1. The present Convention shall be ratified and the instruments of ratification shall be exchanged at Washington as soon as possible.

2. The present Convention shall become effective on the first day of January in the year last preceding the year in which the exchange of the instruments of ratification takes place. It shall continue effective for a period of five years beginning with that date and indefinitely after that period, but may be terminated by either of the Contracting States at the end of the five-year period or any time thereafter, provided that at least six months' prior notice of termination has been given, the termination to become effective on the first day of January following the expiration of the six-month period.

Done at Washington, in duplicate, in the English and Dutch languages, the two texts having equal authenticity, this 29th day of April, 1948.

Convention between the Government of the United States of America and the Government of the Republic of the Philippines with Respect to Taxes on Income, concluded in Manila on October 1, 1976.

The Government of the United States of America and the Government of the Republic of the Philippines, desiring to conclude a convention for the avoidance of double taxation and the prevention of fiscal evasion with respect to taxes on income, have agreed as follows:

Article 1. Taxes Covered

1. The taxes which are the subject of this Convention are:

a. In the case of the United States, the Federal income taxes imposed by the Internal Revenue Code (but not including the tax on improperly accumulated earnings or the personal holding company tax), and

b. In the case of the Philippines, the income tax imposed by Title II of the National Internal Revenue Code (but not including the tax on improperly accumulated earnings or the personal holding company tax).

2. This Convention shall also apply to taxes substantially similar to those covered by paragraph 1 which are imposed in addition to, or in place of, existing taxes after the date of signature of this Convention.

3. The competent authorities of the Contracting States shall notify each other of any amendments of the tax laws referred to in paragraph 1 or 2 and of the adoption of any taxes referred to in paragraph 2 by transmitting the texts of any amendments or new statutes at least once a year.

4. The competent authorities of the Contracting States shall notify each other of the publication by their respective Contracting States of any material concerning the application of this Convention, whether in the form of regulations, rulings, or judicial decisions by transmitting the texts of any such materials at least once a year.

Article 2. General Definitions

1. In this Convention, unless the context otherwise requires:

a. (i) The term 'United States' means the United States of America; and

(ii) When used in a geographical sense, the term 'United States' means the states thereof and the District of Columbia.

b. (i) The term 'Philippines' means the Republic of the Philippines; and

(ii) When used in a geographical sense, the term 'Philippines' means the territory comprising the Republic of the Philippines.

c. The term 'Contracting State' means the United States or the Philippines, as the context requires.

d. The term 'person' includes an individual, a partnership, a corporation, an estate, or a trust.

e. (i) The term 'United States corporation' means a corporation (or any unincorporated entity treated as a corporation for United States tax purposes) which is created or organized in or under the laws of the United States or any state thereof or the District of Columbia; and

(ii) The term 'Philippine corporation' means a corporation (or any unincorporated entity treated as a corporation for Philippine tax purposes) which is created or organized in the Philippines or under its laws.

f. The term 'competent authority' means:

(i) In the case of the United States, the Secretary of the Treasury or his delegate, and

(ii) In the case of the Philippines, the Secretary of Finance or his delegate.

g. The term 'tax' means tax imposed by the United States or the Philippines whichever is applicable, to which this Convention applies by virtue of Article 1 (Taxes Covered).

h. The term 'international traffic' means any transport by a ship or aircraft operated by a resident of one of the Contracting States except where such transport is confined solely to places within a Contracting State.

2. Any other term used in this Convention and not defined in this Convention shall, unless the context otherwise requires, have the meaning which it has under the laws of the Contracting State whose tax is being determined. Notwithstanding the preceding sentence, if the meaning of such a term under the laws of one of the Contracting States is different from the meaning of the term under the laws of the other Contracting State, or if the meaning of such a term is not readily determinable under the laws of one of the Contracting States, the competent authorities of the Contracting States may, in order to prevent double taxation or to further any other purpose of this Convention, establish a common meaning of the term for the purposes of this Convention.

Article 3. Fiscal Residence

1. In this Convention:

a. The term 'resident of the Philippines' means:

(i) A Philippine corporation, and

(ii) Any other person (except a corporation or any entity treated as a corporation for Philippine tax purposes) resident in the Philippines for purposes of Philippine tax, but in the case of a professional partnership, estate, or trust only to the extent that the income derived by such partnership, estate, or trust is subject to Philippine tax as the income of a resident either in the hands of the respective entity or of its partners or beneficiaries.

b. The term 'resident of the United States' means:

(i) A United States corporation, and

(ii) Any other person (except a corporation or any entity treated as a corporation for United States tax purposes) resident in the United States for purposes of United States tax, but in the case of a partnership, estate, or trust only to the extent that the income derived by such partnership, estate, or trust is subject to United States tax as the income of a resident either in the hands of the respective entity or of its partners or beneficiaries.

2. Where by reason of the provisions of paragraph 1 an individual is a resident of both Contracting States:

a. He shall be deemed to be a resident of that Contracting State in which he maintains his permanent home. If he has a permanent home in both Contracting States or in neither of the Contracting States, he shall be deemed to be a resident of that Contracting State with which his personal and economic relations are closest (center of vital interests);

b. If the Contracting State in which he has his center of vital interests cannot be determined, he shall be deemed to be a resident of that Contracting State in which he has a habitual abode;

c. If he has a habitual abode in both Contracting States or in neither of the Contracting States, he shall be deemed to be a resident of the Contracting State of which he is a citizen; and

d. If he is a citizen of both Contracting States or of neither Contracting State, the competent authorities of the Contracting States shall settle the question by mutual agreement.

Article 4. Source of Income

For purposes of this Convention:

1. Dividends shall be treated as income from sources within a Contracting State only if:

a. Paid by a corporation of that Contracting State, or

b. Paid by a corporation of any State if, for the 3-year period ending with the close of such corporation's taxable year preceding the declaration of the dividends (or for such part of that period as such corporation has been in existence), at least 50 per cent of such corporation's gross income from all sources was business profits attributable to a permanent establishment which such corporation had in that Contracting State; but only in an amount which bears the same ratio to such dividends as the amount of the business profits attributable to that permanent establishment bears to the corporation's gross income from all sources.

If a dividend would be treated under this paragraph as income from sources within both Contracting States, it shall be deemed to be income from sources only within the Contracting State described in subparagraph *b.*, to the extent provided therein.

2. Interest shall be treated as income from sources within a Contracting State only if paid by such Contracting State, a political subdivision or a local authority thereof, or by a resident of that Contracting State. Notwithstanding the preceding sentence, if such interest is paid on an indebtedness incurred in connection with a permanent establish-

ment which bears such interest, then such interest shall be deemed to be from sources within the State (whether or not a Contracting State) in which the permanent establishment is situated.

3. Royalties for the use of, or the right to use, property or rights shall be treated as income from sources within a Contracting State only to the extent that such royalties are for the use of, or the right to use, such property or rights within that Contracting State. Notwithstanding the preceding sentence, if such royalty is paid with respect to a liability to pay the royalty that was incurred in connection with a permanent establishment which bears such royalty, then such royalty shall be deemed to be from sources within the State (whether or not a Contracting State) in which the permanent establishment is situated.

4. Income from real property (including royalties) described in Article 7 (Income from Real Property) shall be treated as income from sources within a Contracting State only if such property is situated in that Contracting State.

5. Income received by an individual for his performance of labor or personal services, whether as an employee or in an independent capacity, shall be treated as income from sources within a Contracting State only to the extent that such services are performed in that Contracting State. However, income from personal services performed aboard ships or aircraft operated by a resident of one of the Contracting States in international traffic shall be treated as income from sources within that Contracting State if rendered by a member of the regular complement of the ship or aircraft. Notwithstanding the preceding provisions of this paragraph, remuneration described in Article 20 (Governmental Functions) and payments described in Article 19 (Social Security Payments) paid from the public funds of a Contracting State or a political subdivision or local authority thereof shall be treated as income from sources within that Contracting State only.

6. Notwithstanding paragraphs 1 through 4, business profits which are attributable to a permanent establishment which the recipient, a resident of one of the Contracting States, has in the other Contracting State shall be treated as income from sources within that other Contracting State.

7. Gross revenue from the operation of ships in international traffic shall be treated as from sources within a Contracting State to the extent they are derived from outgoing traffic originating in that State.

8. The source of any item of income to which paragraphs 1 through 7 are not applicable shall be determined by each of the Contracting States in accordance with its own law. Notwithstanding the preceding sentence, if the source of any item of income under the laws of one Contracting State is different from the source of such item of income under the laws of the other Contracting State or if the source of such income is not readily determinable under the laws of one of the Contracting States, the competent authorities of the Contracting States may, in order to prevent double taxation or further any other purpose of this Convention, establish a common source of the item of income for purposes of this Convention.

Article 5. Permanent Establishment

1. For the purpose of this Convention, the term 'permanent establishment' means a fixed place of business through which a resident of one of the Contracting States engages in a trade or business.

2. The term 'fixed place of business' includes but is not limited to:

a. A seat of management;

b. A branch;

c. An office;

d. A store or other sales outlet;

e. A factory;

f. A workshop;

g. A warehouse;

h. A mine, quarry, or other place of extraction of natural resources;

i. A building site or construction or assembly project or supervisory activities in connection therewith, provided such site, project or activity continues for a period of more than 183 days; and

j. The furnishing of services, including consultancy services, by a resident of one of the Contracting States through employees or other personnel, provided activities of that nature continue (for the same or a connected project) within the other Contracting State for a period or periods aggregating more than 183 days.

3. Notwithstanding paragraphs 1, 2, and 4, a permanent establishment shall be deemed not to include any one or more of the following:

a. The use of facilities solely for the purpose of storage, display, or occasional delivery of goods or merchandise belonging to the resident;

b. The maintenance of a stock of goods or merchandise belonging to the resident solely for the purpose of storage, display, or occasional delivery;

c. The maintenance of a stock of goods or merchandise belonging to the resident solely for the purpose of processing by another person;

d. The maintenance of a fixed place of business solely for the purpose of purchasing goods or merchandise, or for collecting information, for the resident;

e. The maintenance of a fixed place of business solely for the purpose of advertising, for the supply of information, for scientific research, or for similar activities which have a preparatory or auxiliary character, for the resident; or

f. The furnishing of services, including the provision of equipment, in one of the Contracting States by a resident of the other Contracting State, including consultancy firms, in accordance with, or in the implementation of, an agreement between the Contracting States regarding technical cooperation.

4. A person acting in one of the Contracting States on behalf of a resident of the other Contracting State, other than an agent of an independent status to whom paragraph 5 applies, shall be deemed to give rise to a permanent establishment in the first-mentioned Contracting State if:

a. Such person has, and habitually exercises in the first-mentioned Contracting State, an authority to conclude contracts in the name of that resident, unless the exercise of such authority is limited to the purchase of goods or merchandise for that resident; or

b. He has no such authority, but habitually maintains in the first-mentioned State a stock of goods or merchandise from which he regularly delivers goods and merchandise on behalf of the resident.

5. An resident of one of the Contracting States shall not be deemed to have a permanent establishment in the other Contracting State merely because such resident carries on business in that other Contracting State through a broker, general commission agent, or any other agent of an independent status, where such broker or agent is acting in the ordinary course of his business. However, when the activities of such an agent are devoted wholly or almost wholly on behalf of that resident, he shall not be considered an agent of independent status within the meaning of this paragraph if the transactions between the agent and the resident were not made under arm's length conditions.

6. Except with respect to reinsurance, a resident of a Contracting State shall be deemed to have a permanent establishment in the other Contracting State if it collects premiums in that other State, or insures risks situated therein, through an employee or representative situated therein who is not an agent of independent status to whom paragraph 5 applies.

7. A resident of one of the Contracting States shall not be deemed to have a permanent establishment in the other Contracting State merely because such resident sells at the termination of a trade fair or convention in such other Contracting State goods or merchandise which such resident displayed at such trade fair or convention.

8. The fact that a corporation of one of the Contracting States controls or is controlled by or is under common control with:

a. A corporation of the other Contracting State or

b. A corporation which carries on business in that other Contracting State (whether through a permanent establishment or otherwise)

shall not be taken into account in determining whether the activities or fixed place of business of either corporation constitutes a permanent establishment of the other corporation.

9. The principles set forth in paragraphs 1 through 8 shall be applied in determining for purposes of this Convention whether there is a permanent establishment in a State other than one of the Contracting States or whether a person other than a resident of one of the Contracting States has a permanent establishment in one of the Contracting States.

Article 6. General Rules of Taxation

1. A resident of one of the Contracting States may be taxed by the other Contracting State on any income from sources within that other Contracting State and only on such income, subject to any limitations set forth in this Convention. For this purpose, the rules set forth in Article 4 (Source of Income) shall be applied to determine the source of income.

2. The provisions of this Convention shall not be construed to restrict in any manner any exclusion, exemption, deduction, credit, or other allowance now or hereafter accorded:

a. By the laws of one of the Contracting States in the determination of the tax imposed by that Contracting State, or

b. By any other agreement between the Contracting States.

3. Notwithstanding any provisions of this Convention except paragraph 4, a Contracting State may tax its residents (as determined under Article 3 (Fiscal Residence)) and its citizens as if this Convention had not come into effect.

4. The provisions of paragraph 3 shall not affect:

a. The benefits conferred by a Contracting State under Articles 19 (Social Security Payments), 23 (Relief from Double Taxation), 24 (Non-Discrimination), and 25 (Mutual Agreement Procedure); and

b. The benefits conferred by a Contracting State under Articles 20 (Governmental Functions), 21 (Teachers), 22 (Students and Trainees), and 28 (Diplomatic and Consular Officers) upon individuals who are neither citizens of, nor have immigrant status in, that Contracting State.

5. The competent authorities of the two Contracting States may each prescribe regulations necessary to carry out the provisions of this Convention.

Article 7. Income from Real Property

1. Income from real property, including royalties and other payments in respect of the exploitation of natural resources and gains derived from the alienation of such property or of the right giving rise to such royalties or other payments, may be taxed by the Contracting State in which such real property or natural resources are situated. For purposes of this Convention, interest on indebtedness secured by real property or secured by a right giving rise to royalties or other payments in respect of the exploitation of natural resources shall not be regarded as income from real property.

2. Paragraph 1 shall apply to income derived from the usufruct, direct use, letting, or use in any other form of real property.

Article 8. Business Profits

1. Business profits of a resident of one of the Contracting States shall be taxable only in that State unless the resident has a permanent establishment in the other Contracting State. If the resident has a permanent establishment in that other Contracting State, tax may be imposed by that other Contracting State on the business profits of the resident but only on so much of them as are attributable to the permanent establishment.

2. Where a resident of one of the Contracting States has a permanent establishment in the other Contracting State, there shall in each Contracting State be attributed to the permanent establishment the business profits which would reasonably be expected to have been derived by it if it were an independent entity engaged in the same or similar activities under the same or similar conditions and dealing

wholly independently with the resident of which it is a permanent establishment.

3. There may also be attributed to that permanent establishment the business profits derived from the sale of goods or merchandise of the same or similar kind as those sold, or from other business activities of the same or similar kind as those affected, through that permanent establishment if the sale or activities had been resorted to in order to avoid taxation.

4. In the determination of the business profits of a permanent establishment, there shall be allowed as deductions ordinary and necessary expenses which are reasonably allocable to such profits, including executive and general administrative expenses, whether incurred in the Contracting State in which the permanent establishment is situated or elsewhere. However, no such deductions shall be allowed in respect of amounts paid or payable (other than reimbursement of actual expenses) by the permanent establishment to the head office of the resident of which it is a permanent establishment or any of its other offices, by way of:

a. Royalties, fees or other similar payments in return for the use of patents or other rights;

b. Commission, for specific services performed or for management; and

c. Interest on moneys lent to the permanent establishment, except in that case of a banking institution.

5. No profits shall be attributed to a permanent establishment of a resident of one of the Contracting States in the other Contracting State merely by reason of the purchase of goods or merchandise by that permanent establishment for the account of the resident.

6. The term ' business profits' means income derived from any trade or business whether carried on by an individual, corporation or any other person, or group of persons, including the rental of tangible personal (movable) property.

7. Where business profits include items of income which are dealt with separately in other articles of this Convention, then the provisions of those articles shall not be affected by the provisions of this article.

Article 9. Shipping and Air Transport

1. Notwithstanding any other provision of this Convention, profits derived by a resident of one of the Contracting States from sources within the other Contracting State from the operation of ships in international traffic may be taxed by both Contracting States; however, the tax imposed by the other Contracting State may be as much as, but shall not exceed, the lesser of:

a. One and one-half per cent of the gross revenues derived from sources in that State; and

b. The lowest rate of Philippine tax that may be imposed on profits of the same kind derived under similar circumstances by a resident of a third State.

2. Nothing in the Convention shall affect the right of a Contracting State to tax, in accordance with domestic laws, profits derived by a resident of the other Contracting State from sources within the first-mentioned Contracting State from the operation of aircraft in international traffic.

3. The provisions of paragraphs 1 and 2 shall also apply to profits derived from the participation in a pool, a joint business or in an international operating agency.

Article 10. Related Persons

1. Where a person subject to the taxing jurisdiction of one of the Contracting States and any other person are related and where such related persons make arrangements or impose conditions between themselves which are different from those which would be made between independent persons, any income, deductions, credits, or allowances which would, but for those arrangements or conditions, have been taken into account in computing the income (or loss) of, or the tax payable by, one of such persons may be taken into account in computing the amount of the income subject to tax and the taxes payable by such person.

2. Where a redetermination has been made by one Contracting State to the income of one of its residents in accordance with paragraph 1, then the other Contracting State shall, if it agrees with such redetermination and if necessary to prevent double taxation, make a corresponding adjustment to the income of a person in such other Contracting State related to such resident. In the event the other Contracting State disagrees with such redetermination, the two Contracting States shall endeavor to reach agreement in accordance with the mutual agreement procedure in paragraph 2 of Article 25 (Mutual Agreement Procedure).

3. For purposes of this Convention, a person is related to another person if either person owns or controls directly or indirectly the other, or if any third person or persons own or control directly or indirectly both. For this purpose, the term 'control' includes any kind of control, whether or not legally enforceable, and however exercised or exercisable.

Article 11. Dividends

1. Dividends derived from sources within one of the Contracting States by a resident of the other Contracting State may be taxed by both Contracting States.

2. The rate of tax imposed by one of the Contracting States on dividends derived from sources within that Contracting State by a resident of the other Contracting State shall not exceed:

a. 25 per cent of the gross amount of the dividend; or

b. When the recipient is a corporation, 20 per cent of the gross amount of the dividend if during the part of the paying corporation's taxable year which precedes the date of payment of the dividend and during the whole of its prior taxable year (if any), at least 10 per cent of the outstanding shares of the voting stock of the paying corporation was owned by the recipient corporation.

3. Dividends paid by a corporation of one of the Contracting States to a person other than a citizen or resident of the other Contracting State may be taxed by the other Contracting State, but only if:

a. Such dividends are treated as income from sources within that other Contracting State and, in the case of the Philippines, the additional tax described in paragraph 6 has not been paid with respect to the earnings distributed, or

b. The recipient of the dividends has a permanent establishment or fixed base in the other Contracting State and the holding in respect of which the dividends are paid is effectively connected with such permanent establishment or fixed base.

4. Paragraph 2 shall not apply if the recipient of dividends derived from sources within one of the Contracting States, being a resident of the other Contracting State, carries on business in the first-mentioned Contracting State through a permanent establishment situated therein or performs in that other State independent personal services from a fixed base situated therein, and the holding in respect of which the dividends are paid is effectively connected with such permanent establishment or fixed base. In such a case, the provisions of Article 8 (Business Profits) or Article 15 (Independent Personal Services), as the case may be, shall apply.

5. The term 'dividends' as used in this Convention means income from shares, mining shares, founders' shares or other rights, not being debt-claims, participating in profits, as well as income from other corporate rights assimilated to income from shares by the taxation law of the State of which the corporation making the distribution is a resident.

6. Nothing in this Convention (except Article 9 (Shipping and Air Transport)) shall be construed as preventing the Philippines from imposing on the earnings of a corporation (other than a Philippines corporation) attributable to a permanent establishment in the Philippines, a tax in addition to the tax which would be chargeable on the earnings of a Philippine corporation, provided that any additional tax so imposed shall not exceed 20 per cent of the amount of such earnings which have not been subjected to such additional tax in previous taxable years. For the purpose of this provision, the term 'earnings' means business profits attributable to a permanent establishment in the Philippines in a year and previous years after deducting therefrom all taxes, other than the additional tax referred to herein, imposed on such profits by the Philippines.

Article 12. Interest

1. Interest derived by a resident of one of the Contracting States from sources within the other Contracting State may be taxed by both Contracting States.

2. Interest derived by a resident of one of the Contracting States from sources within the other Contracting State shall not be taxed by

the other Contracting State at a rate in excess of 15 per cent of the gross amount of such interest.

3. Interest derived by a resident of one of the Contracting States from sources within the other Contracting State with respect to public issues of bonded indebtedness shall not be taxed by the other Contracting State at a rate in excess of 10 per cent of the gross amount of such interest.

4. Notwithstanding paragraphs 1, 2, and 3, interest derived by:

a. One of the Contracting States, or an instrumentality thereof (including the Central Bank of the Philippines, the Federal Reserve Banks of the United States, the Export-Import Bank of the United States, the Overseas Private Investment Corporation of the United States, and such other institutions of either Contracting State as the competent authorities of both Contracting States may determine by mutual agreement), or

b. A resident of one of the Contracting States with respect to debt obligations guaranteed or insured by that Contracting State or an instrumentality thereof,

shall be exempt from tax by the other Contracting State.

5. Paragraphs 2, 3, and 4 shall not apply if the recipient of interest from sources within one of the Contracting States, being a resident of the other Contracting State, carries on business in the first-mentioned Contracting State through a permanent establishment situated therein or performs in that other State independent personal services from a fixed base situated therein and the debt claim in respect of which the interest is paid is effectively connected with such permanent establishment or fixed base. In such a case, the provisions of Article 8 (Business Profits) or Article 15 (Independent Personal Services), as the case may be, shall apply.

6. Where an amount is paid to a related person and would be treated as interest but for the fact that it exceeds an amount which would have been paid to an unrelated person, the provisions of this article shall apply only to so much of the amount as would have been paid to an unrelated person. In such a case the excess amount may be taxed by each Contracting State according to its own law, including the provisions of this Convention where applicable.

7. The term 'interest' as used in this Convention means income from debt-claims of every kind, whether or not secured by mortgage, and whether or not carrying a right to participate in the debtor's profits, and in particular, income from government securities and income from bonds or debentures, including premiums and prizes attaching to such securities, bonds or debentures, as well as income assimilated to income from money lent by the taxation law of the Contracting State in which the income arises, including interest on deferred payment sales.

Article 13. Royalties

1. Royalties derived by a resident of one of the Contracting States from sources within the other Contracting State may be taxed by both Contracting States.

2. However, the tax imposed by that other Contracting State shall not exceed:

a. In the case of the United States, 15 per cent of the gross amount of the royalties, and

b. In the case of the Philippines, the least of:

(i) 25 per cent of the gross amount of the royalties,

(ii) 15 per cent of the gross amount of the royalties, where the royalties are paid by a corporation registered with the Philippine Board of Investments and engaged in preferred areas of activities, and

(iii) The lowest rate of Philippine tax that may be imposed on royalties of the same kind paid under similar circumstances to a resident of a third State.

3. The term 'royalties' as used in this article means payments of any kind received as a consideration for the use of, or the right to use, any copyright of literary, artistic or scientific work, including cinematographic films or films or tapes used for radio or television broadcasting, any patent, trade mark, designs or model, plan, secret formula or process, or other like right or property, or for information concerning industrial, commercial or scientific experience. The term 'royalties' also includes gains derived from the sale, exchange or other disposition of any such right or property which are contingent on the productivity, use, or disposition thereof.

4. The provisions of paragraphs 1 and 2 shall not apply if the recipient of the royalties, being a resident of a Contracting State, carries on business in the other Contracting State in which the royalties arise, through a permanent establishment situated therein, or performs in that other State professional services from a fixed base situated therein, and the right or property in respect of which the royalties are paid is effectively connected with such permanent establishment or fixed base. In such a case, the provisions of Article 8 (Business Profits) or Article 15 (Independent Personal Services), as the case may be, shall apply.

5. Where an amount is paid to a related person and would be treated as a royalty but for the fact that it exceeds an amount which would have been paid to an unrelated person, the provisions of this article shall apply only to so much of the amount as would have been paid to an unrelated person. In such a case, the excess amount may be taxed by each Contracting State according to its own law, including the provisions of this Convention where applicable.

Article 14. Capital Gains

1. Gains from the alienation of tangible personal (movable) property forming part of a business property of a permanent establishment which a resident of a Contracting State has in the other Contracting State or of tangible personal (movable) property pertaining to a fixed base available to a resident of a Contracting State in the other Contracting

State for the purpose of performing independent personal services, including such gains from the alienation of such a permanent establishment (alone or together with the whole enterprise) or of such a fixed base, may be taxed in the other State. However, gains derived by a resident of a Contracting State from the alienation of ships, aircraft or containers operated by such resident in international traffic shall be taxable only in that State, and gains described in Article 13 (Royalties) shall be taxable only in accordance with the provisions of Article 13.

2. Gains from the alienation of any property other than those mentioned in paragraph 1 or in Article 7 (Income From Real Property) shall be taxable only in the Contracting State of which the alienator is a resident.

Article 15. Independent Personal Services

1. Income derived by an individual who is a resident of one of the Contracting States from the performance of personal services in an independent capacity may be taxed by that Contracting State. Except as provided in paragraph 2, such income shall be exempt from tax by the other Contracting State.

2. Income derived by an individual who is a resident of one of the Contracting States from the performance of personal services in an independent capacity in the other Contracting State may be taxed by that other Contracting State, if:

a. He has a fixed base regularly available to him in the other Contracting State for the purpose of performing his activities; in that case, only so much of the income as is attributable to that fixed base may be taxed in that other Contracting State;

b. He is present in that other Contracting State for a period or periods aggregating 90 days or more in the taxable year; or

c. The gross remuneration derived in the taxable year from residents of that other Contracting State for the performance of such services in the other Contracting State exceeds 10,000 United States dollars or its equivalent in Philippine pesos or such higher amount as may be specified and agreed in letters exchanged between the competent authorities of the Contracting States.

3. The term 'income' as used in paragraph 2 means net income.

Article 16. Dependent Personal Services

1. Except as provided in Article 20 (Governmental Functions), wages, salaries, and similar remuneration derived by an individual who is a resident of one of the Contracting States from labor or personal services performed as an employee, including income from services performed by an officer of a corporation, may be taxed by that Contracting State. Except as provided by paragraphs 2 and 3 and in Articles 20 (Governmental Functions), 21 (Teachers), and 22 (Students and Trainees), such remuneration derived from sources within the other Contracting State may also be taxed by that other Contracting State.

2. Remuneration described in paragraph 1 derived by an individual who is a resident of one of the Contracting States shall be exempt from tax by the other Contracting State if:

a. He is present in that other Contracting State for a period or periods aggregating less than 90 days in the taxable year;

b. He is an employee of a resident of, or of a permanent establishment maintained in, the first-mentioned Contracting State; and

c. The remuneration is not borne as such by a permanent establishment which the employer has in that other Contracting State.

3. Notwithstanding the preceding provisions of this article, remuneration derived by an employee of a resident of one of the Contracting States for labor or personal services performed as a member of the regular complement of a ship or aircraft operated in international traffic by a resident of that Contracting State may be taxed only by that Contracting State.

Article 17. Artistes and Athletes

1. Notwithstanding the provisions of Articles 15 (Independent Personal Services) and 16 (Dependent Personal Services), income derived by public entertainers such as theater, motion picture, radio or television artistes, and musicians, and by athletes, from their personal activities as such may be taxed in the Contracting State in which these activities are exercised provided that:

a. Such income exceeds 100 United States dollars or its equivalent in Philippine pesos per day, or

b. Such income exceeds in the aggregate 3,000 United States dollars or its equivalent in Philippine pesos during the taxable year.

2. Where income in respect of personal activities as such of a public entertainer or athlete accrues not to that entertainer or athlete himself but to another person, that income may, notwithstanding the provisions of Articles 8 (Business Profits), 15 (Independent Personal Services) and 16 (Dependent Personal Services), be taxed in the Contracting State in which the activities of the entertainer or athlete are exercised.

3. Notwithstanding the provisions of paragraph 1 and Articles 15 (Independent Personal Services) and 16 (Dependent Personal Services), income derived from activities performed in a Contracting State by public entertainers or athletes shall be exempt from tax in that Contracting State if the visit to that State is substantially supported or sponsored by the other Contracting State and the public entertainer or athlete is certified as qualified under this provision by the competent authority of the sending State.

Article 18. Private Pensions and Annuities

1. Except as provided in Article 20 (Governmental Functions), pensions and other similar remuneration paid to an individual in consideration of past employment shall be taxable by the Contracting State where the service is rendered.

2. Annuities paid to an individual who is a resident of one of the Contracting States shall be taxable only in that Contracting State.

3. Child support payments made by an individual who is a resident of one of the Contracting States to an individual who is a resident of the other Contracting State shall be exempt from tax in that other Contracting State.

4. The term 'pensions and other similar remuneration', as used in this article, includes periodic payments other than social security payments covered in Article 19 (Social Security Payments) made:

a. By reason of retirement or death and in consideration for services rendered or

b. By way of compensation for injuries or sickness received in connection with past employment.

5. The term 'annuities', as used in this article, means a stated sum paid periodically at stated times during life, or during a specified number of years, under an obligation to make the payments in return for adequate and full consideration (other than for services rendered).

6. The term 'child support payments', as used in this article, means periodic payments for the support of a minor child made pursuant to a written separation agreement or a decree of divorce, separate maintenance, or compulsory support.

Article 19. Social Security Payments

Social security payments and other public pensions paid by one of the Contracting States to an individual who is a resident of the other Contracting State (or in the case of such payments by the Philippines to an individual who is a citizen of the United States) shall be taxable only in the first-mentioned Contracting State. This article shall not apply to payments described in Article 20 (Governmental Functions).

Article 20. Governmental Functions

Wages, salaries and similar remuneration, including pensions, annuities, or similar benefits, paid from public funds of one of the Contracting States:

a. To a citizen of that Contracting State, or

b. To a citizen of a State other than a Contracting State who comes to the other Contracting State expressly for the purpose of being employed by the first-mentioned Contracting State

for labor or personal services performed as an employee of the national Government of that Contracting State, or any agency thereof, in the discharge of functions of a governmental nature shall be exempt from tax by the other Contracting State.

Article 21. Teachers

1. Where a resident of one of the Contracting States is invited by the Government of the other Contracting State, a political subdivision, or a local authority thereof, or by a university or other recognized educational institution in that other Contracting State to come to that other Contracting State for a period not expected to exceed 2 years for the purpose of teaching or engaging in research, or both, at a university or other recognized educational institution and such resident comes to

that other Contracting State primarily for such purpose, his income from personal services for teaching or research at such university or educational institution shall be exempt from tax by that other Contracting State for a period not exceeding 2 years from the date of his arrival in that other Contracting State.

2. This article shall not apply to income from research if such research is undertaken not in the general interest but primarily for the private benefit of a specific person or persons.

Article 22. Students and Trainees

1. *a.* An individual who is a resident of one of the Contracting States at the time he becomes temporarily present in the other Contracting State and who is temporarily present in that other Contracting State for the primary purpose of:

(i) Studying at a university or other recognized educational institution in that other Contracting State, or

(ii) Securing training required to qualify him to practice a profession of professional specialty, or

(iii) Studying or doing research as a recipient of a grant, allowance, or award from a governmental, religious, charitable, scientific, literary, or educational organization,

shall be exempt from tax by that other Contracting State with respect to amounts described in subparagraph *b.* for a period not exceeding 5 taxable years from the date of his arrival in that other Contracting State.

b. The amounts referred to in subparagraph *a.* are:

(i) Gifts from abroad for the purpose of his maintenance, education, study, research, or training;

(ii) The grant, allowance, or award; and

(iii) Income from personal services performed in that other Contracting State in an amount not in excess of 3,000 United States dollars or its equivalent in Philippine pesos for any taxable year.

2. An individual who is a resident of one of the Contracting States at the time he becomes temporarily present in the other Contracting State and who is temporarily present in that other Contracting State as an employee of, or under contract with, a resident of the first-mentioned Contracting State, for the primary purpose of:

a. Acquiring technical, professional, or business experience from a person other than that resident of the first-mentioned Contracting State or other than a person related to such resident, or

b. Studying at a university or other recognized educational institution in that other Contracting State,

shall be exempt from tax by that other Contracting State for a period not exceeding 12 consecutive months with respect to his income from personal services in an aggregate amount not in excess of 7,500 United States dollars or its equivalent in Philippine pesos for any taxable year.

3. An individual who is a resident of one of the Contracting States at the time he becomes temporarily present in the other Contracting State and who is temporarily present in that other Contracting State for

a period not exceeding 1 year, as a participant in a program sponsored by the Government of that other Contracting State, for the primary purpose of training, research, or study, shall be exempt from tax by that other Contracting State with respect to his income from personal services in respect of such training, research, or study performed in that other Contracting State in an aggregate amount not in excess of 10,000 United States dollars or its equivalent in Philippine pesos in any taxable year.

4. The benefits provided under Article 21 (Teachers) and paragraph 1 of this article shall, when taken together, extend only for such period of time, not to exceed 5 taxable years from the date of arrival of the individual claiming such benefits, as may reasonably or customarily be required to effectuate the purpose of the visit. The benefits provided under Article 21 (Teachers) shall not be available to an individual if, during the immediately preceding period, such individual enjoyed the benefits of paragraph 1 of this article.

Article 23. Relief from Double Taxation

Double taxation of income shall be avoided in the following manner:

1. In accordance with the provisions and subject to the limitations of the law of the United States (as it may be amended from time to time without changing the general principle hereof), the United States shall allow to a citizen or resident of the United States as a credit against the United States tax the appropriate amount of taxes paid or accrued to the Philippines and, in the case of a United States corporation owning at least 10 per cent of the voting stock of a Philippine corporation from which it receives dividends in any taxable year, shall allow credit for the appropriate amount of taxes paid or accrued to the Philippines by the Philippine corporation paying such dividends with respect to the profits out of which such dividends are paid. Such appropriate amount shall be based upon the amount of tax paid or accrued to the Philippines, but the credit shall not exceed the limitations (for the purpose of limiting the credit to the United States tax on income from sources within the Philippines or on income from sources outside the United States) provided by United States law for the taxable year. For purposes of applying the United States credit in relation to taxes paid or accrued to the Philippines, the rules set forth in Article 4 (Source of Income) shall be applied to determine the source of income. For purposes of applying the United States credit in relation to taxes paid or accrued to the Philippines, the taxes referred to in paragraphs 1*b*. and 2 of Article 1 (Taxes Covered) shall be considered to be income taxes.

2. In accordance with the provisions and subject to the limitations of the law of the Philippines (as it may be amended from time to time without changing the general principle hereof), the Philippines shall allow to a citizen or resident of the Philippines as a credit against Philippine tax the appropriate amount of taxes paid or accrued to the United States and, in the case of a Philippine corporation owning more than 50 per cent of the voting stock of a United States corporation

from which it receives dividends in any taxable year, shall allow credit for the appropriate amount of taxes paid or accrued to the United States by the United States corporation paying such dividends with respect to the profits out of which such dividends are paid. Such appropriate amount shall be based upon the amount of tax paid or accrued to the United States, but the credit shall not exceed the limitations (for the purpose of limiting the credit to the Philippine tax on income from sources within the United States, and on income from sources outside the Philippines) provided by Philippine law for the taxable year. For the purpose of applying the Philippines credit in relation to taxes paid or accrued to the United States, the rules set forth in Article 4 (Source of Income) shall be applied to determine the source of income. For purposes of applying the Philippine credit in relation to taxes paid or accrued to the United States, the taxes referred to in paragraphs 1*a*. and 2 of Article 1 (Taxes Covered) shall be considered to be income taxes.

Article 24. Non-Discrimination

1. A citizen of one of the Contracting States who is a resident of the other Contracting State shall not be subject in that other Contracting State to more burdensome taxes than a citizen of that other Contracting State who is a resident thereof.

2. A permanent establishment which a resident of one of the Contracting States has in the other Contracting State shall not be subject in that other Contracting State to more burdensome taxes than a resident of that other Contracting State carrying on the same activities. This paragraph shall not be construed as obliging a Contracting State to grant to individual residents of the other Contracting State any personal allowances, reliefs, or deductions for taxation purposes on account of civil status or family responsibilities which it grants to its own individual residents.

3. A corporation of one of the Contracting States, the capital of which is wholly or partly owned or controlled, directly or indirectly, by one or more residents of the other Contracting State, shall not be subjected in the first-mentioned Contracting State to any taxation or any requirement connected with taxation which is other or more burdensome than the taxation and requirements to which a corporation of the first-mentioned Contracting State carrying on the same activities, the capital of which is wholly owned or controlled by one or more residents of the first-mentioned Contracting State, is or may be subjected.

4. Notwithstanding any other provision of this Convention, the term 'taxes' or 'taxation' means, for the purpose of this article, taxes or taxation of every kind imposed at the national, state, or local level.

5. With respect to the taxes referred to in Article 1 (Taxes Covered), nothing in this article shall prevent the Philippines from limiting to its citizens or corporations the enjoyment of tax incentives granted under the following enactments:

a. Section 6 of the Investment Incentives Act (Republic Act No. 5186), *b.* Section 5 and Section 7(b) of the Export Incentives Act (Republic Act No. 6135), and

c. Section 9 of the Investment Incentives Program for the Tourism Industry (Presidential Decree No. 535)

so far as they were in force on, and have not been modified since, the date of signature of this Convention, or have been modified only in minor respects so as not to affect their general character.

6. With respect to taxes other than the taxes referred to in Article 1 (Taxes Covered), nothing in this article shall prevent the Philippines or a political subdivision or local authority thereof from limiting to Philippine citizens or corporations the enjoyment of tax incentives for the promotion of industry or business similar to those described in subparagraphs *a.*, *b.*, and *c.* of paragraph 5 so far as they were in force on, and have not been modified since, the date of signature of this Convention, or have been modified only in minor respects so as not to affect their general character.

Article 25. Mutual Agreement Procedure

1. Where a resident or citizen of one of the Contracting States considers that the action of one or both of the Contracting States results or will result for him in taxation not in accordance with this Convention, he may, notwithstanding the remedies provided by the national laws of the Contracting States, present his case to the competent authority of the Contracting State of which he is a resident or citizen. Should the resident's or citizen's claim be considered to have merit by the competent authority of the Contracting State to which the claim is made, it shall endeavor to come to an agreement with the competent authority of the other Contracting State with a view to the avoidance of taxation not in accordance with the provisions of this Convention.

2. The competent authorities of the Contracting States shall endeavor to resolve by mutual agreement any difficulties or doubts arising as to the application of this Convention. In particular, the competent authorities of the Contracting States may agree:

a. To the same attribution of industrial or commercial profits to a resident of one of the Contracting States and its permanent establishment situated in the other Contracting State;

b. To the same allocation of income, deductions, credits, or allowances between a resident of one of the Contracting States and any related persons and to the readjustment of taxes imposed by each Contracting State to reflect such allocation;

c. To the same determination of the source of particular items of income; or

d. To the same characterization of particular items of income.

3. The competent authorities of the Contracting States may communicate with each other directly for the purpose of reaching an agreement in the sense of this article. When it seems advisable for the purpose of reaching agreement, the competent authorities may meet together for an oral exchange of opinions.

4. In the event that the competent authorities reach such an agreement, taxes shall be imposed on such income, and:

a. In the case of the United States, refund or credit of taxes shall be allowed in accordance with such agreement, notwithstanding any procedural rule (including statutes of limitations) applicable under United States law.

b. In the case of the Philippines, refund or credit of taxes shall be allowed in accordance with such agreement, subject to any procedural rule (including statutes of limitations) applicable under Philippine law. However, notwithstanding any such Philippine procedural rule, a tax credit certificate shall be issued if a claim is filed with the competent authority of the Philippines no later than 2 years from the close of the taxable year in which the United States tax imposed under this paragraph is paid and such claim is filed within 5 taxable years from the close of the taxable year in issue. A tax credit certificate shall be issued with respect to a claim filed after the aforementioned 5-year period only if the claim is supported by the books and records of the taxpayer. The amount of the tax credit certificate shall be computed in the same manner as an actual refund (whether or not an actual refund of tax can be made), but may only be used as a credit against Philippine tax liability without giving rise to a refund.

Article 26. Exchange of Information

1. The competent authorities shall exchange such information as is necessary for carrying out the provisions of this Convention or for the prevention of fraud or for the administration of statutory provisions concerning taxes to which this Convention applies provided the information is of a class that can be obtained under the laws and administrative practices of each Contracting State with respect to its own taxes.

2. Any information so exchanged shall be treated as secret, except that such information may be:

a. Disclosed to any person concerned with, or

b. Made part of a public record with respect to,

the assessment, collection, or enforcement of, or litigation with respect to, the taxes to which this Convention applies.

3. No information shall be exchanged which would be contrary to public policy.

4. If information is requested by a Contracting State in accordance with this article, the other Contracting State shall obtain the information to which the request relates from or with respect to its residents or corporations in the same manner and to the same extent as if the tax of the requesting State were the tax of the other State and were being imposed by that other State. A Contracting State may obtain information from or with respect to its residents or corporations in accordance with this paragraph for the sole purpose of assisting the other Contracting State in the determination of the taxes of that other State.

5. If specifically requested by the competent authority of a Contracting State, the competent authority of the other Contracting State shall provide information under this article in the form of depositions

of witnesses and copies of unedited original documents (including books, papers, statements, records, accounts, or writings) to the same extent such depositions and documents can be obtained under the laws and administrative practices of each Contracting State with respect to its own taxes.

6. The exchange of information shall be either on a routine basis or on request with reference to particular cases. The competent authorities of the Contracting States may agree on the list of information which shall be furnished on a routine basis.

Article 27. Assistance in Collection

1. Each of the Contracting States shall endeavor to collect on behalf of the other Contracting State such taxes imposed by that other Contracting State as will ensure that any exemption or reduced rate of tax granted under this Convention by that other Contracting State shall not be enjoyed by persons not entitled to such benefits.

2. In no case shall this article be construed so as to impose upon a Contracting State the obligation to carry out measures at variance with the laws or administrative practices of either Contracting State with respect to the collection of its own taxes.

Article 28. Diplomatic and Consular Officers

Nothing in this Convention shall affect the fiscal privileges of diplomatic and consular officials under the general rules of international law or under the provisions of special agreements.

Article 29. Entry into Force

1. This Convention shall be subject to ratification in accordance with the constitutional procedures of each Contracting State and instruments of ratification shall be exchanged at Washington as soon as possible. It shall enter into force 30 days after the date of exchange of instruments of ratification and shall then have effect for the first time:

a. As respects the rate of withholding tax, to amounts paid on or after the first day of January immediately following the year in which this Convention enters into force.

b. As respects other taxes, to taxable years beginning on or after January 1 of the year following the date on which this Convention enters into force.

2. However, in the case of payments received as a consideration for the use or, or the right to use, a copyright of cinematographic films or films or tapes used for radio or television broadcasting, paragraph 2*b*.(iii) of Article 13 (Royalties) shall not have effect before January 1, 1979.

Article 30. Termination

This Convention shall remain in force until terminated by one of the Contracting States. Either Contracting State may terminate the Convention at any time after 5 years from the date on which this Convention enters into force provided that at least 6 months' prior notice of termination has been given through diplomatic channels. In such event, the Convention shall cease to have force and effect as respects income of calendar years or taxable years beginning (or, in the case of taxes payable at the source, payments made) on or after January 1 next following the expiration of the 6-month period.

Done at Manila in duplicate this first day of October, 1976.

Convention between the United States of America and the Kingdom of Spain for the Avoidance of Double Taxation and the Prevention of Fiscal Evasion with Respect to Taxes on Income, concluded in Madrid on February 22, 1990.

The United States of America and the Kingdom of Spain, desiring to conclude a Convention for the avoidance of double taxation and the prevention of fiscal evasion with respect to taxes on income, have agreed as follows:

Article 1.* General Scope

1. This Convention shall apply to persons who are residents of one or both of the Contracting States, except as otherwise provided in the Convention.

2. The Convention shall not restrict in any manner any exclusion, exemption, deduction, credit, or other allowance now or hereafter accorded:

a. by the laws of either Contracting State; or

b. by any other agreement between the Contracting States.

3. Notwithstanding any provision of the Convention except paragraph 4, a Contracting State may tax its residents (as determined under Article 4 (Residence)), and by reason of citizenship may tax its citizens, as if the Convention had not come into effect.

4. The provisions of paragraph 3 shall not affect

a. the benefits conferred by a Contracting State under paragraph 2 of Article 9 (Associated Enterprises), under paragraph 4 of Article 20 (Pensions, Annuities, Alimony, and Child Support), and under Articles 24 (Relief from Double Taxation), 25 (Non-Discrimination), and 26 (Mutual Agreement Procedure); and

b. the benefits conferred by a Contracting State under Articles 21 (Governmental Service), 22 (Students and Trainees), and 28 (Diplomatic Agents and Consular Officers), upon individuals who are neither citizens of, nor have immigrant status in, that State.

Article 2.* Taxes Covered

1. The existing taxes to which this Convention shall apply are:

a. in Spain:

(i) the Income Tax on Individuals (*el Impuesto sobre la Renta de las Personas Fisicas*), and

(ii) the Corporation Tax (*el Impuesto sobre Sociedades*).

b. in the United States, the Federal income taxes imposed by the Internal Revenue Code (but excluding social security contributions), and the excise taxes imposed on insurance premiums paid to foreign insurers and with respect to private foundations. The Convention shall, however, apply to the excise taxes imposed on insurance premiums paid to foreign insurers only to the extent that the risks covered by such premiums are not reinsured with a person not entitled to exemption from such taxes under this or any other Convention which applies to these taxes.

2. The Convention shall apply also to any identical or substantially similar taxes which are imposed after the date of signature of the Convention in addition to, or in place of, the existing taxes. The competent authorities of the Contracting States shall notify each other of any significant changes which have been made in their respective taxation laws and of any official published material concerning the application of the Convention.

Article 3.* General Definitions

1. For the purpose of this Convention, unless the context otherwise requires:

a. the term 'Spain' means the Spanish State and, when used geographically means the territory of the Spanish State including any area outside the territorial sea in which, in accordance with international law and domestic legislation, the Spanish State may exercise jurisdiction or sovereign rights with respect to the seabed, its subsoil, and superjacent waters and their natural resources.

b. the term 'United States', means the United States of America and, when used geographically means the states thereof, the District of Columbia, the territorial sea, and any area outside the territorial sea in which, in accordance with international law and domestic legislation, the United States may exercise jurisdiction or sovereign rights with respect to the seabed, its subsoil, and superjacent waters and their natural resources.

c. the terms 'a Contracting State' and 'the other Contracting State' mean Spain or the United States as the context requires;

d. the term 'person' includes an individual, a company, and any other body of persons;

e. the term 'company' means any body corporate or any entity which is treated as a body corporate for tax purposes;

f. the terms 'enterprise of a Contracting State' and 'enterprise of the other Contracting State' mean respectively an enterprise carried on by a resident of a Contracting State and an enterprise carried on by a resident of the other Contracting State;

g. the term 'national' means:

(i) any individual possessing the nationality of a Contracting State; and

(ii) any legal person, association, or other entity deriving its status as such from the law in force in a Contracting State;

h. the term 'international traffic' means any transport by a ship or aircraft, except when such transport is solely between places in the other Contracting State;

i. the term 'competent authority' means:

(i) in the case of the United States: the Secretary of the Treasury or his delegate; and

(ii) in the case of Spain: the Minister of Economy and Finance or his authorized representative.

2. As regards the application of the Convention by a Contracting State any term not defined therein shall, unless the context otherwise requires, and subject to the provisions of Article 26 (Mutual Agreement Procedure), have the meaning which it has under the laws of that State concerning the taxes to which the Convention applies.

Article 4.* Residence

1. For the purposes of this Convention, the term 'resident of a Contracting State' means any person who, under the laws of that State, is liable to tax therein by reason of his domicile, residence, place of management, place of incorporation or any other criterion of a similar nature, provided, however, that this term does not include any person who is liable to tax in that State in respect only of income from sources in that State.

2. Where by reason of the provisions of paragraph 1, an individual is a resident of both Contracting States, then his status shall be determined as follows:

a. he shall be deemed to be a resident of the State in which he has a permanent home available to him; if he has a permanent home available to him in both States, he shall be deemed to be a resident of the State with which his personal and economic relations are closer (centre of vital interests);

b. if the State in which he has his centre of vital interests cannot be determined, or if he does not have a permanent home available to him in either State, he shall be deemed to be a resident of the State in which he has an habitual abode;

c. if he has an habitual abode in both States or in neither of them, he shall be deemed to be a resident of the State of which he is a national;

d. If he is a national of both States or of neither of them, the competent authorities of the Contracting States shall settle the question by mutual agreement.

3. Where by reason of the provisions of paragraph 1, a person other than an individual is a resident of both Contracting States, the competent authorities of the Contracting States shall endeavor to settle the question by mutual agreement and determine the mode of application of the Convention to such person. If the competent authorities are unable to make such a determination, the person shall not be treated as a resident of either Contracting State except for the purposes of payments by such person covered by paragraphs 1 through 4 of Article 10 (Dividends), Article 11 (Interest), and Article 12 (Royalties).

Article 5. Permanent Establishment

1. For the purposes of this Convention, the term 'permanent establishment' means a fixed place of business through which the business of an enterprise is wholly or partly carried on.

2. The term 'permanent establishment' includes especially:

a. a place of management;

b. a branch;

c. an office;

d. a factory;

e. a workshop; and

f. a mine, an oil or gas well, a quarry, or any other place of extraction of natural resources.

3. A building site or construction or installation project, or an installation or drilling rig or ship used for the exploration or exploitation of natural resources, constitutes a permanent establishment only if it lasts more than six months.

For the purpose of computing the time limits in this paragraph, activities carried on by an enterprise associated with another enterprise within the meaning of Article 9 (Associated Enterprises) shall be regarded as carried on by the last-mentioned enterprise if the activities of both enterprises are substantially the same, unless they are carried on simultaneously.

4. Notwithstanding the preceding provisions of this Article, the term 'permanent establishment' shall be deemed not to include:

a. the use of facilities solely for the purpose of storage, display, or delivery of goods or merchandise belonging to the enterprise;

b. the maintenance of a stock of goods or merchandise belonging to the enterprise solely for the purpose of storage, display, or delivery;

c. the maintenance of a stock of goods or merchandise belonging to the enterprise solely for the purpose of processing by another enterprise;

d. the maintenance of a fixed place of business solely for the purpose of purchasing goods or merchandise, or of collecting information, for the enterprise;

e. the maintenance of a fixed place of business solely for the purpose of carrying on, for the enterprise, any other activity of a preparatory or auxiliary character;

f. the maintenance of a fixed place of business solely for any combination of the activities mentioned in subparagraphs *a.* to *e.*, provided that the overall activity of the fixed place of business resulting from this combination is of a preparatory or auxiliary character.

5. Notwithstanding the provisions of paragraphs 1 and 2, where a person – other than an agent of an independent status to whom paragraph 6 applies – is acting on behalf of an enterprise and has and habitually exercises in a Contracting State an authority to conclude contracts in the name of the enterprise, that enterprise shall be deemed to have a permanent establishment in that State in respect of any activities which what person undertakes for the enterprise, unless the activities of such person are limited to those mentioned in paragraph 4

which, if exercised through a fixed place of business, would not make this fixed place of business a permanent establishment under the provisions of that paragraph.

6. An enterprise shall not be deemed to have a permanent establishment in a Contracting State merely because it carries on business in that State through a broker, general commission agent, or any other agent of an independent status, provided that such persons are acting in the ordinary course of their business.

7. The fact that a company which is a resident of a Contracting State controls or is controlled by a company which is a resident of the other Contracting State, or which carries on business in that other State (whether through a permanent establishment or otherwise), shall not of itself constitute either company a permanent establishment of the other.

Article 6. Income from Real Property (Immovable Property)

1. Income derived by a resident of a Contracting State from real property (including income from agriculture or forestry) situated in the other Contracting State may be taxed in that other State.

2. The term 'real property' shall have the meaning which it has under the law of the Contracting State in which the property in question is situated. The term in any case shall include property accessory to immovable property, livestock and equipment used in agriculture and forestry, rights to which the provision of general law respecting landed property apply, usufruct of immovable property, and right to variable or fixed payments as consideration for the working of, or the right to work, mineral deposits, sources and other natural resources. Ships, aircraft, and containers used in international traffic shall not be regarded as real property.

3. The provisions of paragraph 1 shall apply to income derived from the direct use, letting, or use in any other form of real property.

4. The provisions of paragraphs 1 and 3 shall also apply to the income from immovable property of an enterprise and to income from immovable property used for the performance of independent personal services.

5. Where the ownership of shares or other rights in a company or other entity entitles the owner of such shares or rights to the enjoyments of real property held by the company or other entity, the income from the direct use, letting, or use in any other form of such right of enjoyment may be taxed in the Contracting State in which the real property is situated.

Article 7. Business Profits

1. The business profits of an enterprise of a Contracting State shall be taxable only in that State unless the enterprise carries on or has carried on business in the other Contracting State through a permanent establishment situated therein. If the enterprise carries on or has carried on business as aforesaid, the business profits of the enterprise may be

taxed in the other State but only so much of them as is attributable to that permanent establishment.

2. Subject to the provisions of paragraph 3, where an enterprise of a Contracting State carries on business in the other Contracting State through a permanent establishment situated therein, there shall in each Contracting State be attributed to that permanent establishment the business profits which it might be expected to make if it were a distinct and independent enterprise engaged in the same or similar activities under the same or similar conditions.

3. In determining the profits of a permanent establishment, there shall be allowed as deductions expenses which are incurred for the purposes of the permanent establishment, including research and development expenses, interest, and other similar expenses and a reasonable amount of executive and general administrative expenses, whether incurred in the State in which the permanent establishment is situated or elsewhere.

4. No business profits shall be attributed to a permanent establishment by reason of the mere purchase by that permanent establishment of goods or merchandise for the enterprise.

5. For the purposes of this Convention, the business profits to be attributed to the permanent establishment shall include only the profits or losses derived from the assets or activities of the permanent establishment and shall be determined by the same method year by year unless there is good and sufficient reason to the contrary.

6. Where business profits include items of income which are dealt with separately in other Articles of the Convention, the provisions of those Articles shall not be affected by the provisions of this Article.

Article 8.* Shipping and Air Transport

1. Profits of an enterprise of a Contracting State from the operation of ships or aircraft in international traffic shall be taxable only in that State.

2. The provisions of paragraph 1 shall also apply to profits from participation in a pool, a joint business, or an international operating agency.

Article 9. Associated Enterprises

1. Where:

a. an enterprise of a Contracting State participates directly or indirectly in the management, control or capital of an enterprise of the other Contracting State, or

b. the same persons participate directly or indirectly in the management, control, or capital of an enterprise of a Contracting State and an enterprise of the other Contracting State,

and in either case conditions are made or imposed between the two enterprises in their commercial or financial relations which differ from those which would be made between independent enterprises, then any profits which, but for those conditions would have accrued to one of the enterprises, but by reason of those conditions have not so accrued, may be included in the profits of that enterprise and taxed accordingly.

2. Where a Contracting State includes in the profits of an enterprise of that State, and taxes accordingly, profits on which an enterprise of the other Contracting State has been charged to tax in that other State, and the profits so included are profits which would have accrued to the enterprise of the first-mentioned State if the conditions made between the two enterprises had been those which would have been made between independent enterprises, then that other State shall make an appropriate adjustment to the amount of tax charged therein on those profits. In determining such adjustment, due regard shall be paid to the other provisions of this Convention and the competent authorities of the Contracting States shall if necessary consult each other.

Article 10.* Dividends

1. Dividends paid by a company which is a resident of a Contracting State to a resident of the other Contracting State may be taxed in that other State.

2. However, such dividends may also be taxed in the Contracting State of which the company paying the dividends is a resident, and according to the laws of that State, but if the beneficial owner of the dividends is a resident of the other Contracting State, the tax so charged shall not exceed:

a. 10 per cent of the gross amount of the dividends if the beneficial owner is a company which owns at least 25 per cent of the voting stock of the company paying the dividends;

b. 15 per cent of the gross amount of the dividends in all other cases.

This paragraph shall not affect the taxation of the company in respect of the profits out of which the dividends are paid.

3. The term 'dividends' as used in this Article means income from shares or other rights, not being debt-claims, participating in profits, as well as income from other corporate rights which is subjected to the same taxation treatment as income from shares by the laws of the State of which the company making the distribution is a resident. The term 'dividends' also includes income from arrangements, including debt obligations, carrying the right to participate in profits, to the extent so characterized under the law of the Contracting State in which the income arises.

4. The provisions of paragraphs 1 and 2 shall not apply if the beneficial owner of the dividends, being a resident of a Contracting State, carries on or has carried on business in the other Contracting State, of which the company paying the dividends is a resident, through a permanent establishment situated therein, or performs or has performed in that other State independent personal services from a fixed base situated therein, and the dividends are attributable to such permanent establishment or fixed base. In such case the provisions of Article 7 (Business Profits) or Article 15 (Independent Personal Services), as the case may be, shall apply.

5. A Contracting State may not impose any tax on dividends paid by a company which is not a resident of that State, except insofar as the dividends are paid to a resident of that State or the dividends are attributable to a permanent establishment or a fixed base situated in that State.

Article 11.* Interest

1. Interest arising in a Contracting State and derived by a resident of the other Contracting State may be taxed in that other State.

2. However, such interest may also be taxed in the Contracting State in which it arises and according to the laws of that State, but if the beneficial owner of the interest is a resident of the other Contracting State, the tax so charged shall not exceed 10 per cent of the gross amount thereof.

3. Notwithstanding the provisions of paragraph 2:

a. interest beneficially owned by a Contracting State, political subdivisions or local authorities thereof, and such government instrumentalities as may be agreed upon by the competent authorities, shall be taxable only in that State;

b. interest on long-term loans (5 or more years) granted by banks or other financial institutions which are residents of a Contracting State shall be taxable only in that State; and

c. interest paid in connection with the sale on credit of any industrial, commercial, or scientific equipment, shall be taxable only in the Contracting State of which the beneficial owner of the interest is a resident.

4. The term 'interest' as used in this Convention means income from debt-claims of every kind, whether or not secured by mortgage, and, subject to paragraph 3 of Article 10 (Dividends), whether or not carrying a right to participate in the debtor's profits, and in particular, income from government securities, and income from bonds or debentures, including premiums or prizes attaching to such securities, bonds, or debentures, as well as all other income that is treated as income from money lent by the taxation law of the Contracting State in which the income arises. Penalty charges for late payment shall not be regarded as interest for the purposes of the Convention.

5. The provisions of paragraphs 1, 2, and 3 shall not apply if the beneficial owner of the interest, being a resident of a Contracting State, carries on or has carried on business in the other Contracting State, in which the interest arises, through a permanent establishment situated therein, or performs or has performed in that other State independent personal services from a fixed base situated therein, and the interest is attributable to such permanent establishment or fixed base. In such case the provisions of Article 7 (Business Profits) or Article 15 (Independent Personal Services), as the case may be, shall apply.

6. For purposes of this Article, interest shall be deemed to arise in a Contracting State when the payer is that State itself or a political subdivision, local authority, or resident of that State. Where, however, the person paying the interest, whether he is a resident of a Contracting

State or not, has in a Contracting State a permanent establishment or a fixed base, and such interest is borne by such permanent establishment or fixed base, then such interest shall be deemed to arise in the State in which the permanent establishment or fixed base is situated.

7. Where, by reason of a special relationship between the payer and the beneficial owner or between both of them and some other person, the amount of the interest, having regard to the debt-claim for which it is paid, exceeds the amount which would have been agreed upon by the payer and the beneficial owner in the absence of such relationship, the provisions of this Article shall apply only to the last-mentioned amount. In such case the excess part of the payments shall remain taxable according to the laws of each Contracting State, due regard being had to the other provisions of the Convention.

Article 12.* Royalties

1. Royalties arising in a Contracting State and derived by a resident of the other Contracting State may be taxed in that other State.

2. However, such royalties may also be taxed in the Contracting State in which they arise and according to the laws of that State, but if beneficial owner is a resident of the other Contracting State, the tax so charged shall not exceed:

a. 5 per cent of the gross amount of royalties for the use of, or the right to use, any copyrights of literary, dramatic, musical, or artistic work;

b. 8 per cent of the gross amount of the royalties received in consideration for the use of, or the right to use, cinematographic films or films, tapes, and other means of transmission or reproduction of image or sound, and of the gross amount of royalties for the use of, or the right to use, industrial, commercial, or scientific equipment, and for any copyright of scientific work; and

c. 10 per cent of the gross amount of all other royalties.

Notwithstanding other provisions of this paragraph, royalties received as a consideration for technical assistance shall be taxable at the rate applying to the royalties stipulated in respect of the rights or property to which the technical assistance is related. To this effect, the taxable base shall be computed net of labor and of material costs incurred in producing such royalties.

3. The term 'royalties' as used in this Convention means payments of any kind received in consideration for the use of, or the right to use, any copyright of literary, dramatic, musical, artistic, or scientific work, including cinematographic films or films, tapes, and other means of image or sound reproduction, any patent, trademark, design or model, plan, secret formula or process, or other like right or property, or for the use of or the right to use industrial, commercial or scientific equipment, or for information concerning industrial, commercial, or scientific experience. It also includes payments for technical assistance performed in a Contracting State by a resident of the other State where such assistance is related to the application of any such right or property. The term 'royalties' also includes gains derived from the alienation of such

right or property to the extent that such gains are contingent on the productivity, use, or disposition thereof.

4. The provisions of paragraphs 1 and 2 shall not apply if the beneficial owner of the royalties, being a resident of a Contracting State, carries on or has carried on business in the other Contracting State, in which the royalties arise, through a permanent establishment situated therein, or performs or has performed in that other State independent personal services from a fixed base situated therein, and the royalties are attributable to such permanent establishment or fixed base. In such case, the provisions of Article 7 (Business Profits) or Article 15 (Independent Personal Services), as the case may be, shall apply.

5. For purposes of this Article, royalties shall be deemed to arise in a Contracting State when the payer is that State itself or a political subdivision or local authority of that State or a person who is a resident of that State. Where, however, the person paying the royalties, whether he is a resident of one of the Contracting States or not, has in one of the Contracting States a permanent establishment or fixed base in connection with which the liability to pay the royalties was incurred, and the royalties are borne by the permanent establishment or fixed base, then the royalties shall be deemed to have their source in the State in which the permanent establishment or fixed base is situated. Where the person paying the royalties is not a resident of either Contracting State, and the royalties are not borne by a permanent establishment or fixed base in either Contracting State, but the royalties relate to the use of, or the right to use, in one of the Contracting States, any property or right described in paragraph 3, the royalties shall be treated as income from sources in that State.

6. Where, by reason of a special relationship between the payer and the beneficial owner or between both of them and some other person, the amount of the royalties, having regard to the use, right, or information for which they are paid, exceeds the amount which would have been agreed upon by the payer and the beneficial owner in the absence of such relationship, the provisions of this Article shall apply only to the last-mentioned amount. In such case, the excess part of the payments shall remain taxable according to the laws of each Contracting State, due regard being had to the other provisions of the Convention.

Article 13.* Capital Gains

1. Gains derived by a resident of a Contracting State from the alienation of real property situated in the other Contracting State may be taxed in that other State.

2. Gains from the alienation of stock, participations, or other rights in a company or other legal person the property of which consists, directly or indirectly mainly of real property situated in Spain, may be taxed in Spain.

3. Gains from the alienation of personal property which are attributable to a permanent establishment which an enterprise of a Contracting State has or had in the other Contracting State, or which are attributable to a fixed base which is or was available to a resident of a Con-

tracting State in the other Contracting State for the purpose of performing independent personal services, and gains from the alienation of such a permanent establishment (alone or with the whole enterprise) or such a fixed base, may be taxed in that other State.

4. In addition to gains taxable under the foregoing paragraphs of this Article, gains derived by a resident of a Contracting State from the alienation of stock, participations, or other rights in the capital of a company or other legal person that is a resident of the other Contracting State may be taxed in that other Contracting State if the recipient of the gain, during the 12-month period preceding such alienation, had a participation, directly or indirectly, of at least 25 per cent in the capital of that company or other legal person. Such gains shall be deemed to arise in that other State to the extent necessary to avoid double taxation.

5. Gains derived by an enterprise of a Contracting State from the alienation of ships, aircraft, or containers operated in international traffic shall be taxable only in that State.

6. Gains described in Article 12 (Royalties) shall be taxable only in accordance with the provisions of Article 12.

7. Gains from the alienation of any property other than property referred to in paragraphs 1 through 6 shall be taxable only in the Contracting State of which the alienator is a resident.

Article 14.* Branch Tax

1. Notwithstanding any other provision of this Convention, a company which is a resident of Spain may be subject in the United States to a tax in addition to the tax allowable under the other provisions of this Convention. Such additional tax may not exceed:

a. 10 per cent of the 'dividend equivalent amount' of the business profits of the company which are effectively connected (or treated as effectively connected) with the conduct of a trade or business within the United States and are either attributable to a permanent establishment in the United States or subject to tax in the United States under Article 6 (Income from Real Property) or paragraph 1 of Article 13 (Capital Gains); and

b. 10 per cent of the excess, if any, of interest deductible in the United States in computing the profits of the company which are either attributable to a permanent establishment in the United States or subject to tax in the United States under Article 6 (Income from Real Property) or paragraph 1 of Article 13 (Capital Gains) over the interest paid by or from that permanent establishment or trade or business in the United States. In the case of a bank which is a resident of Spain the tax imposed under this subparagraph shall not be levied at a rate exceeding 5 per cent.

2. Notwithstanding any other provision of this Convention, where a company which is a resident of the United States conducts business in Spain through a permanent establishment situated therein or derives income subject to tax in Spain under Article 6 (Income from Real Property) or paragraph 1 of Article 13 (Capital Gains), Spain may, in

addition to the tax allowable under the other provisions of this Convention and according to its internal legislation, impose a tax on the profits attributable to the permanent establishment or the income described above, net of the corporation tax on such profits or income, and on interest expenses deductible in computing such profits or income which are comparable to the interest referred to in paragraph 1*b*. The additional tax shall not be charged at a rate exceeding 5 per cent on the deductible interest expenses referred to above in the case of a bank which is a resident of the United States, and 10 per cent in all other cases.

Article 15.* Independent Personal Services

1. Subject to the provisions of Article 7 (Business Profits), income derived by a resident of a Contracting State in respect of professional services or similar activities of an independent character shall be taxable only in that State. However, such income may be taxed in the other Contracting State if such resident has or had a fixed base regularly available to him in the other Contracting State for the purpose of performing those activities. In that case, only so much of the income as is attributable to that fixed base may be taxed in that other Contracting State.

2. The term 'professional services' includes especially independent scientific, literary, artistic, educational, or teaching activities as well as the independent activities of physicians, lawyers, engineers, architects, dentists, and accountants.

Article 16. Dependent Personal Services

1. Subject to the provisions of Articles 20 (Pensions, Annuities, Alimony, and Child Support) and 21 (Government Service), salaries, wages, and other similar remuneration derived by a resident of a Contracting State in respect of an employment shall be taxable only in that State unless the employment is exercised in the other Contracting State. If the employment is so exercised, such remuneration as is derived therefrom may be taxed in that other State.

2. Notwithstanding the provisions of paragraph 1, remuneration derived by a resident of a Contracting State in respect of an employment exercised in the other Contracting State shall be taxable only in the first-mentioned State if:

a. the recipient is present in the other State for a period or periods not exceeding in the aggregate 183 days in any 12 month period;

b. the remuneration is paid by, or on behalf of, an employer who is not a resident of the other State; and

c. the remuneration is not borne by a permanent establishment or a fixed base which the employer has in the other State.

3. Notwithstanding the preceding provisions of this Article, remuneration derived in respect of an employment as a member of the regular complement of a ship or aircraft operated in international traffic by an enterprise of a Contracting State may be taxed in that State.

Article 17.* Limitation on Benefits

1. A person which is a resident of a Contracting State and derives income from the other Contracting State shall be entitled under this Convention to relief from taxation in that other Contracting State only if:

a. such person is an individual; or

b. such person is a Contracting State, a political subdivision or local authority thereof, or a wholly-owned instrumentality thereof; or

c. such person is a non-profit religious, charitable, scientific, literary, or educational private organization or a comparable public institution; or

d. such person is a tax-exempt organization, other than those described in subparagraph *c.*, provided that more than half of the beneficiaries, members, or participants, if any, in such organization are entitled to the benefits of this Convention; or

e. the income derived from the other Contracting State is derived in connection with, or is incidental to, the active conduct by such person of a trade or business in the first-mentioned State (other than the business of making or managing investments, unless these activities are carried on by a bank or insurance company); or

f. the person deriving the income is a company in whose principal class of shares there is substantial and regular trading on a recognized securities exchange, or more than 50 per cent of whose shares of each class is owned by a resident of that Contracting State in whose principal class of shares there is such substantial and regular trading on a recognized securities exchange; or

g. both of the following conditions are satisfied:

(i) more than 50 per cent of the beneficial interest in such person (or in the case of a company, more than 50 per cent of the number of shares of each class of the company's shares) is owned, directly or indirectly, by persons who are entitled to the benefits of the Convention under subparagraphs *a., b., c., d.* or *f.* or who are citizens of the United States;

(ii) the gross income of such person is not used in substantial part, directly or indirectly, to meet liabilities (including liabilities for interest or royalties) other than to persons who are entitled to the benefits of the Convention under subparagraphs *a., b., c., d.* or *f.* or who are citizens of the United States.

2. A person which is not entitled to the benefits of the Convention pursuant to the provisions of paragraph 1 may, nevertheless, demonstrate to the competent authority of the State in which the income arises that such person should be granted the benefits of the Convention. For this purpose, one of the factors the competent authorities shall take into account is whether the establishment, acquisition, and maintenance of such person and the conduct of its operations did not have as one of its principal purposes the obtaining of benefits under the Convention.

3. For purposes of subparagraph *f.* of paragraph 1, the term 'recognized stock exchange' means:

a. the Spanish stock exchanges;

b. the NASDAQ System owned by the National Association of Securities Dealers, Inc. and any stock exchange registered with the Securities and Exchange Commission as a national securities exchange for purposes of the Securities Exchange Act of 1934; and

c. any other stock exchange agreed upon by the competent authorities of the Contracting States.

4. For purposes of subparagraph *g*.(ii) of paragraph 1, the term 'gross income' means gross receipts, or where an enterprise is engaged in a business which includes the manufacture or production of goods, gross receipts reduced by the direct costs of labor and materials attributable to such manufacture or production and paid or payable out of such receipts.

Article 18. Directors' Fees

Directors' fees and similar payments derived by a resident of a Contracting State for services performed outside such Contracting State as a member of the board of directors of a company which is a resident of the other Contracting State may be taxed in that other State.

Article 19.* Artistes and Athletes

1. Notwithstanding the provisions of Articles 15 (Independent Personal Services) and 16 (Dependent Personal Services), income derived by a resident of a Contracting State as an entertainer, such as a theatre, motion picture, radio or television artiste, or a musician, or as an athlete, from his personal activities as such exercised in the other Contracting State, may be taxed in that other State except where the amount of the compensation derived by such entertainer or athlete, including expenses reimbursed to him or borne on his behalf, from such activities does not exceed ten thousand United States dollars ($10,000) or its equivalent in pesetas for the taxable year concerned.

2. Where income in respect of activities exercised by an entertainer or an athlete in his capacity as such accrues not to the entertainer or athlete but to another person, that income of that other person may, notwithstanding the provisions of Articles 7 (Business Profits) and 15 (Independent Personal Services), be taxed in the Contracting State in which the activities of the entertainer or athlete are exercised, unless it is established that neither the entertainer or athlete nor persons related thereto participate directly or indirectly in the profits of that other person in any manner, including the receipt of deferred remuneration, bonuses, fees, dividends, partnership distributions, or other distributions.

3. Notwithstanding the provisions of paragraphs 1 and 2, income derived by a resident of a Contracting State as an entertainer or athlete shall be exempt from tax by the other Contracting State if the visit to that other State is substantially supported by public funds of the first-mentioned Contracting State or a political subdivision or local authority thereof.

Article 20.* Pensions, Annuities, Alimony, and Child Support

1. Subject to the provisions of Article 21 (Government Service):

a. pensions and other similar remuneration derived and beneficially owned by a resident of a Contracting State in consideration of past employment shall be taxable only in that State; and

b. social security benefits paid by a Contracting State to a resident of the other Contracting State or a citizen of the United States may be taxed in the first-mentioned State.

2. Annuities derived and beneficially owned by a resident of a Contracting State shall be taxable only in that State. The term 'annuities' as used in this paragraph means a stated sum paid periodically at stated times during a specific time period, under an obligation to make the payments in return for adequate and full consideration (other than services rendered).

3. Alimony paid to a resident of a Contracting State shall be taxable only in that State. The term 'alimony' as used in this paragraph means periodic payments made pursuant to a written separation agreement or a decree of divorce, separate maintenance, or compulsory support, which payments are taxable to the recipient under the laws of the State of which he is a resident.

4. Periodic payments for the support of a minor child made pursuant to a written separation agreement or a decree of divorce, separate maintenance, or compulsory support, paid by a resident of a Contracting State to a resident of the other Contracting State, shall be taxable only in the first-mentioned State.

Article 21. Government Service

1. *a.* Remuneration, other than a pension, paid by a Contracting State or a political subdivision or a local authority thereof to an individual in respect of services rendered to that State or subdivision or authority shall be taxable only in that State.

b. However, such remuneration shall be taxable only in the other Contracting State if the services are rendered in that other State and the individual is a resident of that State who:

(i) is a national of that State; or

(ii) did not become a resident of that State solely for the purpose of rendering the services.

2. *a.* Any pension paid by, or out of funds created by, a Contracting State or a political subdivision or a local authority thereof to an individual in respect of services rendered to that State or subdivision or authority shall be taxable only in that State.

b. However, such pension shall be taxable only in the other Contracting State if the individual is a resident of, and a national of, that State.

3. The provisions of Articles 15 (Independent Personal Services), 16 (Dependent Personal Services), 18 (Directors' Fees), 19 (Artistes and Athletes), and 20 (Pensions, Annuities, Alimony, and Child Support) shall apply to remuneration and pensions in respect of services

rendered in connection with a business carried on by a Contracting State or a political subdivision or a local authority thereof.

Article 22.* Students and Trainees

1. *a.* An individual who is a resident of a Contracting State at the beginning of his visit to the other Contracting State and who is temporarily present in that other Contracting State for the primary purpose of:

(i) studying at a university or other accredited educational institution in that other Contracting State, or

(ii) securing training required to qualify him to practice a profession or professional specialty, or

(iii) studying or doing research as a recipient of a grant, allowance, or award from a governmental, religious, charitable, scientific, literary, or educational organization,

shall be exempt from tax by that other Contracting State with respect to the amounts described in subparagraph *b.* of this paragraph for a period not exceeding five years from the date of his arrival in that other Contracting State.

b. The amounts referred to in subparagraph *a.* of this paragraph are:

(i) payments from abroad, other than compensation for personal services, for the purpose of his maintenance, education, study, research, or training;

(ii) the grant, allowance, or award; and

(iii) income from personal services performed in that other Contracting State in an aggregate amount not in excess of 5,000 United States dollars or its equivalent in Spanish pesetas for any taxable year.

2. An individual who is a resident of a Contracting State at the beginning of his visit to the other Contracting State and who is temporarily present in that other Contracting State as an employee of, or under contract with, a resident of the first-mentioned Contracting State, for the primary purpose of:

a. acquiring technical, professional, or business experience from a person other than that resident of the first-mentioned Contracting State, or

b. studying at a university or other accredited educational institution in that other Contracting State,

shall be exempt from tax by that other Contracting State for a period of 12 consecutive months with respect to his income from personal services in an aggregate amount not in excess of 8,000 United States dollars or its equivalent in Spanish pesetas.

3. This article shall not apply to income from research if such research is undertaken not in the public interest but primarily for the private benefit of a specific person or persons.

Article 23. Other Income

1. Items of income of a resident of a Contracting State, wherever arising, not dealt with in the foregoing Articles of this Convention shall be taxable only in that Contracting State.

2. The provisions of paragraph 1 shall not apply to income, other than income from real property as defined in paragraph 2 of Article 6 (Income from Real Property (Immovable Property)), if the beneficial owner of the income, being a resident of a Contracting State, carries on or has carried on business in the other Contracting State through a permanent establishment situated therein, or performs or has performed in that other State independent personal services from a fixed base situated therein, and the income is attributable to such permanent establishment or fixed base. In such case the provisions of Article 7 (Business Profits) or Article 15 (Independent Personal Services), as the case may be, shall apply.

Article 24.* Relief from Double Taxation

1. In Spain, double taxation will be avoided, in accordance with the relevant provisions of the law of Spain, as follows:

a. Where a resident of Spain derives income which, in accordance with the provisions of this Convention, may be taxed in the United States, other than solely by reason of citizenship, Spain shall allow as a deduction from the tax on the income of that resident an amount equal to the income tax actually paid to the United States.

Such deduction shall not, however, exceed that part of the income tax, as computed before the deduction is given, which is attributable to the income derived from the United States.

b. In the case of a dividend paid by a company which is a resident of the United States to a company which is a resident of Spain and which holds directly at least 25 per cent of the capital of the company paying the dividend, in the computation of the credit there shall be taken into account, in addition to the tax creditable under subparagraph *a.* of this paragraph, that part of the tax effectively paid by the first-mentioned company on the profits out of which the dividend is paid which relates to such dividend, provided that such amount of tax is included, for this purpose, in the taxable base of the receiving company.

Such deduction, together with the deduction allowable in respect of the dividend under subparagraph *a.* of this paragraph, shall not exceed that part of the income tax, as computed before the deduction is given, which is attributable to the income subject to tax in the United States.

For the application of this subparagraph it shall be required that a 25 per cent or greater participation in the company paying the dividend is held on a continuous basis during the taxable year in which the dividend is paid as well as during the previous taxable year.

c. Where, in accordance with any provision of the Convention, income derived by a resident of Spain is exempt from tax in Spain, Spain may, nevertheless, take into account the exempted income in calculating the amount of tax on the remaining income of such resident.

2. In accordance with the provisions and subject to the limitations of the law of the United States (as it may be amended from time to time without changing the general principle thereof), the United States

shall allow to a resident or citizen of the United States as a credit against the United States tax on income

a. the income tax paid to Spain by or on behalf of such citizen or resident; and

b. in the case of a United States company owning at least 10 per cent of the voting stock of a company which is a resident of Spain and from which the United States company receives dividends, the income tax paid to Spain by or on behalf of the distributing company with respect to the profits out of which the dividends are paid.

3. In the case of an individual who is a citizen of the United States and a resident of Spain, income which may be taxed by the United States by reason of citizenship in accordance with paragraph 3 of Article 1 (General Scope) shall be deemed to arise in Spain to the extent necessary to avoid double taxation, provided that in no event will the tax paid the United States be less than the tax that would be paid if the individual were not a citizen of the United States.

Article 25. Non-Discrimination

1. Nationals of a Contracting State shall not be subjected in the other Contracting State to any taxation or any requirement connected therewith which is other or more burdensome than the taxation and connected requirements to which nationals of that other State in the same circumstances are or may be subjected. This provision shall apply to persons who are not residents of one or both of the Contracting States. However, for the purposes of United States tax, and subject to Article 24 (Relief from Double Taxation), a United States national who is not a resident of the United States and a Spanish national who is not a resident of the United States are not in the same circumstances.

2. The taxation on a permanent establishment which an enterprise of a Contracting State has in the other Contracting State shall not be less favorably levied in that other State than the taxation levied on enterprises of that other State carrying on the same activities. This provision shall not be construed as obliging a Contracting State to grant to residents of the other Contracting State any personal allowances, reliefs, and reductions for taxation purposes on account of civil status or family responsibilities which it grants to its own residents.

3. Nothing in this Article shall be construed as preventing either Contracting State from imposing a tax as described in Article 14 (Branch Tax).

4. Except where the provisions of paragraph 1 of Article 9 (Associated Enterprises), paragraph 7 of Article 11 (Interest), or paragraph 6 of Article 12 (Royalties) apply, interest, royalties, and other disbursements paid by an enterprise of a Contracting State to a resident of the other Contracting State shall, for the purposes of determining the taxable profits of such enterprise, be deductible under the same conditions as if they had been paid to a resident of the first-mentioned State.

5. Enterprises of a Contracting State, the capital of which is wholly or partly owned or controlled, directly or indirectly, by one or more residents of the other Contracting State, shall not be subjected in the

first-mentioned State to any taxation or any requirement connected therewith which is other or more burdensome than the taxation and connected requirements to which other similarly situated enterprises of the first-mentioned State are or may be subjected.

6. The provisions of this Article shall, notwithstanding the provisions of Article 2 (Taxes Covered), apply to taxes of every kind and description imposed by a Contracting State or a political subdivision or local authority thereof.

Article 26.* Mutual Agreement Procedure

1. Where a person considers that the actions of one or both of the Contracting States result or will result for him in taxation not in accordance with the provisions of this Convention, he may, irrespective of the remedies provided by the domestic law of those States, present his case to the competent authority of the Contracting State of which he is a resident or national. The case must be presented within five years from the first notification of the action resulting in taxation not in accordance with the provisions of the Convention.

2. The competent authority shall endeavor, if the objection appears to it to be justified and if it is not itself able to arrive at a satisfactory solution, to resolve the case by mutual agreement with the competent authority of the other Contracting State, with a view to the avoidance of taxation which is not in accordance with the Convention. Any agreement reached shall be implemented notwithstanding any time limits or other procedural limitations in the domestic law of the Contracting States.

3. The competent authorities of the Contracting States shall endeavor to resolve by mutual agreement any difficulties or doubts arising as to the interpretation or application of the Convention. They may also consult together for the elimination of double taxation in cases not provided for in the Convention. In particular, the competent authorities of the Contracting States may agree on the procedures for the application of the limits imposed on the taxation at source of dividends, interest, and royalties by Articles 10 (Dividends), 11 (Interest), and 12 (Royalties), respectively.

4. The competent authorities of the Contracting States may communicate with each other directly for the purpose of reaching an agreement in the sense of the preceding paragraphs.

Article 27.* Exchange of Information and Administrative Assistance

1. The competent authorities of the Contracting States shall exchange such information as is necessary for carrying out the provisions of this Convention or of the domestic laws of the Contracting States concerning taxes covered by the Convention insofar as the taxation thereunder is not contrary to the Convention. The exchange of information is not restricted by Article 1 (General Scope). Any information received by a Contracting State shall be treated as secret in the same manner as information obtained under the domestic laws of that

State and shall be disclosed only to persons or authorities (including courts and administrative bodies) involved in the assessment, collection, or administration of, the enforcement or prosecution in respect of, or the determination of appeals in relation to, the taxes covered by the Convention. Such persons or authorities shall use the information only for such purposes. They may disclose the information in public court proceedings or in judicial decisions.

2. In no case shall the provisions of paragraph 1 be construed so as to impose on a Contracting State the obligation:

a. to carry out administrative measures at variance with the laws and administrative practice of that or of the other Contracting State;

b. to supply information which is not obtainable under the laws or in the normal course of the administration of that or of the other Contracting State;

c. to supply information which would disclose any trade, business, industrial, commercial, or professional secret or trade process, or information the disclosure of which would be contrary to public policy.

Article 28. Diplomatic Agents and Consular Officers

Nothing in this Convention shall affect the fiscal privileges of diplomatic agents or consular officers under the general rules of international law or under the provisions of special agreements.

Article 29.* Entry Into Force

1. This Convention shall be subject to ratification in accordance with the applicable procedures of each Contracting State and instruments of ratification shall be exchanged at Washington as soon as possible.

2. The Convention shall enter into force upon the exchange of instruments of ratification and its provisions shall have effect:

a. in respect of taxes imposed in accordance with Articles 10 (Dividends), 11 (Interest), and 12 (Royalties), for amounts paid or credited on or after the first day of the second month next following the date on which the Convention enters into force;

b. in respect of other taxes, for taxable periods beginning on or after the first day of January next following the date on which the Convention enters into force.

Article 30. Termination

This Convention shall remain in force until terminated by a Contracting State. Either Contracting State may terminate the Convention, through diplomatic channels, by giving notice of termination at least six months before the end of any calendar year following after the period of five years from the date on which the Convention enters into force. In such event, the Convention shall cease to have effect in respect of taxes chargeable for any taxable year beginning on or after the first day of January in the calendar year next following that in which the notice is given.

In witness whereof, the undersigned, being duly authorized by their respective Governments, have signed this Convention.

Done at Madrid, in duplicate, in the English and Spanish languages, both texts being equally authentic, this twenty-second day of February, 1990.

Protocol

At the moment of signing the Convention between the United States of America and the Kingdom of Spain for the Avoidance of Double Taxation and the Prevention of Fiscal Evasion with respect to Taxes on Income, the undersigned have agreed upon the following provisions which shall be an integral part of the Convention.

1. *With reference to paragraph 3 of Article 1 (General Scope)*

For purposes of paragraph 3, the term 'citizen' shall include a former citizen whose loss of citizenship had as one of its principal purposes the avoidance of tax, but only for a period of 10 years following such loss. For the application of this provision to a resident of a Contracting State, the competent authorities shall consult together on the purposes of such loss of citizenship.

2. *With reference to paragraph 1b of Article 2 (Taxes Covered)*

Notwithstanding the provisions of paragraph 1*b*.:

a. a Spanish company shall be exempt from the United States personal holding company tax in any taxable year only if all of its stock is owned by one or more individual, who are not residents or citizens of the United States, in their individual capacities for that entire year; and

b. a Spanish company shall be exempt from the accumulated earnings tax in any taxable year only if it is a company described in paragraph 1*f*. of Article 17 (Limitation on Benefits).

3. *With reference to paragraph 1 of Article 3 (General Definitions)*

The Parties agreed to initiate, as soon as possible, the negotiation of a Protocol to extend the application of this Convention to Puerto Rico, taking into account the special features of the taxes applied by Puerto Rico.

4. *With reference to paragraph 1d of Article 3 (General Definitions)*

The term 'any other body of persons' is understood to include an estate, a trust, or a partnership.

5. *With reference to paragraph 1 of Article 4 (Residence)*

For purposes of paragraph 1 of Article 4 it is understood that:

a. a United States citizen or an alien admitted to the United States for permanent residence (a 'green card' holder) is considered to be a resident of the United States only if the individual has a substantial presence in the United States or would be a resident of the United States and not of another country under the principles of subparagraphs *a.* and *b.* of paragraph 2 of that Article;

b. a partnership, estate, or trust is a resident of a Contracting State only to the extent that the income it derives is subject to tax in that State as the income of a resident; and

c. the term 'resident' also includes a Contracting State or a political subdivision or local authority thereof.

6. *With reference to Article 8 (Shipping and Air Transport)*

For purposes of Article 8, 'income from the operation of ships or aircraft in international traffic' will be defined in accordance with paragraphs 5 through 12 of the Commentary on Article 8 (Shipping, Inland Waterways Transport and Air Transport) of the 1977 Model Convention for the Avoidance of Double Taxation with Respect to Taxes on Income and on Capital of the Organization for Economic Cooperation and Development.

7. *With reference to Article 10 (Dividends)*

a. It is understood that the term dividends includes profits on a liquidation of a company which is a resident of a Contracting State.

b. Subparagraph *a.* of paragraph 2 shall not apply to income attributable, whether distributed or not, to shareholders of the Spanish corporations and entities referred to in Article 12.2 of Law 44/1978 of 8 September 1978 and Article 19 of Law 61/1978 of 27 December 1978 or successor statutes, as long as said income is not subject to the Spanish corporation tax.

c. Subparagraph *a.* of paragraph 2 shall not apply in the case of dividends paid by a Spanish investment institution which is subject to tax in Spain according to Article 34 or Article 35 of Law 46 of December 26, 1984 or successor statutes. Such dividends shall be taxable in Spain at the rate provided by subparagraph *b.* of paragraph 2.

d. Subparagraph *a.* of paragraph 2 shall not apply in the case of dividends paid by a United States Regulated Investment Company or a Real Estate Investment Trust. In the case of dividends from a Regulated Investment Company, subparagraph *b.* of paragraph 2 shall apply. In the case of dividends from a Real Estate Investment Trust, subparagraph *b.* of paragraph 2 shall apply if the beneficial owner of the dividends is an individual holding a less than 25 per cent interest in the Real Estate Investment Trust; otherwise, the rate of withholding applicable under domestic law shall apply.

8. *With reference to Article 11 (Interest)*

In the case of Spain:

a. It is understood that income derived from financial assets covered by Law 14 of 25 May 1985 or successor statues is included in paragraph 4.

b. In the case of the financial assets which, according to the Law referred to in the preceding paragraph, are subject to a unique withholding of tax at the time of issue, the limitation on tax provided by paragraph 2 shall not apply.

9. *With reference to paragraph 2 of Article 12 (Royalties)*

a. Royalties received in consideration for the use of, or the right to use, containers in international traffic, shall be taxable only in the Contracting State of which the recipient is a resident.

b. For purposes of paragraph 2, whether a payment is in consideration for a copyright of a scientific work will be determined in accordance with the domestic law of the Contracting State in which the royalty arises.

10. *With reference to Article 13 (Capital Gains)*

a. For purposes of Article 13, real property situated in the United States includes a United States real property interest.

b. With respect to paragraph 3, it is understood that gains from the alienation of personal property (movable property) which are attributable to a permanent establishment which an enterprise of a Contracting State has or had in the other Contracting State and which is removed from that other Contracting State may be taxed in that other Contracting State in accordance with its law, but only to the extent of the gain that has accrued as of the time of such removal, and may be taxed in the first-mentioned Contracting State in accordance with its law, but only to the extent of the gain accruing subsequent to that time of removal.

c. For purposes of paragraph 4, an alienation does not include a transfer between members of a group of companies that file a consolidated tax return, to the extent that the consideration received by the transferor consists of participations or other rights in the capital of the transferee or of another company resident in the same Contracting State that owns directly or indirectly 80 per cent or more of the voting rights and value of the transferee, if

(i) the transferor and transferee are companies resident in the same Contracting State;

(ii) the transferor or the transferee owns, directly or indirectly, 80 per cent or more of the voting rights and value of the other, or a company resident in the same Contracting State owns directly or indirectly (through companies resident in the same Contracting State) 80 per cent or more of the voting rights and value of each of them; and

(iii) for the purposes of determining gain on any subsequent disposition, the initial cost of the asset for the transferee is determined based on the cost it had for the transferor, increased by any cash or other property paid.

Notwithstanding the foregoing, if cash or property other than such participations or other rights is received, the amount of the gain (limited to the amount of cash or other property received), may be taxed by the other Contracting State.

11. *With reference to Article 14 (Branch Tax)*

a. With reference to the additional tax that may be imposed under Article 14, it is understood that the tax may be imposed on income subject to tax under Article 6 (Income from Real Property) or paragraph 1 of Article 13 (Capital Gains) only when that income is, or has been, subject to tax on a net basis.

b. With reference to paragraph 1*b*. and paragraph 2, it is understood that the term 'a bank' includes a savings bank (*'Cajas de Ahorro'*).

12. *With reference to Article 15 (Independent Personal Services)*

The term 'fixed base' shall be interpreted according to the Commentary on Article 14 (Independent Personal Services) of the 1977 Model Convention for the Avoidance of Double Taxation with Respect to Taxes on Income and on Capital of the Organization for Economic Cooperation and Development, and of any guidelines which, for the application of such Article, may be developed in the future.

13. *With reference to paragraph 1d of Article 17 (Limitation on Benefits)*

The tax-exempt organizations described in paragraph 1*d*. of Article 17 include, but are not limited to, pension funds, pension trusts, private foundations, trade unions, trade associations, and similar organizations. In all events, a pension fund, pension trust, or similar entity organized for purposes of providing retirement, disability, or other employment benefits that is organized under the laws of a Contracting State shall be entitled to the benefits of the Convention if the organization sponsoring such fund, trust, or entity is entitled to the benefits of the Convention under Article 17.

14. *With reference to Article 19 (Artistes and Athletes)*

The provisions of paragraph 1 shall not preclude the imposition of withholding taxes at source in accordance with the domestic laws of the Contracting States. In such case, the provisions of paragraph 1 shall be made effective by way of refunding any excess taxes withheld after the close of the taxable year.

15. *With reference to paragraph 1b of Article 20 (Pensions, Annuities, Alimony, and Child Support)*

The rules applicable to social security benefits also apply to pensions paid from publicly administered funds for non-governmental services (such as payments from the Railroad Retirement Accounts in the United States).

16. *With reference to Article 22 (Students and Trainees)*

The amount of 5,000 United States dollars referred to in paragraph 1*b*. and the amount of 8,000 United States dollars referred to in paragraph 2*b*. includes any amount excluded or exempted from taxation under the laws of that other Contracting State.

17. *With reference to paragraph 1b of Article 24 (Relief from Double Taxation)*

In the case of a company created during the taxable year preceding the payment of the dividend, the previous taxable year, for the purpose of paragraph 1*b*., is deemed to begin on the date of creation of such company.

18. *With reference to paragraph 1 of Article 26 (Mutual Agreement Procedure)*

The term 'first notification' means, in the case of the United States, the Notice of Deficiency as provided for under section 6212 of the Internal Revenue Code and, in the case of Spain, the Notification of the Administrative Act of Assessment. In the case of taxes at source, the 'first notification' means, in the case of both Contracting States, the date on which the tax is withheld or paid.

19. *With reference to Article 27 (Exchange of Information and Administrative Assistance)*

a. Article 27 shall be interpreted consistently with the Commentary on Article 26 (Exchange of Information) of the 1977 Model Convention for the Avoidance of Double Taxation with Respect to Taxes on Income and on Capital of the Organization for Economic Cooperation and Development.

b. The competent authorities of the Contracting States shall, even without previous request, exchange such information as is necessary to ensure that the benefits of the Convention are applied only to those entitled thereto.

20. *With reference to Article 29 (Entry into Force)*

In the event of substantial changes in the domestic legislation of either Contracting State or in their tax relations with other States, either by virtue of new developments in their policy regarding tax treaty negotiations or as a consequence of changes which may occur in the supranational systems of integration to which the Contracting States are Parties, the competent authorities shall consult together on the appropriateness of negotiating modification of the Convention to reflect such changes.

In witness whereof, the undersigned, being duly authorized by their respective Governments, have signed this Convention.

Done at Madrid, in duplicate, in the English and Spanish languages, both texts being equally authentic, this twenty-second day of February, 1990.

Convention between the Government of the United States of America and the Kingdom of Sweden for the Avoidance of Double Taxation and the Establishment of Rules of Reciprocal Administrative Assistance in the Tax of Income and Other Taxes, concluded in Washington on March 23, 1939, as amended by the Protocol of October 22, 1963.

Article I

The taxes referred to in this Convention are:

a. In the case of the United States of America:

(1) The Federal income taxes, including surtaxes and excess-profits taxes.

(2) The Federal capital stock tax.

b. In the case of Sweden:

(1) The National income and property tax, including surtax.

(2) The National special property tax.

(3) The communal income tax.

It is mutually agreed that the present Convention shall also apply to any other or additional taxes imposed by either contracting State, subsequent to the date of signature of this Convention, upon substantially the same bases as the taxes enumerated herein.

The benefits of this Convention shall accrue only to citizens and residents of the United States of America, to citizens and residents of Sweden and to United States or Swedish corporations and other entities.

Article II*

An enterprise of one of the contracting States is not subject to taxation in the other contracting State in respect of its industrial and commercial profits except in respect of such profits allocable to its permanent establishment in the latter State. The income thus taxed in the latter State shall be exempt from taxation in the former State.

No account shall be taken, in determining the tax in one of the contracting States, of the mere purchase of merchandise effected therein by an enterprise of the other State.

The competent authorities of the two contracting States may lay down rules by agreement for the apportionment of industrial and commercial profits.

Article III

When an enterprise of one of the contracting States, by reason of its participation in the management or capital of an enterprise of the other contracting State, makes or imposes on the latter in their commercial or financial relations conditions different from those which would be made with an independent enterprise, any profits which would normally have appeared in the balance sheet of the latter enterprise but which have been in this manner diverted to the former enterprise may, subject to applicable measures of appeal, be incorporated in the taxable profits of the latter enterprise. In such case the consequent rectifications may be made in the accounts of the former enterprise.

Article IV

Income which an enterprise of one of the contracting States derives from the operation of ships or aircraft registered in that State is taxable only in the State in which registered. Income derived by such an enterprise from the operation of ships or aircraft not so registered shall be subject to the provisions of Article II.

Article V

Income of whatever nature derived from real property, including gains derived from the sale of such property, but not including interest from mortgages or bonds secured by real property, shall be taxable only in the contracting State in which the real property is situated.

Article VI

Royalties from real property or in respect of the operation of mines, quarries, or other natural resources shall be taxable only in the contracting State in which such property, mines, quarries, or other natural resources are situated.

Other royalties and amounts derived from within one of the contracting States by a resident or by a corporation or other entity of the other contracting State as consideration for the right to use copyrights, patents, secret processes and formulae, trade-marks and other analogous rights, shall be exempt from taxation in the former State.

Article VII

1. Dividends received from sources within one of the contracting States by a resident, corporation, or other entity of the other State not having a permanent establishment in the former State shall be subject to tax by such former State at a rate not in excess of 15 per cent of the amount of such dividends: *Provided, however,* that such rate of tax shall not exceed 5 per cent of the amount of such dividends paid by a corporation of such former State to a corporation of such other State if:

a. During the part of the payer corporation's taxable year preceding the payment of the dividend and during the whole of the prior taxable year at least 50 per cent of the voting stock of such corporation was owned by the recipient corporation either alone or in association with not more than three other corporations of such other State and at least 10 per cent of the voting stock of the payer corporation was owned by each such recipient corporation; and

b. Not more than 25 per cent of the gross income of the payer corporation (other than a corporation the principal business of which is the making of loans) for such prior taxable year is derived from interest and dividends other than interest and dividends received from a corporation in which it owns at least 50 per cent of the voting stock.

2. When a Swedish corporation or other entity derives dividends from a United States corporation or other entity the dividends thus derived shall be exempt from Swedish tax; provided that in accordance with the laws of Sweden the dividends would be exempt from tax if both corporations or entities had been Swedish corporations or entities.

Article VIII

Interest on bonds, debentures, other securities and notes, or on any other form of indebtedness received from sources within one of the contracting States by a resident or corporation or other entity of the other State not having a permanent establishment in the former State shall be exempt from tax by such former State.

Article IX

Gains derived in one of the contracting States from the sale or exchange of capital assets by a resident or a corporation or other entity of the other contracting State shall be exempt from taxation in the former State, provided such resident or corporation or other entity has no permanent establishment in the former State.

Article X

Wages, salaries and similar compensation – and pensions – paid by one of the contracting States or by the political subdivisions or territories or possessions thereof to individuals residing in the other State shall be exempt from taxation in the latter State.

Private pensions and annuities derived from within one of the contracting States and paid to individuals residing in the other contracting State shall be exempt from taxation in the former State.

Article XI

a. Compensation for labor or personal services, including the practice of the liberal professions, shall be taxable only in the contracting State in which such services are rendered.

b. The provisions of paragraph *a.* are, however, subject to the following exceptions:

A resident of Sweden shall be exempt from United States tax upon compensation for labor or personal services performed within the United States of America if he falls within either of the following classifications:

1. He is temporarily present within the United States of America for a period or periods not exceeding a total of one hundred eighty days during the taxable year and his compensation is received for labor or personal services performed as an employee of, or under contract with, a resident or corporation or such other entity of Sweden; or

2. He is temporarily present in the United States of America for a period or periods not exceeding a total of ninety days during the

taxable year and the compensation received for such services does not exceed $3,000.00 in the aggregate.
In such cases Sweden reserves the right to the taxation of such income.

c. The provisions of paragraph *b.* of this Article shall apply, *mutatis mutandis*, to a resident of the United States of America deriving compensation for personal services performed within Sweden.

d. The provisions of paragraphs *b.* and *c.* of this Article shall have no application to the professional earnings of such individuals as actors, artists, musicians and professional athletes.

e. The provisions of this Article shall have no application to the income to which Article X relates.

Article XII

1. A resident of one of the contracting States who is temporarily present in the other contracting State solely:

a. As a student at a recognized university, college, or school situated in the other contracting State, or

b. As a business apprentice, or

c. As the recipient of a grant, allowance or award which is for the primary purpose of study or research from a religious, charitable, scientific, or educational organization,

shall be exempt from tax by the other State on his remittances from abroad derived as remuneration for employment or for the purposes of his maintenance, education, or training.

2. A resident of one of the contracting States who is temporarily present in the other contracting State, solely for the purpose of training, research, or study, under arrangements with the Government of the other State, shall be exempt from tax by the other State on his remuneration for services directly related to such training, research, or study (including any emoluments or remuneration from his employer abroad), if the amount of such remuneration does not exceed $10,000.

3. *a.* A resident of one of the contracting States who, at the invitation of a university, college, school or other recognized educational institution situated in the other contracting State, is temporarily present in the other State solely for the purpose of teaching, or engaging in research, or both, at the educational institution shall, for a period not exceeding two years from the date of his arrival in such other State, be exempt from tax by the other State on his remuneration for such teaching or research.

b. The preceding subparagraph shall not apply to any remuneration for research carried on for the benefit of any person using or disseminating the results of such research for purposes of profit.

4. An individual who qualifies for exemption under more than one provision of the preceding paragraphs of this Article shall be entitled to claim the exemption most favorable to him.

Article XIII

In the case of taxes on property or increment of property the following provisions shall be applicable:

1. If the property consists of:

a. Immovable property and accessories appertaining thereto;

b. Commercial or industrial enterprises, including maritime shipping and air transport undertakings;

the tax may be levied only in that contracting State which is entitled under the preceding Articles to tax the income from such property.

2. In the case of all other forms of property, the tax may be levied only in that contracting State where the taxpayer has his residence or, in the case of a corporation or other entity, in the contracting State where the corporation or other entity has been created or organized.

The same principles shall apply to the United States capital stock tax with respect to corporations of Sweden having capital or other property in the United States of America.

Article XIV

It is agreed that double taxation shall be avoided in the following manner:

a. Notwithstanding any other provisions of this Convention, the United States of America in determining the income and excess-profits taxes, including all surtaxes, of its citizens or residents or corporations, may include in the basis upon which such taxes are imposed all items of income taxable under the revenue laws of the United States of America as though this Convention had not come into effect. The United States of America shall, however, deduct the amount of the taxes specified in Article I*b*.(1) and (3) of this Convention or other like taxes from the income tax thus computed but not in excess of that portion of the income tax liability which the taxpayer's net income taxable in Sweden bears to his entire net income.

b. (1) Sweden, in determining its taxes specified in Article I of this Convention, shall exclude from the basis upon which its taxes are imposed such items of income and property as are exempt from taxation in Sweden under the provisions of this Convention; but the income and property thus excluded may be taken into account by Sweden in the determination of the graduated rate of Swedish tax to be imposed on Swedish residents or corporations or other entities.

(2) There shall also be allowed by Sweden from its income taxes a deduction offsetting the tax imposed in accordance with this Convention by the United States of America upon such income from sources therein which is not exempt from taxation in Sweden, but in an amount not exceeding that proportion of the Swedish taxes which such income bears to the entire income subject to tax by Sweden.

Article XV

With a view to the more effective imposition of the taxes to which the present Convention relates, each of the contracting States undertakes, subject to reciprocity, to furnish such information in the matter of taxation, which the authorities of the State concerned have at their disposal or are in a position to obtain under their own law, as may be of use to the authorities of the other State in the assessment of the taxes in question and to lend assistance in the service of documents in connection therewith. Such information and correspondence relating to the subject matter of this Article shall be exchanged between the competent authorities of the contracting States in the ordinary course or on demand.

Article XVI

1. In accordance with the preceding Article, the competent authorities of the United States of America shall forward to the competent authorities of Sweden as soon as practicable after the close of each calendar year the following information relating to such calendar year:

a. The names and addresses of all addressees within Sweden deriving from sources within the United States of America dividends, interest, royalties, pensions, annuities, or other fixed or determinable annual or periodical income, showing the amount of such income with respect to each addressee;

b. Any particulars which the competent United States authorities may obtain from banks, savings banks or other similar institutions concerning assets belonging to individuals resident in Sweden or to Swedish corporations or other entities;

c. Any particulars which the competent United States authorities may obtain from inventories in the case of property passing on death concerning debts contracted with individuals resident in Sweden or Swedish corporations or other entities.

2. The competent authorities of Sweden shall forward to the competent authorities of the United States of America as soon as practicable after the close of each calendar year the following information relating to such calendar year:

a. The particulars contained in the forms delivered to the Swedish authorities in connection with the payment to individuals or corporations or other entities whose addresses are within the United States of America of dividends on shares in a corporation or participation certificates in co-operative societies, and interest on bonds or other similar securities;

b. The particulars contained in permits accorded to individuals resident in the United States of America or to United States corporations or other entities to enable them to acquire for business purposes immovable property situated in Sweden;

c. Any particulars which the central Swedish authorities may obtain from banks, savings banks or other similar institutions concerning assets belonging to individuals resident in the United States of America or to United States corporations or other entities;

d. Any particulars which the central Swedish authorities may obtain from inventories in the case of property passing on death, concerning debts contracted with individuals resident in the United States of America, or United States corporations or other entities;

e. A list of the names and addresses of all United States citizens resident in the United States of America who have made declarations to the Central Committee in Stockholm in charge of the taxation of taxpayers not resident in Sweden for purposes of the Swedish tax on income and property;

f. Particulars concerning annuities and pensions, public or private, paid to individuals resident in the United States of America.

Article XVII

Each contracting State undertakes, in the case of citizens or corporations or other entities of the other contracting State, to lend assistance and support in the collection of the taxes to which the present Convention relates, together with interest, costs, and additions to the taxes and fines not being of a penal character. The contracting State making such collection shall be responsible to the other contracting State for the sums thus collected.

In the case of applications for enforcement of taxes, revenue claims of each of the contracting States which have been finally determined shall be accepted for enforcement by the other contracting State and collected in that State in accordance with the laws applicable to the enforcement and collection of its own taxes. The State to which application is made shall not be required to enforce executory measures for which there is no provision in the law of the State making the application.

The applications shall be accompanied by such documents as are required by the laws of the State making the application to establish that the taxes have been finally determined.

If the revenue claim has not been finally determined the State to which application is made may, at the request of the other contracting State, take such measures of conservancy as are authorized by the revenue laws of the former State.

Article XVIII

The competent authority of each of the contracting States shall be entitled to obtain, through diplomatic channels, from the competent authority of the other contracting State, particulars in concrete cases relative to the application to citizens or to corporations or other entities of the former State, of the taxes to which the present Convention relates. With respect to particulars in other cases, the competent authority of each of the contracting States will give consideration to requests from the competent authority of the other contracting State.

Article XIX

In no case shall the provisions of Article XVII, relating to mutual assistance in the collection of taxes, or of Article XVIII, relating to particulars in concrete cases, be construed so as to impose upon either of the contracting States the obligation

1. to carry out administrative measures at variance with the regulations and practice of either contracting State, or
2. to supply particulars which are not procurable under its own legislation or that of the State making application.

The State to which application is made for information or assistance shall comply as soon as possible with the request addressed to it. Nevertheless, such State may refuse to comply with the request for reasons of public policy or if compliance would involve violation of a business, industrial or trade secret or practice. In such case it shall inform, as soon as possible, the State making the application.

Article XX

Where a taxpayer shows proof that the action of the revenue authorities of the contracting States has resulted in double taxation in his case in respect of any of the taxes to which the present Convention relates, he shall be entitled to lodge a claim with the State of which he is a citizen or, if he is not a citizen of either of the contracting States, with the State of which he is a resident, or, if the taxpayer is a corporation or other entity, with the State in which it is created or organized. Should the claim be upheld, the competent authority of such State may come to an agreement with the competent authority of the other State with a view to equitable avoidance of the double taxation in question.

Article XXI

The competent authorities of the two contracting States may prescribe regulations necessary to interpret and carry out the provisions of this Convention. With respect to the provisions of this Convention relating to exchange of information, service of documents and mutual assistance in the collection of taxes, such authorities may, by common agreement, prescribe rules concerning matters of procedure, forms of application and replies thereto, conversion of currency, disposition of amounts collected, minimum amounts subject to collection and related matters.

Article XXII

The present Convention shall be ratified, in the case of the United States of America, by the President, by and with the advice and consent of the Senate, and in the case of Sweden, by his Majesty the King, with the consent of the Riksdag. The ratifications shall be exchanged at Stockholm.

This Convention shall become effective on the first day of January following the exchange of instruments of ratification and shall apply to income realized and property held on or after that date. The Convention shall remain in force for a period of five years and indefinitely thereafter but may be terminated by either contracting State at the end of a five-year period or at any time thereafter, provided at least six months' prior notice of termination has been given, the termination to become effective on the first day of January following the expiration of the six-month period.

In witness whereof the respective Plenipotentiaries have signed this convention and have affixed their seals thereto.

Done in duplicate, in English and Swedish languages, both authentic, at Washington, this twenty-third day of March, 1939.

Protocol

At the moment of signing the Convention for the avoidance of double taxation, and the establishment of rules of reciprocal administrative assistance in the case of income and other taxes, this day concluded between the United States of America and Sweden, the undersigned Plenipotentiaries have agreed that the following provisions shall form an integral part of the Convention:

1. As used in this Convention:

a. The term 'permanent establishment' means a fixed place of business in which the business of the enterprise is wholly or partly carried on. A permanent establishment shall include especially a place of management; a branch; an office; a workshop; a mine, quarry, or other place of extraction of natural resources; a building site, or construction of assembly project, which exists for more than twelve months.

The term 'permanent establishment' shall not be deemed to include:

(i) The use of facilities solely for the purpose of storage, display, or delivery of goods or merchandise belonging to the enterprise;

(ii) The maintenance of a stock of goods or merchandise belonging to the enterprise solely for the purpose of storage, display, or delivery;

(iii) The maintenance of a stock of goods or merchandise belonging to the enterprise solely for the purpose of processing by another enterprise;

(iv) The maintenance of a fixed place of business solely for the purpose of purchasing goods or merchandise or for collecting information, for the enterprise;

(v) The maintenance of a fixed place of business solely for the purpose of advertising, for the supply of information, for scientific research or for similar activities which have a preparatory or auxiliary character, for the enterprise.

A person acting in one of the contracting States on behalf of an enterprise of the other State, other than an agent of independent status to whom the following sentence applies, shall be deemed to be a permanent establishment in the former State if he has, and habitually exercises in that State, an authority to conclude contracts in the name of the enterprise, unless his activities are limited to the purchase of goods or merchandise for the enterprise.

An enterprise of one of the contracting States shall not be deemed to have a permanent establishment in the other State merely because it is carries on business in that other State through a broker, general commission agent, or any other agent of an independent status, where such persons are acting in the ordinary course of their business.

The fact that a corporation of one of the contracting States controls or is controlled by a corporation which is a corporation of the other State, or which carries on business in that other State (whether through a permanent establishment or otherwise), shall not of itself constitute either corporation a permanent establishment of the other.

b. The term 'enterprise' includes every form of undertaking whether carried on by an individual, partnership, corporation, or any other entity.

c. The term 'enterprise of one of the contracting States' means as the case may be, 'United States enterprise' or 'Swedish enterprise'.

d. The term 'United States enterprise' means an enterprise carried on in the United States of America by a resident of the United States of America or by a United States corporation or other entity; the term 'United States corporation or other entity' means a partnership, corporation or other entity created or organized in the United States of America or under the law of the United States of America or of any State or Territory of the United States of America.

e. The term 'Swedish enterprise' is defined in the same manner, *mutatis mutandis*, as the term 'United States enterprise'.

2. The term 'corporation' includes associations, joint-stock companies, and insurance companies.

3. A citizen of one of the contracting States not residing in either shall be deemed, for the purposes of this Convention, to be a resident of the contracting State of which he is a citizen.

When doubt arises with respect to residence or with respect to the taxable status of corporations or other entities, the competent authorities of the two contracting States may settle the question by mutual agreement.

4. The provisions of Swedish law concerning the taxation of the undivided estates of deceased persons shall not apply where the beneficiaries are directly liable to taxation in the United States of America.

5. The term 'life annuities' referred to in Article X of this Convention means a stated sum payable periodically at stated times during life, or during a specified number of years, under an obligation to make the payments in consideration of a gross sum paid for such obligation.

6. The Swedish so-called 'fees tax' (*bevillningsavgift for vissa offentliga forestallningar*) based on gross income in so far as it affects such individuals as actors, artists, musicians and professional athletes shall be deemed to be an income tax for the purpose of Article XIV*a*.

In the application of the provisions of this Convention the benefits of the internal revenue laws of the United States, relating to credits for foreign taxes, shall be accorded.

7. The citizens of one of the contracting States shall not, while resident in the other State, be subject therein to other or more burdensome taxes than are citizens of that other State residing in its territory. The term 'citizens' as used in this paragraph, includes also all legal persons, partnerships, and associations created or organized under the

laws in force in the respective contracting State. In this paragraph the word 'taxes' means taxes of every kind or description, whether Federal, State, or municipal.

8. The provisions of this Convention shall not be construed to deny or affect in any manner the right of diplomatic and consular officers to other or additional exemptions now enjoyed or which may hereafter be granted to such officers, nor to deny to either of the contracting States the right to subject to taxation its own diplomatic and consular officers.

9. The provisions of the present Convention shall not be construed to restrict in any manner any exemption, deduction, credit or other allowance accorded by the laws of one of the contracting States in the determination of tax imposed by such State.

10. In the administration of the provisions of this Convention relating to exchange of information, service of documents, and mutual assistance in collection of taxes, fees and costs incurred in the ordinary course shall be borne by the State to which application is made but extraordinary costs incident to special forms of procedure shall be borne by the applying State.

11. Documents and other communications or information contained therein, transmitted under the provisions of this Convention by one of the contracting States to the other contracting State shall not be published, revealed or disclosed to any person except to the extent permitted under the laws of the latter State with respect to similar documents, communications or information.

12. As used with respect to revenue claims in Article XVII of this Convention the term 'finally determined' shall be deemed to mean:

a. In the case of Sweden, claims which have been finally established, even though still open to revision by exceptional procedure;

b. In the case of the United States of America, claims which are no longer appealable, or which have been determined by decision of a competent tribunal, which decision has become final.

13. As used in this Convention the term 'competent authority' or 'competent authorities' means, in the case of the United States of America, the Secretary of the Treasury or his authorized representative and, in the case of Sweden, the Minister of Finance or his authorized representative.

14. The term 'United States of America' as used in this Convention in a geographical sense includes only the States, the Territories of Alaska and Hawaii, and the District of Columbia.

15. Should any difficulty or doubt arise as to the interpretation or application of the present Convention, or its relationship to Conventions between one of the contracting States and any other State, the competent authorities of the contracting States may settle the question by mutual agreement.

16. The present Convention and Protocol shall not be deemed to affect the exchange of notes between the United States of America and Sweden providing relief from double taxation on shipping profits, signed March 31, 1938.

Sweden

Done at Washington, this twenty-third day of March, 1939.

Convention between the Government of United States of America and the Government of the Swiss Confederation for the Avoidance of Double Taxation with Respect to Taxes on Income, concluded in Washington on May 24, 1951.

Article I

1. The taxes referred to in this Convention are:

a. In the case of the United States of America:

The Federal income taxes, including surtaxes and excess profits taxes.

b. In the case of The Swiss Confederation:

The federal, cantonal and communal taxes on income (total income, earned income, income from property, industrial and commercial profits, etc.).

2. The present Convention shall also apply to any other income or profits tax of a substantially similar character imposed by either contracting State subsequently to the date of signature of the present Convention.

Article II

1. As used in this Convention:

a. The term 'United States' means the United States of America, and when used in a geographical sense means the States, the Territories of Alaska and Hawaii, and the District of Columbia.

b. The term 'Switzerland' means The Swiss Confederation.

c. The term 'permanent establishment' means a branch, office, factory, workshop, warehouse or other fixed place of business, but does not include the casual and temporary use of merely storage facilities, nor does it include an agency unless the agent has and habitually exercises a general authority to negotiate and conclude contracts on behalf of an enterprise or has a stock of merchandise from which he regularly fills orders on its behalf. An enterprise of one of the contracting States shall not be deemed to have a permanent establishment in the other State merely because it carries on business dealing in such other State through a commission agent, broker or custodian or other independent agent acting in the ordinary course of his business as such. The fact that an enterprise of one of the contracting States maintains in the other State a fixed place of business exclusively for the purchase of goods or merchandise shall not of itself constitute such fixed place of business a permanent establishment of such enterprise. The fact that a corporation of one contracting State has a subsidiary corporation which is a corporation of the other State or which is engaged in trade or business in the other State shall not of itself constitute that subsidiary corporation a permanent establishment of its parent corporation. The maintenance within the territory of one of the contracting States by an enterprise of the other contracting State of a warehouse for convenience of delivery and not for purposes of display shall not of itself constitute a permanent establishment within that territory even though offers of purchase have been obtained by an agent of the enterprise in that territory and transmitted by him to the enterprise for acceptance.

d. The term 'enterprise of one of the contracting States' means, as the case may be, 'United States enterprise' or 'Swiss enterprise'.

e. The term 'United States enterprise' means an industrial or commercial enterprise or undertaking carried on in the United States by a resident (including an individual, fiduciary and partnership) of the United States or by a United States corporation or other entity; the term 'United States corporation or other entity' means a corporation or other entity created or organized under the law of the United States or of any State or Territory of the United States.

f. The term 'Swiss enterprise' means an industrial or commercial enterprise or undertaking carried on in Switzerland by an individual resident in Switzerland or by a Swiss corporation or other entity; the term 'Swiss corporation or other entity' means a corporation or institution or foundation having juridical personality, or a partnership (association '*en nom collectif*' or '*en commandite*'), or other association without juridical personality, created or organized under Swiss laws.

g. The term 'competent authorities' means, in the case of the United States, the Commissioner of Internal Revenue as authorized by the Secretary of the Treasury; and in the case of Switzerland, the Director of the Federal Tax Administration as authorized by the Federal Department of Finances and Customs.

h. The term 'industrial or commercial profits' includes manufacturing, mercantile, mining, financial and insurance profits, but does not include income in the form of dividends, interest, rents or royalties, or remuneration for personal services: Provided, however, that such excepted items of income shall, subject to the provisions of this Convention, be taxed separately or together with industrial or commercial profits in accordance with the laws of the contracting States.

2. In the application of the provisions of the present Convention by one of the contracting States any term not otherwise defined shall, unless the context otherwise requires, have the meaning which such term has under its own tax laws.

Article III

1. *a.* An Swiss enterprise shall not be subject to taxation by the United States in respect of its industrial and commercial profits unless it is engaged in trade or business in the United States through a permanent establishment situated therein. If it is so engaged the United States may impose its tax upon the entire income of such enterprise from sources within the United States.

b. A United States enterprise shall not be subject to taxation by Switzerland in respect of its industrial and commercial profits except as to such profits allocable to its permanent establishment situated in Switzerland.

2. No account shall be taken in determining the tax in one of the contracting States of the mere purchase of merchandise therein by an enterprise of the other State.

3. Where an enterprise of one of the contracting States is engaged in trade or business in the territory of the other contracting State through a permanent establishment situated therein, there shall be attributed to such permanent establishment the industrial or commercial profits which it might be expected to derive if it were an independent enterprise engaged in the same or similar activities under the same or similar conditions and dealing at arm's length with the enterprise of which it is a permanent establishment.

4. In the determination of the industrial or commercial profits of the permanent establishment there shall be allowed as deductions all expenses which are reasonably applicable to the permanent establishment, including executive and general administrative expenses so applicable.

5. The competent authorities of the two contracting States may law down rules by agreement for the apportionment of industrial and commercial profits.

Article IV

Where an enterprise of one of the contracting States, by reason of its participation in the management or the financial structure of an enterprise of the other contracting State, makes with or imposes on the latter, in their commercial or financial relations, conditions different from those which would be made with an independent enterprise, any profits which would normally have accrued to one of the enterprises, but by reason of those conditions have not so accrued, may be included in the profits of that enterprise and taxed accordingly.

Article V

Profits which an enterprise of one of the contracting States derives from the operation of ships or aircraft registered in that State shall be taxable only in the State in which such ships or aircraft are registered.

Article VI

1. The rate of tax imposed by one of the contracting States upon dividends derived sources within such State by a resident or corporation of the other contracting State not having a permanent establishment in the former State shall not exceed 15 per cent. Provided, however, that this paragraph shall have no application to Swiss tax in the case of dividends derived from Switzerland by a Swiss citizen (who is not also a citizen of the United States) resident in the United States.

2. It is agreed, however, that such rate of tax shall not exceed five percent if the shareholder is a corporation controlling, directly or indirectly, at least 95 per cent of the entire voting power in the corporation paying the dividend, and if not more than 25 per cent of the gross

income of such paying corporation is derived from interest and dividends, other than interest and dividends received from its own subsidiary corporations. Such reduction of the rate to five per cent shall not apply if the relationship of the two corporations has been arranged or is maintained primarily with the intention of securing such reduced rate.

3. Switzerland may collect its tax without regard to paragraphs 1 and 2 of this Article but it will make refund of the tax so collected in excess of the tax computed at the reduced rates provided in such paragraphs.

Article VII

1. The rate of tax imposed by one of the contracting States on interest on bonds, securities, notes, debentures or on any other form of indebtedness (including mortgages or bonds secured by real property) derived from sources within such contracting State by a resident or corporation or other entity of the other contracting State not having a permanent establishment in the former State shall not exceed five per cent: Provided, however, that this paragraph shall have no application to Swiss tax in the case of interest derived from Switzerland by a Swiss citizen (who is not also a citizen of the United States) resident in the United States.

2. Switzerland may collect its tax without regard to paragraph 1 of this Article but will make refund of the tax so collected in excess of the tax computed at the reduced rate provided in such paragraph.

Article VIII

Royalties and other amounts derived, as consideration for the right to use copyrights, artistic and scientific works, patents, designs, plans, secret processes and formulae, trade-marks, and other like property and rights (including rentals and like payments in respect to motion picture films or for the use of industrial, commercial or scientific equipment), from sources within one of the contracting States by a resident or corporation or other entity of the other contracting State not having a permanent establishment in the former State shall be exempt from taxation in such former State.

Article IX

1. Income from real property (including gains derived from the sale or exchange of such property but not including interest from mortgages or bonds secured by real property) and royalties in respect of the operation of mines, quarries, or other natural resources, shall be taxable only in the contracting State in which such property, mines, quarries, or other natural resources are situated.

2. A resident or corporation or other entity of one of the contracting States deriving any such income from such property within the other contracting State may, for any taxable year, elect to be subject to the tax of such other contracting State, on a net basis, as if such resident or corporation or entity were engaged in trade or business within such other contracting State through a permanent establishment therein during such taxable year.

Article X

1. An individual resident of Switzerland shall be exempt from United States tax upon compensation for labor or personal services performed in the United States (including the practice of the liberal professions and rendition of services as director) if he is temporarily present in the United States for a period or periods not exceeding a total of 183 days during the taxable year and either of the following conditions is met:

a. his compensation is received for such labor or personal services performed as an employee of, or under contract with, resident or corporation or other entity of Switzerland, or

b. his compensation received for such labor or personal services does not exceed $10,000.

2. The provisions of paragraph 1 of this Article shall apply *mutatis mutandis*, to an individual resident of the United States with respect to compensation for such labor or personal services performed in Switzerland.

3. The provisions of this Article shall have no application to the income to which Article XI.1 relates.

4. The provisions of paragraph 1*a*. of this Article shall not apply to the compensation, profits, emoluments or other remuneration of public entertainers such as stage, motion picture or radio artists, musicians and athletes.[1]

Article XI

1. *a.* Wages, salaries and similar compensation, and pensions paid by the United States or by the political subdivisions or territories thereof to an individual (other than a Swiss citizen who is not also a citizen of the United States) shall be exempt from Swiss tax.

b. Wages, salaries and similar compensation and pensions paid by Switzerland or by any agency or instrumentality thereof or by any political subdivisions or other public authorities thereof to an individual (other than a United States citizen who is not also a citizen of Switzerland) shall be exempt from United States tax.

2. Private pensions and life annuities derived from within one of the contracting States and paid to individuals residing in the other contracting State shall be exempt from taxation in the former State.

3. The term 'pensions', as used in this Article, means periodic payments made in consideration for services rendered or by way of compensation for injuries received.

4. The term 'life annuities' as used in this Article, means as stated sum payable periodically at stated times during life, or during a specified number of years, under an obligation to make the payments in return for adequate and full consideration in money or money's worth.

1. The US ratified the convention with a reservation rejecting Art. X.4.

Article XII

A professor or teacher, a resident of one of the contracting States, who temporarily visits the other contracting State for the purpose of teaching for a period not exceeding two years at a university, college, school or other educational institution in the other contracting State, shall be exempted in such other contracting State from tax on his remuneration for such teaching for such period.

Article XIII

A student or apprentice, a resident of one of the contracting States, who temporarily visits the other contracting State exclusively for the purposes of study or for acquiring business or technical experience shall not be taxable in the latter State in respect of remittances received by him from abroad for the purpose of his maintenance or studies.

Article XIV

1. Dividends and interest paid by a corporation other than a United States domestic corporation shall be exempt from United States tax where the recipient is a non-resident alien as to the United States resident in Switzerland or a Swiss corporation, not having a permanent establishment in the United States.

2. Dividends and interest paid by a corporation other than a Swiss corporation shall be exempt from Swiss tax where the recipient is a resident or corporation of the United States, not having a permanent establishment in Switzerland.

Article XV

1. It is agreed that double taxation shall be avoided in the following manner:

a. The United States in determining its taxes specified in Article I of this Convention in the case of its citizens, residents or corporations may, regardless of any other provision of this Convention, include in the basis upon which such taxes are imposed all items of income taxable under the revenue laws of the United States as if this Convention had not come into effect. The United States shall, however, subject to the provisions of section 131, Internal Revenue Code, as in effect on the date of the entry into force of this Convention, deduct from its taxes the amount of Swiss taxes specified in Article I of this Convention. It is agreed that by virtue of the provisions of subparagraph *b.* of this paragraph, Switzerland satisfies the similar credit requirement set forth in section 131(a)(3), Internal Revenue Code.

b. Switzerland, in determining its taxes specified in Article I of this Convention in the case of its residents, corporations or other entities, shall exclude from the basis upon which such taxes are imposed such items of income as are dealt with in this Convention, derived from the United States and not exempt from, and not entitled to the reduced rate of, United States tax under this Convention; but in the case of a citizen of the United States resident in Switzerland there shall be excluded all items of income derived from the United States. Switzerland, however, reserves the right to take into account in the determination of the rate of its taxes also the income excluded as provided in this paragraph.

2. The provisions of this Article shall not be construed to deny the exemptions from United States tax or Swiss tax, as the case may be, granted by Article XI.1 of this Convention.

Article XVI

1. The competent authorities of the contracting States shall exchange such information (being information available under the respective taxation laws of the contracting States) as is necessary for carrying out the provisions of the present Convention or for the prevention of fraud or the like in relation to the taxes which are the subject of the present Convention. Any information so exchanged shall be treated as secret and shall not be disclosed to any person other than those concerned with the assessment and collection of the taxes which are the subject of the present Convention. No information shall be exchanged which would disclose any trade, business, industrial or professional secret or trade process.

2. Each of the contracting States may collect such taxes imposed by the other contracting State as though such taxes were the taxes of the former State as will ensure that the exemption or reduced rate of tax granted under Articles VI, VII, VIII and XI.2 of the present Convention by such State shall not be enjoyed by persons not entitled to such benefits.

3. In no case shall the provisions of this Article be construed so as to impose upon either of the contracting States the obligation to carry out administrative measures at variance with the regulations and practice of either contracting State or which would be contrary to its sovereignty, security or public policy or to supply particulars which are not procurable under its own legislation or that of the State making application.

Article XVII

1. Where a taxpayer shows proof that the action of the tax authorities of the contracting States has resulted, or will result, in double taxation contrary to the provisions of the present Convention, he shall be entitled to present the facts to the State of which he is a citizen or resident, or, if the taxpayer is a corporation or other entity, to the State in which it is created or organized. Should the taxpayer's claim be deemed worthy of consideration, the competent authority of such State shall undertake to come to an agreement with the competent authority of the other State with a view to equitable avoidance of the double taxation in question.

2. Should any difficulty or doubt arise as to the interpretation or application of the present Convention, or its relationship to Conventions between one of the contracting States and any other State, the competent authorities may settle the question by mutual agreement.

Article XVIII

1. The provisions of this Convention shall not be construed to deny or affect in any manner the right of diplomatic and consular officers to other or additional exemptions now enjoyed or which may hereafter be granted to such officers.

2. The provisions of the present Convention shall not be construed to restrict in any manner any exemption, deduction, credit or other allowance now or hereafter accorded by the laws of one of the contracting States in the determination of the tax imposed by such State.

3. The citizens of one of the contracting States shall not, while resident in the other contracting State, be subjected therein to other or more burdensome taxes than are citizens of such other contracting State residing in its territory. The term 'citizens' as used in this Article includes all legal persons, partnerships and associations created or organized under the laws in force in the respective contracting States. In this Article the word 'taxes' means taxes of every kind or description, whether Federal, State, cantonal, municipal, or communal.

Article XIX

1. The competent authorities of the two contracting States may prescribe regulations necessary to carry into effect the present Convention within the respective States.

2. The competent authorities of the two contracting States may communicate with each other directly for the purpose of giving effect to the provisions of this Convention.

Article XX

1. The present Convention shall be ratified and the instruments of ratification shall be exchanged at Berne as soon as possible. It shall have effect for such taxable years beginning on or after the first day of January of the year in which such exchange takes place. Provided, however, that if such exchange takes place on or after October 1 of such year, Article VI (except paragraph 2 thereof) and Article VII of the Convention shall have effect only for taxable years beginning on or after the first day of January of the year immediately following the year in which such exchange takes place.

2. The present Convention shall continue effective for a period of five years beginning with the calendar year in which the exchange of the instruments of ratification takes place and indefinitely after that period, but may be terminated by either of the contracting States at the end of the five-years period or any time thereafter, provided that at least six months' prior notice of termination has been given, and, in such event, the present Convention shall cease to be effective for the taxable years beginning on or after the first day of January next following the expiration of the six-month period.

Done at Washington, in duplicate, in the English and German languages, the two texts having equal authenticity, this 24th day of May, 1951.

Convention between the United States of America and the Union of Soviet Socialist Republics for the Avoidance of Double Taxation of Income, the Prevention of Fiscal Evasion with Respect to Taxes on Income, and the Elimination of Obstacles to International Trade and Investment, concluded in Washington on June 20, 1973.

The President of the United States of America and the Presidium of the Supreme Soviet of the Union of Soviet Socialist Republics, desiring to avoid double taxation and to promote the development of economic, scientific, technical and cultural cooperation between both States, have appointed for this purpose as their respective plenipotentiaries:

The President of the United States of America:

George P. Schulz, Secretary of the Treasury of the USA; and

The Presidium of the Supreme Soviet of the Union of Soviet Socialist Republics:

Nikolai Semenovich Patolichev, Minister of Foreign Trade of the USSR;

Who have agreed as follows:

Article I

1. The taxes which are the subject of this Convention are:

a. In the case of the Union of Soviet Socialist Republics, taxes and dues provided for by the All-Union legislation;

b. In the case of the United States, taxes and dues provided for by the Internal Revenue Code.

2. This Convention shall also apply to taxes and dues substantially similar to those covered by paragraph 1 which are imposed in addition to, or in place of, existing taxes and dues after the signature of this Convention.

Article II

In this Convention, the terms listed below shall have the following meaning:

1. 'Soviet Union' or 'USSR' means the Union of Soviet Socialist Republics and, when used in a geographical sense, means the territories of all the Union Republics. Such term also includes:

a. The territorial sea thereof, and

b. The seabed and subsoil of the submarine areas adjacent to the coast thereof, but beyond the territorial sea, over which the Soviet Union exercises sovereign rights, in accordance with international law, for the purpose of exploration for and exploitation of the natural resources of such areas. However, it is understood that such term includes such areas only to the extent that the person, property, or activity with respect to which the questions of taxation arise is connected with such exploration or exploitation.

2. 'United States' or 'USA' means the United States of America and, when used in a geographical sense, means the territories of all the states and of the District of Columbia. Such term also includes:

a. The territorial sea thereof, and

b. The seabed and subsoil of the submarine areas adjacent to the coast thereof, but beyond the territorial sea, over which the United States exercises sovereign rights, in accordance with international law, for the purpose of exploration for and exploitation of the natural resources of such areas. However, it is understood that such term includes such areas only to the extent that the person, property, or activity with respect to which the questions of taxation arise is connected with such exploration or exploitation.

3. 'Resident of the Soviet Union' means:

a. a legal entity or any other organization treated in the USSR as a legal entity for tax purposes which is created under the laws of the Soviet Union or any Union Republic and

b. an individual resident in the Soviet Union for purposes of its tax.

4. 'Resident of the United States' means:

a. a corporation or any other organization treated in the United States as a corporation for tax purposes which is created or organized under the laws of the United States or any state thereof or of the District of Columbia and

b. an individual resident in the United States for purposes of its tax.

c. 'Contracting State' means the United States or the Soviet Union, as the context requires.

5. The term 'competent authorities' means:

a. in the case of the Soviet Union, the Ministry of Finance;

b. in the case of the United States, the Secretary of the Treasury or his delegate.

Article III

1. The following categories of income derived from sources within one Contracting State by a resident of the other Contracting State shall be subject to tax only in that other Contracting State:

a. rentals, royalties, or other amounts paid as consideration for the use of or the right to use literary, artistic, and scientific works, or for the use of copyrights of such works, as well as the rights to inventions (patents, author's certificates), industrial designs, processes or formulae, computer programs, trademarks, service marks, and other similar property or rights, or for industrial, commercial, or scientific equipment, or for knowledge, experience, or skill (know-how);

b. gains derived from the sale or exchange of any such rights or property, whether or not the amounts realized on sale or exchange are contingent in whole or in part, on the extent and nature of use or disposition of such rights or property;

c. gains from the sale or other disposition of property received as a result of inheritance or gift;

d. income from the furnishing of engineering, architectural, designing, and other technical services in connection with an installation contract with a resident of the first Contracting State which are carried out in a period not exceeding 36 months at one location;

e. income from the sale of goods or the supplying of services through a broker, general commission agent or other agent of independent status, where such broker, general commission agent or other agent is acting in the ordinary course of his business;

f. reinsurance premiums; and

g. interest on credits, loans and other forms of indebtedness connected with the financing of trade between the USA and the USSR except where received by a resident of the other Contracting State from the conduct of a general banking business in the first Contracting State.

2. A Contracting State shall not attribute taxable income to the following activities conducted within that Contracting State by a resident of the other Contracting State:

a. the purchase of goods or merchandise;

b. the use of facilities for the purpose of storage or delivery of goods or merchandise belonging to the resident of the other Contracting State;

c. the display of goods or merchandise belonging to the resident of the other Contracting State, and also the sale of such items on termination of their display;

d. advertising by a resident of the other Contracting State, the collection or dissemination of information, or the conducting of scientific research, or similar activities, which have a preparatory or auxiliary character for the resident.

Article IV

1. Income from commercial activity derived in one Contracting State by a resident of the other Contracting State, shall be taxable in the first Contracting State only if it is derived by a representation.

2. The term 'representation' means:

a. with regard to income derived within the USSR, an office or representative bureau established in the USSR by a resident of the United States in accordance with the laws and regulations in force in the Soviet Union;

b. with regard to income derived within the USA, an office or other place of business established in the USA by a resident of the Soviet Union in accordance with the laws and regulations in force in the United States.

3. In the determination of the profits of a representation, there shall be allowed as deductions from total income the expenses that are connected with the performance of its activity, including executive and general administrative expenses.

4. This article applies to income, other than income of an individual dealt with in Article VI, from the furnishing of tour performances and other public appearances.

5. The provisions of this article shall not affect the exemptions from taxes provided for by Articles III and V.

Article V

1. Income which a resident of the Soviet Union derives from the operation in international traffic of ships or aircraft registered in the USSR and gains which a resident of the USSR derives from the sale, exchange, or other disposition of ships or aircraft operated in international traffic by such resident and registered in the USSR shall be exempt from tax in the United States.

2. Income which a resident of the United States derives from operation in international traffic of ships or aircraft registered in the USA and gains which a resident of the USA derives from the sale, exchange, or other disposition of ships or aircraft operated in international traffic by such resident and registered in the USA shall be exempt from tax in the Soviet Union.

3. Remuneration derived by an individual from the performance of labor or personal services as an employee aboard ships or aircraft operated by one of the Contracting States or a resident thereof in international traffic shall be exempt from tax in the other Contracting State if such individual is a member of the regular complement of the ship or aircraft.

Article VI

1. *Special exemptions*

Income derived by an individual who is a resident of one of the Contracting States shall be exempt from tax in the other Contracting State as provided in subparagraphs *a.* through *f.*

a. Governmental employees:

(1) An individual receiving remuneration from government funds of the Contracting State of which the individual is a citizen for labor or personal services performed as an employee of governmental agencies or institutions of that Contracting State in the discharge of governmental functions shall not be subject to tax on such remuneration in that other Contracting State.

(2) Labor or personal services performed by a citizen of one of the Contracting States shall be treated by the other Contracting State as performed in the discharge of governmental functions if such labor or personal services would be treated under the internal laws of the first Contracting State as so performed. However, it is understood that persons engaging in commercial activity, such as employees or representatives of commercial organizations of the USA and employees or representatives of the foreign trade organizations of the USSR, shall not be considered in the USSR and USA respectively as engaged in the discharge of governmental functions.

(3) The provisions of this Convention shall not affect the fiscal privileges of diplomatic and consular officials under the general rules of international law or under special agreements.

b. Participants in programs of intergovernmental cooperation:

An individual who is a resident of one of the Contracting States and who is temporarily present in the other Contracting State under an exchange program provided for by agreements between the governments of the Contracting States on cooperation in various fields of science and technology shall not be subject to tax in that other Contracting State on remuneration received from sources within either Contracting State.

c. Teachers and researchers:

(1) An individual who is a resident of one of the Contracting States and who is temporarily present in the other Contracting State at the invitation of a governmental agency or institution or an educational or scientific research institution in that other Contracting State for the primary purpose of teaching, engaging in research, or participating in scientific, technical or professional conferences shall not be subject to tax in that other Contracting State on his income from teaching or research or participating in such conferences.

(2) Subparagraph (1) shall not apply to income from research if such research is undertaken primarily for the benefit of a private person or commercial enterprise of the USA or a foreign trade organization of the USSR. However, subparagraph (1) shall apply in all cases where research is conducted on the basis of intergovernmental agreements on cooperation.

d. Students:

An individual who is a resident of one of the Contracting States and who is temporarily present in the other Contracting State for the primary purpose of studying at an educational or scientific research institution or for the purpose of acquiring a profession or a specialty shall be exempt from taxes in the other Contracting State on a stipend, scholarship, or other substitute type of allowance, necessary to provide for ordinary living expenses.

e. Trainees and specialists:

An individual who is a resident of one of the Contracting States and who is temporarily present in the other Contracting State for the primary purpose of acquiring technical, professional, or commercial experience or performing technical services, and who is an employee of, or under contract with, a resident of the first-mentioned Contracting State, shall not be subject to tax in that other Contracting State on remuneration received from abroad. Also, such individual shall not be subject to tax in that other Contracting State on amounts received from sources within that other Contracting State which are necessary to provide for ordinary living expenses.

f. Duration of exemptions:

The exemptions provided for under subparagraphs *b., c., d.*, and *e.* of this article shall extend only for such period of time as is required to effectuate the purpose of the visit, but in no case shall such period of time exceed:

(1) One year in the case of subparagraphs *b.* (Participants in programs of intergovernmental cooperation) and *e.* (Trainees and specialists);

(2) Two years in the case of subparagraph *c.* (Teachers and researchers); and

(3) Five years in the case of subparagraph *d.* (Students).

If an individual qualifies for exemption under more than one of subparagraphs *b., c., d.,* and *e.*, the provisions of that subparagraph which is most favorable to him shall apply. However, in no case shall an individual have the cumulative benefits of subparagraphs *b., c., d.,* and *e.* for more than five taxable years from the date of his arrival in the other Contracting State.

2. *General exemptions*

Income derived by an individual who is a resident of one of the Contracting States from the performance of personal services in the other Contracting State, which is not exempt from tax in accordance with paragraph 1 of this article, may be taxed in that other Contracting State, but only if the individual is present in that other Contracting State for a period aggregating more than 183 days in the taxable year.

Article VII

This Convention shall not restrict the right of a Contracting State to tax a citizen of that Contracting State.

Article VIII

This Convention shall apply only to the taxation of income from activity conducted in a Contracting State in accordance with the laws and regulations in force in such Contracting State.

Article IX

If the income of a resident of one of the Contracting States is exempt from tax in the other Contracting State, in accordance with this Convention, such resident shall also be exempt from any tax which is at present imposed or which may be imposed subsequently in that Contracting State on the transaction giving rise to such income.

Article X

1. A citizen of one of the Contracting States who is a resident of the other Contracting State shall not be subjected in that other Contracting State to more burdensome taxes than a citizen of that other Contracting State who is a resident thereof carrying on the same activities.

2. A citizen of one of the Contracting States who is a resident of the other Contracting State or a representation established by a resident of the first Contracting State in the other Contracting State shall not be subjected in that other Contracting State to more burdensome taxes than are generally imposed in that State on citizens or representations of residents of third States carrying on the same activities. However,

this provision shall not require a Contracting State to grant to citizens or representations of residents of the other Contracting State tax benefits granted by special agreements to citizens or representations of a third State.

3. The provisions of paragraphs 1 and 2 of this article shall apply to taxes of any kind imposed on the Federal or All-Union level, the State or Republic level, and on the local level.

Article XI

1. If a resident of one of the Contracting States considers that the action of one or both of the Contracting States results or will result for him in taxation not in accordance with this Convention, he may, notwithstanding the remedies provided by the laws of the Contracting States, present his case to the competent authorities of the Contracting State of which he is a resident or citizen. Should claim be considered to have merit by the competent authorities of the Contracting State to which the claim is made, they shall endeavor to come to an agreement with the competent authorities of the other Contracting State with a view to the avoidance of taxation not in accordance with the provisions of this Convention.

2. In the event that such an agreement is reached the competent authorities of the Contracting States shall, as necessary, refund the excess amounts paid, allow tax exemptions, or levy taxes.

Article XII

The competent authorities of the Contracting States shall notify each other annually of amendments of the tax legislation referred to in paragraph 1 of Article I and of the adoption of taxes referred to in paragraph 2 of Article I by transmitting the texts of amendments or new statutes and notify each other of any material concerning the application of this Convention.

Article XIII

This Convention shall be subject to ratification and shall enter into force on the thirtieth day after the exchange of instruments of ratification. The instruments of ratification shall be exchanged at Moscow as soon as possible.

The provisions of this Convention shall, however, have effect for income derived on or after January 1 of the year following the year in which the instruments of ratification are exchanged.

Article XIV

1. This Convention shall remain in force for a period of three years after it takes effect and shall remain in force thereafter for an indefinite period. Either of the Contracting States may terminate this Convention at any time after three years from the date on which the Convention enters into force by giving notice of termination through diplomatic channels at least six months before the end of any calendar year. In

such event, the Convention shall cease to have effect beginning on January 1 of the year following the year in which notice is given.

2. Notwithstanding the provisions of paragraph 1 of this article, upon prior notice to be given through diplomatic channels, the provisions of subparagraphs *e.*, *f.*, or *g.* of paragraph 1 of Article III and the provisions of Article IX may be terminated separately by either Contracting State at any time after three years from the date on which this Convention enters into force. In such event such provisions shall cease to have effect beginning on January 1 of the year following the year in which notice is given.

In witness whereof, the plenipotentiaries of the two Contracting States have signed the present Convention and affixed their seals thereto.

Done at Washington, this 20th day of June, 1973, in duplicate, in the English and Russian languages, both texts being equally authentic.

Convention Between the Government of the United States of America and the United Kingdom of Great Britain and Northern Ireland for the Avoidance of Double Taxation and the Prevention of Fiscal Evasion with Respect to Taxes on Income and Capital Gains, concluded in London on December 31, 1975, as amended by the Protocols of August 26, 1976, March 31, 1977, and March 15, 1979.

The Government of the United States of America and the Government of the United Kingdom of Great Britain and Northern Ireland;

Desiring to conclude a new Convention for the avoidance of double taxation and the prevention of fiscal evasion with respect to taxes on income and capital gains,

Have agreed as follows:

Article 1. Personal Scope

1. Except as specifically provided herein, this Convention is applicable to persons who are residents of one or both of the Contracting States.

2. A corporation which is both a resident of the United Kingdom within the meaning of paragraph 1*a*.(ii) of Article 4 (Fiscal Residence), and a resident of the United States within the meaning of paragraph 1*b*.(ii) of Article 4 shall not be entitled to claim any relief or exemption from tax provided by this Convention except that such corporation may claim the benefits of paragraph 2 of Article 8 (Shipping and Air Transport), of Article 23 (Elimination of Double Taxation) with respect to paragraph 1*c*. thereof and the petroleum revenue tax referred to in paragraph 2*b*. of Article 2 (Taxes Covered), of Article 24 (Non-Discrimination) and of Article 28 (Entry into Force) and the provisions of paragraph 7 of Article 11 (Interest) shall apply to it.

3. Notwithstanding any provision of this Convention except paragraph 4 of this Article, a Contracting State may tax its residents (as determined under Article 4 (Fiscal Residence)) and its nationals as if this Convention had not come into effect.

4. Nothing in paragraph 3 of this Article shall affect the application by a Contracting State of:

a. paragraph 4 of Article 4 (Fiscal Residence), paragraph 2 of Article 8 (Shipping and Air Transport), and Articles 9 (Associated Enterprises), 23 (Elimination of Double Taxation), 24 (Non-Discrimination), and 25 (Mutual Agreement Procedure); and

b. Articles 19 (Government Service), 20 (Teachers), 21 (Students and Trainees), and 27 (Effect on Diplomatic and Consular Officials and Domestic Laws), with respect to individuals who are neither nationals of, nor have immigrant status in, that State.

Article 2. Taxes Covered

1. This Convention shall apply to taxes on income imposed by each Contracting State and as hereinafter provided to taxes imposed by its political subdivisions or local authorities.

2. The existing taxes to which this Convention shall apply are:

a. in the case of the United States, the Federal income taxes imposed by the Internal Revenue Code and the tax on insurance premiums paid to foreign insurers; but (except as provided in paragraph 6 of Article 10 (Dividends)) excluding the accumulated earnings tax and the personal holding company tax. The foregoing taxes covered are hereinafter referred to as 'United States tax';

b. in the case of the United Kingdom, the income tax, the capital gains tax, the corporation tax and the petroleum revenue tax. The foregoing taxes covered are hereinafter referred to as 'United Kingdom tax'.

3. This Convention shall also apply to any identical or substantially similar taxes which are imposed by a Contracting State after the date of signature of this Convention in addition to, or in place of, the existing taxes. The competent authorities of the Contracting States shall notify each other of any changes which have been made in their respective taxation laws.

4. For the purpose of Article 24 (Non-Discrimination), this Convention shall also apply to taxes of every kind and description imposed by each Contracting State, or by its political subdivisions or local authorities.

Article 3. General Definitions

1. In this Convention, unless the context otherwise requires:

a. the term 'corporation' means a United States corporation, a United Kingdom corporation, or any body corporate or other entity of a third State which is treated as a body corporate for tax purposes by both Contracting States;

b. (i) The term 'United States corporation' means a corporation (or any unincorporated entity treated as a corporation for United States tax purposes) which is created or organized under the laws of the United States or any state thereof or the District of Columbia; and

(ii) The term 'United Kingdom corporation' means any body corporate or unincorporated association created or organized under the laws of the United Kingdom, but does not include a partnership, a local authority, or a local authority association;

c. the term 'person' includes an individual, a partnership, a corporation, an estate, a trust, or any other body of persons;

d. the term 'enterprise of a Contracting State' means an industrial or commercial undertaking carried on by a resident of a Contracting State;

e. the term 'international traffic' means any transport by a ship or aircraft operated by an enterprise of a Contracting State, except when the ship or aircraft is operated solely between places in the other Contracting State;

f. the term 'competent authority' means:

(i) in the case of the United States, the Secretary of the Treasury or his delegate, and

(ii) in the case of the United Kingdom, the Commissioners of Inland Revenue or their authorized representative;

g. (i) the term 'United States' means the United States of America; and

(ii) when used in a geographical sense, the States thereof and the District of Columbia. Such term also includes:

(aa) the territorial sea thereof, and

(bb) the seabed and subsoil of the submarine areas adjacent to the coast thereof, but beyond the territorial sea, over which the United States exercises sovereign rights, in accordance with international law, for the purpose of exploration for and exploitation of the natural resources of such areas, but only to the extent that the person, property, or activity to which the Convention is being applied is connected with such exploration or exploitation;

h. (i) the term 'United Kingdom' means Great Britain and Northern Ireland, including any area outside the territorial sea of the United Kingdom which in accordance with international law has been or may hereafter be designated, under the laws of the United Kingdom concerning the Continental Shelf, as an area within which the rights of the United Kingdom with respect to the seabed and subsoil and their natural resources may be exercised;

i. the term 'Contracting State' means the United States or the United Kingdom, as the context requires;

j. the term 'third State' means any State or territory other than the United States or the United Kingdom and the term 'enterprise of a third State' shall be construed accordingly;

k. the term 'nationals' means:

(i) in relation to the United Kingdom, all citizens of the United Kingdom and Colonies, British subjects under Sections 2, 13(1) or 16 of the British Nationality Act 1948, and British subjects by virtue of Section 1 of the British Nationality Act 1965, provided they are patrial within the meaning of the Immigration Act 1971, so far as these provisions are in force on the date of entry into force of this Convention or have been modified only in minor respects so as not to affect their general character;

(ii) in relation to the United States, United States citizens.

2. As regards the application of this Convention by a Contracting State any term not otherwise defined shall, unless the context otherwise requires and subject to the provisions of Article 25 (Mutual Agreement Procedure), have the meaning which it has under the laws of that Contracting State relating to the taxes which are the subject of this Convention.

Article 4. Fiscal Residence

1. For the purposes of this Convention:

a. the term 'resident of the United Kingdom' means:

(i) any person, other than a corporation, resident in the United Kingdom for purposes of United Kingdom tax; but in the case of a partnership, estate or trust, only to the extent that the income derived by such partnership, estate or trust is subject to United Kingdom tax as the income of a resident, either in its hands or in the hands of its partners or beneficiaries; and

(ii) a corporation whose business is managed and controlled in the United Kingdom;

b. the term 'resident of the United States' means:

(i) any person, other than a corporation, resident in the United States for the purposes of United States tax; but in the case of a partnership, estate or trust, only to the extent that the income derived by such partnership, estate or trust is subject to United States tax as the income of a resident, either in its hands or in the hands of its partners or beneficiaries; and

(ii) a United States corporation.

2. Where by reason of the provisions of paragraph 1 an individual is a resident of both Contracting States, then the individual's tax status shall be determined as follows:

a. the individual shall be deemed to be a resident of the Contracting State in which he has a permanent home available to him. If the individual has a permanent home available to him in both Contracting States or in neither of the Contracting States, he shall be deemed to be a resident of the Contracting State with which his personal and economic relations are closest (centre of vital interests);

b. if the Contracting State in which the individual's centre of vital interests is located cannot be determined, he shall be deemed to be a resident of the Contracting State in which he has an habitual abode;

c. if the individual has an habitual abode in both Contracting States or in neither of them, he shall be deemed to be a resident of the Contracting State of which he is a national; and

d. if the individual is a national of both Contracting States or of neither of them, the competent authorities of the Contracting States shall settle the question by mutual agreement.

3. Where by reason of the provisions of paragraph 1 an estate or trust may be a resident of both Contracting States, the competent authorities of the Contracting States may settle the question of residence by mutual agreement.

4. A marriage before 1 January 1974 between a woman who is a United States national and a man domiciled within the United Kingdom shall be deemed to have taken place on 1 January 1974 for the purpose of determining her domicile on or after 6 April 1976 for United Kingdom tax purposes.

5. Where under any provision of this Convention income arising in one of the Contracting States is relieved from tax in that Contracting State and, under the law in force in the other Contracting State a person, in respect of the said income, is subject to tax by reference to the amount thereof which is remitted to or received in that other Contracting State and not by reference to the full amount thereof, then the relief

to be allowed under this Convention in the first-mentioned Contracting State shall apply only to so much of the income as is remitted to or received in the other Contracting State.

Article 5. Permanent Establishment

1. For the purposes of this Convention, the term 'permanent establishment' means a fixed place of business through which the business of an enterprise is wholly or partly carried on.

2. The term 'permanent establishment' shall include especially:

a. a branch;

b. an office;

c. a factory;

d. a workshop;

e. a mine, oil or gas well, quarry, or other place of extraction of natural resources; and

f. a building or construction or installation project which exists for more than 12 months.

3. Notwithstanding the provisions of the preceding paragraphs the term 'permanent establishment' shall be deemed not to include a fixed place of business used solely for one or more of the following activities:

a. the storage, display, or delivery of goods or merchandise belonging to the enterprise;

b. the maintenance of a stock of goods or merchandise belonging to the enterprise for the purpose of storage, display or delivery;

c. the maintenance of a stock of goods or merchandise belonging to the enterprise for the purpose of processing by another person;

d. the maintenance of a fixed place of business for the purpose of purchasing goods or merchandise, or for collecting information, for the enterprise;

e. the maintenance of a fixed place of business for the purpose of advertising, for the supply of information, for scientific research, or for similar activities which have a preparatory or auxiliary character, for the enterprise; or

f. a building or construction or installation project which does not exist for more than 12 months.

4. A person acting in a Contracting State on behalf of an enterprise of the other Contracting State – other than an agent of an independent status to whom paragraph 5 applies – shall be deemed to be a permanent establishment of the enterprise in the first-mentioned State if such person has, and habitually exercises in that State, an authority to conclude contracts in the name of the enterprise, unless the contracts are confined to the activities described in paragraph 3 of this Article.

5. An enterprise of a Contracting State shall not be deemed to have a permanent establishment in the other Contracting State merely because it carries on business in that other State through a broker, general commission agent or any other agent of independent status, where such persons are acting in the ordinary course of their business.

6. The fact that a corporation which is a resident of a Contracting State controls or is controlled by a corporation which is a resident of the other Contracting State, or which carries on business in that other State (whether through a permanent establishment or otherwise), shall not of itself constitute either corporation a permanent establishment of the other.

Article 6. Income from Immovable Property (Real Property)

1. Income from immovable property (real property), including income from agriculture or forestry, may be taxed in the Contracting State in which such property is situated.

2. The term 'immovable property' shall be defined in accordance with the law of the Contracting State in which the property in question is situated. The term shall in any case include usufruct of immovable property and rights to variable or fixed payments as consideration for the working of, or the right to work, mineral deposits, sources and other natural resources; ships, boats and aircraft shall not be regarded as immovable property.

3. The provisions of paragraph 1 shall apply to income derived from the direct use, letting, or use in any other form of immovable property.

Article 7. Business Profits

1. The business profits of an enterprise of a Contracting State shall be taxable only in that State unless the enterprise carries on business in the other Contracting State through a permanent establishment situated therein. If the enterprise carries on business as aforesaid, the business profits of the enterprise may be taxed in that other State but only so much of them as is attributable to that permanent establishment.

2. Subject to the provisions of paragraph 3, where an enterprise of a Contracting State carries on business in the other Contracting State through a permanent establishment situated therein, there shall in each Contracting State be attributed to that permanent establishment the profits which it might be expected to make if it were a distinct and separate enterprise engaged in the same or similar activities under the same or similar conditions and dealing wholly independently with the enterprise of which it is a permanent establishment.

3. In the determination of the profits of a permanent establishment, there shall be allowed as deductions those expenses which are incurred for the purposes of the permanent establishment, including a reasonable allocation of executive and general administrative expenses, research and development expenses, interest, and other expenses incurred for the purposes of the enterprise as a whole (or the part thereof which includes the permanent establishment), whether incurred in the State in which the permanent establishment is situated or elsewhere.

4. No business profits shall be attributed to a permanent establishment by reason of the mere purchase by that permanent establishment of goods or merchandise for the enterprise.

5. For the purposes of the preceding paragraphs, the profits to be attributed to the permanent establishment shall be determined by the

same method year by year unless there is good and sufficient reason to the contrary.

6. Where profits include items of income which are dealt with separately in other Articles of this Convention, then the provisions of those Articles shall not be affected by the provisions of this Article.

6A. The United States tax on insurance premiums paid to foreign insurers shall not be imposed on insurance or reinsurance premiums which are the receipts of a business or insurance carried on by an enterprise of the United Kingdom whether or not that business is carried on through a permanent establishment in the United States.

7. For the purposes of this Convention, 'business profits' includes, but is not limited to, income derived from manufacturing, mercantile, banking, insurance, agricultural, fishing or mining activities, the operation of ships or aircraft, the furnishing of services, the rental of tangible personal (movable) property, and the rental or licensing of cinematographic films or films or tapes used for radio or television broadcasting or from copyrights thereof. Such term also includes any other income effectively connected with a permanent establishment which the recipient, being a resident of one of the Contracting States, has in the other Contracting State. Such term does not include the performance of personal services by an individual either as an employee or in an independent capacity.

Article 8. Shipping and Air Transport

1. Profits derived by an enterprise of a Contracting State from the operation of ships or aircraft in international traffic shall be taxable only in that State.

2. Notwithstanding any other provision of this Convention, profits which a national of the United States not resident in the United Kingdom or a United States corporation derives from operating ships documented or aircraft registered under the laws of the United States shall be exempt from United Kingdom tax.

3. For the purpose of this Article, profits from the operation of ships or aircraft include profits derived from the rental on a bareboat basis of ships or aircraft if such rental income is incidental to other income described in paragraph 1 of this Article.

4. Notwithstanding the provisions of Article 7 (Business Profits), profits of an enterprise of a Contracting State from the use, maintenance or rental of containers (including trailers and related equipment for the transport of containers) used for the transport of goods or merchandise shall be taxable only in that State, except where such containers are used for the transport of goods or merchandise solely between places within the other Contracting State.

5. The provisions of this Article shall apply also to profits derived by an enterprise of a Contracting State from participation in a pool, a joint business or an international operating agency.

6. Gains derived by an enterprise of a Contracting State from the alienation of ships, aircraft or containers owned and operated by the

enterprise, the income from which is taxable only in that State, shall be taxed only in that State.

Article 9. Associated Enterprises

1. Where an enterprise of a Contracting State is related to another enterprise and conditions are made or imposed between the two enterprises in their commercial or financial relations which differ from those which would have been made between independent enterprises, then any income, deductions, receipts, or outgoings which would, but for those conditions, have been attributed to one of the enterprises but by reason of those conditions have not been so attributed, may be taken into account in computing the profits or losses of that enterprise and taxed accordingly.

2. Where any income, deductions, receipts, or outgoings which have been taken into account in one Contracting State in computing the profits or losses of an enterprise are also taken into account in the other Contracting State in computing the profits or losses of a related enterprise in accordance with paragraph 1 of this Article, then the first-mentioned State shall make such adjustment as may be appropriate to the amount of tax charged on those profits in that State.

3. If one Contracting State disagrees with the amount of any income, deductions, receipts, or outgoings, taken into account in computing profits or losses in the other in accordance with paragraph 1, the two Contracting States shall endeavour to reach agreement in accordance with the procedure in Article 25 (Mutual Agreement Procedure).

4. Except as specifically provided in this Article:

a. where an enterprise doing business in one Contracting State:

(i) is a resident of the other Contracting State; or

(ii) is controlled, directly or indirectly, by an enterprise which is a resident of the other Contracting State; and

b. where the enterprise which is a resident of the other Contracting State is a corporation, such corporation is neither:

(i) a controlled foreign corporation within the meaning of section 957 of the United States Internal Revenue Code of 1954 (as it may be amended from time to time without changing the principle thereof); nor

(ii) created or organised under the laws of the first-mentioned State or of any third State or controlled, directly or indirectly, by a corporation which is a resident of any third State;

then, in determining the tax liability of the first-mentioned enterprise in the State in which it does business, such State shall not take into account the income, deductions, receipts or outgoings of a related enterprise which is a resident of the other Contracting State or of an enterprise of any third State which is related to the enterprise of the other Contracting State, except that this prohibition shall not apply where the first-mentioned enterprise is a resident of the first-mentioned Contracting State, to the extent that it owns, directly or indirectly, the capital of the related enterprise.

5. For the purposes of this Convention, an enterprise is related to another enterprise if either enterprise directly or indirectly controls the other, or if any third person or persons (related to each other or acting together) control both.

Article 10. Dividends

1. Dividends derived from a Contracting State which is a resident of a Contracting State by a resident of the other Contracting State may be taxed in the other Contracting State. However, such dividends may be taxed in the Contracting State of which the corporation paying the dividends is a resident, but if the beneficial owner is a resident of the other Contracting State, the tax so charged shall not exceed 15 per cent of the gross amount of the dividends.

2. As long as an individual resident in the United Kingdom is entitled under United Kingdom law to a tax credit in respect of dividends paid by a corporation which is resident in the United Kingdom, paragraph 1 of this Article shall not apply. In these circumstances, dividends derived from a corporation which is a resident of a Contracting State by a resident of the other Contracting State may be taxed in the other Contracting State. However, such dividends may be taxed in the Contracting State of which the corporation paying the dividends is a resident, but if the beneficial owner is a resident of the other Contracting State, the tax so charged shall not exceed the tax provided in sub-paragraphs *a.* and *b.* below:

a. In the case of dividends paid by a corporation which is a resident of the United Kingdom:

(i) to a United States corporation which either alone or together with one or more associated corporations controls, directly or indirectly, at least 10 per cent of the voting stock of the corporation which is a resident of the United Kingdom paying the dividend, the United States corporation shall be entitled to a payment from the United Kingdom of a tax credit equal to one-half of the tax credit to which an individual resident in the United Kingdom would have been entitled had he received the dividend, subject to the deduction withheld from such payment and according to the laws of the United Kingdom of an amount not exceeding 5 per cent of the aggregate of the amount or value of the dividend and the amount of the tax credit paid to such corporation;

(ii) in all other cases, the resident of the United States to whom such dividend is paid shall be entitled to a payment from the United Kingdom of the tax credit to which an individual resident in the United Kingdom would have been entitled had he received the dividend, subject to the deduction withheld from such payment and according to the laws of the United Kingdom of an amount not exceeding 15 per cent of the aggregate of the amount or value of the dividend and the amount of the tax credit paid to such resident;

(iii) the aggregate of the amount or value of the dividend and the amount of the tax credit referred to in sub-paragraphs *a.*(i) and (ii) of this paragraph paid by the United Kingdom corporation to the United

States corporation or other resident (without reduction for the 5 or 15 per cent deduction, as the case may be, by the United Kingdom) shall be treated as a dividend for United States tax credit purposes.

b. In the case of dividends paid by a United States corporation:

(i) to a corporation which is a resident of the United Kingdom and controls, directly or indirectly, at least 10 per cent of the voting stock of the United States corporation paying such dividend, the tax charged by the United States shall not exceed 5 per cent of the gross amount of the dividend;

(ii) in all other cases, the tax charged by the United States on payment of a dividend to a resident of the United Kingdom shall not exceed 15 per cent of the gross amount of the dividend.

For the purposes of this paragraph, two corporations shall be deemed to be associated if one controls directly or indirectly more than 50 per cent of the voting power in the other corporation, or a third corporation controls more than 50 per cent of the voting power in both of them.

3. The term 'dividends' for United Kingdom tax purposes includes any item which under the law of the United Kingdom is treated as a distribution and for United States tax purposes includes any item which under the law of the United States is treated as a distribution out of earnings and profits.

4. Paragraphs 1 or 2, as the case may be, shall not apply if the person deriving the dividends, being a resident of a Contracting State, carries on business in the other Contracting State through a permanent establishment situated therein, or performs in that other State independent personal services from a fixed base situated therein, and the holding in respect of which the dividends are paid is effectively connected with such permanent establishment or fixed base. In such a case the provisions of Articles 7 (Business Profits), 14 (Independent Personal Services), or 17 (Artistes and Athletes), as the case may be, shall apply.

5. Where a corporation which is a resident of a Contracting State (and not a resident of the other Contracting State) derives profits or income from the other Contracting State, that other State may not impose any tax on the dividends paid by the corporation, except insofar as such dividends are paid to a resident of that other State (and where that other State is the United States, to a national of the United States) or insofar as the holding in respect of which the dividends are paid is effectively connected with a permanent establishment or fixed base situated in that other State, even if the dividends paid consist wholly or partly of profits or income arising in that other State.

6. A corporation which is a resident of the United Kingdom shall be exempt from United States tax on its accumulated or undistributed earnings, profits, income or surplus, if individuals (other than nationals of the United States) who are residents of the United Kingdom control, directly or indirectly, throughout the last half of the taxable year, more than 50 per cent of the entire voting power in such corporation.

7. *a.* If the beneficial owner of a dividend being a resident of a Contracting State owns 10 per cent or more of the class of shares of

a corporation in respect of which the dividend is paid, then paragraph 1, or as the case may be paragraph 2, of this Article shall not apply to the dividend to the extent that it can have been paid only out of profits which the corporation paying the dividend earned or other income which it received in a period ending 12 months or more before the relevant date. For the purposes of this paragraph the term 'relevant date' means the date on which the beneficial owner of the dividend became the owner of 10 per cent or more of the class of shares in question.

b. Paragraphs 1 and 2 of this Article shall not apply if:

(i) the recipient of the dividend is exempt from tax thereon in the United States; and

(ii) the dividend is paid in such circumstances that, if the recipient were a resident of the United Kingdom exempt from United Kingdom tax, the exemption would be limited or removed.

Provided that this paragraph shall not apply if the beneficial owner of the dividend shows that the shares were acquired for bona fide commercial reasons and not primarily for the purposes of securing the benefit of this Article.

Article 11. Interest

1. Interest derived and beneficially owned by a resident of the United Kingdom shall be exempt from tax by the United States.

2. Interest derived and beneficially owned by a resident of the United States shall be exempt from tax by the United Kingdom.

3. The term 'interest' as used in this Article means income from Government securities, bonds or debentures, whether or not secured by mortgage and whether or not carrying a right to participate in profits, and other debt-claims of every kind as well as other income assimilated to income from money lent by the taxation law of the State in which the income arises but subject to the provisions of paragraph 7 of this Article shall not include any income which is treated as a distribution under the provisions of Article 10 (Dividends). Penalty charges for late payment shall not be regarded as interest for the purpose of this Article.

4. The provisions of paragraphs 1 and 2 shall not apply if the person deriving the interest, being a resident of a Contracting State, carries on business in the other Contracting State through a permanent establishment situated therein, or performs in that other State independent personal services from a fixed base situated therein, and the debt-claim in respect of which the interest is paid is effectively connected with such permanent establishment or fixed base. In such a case, the provisions of Article 7 (Business Profits), Article 14 (Independent Personal Services), or Article 17 (Artistes and Athletes), as the case may be, shall apply.

5. Where, owing to a special relationship between the payer and the person deriving the interest or between both of them and some other person, the amount of the interest paid exceeds for whatever reason the amount which would have been paid in the absence of such relation-

ship, the provisions of this Article shall apply only to the last-mentioned interest. In that case, the excess part of the payments shall remain taxable according to the law of each Contracting State, due regard being had to the other provisions of this Convention.

6. Whether or not a resident of a Contracting State derives profits or income from the other Contracting State, the other State may not impose any tax on the interest paid by that resident, except in so far as such interest is paid to a resident of that other State (and where that other State is the United States, to a national of the United States) or insofar as the debt-claim in respect of which the interest is paid is effectively connected with a permanent establishment or a fixed base of the person deriving interest situated in that other State.

7. Any provision in the law of either Contracting State relating only to interest paid to a non-resident corporation shall not operate so as to require such interest paid to a resident of the other Contracting State to be treated as a distribution by the corporation paying such interest. The preceding sentence shall not apply to interest paid to a corporation of one Contracting State in which more than 50 per cent of the voting power is controlled, directly or indirectly, by a person or persons who are residents of the other Contracting State.

8. The provisions of paragraph 2 of this Article shall not apply if the recipient of the interest is exempt from tax on such income in the United States and such recipient sells or makes a contract to sell the holding from which such interest is derived within three months of the date such recipient acquired such holding.

Article 12. Royalties

1. Royalties derived and beneficially owned by a resident of the United Kingdom shall be exempt from tax by the United States.

2. Royalties derived and beneficially owned by a resident of the United States shall be exempt from tax by the United Kingdom.

3. The term 'royalties' as used in this Article *(a)* means payments of any kind received as a consideration for the use of, or the right to use, any copyright of literary, artistic or scientific work (but not including cinematographic films or films or tapes used for radio or television broadcasting); any patent, trade mark, design or model, plan, secret formula or process, or other like right or property, or for information concerning industrial, commercial or scientific experience; and *(b)* shall include gains derived from the alienation of any such right or property which are contingent on the productivity, use, or disposition thereof; including the supply of assistance of an ancillary and subsidiary nature furnished as a means of enabling the application or enjoyment of any such right or property.

4. The provisions of paragraphs 1 and 2 of this Article shall not apply if the person deriving the royalties, being a resident of a Contracting State, carries on business in the other Contracting State in which the royalties arise, through a permanent establishment situated therein, or performs in that other State independent personal services from a fixed base situated therein, and the right or property in respect

of which the royalties are paid is effectively connected with such permanent establishment or fixed base. In such a case the provisions of Article 7 (Business Profits), Article 14 (Independent Personal Services), or Article 17 (Artistes and Athletes), as the case may be, shall apply.

5. Where, owing to a special relationship between the payer and the person deriving the royalties or between both of them and some other person, the amount of the royalties paid exceeds for whatever reason the amount which would have been paid in the absence of such relationship, the provisions of this Article shall apply only to the last-mentioned interest. In that case, the excess part of the payments shall remain taxable according to the law of each Contracting State, due regard being had to the other provisions of this Convention.

Article 13. Capital Gains

Except as provided in Article 8 (Shipping and Air Transport) of this Convention, each Contracting State may tax capital gains in accordance with the provisions of its domestic law.

Article 14. Independent Personal Services

Income derived by an individual who is a resident of one of the Contracting States from the performance of personal services in an independent capacity may be taxed in that State. Such income may also be taxed in the other Contracting State if:

a. the individual is present in that other State for a period or periods exceeding in the aggregate 183 days in the tax year concerned, but only so much thereof as is attributable to services performed in that State, or

b. the individual has a fixed base regularly available to him in that other State for the purpose of performing his activities, but only so much thereof as is attributable to services performed in that State.

Article 15. Dependent Personal Services

1. Subject to the provisions of Articles 18 (Pensions) and 19 (Government Service), salaries, wages and other similar remuneration derived by a resident of a Contracting State in respect of an employment shall be taxable only in that State unless the employment is exercised in the other Contracting State. If the employment is so exercised, such remuneration as is derived therefrom may be taxed in that other State.

2. Notwithstanding the provisions of paragraph 1, remuneration derived by a resident of a Contracting State in respect of an employment exercised in the other Contracting State shall be taxable only in the first-mentioned State if:

a. the recipient is present in that other State for a period not exceeding in the aggregate 183 days in the tax year concerned; and

b. the remuneration is paid by, or on behalf of, an employer who is not a resident of that other State; and

c. the remuneration is not borne as such by a permanent establishment or a fixed base which the employer has in that other State.

3. Notwithstanding the preceding provisions of this Article, remuneration in respect of an employment as a member of the regular complement of a ship or aircraft in international traffic may be taxed by the Contracting State of which the employer operating the ship or aircraft is a resident.

Article 16. Investment or Holding Companies

1. The provisions of Articles 10 (Dividends), 11 (Interest) or 12 (Royalties) of this Convention shall not apply to a corporation which is a resident of one of the Contracting State and which derives dividends, interest, or royalties arising within the other Contracting State if:

a. (i) the tax imposed on the corporation by the first-mentioned Contracting State in respect of such dividends, interest, or royalties is substantially less than the tax generally imposed by that State on corporate profits; or

(ii) the corporation is a resident of the United States and receives more than eighty per cent of its gross income from sources outside the United States as determined by and for the period prescribed in sections 861(*a*)(1)(B) and (*a*)(2)(A) of the United States Internal Revenue Code of 1954, as they may be amended from time to time in minor respects so as not to affect their general principle; and

b. 25 per cent or more of the capital of such corporation is owned directly or indirectly by one or more persons who are not individual residents of the first-mentioned Contracting State and are not nationals of the United States.

2. Nothing in this Article shall however prevent a claim under the provisions of Articles 10 (Dividends), 11 (Interest) or 12 (Royalties) by a United States corporation where more than 75 per cent of the capital of that corporation is directly or indirectly owned:

a. by a United States corporation which receives 20 per cent or more of its gross income from sources within the United States as determined by and for the period described in subparagraph 1*a*.(ii) of this Article;

b. by a corporation (other than a United States corporation) which by reference to the provisions of section 283 of the United Kingdom Income and Corporation Taxes Act 1970 (as it may be amended from time to time without changing the general principle thereof) would not fail to be treated as a close company; or

c. by a corporation which is a resident of the United Kingdom and in which more than 50 per cent of the voting power is controlled, directly or indirectly, by individuals who are residents of the United Kingdom.

Article 17. Artistes and Athletes

1. Notwithstanding the provisions of Articles 14 (Independent Personal Services) and 15 (Dependent Personal Services), income derived by entertainers, such as theatre, motion picture, radio or television artistes, and musicians, and by athletes, from their personal activities

as such may be taxed in the Contracting State in which these activities are exercised, except where the amount of the gross receipts derived by an entertainer or athlete, including expenses reimbursed to him or borne on his behalf, from such activities do not exceed 15,000 United States dollars or its equivalent in pounds sterling in the tax year concerned.

2. Where income in respect of personal activities as such of an entertainer or athlete accrues not to that entertainer or athlete himself but to another person, that income may, notwithstanding the provisions of Articles 7 (Business Profits), 14 (Independent Personal Services), and 15 (Dependent Personal Services), be taxed in the Contracting State in which the activities of the entertainer or athlete are exercised. For the purposes of the preceding sentence, income of an entertainer or athlete shall be deemed not to accrue to another person if it is established that neither the entertainer or athlete, nor persons related thereto, participate directly or indirectly in the profits of such other person in any manner, including the receipt of deferred remuneration, bonuses, fees, dividends, partnership distributions or other distributions.

Article 18. Pensions

1. Subject to the provisions of paragraph 2 of Article 19 (Government Service), any pension in consideration of past employment and any annuity paid to an individual who is a resident of a Contracting State shall be taxed only in that State.

2. Alimony paid to an individual who is a resident of one of the Contracting States by an individual who is a resident of the other Contracting State shall be exempt from tax in the other Contracting State.

3. The term 'annuity' means a stated sum payable periodically at stated times, during life or during a specified or ascertainable period of time, under an obligation to make the payments in return for adequate and full consideration in money or money's worth.

Article 19. Government Service

1. *a.* Remuneration, other than a pensions, paid by a Contracting State to any individual in respect of services rendered to that State shall be taxable only in that State.

b. However, such remuneration shall be taxable only in the other Contracting State if the services are rendered in that State and the recipient is a resident and a national of that State.

2. *a.* Any pension paid by a Contracting State or a political subdivision or local authority thereof to any individual in respect of services rendered to that State or subdivision or local authority thereof shall be taxable only in that State.

b. However, such pension shall be taxable only in the other Contracting State if the recipient is a national of and a resident of that State.

3. The provisions of Articles 14 (Independent Personal Services) 15 (Dependent Personal Services), 17 (Artistes and Athletes), and 18 (Pensions), as the case may be, shall apply to remuneration and pensions

in respect of services rendered in connection with any business carried on by or on behalf of one of the Contracting States or a political subdivision or local authority thereof.

Article 20. Teachers

1. A professor or teacher who visits one of the Contracting States for a period not exceeding two years for the purpose of teaching or engaging in research at a university, college or other recognized educational institution in that Contracting State and who was immediately before that visit a resident of the other Contracting State, shall be exempted from tax by the first-mentioned Contracting State on any remuneration for such teaching or research for a period not exceeding two years from the date he first visits that State for such purposes.

2. The exemption provided in this Article may be applied by the Contracting State in which the teaching or research is performed to current payments to such professor or teacher in anticipation or fulfilment of the requirements of paragraph 1 or by way of withholding and refund, but in either case exemption shall be conditional upon fulfilment of the requirements of paragraph 1.

3. This Article shall only apply to income from research if such research is undertaken by the professor or teacher in the public interest and not primarily for the benefit of some other private person or persons.

Article 21. Students and Trainees

Payments which a student or business apprentice who was immediately before visiting a Contracting State a resident of the other Contracting State and who is present in the first-mentioned Contracting State for the purpose of his full-time education or training receives for the purpose of his maintenance, education or training shall not be taxed in that State, provided that such payments are made to him from sources outside that State.

Article 22. Other Income

1. Items of income of a resident of a Contracting State, wherever arising, not dealt with in the foregoing Articles of this Convention shall be taxable only in that State. The preceding sentence shall not apply to income paid out of trusts.

2. The provisions of paragraph 1 shall not apply if the person deriving the income, being a resident of a Contracting State, carries on business in the other Contracting State through a permanent establishment situated therein, or performs in that other State independent personal services from a fixed base situated therein, and the right or property in respect of which the income is paid is effectively connected with such permanent establishment or fixed base. In such a case the provisions of Article 7 (Business Profits), Article 14 (Independent Personal Services), or Article 17 (Artistes and Athletes), as the case may be, shall apply.

Article 23. Elimination of Double Taxation

1. In accordance with the provisions and subject to the limitations of the law of the United States (as it may be amended from time to time without changing the general principle hereof), the United States shall allow to a resident or national of the United States as a credit against the United States tax the appropriate amount of tax paid to the United Kingdom; and, in the case of a United States corporation owning at least 10 per cent of the voting stock of a corporation which is a resident of the United Kingdom from it receives dividends in any taxable year, the United States shall allow credit for the appropriate amount of income tax paid to the United Kingdom by that corporation with respect to the profits out of which such dividends are paid. Such appropriate amount shall be based upon the amount of tax paid to the United Kingdom, but the credit shall not exceed the limitations (for the purpose of limiting the credit to the United States tax on income from sources outside of the United States) provided by United States law for the taxable year. For the purposes of applying the United States credit in relation to tax paid to the United Kingdom:

a. the taxes referred to in paragraphs 2*b.* and 3 of Article 2 (Taxes Covered) shall be considered to be income taxes;

b. the amount of 5 or 15 per cent, as the case may be, withheld under paragraph 2*a.*(i) or (ii) of Article 10 (Dividends) from the tax credit paid by the United Kingdom shall be treated as an income tax imposed on the recipient of the dividend; and

c. that amount of tax credit referred to in paragraph 2*a.*(i) of Article 10 (Dividends) which is not paid to the United States corporation but to which an individual resident of the United Kingdom would have been entitled had he received the dividend shall be treated as an income tax imposed on the corporation paying the dividend.

2. Subject to the provisions of the law of the United Kingdom regarding the allowance as a credit against United Kingdom tax of tax payable in a territory outside the United Kingdom (as it may be amended from time to time without changing the general principle hereof):

a. United States tax payable under the laws of the United States and in accordance with the present Convention, whether directly or by deduction, on profits or income from sources within the United States (excluding in the case of a dividend, tax payable in respect of the profits out of which the dividend is paid) shall be allowed as a credit against any United Kingdom tax computed by reference to the same profits or income by reference to which the United States tax is computed;

b. in the case of a dividend paid by a United States corporation to a corporation which is resident in the United Kingdom and which controls directly or indirectly at least 10 per cent of the voting power in the United States corporation, the credit shall take into account (in addition to any United States tax creditable under *a.*) the United States tax payable by the corporation in respect of the profits out of which such dividend is paid.

3. For the purposes of the preceding paragraphs of this Article, income or profits derived by a resident of a Contracting State which may be taxed in the other Contracting State in accordance with this Convention shall be deemed to arise from sources within that other Contracting State, except that where the United States taxes on the basis of citizenship, the United Kingdom shall not be bound to give credit to a United States national who is a resident in the United Kingdom on income from sources outside the United States as determined under the laws of the United Kingdom and the United States shall not be bound to give credit for United Kingdom tax on income received by such national from sources outside the United Kingdom, as determined under the laws of the United States.

4. Notwithstanding subparagraph *a.* of paragraph 1 of this Article, the amount of United Kingdom petroleum revenue tax allowable as a credit against United States tax shall be limited to the amount attributable to United Kingdom source taxable income in the following way, namely:

a. The amount of United Kingdom petroleum revenue tax on income from the extraction of minerals from oil or gas wells in the United Kingdom to be allowed as a credit for a taxable year shall not exceed the amount, if any, by which the product of the maximum statutory United States tax rate applicable to a corporation for such taxable year and the amount of such income exceeds the amount of other United Kingdom tax on such income.

b. The lesser of

(i) the amount of United Kingdom petroleum revenue tax on income from the extraction of minerals from oil or gas wells in the United Kingdom that is not allowable as a credit under the preceding subparagraph, or

(ii) two per cent of such income for the taxable year shall be deemed to be income taxes paid or accrued in the two preceding or five succeeding taxable years, to the extent not deemed paid or accrued in a prior taxable year, and shall be allowable as a credit in the year in which it is deemed paid or accrued subject to the limitation in subparagraph *a.* above.

c. The provisions of subparagraphs *a.* and *b.* above shall apply separately, *mutatis mutandis* (but with the deletion, in the case of *b.*, of the words 'the lesser of (i)' and 'or (ii) two per cent of such income for the taxable year') to the amount of United Kingdom petroleum revenue tax on income from initial transportation, initial treatment and initial storage of minerals from oil or gas wells in the United Kingdom.

Article 24. Non-Discrimination

1. Individuals who are nationals of a Contracting State and who are resident of the other Contracting State shall not be subjected in that other State to any taxation or any requirement connected therewith which is other or more burdensome than the taxation and connected requirements to which nationals of that other State in the same circumstances are or may be subjected.

2. The taxation on a permanent establishment which an enterprise of a Contracting State has in the other Contracting State shall not be less favourably levied in that other State than the taxation levied on enterprises of that other State carrying on the same activities.

3. Subject to the provisions of paragraph 4 of this Article, interest, royalties and other disbursements paid by an enterprise of a Contracting State to a resident of the other Contracting State shall, if reasonable in amount, be deductible for the purpose of determining the taxable profits of such enterprise under the same conditions as if they had been paid to a resident of the first-mentioned State. For the purposes of this paragraph, the term 'other disbursements' shall include charges for amounts expended by such residents for the purposes of such enterprise, including a reasonable allocation of executive and general administrative expenses (except to the extent representing the expenses of a type of activity which is not for the benefit of such enterprise, but constitutes 'stewardship' or 'over-seeing' functions undertaken for such resident's own benefit as an investor in the enterprise), research and development in respect of which such enterprise has the benefits under a cost and risk sharing agreement and other expenses incurred by such resident for the benefit of a group of related enterprises including such enterprise.

4. Paragraph 3 shall not apply to any interest, royalties, or other disbursements to which the provisions of Article 9 (Associated Enterprises), paragraphs 5 and 7 of Article 11 (Interest) or paragraph 5 of Article 12 (Royalties) apply.

5. Enterprises of a Contracting State, the capital of which is wholly or partly owned or controlled, directly or indirectly, by one or more residents of the other Contracting State, shall not be subjected in the first-mentioned Contracting State to any taxation or any requirement connected therewith which is other or more burdensome than the taxation and connected requirements to which other similar enterprises of the first-mentioned State are or may be subjected.

6. Nothing contained in this Article shall be construed as obliging either Contracting State to grant to individuals not resident in that State any of the personal allowances and reliefs which are granted to individuals so resident.

Article 25. Mutual Agreement Procedure

1. Where a resident or national of a Contracting State considers that the actions of one or both of the Contracting States result or will result in taxation not in accordance with this Convention, he may, notwithstanding the remedies provided by the national laws of those States, present his case to the competent authority of the Contracting State of which he is a resident or national.

2. The competent authority shall endeavour, if the objection appears to it to be justified and if it is not itself able to arrive at an appropriate solution, to resolve the case by mutual agreement with the competent authority of the other Contracting State, with a view to the avoidance of taxation not in accordance with the Convention. Where an agreement

has been reached, a refund as appropriate shall be made to give effect to the agreement.

3. The competent authorities of the Contracting States shall endeavour to resolve by mutual agreement any difficulties or doubts arising as to the interpretation or application of the Convention. In particular the competent authorities of the Contracting States may reach agreement on:

a. the attribution of income, deductions, credits, or allowances of an enterprise of a Contracting State to its permanent establishment situated in the other Contracting State;

b. the allocation of income, deductions, credits, or allowances between persons;

c. the nature of particular items of income;

d. the meaning of terms not otherwise defined in this Convention;

e. the place where a particular item of income has its source;

f. the elimination of double taxation in respect of income paid out of trusts.

4. The competent authorities of the Contracting States may communicate with each other directly for the purpose of reaching agreement as contemplated by this Convention.

Article 26. Exchange of Information and Administrative Assistance

1. The competent authorities of the Contracting States shall exchange such information (being information available under the respective taxation laws of the Contracting States) as is necessary for carrying out the provisions of this Convention or for the prevention of fraud or the administration of statutory provisions against legal avoidance in relation to the taxes which are the subject of this Convention. Any information so exchanged shall be treated as secret but may be disclosed to persons (including a court or administrative body) concerned with the assessment, collection, enforcement or prosecution in respect of taxes which are the subject of this Convention. No information shall be exchanged which would disclose any trade, business, industrial or professional secret or any trade process.

2. Each of the Contracting States will endeavour to collect on behalf of the other Contracting State such amounts as may be necessary to ensure that relief granted by this Convention from taxation imposed by such other Contracting State does not enure to the benefit of persons not entitled thereto. The United Kingdom will be regarded as fulfilling this obligation by the continuation of its existing arrangements for ensuring the relief from taxation imposed by the laws of the United States does not enure to the benefits or persons not entitled thereto.

3. Paragraph 2 of this Article shall not impose upon either of the Contracting States the obligation to carry out administrative measures which are of a different nature from those used in the collection of its own tax, or which would be contrary to its sovereignty, security, or public policy. In determining the administrative measures to be carried out, each Contracting State may take into account the administrative

measures and practices of the other Contracting State in recovering taxes on behalf of the first-mentioned Contracting State.

4. The competent authorities of the Contracting States shall consult with each other for the purpose of co-operating and advising in respect of any action to be taken in implementing this Article.

Article 27. Effect on Diplomatic and Consular Officials and Domestic Laws

1. Nothing in this Convention shall affect the fiscal privileges of diplomatic or consular officials under the general rules of international law or under the provisions of special agreements.

2. This Convention shall not restrict in any manner any exclusion, exemption, deduction, credit, or other allowances now or hereafter accorded by the laws of either Contracting State.

Article 27A. Offshore Activities

1. Notwithstanding the provisions of Article 5 (Permanent Establishment) and Article 14 (Independent Personal Services), a person who is a resident of a Contracting State and carries on activities in the other Contracting State in connection with the exploration or exploitation of the seabed and subsoil and their natural resources situated in that other Contracting State shall be deemed to be carrying on in respect of those activities a business in that other Contracting State through a permanent establishment or fixed base situated therein.

2. The provisions of paragraph 1 shall not apply where the activities are carried on for a period not exceeding 30 days in aggregate in any 12 month period. However, for the purpose of this paragraph, activities carried on by an enterprise related to another enterprise shall be regarded as carried on by the enterprise to which it is related if the activities in question are substantially the same as those carried on by the last-mentioned enterprise.

3. The provisions of Article 8 (Shipping and Air Transport) shall not apply to a drilling rig or any vessel the principal function of which is the performance of activities other than the transportation of goods or passengers.

Article 28. Entry into Force

1. This Convention shall be ratified and the instruments of ratification shall be exchanged at Washington as soon as possible.

2. This Convention shall enter into force immediately after the expiration of thirty days following the date on which the instruments of ratification are exchanged and shall thereupon have effect:

a. in the United Kingdom:

(i) in relation to any dividend to which sub-paragraph 2*a*.(ii) of Article 10 (Dividends) applies, in respect of income tax and payment of tax credit, for any year of assessment beginning on or after 6 April 1973. A dividend paid on or after 1 April 1973 and before 6 April 1973 shall be treated for tax credit purposes as paid on 6 April 1973;

(ii) in relation to paragraph 4 of Article 4 (Fiscal Residence), for any year of assessment beginning on or after 6 April 1976;

(iii) in relation to sub-paragraph 2*a*.(i) of Article 10 (Dividends) and any other provision of this Convention, in respect of income tax and payment of tax credit and in respect of capital gains tax, for any year of assessment beginning on or after 6 April 1975;

(iv) in respect of corporation tax, for any financial year beginning on or after 1 April 1975; and

(v) in respect of petroleum revenue, for any chargeable period beginning on or after 1 January 1975;

b. in the United States:

(i) in respect of credits against United States tax allowed under paragraph 1 of Article 23 (Elimination of Double Taxation), for taxes paid to the United Kingdom on or after 1 April 1973;

(ii) in respect of tax withheld at the source, for amounts paid or credited on or after 1 January 1975; and

(iii) in respect of other taxes, for taxable years beginning on or after 1 January 1975.

3. Subject to the provisions of paragraph 4 of this Article the Convention between the United Kingdom of Great Britain and Northern Ireland and the United States of America for the Avoidance of Double Taxation and the Prevention of Fiscal Evasion with respect to Taxes on Income signed in Washington on 16 April 1945, as amended by the Supplementary Protocol signed at Washington on 6 June 1946, by the Supplementary Protocol signed at Washington on 25 May 1954, by the Supplementary Protocol signed at Washington on 19 August 1957 and by the Supplementary Protocol signed at London on 17 March 1966 (hereinafter referred to as 'the 1945 Convention'), shall cease to have effect in respect of taxes to which this Convention in accordance with the provisions of paragraph 2 of this Article applies.

4. Where any provision of the 1945 Convention would have afforded any greater relief from tax any such provision as aforesaid shall continue to have effect:

a. in the United Kingdom, for any year of assessment or financial year; and

b. in the United States, for any taxable year beginning, in either case, before 1 January 1976.

5. The 1945 Convention shall terminate on the last date on which it has effect in accordance with the foregoing provisions of this Article.

6. This Convention shall not affect any Agreement in force extending the 1945 Convention in accordance with Article XXII thereof.

7. Notwithstanding any provisions of the respective domestic laws of the Contracting States imposing time limits for applications for relief from tax, an application for relief under the provisions of this Convention shall have effect, and any consequential refunds of tax made, if the application is made to the competent authority concerned within three years of the end of the calendar year in which this Convention enters into force.

Article 29. Termination

1. This Convention shall remain in force indefinitely but either of the Contracting States may, on or before 30 June in any year after the year 1980, give to the other Contracting State, through diplomatic channels notice of termination and, in such event, the present Convention shall cease to be effective:

a. in respect of United States tax, for the taxable years beginning on or after 1 January in the year next following that in which such notice is given;

b. (i) in respect of United Kingdom income tax and capital gains tax, for any year of assessment beginning on or after 6 April in the year next following that in which such notice is given;

(ii) in respect of United Kingdom corporation tax, for any financial year, beginning on or after 1 April in the year next following that in which such notice is given;

(iii) in respect of United Kingdom petroleum revenue tax, for any chargeable period beginning on or after 1 January in the year next following that in which such notice is given.

2. The termination of the present Convention shall not have the effect of reviving any treaty or arrangement abrogated by the present Convention or by treaties previously concluded between the Contracting States.

In witness whereof the undersigned, duly authorised thereto by their respective Governments, have signed this Convention.

Germany (Estate Tax Treaty)

Convention between the United States of America and the Federal Republic of Germany for the Avoidance of Double Taxation with Respect to Taxes on Estates, Inheritances, and Gifts, concluded at Bonn on 3 December 1980.

The United States of America and the Federal Republic of Germany, desiring to avoid double taxation with respect to taxes on estates, inheritances, and gifts

Have agreed as follows:

Chapter I

Article 1. Scope

This Convention shall apply to:

a. Estates of deceased persons whose domicile at their death was in one or both of the Contracting States, and

b. Gifts of donors whose domicile at the making of a gift was in one or both of the Contracting States.

Article 2. Taxes Covered

1. The existing taxes to which this Convention shall apply are:

a. In the case of the United States: The federal estate tax and the Federal gift tax, including the tax on generation-skipping transfers;

b. In the case of the Federal Republic of Germany: the inheritance and gift tax (*Erbschaftsteuer und Schenkungsteuer*).

2. This Convention shall also apply to any similar taxes on estates, inheritances, and gifts which are imposed after the date of signature of the Convention in addition to, or in place of, the existing taxes.

Chapter II

Article 3. General Definitions

1. In this Convention:

a. The term 'United States of America' when used in a geographical sense means the states thereof and the District of Columbia. Such term also includes the territorial sea thereof and the seabed and subsoil of the submarine areas adjacent to the coast thereof, but beyond the territorial sea over which the United States of America exercises sovereign rights, in accordance with international law, for the purpose of exploration for and exploitation of the natural resources of such areas.

b. The term 'Federal Republic of Germany' when used in a geographical sense means the territory in which the Basic Law for the Federal Republic of Germany is in force as well as any area adjacent to the territorial waters of the Federal Republic of Germany designated, in accordance with international law relating to the rights which the Federal Republic of Germany may exercise with respect to the seabed and subsoil and their natural resources, as domestic area for tax purposes.

c. The term 'enterprise' means an industrial or commercial undertaking.

d. The term 'enterprise of a Contracting State' means an enterprise carried on by a person who is domiciled in a Contracting State.

e. The term 'competent authority' means:

(i) In the case of the United States of America, the Secretary of the Treasury or his delegate, and

(ii) In the case of the Federal Republic of Germany, the Federal Minister of Finance.

2. As regards the application of this Convention by a Contracting State, any term not defined therein shall, unless the context otherwise requires, have the meaning which it has under the law of that Contracting State concerning the taxes to which the Convention applies.

Article 4. Fiscal Domicile

1. For the purposes of this Convention, an individual has a domicile

a. In the United States of America, if he is a resident or citizen thereof;

b. In the Federal Republic of Germany, if he has his domicile (*Wohnsitz*) or habitual abode (*gewöhnlicher Aufenthalt*) therein or if he is deemed for other reasons to be subject to unlimited tax liability for the purposes of the German inheritance and gift tax.

2. Where by reason of the provisions of paragraph 1 an individual was domiciled in both Contracting States, then, subject to the provisions of paragraph 3, this case shall be determined in accordance with the following rules:

a. He shall be deemed to have been domiciled in the Contracting State in which he had a permanent home available to him. If he had a permanent home available to him in both Contracting States, or in neither Contracting State, the domicile shall be deemed to be in the Contracting State with which his personal and economic relations were closest (center of vital interests);

b. If the Contracting State in which he had his center of vital interests cannot be determined, the domicile shall be deemed to be in the Contracting State in which he had an habitual abode;

c. If he had an habitual abode in both Contracting States or in neither of them, the domicile shall be deemed to be in the Contracting State of which he was a citizen;

d. If he was a citizen of both Contracting States or of neither of them, the competent authorities of the Contracting States shall settle the question by mutual agreement.

3. Where an individual, at his death or at the making of a gift, was

a. a citizen of one Contracting State, and not also a citizen of the other Contracting State, and

b. by reason of the provisions of paragraph 1 domiciled in both Contracting States, and

c. by reason of the provisions of paragraph 1 domiciled in the other Contracting State for not more than five years,

then the domicile of that individual and of the members of his family forming part of his household and fulfilling the same requirements shall be deemed, notwithstanding the provisions of paragraph 2, to be in the Contracting State of which they were citizens.

4. An individual who, at his death or at the making of a gift, was a resident of a possession of the United States of America and who became a citizen of the United States of America solely by reason of

a. his being a citizen of a possession, or

b. birth or residence within a possession,

shall be considered as having been neither domiciled in nor a citizen of the United States of America at that time for purposes of this Convention.

5. For the purposes of this Convention the question whether a person other than an individual was domiciled in a Contracting State shall be determined according to the law of that State. Where such person is domiciled in both Contracting States, the competent authorities of the Contracting States shall settle the case by mutual agreement.

Chapter III

Article 5. Immovable Property

1. Immovable property which forms part of the estate or of a gift made by a person domiciled in a Contracting State and which is situated in the other Contracting State may be taxed in that other State.

2. The term 'immovable property' shall have the meaning which it has under the law of the Contracting State in which the property in question is situated. The term shall in any case include property accessory to immovable property, livestock and equipment used in agriculture and forestry, rights to which the provisions of general law respecting landed property apply, usufruct of immovable property, and rights to variable or fixed payments as consideration for the working of, or the right to work, mineral deposits, sources, and other natural resources, ships, boats, and aircraft shall not be regarded as immovable property.

3. The provisions of paragraphs 1 and 2 shall also apply to immovable property of an enterprise and to immovable property used for the performance of independent personal services.

Article 6. Business Property of a Permanent Establishment and Assets Pertaining to a Fixed Base Used for the Performance of Independent Personal Services

1. Except for assets referred to in Articles 5 and 7, assets of an enterprise which form part of the estate of or a gift made by a person domiciled in a Contracting State and forming part of the business property of a permanent establishment situated in the other Contracting State may be taxed in that other State.

2. *a.* The term 'permanent establishment' means a fixed place of business through which the business of an enterprise of a Contracting State is wholly or partly carried on.

b. A permanent establishment shall include especially:

a place of management;

a branch;

an office;

a store or other sales outlet;

a factory;

a workshop;

a mine, quarry, or other place of extraction of natural resources;

a building site or construction or assembly project which exists for more than twelve months.

c. Notwithstanding subparagraph *a.* of this paragraph, a permanent establishment shall be deemed not to include one or more of the following activities:

the use of facilities for the purpose of storage, display, or delivery of goods or merchandise belonging to the enterprise;

the maintenance of a stock of goods or merchandise belonging to the enterprise for the purpose of storage, display or delivery;

the maintenance of a stock of goods or merchandise belonging to the enterprise for the purpose of processing by another enterprise;

the maintenance of a fixed place of business for the purpose of purchasing goods or merchandise, or collecting information, for the enterprise;

the maintenance of a fixed place of business for the purpose of advertising, for the supply of information, for scientific research, or for similar activities, if they have a preparatory or auxiliary character, for the enterprise.

d. Even if an enterprise of a Contracting State does not have a permanent establishment in the other State under subparagraphs *a.* to *c.* of this paragraph, nevertheless it shall be deemed to have a permanent establishment in the latter State if it is engaged in trade or business in that State through an agent who has an authority to conclude contracts in the name of the enterprise and regularly exercises that authority in that State, unless the exercise of authority is limited to the purchase of goods or merchandise for the account of the enterprise.

e. An enterprise of a Contracting State shall not be deemed to have a permanent establishment in the other State merely because it is engaged in trade or business in that other State through a broker, general commission agent, or any other agent of an independent status, where such person is acting in the ordinary course of business.

f. The fact that a resident or a corporation of one of the Contracting States controls, is controlled by, or is under common control with

(i) a corporation of the other State or

(ii) a corporation which is engaged in trade or business in that other State (whether through a permanent establishment or otherwise) shall not be taken into account in determining whether such resident of corporation has a permanent establishment in that other State.

3. Except for assets referred to in Article 5, assets which form part of the estate of or of a gift made by a person domiciled in a Contracting State and pertaining to a fixed base situated in the other Contracting State used for the performance of independent personal services may be taxed in that other State.

Article 7. Ships and Aircraft

Ships and aircraft operated in international traffic and belonging to an enterprise which form part of the estate of or of a gift made by a person domiciled in a Contracting State, and movable property pertaining to the operation of such ships and aircraft, may be taxed only in that State.

Article 8. Interests in Partnerships

An interest in a partnership which forms part of the estate of or of a gift made by a person domiciled in a Contracting State, which partnership owns property described in Article 5 or 6, may be taxed by the State in which such property is situated, but only to the extent that the value of such interest is attributable to such property.

Article 9. Property Not Expressly Mentioned

Property which forms part of the estate of or of a gift made by a person domiciled in a Contracting State, wherever situated, and not dealt with in Article 5, 6, 7, or 8 shall, subject to paragraph 1 of Article 11, be taxable only in that State.

Article 10. Deductions and Exemptions

1. In the case of property which forms part of an estate or gift subject to taxation by a Contracting State solely in accordance with Article 5, 6, or 8, debts shall be allowed as reductions of, or deductions from, the value of such property in an amount no less than:

a. in the case of property referred to in Article 5, debts incurred for purposes of the acquisition, repair, or upkeep of the property;

b. in the case of property referred to in Article 6, debts incurred in connection with the operation of the permanent establishment or fixed base; and

c. in the case of an interest in a partnership referred to in Article 8, debts to which subparagraphs *a.* or *b.* of this paragraph would apply if the property owed by a partnership referred to in that Article were owned directly by the decedent or donor.

2. Property transferred to or for the use of a corporation or organization of a Contracting State organized and operated exclusively for religious, scientific, educational, or public purposes, or to a public body of a Contracting State to be used for such purposes, shall be exempt from tax by the other Contracting State, if and to the extent that such transfer of property to such corporation, organization, or public body

a. is exempt from tax in the first-mentioned Contracting State and

b. would be exempt from tax in the other Contracting State if it were made to a similar corporation, organization, or public body of that other State.

The competent authorities of the Contracting States shall by mutual agreement settle the application of this provision.

3. Pensions, annuities, and other amounts payable by a Contracting State, a state, a Land, or their political subdivisions, or out of a public fund organized under the public laws thereof, or under a plant maintained by a person resident in that State

a. under the Social Security laws of that State, or

b. as consideration for services rendered, or

c. as compensation for injury or damage sustained

shall be exempt from tax by the other Contracting State, to the extent that such pension, annuity, or other amount would be exempt from tax in the first-mentioned Contracting State if the decedent were a domiciliary thereof. The amounts so exempted may, however, be offset against the '*Versorgungsfreibetrag*' according to the provisions of German inheritance and gift tax.

4. Property (other than community property) which passes to the spouse from a decedent or donor who was domiciled in or a citizen of a Contracting State, and which may be taxed by the other Contracting State solely in accordance with Article 5, 6, or 8 shall, for the purpose of determining the tax of that other State, be included in the taxable base only to the extent its value (after taking into account any applicable deductions) exceeds 50 per cent of the value of all property included in the taxable base which may be taxed by that other State. However, the foregoing sentence shall not result in:

a. an exclusion from the taxable base in the Federal Republic of Germany of an amount in excess of the general marital deduction (*Freibetrag des Ehegatten*) granted with respect to transfers to spouses subject to unlimited tax liability under the German inheritance and gift tax;

b. a reduction of the tax due in the United States of America below the tax that would be due by applying to the taxable base determined under that sentence the rates applicable to a person domiciled in the United States of America.

Chapter IV

Article 11. Credits

1. The provisions of this Convention shall not preclude:

a. the United States of America from taxing in accordance with its law the estate of a decedent or the gift of a donor who was at his death or at the making of a gift a citizen of the United States of America; for this purpose the term 'citizen' shall include a former citizen whose loss of citizenship had as one of its principal purposes the avoidance of tax (including, for this purpose, income tax), but only for a period of ten years following such loss;

b. the Federal Republic of Germany from taxing in accordance with its law an heir, a donee, or another beneficiary who was domiciled (within the meaning of Article 4) in the Federal Republic of Germany at the time of the death of the decedent or the making of the gift. The preceding sentence shall not, however, apply to paragraphs 2, 3 and 4 of Article 10, paragraphs 2, 3, 4 and 5 of this Article, and Article 13.

2. Where the United States of America imposes tax by reason of the decedent's or the donor's domicile therein or citizenship thereof, double taxation shall be avoided in the following manner:

a. Where the Federal Republic of Germany imposes tax with respect to property in accordance with Article 5, 6, or 8, the United States of America shall credit against the tax calculated according to its law with respect to such property an amount equal to the tax paid to the Federal Republic of Germany with respect to such property.

b. In addition to any credit allowable under subparagraph *a.* of this paragraph, if the decedent or donor was a citizen of the United States of America and was domiciled in the Federal Republic of Germany at his death or at the making of a gift, then the United States of America shall allow a credit against the tax calculated according to its law with respect to property other than property which the United States of America may tax in accordance with Article 5, 6, or 8, an amount equal to the tax paid to the Federal Republic of Germany with respect to such property.

3. Where the Federal Republic of Germany imposes tax by reason of the domicile therein of the decedent, donor, heir, donee, or other beneficiary, double taxation shall be avoided in the following manner:

a. Where the United States of America imposes tax with respect to property in accordance with Article 5, 6, or 8, the Federal Republic of Germany shall credit against the tax calculated according to its law with respect to such property an amount equal to the tax paid to the United States of America with respect to such property.

b. In addition to any credit allowable under subparagraph *a.* of this paragraph, if the decedent or donor was domiciled in the United States of America and the heir, donee, or other beneficiary was domiciled in the Federal Republic of Germany at the time of the death of the decedent or the making of the gift, then the Federal Republic of Germany shall allow a credit against the tax calculated according to its law with respect to property other than property which the Federal Republic of Germany may tax in accordance with Article 5, 6, or 8, an amount equal to the tax paid to the United States of America with respect to such property.

4. The credits allowed by the Federal Republic of Germany according to the provisions of paragraph 3 shall include taxes levied by political subdivisions of the United States of America. Where a credit is not allowable for such taxes according to the provisions of paragraph 3, the competent authorities may consult for the purpose of avoiding double taxation pursuant to Article 13.

5. In order to avoid double taxation, each Contracting State shall, in allowing credits under paragraphs 2, 3, and 4, take into account in an appropriate way:

a. any tax imposed by the other Contracting State upon a prior gift of property made by the decedent, if such property is included in the estate subject to taxation by the first-mentioned State;

b. any credit allowed by the other Contracting State for estate or gift taxes paid upon prior taxable events.

Difficulties and doubts arising in the application of this provision shall be resolved by the competent authorities under Article 13.

6. Any credits allowed under this Article shall not exceed the part of the tax of a Contracting State, as computed before the credit is given, which is attributable to the property in respect of which a credit is allowable under this Article.

7. Any claim for credit or for refund of tax founded on the provisions of this Article may be made until one year after the final determination (administrative or judicial) and payment of tax for which any credit under this Article is claimed, provided that the determination and payment are made within ten years of the date of death of the decedent or of the date of the making of the gift by the donor. The competent authorities may by mutual agreement extend the ten-year time limit if circumstances beyond the control of the taxpayer prevent the determination within such period of the taxes which are the subject of the claim for credit or for refund. Any refund based solely on the provisions of this Convention shall be made without payment of interest on the amount so refunded.

Article 12. Estates and Trusts

1. The provisions of this Convention shall not preclude either Contracting State from applying its rules governing the recognition of a taxable event, with respect to transfers of property to and from an estate or trust.

2. Where differences in the laws of the Contracting States give rise to taxation at different times of transfers of property to and from an estate or trust, the competent authorities may discuss the case under Article 13 with a view to avoiding hardship, provided that the difference in timing of taxation does not exceed five years.

3. In a case where a transfer of property to an estate or trust results in no taxable transfer at such time under the German inheritance and

gift tax, the beneficiary of the estate or trust may elect within five years after such transfer to be subject to all German taxation (including income taxation) as if a taxable transfer had occurred to him at the time of such transfer.

Article 13. Mutual Agreement Procedure

1. Any person who considers that the actions of one or both of the Contracting States result or will result for him in taxation not in accordance with this Convention may, notwithstanding the remedies provided by the laws of those Contracting States, present his case to the competent authorities of either Contracting State. Such presentation must be made within one year after a claim for exemption, credit, or refund under this Convention has been finally settled or rejected.

2. The competent authority shall endeavor, if the objection appears to it to be justified and if it is not itself able to arrive at a satisfactory solution, to resolve the case by mutual agreement with the competent authority of the other Contracting State, with a view to the avoidance of taxation not in accordance with the Convention.

3. The competent authorities of the Contracting States shall endeavor to resolve by mutual agreement any difficulties or doubts arising as to the interpretation or application of the Convention. They may also consult together for the elimination of double taxation in cases not provided for in this Convention.

4. The competent authorities of the Contracting States may communicate with each other directly for the purpose of reaching an agreement in the sense of this Article. When it seems advisable for the purpose of reaching an agreement, the competent authorities may meet together for an oral exchange of opinions.

5. In the event that the competent authorities reach such an agreement, taxes shall be imposed and, notwithstanding any procedural rule (including statutes of limitations) applicable under the law of either Contracting State, refund or credit of taxes shall be allowed by the Contracting States in accordance with such agreement.

Article 14. Exchange of Information

1. The competent authorities of the Contracting States shall exchange such information as is necessary for the carrying out of this Convention or of the domestic laws of the Contracting States concerning taxes covered by this Convention insofar as the taxation thereunder is not contrary to this Convention. The exchange of information is not restricted by Article 1. Any information received by a Contracting State shall be treated as secret in the same manner as information obtained under the domestic laws of that State and shall be disclosed only to persons or authorities (including courts and administrative bodies) involved in the assessment or collection of, the enforcement or prosecution in respect of, or the determination of appeals in relation to, the taxes which are the subject of the Convention. Such persons or authorities shall use the information only for such purposes. These persons

or authorities may disclose the information in public court proceedings or in judicial decisions.

2. In no case shall the provisions of paragraph 1 be construed to impose on a Contracting State the obligation:

a. to carry out administrative measures at variance with the laws and administrative practice of that or of the other Contracting State;

b. to supply particulars which are not obtainable under the laws or in the normal course of the administration of that or of the other Contracting State;

c. to supply information which would disclose any trade, business, industrial, commercial, or professional secret or trade process, or information the disclosure of which would be contrary to public policy (*ordre public*).

3. If information is requested by a Contracting State in accordance with this Article, the other Contracting State shall obtain the information to which the request relates (including depositions of witnesses and copies of relevant documents) in the same manner and to the same extent as if the tax of the requesting State were the tax of the other State and were being imposed by that other State.

4. If by reason of Article 7 or 9 any property would, without regard to paragraph 1 of Article 11, be taxable only in the Contracting State in which the decedent or donor was domiciled and tax due in that State is not paid, then the competent authorities may agree that tax will be imposed with respect to such property in the other Contracting State notwithstanding Article 7 or 9.

Article 15. Members of Diplomatic Missions or Consular Posts

1. Nothing in this Convention shall affect the fiscal privileges of members of diplomatic missions or consular posts under the general rules of international law or under the provisions of special agreements.

2. This Convention shall not apply to officials of international organizations or members of a diplomatic mission or a consular post of a third State, who were established in a Contracting State and were not treated as being domiciled in either Contracting State in respect of taxes on estates, inheritances, or gifts, as the case may be.

Article 16. Land Berlin

This Convention shall also apply to Land Berlin, provided that the Government of the Federal Republic of Germany does not make a contrary declaration to the Government of the United States of America within three months of the date of entry into force of this Convention.

Chapter V

Article 17. Entry into Force

1. This Convention shall be subject to ratification in accordance with the applicable procedures of each Contracting State and instruments of ratification shall be exchanged at Washington as soon as possible.

2. This Convention shall enter into force upon the exchange of instruments of ratification and its provisions shall apply generally to estates of persons dying and gifts made on or after January 1, 1979.

3. In addition, in the case of estates of persons having died on or after January 1, 1974 and before January 1, 1979, the competent authorities of the Contracting States may consult together with a view to eliminating double taxation not avoided by internal relief measures. To this purpose they may, under the provisions of Article 13, allow taxes of one Contracting State to be credited against taxes of the other Contracting State notwithstanding differences of internal rules regarding situs and domicile.

Article 18. Termination

This Convention shall remain in force until terminated by one of the Contracting States. Either Contracting State may terminate this Convention, through diplomatic channels, at any time after three years from the date on which this Convention enters into force provided that at least six months' prior notice has been given.

In such event, the Convention will not apply to estates of persons dying after or gifts made after the December 31 next following the expiration of the six-month period.

Done at Bonn, in duplicate, in the English and German languages, the two texts having equal authenticity, this third day of December 1980.

For the United States of America:
Walter J. Stoessel, Jr.
For the Federal Republic of Germany:
Guenter van Well

Mexico (Exchange of Information)

Agreement between the United States of America and the United Mexican States for the Exchange of Information with respect to Taxes, concluded in Washington on November 9, 1989.

The United States of America and the United Mexican States, desiring to conclude an Agreement for the exchange of information with respect to taxes (hereinafter referred to as the 'Agreement'), have agreed as follows:

Article 1. Object and Scope

1. The objective of this Agreement is to facilitate the exchange of information between the Contracting States on the assessment and collection of taxes, with a view to better enable them to prevent, within their respective jurisdictions, fiscal evasion and fraud, and develop improved information sources for tax matters.

2. The Contracting States shall cooperate with each other to carry out the objective of this Agreement, in conformity with and subject to the limitations of their respective national laws and regulations.

3. Pursuant to the provision of paragraph 2 of this Article, requests for assistance under this Agreement will be executed, except to the extent that:

a. execution of the request would require the requested State to exceed its legal authority or would otherwise be prohibited by legal provisions in force in that State, or when the information requested is not obtainable under the laws or in the normal course of the administration of the requested State or of the other Contracting State, in which case the competent authorities of both Contracting States shall consult with each other to agree upon alternative lawful means for securing assistance;

b. execution of the request would in the judgment of the requested State be contrary to its national security or public policy;

c. to supply information would disclose any trade, business, industrial, commercial, or professional secret or trade process;

d. to supply information requested by the applicant State to administer or enforce a provision of the tax law of the applicant State, or any requirement connected therewith, would discriminate against a national of the requested State. A provision of tax law, or connected requirement, will be considered to be discriminatory against a national of the requested State if it is more burdensome with respect to a national of the requested State than with respect to a national of the applicant State in the same circumstances. For purposes of the preceding sentence, a national of the applicant State who is subject to tax on worldwide income is not in the same circumstances as a national of the requested State who is not subject to such taxation. The provision of this subparagraph shall not be construed to prevent the exchange of information with respect to the taxes imposed by the United States or Mexico on branch profits or the excess interest of a branch or on the premium income of foreign insurers;

e. the request does not comply with the provisions of this Agreement.

4. The Contracting States shall provide assistance through exchange of information authorized pursuant to Article 4 and such related measures as may be agreed upon by the competent authorities pursuant to Article 5.

5. Information shall be exchanged to fulfill the purpose of this Agreement without regard to whether the person to whom the information relates is, or whether the information is held by, a resident or national of a Contracting State.

Article 2. Taxes Covered

1. This Agreement shall apply to the following taxes imposed by or on behalf of a Contracting State:

a. in the case of the United States of America:

(i) Federal income taxes,
(ii) Federal taxes on employment income,
(iii) Federal taxes on transfers to avoid income tax,
(iv) Federal estate and gift taxes,
(v) Federal excise taxes; and

b. in the case of Mexico:

(i) Federal income taxes,
(ii) Federal taxes on employment income,
(iii) Federal taxes on business assets,
(iv) Federal value added taxes, and
(v) Federal excise taxes.

2. This Agreement shall apply also to any identical or substantially similar taxes imposed after the date of signature of the Agreement in addition to or in place of the existing taxes. The competent authority of each Contracting State shall notify the other of changes in laws which may affect the obligations of that State pursuant to this Agreement.

3. This Agreement shall not apply to the extent that an action or proceeding concerning taxes covered by this Agreement is barred by the applicant State's statute of limitations.

4. This Agreement shall not apply to taxes imposed by states, municipalities or other political subdivisions, or possessions of a Contracting State.

Article 3. Definitions

1. In this Agreement, unless otherwise defined:

a. The term 'competent authority' means:

(i) in the case of the United States of America, the Secretary of the Treasury or his delegate, and

(ii) in the case of Mexico, the Secretary of Finance and Public Credit or his delegate.

b. The term 'national' means:

(i) in the case of the United States, any United States citizen and any legal person, partnership, corporation, trust, estate, association, or other entity deriving its status as such from the laws in force in the United States; and

(ii) in the case of Mexico, any Mexican citizen and any legal person, partnership, corporation, trust, estate, association, or other entity deriving its status as such from the laws in force in Mexico.

c. The term 'person' includes an individual and any legal person, including a partnership, corporation, trust, estate, or association.

d. The term 'tax' means any tax to which the Agreement applies.

e. The term 'information' means any fact or statement, in any form whatever, that may be relevant or material to tax administration and enforcement, including (but not limited to):

(i) testimony of an individual, and

(ii) documents, records or other personal property of a person or Contracting State.

f. The terms 'applicant State' and 'requested State' mean, respectively, the Contracting State applying for or receiving information and the Contracting State providing or requested to provide such information.

g. For purposes of determining the geographical area within which jurisdiction to compel production of information may be exercised, the term 'United States' means the United States of America.

h. For purposes of determining the geographical area within which jurisdiction to compel production of information may be exercised, the term 'Mexico' means the United Mexican States.

2. Any term not defined in this Agreement, unless the context otherwise requires or the competent authorities agree to a common meaning pursuant to the provisions of Article 5, shall have the meaning which it has under the laws of the Contracting State relating to the taxes which are the subject of this Agreement.

Article 4. Exchange of Information

1. The competent authorities of the Contracting States shall exchange information to administer and enforce the domestic laws of the Contracting States concerning taxes covered by this Agreement, including information to effect the determination, assessment, and collection of tax, the recovery and enforcement of tax claims, or the investigation or prosecution of tax crimes or crimes involving the contravention of tax administration.

2. The competent authorities of the Contracting States shall automatically transmit information to each other for the purposes referred to in paragraph 1. The competent authorities shall determine the items of information to be exchanged pursuant to this paragraph and the procedure to be used to exchange such items of information.

3. The competent authority of a Contracting State shall spontaneously transmit to the competent authority of the other State information which has come to the attention of the first-mentioned State and which is likely to be relevant to, and bear significantly on, accomplishment of the purposes referred to in paragraph 1. The competent authorities shall determine the information to be exchanged pursuant to this paragraph and take such measures and implements such procedures as are necessary to ensure that the information is forwarded to the competent authority of the other State.

4. The competent authority of the requested State shall provide information upon request by the competent authority of the applicant State for the purposes referred to in paragraph 1. If the information available in the tax files of the requested State is not sufficient to enable compliance with the request, that State shall take all relevant measures to provide the applicant State with the information requested.

a. The requested State shall have or has the authority to:

(i) examine any books, papers, records, or other tangible property which may be relevant or material to such inquiry;

(ii) question any person having knowledge or in possession, custody or control of information which may be relevant or material to such inquiry;

(iii) compel any person having knowledge or in possession, custody or control of information which may be relevant or material to such inquiry to appear at a stated time and place and testify under oath and produce books, papers, records, or other tangible property;

(iv) take such testimony or any individual under oath.

b. If the United States is requested to obtain the types of information covered by section 3402 of the Right of Financial Privacy Act of 1978 (12 USCA 3402) as in effect at the time of signing this Agreement, it shall obtain the requested information pursuant to that provision. If Mexico is requested to obtain the types of information covered by Article 93 of the Regulatory Law and Banking and Credit Public Service as in effect at the time of signing this Agreement, it shall obtain the requested information pursuant to that provision. Laws or practices of the requested State do not prevent or otherwise affect the authority of the competent authority of the requested State to obtain and provide the types of information covered by the above-cited provisions pursuant to this Agreement.

c. Privileges under the laws or practices of the applicant State shall not apply in the requested State in the execution of a request. Claims of privileges under the laws or practices of the applicant State shall be determined exclusively by the courts of that State, and claims of privilege under the laws or practices of the requested State shall be determined exclusively by the courts of that State.

5. If information is requested by a Contracting State pursuant to paragraph 4, the requested State shall obtain the information requested in the same manner, and provide it in the same form, as if the tax of the applicant State were the tax of the requested State and were being

imposed by the requested State. However, if specifically requested by the competent authority of the applicant State, the requested State shall:

a. specify the time and place for the taking of testimony or the production of books, papers, records, and other tangible property;

b. place the individual giving testimony or producing books, papers, records and other tangible property under oath;

c. permit the presence of individuals designated by the competent authority of the applicant State as being involved in or affected by execution of the request. The individual giving testimony or the accused may be accompanied by his counsel;

d. provide such individuals described in subparagraph *c.* with an opportunity to question the individual giving testimony or producing books, papers, records and other tangible property:

(i) if Mexico is the applicant State, directly or through the executing authority; and

(ii) if the United States is the applicant State, through the executing authority;

e. secure original and unedited books, papers, and records, and other tangible property;

f. secure or produce true and correct copies of original and unedited books, papers and records;

g. determine the authenticity of books, papers, records and other tangible property produced;

h. examine the individual producing books, papers, records and other tangible property regarding the purpose for which and the manner in which the item produced is or was maintained;

i. permit the competent authority of the applicant State to provide written questions through the executing authorities of the requested State to which the individual producing books, papers, records and other tangible property is to respond regarding the item produced;

j. perform any other act not in violation of the laws or at variance with the administrative practice of the requested State;

k. certify either that procedures requested by the competent authority of the applicant State were followed or that the procedures requested could not be followed, with an explanation of the deviation and the reason therefor.

6. The provisions of the preceding paragraphs shall be construed so as to impose on a Contracting State the obligation to use all legal means and its best efforts to execute a request. A Contracting State may, in its discretion, take measures to obtain and transmit to the other State information which, pursuant to paragraph 3 of Article 1, it has not obligation to transmit.

7. Any information received by a Contracting State shall be treated as secret in the same manner as information obtained under the domestic laws of that State and shall be disclosed only to individuals or authorities (including judicial and administrative bodies) involved in the determination, assessment, collection, and administration of, the recovery and collection of claims derived from, the enforcement or prosecution in respect of, or the determination of appeals in respect of, the

taxes which are the subject of this Agreement, or the oversight of the above. Such individuals or authorities shall use the information only for such purposes. These individuals or authorities may disclose the information in public court proceedings or in judicial decisions.

Article 5. Mutual Agreement Procedure

1. The competent authorities of the Contracting States shall agree to implement a program to carry out the purposes of this Agreement. This program may include, in addition to exchanges specified in Article 4, other measures to improve tax compliance, such as exchanges of technical know-how, development of new audit techniques (including simultaneous examinations and simultaneous criminal investigations in their respective jurisdictions and by their respective competent authorities), identification of new areas of non-compliance, and joint studies of non-compliance areas.

2. The competent authorities of the Contracting States shall endeavor to resolve by mutual agreement any difficulties or doubts arising as to the interpretation or application of this Agreement. In particular, the competent authorities may agree to a common meaning of a term and may determine when costs are extraordinary for purposes of Article 6.

3. The competent authorities of the Contracting States may communicate with each other directly for the purposes of reaching an agreement under this Article.

Article 6. Costs

Unless the competent authorities of the Contracting States otherwise agree, ordinary costs incurred in providing assistance shall be borne by the requested State and extraordinary costs incurred in providing assistance shall be borne by the applicant State.

Article 7. Entry into Force

This Agreement shall enter into force upon an exchange of notes by the duly authorized representatives of the Contracting States confirming their mutual agreement that both sides have met all constitutional and statutory requirements necessary to effectuate this Agreement.

Article 8. Termination

This Agreement shall remain in force until terminated by one of the Contracting States. Either Contracting State may terminate the Agreement at any time after the Agreement enters into force provided that at least 3 months prior notice of termination has been given through diplomatic channels.

Done at Washington, D.C. in duplicate, in the English and Spanish languages, the two texts having equal authenticity, this 9th day of November, 1989.

Administrative Assistance

Multilateral Convention on Mutual Administration in Tax Matters, signed by the United States on June 28, 1989.[1]

Chapter I. Scope of the Convention

Article 1. Object of the Convention and Persons covered

1. The Parties shall, subject to the provisions of Chapter IV, provide administrative assistance to each other in tax matters. Such assistance may involve, where appropriate, measures taken by judicial bodies.

2. Such administrative assistance shall comprise:

a. exchange of information, including simultaneous tax examinations and participation in tax examinations abroad;

b. assistance in recovery, including measures of conservancy; and

c. service of documents.

3. A Party shall provide administrative assistance whether the person affected is a resident or national of a Party or of any other State.

Article 2. Taxes covered

1. This Convention shall apply:

a. to the following taxes:

(i) taxes on income or profits,

(ii) taxes on capital gains which are imposed separately from the tax on income or profits,

(iii) taxes on net wealth,

imposed on behalf of a Party; and

b. to the following taxes:

(i) taxes on income, profits, capital gains or net wealth which are imposed on behalf of political subdivisions or local authorities of a Party;

(ii) compulsory social security contributions payable to general government or to social security institutions established under public law;

(iii) taxes in other categories, except customs duties, imposed on behalf of a Party, namely:

A. estate, inheritance or gift taxes;

B. taxes on immovable property;

C. general consumption taxes, such as value-added or sales taxes;

D. specific taxes on goods and services such as excise taxes;

E. taxes on the use or ownership of motor vehicles;

1. Not yet ratified.

F. taxes on the use or ownership of movable property other than motor vehicles;

G. any other taxes.

(iv) taxes in categories referred to in sub-paragraph (iii) above which are imposed on behalf of political subdivisions or local authorities of a Party.

2. The existing taxes to which the Convention shall apply are listed in Annex A in the categories referred to in paragraph 1.

3. The Parties shall notify the Secretary General of the Council of Europe or the Secretary General of OECD (hereinafter referred to as the 'Depositaries') of any change to be made to Annex A as a result of a modification of the list mentioned in paragraph 2. Such changes shall take effect on the first day of the month following the expiration of a period of three months after the date of receipt of such notification by the Depositary.

4. The Convention shall also apply, as from their adoption, to any identical or substantially similar taxes which are imposed in a Contracting State after the entry into force of the Convention in respect of that Party in addition to or in place of the existing taxes listed in Annex A and, in that event, the Party concerned shall notify one of the Depositaries of the adoption of the tax in question.

Chapter II. General Definitions

Article 3. Definitions

1. For the purposes of this Convention, unless the context otherwise requires:

a. the terms 'applicant State' and 'requested State' mean respectively any Party applying for administrative assistance in tax matters and any Party requested to provide such assistance;

b. the term 'tax' means any tax or social security contribution to which the Convention applies pursuant to Article 2;

c. the term 'tax claim' means any amount of tax, as well as interest thereon, related administrative fines and costs incidental to recovery, which are owed and not yet paid;

d. the term 'competent authority' means the persons and authorities listed in Annex B;

e. the term 'nationals' in relation to a Party means:

(i) all individuals possessing the nationality of that Party, and

(ii) all legal persons, partnerships, associations and other entities deriving their status as such from the laws in force in that Party.

For each Party that has made a declaration for that purpose, the terms used above will be understood as defined in Annex C.

2. As regards the application of the Convention by a Party, any term not defined therein shall, unless the context otherwise requires, have the meaning which it has under the law of that Party concerning the taxes covered by the Convention.

3. The Parties shall notify one of the Depositaries of any change to be made to Annexes B and C. Such change shall take effect on the first day of the month following the expiration of a period of three months after the date of receipt of such notification by the Depositary in question.

Chapter III. Forms of Assistance

Section I. Exchange of Information

Article 4. General Provision

1. The Parties shall exchange any information, in particular as provided in this Section, that is foreseeably relevant to:

a. the assessment and collection of tax, and the recovery and enforcement of tax claims, and

b. the prosecution before an administrative authority or the initiation of prosecution before a judicial body.

Information which is unlikely to be relevant to these purposes shall not be exchanged under this Convention.

2. A Party may use information obtained under this Convention as evidence before a criminal court only if prior authorisation has been given by the Party which has supplied the information. However, any two or more Parties may mutually agree to waive the condition of prior authorisation.

3. Any Party may, by a declaration addressed to one of the Depositaries, indicate that, according to its internal legislation, its authorities may inform its resident or national before transmitting information concerning him, in conformity with Articles 5 and 7.

Article 5. Exchange of Information on Request

1. At the request of the applicant State, the requested State shall provide the applicant State with any information referred to in Article 4 which concerns particular persons or transactions.

2. If the information available in the tax files of the requested State is not sufficient to enable it to comply with the request for information, that State shall take all relevant measures to provide the applicant State with the information requested.

Article 6. Automatic Exchange of Information

With respect to categories of cases and in accordance with procedures which they shall determine by mutual agreement, two or more Parties shall automatically exchange the information referred to in Article 4.

Article 7. Spontaneous Exchange of Information

1. A Party shall, without prior request, forward to another Party information of which it has knowledge in the following circumstances:

a. the first-mentioned Party has grounds for supposing that there may be a loss of tax in the other Party;

b. a person liable to tax obtains a reduction in or an exemption from tax in the first-mentioned Party which would give rise to an increase in tax or to liability to tax in the other Party;

c. business dealings between a person liable to tax in a Party and a person liable to tax in another Party are conducted through one or more countries in such a way that a saving in tax may result in one or the other Party or in both;

d. a Party has grounds for supposing that a saving of tax may result from artificial transfers of profits within groups of enterprises;

e. information forwarded to the first-mentioned Party by the other Party has enabled information to be obtained which may be relevant in assessing liability to tax in the latter Party.

2. Each Party shall take such measures and implement such procedures as are necessary to ensure that information described in paragraph 1 will be made available for transmission to another Party.

Article 8. Simultaneous Tax Examinations

1. At the request of one of them, two or more Parties shall consult together for the purposes of determining cases and procedures for simultaneous tax examinations. Each Party involved shall decide whether or not it wishes to participate in a particular simultaneous tax examination.

2. For the purposes of this Convention, a simultaneous tax examination means an arrangement between two or more Parties to examine simultaneously, each in its own territory, the tax affairs of a person or persons in which they have a common or related interest, with a view to exchanging any relevant information which they so obtain.

Article 9. Tax Examinations Abroad

1. At the request of the competent authority of the applicant State, the competent authority of the requested State may allow representatives of the competent authority of the applicant State to be present at the appropriate part of a tax examination in the requested State.

2. If the request is acceded to, the competent authority of the requested State shall, as soon as possible, notify the competent authority of the applicant State about the time and place of the examination, the authority or official designated to carry out the examination and the procedures and conditions required by the requested State for the conduct of the examination. All decisions with respect to the conduct of the examination shall be made by the requested State.

3. A Party shall inform one of the Depositaries of its intention not to accept, as a general rule, such requests as are referred to in paragraph 1. Such a declaration may be made or withdrawn at any time.

Article 10. Conflicting Information

If a Party receives from another Party information about a person's tax affairs which appears to it to conflict with information in its possession, it shall so advise the Party which has provided the information.

Section II. Assistance in Recovery

Article 11. Recovery of Tax Claims

1. At the request of the applicant State the requested State shall, subject to the provisions of Articles 14 and 15, take the necessary steps to recover tax claims of the first-mentioned State as if they were its own tax claims.

2. The provision of paragraph 1 shall apply only to tax claims which form the subject of an instrument permitting their enforcement in the applicant State and, unless otherwise agreed between the Parties concerned, which are not contested.

However, where the claim is against a person who is not a resident of the Applicant State, paragraph 1 shall only apply, unless otherwise agreed between the Parties concerned, where the claim may no longer be contested.

3. The obligation to provide assistance in the recovery of tax claims concerning a deceased person or his estate, is limited to the value of the estate or of the property acquired by each beneficiary of the estate, according to whether the claim is to be recovered from the estate or from the beneficiaries thereof.

Article 12. Measures of Conservancy

At the request of the applicant State the requested State shall, with a view to the recovery of an amount of tax, take measures of conservancy even if the claim is contested or is not yet the subject of an instrument permitting enforcement.

Article 13. Documents Accompanying the Request

1. The request for administrative assistance under this Section shall be accompanied by:

a. a declaration that the tax claim concerns a tax covered by the Convention and, in the case of recovery that, subject to paragraph 2 of Article 11, the tax claim is not or may not be contested;

b. an official copy of the instrument permitting enforcement in the applicant State; and

c. any other document required for recovery or measures of conservancy.

2. The instrument permitting enforcement in the applicant State shall, where appropriate and in accordance with the provisions in force in the requested State, be accepted, recognised, supplemented by or replaced as soon as possible after the date of the receipt of the request for assistance, by an instrument permitting enforcement in the latter State.

Article 14. Time Limits

1. Questions concerning any period beyond which a tax claim cannot be enforced shall be governed by the law of the applicant State. The request for assistance shall give particulars concerning that period.

2. Acts of recovery carried out by the requested State in pursuance of a request for assistance, which, according to the laws of that State, would have the effect of suspending or interrupting the period mentioned in paragraph 1, shall also have this effect under the laws of the applicant State. The requested State shall inform the applicant State about such acts.

3. In any case the requested State is not obliged to comply with a request for assistance which is submitted after a period of 15 years from the date of the original instrument permitting enforcement.

Article 15. Priority

The tax claim in the recovery of which assistance is provided shall not have in the requested State any priority specially accorded to the tax claims of that State even if the recovery procedure used is the one applicable to its own tax claims.

Article 16. Deferral of Payment

The requested State may allow deferral of payment or payment by instalments if its laws or administrative practice permit it to do so in similar circumstances but shall first inform the applicant State.

Section III. Service of Documents

Article 17. Service of Documents

1. At the request of the applicant State the requested State shall serve upon the addressee documents, including those relating to judicial decisions, which emanate from the applicant State and which relate to a tax covered by this Convention.

2. The requested State shall effect service of documents:

a. by a method prescribed by its domestic laws for the service of documents of a substantially similar nature;

b. to the extent possible, by a particular method requested by the applicant State or the closest to such method available under its own laws.

3. A Party may effect service of documents directly through the post on a person within the territory of another Party.

4. Nothing in the Convention shall be construed as invalidating any service of documents by a Party in accordance with its laws.

5. When a document is served in accordance with this Article it need not be accompanied by a translation. However, where it is satisfied that the addressee cannot understand the language of the document the requested State shall arrange to have it translated into or a summary drafted in its or one of its official languages. Alternatively, it may ask the applicant State to have the documents either translated

into or accompanied by a summary in one of the official languages of the requested State, the Council of Europe or the OECD.

Chapter IV. Provisions relating to all Forms of Assistance

Article 18. Information to be provided by the Applicant State

1. A request for assistance shall indicate where appropriate:

a. the authority or agency which initiated the request made by the competent authority;

b. the name, address and any other particulars assisting in the identification of the person in request of whom the request is made;

c. in the case of a request for information, the form in which the applicant State wishes the information to be supplied in order to meet its needs;

d. in the case of a request for assistance in recovery or measures of conservancy, the nature of the tax claim, the components of the tax claim and the assets from which the tax claim may be recovered;

e. in the case of a request for service of documents, the nature and the subject of the document to be served;

f. whether it is in conformity with the law and administrative practice of the applicant State and whether it is justified in the light of the requirements of Article 19.

2. As soon as any other information relevant to the request for assistance comes to its knowledge, the applicant State shall forward it to the requested State.

Article 19. Possibility of Declining a Request

The requested State shall not be obliged to accede to a request if the applicant State has not pursued all means available in its own territory, except where recourse to such means would give rise to disproportionate difficulty.

Article 20. Response to the Request for Assistance

1. If the request for assistance is complied with, the requested State shall inform the applicant State of the action taken and of the result of the assistance as soon as possible.

2. If the request is declined, the requested State shall inform the applicant State of that decision and the reason for it as soon as possible.

3. If, with respect to a request for assistance, the applicant State has specified the form in which it wishes the information to be supplied and the requested State is in a position to do so, the requested State shall supply it in the form requested.

Article 21. Protection of Persons and Limits to the Obligation to provide Assistance

1. Nothing in this Convention shall affect the rights and safeguards secured to persons by the laws or administrative practice of the requested State.

2. Except in the case of Article 14 the provisions of this Convention shall not be construed so as to impose on the requested State the obligation:

a. to carry out measures at variance with its own laws or administrative practice or the laws or administrative practice of the applicant State;

b. to carry out measures which it considers contrary to public policy (*ordre public*) or to its essential interests;

c. to supply information which is not obtainable under its own laws or administrative practice or under the laws of the applicant State or its administrative practice;

d. to supply information which would disclose any trade, business, industrial, commercial or professional secret, or trade process, or information the disclosure of which would be contrary to public policy (*ordre public*) or to its essential interests;

e. to provide administrative assistance if and insofar as it considers the taxation in the applicant State to be contrary to generally accepted taxation principles or to the provisions of a convention for the avoidance of double taxation, or of any other convention which the requested State has concluded with the applicant State;

f. to provide assistance if the application of this Convention would lead to discrimination between a national of the requested State and nationals of the applicant State in the same circumstances.

Article 22. Secrecy

1. Any information obtained by a Party under this Convention shall be treated as secret in the same manner as information obtained under the domestic laws of that Party, or under the conditions of secrecy applying in the supplying Party if such conditions are more restrictive.

2. Such information shall in any case be disclosed only to persons or authorities (including courts and administrative or supervisory bodies) involved in the assessment, collection or recovery of, the enforcement or prosecution in respect of, or the determination of appeals in relation to, taxes of that Party. Only the persons or authorities mentioned above may use the information and then only for such purposes. They may, notwithstanding the provisions of paragraph 1, disclose it in public court proceedings or in judicial decisions relating to such taxes, subject to prior authorisation by the competent authority of the supplying Party. However, any two or more Parties may mutually agree to waive the condition of prior authorisation.

3. If a Party has made a reservation provided for in sub-paragraph *a.* of paragraph 1 of Article 30, any other Party obtaining information from that Party shall not use it for the purpose of a tax in a category subject to the reservation. Similarly the Party making such a reservation

shall not use information obtained under this Convention for the purpose of a tax in a category subject to the reservation.

4. Notwithstanding the provisions of paragraph 1, 2 and 3, information received by a Party may be used for other purposes when such information may be used for such other purposes under the laws of the supplying Party and the competent authority of that Party authorises such use. Information provided by a Party to another Party may be transmitted by the latter to a third Party, subject to prior authorisation by the competent authority of the first-mentioned Party.

Article 23. Proceedings

1. Proceedings relating to measures taken under this Convention by the requested State shall be brought only before the appropriate body of that State.

2. Proceedings relating to measures taken under this Convention by the applicant State, in particular those which, in the field of recovery, concern the existence or the amount of the tax claim or the instrument permitting its enforcement, shall be brought only before the appropriate body of that State. If such proceedings are brought, the applicant State shall inform the requested State which shall suspend the procedure pending the decision of the body in question. However, the requested State shall, if asked by the applicant State, take measures of conservancy to safeguard recovery. The requested State can also be informed of such proceedings by any interested person. Upon receipt of such information the requested State shall consult on the matter, if necessary with the applicant State.

3. As soon as a final decision in the proceedings has been given, the requested State or the applicant State, as the case may be, shall notify the other State of the decision and the implications which it has for the request for assistance.

Chapter V. Special Provisions

Article 24. Implementation of the Convention

1. The Parties shall communicate with each other for the implementation of this convention through their respective competent authorities. The competent authorities may communicate directly for this purpose and may authorise subordinate authorities to act on their behalf. The competent authorities of two or more Parties may mutually agree on the mode of application of the Convention among themselves.

2. Where the requested State considers that the application of this Convention in a particular case would have serious and undesirable consequences, the competent authorities of the requested and of the applicant State shall consult each other and endeavour to resolve the situation by mutual agreement.

3. A co-ordinating body composed of representatives of the competent authorities of the Parties shall monitor the implementation and development of this Convention, under the aegis of the OECD. To that

end, the co-ordinating body shall recommend any action likely to further the general aims of the Convention. In particular it shall act as a forum for the study of new methods and procedures to increase international co-operation in tax matters and, where appropriate, it may recommend revisions or amendments to the Convention. States which have signed but not yet ratified, accepted or approved the Convention are entitled to be represented at the meetings of the co-ordinating body as observers.

4. A Party may ask the co-ordinating body to furnish opinions on the interpretation of the provisions of the Convention.

5. Where difficulties or doubts arise between two or more Parties regarding the implementation or interpretation of the Convention, the competent authorities of those Parties shall endeavour to resolve the matter by mutual agreement. The agreement shall be communicated to the co-ordinating body.

6. The Secretary General of OECD shall inform the Parties, and the Signatory States which have not yet ratified, accepted or approved the Convention, of opinions furnished by the co-ordinating body according to the provisions of paragraph 4 above and of mutual agreements reached under paragraph 5 above.

Article 25. Language

Requests for assistance and answers thereto shall be drawn up in one of the official languages of the OECD and of the Council of Europe or in any other language agreed bilaterally between Contracting States concerned.

Article 26. Costs

Unless otherwise agreed bilaterally by the Parties concerned:

a. ordinary costs incurred in providing assistance shall be borne by the requested State;

b. extraordinary costs incurred in providing assistance shall be borne by the applicant State.

Chapter VI. Final Provisions

Article 27. Other International Agreements or Arrangements

1. The possibilities of assistance provided by this Convention do not limit, nor are they limited by, those contained in existing or future international agreements or other arrangements between the Parties concerned or other instruments which relate to co-operation in tax matters.

2. Notwithstanding the rules of the present Convention, those Parties which are members of the European Economic Community shall apply in their mutual relations the common rules in force in that Community.

Article 28. Signature and Entry into Force of the Convention

1. This Convention shall be open for signature by the member States of the Council of Europe and the Member countries of OECD. It is subject to ratification, acceptance or approval. Instruments of ratification, acceptance or approval shall be deposited with one of the Depositaries.

2. This Convention shall enter into force on the first day of the month following the expiration of a period of three months after the date on which five States have expressed their consent to be bound by the Convention in accordance with the provisions of paragraph 1.

3. In respect of any member State of the Council of Europe or any Member country of OECD which subsequently expresses its consent to be bound by it, the Convention shall enter into force on the first day of the month following the expiration of a period of three months after the date of the deposit of the instrument of ratification, acceptance or approval.

Article 29. Territorial Application of the Convention

1. Each State may at the time of signature, or when depositing its instrument of ratification, acceptance or approval, specify the territory or territories to which this Convention shall apply.

2. Any State may, at any later date, by a declaration addressed to one of the Depositaries, extend the application of this Convention to any other territory specified in the declaration. In respect of such territory the Convention shall enter into force on the first day of the month following the expiration of a period of three months after the date of receipt of such declaration by the Depositary.

3. Any declaration made under either of the two preceding paragraphs may, in respect of any territory specified in such declaration, be withdrawn by a notification addressed to one of the Depositaries. The withdrawal shall become effective on the first day of the month following the expiration of a period of three months after the date of receipt of such notification by the Depositary.

Article 30. Reservations

1. Any State may, at the time of signature or when depositing its instruments of ratification, acceptance or approval or at any later date declare that it reserves the right:

a. not to provide any form of assistance in relation to the taxes of other Parties in any of the categories listed in sub-paragraph *b.* of paragraph 1 of Article 2, provided that it has not included any domestic tax in that category under Annex A of the Convention;

b. not to provide assistance in the recovery of any tax claim, or in the recovery of an administrative fine, for all taxes or only for taxes in one or more of the categories listed in paragraph 1 of Article 2;

c. not to provide assistance in respect of any tax claim, which is in existence at the date of entry into force of the Convention in respect of that State or, where a reservation has previously been made under sub-paragraph *a.* or *b.* above, at the date of withdrawal of such a reservation in relation to taxes in the category in question;

d. not to provide assistance in the service of documents for all taxes or only for taxes in one or more of the categories listed in paragraph 1 of Article 2;

e. not to permit the service of documents through the post as provided for in paragraph 3 of Article 17.

2. No other reservation may be made.

3. After the entry into force of the Convention in respect of a Party, that Party may make one or more of the reservations listed in paragraph 1 which it did not make at the time of ratification, acceptance or approval. Such reservations shall enter into force on the first day of the month following the expiration of a period of three months after the date of receipt of the reservation by one of the Depositaries.

4. Any Party which has made a reservation under paragraphs 1 and 3 may wholly or partly withdraw it by means of a notification addressed to one of the Depositaries. The withdrawal shall take effect on the date of receipt of such notification by the Depositary in question.

5. A Party which has made a reservation in respect of a provision of this Convention may not require the application of that provision by any other Party; it may, however, if its reservation is partial, require the application of that provision insofar as it has itself accepted it.

Article 31. Denunciation

1. Any Party may at any time denounce this Convention by means of a notification addressed to one of the Depositaries.

2. Such denunciation shall become effective on the first day of the month following the expiration of a period of three months after the date of receipt of the notification by the Depositary.

3. Any Party which denounces the Convention shall remain bound by the provisions of Article 22 for as long as it retains in its possession any documents or information obtained under the Convention.

Article 32. Depositaries and their Functions

1. The Depositary with whom an act, notification or communication has been accomplished, shall notify the member States of the Council of Europe and the Member countries of OECD of:

a. any signature;

b. the deposit of any instrument of ratification, acceptance or approval;

c. the date of entry into force of this Convention in accordance with the provisions of Articles 28 and 29;

d. any declaration made in pursuance of the provisions of paragraph 3 of Article 4 or paragraph 3 of Article 9 and the withdrawal of any such declaration;

e. any reservation made in pursuance of the provisions of Article 30 and the withdrawal of any reservation effected in pursuance of the provisions of paragraph 4 of Article 30;

f. any notification received in pursuance of the provisions of paragraph 3 or 4 of Article 2, paragraph 3 of Article 3, Article 29 or paragraph 1 of Article 31;

g. any other act, notification or communication relating to this Convention.

2. The Depositary receiving a communication or making a notification in pursuance of the provisions of paragraph 1 shall inform the other Depositary thereof.

In witness whereof the undersigned, being duly authorised thereto, have signed the Convention.

Done at Strasbourg, the ....
in English and French, both texts being equally authentic, in two copies of which one shall be deposited in the archives of the Council of Europe and the other in the archives of OECD. The Secretaries General of the Council of Europe and of OECD shall transmit certified copies to each member State of the Council of Europe and of the Member countries of OECD.

OECD DRAFT DOUBLE TAXATION CONVENTION ON INCOME AND CAPITAL

1963

TITLE [ ]

Convention between (State A) and (State B) for the avoidance of double taxation with respect to taxes on income and on capital

PREAMBLE[1] [ ]

1. The Preamble of the Convention shall be drafted in accordance with the constitutional procedures of both Contracting States.

OECD MODEL DOUBLE TAXATION CONVENTION ON INCOME AND CAPITAL

1977

TITLE OF THE CONVENTION

Convention between (State A) and (State B) for the avoidance of double taxation with respect to taxes on income and on capital

PREAMBLE OF THE CONVENTION[1]

1. The Preamble of the Convention shall be drafted in accordance with the constitutional procedure of both Contracting States.

Model Double Taxation Conventions

UNITED NATIONS MODEL DOUBLE TAXATION CONVENTION BETWEEN DEVELOPED AND DEVELOPING COUNTRIES

1980

TREASURY DEPARTMENT'S PROPOSED NEW MODEL INCOME TAX TREATY

June 16, 1981

TITLE OF THE CONVENTION

Convention between (State A) and (State B) for the avoidance of double taxation with respect to taxes on income [and on capital].[1]

Convention between the United States of America and . . . for the avoidance of double taxation and the prevention of fiscal evasion with respect to taxes on income and capital.

PREAMBLE OF THE CONVENTION

[ ]

The United States of America and . . . desiring to conclude a convention for the avoidance of double taxation and the prevention of fiscal evasion with respect to taxes on income and capital, have agreed as follows:

1. Throughout the Convention, the words in square brackets are to be deleted if it is not intended to include in the Convention an article on the taxation of capital (see also article 22). The Preamble of the Convention shall be drafted in accordance with the constitutional procedures of both Contracting States.

OECD 1963

CHAPTER I

SCOPE OF THE CONVENTION

Article 1

PERSONAL SCOPE

This Convention shall apply to persons who are residents of one or both of the Contracting States.

OECD 1977

CHAPTER I

SCOPE OF THE CONVENTION

Article 1

PERSONAL SCOPE

This Convention shall apply to persons who are residents of one or both of the Contracting States.

CHAPTER I

[ ]

SCOPE OF THE CONVENTION

[ ]

Article 1

PERSONAL SCOPE

This Convention shall apply to persons who are residents of one or both of the Contracting States.

Article 1

GENERAL SCOPE

1. This Convention shall apply to persons who are residents of one or both of the Contracting States, *except as otherwise provided in the Convention.*

2. The Convention shall not restrict in any manner any exclusion, exemption, deduction, credit, or other allowance now or hereafter accorded

a) by the laws of either Contracting State; or

b) by any other agreement between the Contracting States.

3. Notwithstanding any provision of the Convention except paragraph 4, a Contracting State may tax its residents (as determined under Article 4 (Residence)), and by reason of citizenship may tax its citizens, as if the Convention had not come into effect. For this purpose, the term 'citizen' shall include a former citizen whose loss of citizenship had as one of its principal purposes the avoidance of income tax, but only for a period of 10 years following such loss.

4. The provisions of paragraph 3 shall not affect

a) the benefits conferred by a Contracting State under paragraph 2 of Article 9 (Associated Enterprises), under paragraphs 1b) and 4 of Article 18 (Pensions, Annuities, Alimony, and Child Support), and under Articles 23 (Relief From Double Taxation), 24 (Non-Discrimination), and 25 (Mutual Agreement Procedure); and

b) the benefits conferred by a Contracting State under Articles 19

OECD 1963

Article 2
TAXES COVERED

1. This Convention shall apply to taxes on income and on capital imposed on behalf of *each* Contracting State or of its political subdivisions or local authorities, irrespective of the manner in which they are levied.

2. There shall be regarded as taxes on income and on capital all taxes imposed on total income, on total capital, or on elements of income or of capital, including taxes on gains from the alienation of movable or immovable property, taxes on the total amounts of wages or salaries paid by enterprises, as well as taxes on capital appreciation.

3. The existing taxes to which the Convention shall apply are in particular:

a) *In the case of* (State A): . . .
b) *In the case of* (State B): . . .

OECD 1977

Article 2
TAXES COVERED

1. This Convention shall apply to taxes on income and on capital imposed on behalf of a Contracting State or of its political subdivisions or local authorities, irrespective of the manner in which they are levied.

2. There shall be regarded as taxes on income and on capital all taxes imposed on total income, on total capital, or on elements of income or of capital, including taxes on gains from the alienation of movable or immovable property, taxes on the total amounts of wages or salaries paid by enterprises, as well as taxes on capital appreciation.

3. The existing taxes to which the Convention shall apply are in particular:

a) (in State A): . . . .
b) (in State B): . . . .

(Government Service), 20 (Students and Trainees), and 27 (Diplomatic Agents and Consular Officers), upon individuals who are neither citizens of, nor have immigrant status in, that State.

Article 2
TAXES COVERED

1. This Convention shall apply to taxes on income [and on capital] imposed on behalf of a Contracting State or of its political subdivisions or local authorities, irrespective of the manner in which they are levied.

2. There shall be regarded as taxes on income [and on capital] all taxes imposed on total income, [on total capital,] or on elements of income [or of capital,] including taxes on gains from the alienation of movable or immovable property, taxes on the total amounts of wages or salaries paid by enterprises, as well as taxes on capital appreciation.

3. The existing taxes to which the Convention shall apply are in particular:

a) (in State A): . . . .

b) (in State B): . . . .

Article 2
TAXES COVERED

1. The existing taxes to which this convention shall apply are [ ]

a) *in the United States: the Federal income taxes imposed by the Internal Revenue Code (but excluding the accumulated earnings tax, the personal holding company tax, and social security taxes), and the excise taxes imposed on insurance premiums paid to foreign insurers and with respect to private foundations. The Convention shall, however, apply to the excise taxes imposed on insurance premiums paid to foreign insurers only to the extent that the risks covered by such premiums are not reinsured with a person not entitled to the benefits of this or any other convention which applies to these taxes;*

b) in . . . : . . .

OECD 1963	OECD 1977
4. The Convention shall *also apply* to any identical or substantially similar taxes which are *subsequently* imposed in addition to, or in place of, the existing taxes. At the end of each year, the competent authorities of the Contracting States shall notify each other *any* changes which have been made in their respective taxation laws.	4. The Convention shall apply also to any identical or substantially similar taxes which are imposed after the date of signature of the Convention in addition to, or in place of, the existing taxes. At the end of each year, the competent authorities of the Contracting States shall notify each other of changes which have been made in their respective taxation laws.
CHAPTER II	CHAPTER II
DEFINITIONS	**DEFINITIONS**
Article 3 GENERAL DEFINITIONS	**Article 3** GENERAL DEFINITIONS
1. In this Convention, unless the context otherwise requires: *a) the terms 'a Contracting State' and 'the other Contracting State' mean (State A) or (State B), as the context requires;*	1. For the purposes of this Convention, unless the context otherwise requires:
b) the term 'person' *comprises* an individual, a company and any other body of persons;	a) The term 'person' includes an individual, a company and any other body of persons;
c) the term 'company' means any body corporate or any entity which is treated as a body corporate for tax purposes;	b) The term 'company' means any body corporate or any entity which is treated as a body corporate for tax purposes;
d) the terms 'enterprise of a Contracting State' and 'enterprise of the other Contracting State' mean respectively an enterprise carried on by a resident of a Contracting State and an enterprise carried on by a resident of the other Contracting State;	c) The terms 'enterprise of a Contracting State' and 'enterprise of the other Contracting State' mean respectively an enterprise carried on by a resident of a Contracting State and an enterprise carried on by a resident of the other Contracting State;
	d) The term 'international traffic' means any transport by a ship or aircraft operated by an enterprise

UN:

4. The Convention shall apply also to any identical or substantially similar taxes which are imposed after the date of signature of the Convention in addition to, or in place of, the existing taxes. At the end of each year, the competent authorities of the Contracting States shall notify each other of changes which have been made in their respective taxation laws.

USA:

2. The Convention shall apply also to any identical or substantially similar taxes which are imposed after the date of signature of the Convention in addition to, or in place of, the existing taxes. [ ] The competent authorities of the Contracting States shall notify each other of *any significant* changes which have been made in their respective taxation laws *and of any official published material concerning the application of the Convention, including explanations, regulations, rulings, or judicial decisions*.

CHAPTER II

DEFINITIONS

UN:

Article 3

General Definitions

1. For the purposes of this Convention, unless the context otherwise requires:

a) the term 'person' includes an individual, a company and any other body of persons;

b) the term 'company' means any body corporate or any entity which is treated as a body corporate for tax purposes;

c) the terms 'enterprise of a Contracting State' and 'enterprise of the other Contracting State' mean respectively an enterprise carried on by a resident of a Contracting State and an enterprise carried on by a resident of the other Contracting State;

d) the term 'international traffic' means any transport by a ship or aircraft operated by an enterprise

USA:

Article 3

General Definitions

1. For the purposes of this Convention, unless the context otherwise requires

a) the term 'person' includes an individual, *an estate, a trust, a partnership,* a company, and any other body of persons;

b) the term 'company' means any body corporate or any entity which is treated as a body corporate for tax purposes;

c) the terms 'enterprise of a Contracting State' and 'enterprise of the other Contracting State' mean respectively an enterprise carried on by a resident of a Contracting State and an enterprise carried on by a resident of the other Contracting State;

d) the term 'international traffic' means any transport by a ship or aircraft [ ], except when *such*

OECD 1963	OECD 1977
	which has its place of effective management in a Contracting State, except when the ship or aircraft is operated solely between places in the other Contracting State;
e) the term 'competent authority' means: 1. (in State A): .... 2. (in State B):	e) The term 'competent authority' means: (i) (in State A): .... (ii) (in State B): ....
2. As regards the application of the Convention by a Contracting State any term not *otherwise* defined shall, unless the context otherwise requires, have the meaning which it has under the *laws* of that *Contracting State relating to* the taxes *which are the subject of* the Convention.	2. As regards the application of the Convention by a Contracting State, any term not defined therein shall, unless the context otherwise requires, have the meaning which it has under the law of that State concerning the taxes to which the Convention applies.
Article 4 *Fiscal Domicile* 1. For the purposes of this Convention, the term 'resident of a Contracting State' means any person who, under the *law* of that State, is liable to *taxation* therein by reason of his domicile, residence, place of management or any other criterion of a similar nature. [ ]	**Article 4** Resident 1. For the purposes of this Convention, the term 'resident of a Contracting State' means any person who, under the laws of that State, is liable to tax therein by reason of his domicile, residence, place of management or any other criterion of a similar nature. But this term does not include any person who is liable to tax in that State in respect only of income from sources in that State or capital situated therein.

UN	USA
which has its place of effective management in a Contracting State, except when the ship or aircraft is operated solely between places in the other Contracting State;	*transport is* solely between places in the other Contracting State;
e) the term 'competent authority' means: (i) (in State A): . . . . (ii) (in State B):	e) the term 'competent authority' means (i) in *the United States: the Secretary of the Treasury or his delegate; and* (ii) in . . . *f) the term 'United States' means the United States of America, but does not include Puerto Rico, the Virgin Islands, Guam, or any other United States possession or territory;* *g)* the term . . . means . . .
2. As regards the application of the Convention by a Contracting State any term not defined therein shall, unless the context otherwise requires, have the meaning which it has under the law of that State concerning the taxes to which the Convention applies.	2. As regards the application of the Convention by a Contracting State any term not defined therein shall, unless the context otherwise requires *or the competent authorities agree to a common meaning pursuant to the provisions of Article 25 (Mutual Agreement Procedure)*, have the meaning which it has under the *laws* of that State concerning the taxes to which the Convention applies.
Article 4 RESIDENT	**Article 4** *RESIDENCE*
1. For the purposes of this Convention, the term 'resident of a Contracting State' means any person who, undcr thc laws of that State, is liable to tax therein by reason of his domicile, residence, place of management or any other criterion of a similar nature.[ ]	1. For the purposes of this Convention, the term 'resident of a Contracting State' means any person who, under the laws of that State, is liable to tax therein by reason of his domicile, residence, *citizenship,* place of management, *place of incorporation* or any other criterion of a similar nature, *provided, however, that* *a)* this term does not include any person who is liable to tax in that State in respect only of income from sources in that State or capital situated therein; *and*

OECD 1963	OECD 1977
2. Where by reason of the provisions of paragraph 1 an individual is a resident of both Contracting States, then *this case* shall be determined *in accordance with the following rules:*	2. Where by reason of the provisions of paragraph 1 an individual is a resident of both Contracting States, then his status shall be determined as follows:
a) He shall be deemed to be a resident of the *Contracting* State in which he has a permanent home available to him. If he has a permanent home available to him in both *Contracting* States, he shall be deemed to be a resident of the *Contracting* State with which his personal and economic relations are close*st* (centre of vital interests);	a) he shall be deemed to be a resident of the State in which he has a permanent home available to him; if he has a permanent home available to him in both States, he shall be deemed to be a resident of the State with which his personal and economic relations are closer (centre of vital interests);
b) If the *Contracting* State in which he has his centre of vital interests cannot be determined, or if he has not a permanent home available to him in either *Contracting* State, he shall be deemed to be a resident of the *Contracting* State in which he has an habitual abode;	b) if the State in which he has his centre of vital interests cannot be determined, or if he has not a permanent home available to him in either State, he shall be deemed to be a resident of the State in which he has an habitual abode;
c) If he has an habitual abode in both *Contracting* States or in neither of them, he shall be deemed to be a resident of the *Contracting* State of which he is a national;	c) if he has an habitual abode in both States or in neither of them, he shall be deemed to be a resident of the State of which he is a national;
d) If he is a national of both *Contracting* States or of neither of them, the competent authorities of the Contracting States shall settle the question by mutual agreement.	d) if he is a national of both States or of neither of them, the competent authorities of the Contracting States shall settle the question by mutual agreement.
3. Where by reason of the provisions of paragraph 1 a person other than an individual is a resident of both Contracting States,	3. Where by reason of the provisions of paragraph 1 a person other than an individual is a resident of both Contracting States,

b) in the case of income derived or paid by a partnership, estate, or trust, this term applies only to the extent that the income derived by such partnership, estate, or trust is subject to tax in that State as the income of a resident, either in its hands or in the hands of its partners or beneficiaries.

UN	USA
2. Where by reason of the provisions of paragraph 1 an individual is a resident of both Contracting States, then his status shall be determined as follows:	2. Where by reason of the provisions of paragraph 1, an individual is a resident of both Contracting States, then his status shall be determined as follows:
a) He shall be deemed to be a resident of the State in which he has a permanent home available to him: if he has a permanent home available to him in both States, he shall be deemed to be a resident of the State with which his personal and economic relations are closer (centre of vital interests);	a) he shall be deemed to be a resident of the State in which he has a permanent home available to him; if he has a permanent home available to him in both States, he shall be deemed to be a resident of the State with which his personal and economic relations are closer (center of vital interests);
b) If the State in which he has his centre of vital interests cannot be determined, or if he has not a permanent home available to him in either State, he shall be deemed to be a resident of the State in which he has an habitual abode;	b) if the State in which he has his cent*er* of vital interests cannot be determined, or if he *does* not *have* a permanent home available to him in either State, he shall be deemed to be a resident of the State in which he has an habitual abode;
c) If he has an habitual abode in both States or in neither of them, he shall be deemed to be a resident of the State of which he is a national;	c) if he has an habitual abode in both States or in neither of them, he shall be deemed to be a resident of the State of which he is a national;
d) If he is a national of both States or of neither of them, the competent authorities of the Contracting States shall settle the question by mutual agreement.	d) if he is a national of both States or of neither of them, the competent authorities of the Contracting States shall settle the question by mutual agreement.
3. Where by reason of the provisions of paragraph 1 a person other than an individual is a resident of both Contracting States,	3. Where by reason of the provisions of paragraph 1 a *company* is a resident of both Contracting States, then *if it is created under*

OECD 1963

then it shall be deemed to be a resident of the *Contracting* State in which its place of effective management is situated.

Article 5

PERMANENT ESTABLISHMENT

1. For the purposes of this Convention, the term 'permanent establishment' means a fixed place of business *in* which the business of the enterprise is wholly or partly carried on.

2. The term 'permanent establishment' *shall include* especially:

a) a place of management;

b) a branch;

c) an office;

d) a factory;

e) a workshop; [ ]

f) a mine, [ ] quarry or [ ] other place of extraction of natural resources;

g) a building site or construction or *assembly* project *which exists for* more than twelve months.

OECD 1977

then it shall be deemed to be a resident of the State in which its place of effective management is situated.

Article 5

PERMANENT ESTABLISHMENT

1. For the purposes of this Convention, the term 'permanent establishment' means a fixed place of business through which the business of an enterprise is wholly or partly carried on.

2. The term 'permanent establishment' includes especially:

a) a place of management;

b) a branch;

c) an office;

d) a factory;

e) a workshop; and

f) a mine, an oil or gas well, a quarry or any other place of extraction of natural resources.

3. A building site or construction or installation project constitutes a permanent establishment only if it lasts more than twelve months.

UN

then it shall be deemed to be a resident of the State in which its place of effective management is situated.

Article 5

PERMANENT ESTABLISHMENT

1. For the purposes of this Convention, the term 'permanent establishment' means a fixed place of business through which the business of an enterprise is wholly or partly carried on.

2. The term 'permanent establishment' includes especially:

a) A place of management;

b) A branch;

c) An office;

d) A factory;

e) A workshop;

f) A mine, an oil or gas well, a quarry or any other place of extraction of natural resources.

3. *The term 'permanent establishment' likewise encompasses:*

a) A building site, a construction, *assembly* or installation project *or supervisory activities in connexion therewith, but only where such site, project or activities continue for a period of more than six months;*

b) The furnishing of services, including consultancy services, by an enterprise through employees or other personnel engaged by the enterprise for such purpose, but only where activities of that nature continue (for the same or a con-

USA

the laws of a Contracting State or a political subdivision thereof, it shall be deemed to be a resident of *that State.*

4. Where by reason of the provisions of paragraph 1 a person other than an individual or a company is a resident of both Contracting States, the competent authorities of the Contracting States settle the question by mutual agreement and determine the mode of application of the Convention to such person.

Article 5

PERMANENT ESTABLISHMENT

1. For the purposes of this Convention, the term 'permanent establishment' means a fixed place of business through which the business of an enterprise is wholly or partly carried on.

2. The term 'permanent establishment' includes especially

a) a place of management;

b) a branch;

c) an office;

d) a factory;

e) a workshop; and

f) a mine, an oil or gas well, a quarry, or any other place of extraction of natural resources.

3. A building site or construction or installation project, *or an installation or drilling rig or ship used for the exploration or exploitation of natural resources,* constitutes a permanent establishment only if it lasts more than twelve months.

OECD 1963

3. [ ] The term 'permanent establishment' shall not be deemed to include:

a) the use of facilities solely for the purpose of storage, display or delivery of goods or merchandise belonging to the enterprise;

b) the maintenance of a stock of goods or merchandise belonging to the enterprise solely for the purpose of storage, display or delivery;

c) the maintenance of a stock of goods or merchandise belonging to the enterprise solely for the purpose of processing by another enterprise;

d) the maintenance of a fixed place of business solely for the purpose of purchasing goods or merchandise or *for* collecting information, for the enterprise;

e) the maintenance of a fixed place of business solely for the purpose of *advertising, for the supply of information, for scientific research or for similar activities which have* a preparatory or auxiliary character, for the enterprise.

4. [ ] A person acting in a Contracting State on behalf of an enterprise *of the other Contracting State* – other than an agent of an independent status to whom paragraph 5 applies – shall be deemed to *be* a permanent establishment in the *first-mentioned* State [ ] if he has, and habitually exercises in

OECD 1977

4. Notwithstanding the preceding provisions of this article, the term 'permanent establishment' shall be deemed not to include:

a) the use of facilities solely for the purpose of storage, display or delivery of goods or merchandise belonging to the enterprise;

b) the maintenance of a stock of goods or merchandise belonging to the enterprise solely for the purpose of storage, display or delivery;

c) the maintenance of a stock of goods or merchandise belonging to the enterprise solely for the purpose of processing by another enterprise;

d) the maintenance of a fixed place of business solely for the purpose of purchasing goods or merchandise or of collecting information, for the enterprise;

e) the maintenance of a fixed place of business solely for the purpose of carrying on, for the enterprise, any other activity of a preparatory or auxiliary character;

f) the maintenance of a fixed place of business solely for any combination of activities, mentioned in subparagraphs a) to e), provided that the overall activity of the fixed place of business resulting from this combination is of a preparatory or auxiliary character.

5. Notwithstanding the provisions of paragraphs 1 and 2, where a person – other than an agent of an independent status to whom paragraph 6 applies – is acting on behalf of an enterprise and has, and habitually exercises, in a Contracting State an authority to conclude contracts in the name of the enter-

UN

nected project) within the country for a period or periods aggregating more than six months within any 12-month period.

4. Notwithstanding the preceding provisions of this article, the term 'permanent establishment' shall be deemed not to include:

a) The use of facilities solely for the purpose of storage *or* display [ ] of goods or merchandise belonging to the enterprise;

b) The maintenance of a stock of goods or merchandise belonging to the enterprise solely for the purpose of storage *or* display [ ];

c) The maintenance of a stock of goods or merchandise belonging to the enterprise solely for the purpose of processing by another enterprise;

d) The maintenance of a fixed place of business solely for the purpose of purchasing goods or merchandise or of collecting information, for the enterprise;

e) The maintenance of a fixed place of business solely for the purpose of carrying on, for the enterprise, any other activity of a preparatory or auxiliary character;

5.* Notwithstanding the provisions of paragraphs 1 and 2, where a person – other than an agent of

USA

4. Notwithstanding the preceding provisions of this Article, the term 'permanent establishment' shall be deemed not to include

a) the use of facilities solely for the purpose of storage, display, or delivery of goods or merchandise belonging to the enterprise;

b) the maintenance of a stock of goods or merchandise belonging to the enterprise solely for the purpose of storage, display, or delivery;

c) the maintenance of a stock of goods or merchandise belonging to the enterprise solely for the purpose of processing by another enterprise;

d) the maintenance of a fixed place of business solely for the purpose of purchasing goods or merchandise, or of collecting information, for the enterprise;

e) the maintenance of a fixed place of business solely for the purpose of carrying on, for the enterprise, any other activity of a preparatory or auxiliary character;

f) the maintenance of a fixed place of business solely for any combination of *the* activities mentioned in subparagraphs a) to e) [ ].

5. Notwithstanding the provisions of paragraphs 1 and 2, where a person – other than an agent of

---

Editor's note: the text of paragraph 5, beginning and under a), is, although organized differently, in substance identical to paragraph 5 of the 1977 OECD text.

OECD 1963	OECD 1977
that State, an authority to conclude contracts in the name of the enterprise, unless *his* activities are limited to *the purchase of goods or merchandise for the enterprise.*	prise, that enterprise shall be deemed to have a permanent establishment in that State in respect of any activities which that person undertakes for the enterprise, unless the activities of such person are limited to those mentioned in paragraph 4 which, if exercised through a fixed place of business, would not make this fixed place of business a permanent establishment under the provisions of that paragraph.
5. An enterprise *of a Contracting State* shall not be deemed to have a permanent establishment in *the other* Contracting State merely because it carries on business in that *other* State through a broker, general commission agent or any	6. An enterprise shall not be deemed to have a permanent establishment in a Contracting State merely because it carries on business in that State through a broker, general commission agent or any other agent of an independent

UN

an independent status to whom paragraph 7 applies – is acting in a Contracting State on behalf of an enterprise of the other Contracting State, that enterprise shall be deemed to have a permanent establishment in the first-mentioned Contracting State in respect of any activities which that person undertakes for the enterprise, if such a person:

a) Has and habitually exercises in that State an authority to conclude contracts in the name of the enterprise, unless the activities of such person are limited to those mentioned in paragraph 4 which, if exercised through a fixed place of business, would not make this fixed place of business a permanent establishment under the provisions of that paragraph; *or*

b) Has no such authority, but habitually maintains in the first-mentioned State a stock of goods or merchandise from which he regularly delivers goods or merchandise on behalf of that enterprise.

6. Notwithstanding the preceding provisions of this article, an insurance enterprise of a Contracting State shall, except in regard to re-insurance, be deemed to have a permanent establishment in the other Contracting State if it collects premiums in the territory of that other State or insures risks situated therein through a person other than an agent of an independent status to whom paragraph 7 applies.

7. An enterprise *of a Contracting State* shall not be deemed to have a permanent establishment in *the other* Contracting State merely because it carries on business in that State through a broker, general commission agent, or any other

USA

an independent status to whom paragraph 6 applies – is acting on behalf of an enterprise and has and habitually exercises in a Contracting State an authority to conclude contracts in the name of the enterprise, that enterprise shall be deemed to have a permanent establishment in that State in respect of any activities which that person undertakes for the enterprise, unless the activities of such person are limited to those mentioned in paragraph 4 which, if exercised through a fixed place of business, would not make this fixed place of business a permanent establishment under the provisions of that paragraph.

6. An enterprise shall not be deemed to have a permanent establishment in a Contracting State merely because it carries on business in that State through a broker, general commission agent, or any other agent of an independent

OECD 1963

other agent of an independent status, *where* such persons are acting in the ordinary course of their business.

6. The fact that a company which is a resident of a Contracting State controls or is controlled by a company which is a resident of the other Contracting State, or which carries on business in that other State (whether through a permanent establishment or otherwise), shall not of itself constitute either company a permanent establishment of the other.

CHAPTER III

TAXATION OF INCOME

Article 6

INCOME FROM IMMOVABLE PROPERTY

1. Income [ ] from immovable property [ ] may be taxed in *the Contracting* State *in which such property is situated.*

2. The term 'immovable property' shall *be defined in accordance with* the law of the Contracting State in which the property in question is situated. The term shall in any case include property accessory to immovable property, livestock and equipment used in agriculture and forestry, rights to which the provisions of general law respecting landed property apply, usufruct of immovable

OECD 1977

status, provided that such persons are acting in the ordinary course of their business.

7. The fact that a company which is a resident of a Contracting State controls or is controlled by a company which is a resident of the other Contracting State, or which carries on business in that other State (whether through a permanent establishment or otherwise), shall not of itself constitute either company a permanent establishment of the other.

CHAPTER III

TAXATION OF INCOME

Article 6

INCOME FROM IMMOVABLE PROPERTY

1. Income derived by a resident of a Contracting State from immovable property (including income from agriculture or forestry) situated in the other Contracting State may be taxed in that other State.

2. The term 'immovable property' shall have the meaning which it has under the law of the Contracting State in which the property in question is situated. The term shall in any case include property accessory to immovable property, livestock and equipment used in agriculture and forestry, rights to which the provisions of general law respecting landed property apply, usufruct of immov-

UN

agent of an independent status, provided that such persons are acting in the ordinary course of their business. *However, when the activities of such an agent are devoted wholly or almost wholly on behalf of that enterprise, he will not be considered an agent of an independent status within the meaning of this paragraph.*

8. The fact that a company which is a resident of a Contracting State controls or is controlled by a company which is a resident of the other Contracting State, or which carries on business in that other State (whether through a permanent establishment or otherwise), shall not of itself constitute either company a permanent establishment of the other.

USA

status, provided that such persons are acting in the ordinary course of their business.

7. The fact that a company which is a resident of a Contracting State controls or is controlled by a company which is a resident of the other Contracting State, or which carries on business in that other State (whether through a permanent establishment or otherwise), shall not of itself constitute either company a permanent establishment of the other.

CHAPTER III

TAXATION OF INCOME

UN

Article 6

INCOME FROM IMMOVABLE PROPERTY

1. Income derived by a resident of a Contracting State from immovable property (including income from agriculture or forestry) situated in the other Contracting State may be taxed in that other State.

2. The term 'immovable property' shall have the meaning which it has under the law of the Contracting State in which the property in question is situated. The term shall in any case include property accessory to immovable property, livestock and equipment used in agriculture and forestry, rights to which the provisions of general law respecting landed property apply, usufruct of immov-

USA

Article 6

INCOME FROM *REAL PROPERTY* (IMMOVABLE PROPERTY)

1. Income derived by a resident of a Contracting State from *real* property (including income from agriculture or forestry) situated in the other Contracting State may be taxed in that other State.

2. The term '*real* property' shall have the meaning which it has under the law of the Contracting State in which the property in question is situated.[ ]

OECD 1963

property and rights to variable or fixed payments as consideration for the working of, or the right to work, mineral deposits, sources and other natural resources; ships, boats and aircraft shall not be regarded as immovable property.

3. The provisions of paragraph 1 shall apply to income derived from the direct use, letting, or use in any other form of immovable property.

4. The provisions of paragraphs 1 and 3 shall also apply to the income from immovable property of an enterprise and to income from immovable property used for the performance of *professional* services.

OECD 1977

able property and rights to variable or fixed payments as consideration for the working of, or the right to work, mineral deposits, sources and other natural resources; ships, boats and aircraft shall not be regarded as immovable property.

3. The provisions of paragraph 1 shall apply to income derived from the direct use, letting, or use in any other form of immovable property.

4. The provisions of paragraphs 1 and 3 shall also apply to the income from immovable property of an enterprise and to income from immovable property used for the performance of independent personal services.

Article 7

BUSINESS PROFITS

1. The profits of an enterprise of a Contracting State shall be taxable only in that State unless the enterprise carries on business in the other Contracting State through a permanent establishment situated therein. If the enterprise

Article 7

BUSINESS PROFITS

1. The profits of an enterprise of a Contracting State shall be taxable only in that State unless the enterprise carries on business in the other Contracting State through a permanent establishment situated therein. If the enterprise

UN

able property and rights to variable or fixed payments as consideration for the working of, or the right to work, mineral deposits, sources and other natural resources: ships, boats and aircraft shall not be regarded as immovable property.

3. The provisions of paragraph 1 shall also apply to income derived from the direct use, letting, or use in any other form of immovable property.

4. The provisions of paragraphs 1 and 3 shall also apply to the income from immovable property of an enterprise and to income from immovable property used for the performance of independent personal services.

USA

3. The provisions of paragraph 1 shall apply to income derived from the direct use, letting, or use in any other form of *real* property.

4. The provisions of paragraphs 1 and 3 shall also apply to the income from *real* property of an enterprise and to income from *real* property used for the performance of independent personal services.

5. A resident of a Contracting State who is liable to tax in the other Contracting State on income from real property situated in the other Contracting State may elect for any taxable year to compute the tax on such income on a net basis as if such income were attributable to a permanent establishment in such other State. Any such election shall be binding for the taxable year of the election and all subsequent taxable years unless the competent authorities of the Contracting States, pursuant to a request by the taxpayer made to the competent authority of the Contracting State in which the taxpayer is a resident, agree to terminate the election.

UN

Article 7

BUSINESS PROFITS

1. The profits of an enterprise of a Contracting State shall be taxable only in that State unless the enterprise carries on business in the other Contracting State through a permanent establishment situated therein. If the enterprise

USA

Article 7

BUSINESS PROFITS

1. The *business* profits of an enterprise of a Contracting State shall be taxable only in that State unless the enterprise carries on business in the other Contracting State through a permanent establishment situated therein. If the

OECD 1963

carries on business as aforesaid, the profits of the enterprise may be taxed in the other State but only so much of them as is attributable to that permanent establishment.

2. [ ] Where an enterprise of a Contracting State carries on business in the other Contracting State through a permanent establishment situated therein, there shall in each Contracting State be attributed to that permanent establishment the profits which it might be expected to make if it were a distinct and separate enterprise engaged in the same or similar activities under the same or similar conditions and dealing wholly independently with the enterprise of which it is a permanent establishment.

3. In *the determination of* the profits of a permanent establishment, there shall be allowed as deductions expenses which are incurred for the purposes of the permanent establishment including executive and general administrative expenses so incurred, whether in the State in which the permanent establishment is situated or elsewhere.

OECD 1977

carries on business as aforesaid, the profits of the enterprise may be taxed in the other State but only so much of them as is attributable to that permanent establishment.

2. Subject to the provisions of paragraph 3, where an enterprise of a Contracting State carries on business in the other Contracting State through a permanent establishment situated therein, there shall in each Contracting State be attributed to that permanent establishment the profits which it might be expected to make if it were a distinct and separate enterprise engaged in the same or similar activities under the same or similar conditions and dealing wholly independently with the enterprise of which it is a permanent establishment.

3. In determining the profits of a permanent establishment, there shall be allowed as deductions expenses which are incurred for the purposes of the permanent establishment, including executive and general administrative expenses so incurred, whether in the State in which the permanent establishment is situated or elsewhere.

UN

carries on business as aforesaid, the profits of the enterprise may be taxed in the other State but only so much of them as is attributable to *(a)* that permanent establishment; *(b) sales in that other State of goods or merchandise of the same or similar kind as those sold through that permanent establishment; or (c) other business activities carried on in that other State of the same or similar kind as those effected through that permanent establishment.*

2. Subject to the provisions of paragraph 3, where an enterprise of a Contracting State carries on business in the other Contracting State through a permanent establishment situated therein, there shall in each Contracting State be attributed to that permanent establishment the profits which it might be expected to make if it were a distinct and separate enterprise engaged in the same or similar activities under the same or similar conditions and dealing wholly independently with the enterprise of which it is a permanent establishment.

3. In *the determination of* the profits of a permanent establishment, there shall be allowed as deductions expenses which are incurred for the purposes of *the business of* the permanent establishment, including executive and general administrative expenses so incurred, whether in the State in which the permanent establishment is situated or elsewhere. *However, no such deduction shall be allowed in respect of amounts, if any, paid (otherwise than towards reimbursement of actual expenses) by the permanent establishment to the head office of the enterprise or any of its other offices, by way of*

USA

enterprise carries on business as aforesaid, the *business* profits of the enterprise may be taxed in the other State but only so much of them as is attributable to that permanent establishment.

2. Subject to the provisions of paragraph 3, where an enterprise of a Contracting State carries on business in the other Contracting State through a permanent establishment situated therein, there shall in each Contracting State be attributed to that permanent establishment the *business* profits which it might be expected to make if it were a distinct and *independent* enterprise engaged in the same or similar activities under the same or similar conditions [ ].

3. In determining the *business* profits of a permanent establishment, there shall be allowed as deductions expenses which are incurred for the purposes of the permanent establishment, including *a reasonable allocation of* executive and general administrative expenses, *research and development expenses, interest, and other expenses incurred for the purposes of the enterprise as a whole (or the part thereof which includes the permanent establishment)*, whether incurred in the State in which the permanent establishment is situated or elsewhere.

OECD 1963	OECD 1977
4. Insofar as it has been customary in a Contracting State to determine the profits to be attributed to a permanent establishment on the basis of an apportionment of the total profits of the enterprise to its various parts, nothing in paragraph 2 shall preclude that Contracting State from determining the profits to be taxed by such an apportionment as may be customary; the method of apportionment adopted shall, however, be such that the result shall be in accordance with the principles *laid down* in this Article.	4. Insofar as it has been customary in a Contracting State to determine the profits to be attributed to a permanent establishment on the basis of an apportionment of the total profits of the enterprise to its various parts, nothing in paragraph 2 shall preclude that Contracting State from determining the profits to be taxed by such an apportionment as may be customary; the method of apportionment adopted shall, however, be such that the result shall be in accordance with the principles contained in this Article.
5. No profits shall be attributed to a permanent establishment by reason of the mere purchase by that permanent establishment of goods or merchandise for the enterprise.	5. No profits shall be attributed to a permanent establishment by reason of the mere purchase by that permanent establishment of goods or merchandise for the enterprise.

royalties, fees or other similar payments in return for the use of patents or other rights, or by way of commission, for specific services performed or for management, or, except in the case of a banking enterprise, by way of interest on moneys lent to the permanent establishment. Likewise, no account shall be taken, in the determination of the profits of a permanent establishment, for amounts charged (otherwise than towards reimbursement of actual expenses), by the permanent establishment to the head office of the enterprise or any of its other offices, by way of royalties, fees or other similar payments in return for the use of patents or other rights, or by way of commission, for specific services performed or for management, or, except in the case of a banking enterprise, by way of interest on moneys lent to the head office of the enterprise of any of its other offices.

4. In so far as it has been customary in a Contracting State to determine the profits to be attributed to a permanent establishment on the basis of an apportionment of the total profits of the enterprise to its various parts, nothing in paragraph 2 shall preclude that Contracting State from determining the profits to be taxed by such an apportionment as may be customary; the method of apportionment adopted shall, however, be such that the result shall be in accordance with the principles contained in this article.

(Note: the question of whether profits should be attributed to a permanent establishment by reason of the mere purchase by that permanent establishment of goods and merchandise for the enterprise was

4. No *business* profits shall be attributed to a permanent establishment by reason of the mere purchase by that permanent establishment of goods or merchandise for the enterprise.

OECD 1963	OECD 1977
6. For the purposes of the preceding paragraphs, the profits to be attributed to the permanent establishment shall be determined by the same method year by year unless there is good and sufficient reason to the contrary.	6. For the purposes of the preceding paragraphs, the profits to be attributed to the permanent establishment shall be determined by the same method year by year unless there is good and sufficient reason to the contrary.
7. Where profits include items of income which are dealt with separately in other Articles of this Convention, then the provisions of those Articles shall not be affected by the provisions of this Article.	7. Where profits include items of income which are dealt with separately in other Articles of this Convention, then the provisions of those Articles shall not be affected by the provisions of this Article.
Article 8 SHIPPING, INLAND WATERWAYS TRANSPORT AND AIR TRANSPORT	**Article 8** SHIPPING, INLAND WATERWAYS TRANSPORT AND AIR TRANSPORT
1. Profits from the operation of ships or aircraft in international traffic shall be taxable only in the Contracting State in which the place of effective management of the enterprise is situated. 2. Profits from the operation of boats engaged in inland waterways transport shall be taxable only in the Contracting State in which the place of effective management of the enterprise is situated.	1. Profits from the operation of ships or aircraft in international traffic shall be taxable only in the Contracting State in which the place of effective management of the enterprise is situated. 2. Profits from the operation of boats engaged in inland waterways transport shall be taxable only in the Contracting State in which the place of effective management of the enterprise is situated.

UN

not resolved. It should therefore be settled in bilateral negotiations.)

5. For the purposes of the preceding paragraphs, the profits to be attributed to the permanent establishment shall be determined by the same method year by year unless there is good and sufficient reason to the contrary.

6. Where profits include items of income which are dealt with separately in other articles of this Convention, then the provisions of those articles shall not be affected by the provisions of this article.

USA

5. For the purposes of *this Convention*, the *business* profits to be attributed to the permanent establishment *shall include only the profits derived from the assets or activities of the permanent establishment and* shall be determined by the same method year by year unless there is good and sufficient reason to the contrary.

6. Where *business* profits include items of income which are dealt with separately in other Articles of *the* Convention, then the provisions of those Articles shall not be affected by the provisions of this Article.

7. For the purposes of the Convention, the term 'business profits' means income derived from any trade or business, including the rental of tangible personal property and the rental or licensing of cinematographic films or tapes used for radio or television broadcasting.

UN

Article 8

SHIPPING, INLAND WATERWAYS TRANSPORT AND AIR TRANSPORT

Article 8A (alternative A)

1. Profits from the operation of ships or aircraft in international traffic shall be taxable only in the Contracting State in which the place of effective management of the enterprise is situated.

2. Profits from the operation of boats engaged in inland waterways transport shall be taxable only in the Contracting State in which the place of effective management of the enterprise is situated.

USA

Article 8

SHIPPING [ ] AND AIR TRANSPORT

1. Profits *of an enterprise of a Contracting State* from the operation of ships or aircraft in international traffic shall be taxable only in *that* State [ ].

2. *For the purposes of this Article, profits from the operation of ships or aircraft in international traffic include profits derived from the rental of ships or aircraft if such ships or aircraft are operated in international traffic by the lessee or if such rental profits are incidental to other profits described in*

OECD 1963	OECD 1977
3. If the place of effective management of a shipping enterprise or of an inland waterways transport enterprise is aboard a ship or boat, then it shall be deemed to be situated in the Contracting State in which the home harbour of the ship or boat is situated, or, if there is no such home harbour, in the Contracting State of which the operator of the ship or boat is a resident.	3. If the place of effective management of a shipping enterprise or of an inland waterways transport enterprise is aboard a ship or boat, then it shall be deemed to be situated in the Contracting State in which the home harbour of the ship or boat is situated, or, if there is no such home harbour, in the Contracting State of which the operator of the ship or boat is a resident.
	4. The provisions of paragraph 1 shall also apply to profits from the participation in a pool, a joint business or an international operating agency.

paragraph 1.

UN	USA
3. If the place of effective management of a shipping enterprise or of an inland waterways transport enterprise is aboard a ship or a boat, then it shall be deemed to be situated in the Contracting State in which the home harbour of the ship or boat is situated, or, if there is no such home harbour, in the Contracting State of which the operator of the ship or boat is a resident.	3. *Profits of an enterprise of a Contracting State from the use, maintenance, or rental of containers (including trailers, barges, and related equipment for the transport of containers) used in international traffic shall be taxable only in that State.*
4. The provisions of paragraphs 1 shall also apply to profits from the participation in a pool, a joint business or an international operating agency.	4. The provisions of paragraphs 1 *and 3* shall also apply to profits from [ ] participation in a pool, a joint business, or an international operating agency.

Article 8B (alternative B)

1. Profits from the operation of [ ] aircraft in international traffic shall be taxable only in the Contracting State in which the place of effective management of the enterprise is situated.

2. *Profits from the operation of ships in international traffic shall be taxable only in the Contracting State in which the place of effective management of the enterprise is situated unless the shipping activities arising from such operation in the other Contracting State are more than casual. If such activities are more than casual, such profits may be taxed in that other State. The profits so taxed in that other State shall be determined on the basis of an appropriate allocation of the over-all net profits derived by the enterprise from its shipping operations. The tax computed in accordance with such allocation shall then be reduced by . . . per cent. (The percentage is to be established through bilateral negotiations.)*

OECD 1963

Article 9

Associated Enterprises

Where

a) an enterprise of a Contracting State participates directly or indirectly in the management, control or capital of an enterprise of the other Contracting State, or

b) the same persons participate directly or indirectly in the management, control or capital of an enterprise of a Contracting State and an enterprise of the other Contracting State,

and in either case conditions are made or imposed between the two enterprises in their commercial or financial relations which differ from those which would be made between independent enterprises, then any profits which would, but for those conditions, have accrued to one of the enterprises, but, by

OECD 1977

Article 9

Associated Enterprises

1. Where

a) an enterprise of a Contracting State participates directly or indirectly in the management, control or capital of an enterprise of the other Contracting State, or

b) the same persons participate directly or indirectly in the management, control or capital of an enterprise of a Contracting State and an enterprise of the other Contracting State,

and in either case conditions are made or imposed between the two enterprises in their commercial or financial relations which differ from those which would be made between independent enterprises, then any profits which would, but for those conditions, have accrued to one of the enterprises, but, by

UN

3. Profits from the operation of boats engaged in inland waterways transport shall be taxable only in the Contracting State in which the place of effective management of the enterprise is situated.

4. If the place of effective management of a shipping enterprise or of an inland waterways transport enterprise is aboard a ship or boat, then it shall be deemed to be situated in the Contracting State in which the home harbour of the ship or boat is situated, or, if there is no such home harbour, in the Contracting State in which the operator of the ship or boat is a resident.

5. The provisions of paragraphs 1 *and 2* shall also apply to profits from the participation in a pool, a joint business or an international operating agency.

Article 9

ASSOCIATED ENTERPRISES

1. Where

a) An enterprise of a Contracting State participates directly or indirectly in the management, control or capital of an enterprise of the other Contracting State, or

b) The same persons participate directly or indirectly in the management, control or capital of an enterprise of a Contracting State and an enterprise of the other Contracting State,

and in either case conditions are made or imposed between the two enterprises in their commercial or financial relations which differ from those which would be made between independent enterprises, then any profits which would, but for those conditions, [have accrued to one of the enterprises, but, by

USA

Article 9

ASSOCIATED ENTERPRISES

1. Where:

a) an enterprise of a Contracting State participates directly or indirectly in the management, control or capital of an enterprise of the other Contracting State, or

b) the same persons participate directly or indirectly in the management, control, or capital of an enterprise of a Contracting State and an enterprise of the other Contracting State,

and in either case conditions are made or imposed between the two enterprises in their commercial or financial relations which differ from those which would be made between independent enterprises, then any profits which, but for those conditions would have accrued to one of the enterprises,

OECD 1963

reason of those conditions, have not so accrued, may be included in the profits of that enterprise and taxed accordingly.

OECD 1977

reason of those conditions, have not so accrued, may be included in the profits of that enterprise and taxed accordingly.

2. Where a Contracting State includes in the profits of an enterprise of that State – and taxes accordingly – profits on which an enterprise of the other Contracting State has been charged to tax in that other State and the profits so included are profits which would have accrued to the enterprise of the first-mentioned State if the conditions made between the two enterprises had been those which would have been made between independent enterprises, then that other State shall make an appropriate adjustment to the amount of the tax charged therein on those profits. In determining such adjustment, due regard shall be had to the other provisions of this Convention and the competent authorities of the Contracting States shall if necessary consult each other.

UN	USA
reason of those conditions,]* have not so accrued, may be included in the profits of that enterprise and taxed accordingly.	but by reason of those conditions have not so accrued, may be included in the profits of that enterprise and taxed accordingly.
2. Where a Contracting State includes in the profits of an enterprise of that State – and taxes accordingly – profits on which an enterprise of the other Contracting State has been charged to tax in that other State and the profits so included are profits which would have accrued to the enterprise of the first-mentioned State if the conditions made between the two enterprises had been those which would have been made between independent enterprises, then that other State shall make an appropriate adjustment to the amount of tax charged therein on those profits. In determining such adjustment, due regard shall be had to the other provisions of *the* Convention and the competent authorities of the Contracting States shall, if necessary, consult each other.	2. Where a Contracting State includes in the profits of an enterprise of that State, and taxes accordingly, profits on which an enterprise of the other Contracting State has been charged to tax in that other State, and the profits so included are profits which would have accrued to the enterprise of the first-mentioned State if the conditions made between the two enterprises had been those which would have been made between independent enterprises, then that other State shall make an appropriate adjustment to the amount of tax charged therein on those profits. In determining such adjustment, due regard shall be *paid* to the other provisions of this Convention and the competent authorities of the Contracting States shall, if necessary, consult each other.
	3. The provisions of paragraph 1 shall not limit any provision of the law of either Contracting State which permit the distribution, apportionment, or allocation of income, deductions, credits, or allowances between persons, whether or not residents of a Contracting State, owned or controlled directly or indirectly by the same interests when necessary in order to prevent evasion of taxes or clearly to reflect the income of any of such persons.

* *Editor's note:* the language in square brackets is apparently erroneously omitted in the official text.

OECD 1963	OECD 1977
Article 10 DIVIDENDS	**Article 10** DIVIDENDS
1. Dividends paid by a company which is a resident of a Contracting State to a resident of the other Contracting State may be taxed in that other State.	1. Dividends paid by a company which is a resident of a Contracting State to a resident of the other Contracting State may be taxed in that other State.
2. However, such dividends may [ ] be taxed in the Contracting State of which the company paying the dividends is a resident and according to the *law* of that State, but [ ] the tax so charged shall not exceed:	2. However, such dividends may also be taxed in the Contracting State of which the company paying the dividends is a resident and according to the laws of that State, but if the recipient is the beneficial owner of the dividends the tax so charged shall not exceed:
a) 5 per cent of the gross amount of the dividends if the *recipient* is a company (*excluding* partnership) which holds directly at least 25 per cent of the capital of the company paying the dividends;	a) 5 percent of the gross amount of the dividends if the beneficial owner is a company (other than a partnership) which holds directly at least 25 percent of the capital of the company paying the dividends;
b) in all other cases, 15 per cent of the gross amount of the dividends.	b) 15 percent of the gross amount of the dividends in all other cases.
The competent authorities of the Contracting States shall by mutual agreement settle the mode of application of these limitations.	The competent authorities of the Contracting States shall by mutual agreement settle the mode of application of these limitations.
This paragraph shall not affect the taxation of the company in respect of the profits out of which the dividends are paid.	This paragraph shall not affect the taxation of the company in respect of the profits out of which the dividends are paid.
3. The term 'dividends' as used in this Article means income from shares, 'jouissance' shares or 'jouissance' rights, mining shares, founders' shares or other rights, not being debt-claims, participating in profits, as well as income from other corporate rights *assimilated to* income from shares by the *taxation law* of the State of which	3. The term 'dividends' as used in this Article means income from shares, 'jouissance' shares or 'jouissance' rights, mining shares, founders' shares or other rights, not being debt-claims, participating in profits, as well as income from other corporate rights which is subjected to the same taxation treatment as income from shares by the laws of the State of which

UN

Article 10

DIVIDENDS

1. Dividends paid by a company which is a resident of a Contracting State to a resident of the other Contracting State may be taxed in that other State.

2. However, such dividends may also be taxed in the Contracting State of which the company paying the dividends is a resident and according to the laws of that State, but if the recipient is the beneficial owner of the dividends the tax so charged shall not exceed:

a) . . . per cent *(the percentage is to be established through bilateral negotiations)* of the gross amount of the dividends if the beneficial owner is a company (other than a partnership) which holds directly at least *10* per cent of the capital of the company paying the dividends;

b) . . . per cent *(the percentage is to be established through bilateral negotiations)* of the gross amount of the dividends in all other cases.

The competent authorities of the Contracting States shall by mutual agreement settle the mode of application of these limitations.

This paragraph shall not affect the taxation of the company in respect of the profits out of which the dividends are paid.

3. The term 'dividends' as used in this article means income from shares, 'jouissance' shares or 'jouissance' rights, mining shares, founders' shares or other rights, not being debt-claims, participating in profits, as well as income from other corporate rights which is subjected to the same taxation treatment as income from shares by the laws of the State of which

USA

Article 10

DIVIDENDS

1. Dividends paid by a company which is a resident of a Contracting State to a resident of the other Contracting State may be taxed in that other State.

2. However, such dividends may also be taxed in the Contracting State of which the company paying the dividends is a resident and according to the laws of that State, but if [ ] the beneficial owner of the dividends *is a resident of the other Contracting State,* the tax so charged shall not exceed:

a) 5 percent of the gross amount of the dividends *if* the beneficial owner is a company [ ] which *owns* [ ] at least *10 percent* of the *voting stock* of the company paying the dividends;

b) 15 percent of the gross amount of the dividends in all other cases.

[ ]

This paragraph shall not affect the taxation of the company in respect of the profits out of which the dividends are paid.

3. The term 'dividends' as used in this Article means income from shares [ ] or other rights, not being debt-claims, participating in profits, as well as income from other corporate rights which is subjected to the same taxation treatment as income from shares by the laws of the State of which the company making the distribution is a resident.

OECD 1963	OECD 1977
the company making the distribution is a resident.	the company making the distribution is a resident.
4. The provisions of paragraphs 1 and 2 shall not apply if the *recipient* of the dividends, being a resident of a Contracting State, *has* in the other Contracting State, of which the company paying the dividends is a resident, [ ] a permanent establishment [ ] *with which* the holding *by virtue* of which the dividends are paid is effectively connected [ ]. In such a case, the provisions of Article 7 [ ] shall apply.	4. The provisions of paragraphs 1 and 2 shall not apply if the beneficial owner of the dividends, being a resident of a Contracting State, carries on business in the other Contracting State of which the company paying the dividends is a resident, through a permanent establishment situated therein, or performs in that other State independent personal services from a fixed base situated therein, and the holding in respect of which the dividends are paid is effectively connected with such permanent establishment or fixed base. In such case the provisions of Article 7 or Article 14, as the case may be, shall apply.
5. Where a company which is a resident of a Contracting State derives profits or income from the other Contracting State, that other State may not impose any tax on the dividends paid by the company *to persons who are not* residents of that other State, or [ ] subject the company's undistributed profits to a tax on [ ] undistributed profits, even if the dividends paid or the undistributed profits consist wholly or partly of profits or income arising in such other State.	5. Where a company which is a resident of a Contracting State derives profits or income from the other Contracting State, that other State may not impose any tax on the dividends paid by the company, except insofar as such dividends are paid to a resident of that other State or insofar as the holding in respect of which the dividends are paid is effectively connected with a permanent establishment or a fixed base situated in that other State, nor subject the company's undistributed profits to a tax on the company's undistributed profits, even if the dividends paid or the undistributed profits consist wholly or partly of profits or income arising in such other State.
Article 11	**Article 11**
INTEREST	INTEREST
1. Interest arising in a Contracting State and paid to a resident of the other Contracting State may be	1. Interest arising in a Contracting State and paid to a resident of the other Contracting State may be

the company making the distribution is a resident.

4. The provisions of paragraphs 1 and 2 shall not apply if the beneficial owner of the dividends, being a resident of a Contracting State, carries on business in the other Contracting State of which the company paying the dividends is a resident, through a permanent establishment situated therein, or performs in that other State independent personal services from a fixed base situated therein, and the holding in respect of which the dividends are paid is effectively connected with such permanent establishment or fixed base. In such case the provisions of article 7 or article 14, as the case may be, shall apply.

5. Where a company which is a resident of a Contracting State derives profits or income from the other Contracting State, that other State may not impose any tax on the dividends paid by the company, except in so far as such dividends are paid to a resident of that other State or in so far as the holding in respect of which the dividends are paid is effectively connected with a permanent establishment or a fixed base situated in that other State, nor subject the company's undistributed profits to a tax on the company's undistributed profits, even if the dividends paid or the undistributed profits consist wholly or partly of profits or income arising in such other State.

4. The provisions of paragraph [ ] 2 shall not apply if the beneficial owner of the dividends, being a resident of a Contracting State, carries on business in the other Contracting State, of which the company paying the dividends is a resident, through a permanent establishment situated therein, or performs in that other State independent personal services from a fixed base situated therein, and the *dividends are attributable to* such permanent establishment or fixed base. In such case the provisions of Article 7 *(Business Profits)* or Article 14 *(Independent Personal Services)*, as the case may be, shall apply.

5. A Contracting State may not impose any tax on dividends paid by a company which is not a resident of that State, except insofar as

a) such dividends are paid to a resident of that State,

b) the dividends are attributable to a permanent establishment, or a fixed base situated in that State, or

c) the dividends are paid out of profits attributable to one or more permanent establishments of such company in that State, provided that the gross income of the company attributable to such permanent establishment constituted at least 50% of the company's gross income from all sources.

Where subparagraph c) applies and subparagraphs a) and b) do not apply, the tax shall be subject to the limitations of paragraph 2.

Article 11
INTEREST

1. Interest arising in a Contracting State and paid to a resident of the other Contracting State may be

Article 11
INTEREST

1. Interest *derived and beneficially owned by* a resident of *a* Contracting State *shall be taxable*

OECD 1963	OECD 1977
taxed in that other State.	taxed in that other State.
2. However, such interest may be taxed in the Contracting State in which it arises and according to the *law* of that State, but [ ] the tax so charged shall not exceed 10 per cent of the [ ] amount of the interest. The competent authorities of the Contracting States shall by mutual agreement settle the mode of application of this limitation.	2. However, such interest may also be taxed in the Contracting State in which it arises and according to the laws of that State, but if the recipient is the beneficial owner of the interest the tax so charged shall not exceed 10 percent of the gross amount of the interest. The competent authorities of the Contracting States shall by mutual agreement settle the mode of application of this limitation.
3. The term 'interest' as used in this Article means income from Government securities, bonds or debentures whether or not secured by mortgage and whether or not carrying a right to participate in [ ] profits, *and debt-claims of every kind as well as all other income assimilated to income from money lent by the taxation law of the State in which the income arises.* [ ]	3. The term 'interest' as used in this Article means income from debt-claims of every kind, whether or not secured by mortgage and whether or not carrying a right to participate in the debtor's profits, and in particular, income from government securities and income from bonds or debentures, including premiums or prizes attaching to such securities, bonds, or debentures. Penalty charges for late payment shall not be regarded as interest for the purposes of this Article.
4. The provisions of paragraphs 1 and 2 shall not apply if the *recipient* of the interest, being a resident of a Contracting State, *has* in the other Contracting State in which the interest arises a permanent establishment with which the debt-claim from which the interest arises is effectively connected. [ ] In such *a* case the provisions of Article 7 shall apply.	4. The provisions of paragraphs 1 and 2 shall not apply if the beneficial owner of the interest, being a resident of a Contracting State, carries on business in the other Contracting State in which the interest arises, through a permanent establishment situated therein, or performs in that other State independent personal services from a fixed base situated therein, and the debt-claim in respect of which the interest is paid is effectively connected with such permanent establishment or fixed base. In such case the provisions of Article 7 or Article 14, as the case may be, shall apply.

UN

taxed in that other State.

2. However, such interest may also be taxed in the Contracting State in which it arises and according to the laws of that State, but if the recipient is the beneficial owner of the interest the tax so charged shall not exceed . . . per cent *(the percentage is to be established through bilateral negotiations)* of the gross amount of the interest. The competent authorities of the Contracting States shall by mutual agreement settle the mode of application of this limitation.

3. The term 'interest' as used in this article means income from debt-claims of every kind, whether or not secured by mortgage and whether or not carrying a right to participate in the debtor's profits, and in particular, income from government securities and income from bonds or debentures, including premiums or prizes attaching to such securities, bonds, or debentures. Penalty charges for late payment shall not be regarded as interest for the purposes of this article.

4. The provisions of paragraphs 1 and 2 shall not apply if the beneficial owner of the interest, being a resident of a Contracting State, carries on business in the other Contracting State in which the interest arises, through a permanent establishment situated therein, or performs in that other State independent personal services from a fixed base situated therein, and the debt-claim in respect of which the interest is paid is effectively connected with *(a)* such permanent establishment or fixed base, *or with (b) business activities referred to under (c) of paragraph 1 of article* 7. In such case the provisions of article 7 or article 14, as the case

USA

only in that [ ] State.

2. The term 'interest' as used in this *Convention* means income from debt-claims of every kind, whether or not secured by mortgage, and whether or not carrying a right to participate in the debtor's profits, and in particular, income from government securities, and income from bonds or debentures, including premiums or prizes attaching to such securities, bonds, or debentures. Penalty charges for late payment shall not be regarded as interest for the purposes of the *Convention*.

3. The provisions of paragraph 1 [ ] shall not apply if the beneficial owner of the interest, being a resident of a Contracting State, carries on business in the other Contracting State, in which the interest arises, through a permanent establishment situated therein, or performs in that other State independent personal services from a fixed base situated therein, and the *interest is attributable to* such permanent establishment or fixed base. In such case the provisions of Article 7 *(Business Profits)* or Article 14 *(Independent Personal Services)*, as the case may be, shall apply.

OECD 1963

5. Interest shall be deemed to arise in a Contracting State when the payer is that State itself, a political subdivision, a local authority or a resident of that State. Where, however, the person paying the interest, whether he is a resident of a Contracting State or not, has in a Contracting State a permanent establishment [ ] in connection with which the indebtedness on which the interest is paid was incurred, and such interest is borne by such permanent establishment [ ], then such interest shall be deemed to arise in the *Contracting* State in which the permanent establishment [ ] is situated.

6. Where, *owing to* a special relationship between the payer and the *recipient* or between both of them and some other person, the amount of the interest paid, having regard to the debt-claim for which it is paid, exceeds the amount which would have been agreed upon by the payer and the *recipient* in the absence of such relationship, the provisions of this Article shall apply only to the last-mentioned amount. In *that* case, the excess part of the payments shall remain taxable according to the *law* of each Contracting State, due regard being had to the other provisions of this Convention.

OECD 1977

5. Interest shall be deemed to arise in a Contracting State when the payer is that State itself, a political subdivision, a local authority or a resident of that State. Where, however, the person paying the interest, whether he is a resident of a Contracting State or not, has in a Contracting State a permanent establishment or a fixed base in connection with which the indebtedness on which the interest is paid was incurred, and such interest is borne by such permanent establishment or fixed base, then such interest shall be deemed to arise in the State in which the permanent establishment or fixed base is situated.

6. Where, by reason of a special relationship between the payer and the beneficial owner or between both of them and some other person, the amount of the interest, having regard to the debt-claim for which it is paid, exceeds the amount which would have been agreed upon by the payer and the beneficial owner in the absence of such relationship, the provisions of this Article shall apply only to the last-mentioned amount. In such case, the excess part of the payments shall remain taxable according to the laws of each Contracting State, due regard being had to the other provisions of this Convention.

may be, shall apply.

5. Interest shall be deemed to arise in a Contracting State when the payer is that State itself, a political subdivision, a local authority, or a resident of that State. Where, however, the person paying the interest, whether he is a resident of a Contracting State or not, has in a Contracting State a permanent establishment or a fixed base in connection with which the indebtedness on which the interest is paid was incurred, and such interest is borne by such permanent establishment or fixed base, then such interest shall be deemed to arise in the State in which the permanent establishment or fixed base is situated.

6. Where, by reason of a special relationship between the payer and the beneficial owner or between both of them and some other person, the amount of the interest, having regard to the debt-claim for which it is paid, exceeds the amount which would have been agreed upon by the payer and the beneficial owner in the absence of such relationship, the provisions of this article shall apply only to the last-mentioned amount. In such case, the excess part of the payments shall remain taxable according to the laws of each Contracting State, due regard being had to the other provisions of the Convention.

4. Interest shall be deemed to arise in a Contracting State when the payer is that State itself or a political subdivision, [ ] local authority, or [ ] resident of that State. Where, however, the person paying the interest, whether he is a resident of a Contracting State or not, has in a Contracting State a permanent establishment or a fixed base in connection with which the indebtedness on which the interest is paid was incurred, and such interest is borne by such permanent establishment or fixed base, then such interest shall be deemed to arise in the State in which the permanent establishment or fixed base is situated.

5. Where, by reason of a special relationship between the payer and the beneficial owner or between both of them and some other person, the amount of the interest, having regard to the debt-claim for which it is paid, exceeds the amount which would have been agreed upon by the payer and the beneficial owner in the absence of such relationship, the provisions of this Article shall apply only to the last-mentioned amount. In such case the excess part of the payments shall remain taxable according to the laws of each Contracting State, due regard being had to the other provisions of the Convention.

6. A Contracting State may not impose any tax on interest paid by a resident of the other Contracting State, except insofar as

a) the interest is paid to a resident of the first-mentioned State;

b) the interest is attributable to a permanent establishment or a fixed base situated in the first-mentioned State;

OECD 1963	OECD 1977
Article 12 ROYALTIES 1. Royalties arising in a Contracting State and paid to a resident of the other Contracting State shall be taxable only in that other State [ ].	**Article 12** ROYALTIES 1. Royalties arising in a Contracting State and paid to a resident of the other Contracting State shall be taxable only in that other State if such resident is the beneficial owner of the royalties.
2. The term 'royalties' as used in this Article means payments of any kind received as a consideration for the use of, or the right to use, any copyright of literary, artistic or scientific work including cinematograph films, any patent, trade mark, design or model, plan, secret formula or process, or for the use of, or the right to use, industrial, commercial, or scientific equipment, or for information concerning industrial, commercial, or scientific experience.	2. The term 'royalties' as used in this Article means payments of any kind received as a consideration for the use of, or the right to use, any copyright of literary, artistic or scientific work including cinematograph films, any patent, trade mark, design or model, plan, secret formula or process, or for the use of, or the right to use, industrial, commercial, or scientific equipment, or for information concerning industrial, commercial, or scientific experience.
3. The provisions of paragraph 1 shall not apply if the *recipient* of	3. The provisions of paragraph 1 shall not apply if the beneficial

c) the interest arises in the first-mentioned State and is not paid to a resident of the other State.

Article 12
ROYALTIES

1. Royalties arising in a Contracting State and paid to a resident of the other Contracting State *may be taxed* in that other State [ ].

2. *However, such royalties may also be taxed in the Contracting State in which they arise and according to the laws of that State, but if the recipient is the beneficial owner of the royalties, the tax so charged shall not exceed ... per cent (the percentage is to be established through bilateral negotiations) of the gross amount of the royalties. The competent authorities of the Contracting States shall by mutual agreement settle the mode of application of this limitation.*

Article 12
ROYALTIES

1. Royalties *derived and beneficially owned by* a resident of *a* Contracting State shall be taxable only in that [ ] State.

3. The term 'royalties' as used in this article means payments of any kind received as a consideration for the use of, or the right to use, any copyright of literary, artistic or scientific work including cinematograph films, *or films or tapes used for radio or television broadcasting*, any patent, trade mark, design or model, plan, secret formula or process, or for the use of, or the right to use, industrial, commercial, or scientific equipment, or for information concerning industrial, commercial or scientific experience.

2. The term 'royalties' as used in this Convention means payments of any kind received as a consideration for the use of, or the right to use, any copyright of literary, artistic, or scientific work (*but not* including cinematograph*ic* films *or films or tapes used for radio or television broadcasting)*, any patent, trademark, design or model, plan, secret formula or process, or *other like right or property, or for information concerning* industrial, commercial, or scientific experience. *The term 'royalties' also includes gains derived from the alienation of any such right or property which are contingent on the productivity, use, or disposition thereof.*

4. The provisions of paragraphs 1 *and 2* shall not apply if the ben-

3. The provisions of paragraph 1 shall not apply if the beneficial

OECD 1963	OECD 1977
the royalties, being a resident of a Contracting State, *has* in the other Contracting State in which the royalties arise [ ] a permanent establishment *with which* the right or property *giving rise to* the royalties [ ] is *effectively connected* [ ]. In such *a* case, the provisions of Article 7 [ ] shall apply.	owner of the royalties, being a resident of a Contracting State, carries on business in the other Contracting State in which the royalties arise, through a permanent establishment situated therein, or performs in that other State independent personal services from a fixed base situated therein, and the right or property in respect of which the royalties are paid is effectively connected with such permanent establishment or fixed base. In such case the provisions of Article 7 or Article 14, as the case may be, shall apply.
4. Where, *owing to* a special relationship between the payer and the *recipient* or between both of them and some other person, the amount of the royalties paid, having regard to the use, right, or information for which they are paid, exceeds the amount which would have been agreed upon by the payer and the *recipient* in the absence of such relationship, the	4. Where, by reason of a special relationship between the payer and the beneficial owner or between both of them and some other person, the amount of the royalties, having regard to the use, right, or information for which they are paid, exceeds the amount which would have been agreed upon by the payer and the beneficial owner in the absence of such relationship,

UN

eficial owner of the royalties, being a resident of a Contracting State, carries on business in the other Contracting State in which the royalties arise, through a permanent establishment situated therein, or performs in that other State independent personal services from a fixed base situated therein, and the right or property in respect of which the royalties are paid is effectively connected with *(a)* such permanent establishment or fixed base, *or with (b) business activities referred to under (c) of paragraph 1 of article 7*. In such cases the provisions of article 7 or article 14, as the case may be, shall apply.

5. Royalties shall be deemed to arise in a Contracting State when the payer is that State itself, a political subdivision, a local authority or a resident of that State. Where, however, the person paying the royalties, whether he is a resident of a Contracting State or not, has in a Contracting State a permanent establishment or a fixed base in connexion with which the liability to pay the royalties was incurred, and such royalties are borne by such permanent establishment or fixed base, then such royalties shall be deemed to arise in the State in which the permanent establishment or fixed base is situated.

6. Where, by reason of a special relationship between the payer and the beneficial owner or between both of them and some other person, the amount of the royalties, having regard to the use, right, or information for which they are paid, exceeds the amount which would have been agreed upon by the payer and the beneficial owner in the absence of such relationship,

USA

owner of the royalties, being a resident of a Contracting State, carries on business in the other Contracting State, in which the royalties arise, through a permanent establishment situated therein, or performs in that other State independent personal services from a fixed base situated therein, and the *royalties are attributable to* such permanent establishment or fixed base. In such case the provisions of Article 7 *(Business Profits)* or Article 14 *(Independent Personal Services)*, as the case may be, shall apply.

4. Where, by reason of a special relationship between the payer and the beneficial owner or between both of them and some other person, the amount of the royalties, having regard to the use, right, or information for which they are paid, exceeds the amount which would have been agreed upon by the payer and the beneficial owner in the absence of such relationship,

OECD 1963

provisions of this Article shall apply only to the last-mentioned amount. In *that* case, the excess part of the payments shall remain taxable according to the *law* of each Contracting State, due regard being had to the other provisions of the Convention.

Article 13
CAPITAL GAINS

1. Gains [ ] from the alienation of immovable property, *as defined in paragraph 2 of* Article 6, [ ] may be taxed in the [ ] Contracting State *in which such property is situated.*

2. Gains from the alienation of movable property forming part of the business property of a permanent establishment which an enterprise of a Contracting State has in the other Contracting State or of movable property pertaining to a fixed base available to a resident of a Contracting State in the other Contracting State for the purpose of performing *professional* ser-

OECD 1977

the provisions of this Article shall apply only to the last-mentioned amount. In such case, the excess part of the payments shall remain taxable according to the laws of each Contracting State, due regard being had to the other provisions of the Convention.

Article 13
CAPITAL GAINS

1. Gains derived by a resident of a Contracting State from the alienation of immovable property referred to in Article 6 and situated in the other Contracting State may be taxed in that other State.

2. Gains from the alienation of movable property forming part of the business property of a permanent establishment which an enterprise of a Contracting State has in the other Contracting State or of movable property pertaining to a fixed base available to a resident of a Contracting State in the other Contracting State for the purpose of performing independent per-

the provisions of this article shall apply only to the last-mentioned amount. In such case, the excess part of the payments shall remain taxable according to the laws of each Contracting State, due regard being had to the other provisions of the Convention.

Article 13

CAPITAL GAINS

1. Gains derived by a resident of a Contracting State from the alienation of immovable property referred to in article 6 and situated in the other Contracting State may be taxed in that other State.

2. Gains from the alienation of movable property forming part of the business property of a permanent establishment which an enterprise of a Contracting State has in the other Contracting State or of movable property pertaining to a fixed base available to a resident of a Contracting State in the other Contracting State for the purpose of performing independent per-

the provisions of this Article shall apply only to the last-mentioned amount. In such case the excess part of the payments shall remain taxable according to the laws of each Contracting State, due regard being had to the other provisions of the Convention.

Article 13

[ ] GAINS

1. Gains derived by a resident of a Contracting State from the alienation of *real* property referred to in Article 6 *(Income from Real Property (Immovable Property))* and situated in the other Contracting State may be taxed in that other State.

2. Gains from the alienation of

a) shares of the stock of a company (whether or not a resident of a Contracting State) the property of which consists principally of real property situated in a Contracting State; or

b) an interest in a partnership, trust, or estate (whether or not a resident of a Contracting State) to the extent attributable to real property situated in a Contracting State may be taxed in that State. For the purposes of this paragraph, the term 'real property' includes the shares of a company referred to in subparagraph a) or an interest in a partnership, trust, or estate referred to in subparagraph b).

3. Gains from the alienation of *personal* property *which are attributable to* a permanent establishment which an enterprise of a Contracting State has in the other Contracting State, or *which are attributable to* a fixed base available to a resident of a Contracting State in the other Contracting State for the purpose of performing independent personal services, *and*

OECD 1963

vices, including such gains from the alienation of such a permanent establishment (alone or *together* with the whole enterprise) or of such *a* fixed base, may be taxed in that other State. *However, gains from the alienation of movable property of the kind referred to in paragraph 3 of Article 22 shall be taxable only in the Contracting State in which such movable property is taxable according to the said Article.*

OECD 1977

sonal services, including such gains from the alienation of such a permanent establishment (alone or with the whole enterprise) or of such fixed base, may be taxed in that other State.

3. Gains from the alienation of ships or aircraft operated in international traffic, boats engaged in inland waterways transport or movable property pertaining to the operation of such ships, aircraft or boats, shall be taxable only in the Contracting State in which the place of effective management of the enterprise is situated.

OECD 1963

3. Gains from the alienation of any property other than *those mentioned* in paragraphs 1 and 2 [ ], shall be taxable only in the Contracting State of which the alienator is a resident.

Article 14

INDEPENDENT PERSONAL SERVICES

1. Income derived by a resident of a Contracting State in respect of professional services or other *independent* activities of *a similar* character shall be taxable only in that State unless he has a fixed base regularly available to him in the other Contracting State for the

OECD 1977

4. Gains from the alienation of any property other than that referred to in paragraphs 1, 2 and 3, shall be taxable only in the Contracting State of which the alienator is a resident.

Article 14

INDEPENDENT PERSONAL SERVICES

1. Income derived by a resident of a Contracting State in respect of professional services or other activities of an independent character shall be taxable only in that State unless he has a fixed base regularly available to him in the other Contracting State for the purpose of

UN

sonal services, including such gains from the alienation of such a permanent establishment (alone or with the whole enterprise) or of such fixed base, may be taxed in that other State.

3. Gains from the alienation of ships or aircraft operated in international traffic, boats engaged in inland waterways transport or movable property pertaining to the operation of such ships, aircraft or boats, shall be taxable only in the Contracting State in which the place of effective management of the enterprise is situated.

4. Gains from the alienation of shares of the capital stock of a company the property of which consists directly or indirectly principally of immovable property situated in a Contracting State may be taxed in that State.

5. Gains from the alienation of shares other than those mentioned in paragraph 4 representing a participation of . . . per cent (the percentage is to be established through bilateral negotiations) in a company which is a resident of a Contracting State may be taxed in that State.

6. Gains from the alienation of any property other than that referred to in paragraphs 1, 2, 3, *4* and 5 shall be taxable only in the Contracting State of which the alienator is a resident.

Article 14

INDEPENDENT PERSONAL SERVICES

1. Income derived by a resident of a Contracting State in respect of professional services or other activities of an independent character shall be taxable only in that State *except in the following circumstances, when such income may also be taxed in the other Con-*

USA

gains from the alienation of such a permanent establishment (alone or with the whole enterprise) or such a fixed base, may be taxed in that other State.

4. Gains *derived by an enterprise of a Contracting State* from the alienation of ships, aircraft, *or containers* operated in international traffic [ ] shall be taxable only in *that State.*

5. Gains described in Article 12 (Royalties) shall be taxable only in accordance with the provisions of Article 12.

6. Gains from the alienation of any property other than property referred to in paragraphs 1 *through* 5 shall be taxable only in the Contracting State of which the alienator is a resident.

Article 14

INDEPENDENT PERSONAL SERVICES

Income derived by *an individual who is* a resident of a Contracting State *from the performance of personal* services *in* an independent *capacity* shall be taxable only in that State, unless *such services are performed in the other Contracting State and the income is attributable*

OECD 1963

purpose of performing his activities. If he has such a fixed base, the income may be taxed in the other State but only so much of it as is attributable to that fixed base.

2. The term 'professional services' includes especially independent scientific, literary, artistic, educational or teaching activities as well as the independent activities of physicians, lawyers, engineers, architects, dentists and accountants.

Article 15

DEPENDENT PERSONAL SERVICES

1. Subject to the provisions of Articles 16, 18 and 19, salaries, wages, and other similar remuneration derived by a resident of a Contracting State in respect of an employment shall be taxable only in that State unless the employment is exercised in the other Contracting State. If the employment is so exercised, such remun-

OECD 1977

performing his activities. If he has such a fixed base, the income may be taxed in the other State but only so much of it as is attributable to that fixed base.

2. The term 'professional services' includes especially independent scientific, literary, artistic, educational or teaching activities as well as the independent activities of physicians, lawyers, engineers, architects, dentists and accountants.

Article 15

DEPENDENT PERSONAL SERVICES

1. Subject to the provisions of Articles 16, 18 and 19, salaries, wages, and other similar remuneration derived by a resident of a Contracting State in respect of an employment shall be taxable only in that State unless the employment is exercised in the other Contracting State. If the employment is so exercised, such remun-

tracting State:

a) If he has [ ] a fixed base *regularly available to him in the other Contracting State for the purpose of performing his activities; in that case,* only so much of *the income* as is attributable to that fixed base *may be taxed in that other Contracting State; or*

b) If his stay in the other Contracting State is for a period or periods amounting to or exceeding in the aggregate 183 days in the fiscal year concerned; in that case, only so much of the income as is derived from his activities performed in that other State may be taxed in that other State; or

c) If the remuneration for his activities in the other Contracting State is paid by a resident of that Contracting State or is borne by a permanent establishment or a fixed base situated in that Contracting State and exceeds in the fiscal year . . . (the amount is to be established through bilateral negotiations).

2. The term 'professional services' includes especially independent scientific, literary, artistic, educational or teaching activities as well as the independent activities of physicians, lawyers, engineers, architects, dentists and accountants.

to a fixed base regularly available to *the individual* in *that* other State for the purpose of performing his activities.[ ]

Article 15

DEPENDENT PERSONAL SERVICES

1. Subject to the provisions of articles 16, 18 and 19, salaries, wages, and other similar remuneration derived by a resident of a Contracting State in respect of an employment shall be taxable only in that State unless the employment is exercised in the other Contracting State. If the employment is so exercised, such remun-

Article 15

DEPENDENT PERSONAL SERVICES

1. Subject to the provisions of Articles [ ] 18 *(Pensions, Annuities, Alimony, and Child Support)* and 19 *(Government Service)*, salaries, wages, and other similar remuneration derived by a resident of a Contracting State in respect of an employment shall be taxable only in that State unless the employment is exercised in the other

OECD 1963

eration as is derived therefrom may be taxed in that other State.

2. Notwithstanding the provisions of paragraph 1, remuneration derived by a resident of a Contracting State in respect of an employment exercised in the other Contracting State shall be taxable only in the first-mentioned State if:

a) the recipient is present in the other State for a period or periods not exceeding in the aggregate 183 days in the fiscal year concerned, and

b) the remuneration is paid by, or on behalf of, an employer who is not a resident of the other State; and

c) the remuneration is not borne by a permanent establishment or a fixed base which the employer has in the other State.

3. Notwithstanding the preceding provisions of this Article, remuneration [ ] in respect of an employment exercised aboard a ship or aircraft [ ] in international traffic, or aboard a boat engaged in inland waterways transport, may be taxed in the Contracting State in which the place of effective management of the enterprise is situated.

OECD 1977

eration as is derived therefrom may be taxed in that other State.

2. Notwithstanding the provisions of paragraph 1, remuneration derived by a resident of a Contracting State in respect of an employment exercised in the other Contracting State shall be taxable only in the first-mentioned State if:

a) the recipient is present in the other State for a period or periods not exceeding in the aggregate 183 days in the fiscal year concerned, and

b) the remuneration is paid by, or on behalf of, an employer who is not a resident of the other State; and

c) the remuneration is not borne by a permanent establishment or a fixed base which the employer has in the other State.

3. Notwithstanding the preceding provisions of this Article, remuneration derived in respect of an employment exercised aboard a ship or aircraft operated in international traffic, or aboard a boat engaged in inland waterways transport, may be taxed in the Contracting State in which the place of effective management of the enterprise is situated.

UN	USA
eration as is derived therefrom may be taxed in that other State.	Contracting State. If the employment is so exercised, such remuneration as is derived therefrom may be taxed in that other State.
2. Notwithstanding the provisions of paragraph 1, remuneration derived by a resident of a Contracting State in respect of an employment exercised in the other Contracting State shall be taxable only in the first-mentioned State if:	2. Notwithstanding the provisions of paragraph 1, remuneration derived by a resident of a Contracting State in respect of an employment exercised in the other Contracting State shall be taxable only in the first-mentioned State if
a) The recipient is present in the other State for a period or periods not exceeding in the aggregate 183 days in the fiscal year concerned, and	a) the recipient is present in the other State for a period or periods not exceeding in the aggregate 183 days in the *taxable* year concerned;
b) The remuneration is paid by, or on behalf of, an employer who is not a resident of the other State; and	b) the remuneration is paid by, or on behalf of, an employer who is not a resident of the other State; and
c) The remuneration is not borne by a permanent establishment or a fixed base which the employer has in the other State.	c) the remuneration is not borne by a permanent establishment or a fixed base which the employer has in the other State.
3. Notwithstanding the preceding provisions of this Article, remuneration derived in respect of an employment exercised aboard a ship or aircraft operated in international traffic, or aboard a boat engaged in inland waterways transport, may be taxed in the Contracting State in which the place of effective management of the enterprise is situated.	3. Notwithstanding the preceding provisions of this Article, remuneration derived *by a resident of a Contracting State* in respect of an employment *as a member of the regular complement* of a ship or aircraft operated in international traffic [ ] may be taxed *only in that State*.

(USA)

* An alternative draft was published on December 23, 1981. It reads:

Article 16
INVESTMENT OR HOLDING COMPANIES

1. A corporation which is a resident of a Contracting State shall not be entitled under this Convention to relief from taxation in the other Contracting State with respect to an item of income, gains or profits unless the corporation establishes that:

a) its stock of any class is listed on an approved stock exchange in a Contracting State, or that it is wholly owned, directly or through one or more corporations each of which is a resident of a Contracting State, by a corporation the stock of which of any class is so listed; or

b) it is not controlled by a person or persons who are not residents of a Contracting State, other than citizens of the United States; or

c) it was not a principal purpose of the corporation or of the conduct of its business or of the acquisition or maintenance by it of the shareholding or other property from which the income in question is derived to obtain any of such benefits.

2. For the purposes of this Article:

a) an approved stock exchange in .... means: ....

b) an approved stock exchange in the United States means the NASDAQ System owned by the National Association of Securities Dealers, Inc. and any stock exchange registered with the Securities and Exchange Commission as a national securities exchange for the purposes of the Securities Exchange Act of 1934;

c) a person or persons shall be treated as having control of a corporation if under the income tax laws of the Contracting State in which the income arises the person or persons could be treated as having direct or indirect control of the corporation for any purpose;

d) notwithstanding subparagraph c) of this paragraph, a corporation is presumed to meet the requirements of subparagraph b) of paragraph 1 of this Article if the corporation establishes that individuals who are:

i) citizens of the United States;

ii) residents of a Contracting State; or

iii) residents of States that have income tax conventions in force with the Contracting State from which relief from taxation is claimed and such conventions provide relief from taxation not less than the relief from taxation claimed under this Convention;

own directly more than 75 percent of the total combined voting power of all classes of the corporation's stock entitled to vote and more than 75 percent of the number of shares of each other class of the corporation's stock;

e) a corporation is presumed to meet the requirements of subparagraph c) of paragraph 1 of this Article, in particular, where:

i) the reduction in tax claimed is not greater than the tax actually imposed by the Contracting State of which the corporation is resident;

ii) the corporation engaged in business operations in the Contracting State of which it is a resident and the relief from taxation claimed from the other Contracting State is with respect to income which is incidental to or derived in connection with such business.

Article 16* (see facing page for note)
LIMITATION ON BENEFITS

1. A person (other than an individual) which is a resident of a Contracting State shall not be entitled under this Convention to relief from taxation in the other Contracting State unless

a) more than 75 percent of the beneficial interest in such person is owned, directly or indirectly, by one or more individual residents of the first-mentioned Contracting State; and

b) the income of such person is not used in substantial part, directly or indirectly, to meet liabilities (including liabilities for interest or royalties) to persons who are residents of a State other than a Contracting State and who are not citizens of the United States.

For the purposes of subparagraph a), a company that has substantial trading in its stock on a recognized stock exchange in a Contracting State is presumed to be owned by individual residents of that Contracting State.

2. Paragraph 1 shall not apply if it is determined that the acquisition or maintenance of such person and the conduct of its operations did not have as a principal purpose obtaining benefits under the convention.

3. Any relief from tax provided by a Contracting State to a resident of the other Contracting State under the Convention shall be inapplicable to the extent that, under the law in force in that other State, the income to which the relief relates bears significantly lower tax than similar income arising within that other State derived by residents of that other State.

OECD 1963

Article 16
DIRECTORS' FEES

Directors' fees and [ ] similar payments derived by a resident of a Contracting State in his capacity as a member of the board of directors of a company which is a resident of the other Contracting State may be taxed in that other State.

Article 17
ARTISTES AND ATHLETES

Notwithstanding the provisions of Articles 14 and 15, income derived by [ ] *public* entertainer*s*, such as [ ] theatre, motion picture, radio, or television artiste*s*, *and* musician*s*, *and by* athlete*s*, from *their* personal activities as such may be taxed in *the Contracting State in which these activities are exercised.*

OECD 1977

Article 16
DIRECTORS' FEES

Directors' fees and other similar payments derived by a resident of a Contracting State in his capacity as a member of the board of directors of a company which is a resident of the other Contracting State may be taxed in that other State.

Article 17
ARTISTES AND ATHLETES

1. Notwithstanding the provisions of Articles 14 and 15, income derived by a resident of a Contracting State as an entertainer, such as a theatre, motion picture, radio, or television artiste, or a musician, or as an athlete, from his personal activities as such exercised in the other Contracting State, may be taxed in that other State.

2. Where income in respect of personal activities exercised by an entertainer or an athlete in his capacity as such accrues not to the

UN

Article 16

DIRECTORS' FEES *AND REMUNERATION OF TOP LEVEL MANAGERIAL OFFICIALS*

1. Directors' fees and other similar payments derived by a resident of a Contracting State in his capacity as a member of the *B*oard of *D*irectors of a company which is a resident of the other Contracting State may be taxed in that other State.

2. *Salaries, wages and other similar remuneration derived by a resident of a Contracting State in his capacity as an official in a top-level managerial position of a company which is a resident of the other Contracting State may be taxed in that other State.*

Article 17

INCOME EARNED BY ENTERTAINERS AND ATHLETES

1. Notwithstanding the provisions of articles 14 and 15, income derived by a resident of a Contracting State as an entertainer, such as a theatre, motion picture, radio, or television artiste, or a musician, or as an athlete, from his personal activities as such exercised in the other Contracting State, may be taxed in that other State.

2. Where income in respect of personal activities exercised by an entertainer or an athlete in his capacity as such accrues not to the

USA

Article 17

ARTISTES AND ATHLETES

1. Notwithstanding the provisions of Articles 14 *(Independent Personal Services)* and 15 *(Dependent Personal Services)*, income derived by a resident of a Contracting State as an entertainer, such as a theatre, motion picture, radio, or television artiste, or a musician, or as an athlete, from his personal activities as such exercised in the other Contracting State, may be taxed in that other State, *except where the amount of the gross receipts derived by such entertainer or athlete, including expenses reimbursed to him or borne on his behalf, from such activities does not exceed twenty thousand United States dollars ($ 20,000) or its equivalent in . . . for the taxable year concerned.*

2. Where income in respect of [ ] activities exercised by an entertainer or an athlete in his capacity as such accrues not to the enter-

OECD 1977:

entertainer or athlete himself but to another person, that income may, notwithstanding the provisions of Articles 7, 14 and 15, be taxed in the Contracting State in which the activities of the entertainer or athlete are exercised.

OECD 1963:

Article 18
PENSIONS

Subject to the provisions of paragraph *1* of Article 19, pensions and other similar remuneration paid to a resident of a Contracting State in consideration of past employment shall be taxable only in that State.

OECD 1977:

Article 18
PENSIONS

Subject to the provisions of paragraph 2 of Article 19, pensions and other similar remuneration paid to a resident of a Contracting State in consideration of past employment shall be taxable only in that State.

UN

entertainer or athlete himself but to another person, that income may, notwithstanding the provisions of articles 7, 14 and 15, be taxed in the Contracting State in which the activities of the entertainer or athlete are exercised.

USA

tainer or athlete [ ] but to another person, that income *of that other person* may, notwithstanding the provisions of Articles 7 *(Business Profits)* and 14 *(Independent Personal Services)*, [ ], be taxed in the Contracting State in which the activities of the entertainer or athlete are exercised, *unless it is established that neither the entertainer or athlete nor persons related thereto participate directly or indirectly in the profits of that other person in any manner, including the receipt of deferred remuneration, bonuses, fees, dividends, partnership distributions, or other distributions.*

UN

Article 18

PENSIONS *AND SOCIAL SECURITY PAYMENTS*

Article 18A (alternative A)

1. Subject to the provisions of paragraph 2 of article 19, pensions and other similar remuneration paid to a resident of a Contracting State in consideration of past employment shall be taxable only in that State.

USA

Article 18

PENSIONS , *ANNUITIES , ALIMONY AND CHILD SUPPORT*

1. Subject to the provisions of [ ] Article 19 *(Government Service)*

a) pensions and other similar remuneration *derived and beneficially owned by* a resident of a Contracting State in consideration of past employment shall be taxable only in that State*; and*

b) social security benefits and other public pensions paid by a Contracting State to a resident of the other Contracting State or a citizen of the United States shall be taxable only in the first mentioned State.

2. Annuities derived and beneficially owned by a resident of a Contracting State shall be taxable only in that State. The term 'annuities' as used in this paragraph means a stated sum paid periodically at stated times during a specified number of years, under an obligation to make the payments in return for adequate and full

consideration (other than services rendered).

3. Alimony paid to a resident of a Contracting State shall be taxable only in that State. The term 'alimony' as used in this paragraph means periodic payments made pursuant to a written separation agreement or a decree of divorce, separate maintenance, or compulsory support, which payments are taxable to the recipient under the laws of the State of which he is a resident.

4. Periodic payments for the support of a minor child made pursuant to a written separation agreement or a decree of divorce, separate maintenance or compulsory support, paid by a resident of a Contracting State to a resident of the other Contracting State, shall be taxable only in the first-mentioned State.

2. Notwithstanding the provisions of paragraph 1, pensions paid and other payments made under a public scheme which is part of the social security system of a Contracting State or a political subdivision or a local authority thereof shall be taxable only in that State.

Article 18B (alternative B)

1. Subject to the provisions of paragraph 2 of article 19, pensions and other similar remuneration paid to a resident of a Contracting State in consideration of past employment *may be taxed* in that State.

2. However, such pensions and other similar remuneration may also be taxed in the other Contracting State if the payment is made by a resident of that other

OECD 1963

Article 19
GOVERNMENT*AL* *FUNCTIONS*

1. Remuneration, *including* pensions, paid by, *or out of funds created by,* a Contracting State or a political subdivision or a local authority thereof to any individual in respect of services rendered to that State or subdivision or *local* authority *thereof in the discharge of functions of a governmental nature may* be *taxed* in that State.

2. The provisions of Articles 15, 16 and 18 shall apply to re-

OECD 1977

Article 19
GOVERNMENT SERVICE

1. a) Remuneration, other than a pension, paid by a Contracting State or a political subdivision or a local authority thereof to an individual in respect of services rendered to that State or subdivision or authority shall be taxable only in that State.

b) However, such remuneration shall be taxable only in the other Contracting State if the services are rendered in that State and the individual is a resident of that State who:

(i) is a national of that State; or

(ii) did not become a resident of that State solely for the purpose of rendering the services.

2. a) Any pension paid by, or out of funds created by, a Contracting State or a political subdivision or a local authority thereof to an individual in respect of services rendered to that State or subdivision or authority shall be taxable only in that State.

b) However, such pension shall be taxable only in the other Contracting State if the individual is a resident of, and a national of, that State.

3. The provisions of Articles 15, 16 and 18 shall apply to remuner-

UN:

State or a permanent establishment situated therein.

3. Notwithstanding the provisions of paragraphs 1 and 2, pensions paid and other payments made under a public scheme which is part of the social security system of a Contracting State or a political subdivision or local authority thereof shall be taxable only in that State.

Article 19

REMUNERATION AND PENSIONS IN RESPECT OF GOVERNMENT SERVICE

1. a) Remuneration, other than a pension, paid by a Contracting State or a political subdivision or a local authority thereof to an individual in respect of services rendered to that State or subdivision or authority shall be taxable only in that State.

b) However, such remuneration shall be taxable only in the other Contracting State if the services are rendered in that *other* State and the individual is a resident of that State who:

(i) Is a national of that State; or

(ii) Did not become a resident of that State solely for the purpose of rendering the services.

2. a) Any pension paid by, or out of funds created by, a Contracting State or a political subdivision or a local authority thereof to an individual in respect of services rendered to that State or subdivision or authority shall be taxable only in that State.

b) However, such pension shall be taxable only in the other Contracting State if the individual is a resident of, and a national of, that *other* State.

3. The provisions of articles 15, 16 and 18 shall apply to remuner-

USA:

Article 19

GOVERNMENT SERVICE

Remuneration, *including* a pension, paid *from the public funds of* a Contracting State or a political subdivision or local authority thereof to *a citizen of the State* in respect of services rendered *in the discharge of functions of a governmental nature* shall be taxable only in that State.

[ ]

However, the provisions of *Article 14 (Independent Personal Ser-*

OECD 1963	OECD 1977
muneration and pensions in respect of services rendered in connection with *any trade or* business carried on by *one of the* Contracting State*s* or a political subdivision or a local authority thereof.	ation and pensions in respect of services rendered in connection with a business carried on by a Contracting State or a political subdivision or a local authority thereof.
Article 20 STUDENTS	**Article 20** STUDENTS
Payments which a student or business apprentice who is or was *formerly* a resident of *a* Contracting State and who is present in the *other Contracting* State solely for the purpose of his education or training receives for the purpose of his maintenance, education or training shall not be taxed in that *other* State, provided that such payments *are made to him* from sources outside that *other* State.	Payments which a student or business apprentice who is or was immediately before visiting a Contracting State a resident of the other Contracting State and who is present in the first-mentioned State solely for the purpose of his education or training receives for the purpose of his maintenance, education or training shall not be taxed in that State, provided that such payments arise from sources outside that State.
Article 21 INCOME *NOT EXPRESSLY MENTIONED*	**Article 21** OTHER INCOME
Items of income of a resident of a Contracting State [ ] *which are* not *expressly mentioned* in the foregoing Articles of this Convention shall be taxable only in that State.	1. Items of income of a resident of a Contracting State, wherever arising, not dealt with in the foregoing Articles of this Convention shall be taxable only in that State.

ation and pensions in respect of services rendered in connexion with a business carried on by a Contracting State or a political subdivision or a local authority thereof.

vices), Article 15 *(Dependent Personal Services)* [ ] *or Article 17 (Artistes and Athletes), as the case may be,* shall apply, *and the preceding sentence shall not apply,* to remuneration *paid* in respect of services rendered in connection with a business carried on by a Contracting State or a political subdivision or local authority thereof.

Article 20
PAYMENTS RECEIVED BY STUDENTS *AND APPRENTICES*

1. Payments which a student or business apprentice who is or was immediately before visiting a Contracting State a resident of the other Contracting State and who is present in the first-mentioned State solely for the purpose of his education or training receives for the purpose of his maintenance, education, or training shall not be taxed in that State, provided that such payments arise from sources outside that State.

2. In respect of grants, scholarships and remuneration from employment not covered by paragraph 1, a student or business apprentice described in paragraph 1 shall, in addition, be entitled during such education or training to the same exemptions, reliefs or reductions in respect of taxes available to residents of the State which he is visiting.

Article 20
STUDENTS *AND TRAINEES*

Payments *received for the purpose of maintenance, education, or training by* a student, [ ] apprentice, *or business trainee* who is or was immediately before visiting a Contracting State a resident of the other Contracting State and who is present in the first-mentioned State [ ] for the purpose of his *full-time* education or training [ ] shall not be taxed in that State, provided that such payments arise [ ] outside that State.

Article 21
OTHER INCOME

1. Items of income of a resident of a Contracting State, wherever arising, not dealt with in the foregoing Articles of this Convention shall be taxable only in that State.

Article 21
OTHER INCOME

1. Items of income of a resident of a Contracting State, wherever arising, not dealt with in the foregoing Articles of this Convention shall be taxable only in that State.

OECD 1963	OECD 1977
	2. The provisions of paragraph 1 shall not apply to income, other than income from immovable property as defined in paragraph 2 of Article 6, if the recipient of such income, being a resident of a Contracting State, carries on business in the other Contracting State through a permanent establishment situated therein, or performs in that other State independent personal services from a fixed base situated therein, and the right or property in respect of which the income is paid is effectively connected with such permanent establishment or fixed base. In such case the provisions of Article 7 or Article 14, as the case may be, shall apply.
CHAPTER IV	CHAPTER IV
TAXATION OF CAPITAL	**TAXATION OF CAPITAL**
Article 22 CAPITAL	**Article 22** CAPITAL
1. Capital represented by immovable property *as defined in paragraph 2 of* Article 6, [ ] may be taxed in *the* Contracting State *in which such property is situated.*	1. Capital represented by immovable property referred to in Article 6, owned by a resident of a Contracting State and situated in the other Contracting State, may be taxed in that other State.
2. Capital represented by movable property forming part of the business property of a permanent establishment *of* an enterprise, [ ]	2. Capital represented by movable property forming part of the business property of a permanent establishment which an enterprise

UN

2. The provisions of paragraph 1 shall not apply to income, other than income from immovable property as defined in paragraph 2 of Article 6, if the recipient of such income, being a resident of a Contracting State, carries on business in the other Contracting State through a permanent establishment situated therein, or performs in that other State independent personal services from a fixed base situated therein, and the right or property in respect of which the income is paid is effectively connected with such permanent establishment or fixed base. In such case the provisions of article 7 or article 14, as the case may be, shall apply.

3. Notwithstanding the provisions of paragraphs 1 and 2, items of income of a resident of a Contracting State not dealt with in the foregoing articles of this Convention and arising in the other Contracting State may also be taxed in that other State.

USA

2. The provisions of paragraph 1 shall not apply to income, other than income from *real* property as defined in paragraph 2 of Article 6 *(Income from Real Property (Immovable Property))*, if *the beneficial owner* of *the* income, being a resident of a Contracting State, carries on business in the other Contracting State through a permanent establishment situated therein, or performs in that other State independent personal services from a fixed base situated therein, and [ ] the income *is attributable to* such permanent establishment or fixed base. In such case the provisions of Article 7 *(Business Profits)* or Article 14 *(Independent Personal Services)*, as the case may be, shall apply.

CHAPTER IV

TAXATION OF CAPITAL

UN

Article 22
CAPITAL

1. [Capital represented by immovable property referred to in article 6, owned by a resident of a Contracting State and situated in the other Contracting State, may be taxed in that other State.]

2. [Capital represented by movable property forming part of the business property of a permanent establishment which an enterprise

USA

Article 22
CAPITAL

1. Capital represented by *real* property referred to in Article 6 *(Income from Real Property (Immovable Property))*, owned by a resident of a Contracting State and situated in the other Contracting State, may be taxed in that other State.

2. Capital represented by *personal* property forming part of the business property of a permanent establishment which an enterprise

OECD 1963

or by movable property pertaining to a fixed base *used for the performance of professional services,* may be taxed in *the Contracting* State *in which the permanent establishment or fixed base is situated.*

3. [ ] Ships and aircraft operated in international traffic and boats engaged in inland waterways transport, and movable property pertaining to the operation of such ships, aircraft and boats, shall be taxable only in the Contracting State in which the place of effective management of the enterprise is situated.

4. All other elements of capital of a resident of a Contracting State shall be taxable only in that State.

CHAPTER V

METHODS FOR ELIMINATION OF DOUBLE TAXATION

Article 23A

EXEMPTION METHOD

1. Where a resident of a Contracting State derives income or

OECD 1977

of a Contracting State has in the other Contracting State or by movable property pertaining to a fixed base available to a resident of a Contracting State in the other Contracting State for the purpose of performing independent personal services, may be taxed in that other State.

3. Capital represented by ships and aircraft operated in international traffic and by boats engaged in inland waterways transport, and by movable property pertaining to the operation of such ships, aircraft and boats shall be taxable only in the Contracting State in which the place of effective management of the enterprise is situated.

4. All other elements of capital of a resident of a Contracting State shall be taxable only in that State.

CHAPTER V

METHODS FOR ELIMINATION OF DOUBLE TAXATION

Article 23A

EXEMPTION METHOD

1. Where a resident of a Contracting State derives income or

UN

of a Contracting State has in the other Contracting State or by movable property pertaining to a fixed base available to a resident of a Contracting State in the other Contracting State for the purpose of performing independent personal services, may be taxed in that other State.]

3. [Capital represented by ships and aircraft operated in international traffic and by boats engaged in inland waterways transport, and by movable property pertaining to the operation of such ships, aircraft and boats, shall be taxable only in the Contracting State in which the place of effective management of the enterprise is situated.]

4. [All other elements of capital of a resident of a Contracting State shall be taxable only in that State.]

(The Group decided to leave to bilateral negotiations the question of the taxation of the capital represented by immovable property and movable property and of all other elements of capital of a resident of a Contracting State. Should the negotiating parties decide to include in the Convention an article on the taxation of capital, they will have to determine whether to use the wording of paragraph 4 as shown or wording that leaves taxation to the State in which the capital is located.)

CHAPTER V

METHODS FOR THE ELIMINATION OF DOUBLE TAXATION

Article 23A

EXEMPTION METHOD

1. Where a resident of a Contracting State derives income [or

USA

of a Contracting State has in the other Contracting State, or by *personal* property pertaining to a fixed base available to a resident of a Contracting State in the other Contracting State for the purpose of performing independent personal services, may be taxed in that other State.

3. Capital represented by ships, aircraft, *and containers owned by a resident of a Contracting State and* operated in international traffic [ ], and by *personal* property pertaining to the operation of such ships, aircraft, and *containers* shall be taxable only in *that* State [ ].

4. All other elements of capital of a resident of a Contracting State shall be taxable only in that State.

OECD 1963	OECD 1977
owns capital which, in accordance with the provisions of this Convention, may be taxed in the other Contracting State, the first-mentioned State shall, subject to the provisions of paragraph 2 [ ], exempt such income or capital from tax *but may, in calculating tax on the remaining income or capital of that person, apply the rate of tax which would have been applicable if the exempted income or capital had not been so exempted.*	owns capital which, in accordance with the provisions of this Convention, may be taxed in the other Contracting State, the first-mentioned State shall, subject to the provisions of paragraphs 2 and 3, exempt such income or capital from tax.
2. Where a resident of a Contracting State derives [ ] income which, in accordance with the provisions of Articles 10 and 11, may be taxed in the other Contracting State, the first-mentioned State shall allow as a deduction from the tax on the income of that *person* an amount equal to the tax paid in that other *Contracting* State. Such deduction shall not, however, exceed that part of the tax, as computed before the deduction is given, which is *appropriate* to *the* income derived from that other *Contracting* State.	2. Where a resident of a Contracting State derives items of income which, in accordance with the provisions of Articles 10 and 11, may be taxed in the other Contracting State, the first-mentioned State shall allow as a deduction from the tax on the income of that resident an amount equal to the tax paid in that other State. Such deduction shall not, however, exceed that part of the tax, as computed before the deduction is given, which is attributable to such items of income derived from that other State.
	3. Where in accordance with any provision of the Convention income derived or capital owned by a resident of a Contracting State is exempt from tax in that State, such State may nevertheless, in calculating the amount of tax on the remaining income or capital of such resident, take into account the exempted income or capital.
Article 23B CREDIT METHOD	**Article 23B** CREDIT METHOD
1. Where a resident of a Contracting State derives income or owns capital which, in accordance with the provisions of this Convention, may be taxed in the other	1. Where a resident of a Contracting State derives income or owns capital which, in accordance with the provisions of this Convention, may be taxed in the other

owns capital] which, in accordance with the provisions of this Convention, may be taxed in the other Contracting State, the first-mentioned State shall, subject to the provisions of paragraphs 2 and 3, exempt such income [or capital] from tax.

2. Where a resident of a Contracting State derives items of income which, in accordance with the provisions of articles 10, 11 *and 12*, may be taxed in the other Contracting State, the first-mentioned State shall allow as a deduction from the tax on the income of that resident an amount equal to the tax paid in that other State. Such deduction shall not, however, exceed that part of the tax, as computed before the deduction is given, which is attributable to such items of income derived from that other State.

3. Where in accordance with any provision of *this* Convention income derived [or capital owned] by a resident of a Contracting State is exempt from tax in that State, such State may nevertheless, in calculating the amount of tax on the remaining income [or capital] of such resident, take into account the exempted income [or capital].

Article 23B
CREDIT METHOD

1. Where a resident of a Contracting State derives income [or owns capital] which, in accordance with the provisions of this Convention, may be taxed in the other

Article 23
RELIEF FROM DOUBLE TAXATION

1. In accordance with the provisions and subject to the limitations of the law of the United States (as it may be amended from time to time without changing the

OECD 1963	OECD 1977
Contracting State, the first-mentioned State shall allow:	Contracting State, the first-mentioned State shall allow:
a) as a deduction from the tax on the income of that *person,* an amount equal to the income tax paid in that other *Contracting* State;	a) as a deduction from the tax on the income of that resident, an amount equal to the income tax paid in that other State;
b) as a deduction from the tax on the capital of that *person,* an amount equal to the capital tax paid in that other *Contracting* State.	b) as a deduction from the tax on the capital of that resident, an amount equal to the capital tax paid in that other State.
2. The deduction in either case shall not, however, exceed that part of the income tax or capital tax, *respectively,* as computed before the deduction is given, which is *appropriate,* as the case may be, to the income or the capital which may be taxed in *the* other *Contracting* State.	Such deduction in either case shall not, however, exceed that part of the income tax or capital tax, as computed before the deduction is given, which is attributable, as the case may be, to the income or the capital which may be taxed in that other State.
	2. Where, in accordance with any provision of the Convention income derived or capital owned by a resident of a Contracting State is exempt from tax in that State, such State may, nevertheless, in calculating the amount of tax on the remaining income or capital of such resident, take into account the exempted income or capital.

Contracting State, the first-mentioned State shall allow as a deduction from the tax on the income of that resident an amount equal to the income tax paid in that other State [; and as a deduction from the tax on the capital of that resident, an amount equal to the capital tax paid in that other State]. Such deduction [in either case] shall not, however, exceed that part of the income tax [or capital tax,] as computed before the deduction is given, which is attributable, as the case may be, to the income [or the capital] which may be taxed in that other State.

general principle hereof), the United States shall allow to a resident or citizen of the United States as a credit against the United States tax on income

a) the income tax paid to . . . by or on behalf of such citizen or resident; and

b) in the case of a United States company owning at least 10 percent of the voting stock of a company which is a resident of. . . and from which the United States company receives dividends, the income tax paid to . . . by or on behalf of the distributing company with respect to the profits out of which the dividends are paid.

For the purposes of this paragraph, the taxes referred to in paragraphs 1b) and 2 of Article 2 (Taxes Covered) shall be considered income taxes. Credits allowed solely by reason of the preceding sentence, when added to otherwise allowable credits for taxes referred to in paragraphs 1b) and 2 of Article 2, shall not in any taxable year exceed that proportion of the United States tax on income which taxable income arising in . . . bears to total taxable income.

2. Where, in accordance with any provision of this Convention income derived [or capital owned] by a resident of a Contracting State is exempt from tax in that State, such State may nevertheless, in calculating the amount of tax on the remaining income [or capital] of such resident, take into account the exempted income [or capital].

2. *In accordance with the provisions and subject to the limitations of. . . (as it may be amended from time to time without amending the general principle hereof) . . . shall allow to a resident or citi-*

CHAPTER VI

SPECIAL PROVISIONS

Article 24

NON-DISCRIMINATION

1. *The* nationals of a Contracting State shall not be subjected in the other Contracting State to any taxation or any requirement connected therewith which is other or more burdensome than the taxation and connected requirements to which nationals of that other State in the same circumstances are or may be subjected. [ ]

CHAPTER VI

SPECIAL PROVISIONS

Article 24

NON-DISCRIMINATION

1. Nationals of a Contracting State shall not be subjected in the other Contracting State to any taxation or any requirement connected therewith, which is other or more burdensome than the taxation and connected requirements to which nationals of that other State in the same circumstances are or may be subjected. This provision shall, notwithstanding the provisions of Article 1, also apply to persons who are not residents of one or

zen of . . . as a credit against the . . . tax on income . . .

3. For the purposes of allowing relief from double taxation pursuant to this Article, income shall be deemed to arise exclusively as follows:

a) income derived by a resident of a Contracting State which may be taxed in the other Contracting State in accordance with this Convention (other than solely by reason of citizenship in accordance with paragraph 2 of Article 1 (General Scope) shall be deemed to arise in that other State;

b) income derived by a resident of a Contracting State which may not be taxed in the other Contracting State in accordance with the Convention shall be deemed to arise in the first-mentioned State.

The rules of this paragraph shall not apply in determining credits against United States tax for foreign taxes other than the taxes referred to in paragraphs 1b) and 2 of Article 2 (Taxes Covered).

UN	USA
CHAPTER VI	[ ]
SPECIAL PROVISIONS	[ ]
Article 24 NON-DISCRIMINATION	**Article 24** NON-DISCRIMINATION
1. Nationals of a Contracting State shall not be subjected in the other Contracting State to any taxation or any requirement connected therewith which is other or more burdensome than the taxation and connected requirements to which nationals of that other State in the same circumstances are or may be subjected. This provision shall, notwithstanding the provisions of article 1, also apply to persons who are not residents of one or	1. Nationals of a Contracting State shall not be subjected in the other Contracting State to any taxation or any requirement connected therewith which is other or more burdensome than the taxation and connected requirements to which nationals of that other State in the same circumstances are or may be subjected. This provision shall [ ] apply to persons who are not residents of one or both of the Contracting States. *However, for*

OECD 1963	OECD 1977
	both of the Contracting States.
2. The term 'nationals' means:	2. The term 'nationals' means:
a) all individuals possessing the nationality of a Contracting State;	a) all individuals possessing the nationality of a Contracting State;
b) all legal persons, partnerships and associations deriving their status as such from the *law* in force in a Contracting State.	b) all legal persons, partnerships and associations deriving their status as such from the laws in force in a Contracting State.
3. Stateless persons [ ] shall not be subjected in *a* Contracting State to any taxation or any requirement connected therewith which is other or more burdensome than the taxation and connected requirements to which nationals of *that* State in the same circumstances are or may be subjected.	3. Stateless persons who are residents of a Contracting State shall not be subjected in either Contracting State to any taxation or any requirement connected therewith, which is other or more burdensome than the taxation and connected requirements to which nationals of the State concerned in the same circumstances are or may be subjected.
4. The taxation on a permanent establishment which an enterprise of a Contracting State has in the other Contracting State shall not be less favourably levied in that other State than the taxation levied on enterprises of that other State carrying on the same activities.	4. The taxation on a permanent establishment which an enterprise of a Contracting State has in the other Contracting State shall not be less favourably levied in that other State than the taxation levied on enterprises of that other State carrying on the same activities.
This provision shall not be construed as obliging a Contracting State to grant to residents of the other Contracting State any personal allowances, reliefs and reductions for taxation purposes on account of civil status or family responsibilities which it grants to its own residents.	This provision shall not be construed as obliging a Contracting State to grant to residents of the other Contracting State any personal allowances, reliefs and reductions for taxation purposes on account of civil status or family responsibilities which it grants to its own residents.
	5. Except where the provisions of paragraph 1 of Article 9, paragraph 6 of Article 11, or paragraph 4 of Article 12 apply, interest, royalties, and other disbursements paid by an enterprise of a Contracting State to a resident of the other Contracting State shall, for the

both of the Contracting States.

2. The term 'nationals' means:

a) All individuals possessing the nationality of a Contracting State;

b) All legal persons, partnerships and associations deriving their status as such from the laws in force in a Contracting State.

3. Stateless persons who are residents of a Contracting State shall not be subjected in either Contracting State to any taxation or any requirement connected therewith, which is other or more burdensome than the taxation and connected requirements to which nationals of the State concerned in the same circumstances are or may be subjected.

4. The taxation on a permanent establishment which an enterprise of a Contracting State has in the other Contracting State shall not be less favourably levied in that other State than the taxation levied on enterprises of that other State carrying on the same activities. This provision shall not be construed as obliging a Contracting State to grant to residents of the other Contracting State any personal allowances, reliefs and reductions for taxation purposes on account of civil status or family responsibilities which it grants to its own residents.

5. Except where the provisions of paragraph 1 of article 9, paragraph 6 of article 11, or paragraph 6 of article 12 apply, interest, royalties, and other disbursements paid by an enterprise of a Contracting State to a resident of the other Contracting State shall, for

the purposes of United States tax, a United States national who is not a resident of the United States and a . . . national who is not a resident of the United States are not in the same circumstances.

2. *For the purposes of this Convention,* the term 'nationals' means

a) *in relation to . . ., . . .;* and

b) *in relation to the United States, United States citizens.*

3. The taxation on a permanent establishment which an enterprise of a Contracting State has in the other Contracting State shall not be less favorably levied in that other State than the taxation levied on enterprises of that other State carrying on the same activities. This provision shall not be construed as obliging a Contracting State to grant to residents of the other Contracting State any personal allowances, reliefs, and reductions for taxation purposes on account of civil status or family responsibilities which it grants to its own residents.

4. Except where the provisions of paragraph 1 of Article 9 *(Associated Enterprises)*, paragraph *5* of Article 11 *(Interest)*, or paragraph *4* of Article 12 *(Royalties)* apply, interest, royalties, and other disbursements paid by *a resident* of a Contracting State to a resident

OECD 1963	OECD 1977
	purposes of determining the taxable profits of such enterprise, be deductible under the same conditions as if they had been paid to a resident of the first-mentioned State. Similarly, any debts of an enterprise of a Contracting State to a resident of the other Contracting State shall, for the purpose of determining the taxable capital of the such enterprise, be deductible under the same conditions as if they had been contracted to a resident of the first-mentioned State.
5. Enterprises of a Contracting State, the capital of which is wholly or partly owned or controlled, directly or indirectly, by one or more residents of the other Contracting State, shall not be subjected in the first-mentioned *Contracting* State to any taxation or any requirement connected therewith which is other or more burdensome than the taxation and connected requirements to which other similar enterprises of *that* first-mentioned State are or may be subjected.	6. Enterprises of a Contracting State, the capital of which is wholly or partly owned or controlled, directly or indirectly, by one or more residents of the other Contracting State, shall not be subjected in the first-mentioned State to any taxation or any requirement connected therewith which is other or more burdensome than the taxation and connected requirements to which other similar enterprises of the first-mentioned State are or may be subjected.
6. *In* this Article *the term 'taxation' means* taxes of every kind and description.	7. The provisions of this Article shall, notwithstanding the provisions of Article 2, apply to taxes of every kind and description.
Article 25 MUTUAL AGREEMENT PROCEDURE	**Article 25** MUTUAL AGREEMENT PROCEDURE
1. Where a *resident of a Contracting State* considers that the actions of one or both of the Contracting States result or will result for him in taxation not in accordance with [ ] this Convention, he may, *notwithstanding* the remedies	1. Where a person considers that the actions of one or both of the Contracting States result or will result for him in taxation not in accordance with the provisions of this Convention, he may, irrespective of the remedies provided

the purposes of determining the taxable profits of such enterprise, be deductible under the same conditions as if they had been paid to a resident of the first-mentioned State. [Similarly, any debts of an enterprise of a Contracting State to a resident of the other Contracting State shall, for the purposes of determining the taxable capital of the such enterprise, be deductible under the same conditions as if they had been contracted to a resident of the first-mentioned State.]

of the other Contracting State shall, for the purposes of determining the taxable profits of *the first-mentioned resident*, be deductible under the same conditions as if they had been paid to a resident of the first-mentioned State. Similarly, any debts of *a resident* of a Contracting State to a resident of the other Contracting State shall, for the purposes of determining the taxable capital of the *first-mentioned resident*, be deductible under the same conditions as if they had been contracted to a resident of the first-mentioned State.

6. Enterprises of a Contracting State, the capital of which is wholly or partly owned or controlled, directly or indirectly, by one or more residents of the other Contracting State, shall not be subjected in the first-mentioned State to any taxation or any requirement connected therewith which is other or more burdensome than the taxation and connected requirements to which other similar enterprises of the first-mentioned State are or may be subjected.

5. Enterprises of a Contracting State, the capital of which is wholly or partly owned or controlled, directly or indirectly, by one or more residents of the other Contracting State, shall not be subjected in the first-mentioned State to any taxation or any requirement connected therewith which is other or more burdensome than the taxation and connected requirements to which other similar enterprises of the first-mentioned State are or may be subjected.

7. The provisions of this article shall, notwithstanding the provisions of article 2, apply to taxes of every kind and description.

6. The provisions of this Article shall, notwithstanding the provisions of Article 2 *(Taxes Covered)*, apply to taxes of every kind and description *imposed by a Contracting State or a political subdivision or local authority thereof.*

Article 25

MUTUAL AGREEMENT PROCEDURE

1. Where a person considers that the actions of one or both of the Contracting States result or will result for him in taxation not in accordance with the provisions of this Convention, he may, irrespective of the remedies provided

Article 25

MUTUAL AGREEMENT PROCEDURE

1. Where a person considers that the actions of one or both of the Contracting States result or will result for him in taxation not in accordance with the provisions of this Convention, he may, irrespective of the remedies provided

OECD 1963	OECD 1977
provided by the *national* laws of those States, present his case to the competent authority of the Contracting State of which he is a resident [ ].	by the domestic law of those States, present his case to the competent authority of the Contracting State of which he is a resident or, if his case comes under paragraph 1 of Article 24, to that of the Contracting State of which he is a national. The case must be presented within three years from the first notification of the action resulting in taxation not in accordance with the provisions of the Convention.
2. The competent authority shall endeavour, if the objection appears to it to be justified and if it is not itself able to arrive at an *appropriate* solution, to resolve the case by mutual agreement with the competent authority of the other Contracting State, with a view to the avoidance of taxation [ ] not in accordance with the Convention. [ ]	2. The competent authority shall endeavour, if the objection appears to it to be justified and if it is not itself able to arrive at a satisfactory solution, to resolve the case by mutual agreement with the competent authority of the other Contracting State, with a view to the avoidance of taxation which is not in accordance with the Convention. Any agreement reached shall be implemented notwithstanding any time limits in the domestic law of the Contracting States.
3. The competent authorities of the Contracting States shall endeavour to resolve by mutual agreement any difficulties or doubts arising as to the interpretation or application of the Convention. They may also consult together for the elimination of double taxation in cases not provided for in the Convention.	3. The competent authorities of the Contracting States shall endeavour to resolve by mutual agreement any difficulties or doubts arising as to the interpretation or application of the Convention. They may also consult together for the elimination of double taxation in cases not provided for in the Convention.

UN

by the domestic law of those States, present his case to the competent authority of the Contracting State of which he is a resident or, if his case comes under paragraph 1 of article 24, to that of the Contracting State of which he is a national. The case must be presented within three years from the first notification of the action resulting in taxation not in accordance with the provisions of the Convention.

2. The competent authority shall endeavour, if the objection appears to it to be justified and if it is not itself able to arrive at a satisfactory solution, to resolve the case by mutual agreement with the competent authority of the other Contracting State, with a view to the avoidance of taxation which is not in accordance with *this* Convention. Any agreement reached shall be implemented notwithstanding any time-limits in the domestic law of the Contracting States.

3. The competent authorities of the Contracting States shall endeavour to resolve by mutual agreement any difficulties or doubts arising as to the interpretation or application of the Convention. They may also consult together for the elimination of double taxation in cases not provided for in the Convention.

USA

by the domestic law of those States, present his case to the competent authority of the Contracting State of which he is a resident or [ ] national.[ ]

2. The competent authority shall endeavor, if the objection appears to it to be justified and if it is not itself able to arrive at a satisfactory solution, to resolve the case by mutual agreement with the competent authority of the other Contracting State, with a view to the avoidance of taxation which is not in accordance with the Convention. Any agreement reached shall be implemented notwithstanding any time limits *or other procedural limitations* in the domestic law of the Contracting States.

3. The competent authorities of the Contracting States shall endeavor to resolve by mutual agreement any difficulties or doubts arising as to the interpretation or application of the Convention. *In particular the competent authorities of the Contracting States may agree*

a) to the same attribution of income, deductions, credits, or allowances of an enterprise of a Contracting State to its permanent establishment situated in the other Contracting State;

b) to the same allocation of income, deductions, credits, or allowances between persons;

c) to the same characterization of particular items of income;

d) to the same application of source rules with respect to par-

OECD 1963	OECD 1977
4. The competent authorities of the Contracting States may communicate with each other directly for the purpose of reaching an agreement in the sense of the preceding paragraphs. When it seems advisable in order to reach agreement to have an oral exchange of opinions, such exchange may take place through a Commission consisting of the competent authorities of the Contracting States.	4. The competent authorities of the Contracting States may communicate with each other directly for the purpose of reaching an agreement in the sense of the preceding paragraphs. When it seems advisable in order to reach agreement to have an oral exchange of opinions, such exchange may take place through a Commission consisting of the competent authorities of the Contracting States.
Article 26 EXCHANGE OF INFORMATION	**Article 26** EXCHANGE OF INFORMATION
1. The competent authorities of the Contracting States shall exchange such information as is necessary for *the* carrying out [ ] of this Convention *and* of the domestic laws of the Contracting States concerning taxes covered by *this* Convention insofar as the taxation thereunder is *in accordance with this* Convention. [ ] Any	1. The competent authorities of the Contracting States shall exchange such information as is necessary for carrying out the provisions of this Convention or of the domestic laws of the Contracting States concerning taxes covered by the Convention insofar as the taxation thereunder is not contrary to the Convention. The

ticular items of income;

e) to a common meaning of a term;

f) to increases in any specific amounts referred to in the Convention to reflect economic or monetary developments; and

g) to the application of the provisions of domestic law regarding penalties, fines, and interest in a manner consistent with the purposes of the Convention.

They may also consult together for the elimination of double taxation in cases not provided for in the Convention.

4. The competent authorities of the Contracting States may communicate with each other directly for the purpose of reaching an agreement in the sense of the preceding paragraphs. *The competent authorities, through consultations, shall develop appropriate bilateral procedures, conditions, methods and techniques for the implementation of the mutual agreement procedure provided for in this article. In addition, a competent authority may devise appropriate unilateral procedures, conditions, methods and techniques to facilitate the above-mentioned bilateral actions and the implementation of the mutual agreement procedure.*

4. The competent authorities of the Contracting States may communicate with each other directly for the purpose of reaching an agreement in the sense of the preceding paragraphs. [ ]

Article 26

EXCHANGE OF INFORMATION

1. The competent authorities of the Contracting States shall exchange such information as is necessary for carrying out the provisions of this Convention or of the domestic laws of the Contracting States concerning taxes covered by the Convention in so far as the taxation thereunder is not contrary to the Convention, *in*

Article 26

EXCHANGE OF INFORMATION *AND ADMINISTRATIVE ASSISTANCE*

1. The competent authorities of the Contracting States shall exchange such information as is necessary for carrying out the provisions of this Convention or of the domestic laws of the Contracting States concerning taxes covered by the Convention insofar as the taxation thereunder is not contrary to the Convention. The

OECD 1963

information *so exchanged* shall be treated as secret [ ] and *shall not be disclosed to any persons or authorities other than those concerned with the assessment or collection of the taxes which are the subject of the Convention.* [ ]

2. In no case shall the provisions of paragraph 1 be construed so as to impose on *one of the* Contracting State*s* the obligation:

a) to carry out administrative measures at variance with the laws *or the* administrative practice of that or of the other Contracting State;

b) to supply *particulars* which *are* not obtainable under the laws or in the normal course of the administration of that or of the other Contracting State;

c) to supply information which would disclose any trade, business,

OECD 1977

exchange of information is not restricted by Article 1. Any information received by a Contracting State shall be treated as secret in the same manner as information obtained under the domestic laws of that State and shall be disclosed only to persons or authorities (including courts and administrative bodies) involved in the assessment or collection of, the enforcement or prosecution in respect of, or the determination of appeals in relation to, the taxes covered by the Convention. Such persons or authorities shall use the information only for such purposes. They may disclose the information in public court proceedings or in judicial decisions.

2. In no case shall the provisions of paragraph 1 be construed so as to impose on a Contracting State the obligation:

a) to carry out administrative measures at variance with the laws and administrative practice of that or of the other Contracting State;

b) to supply information which is not obtainable under the laws or in the normal course of the administration of that or of the other Contracting State;

c) to supply information which would disclose any trade, business, industrial, commercial, or profes-

UN	USA
particular for the prevention of fraud or evasion of such taxes. The exchange of information is not restricted by article 1. Any information received by a Contracting State shall be treated as secret in the same manner as information obtained under the domestic laws of that State. *However, if the information is originally regarded as secret in the transmitting State* it shall be disclosed only to persons or authorities (including courts and administrative bodies) involved in the assessment or collection of, the enforcement or prosecution in respect of, or the determination of appeals in relation to, the taxes *which are the subject of* the Convention. Such persons or authorities shall use the information only for such purposes *but* may disclose the information in public court proceedings or in judicial decisions. *The competent authorities shall, through consultation, develop appropriate conditions, methods and techniques concerning the matters in respect of which such exchanges of information shall be made, including, where appropriate, exchanges of information regarding tax avoidance.*	exchange of information is not restricted by Article 1 *(General Scope)*. Any information received by a Contracting State shall be treated as secret in the same manner as information obtained under the domestic laws of that State and shall be disclosed only to persons or authorities (including courts and administrative bodies) involved in the assessment, collection, *or administration* of, the enforcement or prosecution in respect of, or the determination of appeals in relation to, the taxes covered by the Convention. Such persons or authorities shall use the information only for such purposes. They may disclose the information in public court proceedings or in judicial decisions.
2. In no case shall the provisions of paragraph 1 be construed so as to impose on a Contracting State the obligation:	2. In no case shall the provisions of paragraph 1 be construed so as to impose on a Contracting State the obligation
a) To carry out administrative measures at variance with the laws and administrative practice of that or of the other Contracting State;	a) to carry out administrative measures at variance with the laws and administrative practice of that or of the other Contracting State;
b) To supply information which is not obtainable under the laws or in the normal course of the administration of that or of the other Contracting State;	b) to supply information which is not obtainable under the laws or in the normal course of the administration of that or of the other Contracting State;
c) To supply information which would disclose any trade, business, industrial, commercial or profes-	c) to supply information which would disclose any trade, business, industrial, commercial, or profes-

OECD 1963	OECD 1977
industrial, commercial or professional secret or trade process, or information, the disclosure of which would be contrary to public policy (ordre public).	sional secret or trade process, or information, the disclosure of which would be contrary to public policy (ordre public).

UN	USA
sional secret or trade process, or information, the disclosure of which would be contrary to public policy (ordre public).	sional secret or trade process, or information the disclosure of which would be contrary to public policy (ordre public).
	3. If information is requested by a Contracting State in accordance with this Article, the other Contracting State shall obtain the information to which the request relates in the same manner and to the same extent as if the tax of the first-mentioned State were the tax of that other State and were being imposed by that other State. If specifically requested by the competent authority of a Contracting State, the competent authority of the other Contracting State shall provide information under this Article in the form of depositions of witnesses and authenticated copies of unedited original documents (including books, papers, statements, records, accounts, and writings), to the same extent such depositions and documents can be obtained under the laws and administrative practices of that other State with respect to its own taxes.
	4. Each of the Contracting States shall endeavor to collect on behalf of the other Contracting State such amounts as may be necessary to ensure that relief granted by the Convention from taxation imposed by that other State does not enure to the benefit of persons not entitled thereto.
	5. Paragraph 4 of this Article shall not impose upon either of the Contracting States the obligation to carry out administrative measures which are of a different nature from those used in the collection of its own taxes, or which would be contrary to its sovereignty, security, or public policy.
	6. For the purposes of this

OECD 1963

Article 27

DIPLOMATIC [ ] AND CONSULAR *OFFICIALS*

Nothing in this Convention shall affect the fiscal privileges of diplomatic [ ] or consular *officials* under the general rules of international law or under the provisions of special agreements.

Article 28

TERRITORIAL EXTENSION

1. This Convention may be extended, either in its entirety or with any necessary modifications, [to any part of the territory of (State A) or of (State B) which is specifically excluded from the application of the Convention or], to any State or territory for whose international relations (State A) or (State B) is responsible, which imposes taxes substantially similar in character to those to which the Convention applies. Any such extension shall take effect from such date and subject to such modification and conditions, including conditions as to termination, as may be specified and agreed between the Contracting States in notes to be exchanged through diplomatic channels or in any other manner in accordance with their constitutional procedures.

Note: The words between brackets are of relevance when, by special provision, a part of the territory of a Contracting State is excluded from the application of the Convention.

OECD 1977

Article 27

DIPLOMATIC AGENTS AND CONSULAR OFFICERS

Nothing in this Convention shall affect the fiscal privileges of diplomatic agents or consular officers under the general rules of international law or under the provisions of special agreements.

Article 28

TERRITORIAL EXTENSION

1. This Convention may be extended, either in its entirety or with any necessary modifications, [to any part of the territory of (State A) or of (State B) which is specifically excluded from the application of the Convention or], to any State or territory for whose international relations (State A) or (State B) is responsible, which imposes taxes substantially similar in character to those to which the Convention applies. Any such extension shall take effect from such date and subject to such modification and conditions, including conditions as to termination, as may be specified and agreed between the Contracting States in notes to be exchanged through diplomatic channels or in any other manner in accordance with their constitutional procedures.

Note: The words between brackets are of relevance when, by special provision, a part of the territory of a Contracting State is excluded from the application of the Convention.

Article, the Convention shall apply, notwithstanding the provisions of Article 2 (Taxes Covered), to taxes of every kid imposed by a Contracting State.

Article 27

DIPLOMATIC [ ] AND CONSULAR *OFFICIALS*

Nothing in this Convention shall affect the fiscal privileges of diplomatic agents or consular officers under the general rules of international law or under the provisions of special agreements.

Article 27

DIPLOMATIC AGENTS AND CONSULAR OFFICERS

Nothing in this Convention shall affect the fiscal privileges of diplomatic agents or consular officers under the general rules of international law or under the provisions of special agreements.

OECD 1963

2. Unless otherwise agreed by both Contracting States, the *denunciation* of the Convention by one of them under Article 30 shall [ ] terminate, in the manner provided for in that Article, the application of the Convention [to any part of the territory of (State A) or of (State B) or] to any State or territory to which it has been extended under this Article.

CHAPTER VII

FINAL PROVISIONS

Article 29

ENTRY INTO FORCE

1. This Convention shall be ratified and the instruments of ratification shall be exchanged at . . . as soon as possible.

2. The Convention shall enter into force upon the exchange of instruments of ratification and its provisions shall have effect:

a) in (State A) . . . .

b) in (State B) . . . .

Article 30

TERMINATION

This Convention shall remain in force until *denounced* by *one of the* Contracting State*s*. Either Contracting State may *denounce* the Convention, through diplomatic

OECD 1977

2. Unless otherwise agreed by both Contracting States, the termination of the Convention by one of them under Article 30 shall also terminate, in the manner provided for in that Article, the application of the Convention [to any part of the territory of (State A) or of (State B) or] to any State or territory to which it has been extended under this Article.

CHAPTER VII

FINAL PROVISIONS

Article 29

ENTRY INTO FORCE

1. This Convention shall be ratified and the instruments of ratification shall be exchanged at . . . as soon as possible.

2. The Convention shall enter into force upon the exchange of instruments of ratification and its provisions shall have effect:

a) (in State A) . . . .

b) (in State B) . . . .

Article 30

TERMINATION

This Convention shall remain in force until terminated by a Contracting State. Either Contracting State may terminate the Convention, through diplomatic channels,

CHAPTER VII

FINAL PROVISIONS

UN

Article 28
ENTRY INTO FORCE

1. This Convention shall be ratified and the instruments of ratification shall be exchanged at . . . as soon as possible.

2. The Convention shall enter into force upon the exchange of instruments of ratification and its provisions shall have effect:

a) (In State A) . . . .

b) (In State B) . . . .

USA

Article 28
ENTRY INTO FORCE

1. This Convention shall be *subject to ratification in accordance with the applicable procedures of each Contracting State* and [ ] instruments of ratification shall be exchanged at . . . as soon as possible.

2. The Convention shall enter into force upon the exchange of instruments of ratification and its provisions shall have effect:

a) *in respect of taxes withheld at source, for amounts paid or credited on or after the first day of the second month next following the date on which the Convention enters into force;*

b) *in respect of other taxes for taxable periods, beginning on or after the first day of January next following the date on which the Convention enters into force.*

UN

Article 29
TERMINATION

1. This Convention shall remain in force until terminated by a Contracting State. Either Contracting State may terminate the Convention, through diplomatic channels,

USA

Article 29
TERMINATION

1. This Convention shall remain in force until terminated by a Contracting State. Either Contracting State may terminate the Convention *at any time after 5 years from*

OECD 1963

channels, by giving notice of termination at least six months before the end of any calendar year after the year . . . In such event, the Convention shall cease to have effect:

a) in (State A) . . . .
b) in (State B) . . . .

TERMINAL CLAUSE[1]

1. The terminal clause concerning the signing shall be drafted in accordance with the constitutional procedure of both Contracting States.

OECD 1977

by giving notice of termination at least six months before the end of any calendar year after the year . . . In such event, the Convention shall cease to have effect:

a) (in State A) . . . .
b) (in State B) . . . .

TERMINAL CLAUSE[1]

1. The terminal clause concerning the signing shall be drafted in accordance with the constitutional procedure of both Contracting States.

by giving notice of termination at least six months before the end of any calendar year after the year . . . In such event, the Convention shall cease to have effect:

a) (In State A) . . . .

b) (In State B) . . . .

the date on which the Convention enters into force, provided that at least 6 months prior notice of termination has been given through diplomatic channels. In such event, the Convention shall cease to have effect

a) *in respect of taxes withheld at source, for amounts paid or credited on or after the first day of January next following the expiration of the 6 months period;*

b) *in respect of other taxes, for taxable periods beginning on or after the first day of January next following the expiration of the 6 months period.*

TERMINAL CLAUSE

Done at . . . in duplicate, in the English and . . . languages, the two texts having equal authenticity, this . . . day of . . . 19. . .

For the United States of America:

For . . .

Note: The provisions relating to the entry into force and termination and the terminal clause concerning the signing of the Convention shall be drafted in accordance with the constitutional procedure of both Contracting States.

Selections from the 1977 OECD Commentary

Commentary on Article 1 concerning the Personal Scope of the Convention

1. Whereas the earliest conventions in general were applicable to 'citizens' of the Contracting States, more recent conventions usually apply to 'residents' of one or the both of the Contracting States without distinctions of nationality. Some conventions were of even wider scope inasmuch as they apply more generally to 'taxpayers' of the Contracting States; they are, therefore, also applicable to persons, who, although not residing in either State, are nevertheless liable to tax on part of their income or capital in each of them. The Convention is intended to be applied between OECD Member countries and it has been deemed preferable for practical reasons to provide that the Convention is to apply to persons who are residents of one or both of the Contracting States. It is recalled that the meaning of the term 'resident' is defined in Article 4.

Application of the Convention to Partnerships

2. The domestic laws of the various OECD Member countries differ in the treatment of partnerships. The main issue of such differences is founded on the fact that some countries treat partnerships as taxable units (sometimes even as companies) whereas other countries disregard the partnership and tax only the individual partners on their share of the partnership income.

3. These differences in views have many effects on the application of the Convention in the case of partnerships, especially where one or more partners are not residents of the State in which the partnership was created or organised. First the question arises, whether a partnership as such may invoke the provisions of the Convention. Where a partnership is treated as a company or taxed in the same way, it may reasonably be argued that the partnership is a resident of the Contracting State taxing the partnership on the grounds mentioned in paragraph 1 of Article 4 and therefore, falling under the scope of the Convention, is entitled to the benefits of the Convention. In the other instances mentioned in paragraph 2 above, the application of the Convention to the partnership as such might be refused, at least if no special rule is provided for in the Convention covering partnerships.

4. Moreover, different rules of the Convention may be applied in the Contracting States to income derived by a partner from the partnership, depending on the approach of such States. In States, where part-

nerships are treated as companies, distributions of profits to the partners may be considered to be dividends (paragraph 3 of Article 10), whilst for other States all profits of a partnership, whether distributed or not, are considered as business profits of the partners (Article 7). In many States, business profits of partnerships include, for tax purposes, all or some special remuneration paid by a partnership to its partners (such as rents, interest, royalties, remuneration for services), whilst in other States such payments are not dealt with as business profits (Article 7) but under other headings (in the above-mentioned examples: Articles 6, 11, 12, 14 or 15, respectively).

5. Finally the capital invested in a partnership or the alienation of a participation in a partnership may be treated, depending on the approach, under paragraph 2 of Articles 22 and 13 (permanent establishment) or paragraph 4 of Articles 22 and 13 (other movable property).

6. The concurrent application of different Articles of the Convention in the two Contracting States (or even the non-application of the Convention in one of them) may not only result in double taxation, but also in non-taxation. However, the practical application of double taxation conventions, whether or not based on the 1963 Draft Convention, and the discussions on the revision of the 1963 Draft Convention have shown that the opinions of the OECD Member countries differ too much and that it is extremely difficult to find a uniform solution which would be acceptable to all or even to the great majority of Member countries. The Convention does not, therefore, contain any special provisions relating to partnerships. Contracting States are however left free to examine the problems of partnerships in their bilateral negotiations and to agree upon such special provisions as they may find necessary and appropriate.

Improper Use of the Convention

7. The purpose of double taxation conventions is to promote, by eliminating international double taxation, exchanges of goods and services, and the movement of capital and persons; they should not, however, help tax avoidance or evasion. True, taxpayers have the possibility, double taxation conventions being left aside, to exploit the differences in tax levels as between States and the tax advantages provided by various countries' taxation laws, but it is for the States concerned to adopt provisions in their domestic laws to counter possible manoeuvres. Such States will then wish, in their bilateral double taxation conventions, to preserve the application of provisions of this kind contained in their domestic laws.

8. Moreover, the extension of the network of double taxation conventions still reinforces the impact of such manoeuvres as they make it possible, through the creation of usually artificial legal constructions, to benefit both from the tax advantages available under certain domestic laws and the reliefs from tax provided for in double taxation conventions.

9. This would be the case, for example, if a person (whether or not a resident of a Contracting State), acted through a legal entity created in a State essentially to obtain treaty benefits which would not be available directly to such person. Another case would be one of an individual having in a Contracting State both his permanent home and all his economic interests, including a substantial participation in a company of that State, and who, essentially in order to sell the participation and escape taxation in that State on the capital gains from the alienation (by virtue of paragraph 4 of Article 13), transferred his permanent home to the other Contracting State, where such gains were subject to little or no tax.

10. Some of these situations are dealt with in the Convention, e.g. by the introduction of the concept of 'beneficial owner' (in Articles 10, 11 and 12) and of special provisions, for so-called artiste-companies (paragraph 2 of Article 17). Such problems are also mentioned in the Commentaries on Article 10 (paragraph 17 and 22), Article 11 (paragraph 12), Article 12 (paragraph 7). It may be appropriate for Contracting States to agree in bilateral negotiations that any relief from tax should not apply in certain cases, or to agree that the application of the provisions of domestic laws against tax avoidance should not be affected by the Convention.

Reservation on the Article:

11. The *United States* reserves the right to tax its citizens and residents (with certain exceptions) without regard to the Convention.

Commentary on Article 2 concerning Taxes Covered by the Convention

1. This Article is intended to make the terminology and nomenclature relating to the taxes covered by the Convention more acceptable and precise, to ensure identification of the Contracting States' taxes covered by the Convention, to widen as much as possible the field of application of the Convention by including, as far as possible, and in harmony with the domestic laws of the Contracting States, the taxes imposed by their political subdivisions or local authorities, and to avoid the necessity of concluding a new convention whenever the Contracting States' domestic laws are modified, by means of the periodical exchange of lists and through a procedure for mutual consultation.

Paragraph 1

2. This paragraph defines the scope of application of the Convention; taxes on income and on capital; the term 'direct taxes' which is far too imprecise has therefore been avoided. It is immaterial on behalf of which authorities such taxes are imposed; it may be the State itself or its political subdivisions or local authorities (constituent States,

regions, provinces, '*départements*', cantons, districts, '*arrondissements*', '*Kreise*', municipalities or groups of municipalities, etc.). The method of levying the taxes is equally immaterial: by direct assessment or by deduction at the source, in the form of surtaxes or surcharges, or as additional taxes ('*centimes additionnels*'), etc.

Paragraph 2

3. This paragraph gives a definition of taxes on income and on capital. Such taxes comprise taxes on total income and on elements of income, on total capital and on elements of capital. They also include taxes on profits and gains derived from the alienation of movable and immovable property, as well as taxes on capital appreciation. Finally, the definition extends to taxes on the total amounts of wages or salaries paid by undertakings ('payroll taxes'; in Germany '*Lohnsummensteuer*'; in France '*taxe sur les salaires*'). Social security charges, or any other charges paid where there is a direct connection between the levy and the individual benefits to be received, shall not be regarded as 'taxes on the total amount of wages'.

4. Clearly a State possessing taxing powers – and it alone – may levy the taxes imposed by its legislation together with any duties or charges accessory to them: increases, costs, interest, etc. It has not been considered necessary to specify this in the Article, as it is obvious that in the levying of the tax the accessory duties or charges depend on the same rule as the principal duty.

5. The Article does not mention 'ordinary taxes' or 'extraordinary taxes'. Normally, it might be considered justifiable to include extraordinary taxes in a Model Convention, but experience has shown that such taxes are generally imposed in very special circumstances. In addition, it would be difficult to define them. They may be extraordinary for various reasons; their imposition, the manner in which they are levied, their rates, their objects, etc. This being so, it seems preferable not to include extraordinary taxes in the Article. But, as it is not intended to exclude extraordinary taxes from all conventions, ordinary taxes have not been mentioned either. The Contracting States are thus free to restrict the convention's field of application to ordinary taxes, to extend it to extraordinary taxes, or even to establish special provisions.

Paragraph 3

6. This paragraph lists the taxes in force at the times of signature of the convention. The list is not exhaustive. It serves to illustrate the preceding paragraphs of the Article. In principle, however, it will be a complete list of taxes imposed in each State at the time of signature and covered by the convention.

Paragraph 4

7. This paragraph provides, since the list of taxes in paragraph 3 is purely declaratory, that the Convention is also to apply to all identical or substantially similar taxes which are imposed after the date of signature of the Convention in addition to, or in place of, the

existing taxes. This provision is necessary to prevent the Convention from becoming inoperative in the event of one of the States modifying its taxation laws.

8. Each State undertakes to notify the other of any amendments made to its taxation laws by communicating to it at the end of each year, when necessary, a list of new or substituted taxes, imposed during that year.

Observation on the Commentary

9. [Omitted]

Reservations on the Article:

10. *Australia, Canada* and the *United States* reserve their positions on that part of paragraph 1 which states that the Convention should apply to taxes of political subdivisions or local authorities.

11. [Omitted]

Commentary on Article 3 concerning General Definitions

1. This Article groups together a number of general provisions required for the interpretation of the terms used in the Convention. It should be observed, however, that the meaning of some important terms is explained elsewhere in the Convention. Thus the terms 'resident' and 'permanent establishment' are defined in Articles 4 and 5 respectively, while the interpretation of certain terms appearing in the Articles on special categories of income ('immovable property', 'dividends', etc.) is clarified by provisions embodied in those Articles. In addition to the definitions contained in the Article, Contracting States are free to agree bilaterally on definitions of the terms 'a Contracting State' and 'the other Contracting State'. Furthermore, Contracting States are free to agree bilaterally to include in the possible definitions of 'Contracting States' a reference to continental shelves.

Paragraph 1

The term 'person'

2. The definition of the term 'person' given in sub-paragraph *a.* is not exhaustive and should be read as indicating that the term 'person' is used in a very wide sense (cf. especially Articles 1 and 4). The definition explicitly mentions individuals, companies and other bodies of persons. From the meaning assigned to the term 'company' by the definition contained in sub-paragraph *b.* it follows that, in addition, the term 'person' includes any entity which, although itself not a body of

persons, is treated as a body corporate for tax purposes. Thus, e.g. a foundation (*'fondation'*, *'Stiftung'*) may fall within the meaning of the term 'person'. Special considerations for the application of the Convention to partnerships are found in paragraphs 2 to 6 of the Commentary on Article 1.

The term company

3. The term 'company' means in the first place any body corporate. In addition, the term covers any other taxable unit which is treated as a body corporate according to the tax laws of the Contracting State in which it is organised. The definition is drafted with special regard to the Article on dividends. It should be noted that the term 'company' has a bearing only on that Article, paragraph 7 of Article 5 and Article 16.

The term 'enterprise'

4. The question whether an activity is performed within the framework of an enterprise or is deemed to constitute in itself an enterprise has always been interpreted according to the provisions of the domestic laws of the Contracting States. No definition, properly speaking, of the term 'enterprise' has therefore been attempted in this Article.

The term 'international traffic'

5. The definition of the term 'international traffic' is based on the principle as set forth in paragraph 1 of Article 8 that the right to tax profits from the operation of ships or aircraft in international traffic resides only in the Contracting State in which the place of effective management is situated in view of the special nature of the international traffic business. However, as stated in the Commentary on paragraph 1 of Article 8, the Contracting States are free on a bilateral basis to insert in sub-paragraph *d.* the reference to residence, in order to be consistent with the general pattern of the other Articles. In such a case, the words 'an enterprise which has its place of effective management in a Contracting State' should be replaced, by 'an enterprise of a Contracting State' or 'a resident of a Contracting State'.

6. It is to be noted that the definition of the term 'international traffic' is broader than the term normally signifies. However, this has been deliberate in order to preserve for the State of the place of effective management the right to tax purely domestic traffic as well as international traffic between third States, and to allow the other Contracting State to tax traffic solely within its borders. This intention may be clarified by the following illustration. Suppose an enterprise of a Contracting State or an enterprise which has its place of effective management in a Contracting State, through an agent in the other Contracting State, sells tickets for a passage which is confined wholly within the first-mentioned State or, alternatively, within a third State. The

Article does not permit the other State to tax the profits of either voyage. The other State is allowed to tax such an enterprise of the first-mentioned State only where the operations are confined solely to places in that other State.

The term 'competent authority'

7. The definition of the term 'competent authority' has regard to the fact that in some OECD Member countries the execution of double taxation conventions does not exclusively fall within the competence of the highest tax authorities but that some matters are reserved or may be delegated to other authorities. The present definition enables each Contracting State to nominate one or more authorities as being competent.

Paragraph 2

8. This paragraph provides a general rule of interpretation in respect of terms used in the Convention but not defined therein

Observation on the Commentary

9. [Omitted]

Reservation on the Article:

10. [Omitted]

Commentary on Article 4 concerning the Definition of Resident

I. PRELIMINARY REMARKS

1. The concept of 'resident of a Contracting State' has various functions and is of importance in three cases:

a. in determining a convention's personal scope of application;

b. in solving cases where double taxation arises in consequence of double residence;

c. in solving cases where double taxation arises as a consequence of taxation in the State of residence and in the State of source or situs.

2. The Article is intended to define the meaning of the term 'resident of a Contracting State' and to solve cases of double residence. To clarify the scope of the Article some general comments are made below referring to the two typical cases of conflict, i.e. between two residences and between residence and source or situs. In both cases the conflict arises because, under their domestic laws, one or both Contracting States claim that the person concerned is resident in their territory.

3. Generally the domestic laws of the various States impose a comprehensive liability to tax – 'full tax liability' – based on the taxpayers' personal attachment to the State concerned (the 'State of residence'). This liability to tax is not imposed only on persons who are 'domiciled' in a State in the sense in which 'domicile' is usually taken in the legislations (private law). The cases of full liability to tax are extended to comprise also, for instance, persons who stay continually, or maybe only for a certain period, in the territory of the State. Some legislations impose full liability to tax on individuals who perform services on board ships which have their home harbour in the State.

4. Conventions for the avoidance of double taxation do not normally concern themselves with the domestic laws of the Contracting States laying down the conditions under which a person is to be treated fiscally as 'resident' and, consequently, is fully liable to tax in that State. They do not lay down standards which the provisions of the domestic laws on 'residence' have to fulfil in order that claims for full tax liability can be accepted between the Contracting States. In this respect the States take their stand entirely on the domestic laws.

5. This manifests itself quite clearly in the cases where there is no conflict at all between two residences, but where the conflict exists only between residence and source or situs. But the same view applies in conflicts between two residences. The special point in these cases is only that no solution of the conflict can be arrived at by reference to the concept of residence adopted in the domestic laws of the States concerned. In these cases special provisions must be established in the Convention to determine which of the two concepts of residence is to be given preference.

6. An example will elucidate the case. An individual has his permanent home in State A, where his wife and children live. He has had a stay of more than six months in State B and according to the legislation of the latter State he is, in consequence of the length of the stay, taxed as being a resident of that State. Thus, both States claim that he is fully liable to tax. This conflict has to be solved by the Convention.

7. In this particular case the Article (under paragraph 2) gives preference to the claim of State A. This does not, however, imply that the Article lays down special rules on 'residence' and that the domestic laws of State B are ignored because they are incompatible with such rules. The fact is quite simply that in the case of such conflict a choice must necessarily be made between the two claims, and it is on this point that the Article proposes special rules.

II. COMMENTARY ON THE PROVISIONS OF THE ARTICLE

Paragraph 1

8. Paragraph 1 provides a definition of the expression 'resident of a Contracting State' for the purposes of the Convention. The definition refers to the concept of residence adopted in the domestic laws (cf. Preliminary Remarks). As criteria for the taxation as a resident the definition mentions: domicile, residence, place of management or any

other criterion of a similar nature. As far as individuals are concerned, the definition aims at covering the various forms of personal attachment to a State which, in the domestic taxation laws, form the basis of a comprehensive taxation (full liability to tax). It also covers cases where a person is deemed, according to the taxation laws of a State, to be a resident of that State and on account thereof is fully liable to tax therein (e.g. diplomats or other persons in government service). In accordance with the provisions of the second sentence of paragraph 1, however, a person is not to be considered a 'resident of a Contracting State' in the sense of the Convention if, although not domiciled in that State, he is considered to be a resident according to the domestic laws but is subject only to a taxation limited to the income from sources in that State or to capital situated in that State. That situation exists in some States in relation to individuals, e.g. in the case of foreign diplomatic and consular staff serving in their territory.

Paragraph 2

9. This paragraph relates to the case where, under the provisions of paragraph 1, an individual is a resident of both Contracting States.

10. To solve this conflict special rules must be established which give the attachment to one State a preference over the attachment to the other State. As far as possible, the preference criterion must be of such a nature that there can be no question but that the person concerned will satisfy it in one State only, and at the same time it must reflect such an attachment that it is felt to be natural that the right to tax devolves upon that particular State.

11. The Article gives preference to the Contracting State in which the individual has a permanent home available to him. This criterion will frequently be sufficient to solve the conflict, e.g. where the individual has a permanent home in one Contracting State and has only made a stay of some length in the other Contracting State.

12. Sub-paragraph *a.* means, therefore, that in the application of the Convention (that is, where there is a conflict between the laws of the two States) it is considered that the residence is that place where the individual owns or possesses a home; this home must be permanent, that is to say, the individual must have arranged and retained it for his permanent use as opposed to staying at a particular place under such conditions that it is evident that the stay is intended to be of short duration.

13. As regards the concepts of home, it should be observed that any form of home may be taken into account (house or department belonging to or rented by the individual, rented furnished room). But the permanence of the home is essential; this means that the individual has arranged to have the dwelling available to him at all times continuously, and not occasionally for the purpose of a stay which, owing to the reasons for it, is necessarily of short duration (travel for pleasure, business travel, educational travel, attending a course at a school, etc.).

14. If the individual has a permanent home in both Contracting States, paragraph 2 gives preference to the State with which the per-

sonal and economic relations of the individual are closer, this being understood as the centre of vital interests. In the cases where the residence cannot be determined by reference to this rule, paragraph 2 provides as subsidiary criteria, first, habitual abode, and then nationality. If the individual is a national of both States or of neither of them, the question shall be solved by mutual agreement between the States concerned according to the procedure laid down in Article 25.

15. If the individual has a permanent home in both Contracting States, it is necessary to look at the facts in order to ascertain with which of the two States his personal and economic relations are closer. Thus, regard will be had to his family and social relations, his occupations, his political, cultural or other activities, his place of business, the place from which he administers his property, etc. The circumstances must be examined as a whole, but it is nevertheless obvious that considerations based on personal acts of the individual must receive special attention. If a person who has a home in one State sets up a second in the other State while retaining the first, the fact that he retains the first in the environment where he has always lived, where he has worked, and where he has his family and possessions, can, together with other elements, go to demonstrate that he has retained his centre of vital interests in the first State.

16. Sub-paragraph *b.* establishes a secondary criterion for two quite distinct and different situations:

a. the case where the individual has a permanent home available to him in both Contracting States and it is not possible to determine in which one he has his centre of vital interests;

b. the case where the individual has a permanent home available to him in neither Contracting State.

Preference is given to the Contracting State where the individual has an habitual abode.

17. In the first situation, the case where the individual has a permanent home available to him in both States, the fact of having an habitual abode in one State rather than in the other appears therefore as the circumstance which, in case of doubt as to where the individual has his centre of vital interests, tips the balance towards the State where he stays more frequently. For this purpose regard must be had to stays made by the individual not only at the permanent home in the State in question but also at any other place in the same State.

18. The second situation is the case of an individual who has a permanent home available to him in neither Contracting State, as for example, a person going from one hotel to another. In this case also all stays made in a State must be considered without it being necessary to ascertain the reasons for them.

19. In stipulating that in the two situations which it contemplates preference is given to the Contracting State where the individual has an habitual abode, sub-paragraph *b.* does not specify over what length of time the comparison must be made. The comparison must cover a sufficient length of time for it to be possible to determine whether the

residence in each of the two States is habitual and to determine also the intervals at which the stays take place.

20. Where, in the two situations referred to in sub-paragraph *b.* the individual has an habitual abode in both Contracting States or in neither, preference is given to the State of which he is a national. If, in these cases still, the individual is a national of both Contracting States or of neither of them the sub-paragraph *d.* assigns to the competent authorities the duty of resolving the difficulty by mutual agreement according to the procedure established in Article 25.

Paragraph 3

21. This paragraph concerns companies and other bodies of persons, irrespective of whether they are or not legal persons. It may be rare in practice for a company, etc. to be subject to tax as a resident in more than one State, but it is, of course, possible if, for instance, one State attaches importance to the registration and the other State to the place of effective management. So, in the case of companies, etc., also, special rules as to the preference must be established.

22. It would not be an adequate solution to attach importance to a purely formal criterion like registration. Therefore paragraph 3 attaches importance to the place where the company, etc.is actually managed.

23. The formulation of the preference criterion in the case of persons other than individuals was considered in particular in connection with the taxation of income from shipping, inland waterways transport and air transport. A number of conventions for the avoidance of double taxation on such income accord the taxing power to the State in which the 'place of management' of the enterprise is situated; other conventions attach importance to its 'place of effective management', others again to the 'fiscal domicile of the operator'. Concerning conventions concluded by the United Kingdom which provide that a company shall be regarded as resident in the State in which 'its business is managed and controlled', it has been made clear, on the United Kingdom side, that this expression means the 'effective management' of the enterprise.

24. As a result of these considerations, the 'place of effective management' has been adopted as the preference criterion for persons other than individuals.

Observation on the Commentary

25. [Omitted]

Reservations on the Article:

26. *Canada* and the *United States* reserve the right to use as the test for paragraph 3 the place of incorporation or organisation with respect to a company.

27. [Omitted]

28. [Omitted]

Commentary on Article 5 concerning the Definition of Permanent Establishment

1. The main use of the concept of a permanent establishment is to determine the right of a Contracting State to tax the profits of an enterprise of the other Contracting State. Under Article 7 a Contracting State cannot tax the profits of an enterprise of the other Contracting State unless it carries on its business through a permanent establishment situated therein.

Paragraph 1

2. Paragraph 1 gives a general definition of the term 'permanent establishment' which brings out its essential characteristics of a permanent establishment in the sense of the Convention, i.e. a distinct 'situs', a 'fixed place of business'. The paragraph defines the term 'permanent establishment' as a fixed place of business, through which the business of an enterprise is wholly or partly carried on. This definition, therefore, contains the following conditions:

- the existence of a 'place of business', i.e. a facility such as premises or, in certain instances, machinery or equipment;
- this place of business must be 'fixed', i.e. it must be established at a distinct place with a certain degree of permanence;
- the carrying on of the business of the enterprise through this fixed place of business. This means usually that persons who, in one way or another, are dependent on the enterprise (personnel) conduct the business of the enterprise in the State in which the fixed place is situated.

3. It could perhaps be argued that in the general definition some mention should also be made of the other characteristic of a permanent establishment to which some importance has sometimes been attached in the past, namely that the establishment must have a productive character – i.e. contribute to the profits of the enterprise. In the present definition this course has not been taken. Within the framework of a well-run business organisation it is surely axiomatic to assume that each part contributes to the productivity of the whole. It does not, of course, follow in every case that because in the wider context of the whole organisation a particular establishment has a 'productive character' it is consequently a permanent establishment to which profits can properly be attributed for the purpose of tax in a particular territory (cf. Commentary on paragraph 4).

4. The term 'place of business' covers any premises, facilities or installations used for carrying on the business of the enterprise whether or not they are used exclusively for that purpose. A place of business may also exist where no premises are available or required for carrying on the business of the enterprise and it simply has a certain amount of space at its disposal. It is immaterial whether the premises, facilities or installations are owned or rented by or otherwise at the disposal of the enterprise. A place of business may thus be constituted by a pitch

in a market place, or by a certain permanently used area in a Customs depot (e.g. for the storage of dutiable goods). Again the place of business may be situated in the business facilities of another enterprise. This may be the case, for instance where the foreign enterprise has at its constant disposal certain premises or a part thereof owned by the other enterprise.

5. According to the definition, the place of business has to be a 'fixed one'. Thus in the normal way there has to be a link between the place of business and a specific geographical point. It is immaterial how long an enterprise of a Contracting State operates in the other Contracting State if it does not do so at a distinct place, but this does not mean that the equipment constituting the place of business has to be actually fixed to the soil on which it stands. It is enough that the equipment remains on a particular site (but cf. paragraph 19 below).

6. Since the place of business must be fixed, it also follows that a permanent establishment can be deemed to exist only if the place of business has a certain degree of permanency, i.e. if it is not of a purely temporary nature. If the place of business was not set up merely for a temporary purpose, it can constitute a permanent establishment, even though it existed, in practice, only for a very short period of time because of the special nature of the activity of the enterprise or because, as a consequence of special circumstances (e.g. death of the taxpayer, investment failure), it was prematurely liquidated. Where a place of business which was, at the outset, designed for a short temporary purpose only, is maintained for such a period that it cannot be considered as a temporary one, it becomes a fixed place of business and thus – retrospectively – a permanent establishment.

7. For a place of business to constitute a permanent establishment the enterprise using it must carry on its business wholly or partly through it. As stated in paragraph 3 above, the activity need not be of a productive character. Furthermore, the activity need not be permanent in the sense that there is no interruption of operation, but operations must be carried out on a regular basis.

8. Where tangible property such as facilities, equipment, buildings, or intangible property such as patents, procedures and similar property, are let or leased to third parties through a fixed place of business maintained by an enterprise of a Contracting State in the other State, this activity will, in general, render the place of business a permanent establishment. The same applies if capital is made available through a fixed place of business. If an enterprise of a State lets or leases facilities, equipment, buildings or intangible property to an enterprise of the other State without maintaining for such letting or leasing activity a fixed place of business in the other State, the leased facility, equipment, building or intangible property, as such, will not constitute a permanent establishment of the lessor provided the contract is limited to the mere leasing of the equipment etc. This remains the case when, for example, the lessor supplies personnel after installation to operate the equipment provided that their responsibility is limited solely to the operation or maintenance of the equipment under the direction, responsibility and

control of the lessee. If the personnel have wider responsibilities, for example, participation in the decisions regarding the work for which the equipment is used, the activity of the lessor may go beyond the mere leasing of equipment and may constitute an entrepreneurial activity. In such a case a permanent establishment could be deemed to exist if the criterion of permanency is met. When such activity is connected with, or is similar in character to, those mentioned in paragraph 3, the time limit of twelve months applies. Other cases have to be determined according to the circumstances.

9. The business of an enterprise is carried on mainly by the entrepreneur or persons who are in paid-employment relationship with the enterprise (personnel). This personnel includes employees and other persons receiving instructions from the enterprise (e.g. dependent agents). The powers of such personnel in its relationship with third parties are irrelevant. It makes no difference whether or not the dependent agent is authorised to conclude contracts if he works at the fixed place of business (cf. paragraph 34 below). But a permanent establishment may nevertheless exist if the business of the enterprise is carried on mainly through automatic equipment, the activities of the personnel being restricted to setting up operating, controlling and maintaining such equipment. Whether or not gaming and vending machines and the like set up by an enterprise of a State in the other State constitute a permanent establishment thus depends on whether or not the enterprise carries on a business activity besides the initial setting up of the machines. A permanent establishment does not exist if the enterprise merely sets up the machines and then leases the machines to other enterprises. A permanent establishment may exist, however, if the enterprise which sets up the machines also operates and maintains them for its own account. This also applies if the machines are operated and maintained by an agent dependent on the enterprise.

10. A permanent establishment begins to exist as soon as the enterprise commences to carry on its business through a fixed place of business. This is the case once the enterprise prepares, at the place of business, the activity for which the place of business is to serve permanently. The period of time during which the fixed place of business itself is being set up by the enterprise should not be counted, provided that this activity differs substantially from the activity for which the place of business is to serve permanently. The permanent establishment ceases to exist with the disposal of the fixed place of business or with the cessation of any activity through it, that is when all acts and measures connected with the former activities of the permanent establishment are terminated (winding up current business transactions, maintenance and repair of facilities). A temporary interruption of operations, however, cannot be regarded as a closure. If the fixed place of business is leased to another enterprise, it will normally only serve the activities of that enterprise instead of the lessor's; in general, the lessor's permanent establishment ceases to exist, except where he continues carrying on a business activity of his own through the fixed place of business.

Paragraph 2

11. This paragraph contains a list, by no means exhaustive, of examples, each of which can be regarded, prima facie, as constituting a permanent establishment. As these examples are to be seen against the background of the general definition given in paragraph 1, it is assumed that the Contracting States interpret the terms listed, 'a place of management', 'a branch', 'an office', etc. in such a way that such places of business constitute permanent establishments only if they meet the requirements of paragraph 1.

12. The term 'place of management' has been mentioned separately because it is not necessarily an 'office'. However, where the laws of the two Contracting States do not contain the concept of 'a place of management' as distinct from an 'office', there will be no need to refer to the former term in their bilateral convention.

13. Sub-paragraph *f.* provides that mines, oil or gas wells, quarries or any other place of extraction of natural resources are permanent establishments. The term 'any other place of extraction of natural resources' should be interpreted broadly. It includes, for example, all places of extraction of hydrocarbons whether on or off-shore.

14. Sub-paragraph *f.* refers to the extraction of natural resources, but does not mention the exploration of such resources, whether on or off-shore. Therefore, whenever income from such activities is considered to be business profits, the question whether these activities are carried on through a permanent establishment is governed by paragraph 1. Since, however, it has not been possible to arrive at a common view on the basic questions of the attribution of taxation rights and of the qualification of the income from exploration activities, the Contracting States may agree upon the insertion of specific provisions. They may agree, for instance, that an enterprise of a Contracting State, as regards its activities of exploration of natural resources in a place or area in the other Contracting State:

a. shall be deemed not to have a permanent establishment in that other State; or

b. shall be deemed to carry on such activities through a permanent establishment in that other State; or

c. shall be deemed to carry on such activities through a permanent establishment in that other State if such activities last longer than a specified period of time.

The Contracting States may moreover agree to submit the income from such activities to any other rule.

Paragraph 3

15. This paragraph provides expressly that a building site or construction or installation project constitutes a permanent establishment only if it lasts more than twelve months. Any of those items which does not meet this condition does not of itself constitute a permanent establishment, even if there is within it an installation, for instance an office or a workshop within the meaning of paragraph 2, associated with the construction activity.

16. The term 'building site or construction or installation project' includes not only the construction of buildings but also the construction of roads, bridges or canals, the laying of pipe-lines and excavating and dredging. Planning and supervision of the erection of a building are covered by this term, if carried out by the building contractor. However, planning and supervision is not included if carried out by another enterprise whose activities in connection with the construction concerned are restricted to planning and supervising the work. If that other enterprise has an office which it uses only for planning or supervision activities relating to a site or project which does not constitute a permanent establishment, such office does not constitute a fixed place of business within the meaning of paragraph 1, because its existence has not a certain degree of permanence.

17. The twelve month test applies to each individual site or project. In determining how long the site or project has existed, no account should be taken of the time previously spent by the contractor concerned on other sites or projects which are totally unconnected with it. A building site should be regarded as a single unit, even if it is based on several contracts, provided that it forms a coherent whole commercially and geographically. Subject to this proviso, a building site forms a single unit even if the orders have been placed by several persons (e.g. for a row of houses).

18. A site exists from the date on which the contractor begins his work, including any preparatory work, in the country where the construction is to be established, e.g. if he installs a planning office for the construction. In general, it continues to exist until the work is completed or permanently abandoned. A site should not be regarded as ceasing to exist when work is temporarily discontinued. Seasonal or other temporary interruptions should be included in determining the life of a site. Seasonal interruptions include interruptions due to bad weather. Temporary interruption could be caused, for example, by shortage of material or labour difficulties. Thus, for example, if a contractor started work on a road on 1st May, stopped on 1st November because of bad weather conditions or lack of materials but resumed work on 1st February the following year, completing the road on 1st June, his construction project should be regarded as a permanent establishment because thirteen months elapsed between the date he first commenced work (1st May) and the date he finished (1st June of the following year). If an enterprise (general contractor) which has undertaken the performance of a comprehensive project sub-contracts parts of such project to other enterprises (sub-contractors), the period spent by the sub-contractor working on the building site must be considered as being time spent by the general contractor on the building project. The sub-contractor himself has a permanent establishment at the site if his activities there last more than twelve months.

19. The very nature of a construction or installation project may be such that the contractor's activity has to be relocated continuously or at least from time to time, as the project progresses. This would be the case for instance where roads or canals were being constructed, water-

ways dredged, or pipe-lines laid. In such a case, the fact that the work force is not present for twelve months in one particular place is immaterial. The activities performed at each particular spot are part of a single project, and that project must be regarded as a permanent establishment if, as a whole, it lasts more then twelve months.

Paragraph 4

20. This paragraph lists a number of business activities which are treated as exceptions to the general definition laid down in paragraph 1 and which are not permanent establishments, even if the activity is carried on through a fixed place of business. The common feature of these activities is that they are, in general, preparatory or auxiliary activities. This is laid down explicitly in the case of the exception mentioned in sub-paragraph *e.*, which actually amounts to a general restriction of the scope of the definition contained in paragraph 1. Moreover sub-paragraph *f.* provides that combinations of activities mentioned in sub-paragraph *a.* to *e.* in the same fixed place of business shall be deemed not to be a permanent establishment, provided that the overall activity of the fixed place of business resulting from this combination is of a preparatory or auxiliary character. Thus the provisions of paragraph 4 are designed to prevent an enterprise of one State from being taxed in the other State, if it carries on in that other State, activities of a purely preparatory or auxiliary character.

21. Sub-paragraph *a.* relates only to the case in which an enterprise acquires the use of facilities for storing, displaying or delivering its own goods or merchandise. Sub-paragraph *b.* relates to the stock of merchandise itself and provides that the stock, as such, shall not be treated as a permanent establishment if it is maintained for the purpose of storage, display or delivery. Sub-paragraph *c.* covers the case in which a stock of goods or merchandise belonging to one enterprise is processed by a second enterprise, on behalf of, or for the account of, the first-mentioned enterprise. The reference to the collection of information in sub-paragraph *d.* is intended to include the case of the newspaper bureau which has no purpose other than to act as one of many 'tentacles' of the parent body; to exempt such a bureau is to do no more than to extend the concept of 'mere purchase'.

22. Sub-paragraph *e.* provides that a fixed place of business through which the enterprise exercises solely an activity which has for the enterprise a preparatory or auxiliary character, is deemed not to be a permanent establishment. The wording of this sub-paragraph makes it unnecessary to produce an exhaustive list of exceptions. Furthermore, this sub-paragraph provides a generalised exception to the general definition in paragraph 1 and, when read with that paragraph, provides a more selective test, by which to determine what constitutes a permanent establishment. To a considerable degree it limits that definition and excludes from its rather wide scope a number of forms of business organisations which, although they are carried on through a fixed place of business, should not be treated as permanent establishments. It is recognised that such a place of business may well contribute to the

productivity of the enterprise, but the services it performs are so remote from the actual realisation of profits that it is difficult to allocate any profit to the fixed place of business in question. Examples are fixed places of business solely for the purpose of advertising or for the supply of information or for scientific research or for the servicing of a patent or a know-how contract, if such activities have a preparatory or auxiliary character.

23. It is often difficult to distinguish activities which have a preparatory or auxiliary character and those which have not. The decisive criterion is whether or not the activity of the fixed place of business in itself forms an essential and significant part of the activity of the enterprise as a whole. Each individual case will have to be examined on its own merits. In any case, a fixed place of business whose general purpose is one which is identical to the general purpose of the whole enterprise, does not exercise a preparatory or auxiliary activity. Where, for example, the servicing of patents and know-how is the purpose of an enterprise, a fixed place of business of such enterprise exercising such an activity cannot get the benefits of sub-paragraph *e.* A fixed place of business which has the function of managing an enterprise or even only a part of an enterprise or of a group of the concern cannot be regarded as doing a preparatory or auxiliary activity, for such managerial activity exceeds this level. If enterprises with international ramifications establish a so-called 'management office' in States in which they maintain subsidiaries, permanent establishments, agents or licensees, such office having supervisory and co-ordinating functions for all departments of the enterprise located within the region concerned, a permanent establishment will normally be deemed to exist, because the management office may be regarded as an office within the meaning of paragraph 2. Where a big international concern has delegated all management functions to its regional management offices so that the functions of the head office of the concern are restricted to general supervision (so-called polycentric enterprises), the regional management offices even have to be regarded as a 'place of management' within the meaning of sub-paragraph *a.* of paragraph 2. The function of managing an enterprise, even if it only covers a certain area of the operations of the concern, constitutes an essential part of the business operations of the enterprise and therefore can in no way be regarded as an activity which has a preparatory or auxiliary character within the meaning of sub-paragraph *e.* of paragraph 4.

24. A permanent establishment could also be constituted if an enterprise maintains a fixed place of business in order to supply spare parts to customers for the machinery supplied to such customers, and to maintain and repair such machinery, as this goes beyond the pure delivery mentioned in sub-paragraph *a.* of paragraph 4. Since these after-sale organisations perform an essential and significant part of the services of an enterprise vis-à-vis its customers, their activities are not merely auxiliary ones. Sub-paragraph *e.* applies only if the activity of the fixed place of business is limited to a preparatory or auxiliary one. This would not be the case where, for example, the fixed place of

business does not only give information but also furnishes plans etc. specially developed for the purposes of the individual customer. Nor would it be the case if a research establishment were to concern itself with manufacture.

25. Moreover, sub-paragraph *e.* makes it clear that the activities of the fixed place of business must be carried on for the enterprise. A fixed place of business which renders services not only to its enterprise but also directly to other enterprises, for example to other companies of a group to which the company owning the fixed place belongs, would not fall within the scope of sub-paragraph *e.*

26. As already mentioned in paragraph 20 above, paragraph 4 is designed to provide for exceptions to the general definition of paragraph 1 in respect of fixed places of business which are engaged in activities having a preparatory or auxiliary character. Therefore, according to sub-paragraph *f.* of paragraph 4, the fact that one fixed place of business combines any of the activities mentioned in the sub-paragraphs *a.* to *e.* of paragraph 4 does not mean of itself that a permanent establishment exists. As long as the combined activity of such a fixed place of business is merely preparatory or auxiliary a permanent establishment should be deemed not to exist. Such combinations should not be viewed on rigid lines, but should be considered in the light of the particular circumstances. The criterion 'preparatory or auxiliary character' is to be interpreted in the same way as is set out for the same criterion of sub-paragraph *e.* (cf. paragraphs 23 and 24 above). Sub-paragraph *f.* is of no importance in a case where an enterprise maintains several fixed places of business within the meaning of the sub-paragraphs *a.* to *e.* provided that they are separated from each other locally and organisationally, as in such a case each place of business has to be viewed separately and in isolation for deciding the question whether or not a permanent establishment exists. States which want to allow any combination of the items mentioned in sub-paragraphs *a.* to *e.*, disregarding whether or not the criterion of the preparatory or auxiliary character of such a combination is met, are free to do so by deleting the words 'provided' to 'character' in sub-paragraph *f.*

27. The fixed places of business mentioned in paragraph 4 cannot be deemed to constitute permanent establishments so long as their activities are restricted to the functions which are the prerequisite for assuming that the fixed place of business is not a permanent establishment. This will be the case even if the contracts necessary for establishing and carrying on the business are concluded by those in charge of the places of business themselves. The employees of places of business within the meaning of paragraph 4 who are authorised to conclude such contracts should not be regarded as agents within the meaning of paragraph 5. A case in point would be a research institution the manager of which is authorised to conclude the contracts necessary for maintaining the institution and who exercises this authority within the framework of the functions of the institution. A permanent establishment, however, exists if the fixed place of business exercising any of the functions listed in paragraph 4 were to exercise them not only on

behalf of the enterprise to which it belongs but also on behalf of other enterprises. If, for instance, an advertising agency maintained by an enterprise were also to engage in advertising for other enterprises, it would be regarded as a permanent establishment of the enterprise by which it is maintained.

28. If a fixed place of business under paragraph 4 is deemed not to be a permanent establishment, this exception applies likewise to the disposal of movable property forming part of the business property of the place of business at the termination of the enterprise's activity in such installation (cf. paragraph 10 above and paragraph 2 of Article 13). Since, for example, the display of merchandise is excepted under sub-paragraphs *a.* and *b.*, the sale of the merchandise at the termination of a trade fair or convention is covered by this exception. The exception does not, of course, apply to sales of merchandise not actually displayed at the trade fair or convention.

29. A fixed place of business used both for activities which rank as exceptions (paragraph 4) and for other activities would be regarded as a single permanent establishment and taxable as regards both types of activities. This would be the case, for instance, where a store maintained for the delivery of goods also engaged in sales.

Paragraph 5

30. It is a generally accepted principle that an enterprise should be treated as having a permanent establishment in a State if there is under certain conditions a person acting for it, even though the enterprise may not have a fixed place of business in that State within the meaning of paragraphs 1 and 2. This provision intends to give that State the right to tax in such cases. Thus paragraph 5 stipulates the conditions under which an enterprise is deemed to have a permanent establishment in respect of any activity of a person acting for it. The paragraph has been redrafted to clarify the intention of the corresponding provision of the 1963 Draft Convention without altering its substance apart from an extension of the excepted activities of the person.

31. Persons whose activities may create a permanent establishment for the enterprise are so-called dependent agents i.e. persons, whether employees or not, who are not independent agents falling under paragraph 6. Such persons may be either individuals or companies. It would not have been in the interest of international economic relations to provide that the maintenance of any dependent person would lead to a permanent establishment for the enterprise. Such treatment is to be limited to persons who in view of the scope of their authority or the nature of their activity involve the enterprise to a particular extent in business activities in the State concerned. Therefore, paragraph 5 proceeds on the basis that only persons having the authority to conclude contracts can lead to a permanent establishment for the enterprise maintaining them. In such a case the person has sufficient authority to bind the enterprise's participation in the business activity in the State concerned. The use of the term 'permanent establishment' in this context

presupposes, of course, that that person makes use of this authority repeatedly and not merely in isolated cases.

32. The authority to conclude contracts must cover contracts relating to operations which constitute the business proper of the enterprise. It would be irrelevant, for instance, if the person had authority to engage employees for the enterprise to assist that person's activity for the enterprise or if the person were authorised to conclude, in the name of the enterprise, similar contracts relating to internal operations only. Moreover the authority has to be habitually exercised in the other State; whether or not this is the case should be determined on the basis of the commercial realities of the situation. A person who is authorised to negotiate all elements and details of a contract in a way binding on the enterprise can be said to exercise this authority 'in that State', even if the contract is signed by another person in the State in which the enterprise is situated. Since, by virtue of paragraph 4, the maintenance of a fixed place of business solely for purposes listed in that paragraph is deemed not to constitute a permanent establishment, a person whose activities are restricted to such purposes does not create a permanent establishment either.

33. Where the requirements set out in paragraph 5 are met, a permanent establishment of the enterprise exists to the extent that the person acts for the latter, i.e. not only to the extent that such a person exercises the authority to conclude contracts in the name of the enterprise.

34. Under paragraph 5, only those persons who meet the specific conditions, may create a permanent establishment; all other persons are excluded. It should be borne in mind, however, that paragraph 5 simply provides an alternative test of whether an enterprise has a permanent establishment in a State. If it can be shown that the enterprise has a permanent establishment within the meaning of paragraphs 1 and 2 (subject to the provisions of paragraph 4), it is not necessary to show that the person in charge is one who would fall under paragraph 5.

Paragraph 6

35. Where an enterprise of a Contracting State carries on business dealings through a broker, general commission agent or any other agent of an independent status, it cannot be taxed in the other Contracting State in respect of those dealings if the agent is acting in the ordinary course of his business (cf. paragraph 31 above). Although it stands to reason that such an agent, representing a separate enterprise, cannot constitute a permanent establishment of the foreign enterprise, paragraph 6 has been inserted in the Article for the sake of clarity and emphasis.

36. A person will come within the scope of paragraph 6 – i.e. he will not constitute a permanent establishment of the enterprise on whose behalf he acts – only if

a. he is independent of the enterprise both legally and economically, and *b.* he acts in the ordinary course of this* business when acting on behalf of the enterprise.

37. Whether a person is independent of the enterprise represented depends on the extent of the obligations which this person has vis-à-vis the enterprise. Where the person's commercial activities for the enterprise are subject to detailed instructions or to comprehensive control by it, such person cannot be regarded as independent of the enterprise. Another important criterion will be whether the entrepreneurial risk has to be borne by the person or by the enterprise the person represents. A subsidiary is not to be considered dependent on its parent company solely because of the parent's ownership of the share capital. Persons cannot be said to act in the ordinary course of their own business if, in place of the enterprise, such persons perform activities which, economically, belong to the sphere of the enterprise rather than to that of their own business operations. Where, for example, a commission agent not only sells the goods or merchandise of the enterprise in his own name but also habitually acts, in relation to that enterprise, as a permanent agent having an authority to conclude contracts, he would be deemed in respect of this particular activity to be a permanent establishment, since he is thus acting outside the ordinary course of his own trade or business (namely that of a commission agent), unless his activities are limited to those mentioned at the end of paragraph 5.

38. According to the definition of the term 'permanent establishment' an insurance company of one State may be taxed in the other State on its insurance business, if it has a fixed place of business within the meaning of paragraph 1 or if it carries on business through a person within the meaning of paragraph 5. Since agencies of foreign insurance companies sometimes do not meet either of the above requirements, it is conceivable that these companies do large-scale business in a State without being taxed in that State on their profits arising from such business. In order to obviate this possibility, various conventions concluded by OECD Member countries include a provision which stipulates that insurance companies of a State are deemed to have a permanent establishment in the other State if they collect premiums in that other State through an agent established there – other than an agent who already constitutes a permanent establishment by virtue of paragraph 5 – or insure risks situated in that territory through such an agent. The decision as to whether or not a provision along these lines should be included in a convention will depend on the factual and legal situation prevailing in the Contracting States concerned. Frequently, therefore, such a provision will not be comtemplated.** In view of this fact, it did not seem advisable to insert a provision along these lines in the Model Convention.

---

* *Read:* 'his' (*ed.*)

** *Read:* 'contemplated' (*ed.*)

Paragraph 7

39. It is generally accepted that the existence of a subsidiary company does not, of itself, constitute that subsidiary company a permanent establishment of its parent company. This follows from the principle that, for the purpose of taxation, such a subsidiary company constitutes an independent legal entity. Even the fact that the trade or business carried on by the subsidiary company is managed by the parent company does not constitute the subsidiary company a permanent establishment of the parent company.

40. However, a subsidiary company will constitute a permanent establishment for its parent company under the same conditions stipulated in paragraph 5 as are valid for any other unrelated company, i.e. if it cannot be regarded as an independent agent in the meaning of paragraph 6, and if it has and habitually exercises an authority to conclude contracts in the name of the parent company. And the effects would be the same as for any other unrelated company to which paragraph 5 applies.

41. The same rules should apply to activities which one subsidiary carries on for any other subsidiary of the same company.

Observations on the Commentary

42.-48. [Omitted]

Commentary on Article 6 concerning the Taxation of Income from Immovable Property

1. Paragraph 1 gives the right to tax income from immovable property to the State of source, that is, the State in which the property producing such income is situated. This is due to the fact that there is always a very close economic connection between the source of this income and the State of source. Although income from agriculture or forestry is included in Article 6, Contracting States are free to agree in their bilateral conventions to treat such income under Article 7. Article 6 deals only with income which a resident of a Contracting State derives from immovable property situated in the other Contracting State. It does not, therefore, apply to income from immovable property situated in the Contracting State of which the recipient is a resident within the meaning of Article 4 or situated in a third State; the provisions of paragraph 1 of Article 21 shall apply to such income.

2. Defining the concept of immovable property by reference to the law of the State in which the property is situated, as is provided in paragraph 2, will help to avoid difficulties of interpretation over the question whether an asset or a right is to be regarded as immovable property or not. The paragraph, however, specifically mentions the assets and rights which must always be regarded as immovable property. In fact such assets and rights are already treated as immovable

property according to the laws or the taxation rules of most OECD Member countries. Conversely, the paragraph stipulates that ships, boats and aircraft shall never be considered as immovable property. No special provision has been included as regards income from indebtedness secured by immovable property, as this question is settled by Article 11.

3. Paragraph 3 indicates that the general rule applies irrespective of the form of exploitation of the immovable property. Paragraph 4 makes it clear that the provisions of paragraphs 1 and 3 apply also to income from immovable property of industrial, commercial and other enterprises and to income from immovable property used for the performance of independent personal services.

4. It should be noted in this connection that the right to tax of the State of source has priority over the right to tax of the other State and applies also where, in the case of an enterprise or of non-industrial and non-commercial activities, income is only indirectly derived from immovable property. This does not prevent income from immovable property, when derived through a permanent establishment, from being treated as income of an enterprise, but secures that income from immovable property will be taxed in the State in which the property is situated also in the case where such property is not part of a permanent establishment situated in that State. It should further be noted that the provisions of the Article do not prejudge the application of domestic law as regards the manner in which income from immovable property is to be taxed.

Reservations on the Article:

5.-6. [Omitted]

Commentary on Article 7 concerning the Taxation of Business Profits

I. PRELIMINARY REMARKS

1. This Article is in many respects a continuation of, and a corollary to, Article 5 on the definition of the concept of permanent establishment. The permanent establishment criterion is commonly used in international double taxation conventions to determine whether a particular kind of income shall or shall not be taxed in the country from which it originates but the criterion does not of itself provide a complete solution to the problem of the double taxation of business profits; in order to prevent such double taxation it is necessary to supplement the definition of permanent establishment by adding to it an agreed set of rules of reference to which the profits made by the permanent establishment, or by an enterprise trading with a foreign member of the same group of enterprises, are to be calculated. To put the matter in

a slightly different way, when an enterprise of a Contracting State carries on business in the other Contracting State the authorities of that second State have to ask themselves two questions before they levy tax on the profits of the enterprise: the first question is whether the enterprise has a permanent establishment in their country: if the answer is in the affirmative the second question is what, if any, are the profits on which that permanent establishment should pay tax. It is with the rules to be used in determining the answer to this second question that Article 7 is concerned. Rules for ascertaining the profits of an enterprise of a Contracting State which is trading with an enterprise of the other Contracting State when both enterprises are members of the same group of enterprises or are under the same effective control are dealt with in Article 9.

2. It should perhaps be said at this point that neither Article is strikingly novel or particularly detailed. The question of what criteria should be used in attributing profits to a permanent establishment, and of how to allocate profits from transactions between enterprises under common control, has had to be dealt with in a large number of double taxation conventions and it is fair to say that the solutions adopted have generally conformed to a standard pattern. It is generally recognised that the essential principles on which this standard pattern is based are well founded, and it has been thought sufficient to restate them with some slight amendments and modifications primarily aimed at producing greater clarity. The two Articles incorporate a number of directives. They do not, nor in the nature of things could they be expected to, lay down a series of precise rules for dealing with every kind of problem that may arise when an enterprise of one State makes profits in another. Modern commerce organises itself in an infinite variety of ways, and it would be quite impossible within the fairly narrow limits of an Article in a double taxation convention to specify an exhaustive set of rules for dealing with every kind of problem that may arise. This, however, is a matter of relatively minor importance, if there is agreement on general lines. Special cases may require special consideration, but it should not be difficult to find an appropriate solution if the problem is approached within the framework of satisfactory rules based on agreed principles.

II. COMMENTARY ON THE PROVISIONS OF THE ARTICLE

Paragraph 1

3. This paragraph is concerned with two questions. First, it restates the generally accepted principle of double taxation conventions that an enterprise of one State shall not be taxed in the other State unless it carries on business in that other State through a permanent establishment situated therein. It is hardly necessary to argue here the merits of this principle. It is perhaps sufficient to say that it has come to be accepted in international fiscal matters that until an enterprise of one State sets up a permanent establishment in another State it should not properly be regarded as participating in the economic life of that other

State to such an extent that it comes within the jurisdiction of that other State's taxing rights.

4. The second and more important point is that it is laid down – in the second sentence – that when an enterprise carries on business through a permanent establishment in another State that State may tax the profits of the enterprise but only so much of them as is attributable to the permanent establishment; in other words that the right to tax does not extend to profits that the enterprise may derive from that State otherwise than through the permanent establishment. This is a question on which there may be differences of view. Some countries have taken the view that when a foreign enterprise has set up a permanent establishment within their territory it has brought itself within their fiscal jurisdiction to such a degree that they can properly tax all profits that the enterprise derives from their territory, whether the profits come from the permanent establishment or from other activities in that territory. But it is thought that it is preferable to adopt the principle contained in the second sentence of paragraph 1, namely that the test that business profits should not be taxed unless there is a permanent establishment is one that should properly be applied not to the enterprise itself but to its profits. To put the matter another way, the principle laid down in the second sentence of paragraph 1 is based on the view that in taxing the profits that a foreign enterprise derives from a particular country, the fiscal authorities of that country should look at the separate sources of profit that the enterprise derives from their country and should apply to each the permanent establishment test. This is of course without prejudice to other Articles.

5. On this matter, naturally, there is room for differences of view, and since it is an important question it may be useful to set out the arguments for each point of view.

6. Apart from the background question of fiscal jurisdiction, the main argument commonly put forward against the solution advocated above is that there is a risk that it might facilitate avoidance of tax. This solution, the argument runs, might leave it open to an enterprise to set up in a particular country a permanent establishment which made no profits, was never intended to make profits, but existed solely to supervise a trade, perhaps of an extensive nature, that the enterprise carried on in that country through independent agents and the like. Moreover, the argument goes, although the whole of this trade might be directed and arranged by the permanent establishment, it might be difficult in practice to prove that that was the case. If the rates of tax are higher in that country than they are in the country in which the head office is situated, then the enterprise has a strong incentive to see that it pays as little tax as possible in the other territory: the main criticism of the solution advocated above is that it might conceivably provide the enterprise with a means of ensuring that result.

7. Apart again from the question of the proper extent of fiscal jurisdiction, the main argument in favour of the proposed solution is that it is conducive to simple and efficient administration, and that it is more closely adapted to the way in which business is commonly trans-

acted. The organisation of modern business is highly complex. In OECD Member countries, there are a considerable number of companies each of which is engaged in a wide diversity of activities and is carrying on business extensively in many countries. It may be that such a company may have set up a permanent establishment in a second country and may be transacting a considerable amount of business through that permanent establishment in one particular kind of manufacture; that a different part of the same company may be selling quite different goods or manufactures in that second country through independent agents; and that the company may have perfectly genuine reasons for taking this course – reasons based, for example, either on the historical pattern of its business or on commercial convenience. It is desirable that the fiscal authorities should go so far as to insist on trying to search out the profit element of each of the transactions carried on through independent agents, with a view to aggregating that profit with the profits of the permanent establishment? Such an Article might interfere seriously with ordinary commercial processes, and so be out of keeping with the aims of the Convention.

8. It is no doubt true that evasion of tax could be practised by undisclosed channelling of profits away from a permanent establishment and that this may sometimes need to be watched, but it is necessary in considering this point to preserve a sense of proportion and to bear in mind what is said above. It is not, of course, sought in any way to sanction any such malpractice, or to shelter any concern thus evading tax from the consequences that would follow from detection by the fiscal authorities concerned. It is fully recognised that Contracting States should be free to use all methods at their disposal to fight fiscal evasion.

9. For the reasons given above, it is thought that the argument that the solution advocated might lead to increased avoidance of tax by foreign enterprises should not be given undue weight. Much more importance is attached to the desirability of interfering as little as possible with existing business organisations and of refraining from inflicting demands for information on foreign enterprises which are unnecessarily onerous.

Paragraph 2

10. This paragraph contains the central directive on which the allocation of profits to a permanent establishment is intended to be based. The paragraph incorporates the view, which is generally contained in bilateral conventions, that the profits to be attributed to a permanent establishment are those which that permanent establishment would have made if, instead of dealing with its head office, it had been dealing with an entirely separate enterprise under conditions and at prices prevailing in the ordinary market. Normally, these would be the same profits that one would expect to be determined by the ordinary processes of good business accountancy. This principle also extends to the allocation of profits which the permanent establishment may derive from transactions with other permanent establishments of the enterprise

and with associated companies and their permanent establishments; but Contracting States which consider that the existing paragraph does not in fact cover these more general transactions may, in their bilateral negotiations, agree upon more detailed provisions.

11. In the great majority of cases, trading accounts of the permanent establishment – which are commonly available if only because a well-run business organisation is normally concerned to know what is the profitability of its various branches – will be used by the taxation authorities concerned to ascertain the profit properly attributable to that establishment. Exceptionally there may be no separate accounts (cf. paragraphs 23 to 27 below). But where there are such accounts they will naturally form the starting point for any processes of adjustment in case adjustment is required to produce the amount of properly attributable profits. It should perhaps be emphasized that the directive contained in paragraph 2 is no justification for tax administrations to construct hypothetical profit figures in vacuo; it is always necessary to start with the real facts of the situation as they appear from the business records of the permanent establishment and to adjust as may be shown to be necessary the profit figures which those facts produce. It should also be noted that the principle set out in paragraph 2 is subject to the provisions contained in paragraph 3, especially as regards the treatment of payments which, under the name of interest, royalties, etc. are made by a permanent establishment to its head office in return for money loaned, or patent rights conceded by the latter to the permanent establishment (cf. paragraphs 16 below and following).

12. Even where a permanent establishment is able to produce proper accounts which purport to show the profits arising from its activities, it may still be necessary for the taxation authorities of the country concerned to rectify those accounts, in accordance with the general directive laid down in paragraph 2. Adjustment of this kind may be necessary, for example, because goods have been invoiced from the head office to the permanent establishment at prices which are not consistent with this directive, and profits have thus been diverted from the permanent establishment to the head office, or vice versa.

13. In such cases, it will usually be appropriate to substitute for the prices used ordinary market prices for the same or similar goods supplied on the same or similar conditions. Clearly the price at which goods can be bought on open market terms varies with the quantity required and the period over which they will be supplied; such factors would have to be taken into account in deciding the open market price to be used. It is perhaps only necessary to mention at this point that there may sometimes be perfectly good commercial reasons for an enterprise invoicing its goods at prices less than those prevailing in the ordinary market; this may, for example, be a perfectly normal commercial method of establishing a competitive position in a new market and should not then be taken as evidence of an attempt to divert profits from one country to another. Difficulties may also occur in the case of proprietary goods produced by an enterprise all of which are sold through its permanent establishments; if in such circumstances there

is no open market price and it is thought that the figures in the accounts are unsatisfactory, it may be necessary to calculate the permanent establishment's profits by other methods, for example, by applying an average ratio of gross profit to the turnover of the permanent establishment and then deducting from the figure so obtained the proper amount of expenses incurred. Clearly many special problems of this kind may arise in individual cases but the general rule should always be that the profits attributed to a permanent establishment should be based on that establishment's accounts insofar as accounts are available which represent the real facts of the situation. If available accounts do not represent the real facts then new accounts will have to be constructed, or the original ones rewritten, and for this purpose the figures to be used will be those prevailing in the open market.

14. Some States consider that there is a realisation of a taxable profit when an asset, other than trading stock, forming part of the business property of a permanent establishment situated within their territory is transferred to a permanent establishment or the head office of the same enterprise situated in another State. Article 7 allows such States to tax profits deemed to arise in connection with such a transfer. Such profits may be determined as indicated in paragraphs 10 to 13 above.

Paragraph 3

15. This paragraph clarifies, in relation to the expenses of a permanent establishment, the general directive laid down in paragraph 2. The paragraph specifically recognises that in calculating the profits of a permanent establishment allowance is to be made for expenses, wherever incurred, that were incurred for the purposes of the permanent establishment. Clearly in some cases it will be necessary to estimate or to calculate by conventional means the amount of expenses to be taken into account. In the case, for example, of general administrative expenses incurred at the head office of the enterprise, it may be appropriate to take into account a proportionate part based on the ratio that the permanent establishment's turnover (or perhaps gross profits) bears to that of the enterprise as a whole. Subject to this, it is considered that the amount of expenses to be taken into account as incurred for the purposes of the permanent establishment should be the actual amount so incurred. The deduction allowable to the permanent establishment for any of the expenses of the enterprise attributed to it does not depend upon the actual reimbursement of such expenses by the permanent establishment.

16. Apart from what may be regarded as ordinary expenses, there are some classes of payments between permanent establishments and head offices which give rise to special problems, and it is convenient to deal with them at this point. The next paragraphs discuss three specific cases of this kind and give solutions for them. It should not, of course, be inferred that it is only in relation to the three classes of payments mentioned in these paragraphs that problems may arise; there may well be payments of other kinds to which similar considerations apply.

17. The first of these cases relates to payments which under the name of interest, royalties etc. are made by a permanent establishment to its head office in return for money loaned, or patent rights conceded, by the latter to the permanent establishment. In such a case, it is considered that the payments should not be allowed as deductions in computing the permanent establishment's taxable profits. Equally, such payments made to a permanent establishment by the head office should be excluded from the computation of the permanent establishment's taxable profits. It is, however, recognised that special considerations apply to payments of interest made by different parts of a financial enterprise (e.g. a bank) to each other on advances etc. (as distinct from capital allotted to them), in view of the fact that making and receiving advances is narrowly related to the ordinary business of such enterprises. Furthermore, if an enterprise makes payments of interest, etc. to a third party and these payments in part relate to the activities of the permanent establishment, then a proportionate part of them should naturally be taken into account in calculating the permanent establishment's profits insofar as they can properly be regarded as expenses incurred for the purposes of the permanent establishment.

18. The second case relates to the performance of ancillary services by a permanent establishment on behalf of its head office or vice versa. Consider, for example, the case of a large company with a varied business, part of which it carries on in another country through a permanent establishment. In addition, that permanent establishment advertises on behalf of its head office goods which that enterprise produces but which the permanent establishment itself does not handle. Clearly, in calculating for tax purposes the profits of the permanent establishment, the profits should be increased by the amount of the expense it has incurred on behalf of the head office (unless, of course, such an adjustment has already been made in drawing up the accounts of the permanent establishment). In fact if the permanent establishment and its head office were entirely separate and independent, the permanent establishment would ordinarily carry out services for the head office only if it were paid a commission as well as reimbursed the actual expenses incurred. It is, therefore, necessary to decide whether the calculation should be made on the basis of account being taken not only of any expenses borne by a permanent establishment by reason of services performed for the head office but also of a notional commission increasing the profits of the permanent establishment.

19. After consideration of this question, it is thought that in such circumstances the profits of the permanent establishment should not be increased by the addition of a 'commission' figure. While, on one view, to include a 'commission' figure in the profits of every permanent establishment that has performed services otherwise than for its own purposes could be looked at in theory as a consequential application of the fiction of separate enterprise, it would inevitably be found exceedingly cumbersome in practice. There would be scope for lengthy argument about, and usually no concrete basis for determining, the percentage to be used in calculating the amount of notional 'commis-

sion'. In the great majority of cases the accounts of the permanent establishment would doubtless take into consideration actual expenses incurred: in other words they would not normally include any credit for 'commission'. If as a general rule the 'separate enterprise' test were to be applied to services performed by a permanent establishment on behalf of its head office and a notional 'commission' profit were to be included in the profits of the permanent establishment, it would, therefore, be necessary in the great majority of cases first to settle how the 'commission' element was to be calculated and then re-write the accounts of the permanent establishment. Considerations of practical administration weigh heavily against such a course. Therefore no 'commission' element should in such cases be included in the profits of the permanent establishment. Similarly, in the converse case where the head office undertakes services on behalf of the permanent establishment, no 'commission' element should be deducted in determining the profits of the permanent establishment.

20. The third case is related to the question whether any part of the total profits of an enterprise should be deemed to arise from the exercise of good management. Consider the case of a company that has its office in one country but carries on all its business through a permanent establishment situated in another country. In the extreme case it might well be that only the directors' meetings were held at the head office and that all other activities of the company, apart from purely formal legal activities, were carried on in the permanent establishment. In such a case there is something to be said for the view that at least part of the profits of the whole enterprise arose from the skilful management and business acumen of the directors and that part of the profits of the enterprise ought, therefore, to be attributed to the country in which the head office was situated. If the company has been managed by a managing agency, then that agency would doubtless have charged a fee for its services and the fee might well have been a simple percentage participation in the profits of the enterprise. But, once again, whatever the theoretical merits of such a course, practical considerations weigh heavily against it. In the kind of case quoted the expenses of management would, of course, be set against the profits of the permanent establishment in accordance with the provisions of paragraph 3, but when the matter is looked at as a whole, it is thought that it would not be right to go further by deducting and taking into account some notional figure for 'profits of management'. In cases identical to the extreme case mentioned above, no account should therefore be taken in determining taxable profits of the permanent establishment of any notional figure such as profits of management.

21. It may be, of course, that countries where it has been customary to allocate some proportion of the total profits of an enterprise to the head office of the enterprise to represent the profits of good management will wish to continue to make such an allocation. Nothing in the Article is designed to prevent this. Nevertheless it follows from what is said in paragraph 20 above that a country in which a permanent establishment is situated is in no way required to deduct when calculat-

ing the profits attributable to that permanent establishment an amount intended to represent a proportionate part of the profits of management attributable to the head office.

22. It might well be that if the country in which the head office of an enterprise is situated allocates to the head office some percentage of the profits of the enterprise only in respect of good management, while the country in which the permanent establishment is situated does not, the resulting total of the amounts charged to tax in the two countries would be greater than it should be. In any such case the country in which the head office of the enterprise is situated should take the initiative in arranging for such adjustments to be made in computing the taxation liability in that country as may be necessary to ensure that any double taxation is eliminated.

23. It is usually found that there are, or there can be constructed, adequate accounts for each part or section of an enterprise so that profits and expenses, adjusted as may be necessary, can be allocated to a particular part of the enterprise with a considerable degree of precision. This method of allocation is, it is thought, to be preferred in general wherever it is reasonably practicable to adopt it. There are, however, circumstances in which this may not be the case and paragraphs 2 and 3 are in no way intended to imply that other methods cannot properly be adopted where appropriate in order to arrive at the profits of a permanent establishment on a 'separate enterprise' footing. It may well be, for example, that profits of insurance enterprises can most conveniently be ascertained by special methods of computation, e.g. by applying appropriate co-efficients to gross premiums received from policy holders in the country concerned. Again, in the case of a relatively small enterprise operating on both sides of the border between two countries, there may be no proper accounts for the permanent establishment nor means of constructing them. There may, too, be other cases where the affairs of the permanent establishment are so closely bound up with those of the head office that it would be impossible to disentangle them on any strict basis of branch accounts. Where it has been customary in such cases to estimate the arm's length profit of a permanent establishment by reference to suitable criteria, it may well be reasonable that that method should continue to be followed, notwithstanding that the estimate thus made may not achieve as high a degree of accurate measurement of the profit as adequate accounts. Even where such a course has not been customary, it may, exceptionally, be necessary for practical reasons to estimate the arm's length profits.

Paragraph 4

24. It has in some cases been the practice to determine the profits to be attributed to a permanent establishment not on the basis of separate accounts or by making an estimate of arm's length profit, but simply by apportioning the total profits of the enterprise by reference to various formulae. Such a method differs from those envisaged in paragraph 2, since it contemplates not an attribution of profits on a separate

enterprise footing, but an apportionment of total profits; and indeed it might produce a result in figures which would differ from that which would be arrived at by a computation based on separate accounts. Paragraph 4 makes it clear that such a method may continue to be employed by a Contracting State if it has been customary in that State to adopt it, even though the figure arrived at may at times differ to some extent from that which would be obtained from separate accounts, provided that the result can fairly be said to be in accordance with the principles contained in the Article. It is emphasized, however, that in general the profits to be attributed to a permanent establishment should be determined by reference to the establishment's accounts if these reflect the real facts. It is considered that a method of allocation which is based on apportioning total profits is generally not as appropriate as a method which has regard only to the activities of the permanent establishment and should be used only where, exceptionally, it has as a matter of history been customary in the past and is accepted in the country concerned both by the taxation authorities and taxpayers generally there as being satisfactory. It is understood that paragraph 4 may be deleted where neither State uses such a method. Where, however, Contracting States wish to be able to use a method which has not been customary in the past the paragraph should be amended during the bilateral negotiations to make this clear.

25. It would not, it is thought, be appropriate within the framework of this Commentary to attempt to discuss at length the many various methods involving apportionment of total profits that have been adopted in particular fields for allocating profits. These methods have been well documented in treatises on international taxation. It may, however, not be out of place to summarise briefly some of the main types and to lay down some very general directives for their use.

26. The essential character of a method involving apportionment of total profits is that a proportionate part of the profits of the whole enterprise is allocated to a part thereof, all parts of the enterprise being assumed to have contributed on the basis of the criterion or criteria adopted to the profitability of the whole. The difference between one such method and another arises for the most part from the varying criteria used to determine what is the correct proportion of the total profits. It is fair to say that the criteria commonly used can be grouped into three main categories, namely those which are based on the receipts of the enterprise, its expenses or its capital structure. The first category covers allocation methods based on turnover or on commission, the second on wages and the third on the proportion of the total working capital of the enterprise allocated to each branch or part. It is not, of course, possible to say in vacuo that any of these methods is intrinsically more accurate than the others; the appropriateness of any particular method will depend on the circumstances to which it is applied. In some enterprises, such as those providing services or producing proprietary articles with a high profit margin, net profits will depend very much on turnover. For insurance enterprises it may be appropriate to make an apportionment of total profits by reference to

premiums received from policy-holders in each of the countries concerned. In the case of an enterprise manufacturing goods with a high cost raw material or labour content, profits may be found to be related more closely to expenses. In the case of banking and financial concerns the proportion of total working capital may be the most relevant criterion. It is considered that the general aim of any method involving apportionment of total profits ought to be to produce figures of taxable profit that approximate as closely as possible to the figures that would have been produced on a separate accounts basis, and that it would not be desirable to attempt in this connection to lay down any specific directive other than that it should be the responsibility of the taxation authority, in consultation with the authorities of other countries concerned, to use the method which in the light of all the known facts seems most likely to produce that result.

27. The use of any method which allocates to a part of an enterprise a proportion of the total profits of the whole does, of course, raise the question of the method to be used in computing the total profits of the enterprise. This may well be a matter which will be treated differently under the laws of different countries. This is not a problem which it would seem practicable to attempt to resolve by laying down any rigid rule. It is scarcely to be expected that it would be accepted that the profits to be apportioned should be the profits as they are computed under the laws of one particular country; each country concerned would have to be given the right to compute the profits according to the provisions of its own laws.

Paragraph 5

28. In paragraph 4 of Article 5 there are listed a number of examples of activities which, even though carried on at a fixed place of business, are deemed not to be included in the term 'permanent establishment'. In considering rules for the allocation of profits to a permanent establishment the most important of these examples is the activity mentioned in paragraph 5 of this Article, i.e. the purchasing office.

29. Paragraph 5 is not, of course, concerned with the organisation established solely for purchasing; such an organisation is not a permanent establishment and the profits allocation provisions of this Article would not therefore come into play. The paragraph is concerned with a permanent establishment which although carrying on other business also carries on purchasing for its head office. In such a case the paragraph provides that the profits of the permanent establishment shall not be increased by adding to them a notional figure for profits from purchasing. It follows, of course, that any expenses that arise from the purchasing activities will also be excluded in calculating the taxable profits of the permanent establishment.

Paragraph 6

30. This paragraph is intended to lay down clearly that a method of allocation once used should not be changed merely because in a particular year some other method produces more favourable results. One

of the purposes of a double taxation convention is to give an enterprise of a Contracting State some degree of certainty about the tax treatment that will be accorded to its permanent establishment in the other Contracting State as well as to the part of it in its home State which is dealing with the permanent establishment; for this reason, paragraph 6 gives an assurance of continuous and consistent tax treatment.

Paragraph 7

31. Although it has not been found necessary in the Convention to define the term 'profits', it should nevertheless be understood that the term when used in this Article and elsewhere in the Convention has a broad meaning including all income derived in carrying on an enterprise. Such a broad meaning corresponds to the use of the term made in the tax laws of most OECD Member countries.

32. This interpretation of the term 'profits', however, may give rise to some uncertainty as to the application of the Convention. If the profits of an enterprise include categories of income which are treated separately in other Articles of the Convention, e.g. dividends, it may be asked whether the taxation of those profits is governed by the special Article on dividends etc., or by the provisions of this Article.

33. To the extent that an application of this Article and the special Article concerned would result in the same tax treatment, there is little practical significance to this question. Further, it should be noticed that some of the special Articles contain specific provisions giving priority to a specific Article (cf. paragraph 4 of Article 6, paragraph 4 of Articles 10 and 11, paragraph 3 of Article 12, and paragraph 2 of Article 21).

34. It has seemed desirable, however, to lay down a rule of interpretation in order to clarify the field of application of the present Article in relation to the other Articles dealing with a specific category of income. In conformity with the practice generally adhered to in existing bilateral conventions, paragraph 7 gives first preference to the special Articles on dividends, interest etc. It follows from the rule that this Article will be applicable to industrial and commercial income which does not belong to categories of income covered by the special Articles, and, in addition, to dividends, interest etc. which under paragraph 4 of Articles 10 and 11, paragraph 3 of Article 12 and paragraph 2 of Article 21, fall within this Article. It is understood that the items of income covered by the special Articles may, subject to the provisions of the Convention, be taxed either separately, or as industrial and commercial profits, in conformity with the tax laws of the Contracting States.

35. It is open to Contracting States to agree bilaterally upon special explanations or definitions concerning the term 'profits' with a view to clarifying the distinction between this term and e.g. the concept of dividends. It may in particular be found appropriate to do so where in a convention under negotiation a deviation has been made from the definitions in the special Articles on dividends, interest and royalties. It may also be deemed desirable if the Contracting States wish to place

on notice, that, in agreement with the domestic tax laws of one or both of the States, the term 'profits' includes special classes of receipts such as income from the alienation or the letting of a business or of movable property used in a business. In this connection it may have to be considered whether it would be useful to include also additional rules for the allocation of such special profits.

Observations on the Commentary

36.-39. [Omitted]

40. The *United States* believes it appropriate to provide in paragraph 2 for arm's length treatment not only with the head office of the enterprise, but also with any person controlling, controlled by, or subject to the same common control as, the enterprise. This can be accomplished by changing the phrase 'separate enterprise' to 'independent enterprise' and by deleting the last fourteen words.

Commentary on Article 8 concerning the Taxation of Profits from Shipping, Inland Waterways Transport and Air Transport

Paragraph 1

1. The object of paragraph 1 concerning profits from the operation of ships or aircraft in international traffic is to secure that such profits will be taxed in one State alone. The provision is based on the principle that the taxing right shall be left to the Contracting State in which the place of effective management of the enterprise is situated. The term 'international traffic' is defined in sub-paragraph *d.* of paragraph 1 of Article 3.

2. In certain circumstances the Contracting State in which the place of effective management is situated may not be the State of which an enterprise operating ships or aircraft is a resident, and some States therefore prefer to confer the exclusive taxing right on the State of residence. Such States are free to substitute a rule on the following lines:

> 'Profits of an enterprise of a Contracting State from the operation of ships or aircraft in international traffic shall be taxable only in that State.'

3. Some other States, on the other hand, prefer to use a combination of the residence criterion and the place of effective management criterion by giving the primary right to tax to the State in which the place of effective management is situated while the State of residence eliminates double taxation in accordance with Article 23, so long as the former State is able to tax the total profits of the enterprise, and by giving the primary right to tax to the State of residence when the State of effective management is not able to tax total profits. States

wishing to follow that principle are free to substitute a rule on the following lines:

> 'Profits of an enterprise of a Contracting State from the operation of ships or aircraft, other than those from transport by ships or aircraft, operated solely between places in the other Contracting State, shall be taxable only in the first-mentioned State. However, where the place of effective management of the enterprise is situated in the other State and that other State imposes tax on the whole of the profits of the enterprise from the operation of ships or aircraft, the profits from the operation of ships or aircraft, other than those from transport by ships or aircraft operated solely between places in the first-mentioned State, may be taxed in that other State.'

4. The profits covered consist in the first place of the profits obtained by the enterprise from the carriage of passengers or cargo. With this definition, however the provision would be unduly restrictive, in view of the development of shipping and air transport, and for practical considerations also. The provision therefore covers other classes of profits as well, i.e. those which by reason of their nature or their close relationship with the profits directly obtained from transport may all be placed in a single category. Some of these classes of profits are mentioned in the following paragraphs.

5. Profits obtained by leasing a ship or aircraft on charter fully equipped, manned and supplied must be treated like the profits from the carriage of passengers or cargo. Otherwise, a great deal of business of shipping or air transport would not come within the scope of the provision. The Article does not apply to profits from leasing a ship or aircraft on a bare boat charter basis except when it is an occasional source of income for an enterprise engaged in the international operation of ships or aircraft.

6. The principle that the taxing right should be left to one Contracting State alone makes it unnecessary to devise detailed rules, e.g. for defining the profits covered, this being rather a question of applying general principles of interpretation.

7. Shipping and air transport enterprises – particularly the latter – often engage in additional activities more or less closely connected with the direct operation of ships and aircraft. Although it would be out of the question to list here all the auxiliary activities which could properly be brought under the provision, nevertheless a few examples may usefully be given.

8. The provision applies, inter alia, to the following activities:

a. the sale of passage tickets on behalf of other enterprises;

b. the operation of a bus service connecting a town with its airport;

c. advertising and commercial propaganda;

d. transportation of goods by truck connecting a depot with a port or airport.

9. If an enterprise engaged in international transport undertakes to see to it that, in connection with such transport, goods are delivered directly to the consignee in the other Contracting State, such inland transportation is considered to fall within the scope of the international

operation of ships or aircraft and, therefore, is covered by the provisions of this Article.

10. Recently, 'containerisation' has come to play an increasing role in the field of international transport. Such containers frequently are also used in inland transport. Profits derived by an enterprise engaged in international transport from the lease of containers which is supplementary or incidental to its international operation of ships or aircraft fall within the scope of this Article.

11. On the other hand, the provision does not cover a clearly separate activity, such as the keeping of a hotel as a separate business; the profits from such an establishment are in any case easily determinable. In certain cases, however, circumstances are such that the provision must apply even to a hotel business, e.g. the keeping of a hotel for no other purpose than to provide transit passengers with night accommodation, the cost of such a service being included in the price of the passage ticket. In such a case, the hotel can be regarded as a kind of waiting room.

12. There is another activity which is excluded from the field of application of the provision, namely a shipbuilding yard operated in one country by a shipping enterprise having its place of effective management in another country.

13. It may be agreed bilaterally that profits from the operation of vessels engaged in fishing, dredging or hauling activities on the high seas be treated as income falling under this Article.

14. Investment income of shipping, inland waterways or air transport enterprises (e.g. income from stocks, bonds, shares or loans) is to be subjected to the treatment ordinarily applied to this class of income.

Paragraph 2

15. The rules with respect to the taxing right of the State of residence as set forth in paragraphs 2 and 3 above apply also to this paragraph of the Article.

16. The object of this paragraph is to apply the same treatment to transport on rivers, canals and lakes as to shipping and air transport in international traffic. The provision applies not only to inland waterways transport between two or more countries, but also to inland waterways transport carried on by an enterprise of one country between two points in another country.

17. The provision does not prevent specific tax problems which may arise in connection with inland waterways transport, in particular between adjacent countries, from being settled specially by bilateral agreement.

Enterprises not Exclusively Engaged in Shipping, Inland Waterways Transport or Air Transport

18. It follows from the wording of paragraphs 1 and 2 that enterprises not exclusively engaged in shipping, inland waterways transport or air transport nevertheless come within the provisions of these para-

graphs as regards profits arising to them from the operation of ships, boats or aircraft belonging to them.

19. If such an enterprise has in a foreign country permanent establishments exclusively concerned with the operation of its ships or aircraft, there is no reason to treat such establishments differently from the permanent establishments of enterprises engaged exclusively in shipping, inland waterways transport or air transport.

20. Nor does any difficulty arise in applying the provisions of paragraphs 1 and 2 if the enterprise has in another State a permanent establishment which is not exclusively engaged in shipping, inland waterways transport or air transport. If its goods are carried in its own ships to a permanent establishment belonging to it in a foreign country, it is right to say that none of the profit obtained by the enterprise through acting as its own carrier can properly be attributed to the permanent establishment. The same must be true even if the permanent establishment maintains installations for operating the ships or aircraft (e.g. consignment wharves) or incurs other costs in connection with the carriage of the enterprise's goods (e.g. staff costs). In this case, the permanent establishment's expenditure in respect of the operation of the ships, boats or aircraft should be attributed not to the permanent establishment but to the enterprise itself, since none of the profit obtained through the carrying benefits the permanent establishment.

21. Where the enterprise's ships or aircraft are operated by a permanent establishment which is not the place of effective management of the whole enterprise (e.g. ships or aircraft put into service by the permanent establishment and figuring on its balance sheet), then the effective management for the purposes of paragraphs 1 and 2 must be considered, as regards the operation of the ships or aircraft, as being in the Contracting State in which the permanent establishment is situated.

Paragraph 3

22. This paragraph deals with the particular case where the place of effective management of the enterprise is aboard a ship or a boat. In this case tax will only be charged by the State where the home harbour of the ship or boat is situated. It is provided that if the home harbour cannot be determined, tax will be charged only in the Contracting State of which the operator of the ship or boat is a resident.

Paragraph 4

23. Various forms of international co-operation exist in shipping or air transport. In this field international co-operation is secured through pooling agreements or other conventions of a similar kind which lay down certain rules for apportioning the receipts (or profits) from the joint business.

24. In order to clarify the taxation position of the participant in a pool, joint business or in an international operating agency and to cope with any difficulties which may arise the Contracting States may bilaterally add the following, if they find it necessary:

'but only to so much of the profits so derived as is attributable to the participant in proportion to its share in the joint operation'.

Special Derogation

25. In view of its particular situation in relation to shipping, Greece will retain its freedom of action with regard to the provisions in the Convention relating to profits from the operation of ships in international traffic, to remuneration of crews of such ships, to capital represented by ships in international traffic and by movable property pertaining to the operation of such ships, and to capital gains from the alienation of such ships and assets.

Observations on the Commentary

26.-30. [Omitted]

31. *Canada, Turkey* and the *United States* reserve the right not to extend the scope of the Article to cover inland transportation in bilateral conventions (paragraph 2 of the Article).

Commentary on Article 9 concerning the Taxation of Associated Enterprises

Paragraph 1

1. This Article deals with associated enterprises (parent and subsidiary companies and companies under common control) and its paragraph 1 provides that in such cases the taxation authorities of a Contracting State may for the purpose of calculating tax liabilities re-write the accounts of the enterprises if as a result of the special relations between the enterprises the accounts do not show the true taxable profits arising in that State. It is evidently appropriate that adjustment should be sanctioned in such circumstances, and this paragraph seems to call for very little comment. It should perhaps be mentioned that the provisions of this paragraph apply only if special conditions have been made or imposed between the two enterprises. No re-writing of the accounts of associated enterprises is authorised if the transactions between such enterprises have taken place on normal open market commercial terms (on an arm's length basis).

Paragraph 2

2. The re-writing of transactions between associated enterprises in the situation envisaged in paragraph 1 may give rise to economic double taxation (taxation of the same income in the hands of different persons), insofar as an enterprise of State A whose profits are revised upwards will be liable to tax on an amount of profit which has already been taxed in the hands of its associated enterprise in State B. Para-

graph 2 provides that in these circumstances, State B shall make an appropriate adjustment so as to relieve the double taxation.

3. It should be noted, however, that an adjustment is not automatically to be made in State B simply because the profits in State A have been increased; the adjustment is due only if State B considers that the figure of adjusted profits correctly reflects what the profits would have been if the transactions had been at arm's length. In other words, the paragraph does not seek to avoid a double charge to tax which arises where the profits of one associated enterprise are increased to a level which exceeds what they would have been if they had been correctly computed on arm's length basis. State B is therefore committed to make an adjustment of the profits of the affiliated company only if it considers that the adjustment made in State A is justified both in principle and as regards the amount.

4. The paragraph does not specify the method by which an adjustment is to be made. OECD Member countries use different methods to provide relief in these circumstances and it is therefore left open for Contracting States to agree bilaterally on any specific rules which they wish to add to the Article. Some States, for example, would prefer the system under which, where the profits of enterprise X in State A are increased to what they would have been on an arm's length basis, the adjustment would be made by re-opening the assessment on the associated enterprise Y in State B containing the doubly taxed profits in order to reduce the taxable profit by an appropriate amount. Some other States, on the other hand, would prefer to provide that, for the purposes of Article 23, the doubly taxed profits should be treated in the hands of enterprise Y of State B as if they may be taxed in State A; accordingly, the enterprise of State B is entitled to relief in State B, under Article 23, in respect of tax paid by its associate enterprise in State A.

5. It is not the purpose of the paragraph to deal with what might be called 'secondary adjustments'. Suppose that an upward revision of taxable profits of enterprise X in State A has been made in accordance with the principle laid down in paragraph l; and suppose also that an adjustment is made to the profits of enterprise Y in State B in accordance with the principle laid down in paragraph 2. The position has still not been restored exactly to what it would have been had the transactions taken place at arm's length prices because, as a matter of fact the money representing the profits which are the subject of the adjustment is found in the hands of enterprise Y instead of in those of enterprise X. It can be argued that if arm's length pricing had operated and enterprise X had subsequently wished to transfer these profits to enterprise Y, it would have done so in the form of, for example, a dividend or a royalty (if enterprise Y were the parent of enterprise X) or in the form of, for example, a loan (if enterprise X were the parent of enterprise Y); and that in those circumstances there could have been other tax consequences (e.g. the operation of a withholding tax) depending upon the type of income concerned and the provisions of the Article dealing with such income.

6. These secondary adjustments, which would be required to establish the situation exactly as it would have been if transactions had been at arm's length, depend on the facts of the individual case. It should be noted that nothing in paragraph 2 prevents such secondary adjustments from being made where they are permitted under the domestic laws of Contracting States.

7. The paragraph also leaves open the question whether there should be a period of time after the expiration of which State B would not be obliged to make an appropriate adjustment to the profits of enterprise Y following an upward revision of the profits of enterprise X in State A. Some States consider that State B's commitment should be open-ended – in other words, that however many years State A goes back to revise assessments, enterprise Y should in equity be assured of an appropriate adjustment in State B. Other States consider that an open-ended commitment of this sort is unreasonable as a matter of practical administration. In the circumstances, therefore, this problem has not been dealt with in the text of the Article; but Contracting States are left free in bilateral conventions to include, if they wish, provisions dealing with the length of time during which State B is to be under obligation to make an appropriate adjustment.

8. If there is a dispute between the interested parties over the character and amount of the appropriate adjustment, the matter will be dealt with in the same way as any other question of fact; if necessary the competent authorities may consult each other.

Observations on the Commentary

9.-11. [Omitted]

Commentary on Article 10 concerning the Taxation of Dividends

I. PRELIMINARY REMARKS

1. By 'dividends' is generally meant the distribution of profits to the shareholders by companies limited by shares,[1] limited partnerships with share capital,[2] limited liability companies[3] or other joint stock companies.[4] Under the laws of the OECD Member countries, such joint stock companies are legal entities with a separate juridical personality distinct from all their shareholders. On this point, they differ from

1. *'Sociétés anonymes'*.
2. *'Sociétés en commandite par actions'*.
3. *'Sociétés à responsabilité limitée'*.
4. *'Sociétés de capitaux'*.

partnerships insofar as the latter do not have juridical personality in most countries.

2. The profits of a business carried on by a partnership are the partners' profits derived from their own exertions; for them they are industrial or commercial profits. So the partner is ordinarily taxed personally on his share of the partnership capital and partnership profits.

3. The position is different for the shareholder; he is not a trader and the company's profits are not his; so they cannot be attributed to him. He is personally taxable only on those profits which are distributed by the company (apart from the provisions in certain countries' laws relating to the taxation of undistributed profits in special cases). From the shareholders' standpoint, dividends are income from the capital which they have made available to the company as its shareholders.

II. COMMENTARY ON THE PROVISIONS OF THE ARTICLE

Paragraph 1

4. Paragraph I does not prescribe the principle of taxation of dividends either exclusively in the State of the beneficiary's residence or exclusively in the State of which the company paying the dividends is a resident.

5. Taxation of dividends exclusively in the State of source is not acceptable as a general rule. Furthermore, there are some States which do not have taxation of dividends at the source, while as a general rule, all the States tax residents in respect of dividends they receive from non-resident companies.

6. On the other hand, taxation of dividends exclusively in the State of the beneficiary's residence is not feasible as a general rule. It would be more in keeping with the nature of dividends, which are investment income, but it would be unrealistic to suppose that there is any prospect of it being agreed that all taxation of dividends at the source should be relinquished.

7. For this reason, paragraph 1 states simply that dividends may be taxed in the State of the beneficiary's residence. The term 'paid' has a very wide meaning, since the concept of payment means the fulfilment of the obligation to put funds at the disposal of the shareholder in the manner required by contract or by custom.

8. The Article deals only with dividends paid by a company which is a resident of a Contracting State to a resident of the other Contracting State. It does not, therefore, apply to dividends paid by a company which is a resident of a third State or to dividends paid by a company which is a resident of a Contracting State which are attributable to a permanent establishment which an enterprise of that State has in the other Contracting State (for these cases, cf. paragraphs 4 to 6 of the Commentary on Article 21).

Paragraph 2

9. Paragraph 2 reserves a right to tax to the State of source of the dividends, i.e. to the State of which the company paying the dividends is a resident; this right to tax, however, is limited considerably. The rate of tax is limited to 15 per cent, which appears to be a reasonable maximum figure. A higher rate could hardly be justified since the State of source can already tax the company's profits.

10. On the other hand, a lower rate (5 per cent) is expressly provided in respect of dividends paid by a subsidiary company to its parent company. If a company of one of the States owns directly a holding of at least 25 per cent in a company of the other State, it is reasonable that payments of profits by the subsidiary to the foreign parent company should be taxed less heavily to avoid recurrent taxation and to facilitate international investment. The realisation of this intention depends on the fiscal treatment of the dividends in the State of which the parent company is a resident (cf. paragraphs 49 to 54 of the Commentary on Articles 23A and 23B).

11. If a partnership is treated as a body corporate under the domestic laws applying to it, the two Contracting States may agree to modify sub-paragraph *a.* of paragraph 2 in a way to give the benefits of the reduced rate provided for parent companies also to such partnership.

12. Under paragraph 2, the limitation of tax in the State of source is not available when an intermediary, such as an agent or nominee, is interposed between the beneficiary and the payer, unless the beneficial owner is a resident of the other Contracting State. States which wish to make this more explicit are free to do so during bilateral negotiations.

13. The tax rates fixed by the Article for the tax in the State of source are maximum rates. The States may agree, in bilateral negotiations, on lower rates or even on taxation exclusively in the State of the beneficiary's residence. The reduction of rates provided for in paragraph 2 refers solely to the taxation of dividends and not to the taxation of the profits of the company paying the dividends.

14. The two Contracting States may also, during bilateral negotiations, agree to a holding percentage lower than that fixed in the Article. A lower percentage is, for instance, justified in cases where the State of residence of the parent company, in accordance with its domestic law, grants exemption to such a company for dividends derived from a holding of less than 25 per cent in a non-resident subsidiary.

15. In sub-paragraph *a.* of paragraph 2, the term 'capital' is used in relation to the taxation treatment of dividends, i.e. distributions of profits to shareholders. The use of this term in this context implies that, for the purposes of sub-paragraph *a.*, it should be used in the sense in which it is used for the purposes of distribution to the shareholder (in the particular case, the parent company).

a. As a general rule, therefore, the term 'capital' in sub-paragraph *a.* should be understood as it is understood in company law. Other elements, in particular the reserves, are not to be taken into account.

b. Capital, as understood in company law, should be indicated in terms of par value of all shares which in the majority of cases will be shown as capital in the company's balance sheet.

c. No account need be taken of differences due to the different classes of shares issued (ordinary shares, preference shares, plural voting shares, non-voting shares, bearer shares, registered shares, etc.), as such differences relate more to the nature of the shareholder's right than to the extent of his ownership of the capital.

d. When a loan or other contribution to the company does not, strictly speaking, come as capital under company law but when on the basis of internal law or practice ('thin capitalisation', or assimilation of a loan to share capital), the income derived in respect thereof is treated as dividend under Article 10, the value of such loan or contribution is also to be taken as 'capital' within the meaning of sub-paragraph *a.*

e. In the case of bodies which do not have a capital within the meaning of company law, capital for the purpose of sub-paragraph *a.* is to be taken as meaning the total of all contributions to the body which are taken into account for the purpose of distributing profits.

In bilateral negotiations, Contracting States may depart from the criterion of 'capital' used in sub-paragraph *a.* of paragraph 2 and use instead the criterion of 'voting power'.

16. Sub-paragraph *a.* of paragraph 2 does not require that the company receiving the dividends must have owned at least 25 per cent of the capital for a relatively long time before the date of the distribution. This means that all that counts regarding the holding is the situation prevailing at the time material for the coming into existence of the liability to the tax to which paragraph 2 applies, i.e. in most cases the situation existing at the time when the dividends become legally available to the shareholders. The primary reason for this resides in the desire to have a provision which is applicable as broadly as possible. To require the parent company to have possessed the minimum holding for a certain time before the distribution of the profits could involve extensive inquiries. Internal laws of certain OECD Member countries provide for a minimum period during which the recipient company must have held the shares to qualify for exemption or relief in respect of dividends received. In view of this, Contracting States may include a similar condition in their conventions.

17. The reduction envisaged in sub-paragraph *a.* of paragraph 2 should not be granted in cases of abuse of this provision, for example, where a company with a holding of less than 25 per cent has, shortly before the dividends become payable, increased its holding primarily for the purpose of securing the benefits of the above-mentioned provision, or otherwise, where the qualifying holding was arranged primarily in order to obtain the reduction. To counteract such manoeuvres Contracting States may find it appropriate to add to sub-paragraph *a.* a provision along the following lines:

> 'provided that this holding was not acquired primarily for the purpose of taking advantage of this provision'.

18. Paragraph 2 lays down nothing about the mode of taxation in the State of source. It therefore leaves that State free to apply its own laws and, in particular, to levy the tax either by deduction at source or by individual assessment.

19. The paragraph does not settle procedural questions. Each State should be able to use the procedure provided in its own laws. It can either forthwith limit its tax to the rates given in the Article or tax in full and make a refund.

20. It does not specify whether or not the relief in the State of source should be conditional upon the dividends being subject to tax in the State of residence. This question can be settled by bilateral negotiations.

21. The Article contains no provisions as to how the State of the beneficiary's residence should make allowance for the taxation in the State of source of the dividends. This question is dealt with in Articles 23A and 23B.

22. Attention is drawn generally to the following case: the beneficial owner of the dividends arising in a Contracting State is a company resident of the other Contracting State; all or part of its capital is held by shareholders resident outside that other State; its practice is not to distribute its profits in the form of dividends; and it enjoys preferential taxation treatment (private investment company, base company). The question may arise whether in the case of such a company it is justifiable to allow in the State of source of the dividends the limitation of tax which is provided in paragraph 2. It may be appropriate, when bilateral negotiations are being conducted, to agree upon special exceptions to the taxing rule laid down in this Article, in order to define the treatment applicable to such companies.

Paragraph 3

23. In view of the great differences between the laws of OECD Member countries, it is impossible to define 'dividends' fully and exhaustively. Consequently, the definition merely mentions examples which are to be found in the majority of the Member countries' laws and which, in any case, are not treated differently in them. The enumeration is followed up by a general formula. In the course of the revision of the 1963 Draft Convention, a thorough study has been undertaken to find a solution which does not refer to domestic laws. This study has led to the conclusion that, in view of the still remaining dissimilarities between Member countries in the field of company law and taxation law, it does not yet appear to be possible to work out a definition of the concept of dividends that would be independent of domestic laws. It is open to the Contracting States, through bilateral negotiations, to make allowance for peculiarities of their laws and to agree to bring under the definition of 'dividends' other payments by companies falling under the Article.

24. The notion of dividends basically concerns distributions by companies within the meaning of sub-paragraph *b.* of paragraph 1 of Article 3. Therefore the definition relates, in the first instance, to dis-

tributions of profits the title to which is constituted by shares, that is holdings in a company limited by shares (joint stock company). The definition assimilates to shares all securities issued by companies which carry a right to participate in the companies' profits without being debt-claims; such are, for example, 'jouissance' shares or 'jouissance' rights, founders' shares or other rights participating in profits. In bilateral conventions, of course, this enumeration may be adapted to the legal situation in the Contracting States concerned. This may be necessary in particular, as regards income from 'jouissance' shares and founders' shares. On the other hand, debt-claims participating in profits do not come into this category (cf. paragraph 18 of the commentary on Article 11); likewise interest on convertible debentures is not a dividend.

25. The laws of many of the States put participations in a '*Societé à responsabilité limitée*' (limited liability company) on the same footing as shares. Likewise, distributions of profits by co-operative societies are generally regarded as dividends.

26. Distributions of profits by partnerships are not dividends within the meaning of the definition, unless the partnerships are subject, in the State where their place of effective management is situated, to a fiscal treatment substantially similar to that applied to companies limited by shares (for instance, in Belgium, Portugal and Spain, also in France as regards distributions to '*commanditaires*' in the '*sociétés en commandite simple*') . On the other hand, clarification in bilateral conventions may be necessary in cases where the taxation law of a Contracting State gives the owner of holdings in a company a right to opt, under certain conditions, for being taxed as a partner of a partnership, or, vice versa, gives the partner of a partnership the right to opt for taxation as the owner of holdings in a company.

27. Payments regarded as dividends may include not only distributions of profits decided by annual general meetings of shareholders, but also other benefits in money or money's worth, such as bonus shares, bonuses, profits on a liquidation and disguised distributions of profits. The reliefs provided in the Article apply so long as the State of which the paying company is a resident taxes such benefits as dividends. It is immaterial whether any such benefits are paid out of current profits made by the company or are derived, for example, from reserves, i.e. profits of previous financial years. Normally, distributions by a company which have the effect of reducing the membership rights, for instance, payments constituting a reimbursement of capital in any form whatever are not regarded as dividends.

28. The benefits to which a holding in a company confer entitlement are, as a general rule, available solely to the shareholders themselves. Should, however, certain of such benefits be made available to persons who are not shareholders within the meaning of company law, they may constitute dividends if:

- the legal relations between such persons and the company are assimilated to a holding in a company ('concealed holdings') and
- the persons receiving such benefits are closely connected with a shareholder; this is the case, for example, where the recipient is a

relative of the shareholder or is a company belonging to the same group as the company owning the shares.

29. When the shareholder and the person receiving such benefits are residents of two different States with which the State of source has concluded conventions, differences of views may arise as to which of these conventions is applicable. A similar problem may arise when the State of source has concluded a convention with one of the States but not with the other. This, however, is a conflict which may affect other types of income, and the solution to it can be found only through an arrangement under the mutual agreement procedure.

Paragraph 4

30. Certain States consider that dividends, interest and royalties arising from sources in their territory and payable to individuals or legal persons who are residents of other States fall outside the scope of the arrangement made to prevent them from being taxed both in the State of source and in the State of the beneficiary's residence when the beneficiary has a permanent establishment in the former State. Paragraph 4 is not based on such a conception which is sometimes referred to as 'the force of attraction of the permanent establishment'. It does not stipulate that dividends flowing to a resident of a Contracting State from a source situated in the other State must, by a kind of legal presumption, or fiction even, be related to a permanent establishment which that resident may have in the latter State, so that the said State would not be obliged to limit its taxation in such a case. The paragraph merely provides that in the State of source the dividends are taxable as part of the profits of the permanent establishment there owned by the beneficiary which is a resident of the other State, if they are paid in respect of holdings forming part of the assets of the permanent establishment or otherwise effectively connected with that establishment. In that case, paragraph 4 relieves the State of source of the dividends from any limitations under the Article. The foregoing explanations accord with those in the Commentary on Article 7.

31. The rules set out above apply where the beneficiary of the dividends has in the other Contracting State, for the purpose of performing any of the kinds of independent personal services mentioned in Article 14, a fixed base with which the holding in respect of which the dividends are paid is effectively connected.

Paragraph 5

32. The Article deals only with dividends paid by a company which is a resident of a Contracting State to a resident of the other State. Certain States, however, tax not only dividends paid by companies resident therein – but even distributions by non-resident companies of profits arising within their territory. Each State, of course, is entitled to tax profits arising in its territory which are made by non-resident companies, to the extent provided in the Convention (in particular in Article 7). The shareholders of such companies should not be taxed as

well at any rate, unless they are residents of the State and so naturally subject to its fiscal sovereignty.

33. Paragraph 5 rules out the extra-territorial taxation of dividends, i.e. the practice by which States tax dividends distributed by a non-resident company solely because the corporate profits from which the distributions are made originated in their territory (for example, realised through a permanent establishment situated therein). There is, of course, no question of extra-territorial taxation when the country of source of the corporate profits taxes the dividends because they are paid to a shareholder who is a resident of that State or to a permanent establishment or fixed base situated in that State.

34. Moreover, it can be argued that such a provision does not aim at, or cannot result in, preventing a State from subjecting the dividends to a withholding tax when distributed by foreign companies if they are cashed in its territory. Indeed, in such a case, the criterion for tax liability is the fact of the payment of the dividends, and not the origin of the corporate profits allotted for distribution. But if the person cashing the dividends in a Contracting State is a resident of the other Contracting State (of which the distributing company is a resident), he may under Article 21 obtain exemption from, or refund of, the withholding tax of the first-mentioned State. Similarly, if the beneficiary of the dividends is a resident of a third State which had concluded a double taxation convention with the State where the dividends are cashed, he may, under Article 21 of that convention, obtain exemption from, or refund of, the withholding tax of the last-mentioned State.

35. Paragraph 5 further provides that non-resident companies are not to be subjected to special taxes on undistributed profits.

III. EFFECTS OF SPECIAL FEATURES OF THE DOMESTIC TAX LAWS OF CERTAIN COUNTRIES

36.-79. [Omitted]

Paragraph 5

80.-82. [Omitted]

83. The *United States* believes that the text should clarify that the prohibition of paragraph 5 will apply regardless of whether the company derives profits or income from the other Contracting State.

84. The *United States* reserves the right to impose its accumulated earnings tax and personal holding company tax, to prevent tax avoidance.

85. The *United States* reserves the right to apply its dividend withholding tax to dividends paid by a company which is incorporated outside the United States, if at least one-half of the company's income consists of profits attributable to a permanent establishment in the United States.

Commentary on Article 11 concerning the Taxation of Interest

I. PRELIMINARY REMARKS

1. 'Interest' is generally taken to mean remuneration on money lent, being remuneration coming within the category of 'income from movable capital' (*revenus de capitaux mobiliers*). Unlike dividends, interest does not suffer economic double taxation, that is, it is not taxed both in the hands of the debtor and in the hands of the creditor. Unless it is provided to the contrary by the contract, payment of the tax charged on interest falls on the recipient. If it happens that the debtor undertakes to bear any tax chargeable at the source, this is as though he had agreed to pay his creditor additional interest corresponding to such tax.

2. But, like dividends, interest on bonds or debentures or loans usually attracts tax charged by deduction at the source when the interest is paid. This method is, in fact, commonly used for practical reasons, as the tax charged at the source can constitute an advance of the tax payable by the recipient in respect of his total income or profits. If in such a case the recipient is a resident of the country which practises deduction at the source, any double taxation he suffers is remedied by internal measures. But the position is different if he is a resident of another country: he is then liable to be taxed twice on the interest, first by the State of source and then by the State of which he is a resident. It is clear that his double charge of tax can reduce considerably the interest on the money lent and so hamper the movement of capital and the development of international investment.

3. A formula reserving the exclusive taxation of interest to one State, whether the State of the beneficiary's residence or the State of source, could not be sure of receiving general approval. Therefore a compromise solution was adopted. It provides that interest may be taxed in the State of residence – but leaves to the State of source the right to impose a tax if its laws so provide, it being implicit in this right that the State of source is free to give up all taxation on interest paid to non-residents. Its exercise of this right will however be limited by a ceiling which its tax cannot exceed but, it goes without saying, the Contracting States can agree to adopt an even lower rate of taxation in the State of source. The sacrifice that the latter would accept in such conditions will be matched by a relief to be given by the State of residence, in order to take into an account the tax levied in the State of source (cf. Article 23A or 23B).

4. Certain countries do not allow interest paid to be deducted for the purposes of the payer's tax unless the recipient also resides in the same State or is taxable in that State. Otherwise they forbid the deduction. The question whether the deduction should also be allowed in cases where the interest is paid by a resident of a Contracting State to a resident of the other State, is dealt with in paragraph 5 of Article 24.

II. COMMENTARY ON THE PROVISIONS OF THE ARTICLE

Paragraph 1

5. Paragraph 1 lays down the principle that interest arising in a Contracting State and paid to a resident of the other Contracting State may be taxed in the latter. In doing so, it does not stipulate an exclusive right to tax in favour of the State of residence. The term 'paid' has a very wide meaning, since the concept of payment means the fulfilment of the obligation to put funds at the disposal of the creditor in the manner required by contract or by custom.

6. The Article deals only with interest arising in a Contracting State and paid to a resident of the other Contracting State. It does not, therefore, apply to interest arising in a third State or to interest arising in a Contracting State which is attributable to a permanent establishment which an enterprise of that State has in the other Contracting State (for these cases, cf. paragraphs 4 to 6 of the Commentary on Article 21).

Paragraph 2

7. Paragraph 2 reserves a right to tax interest to the State in which the interest arises, but it limits the exercise of that right by determining a ceiling for the tax, which may not exceed 10 per cent. This rate may be considered a reasonable maximum bearing in mind that the State of source is already entitled to tax profits or income produced on its territory by investments financed out of borrowed capital. The Contracting States may agree in bilateral negotiations upon a lower tax or even on exclusive taxation in the State of the beneficiary's residence.

8. Under paragraph 2, the limitation of tax in the State of source is not available when an intermediary, such as an agent or nominee, is interposed between the beneficiary and the payer, unless the beneficial owner is a resident of the other Contracting State. States which wish to make this more explicit are free to do so during bilateral negotiations.

9. The paragraph lays down nothing about the mode of taxation in the State of source. It therefore leaves that State free to apply its own laws and, in particular, to levy the tax either by deduction at source or by individual assessment.

10. It does not specify whether or not the relief in the State of source should be conditional upon the interest being subject to tax in the State of residence. This question can be settled by bilateral negotiations.

11. The Article contains no provisions as to how the State of the beneficiary's residence should make allowance for the taxation in the State of source of the interest. This question is dealt with in Articles 23A and 23B.

12. Attention is drawn generally to the following case: the beneficial owner of interest arising in a Contracting State is a company resident in the other Contracting State; all or part of its capital is held by shareholders resident outside that other State; its practice is not to distribute its profits in the form of dividends; and it enjoys preferential taxation

treatment (private investment company, base company). The question may arise whether, in the case of such a company, it is justifiable to allow in the State of source of the interest the limitation of tax which is provided in paragraph 2. It may be appropriate, when bilateral negotiations are being conducted, to agree upon special exceptions to the taxing rule laid down in this Article, in order to define the treatment applicable to such companies.

13. It should, however, be pointed out that the solution adopted, given the combined effect of the right to tax accorded to the State of source and the allowance to be made for the tax levied there against that due in the State of residence, could, in certain cases result in maintaining partial double taxation and lead to adverse economic consequences. In fact, when the beneficiary of the interest has himself had to borrow in order to finance the operation which earns him interest the profit he will realise by way of interest will be much smaller than the nominal amount of interest he receives; if the interest he pays and that which he receives balance, there will be no profit at all. In such a case, the allowance to be made under paragraph 2 of Article 23A, or paragraph 1 of Article 23B, raises a difficult and sometimes insoluble problem in view of the fact that the tax levied in the State where the interest arises is calculated on the gross amount thereof, whereas the same interest is reflected in the beneficiary's business results at its net amount only. The result of this is that part, or sometimes even the whole amount, of the tax levied in the State where the interest arises cannot be allowed as a credit in the beneficiary's State of residence and so constitutes an excess charge for the beneficiary, who, to that extent, suffers double taxation. Moreover, the latter, in order to avoid the disadvantage just mentioned, will tend to increase the rate of interest he charges his debtor, whose financial burden would then be increased to a corresponding extent. Thus in certain cases the practice of taxation at the source can constitute an obstacle to international trade. Furthermore, if the payer of the interest happens to be the State itself, a public sector institution, or an enterprise guaranteed by the State, the end result may well be that the tax levied at source is actually borne by the Treasury of the debtor's State, which latter thus derived no real benefit from its own taxation.

14. The disadvantages just mentioned arise in business, particularly with the sale on credit of equipment, other commercial credit sales, and loans granted by banks. The supplier in such cases very often merely passes on to the customer, without any additional charge, the price he will himself have had to pay to a bank or an export finance agency to finance the credit; similarly, the banker generally finances the loan which he grants with funds lent to his bank and, in particular, funds accepted by him on deposit. In the case especially of the person selling equipment on credit, the interest is more an element of the selling price than income from invested capital.

15. If two Contracting States, in order to eliminate all risks of double taxation, should desire to avoid the imposition of a tax in the State of source on interest arising from the above-mentioned categories

of debts, their common intention can be expressed by an additional paragraph which would follow paragraph 2 of the Article, and which might be in the following terms:

'3. Notwithstanding the provisions of paragraph 2, any such interest as is mentioned in paragraph 1 shall be taxable only in the Contracting State of which the recipient is a resident, if such recipient is the beneficial owner of the interest and if such interest is paid:

a. in connection with the sale on credit of any industrial, commercial or scientific equipment,

b. in connection with the sale on credit of any merchandise by one enterprise to another enterprise, or

c. on any loan of whatever kind granted by a bank.'

16. As regards, more particularly, the types of credit sale referred to in subparagraph *a.* of the text suggested above, they comprise not only sales of complete units, but also sales of separate components thereof. Furthermore, as regards credit sales of the types referred to in sub-paragraphs *a.* and *b.* of the suggested text, it is immaterial whether the interest is stipulated separately and as additional to the sale price, or is included from the outset in the price payable by instalments.

17. Contracting States may add to the categories of interest enumerated in the text suggested in paragraph 15 above, other categories in regard to which the imposition of a tax in the State of source might appear to them to be undesirable. They may also agree that the exclusion of a right to tax in the State of source shall be limited to certain of the categories of interest mentioned.

Paragraph 3

18. Paragraph 3 specifies the meaning to be attached to the term 'interest' for the application of the taxation treatment defined by the Article. The term designates, in general, income from debt-claims of every kind, whether or not secured by mortgage and whether or not carrying a right to participate in profits. The term 'debt-claims of every kind' obviously embraces cash deposits and security in the form of money, as well as Government securities, and bonds and debentures, although the three latter are specially mentioned because of their importance and of certain peculiarities that they may present. It is recognised, on the one hand, that mortgage interest comes within the category of income from movable capital (*'revenus de capitaux mobiliers'*), even though certain countries assimilate it to income from immovable property. On the other hand, debt-claims, and bonds and debentures in particular, which carry a right to participate in the debtor's profits are nonetheless regarded as loans if the contract by its general character clearly evidences a loan at interest. In the contrary case, where the participation in profits rests upon a provision of funds that is subject to the hazards of the enterprise's business, the operation is not in the nature of a loan and Article 11 does not apply. As regards, more particularly, Government securities, and bonds and debentures, the text specifies that premiums or prizes attaching thereto constitute interest. Generally speaking, what constitutes interest yielded by a loan

security, and may properly be taxed as such in the State of source, is all that the institution issuing the loan pays over and above the amount paid by the subscriber, that is to say, the interest accruing plus any premium paid at redemption or at issue. It follows that when a bond or debenture has been issued at a premium, the excess of the amount paid by the subscriber over that repaid to him may constitute negative interest which should be deducted from the interest that is taxable. On the other hand, any profit or loss which a holder of such a security realises by the sale thereof to another person does not enter into the concept of interest. Such profit or loss may, depending on the case, constitute either a business profit or a loss, a capital gain or a loss, or income falling under Article 21.

19. Moreover, the definition of interest in the first sentence of paragraph 3 is, in principle, exhaustive. It has seemed preferable not to include a subsidiary reference to domestic laws in the text; this is justified by the following considerations:

a. the definition covers practically all the kinds of income which are regarded as interest in the various domestic laws;

b. the formula employed offers greater security from the legal point of view and ensures that conventions would be unaffected by future changes in any country's domestic laws;

c. in the Model Convention references to domestic laws should as far as possible be avoided.

It nevertheless remains understood that in a bilateral convention two Contracting States may widen the formula employed so as to include in it any income which is taxed as interest under either of their domestic laws but which is not covered by the definition and in these circumstances may find it preferable to make reference to their domestic laws.

20. The second sentence of paragraph 3 excludes from the definition of interest penalty charges for late payment but Contracting States are free to omit this sentence and treat penalty charges as interest in their bilateral conventions. Penalty charges, which may be payable under the contract, or by customs or by virtue of a judgment, consist either of payments calculated pro rata temporis or else of fixed sums; in certain cases they may combine both forms of payment. Even if they are determined pro rata temporis they constitute not so much income from capital as a special form of compensation for the loss suffered by the creditor through the debtor's delay in meeting his obligations. Moreover, considerations of legal security and practical convenience make it advisable to place all penalty charges of this kind, in whatever form they be paid, on the same footing for the purposes of their taxation treatment. On the other hand, two Contracting States may exclude from the application of Article 11 any kinds of interest which they intend to be treated as dividends.

21. Finally, the question arises whether annuities ought to be assimilated to interest; it is considered that they ought not to be. On the one hand, annuities granted in consideration of past employment are referred to in Article 18 and are subject to the rules governing pensions. On the other hand, although it is true that instalments of pur-

chased annuities include an interest element on the purchase capital as well as return of capital, such instalments thus constituting *'fruits civils'* which accrue from day to day, it would be difficult for many countries to make a distinction between the element representing income from capital and the element representing a return of capital in order merely to tax the income element under the same category as income from movable capital. Taxation laws often contain special provisions classifying annuities in the category of salaries, wages and pensions, and taxing them accordingly.

Paragraph 4

22. Certain States consider that dividends, interest and royalties arising from sources in their territory and payable to individuals or legal persons who are residents of other States fall outside the scope of the arrangement made to prevent them from being taxed both in the State of source and in the State of the beneficiary's residence when the beneficiary has a permanent establishment in the former State. Paragraph 4 is not based on such a conception which is sometimes referred to as the force of attraction of the permanent establishment. It does not stipulate that interest arising to a resident of a Contracting State from a source situated in the other State must, by a kind of legal presumption, or fiction even, be related to a permanent establishment which that resident may have in the latter State, so that the said State would not be obliged to limit its taxation in such a case. The paragraph merely provides that in the State of source the interest is taxable as part of the profits of the permanent establishment there owned by the beneficiary which is a resident in the other State, if it is paid in respect of debt-claims forming part of the assets of the permanent establishment or otherwise effectively connected with that establishment. In that case, paragraph 4 relieves the State of source of the interest from any limitation under the Article. The foregoing explanations accord with those in the Commentary on Article 7.

23. The rules set out above also apply where the beneficiary of the interest has in the other Contracting State, for the purpose of performing any of the kinds of independent personal services mentioned in Article 14, a fixed base with which the debt-claim in respect of which the interest is paid is effectively connected.

Paragraph 5

24. This paragraph lays down the principle that the State of source of the interest is the State of which the payer of the interest is a resident, who may, moreover, be that State itself or one of its political subdivisions or local authorities. It provides, however, for an exception to this rule in the case of interest-bearing loans which have an obvious economic link with a permanent establishment owned in the other Contracting State by the payer of the interest. If the loan was contracted for the requirements of that establishment and the interest is borne by the latter, the paragraph determines that the source of the interest is in the Contracting State in which the permanent establishment is

situated, leaving aside the place of residence of the owner of the permanent establishment, even when he resides in a third State.

25. In the absence of an economic link between the loan on which the interest arises and the permanent establishment, the State where the latter is situated cannot on that account be regarded as the State where the interest arises; it is not entitled to tax such interest, not even within the limits of a 'taxable quota' proportional to the importance of the permanent establishment. Such a practice would be incompatible with paragraph 5. Moreover, any departure from the rule fixed in the first sentence of paragraph 5 is justified only where the economic link between the loan and the permanent establishment is sufficiently clear-cut. In this connection, a number of possible cases may be distinguished:

a. The management of the permanent establishment has contracted a loan which it uses for the specific requirements of the permanent establishment; it shows it among its liabilities and pays the interest thereon directly to the creditor.

b. The head office of the enterprise has contracted a loan the proceeds of which are used solely for the purposes of a permanent establishment situated in another country. The interest is serviced by the head office but is ultimately borne by the permanent establishment.

c. The loan is contracted by the head office of the enterprise and its proceeds are used for several permanent establishments situated in different countries.

In cases *a.* and *b.* the conditions laid down in the second sentence of paragraph 5 are fulfilled, and the State where the permanent establishment is situated is to be regarded as the State where the interest arises. Case *c.*, however, falls outside the provisions of paragraph 5, the text of which precludes the attribution of more than one source to the same loan. Such a solution, moreover, would give rise to considerable administrative complications and make it impossible for lenders to calculate in advance the taxation that interest would attract. It is, however, open to two Contracting States to restrict the application of the final provision in paragraph 5 to case *a.* or to extend it to case *c.*

26. Paragraph 5 provides no solution for the case, which it excludes from its provisions, where both the beneficiary and the payer are indeed residents of the Contracting States, but the loan was borrowed for the requirements of a permanent establishment owned by the payer in a third State and the interest is borne by that establishment. As paragraph 5 now stands, therefore, only its first sentence will apply in such a case. The interest will be deemed to arise in the Contracting State of which the payer is a resident and not in the third State in whose territory is situated the permanent establishment for the account of which the loan was effected and by which the interest is payable. Thus the interest will be taxed both in the Contracting State of which the payer is a resident and in the Contracting State of which the beneficiary is a resident. But, although double taxation will be avoided between these two States by the arrangements provided in the Article, it will not be avoided between them and the third State if the latter

taxes the interest on the loan at the source when it is borne by the permanent establishment in its territory.

27. It has not, however, been considered possible to refer to such a case in a bilateral convention and provide for it a solution consisting, for example, in obliging the Contracting State of the payer's residence to relinquish its tax at the source in favour of the third State in which is situated the permanent establishment for the account of which the loan was effected and by which the interest is borne. The risk of double taxation just referred to can only be fully avoided through a bilateral convention containing a similar provision to that in paragraph 5, between the Contracting State of which the payer of the interest is a resident and the third State in which the permanent establishment paying the interest is situated, or through a multilateral convention containing such a provision.

28. Moreover, in the case – not settled in paragraph 5 – where whichever of the two Contracting States is that of the payer's residence and the third State in which is situated the permanent establishment for the account of which the loan is effected and by which the interest is borne, together claim the right to tax the interest at the source, there would be nothing to prevent those two States – together with, where appropriate, the State of the beneficiary's residence – from concerting measures to avoid the double taxation that would result from such claims. The proper remedy, it must be said again, would be the establishment between these different States of bilateral conventions, or a multilateral convention, containing a provision similar to that in paragraph 5. Another solution would be for two Contracting States to word the second sentence of paragraph 5 in the following way:

> 'Where, however, the person paying the interest, whether he is a resident of a Contracting State or not, has in a State other than that of which he is a resident a permanent establishment or a fixed base in connection with which the indebtedness on which the interest is paid was incurred, and such interest is borne by such permanent establishment or fixed base, then such interest shall be deemed to arise in the State in which the permanent establishment or fixed base is situated.'

29. If two Contracting States agree in bilateral negotiations to reserve to the State where the beneficiary of the income resides the exclusive right to tax such income, then ipso facto there is no value in inserting in the convention which fixes their relations that provision in paragraph 5 which defines the State of source of such income. But it is equally obvious that double taxation would not be fully avoided in such a case if the payer of the interest owned, in a third State which charged its tax at the source on the interest, a permanent establishment for the account of which the loan had been borrowed and which bore the interest payable on it. The case would then be just the same as is contemplated in paragraphs 26 to 28 above.

Paragraph 6

30. The purpose of this paragraph is to restrict the operation of the provisions concerning the taxation of interest in cases where, by reason of a special relationship between the payer and the beneficial owner or between both of them and some other person, the amount of the interest paid exceeds the amount which would have been agreed upon by the payer and the beneficial owner had they stipulated at arm's length. It provides that in such a case the provisions of the Article apply only to that last-mentioned amount and that the excess part of the interest shall remain taxable according to the laws of the two Contracting States, due regard being had to the other provisions of the Convention.

31. It is clear from the text that for this clause to apply the interest held excessive must be due to a special relationship between the payer and the beneficial owner or between either of them and some other person. There may be cited as examples cases where interest is paid to an individual or legal person who directly or indirectly controls the payer, or who is directly or indirectly controlled by him or is subordinate to a group having common interest with him. These examples, moreover, are similar or analogous to the cases contemplated by Article 9.

32. On the other hand, the concept of special relationship also covers relationship by blood or marriage and, in general, any community of interests as distinct from the legal relationship giving rise to the payment of the interest.

33. With regard to the taxation treatment to be applied to the excess part of the interest, the exact nature of such excess will need to be ascertained according to the circumstances of each case, in order to determine the category of income in which it should be classified for the purposes of applying the provisions of the tax laws of the States concerned and the provisions of the Convention. If two Contracting States should have difficulty in determining the other provisions of the Convention applicable, as cases require, to the excess part of the interest, there would be nothing to prevent them from introducing additional clarifications in the last sentence of paragraph 6, as long as they do not alter its general purport.

34. Should the principles and rules of their respective laws oblige the two Contracting States to apply different Articles of the Convention for the purpose of taxing the excess, it will be necessary to resort to the mutual agreement procedure provided by the Convention in order to resolve the difficulty.

Observations on the Commentary

35. [Omitted]

36. The *United States* observes that the Article does not limit the taxation by internal law of interest not attributable to a United States permanent establishment in cases where 50 per cent of more of a non-resident payer's gross income is effectively connected with a trade or

business in the United States. The United States is willing, in appropriate situations, to limit such taxation by making appropriate modifications in the text of the Article.

Reservations on the Article:

Paragraph 2

37.-39. [Omitted]

Paragraph 4

40. [Omitted]

Commentary on Article 12 concerning the Taxation of Royalties

I. PRELIMINARY REMARKS

1. In principle, royalties in respect of licences to use patents and similar property and similar payments are income to the recipient from a letting. The letting may be granted in connection with an industrial or commercial enterprise (e.g. the use of literary copyright granted by a publisher) or an independent profession (e.g. use of a patent granted by the inventor) or quite independently of any activity of the grantor (e.g. use of a patent granted by the inventor's heirs).

2. Certain countries do not allow royalties paid to be deducted for the purposes of the payer's tax unless the recipient also resides in the same State or is taxable in that State. Otherwise they forbid the deduction. The question whether the deduction should also be allowed in cases where the royalties are paid by a resident of a Contracting State to a resident of the other State, is dealt with in paragraph 5 of Article 24.

II. COMMENTARY ON THE PROVISIONS OF THE ARTICLE

Paragraph 1

3. Paragraph 1 lays down the principle of exclusive taxation of royalties in the State of the beneficial owner's residence. The only exception to this principle is that made in the cases dealt with in paragraph 3.

4. Under paragraph 1, the exemption from tax in the State of source is not available when an intermediary, such as an agent or nominee, is interposed between the beneficiary and the payer, unless the beneficial owner is a resident of the other Contracting State. States which wish to make this more explicit are free to do so during bilateral negotiations. The term 'paid' has a very wide meaning, since the concept of payment means the fulfilment of the obligation to put funds at the

disposal of the creditor in the manner required by contract or by custom.

5. The Article deals only with royalties arising in a Contracting State and paid to a resident of the other Contracting State. It does not, therefore, apply to royalties arising in a third State as well as to royalties arising in a Contracting State which are attributable to a permanent establishment which an enterprise of that State has in the other Contracting State (for these cases cf. paragraphs 4 to 6 of the Commentary on Article 21).

6. The paragraph does not specify whether or not the exemption in the State of source should be conditional upon the royalties being subject to tax in the State of residence. This question can be settled by bilateral negotiations.

7. Attention is drawn generally to the following case: the beneficial owner of royalties arising in a Contracting State is a company resident in the other Contracting State; all or part of its capital is held by shareholders resident outside that other State; its practice is not to distribute its profits in the form of dividends; and it enjoys preferential taxation treatment (private investment company, base company). The question may arise whether in the case of such a company it is justifiable to allow in the State of source of the royalties the tax exemption which is provided in paragraph 1 . It may be appropriate, when bilateral negotiations are being conducted, to agree upon special exceptions to the taxing rule laid down in this Article, in order to define the treatment applicable to such companies.

Paragraph 2

8. Paragraph 2 contains a definition of the term 'royalties'. These relate, in general, to rights or property constituting the different forms of literary and artistic property, the elements of industrial and commercial property specified in the text and information concerning industrial, commercial or scientific experience. The definition applies to payments for the use of, or the entitlement to use, rights of the kind mentioned, whether or not they have been, or are required to be, registered in a public register. The definition covers both payments made under a licence and compensation which a person would be obliged to pay for fraudulently copying of infringing the right. As a guide, certain explanations are given below in order to define the scope of Article 12 in relation to that of other Articles of the Convention, as regards, in particular, equipment renting and the provision of information.

9. A clear distinction must be made between royalties paid for the use of equipment, which fall under Article 12, and payments constituting consideration for the sale of equipment, which may, depending on the case, fall under Articles 7, 13, 14 or 21. Some contracts combine the hire element and the sale element, so that it sometimes proves difficult to determine their true legal import. In the case of credit sale agreements and hire-purchase agreements, it seems clear that the sale element is the paramount use, because the parties have from the outset agreed that the ownership of the property in question shall be trans-

ferred from one to the other, although they have made this dependent upon the payment of the last instalment. Consequently, the instalments paid by the purchaser/hirer do not, in principle, constitute royalties. In the case, however, of lend-lease, and of leasing in particular, the sole, or at least the principal, purpose of the contract is normally that of hire, even if the hirer has the right thereunder to opt during its term to purchase the equipment in question outright. Article 12 therefore applies in the normal case to the rentals paid by the hirer, including all rentals paid by him up to the date he exercises any right to purchase.

10. Rents in respect of cinematograph films are also treated as royalties, whether such films are exhibited in cinemas or on the television. It may, however, be agreed through bilateral negotiations that rents in respect of cinematograph films shall be treated as industrial and commercial profits and, in consequence, subjected to the provisions of Articles 7 and 9.

11. The rules set out above in regard to rents in respect of cinematograph films could also be applied in regard to rentals derived by a shipping enterprise from the hire of its containers for the conveyance of goods on land after leaving the ship. It is considered, however, that where the hire of the containers is a supplementary or incidental activity of a transport company, the income should be treated as profits falling under Article 8.

12. In classifying as royalties payments received as consideration for information concerning industrial, commercial or scientific experience, paragraph 2 alludes to the concept of 'know-how'. Various specialist bodies and authors have formulated definitions of know-how which do not differ intrinsically. One such definition, given by the '*Association des Bureaux pour la Protection de la Propriété Industrielle*' (ANBPPI) states that 'know-how is all the undivulged technical information, whether capable of being patented or not, that is necessary for the industrial reproduction of a product or process, directly and under the same conditions; inasmuch as it is derived from experience, know-how represents what a manufacturer cannot know from mere examination of the product and mere knowledge of the progress of technique.' In the know-how contract, one of the parties agrees to impart to the other, so that he can use them for his own account, his special knowledge and experience which remain unrevealed to the public. It is recognised that the grantor is not required to play any part himself in the application of the formulae granted to the licensee and that he does not guarantee the result thereof. This type of contract thus differs from contracts for the provision of services, in which one of the parties undertakes to use the customary skills of his calling to execute work himself for the other party. Thus, payments obtained as consideration for after-sales service, for services rendered by a seller to the purchaser under a guarantee, for pure technical assistance, or for an opinion given by an engineer, an advocate or an accountant, do not constitute royalties within the meaning of paragraph 2. Such payments generally fall under Article 7 or Article 14. In business practice, contracts are encountered which cover both know-how and the provision of technical assistance. One

example, amongst others, of contracts of this kind is that of franchising, where the franchisor imparts his knowledge and experience to the franchisee and, in addition, provides him with varied technical assistance, which, in certain cases, is backed up with financial assistance and the supply of goods. The appropriate course to take with a mixed contract is, in principle, to break down, on the basis of the information contained in the contract or by means of a reasonable apportionment, the whole amount of the stipulated consideration according to the various parts of what is being provided under the contract, and then to apply to each part of it so determined the taxation treatment proper thereto. If, however, one part of what is being provided constitutes by far the principal purpose of the contract and the other parts stipulated therein are only of an ancillary and largely unimportant character, then it seems possible to apply to the whole amount of the consideration the treatment applicable to the principal part.

13. The suggestions made above regarding mixed contracts could also be applied in regard to certain performances by artists and, in particular, in regard to an orchestral concert given by a conductor or a recital given by a musician. The fee for the musical performance, together with that paid for any simultaneous radio broadcasting thereof, seems to fall to be treated under Article 17. Where, whether under the same contract or under a separate one, the musical performance is recorded and the artist has stipulated that he be paid royalties on the sale or public playing of the records, then so much of the payment received by him as consists of such royalties falls to be treated under Article 12.

14. It is further pointed out that variable or fixed payments for the working of mineral deposits, sources or other natural resources are governed by Article 6 and do not, therefore, fall within the present Article. If two Contracting States should have difficulty from the legal standpoint in applying this distinction in regard to consideration for the use of, or the right to use, equipment, they could add to the text of paragraph 2, after the words 'industrial, commercial or scientific equipment', the words 'not constituting immovable property referred to in Article 6'.

Paragraph 3

15. Certain States consider that dividends, interest and royalties arising from sources in their territory and payable to individuals or legal persons who are residents of other States fall outside the scope of the arrangement made to prevent them from being taxed both in the State of source and in the State of the beneficiary's residence when the beneficiary has a permanent establishment in the former State. Paragraph 3 is not based on such a conception which is sometimes referred to as 'the force of attraction of the permanent establishment'. It does not stipulate that royalties arising to a resident of a Contracting State from a source situated in the other State must, by a kind of legal presumption, or fiction even, be related to a permanent establishment which that resident may have in the latter State, so that the said State would not

be obliged to limit its taxation in such a case. The paragraph merely provides that in the State of source the royalties are taxable as part of the profits of the permanent establishment there owned by the beneficiary which is a resident of the other State, if they are paid in respect of rights or property forming part of the assets of the permanent establishment or otherwise effectively connected with that establishment. In that case, paragraph 3 relieves the State of source of the royalties from any limitations under the Article. The foregoing explanations accord with those in the Commentary on Article 7.

16. The rules set out above also apply where the beneficiary of the royalties has in the other Contracting State, for the purpose of performing any of the kinds of independent personal services mentioned in Article 14, a fixed base with which the right or property in respect of which the royalties are paid is effectively connected.

Paragraph 4

17. The purpose of this paragraph is to restrict the operation of the provisions concerning the taxation of royalties in cases where, by reason of a special relationship between the payer and the beneficial owner or between both of them and some other person, the amount of the royalties paid exceeds the amount which would have been agreed upon by the payer and the beneficial owner had they stipulated at arm's length. It provides that in such a case the provisions of the Article apply only to that last-mentioned amount and that the excess part of the royalty shall remain taxable according to the laws of the two Contracting States, due regard being had to the other provisions of the Convention.

18. It is clear from the text that for this clause to apply the payment held excessive must be due to a special relationship between the payer and the beneficial owner or between both of them and some other person. There may be cited as examples cases where royalties are paid to an individual or legal person who directly or indirectly controls the payer, or who is directly or indirectly controlled by him or is subordinate to a group having common interest with him. These examples, moreover, are similar or analogous to the cases contemplated by Article 9.

19. On the other hand, the concept of special relationship also covers relationship by blood or marriage and, in general, any community of interests as distinct from the legal relationship giving rise to the payment of the royalty.

20. With regard to the taxation treatment to be applied to the excess part of the royalty, the exact nature of such excess will need to be ascertained according to the circumstances of each case, in order to determine the category of income in which it should be classified for the purpose of applying the provisions of the tax laws of the States concerned and the provisions of the Convention. If two Contracting States should have difficulty in determining the other provisions of the Convention applicable, as cases required, to the excess part of the royalties, there would be nothing to prevent them from introducing

additional clarifications in the last sentence of paragraph 4, as long as they do not alter its general purport.

21. Should the principles and rules of their respective laws oblige the two Contracting States to apply different Articles of the Convention for the purpose of taxing the excess, it will be necessary to resort to the mutual agreement procedure provided by the Convention in order to resolve the difficulty.

Observation on the Commentary

22. [Omitted]

Reservations on the Article:

Paragraph 1
23.-29. [Omitted]

Paragraph 3
30. Italy reserves the right to subject royalties and profits from the alienation of rights or property giving rise to royalties to the taxes imposed by its law whenever the recipient thereof has a permanent establishment in Italy, even if the rights or property in respect of which the royalties are paid is not effectively connected with such permanent establishment.

31. [Omitted]

Commentary on Article 13 concerning the Taxation of Capital Gains

I. PRELIMINARY REMARKS

1. A comparison of the tax laws of the OECD Member countries shows that the taxation of capital gains varies considerably from country to country:
- in some countries capital gains are not deemed to be taxable income;
- in other countries capital gains accrued to an enterprise are taxed, but capital gains made by an individual outside the course of his trade or business are not taxed;
- even where capital gains made by an individual outside the course of his trade or business are taxed, such taxation often applies only in specified cases, e.g. profits from the sale of immovable property or speculative gains (where an asset was bought to be resold).

2. Moreover, the taxes on capital gains vary from country to country. In some OECD Member countries capital gains are taxed as ordinary income and therefore added to the income from other sources. This applies especially to the capital gains made by the alienation of assets of an enterprise. In a number of OECD Member countries, however,

capital gains are subjected to special taxes, such as taxes on profits from the alienation of immovable property, or general capital gains taxes, or taxes on capital appreciation (increment taxes). Such taxes are levied on each capital gain or on the sum of the capital gains accrued during a year, mostly at special rates, which do not take into account the other income (or losses) of the taxpayer. It does not seem necessary to describe all those taxes.

3. The Article does not deal with the above-mentioned questions. It is left to the domestic law of each Contracting State to decide whether capital gains should be taxed and, if they are taxable, how they are to be taxed. The Article can in no way be construed as giving a State the right to tax capital gains if such right is not provided for in its domestic law. The Article does not specify to what kind of tax it applies. It is understood that the Article must apply to all kinds of taxes levied by a Contracting State on capital gains. The wording of Article 2 is large enough to achieve this aim and to include also special taxes on capital gains.

II. COMMENTARY ON THE PROVISIONS OF THE ARTICLE

General Remarks

4. It is normal to give the right to tax capital gains on a property of a given kind to the State which under the Convention is entitled to tax both the property and the income derived therefrom. The right to tax a gain from the alienation of a business asset must be given to the same State without regard to the question whether such gain is a capital gain or a business profit. Accordingly, no distinction between capital gains and commercial profits is made nor is it necessary to have special provisions as to whether the Article on capital gains or Article 7 on the taxation of business profits should apply. It is however left to the domestic law of the taxing State to decide whether a tax on capital gains or on ordinary income must be levied. The Convention does not prejudge this question.

5. The Article does not give a detailed definition of capital gains. This is not necessary for the reasons mentioned above. The words 'alienation of property' are used to cover in particular capital gains resulting from the sale or exchange of property and also from a partial alienation, the expropriation, the transfer to a company in exchange for stock, the sale of a right, the gift and even the passing of property on death.

6. Most States taxing capital gains do so when an alienation of capital assets takes place. Some of them, however, tax only so-called realised capital gains. Under certain circumstances, though there is an alienation no realised capital gain is recognised for tax purposes (e.g. when the alienation proceeds are used for acquiring new assets). Whether or not there is a realisation has to be determined according to the applicable domestic tax law. No particular problems arise when

the State which has the right to tax does not exercise it at the time the alienation takes place.

7. As a rule, appreciation in value not associated with the alienation of a capital asset is not taxed, since, as long as the owner still holds the asset in question, the capital gain exists only on paper. There are, however, tax laws under which capital appreciation and revaluation of business assets are taxed even if there is no alienation.

8. Special circumstances may lead to the taxation of the capital appreciation of an asset that has not been alienated. This may be the case if the value of a capital asset has increased in such a manner that the owner proceeds to the revaluation of this asset in his books. Such revaluation of assets in the books may also occur in the case of a depreciation of the national currency. A number of States levy special taxes on such book profits, amounts put into reserve, an increase in the paid-up capital and other revaluations resulting from the adjustment of the book-value to the intrinsic value of a capital asset. These taxes on capital appreciation (increment taxes) are covered by the Convention according to Article 2.

9. Where capital appreciation and revaluation of business assets are taxed, the same principle should, as a rule, apply as in the case of the alienation of such assets. It has not been found necessary to mention such cases expressly in the Article or to lay down special rules. The provisions of the Article as well as those of Articles 6, 7 and 21, seem to be sufficient. As a rule, the right to tax is conferred by the above-mentioned provisions on the State of which the alienator is a resident, except that in the cases of immovable property or of movable property forming part of the business property of a permanent establishment or pertaining to a fixed base, the prior right to tax belongs to the State where such property is situated. Special attention must be drawn, however, to the cases dealt with in paragraphs 13 to 17 below.

10. In some States the transfer of an asset from a permanent establishment situated in the territory of such State to a permanent establishment or the head office of the same enterprise situated in another State is assimilated to an alienation of property. The Article does not prevent these States from taxing profits or gains deemed to arise in connection with such a transfer, provided, however, that such taxation is in accordance with Article 7.

11. The Article does not distinguish as to the origin of the capital gain. Therefore all capital gains, those accruing over a long term, parallel to a steady improvement in economic conditions, as well as those accruing in a very short period (speculative gains) are covered. Also capital gains which are due to depreciation of the national currency are covered. It is, of course, left to each State to decide whether or not such gains should be taxed.

12. The Article does not specify how to compute a capital gain, this being left to the domestic law applicable. As a rule, capital gains are calculated by deducting the cost from the selling price. To arrive at cost all expenses incidental to the purchase and all expenditure for improvements are added to the purchase price. In some cases the cost

after deduction of the depreciation allowances already given is taken into account. Some tax laws prescribe another base instead of cost, e.g. the value previously reported by the alienator of the asset for capital tax purposes.

13. Special problems may arise when the basis for the taxation of capital gains is not uniform in the two Contracting States. The capital gain from the alienation of an asset computed in one State according to the rules mentioned in paragraph 12 above, may not necessarily coincide with the capital gain computed in the other State under the accounting rules used there. This may occur when one State has the right to tax capital gains because it is the State of situs while the other State has the right to tax because the enterprise is a resident of that other State.

14. The following example may illustrate this problem: an enterprise of State A bought immovable property situated in State B. The enterprise may have entered depreciation allowances in the books kept in State A. If such immovable property is sold at a price which is above cost, a capital gain may be realised and, in addition, the depreciation allowances granted earlier may be recovered. State B in which the immovable property is situated and where no books are kept does not have to take into account, when taxing the income from the immovable property, the depreciation allowances booked in State A. Neither can State B substitute the value of the immovable property shown in the books kept in State A for the cost at the time of the alienation. State B cannot, therefore, tax the depreciation allowances realised in addition to the capital gain as mentioned in paragraph 12 above.

15. On the other hand, State A of which the alienator is a resident, cannot be obliged in all cases to exempt such book profits fully from its taxes under paragraph 1 of the Article and Article 23A (there will be hardly any problems for States applying the tax credit method). To the extent that such book profits are due to the realisation of the depreciation allowances previously claimed in State A and which had reduced the income or profits taxable in such State A, that State cannot be prevented from taxing such book profits. The situation corresponds to that dealt with in paragraph 44 of the Commentary on Article 23A.

16. Further problems may arise in connection with profits due to changes of the rate of exchange between the currencies of State A and State B. After the devaluation of the currency of State A, enterprises of such State A may, or may have to, increase the book value of the assets situated outside the territory of State A. Apart from any devaluation of the currency of a State, the usual fluctuations of the rate of exchange may give rise to so-called currency gains or losses. Take for example an enterprise of State A having bought and sold immovable property situated in State B. If the cost and the selling price, both expressed in the currency of State B, are equal, there will be no capital gain in State B. When the value of the currency of State B has risen between the purchase and the sale of the asset in relation to the currency of State A, in the currency of that State a profit will accrue to such enterprise. If the value of the currency of State B has fallen in the

meantime, the alienator will sustain a loss which will not be recognised in State B. Such currency gains or losses may also arise in connection with claims and debts contracted in a foreign currency. If the balance-sheet of a permanent establishment situated in State B of an enterprise of State A shows claims and debts expressed in the currency of State B, the books of the permanent establishment do not show any gain or loss when repayments are made. Changes of the rate of exchange may be reflected, however, in the accounts of the head office. If the value of the currency of State B has risen (fallen) between the time the claim has originated and its repayment, the enterprise, as a whole, will realise a gain (sustain a loss). This is true also with respect to debts if between the time they have originated and their repayment, the currency of State B has fallen (risen) in value.

17. The provisions of the Article do not settle all questions regarding the taxation of such currency gains. Such gains are in most cases not connected with an alienation of the asset; they may often not even be determined in the State on which the right to tax capital gains is conferred by the Article. Accordingly, the question, as a rule, is not whether the State in which a permanent establishment is situated has a right to tax, but whether the State of which the taxpayer is a resident must, if applying the exemption method, refrain from taxing such currency gains which, in many cases, cannot be shown but in the books kept in the head office. The answer to that latter question depends not only on the Article but also on Article 7 and on Article 23A. If in a given case differing opinions of two States should result in an actual double taxation, the case should be settled under the mutual agreement procedure provided for by Article 25.

18. Moreover the question arises which Article should apply when there is paid for property sold an annuity during the lifetime of the alienator and not a fixed price. Are such annuity payments, as far as they exceed costs, to be dealt with as a gain from the alienation of the property or as 'income not dealt with' according to Article 21? Both opinions may be supported by arguments of equivalent weight, and it seems difficult to give one rule on the matter. In addition such problems are rare in practice, so it therefore seems unnecessary to establish a rule for insertion in the Convention. It may be left to Contracting States, who may be involved in such a question, to adopt a solution in the mutual agreement procedure provided for by Article 25.

19. The Article is not intended to apply to prizes in a lottery or to premiums and prizes attaching to bonds or debentures.

20. The Article deals first with the gains which may be taxed in the State where the alienated property is situated. For all other capital gains, paragraph 4 gives the right to tax to the State of which the alienator is a resident.

21. As capital gains are not taxed by all States, it may be considered reasonable to avoid only actual double taxation of capital gains. Therefore, Contracting States are free to supplement their bilateral convention in such a way that a State has to forego its right to tax conferred on it by the domestic laws only if the other State on which the right

to tax is conferred by the Convention makes use thereof. In such a case, paragraph 4 of the Article should be supplemented accordingly. Besides, a modification of Article 23A as suggested in paragraph 35 of the Commentary on Article 23A is needed.

Paragraph 1

22. Paragraph 1 states that gains from the alienation of immovable property may be taxed in the State in which it is situated. This rule corresponds to the provisions of Article 6 and of paragraph 1 of Article 22. It applies also to immovable property forming part of the assets of an enterprise or used for performing independent personal services. For the definition of immovable property paragraph 1 refers to Article 6. Paragraph 1 of Article 13 deals only with gains which a resident of a Contracting State derives from the alienation of immovable property situated in the other Contracting State. It does not, therefore, apply to gains derived from the alienation of immovable property situated in the Contracting State of which the alienator is a resident un the meaning of Article 4 or situated in a third State; the provisions of paragraph 1 of the Article 21 shall apply to such gains.

23. Certain tax laws assimilate the alienation of all part of the shares in a company, the exclusive or main aim of which is to hold immovable property, to the alienation of such immovable property. In itself paragraph 1 does not allow the practice: a special provision in the bilateral convention can alone provide for such an assimilation. Contracting States are of course free either to include in their bilateral conventions such special provision, or to confirm expressly that the alienation of shares cannot be assimilated to the alienation of the immovable property.

Paragraph 2

24. Paragraph 2 deals with movable property forming part of the business property of a permanent establishment of an enterprise or pertaining to a fixed base used for performing independent personal services. The term 'movable property' means all property other than immovable property which is dealt with in paragraph 1. It includes also incorporeal property, such as goodwill, licences, etc. Gains from the alienation of such assets may be taxed in the State in which the permanent establishment or fixed base is situated, which corresponds to the rules for business profits and for income from independent personal services (Article 7 and 14).

25. The paragraph makes clear that its rules apply when movable property of a permanent establishment or fixed base is alienated as well as when the permanent establishment as such (alone or with the whole enterprise) or the fixed base as such is alienated. If the whole enterprise is alienated, then the rule applies to such gains which are deemed to result from the alienation of movable property forming part of the business property of the permanent establishment. The rules of Article 7 should then apply mutatis mutandis without express reference thereto. For the transfer of an asset from a permanent establishment in one

State to a permanent establishment (or the head office) in another State, cf. paragraph 10 above.

26. On the other hand, paragraph 2 may not always be applicable to capital gains from the alienation of a participation in an enterprise. The provision applies only to property which was owned by the alienator, either wholly or jointly with another person. Under the laws of some countries, capital assets of a partnership are considered to be owned by the partners. Under some other laws, however, partnerships and other associations are treated as body corporate for tax purposes, distinct from their partners (members), which means that participations in such entities are dealt with in the same way as shares in a company. Capital gains from the alienation of such participations like capital gains from the alienation of shares, are therefore taxable only in the State of residence of the alienator. Contracting States may agree bilaterally on special rules governing the taxation of capital gains from the alienation of a participation in a partnership.

27. Certain States consider that all capital gains arising from sources in their territory should be subject to their taxes according to their domestic laws, if the alienator has a permanent establishment within their territory. Paragraph 2 is not based on such a conception which is sometimes referred to as 'the force of attraction of the permanent establishment'. The paragraph merely provides that gains from the alienation of movable property forming part of the business property of a permanent establishment or of movable property pertaining to a fixed base used for performing independent personal services may be taxed in the State where the permanent establishment or the fixed base is situated. The gains from the alienation of all other movable property are taxable only in the State of residence of the alienator as provided in paragraph 4. The foregoing explanations accord with those in the Commentary on Article 7.

Paragraph 3

28. An exception from the rule of paragraph 2 is provided for ships and aircraft operated in international traffic and for boats engaged in inland waterways transport and movable property pertaining to the operation of such ships, aircraft and boats. Gains from the alienation of such assets are taxable only in the State in which the place of effective management of the enterprise operating such ships, aircraft and boats is situated. This rule corresponds to the provisions of Article 8 and of paragraph 3 of Article 22. It is understood that paragraph 3 of Article 8 is applicable if the place of effective management of such enterprise is aboard a ship or a boat. Contracting States which would prefer to confer the exclusive taxing right on the State of residence or to use a combination of the residence criterion and the place of effective management criterion are free, in bilateral conventions, to substitute to paragraph 3 a provision corresponding to those proposed in paragraphs 2 and 3 of the Commentary on Article 8.

Paragraph 4

29. As regards gains from the alienation of any property other than that referred to in paragraphs 1, 2 and 3, paragraph 4 provides that they are taxable only in the State of which the alienator is a resident. This corresponds to the rules laid down in Article 22.

30. The Article does not contain special rules for gains from the alienation of shares in a company or of securities, bonds, debentures and the like. Such gains are, therefore, taxable only in the State of which the alienator is a resident.

31. If shares are sold by a shareholder to the issuing company in connection with the liquidation of such company or the reduction of its paid-up capital, the difference between the selling price and the par value of the shares may be treated in the State of which the company is a resident as a distribution of accumulated profits and not as a capital gain. The Article does not prevent the State of residence of the company from taxing such distributions at the rates provided for in Article 10: such taxation is permitted because such difference is covered by the definition of the term 'dividends' contained in paragraph 3 of Article 10 and interpreted in paragraph 27 of the Commentary relating thereto. The same interpretation may apply if bonds or debentures are redeemed by the debtor at a price which is higher than the par value or the value at which the bonds or debentures have been issued; in such a case, the difference may represent interest and, therefore, be subjected to a limited tax in the State of source of the interest in accordance with Article 11 (cf. also paragraphs 18 and 19 of the Commentary on Article 11).

Special Derogation

32.-40. [Omitted]

Commentary on Article 14 concerning the Taxation of Independent Personal Services

1. The Article is concerned with what are commonly known as professional services and with other activities of an independent character. This excludes industrial and commercial activities and also professional services performed in employment, e.g. a physician serving as a medical officer in a factory. It should, however, be observed that the Article does not concern independent activities of entertainers and athletes, these being covered by Article 17.

2. The meaning of the term 'professional services' is illustrated by some examples of typical liberal professions. The enumeration has an explanatory character only and is not exhaustive. Difficulties of interpretation which might arise in special cases may be solved by mutual agreement between the competent authorities of the Contracting States concerned.

3. The provisions of the Article are similar to those for business profits and rest in fact on the same principles as those of Article 7. The provisions of Article 7 and the Commentary thereon could therefore be used as guidance for interpreting and applying Article 14. Thus the principles laid down in Article 7 for instance as regards allocation of profits between head office and permanent establishment could be applied also in apportioning income between the State of residence of a person performing independent personal services and the State where such services are performed from a fixed base. Equally, expenses incurred for the purposes of a fixed base, including executive and general expenses, should be allowed as deductions in determining the income attributable to a fixed base in the same way as such expenses incurred for the purposes of a permanent establishment (cf. paragraph 3 of Article 7). Also in other respects Article 7 and the Commentary thereon could be of assistance for the interpretation of Article 14.

4. Even if Article 7 and 14 are based on the same principles, it was thought that the concept of permanent establishment should be reserved for commercial and industrial activities. The term 'fixed base' has therefore been used. It has not been thought appropriate to try to define it, but it would cover, for instance, a physician's consulting room or the office of an architect or a lawyer. A person performing independent personal services would probably not as a rule have premises of this kind in any other State than of his residence. But if there is in another State a centre of activity of a fixed or a permanent character, then that State should be entitled to tax the person's activities.

Reservations on the Article:

5.-6. [Omitted]

7. The *United States* reserves the right to tax services performed by individuals who are present in the United States for more than 183 days during the taxable year. The United States also believes that this Article should be limited to individuals and to income from the performance of personal services.

Commentary on Article 15 concerning the Taxation of Dependent Personal Services

1. Paragraph 1 establishes the general rule as to the taxation of income from employment (other than pensions), namely, that such income is taxable in the State where the employment is actually exercised. One consequence of this would be that a resident of a Contracting State who derived remuneration, in respect of an employment, from sources in the other State could not be taxed in that other State in respect of that remuneration merely because the results of this work were exploited in that other State.

2. The general rule is subject to exception only in the case of pensions (Article 18) and of remuneration and pensions in respect of government service (Article 19). Remuneration of members of boards of directors of companies is the subject of Article 16.

3. Paragraph 2 contains, however, a general exception to the rule in paragraph 1. This exception, which concerns employment of short duration abroad, is mainly intended to facilitate the international movement of qualified personnel, as in the case of firms which sell capital goods and are responsible for installing and assembling them abroad. The three conditions prescribed in this paragraph must be satisfied for the remuneration to qualify for the exemption. The exemption is limited to the 183-day period. It is further stipulated that this time period may not be exceeded 'in the fiscal year concerned'. The formulation used may create difficulties in cases where the fiscal years of the Contracting States do not coincide. In order to avoid these difficulties such Contracting States may prefer to use another phrasing, for instance 'fiscal year of that other State' or 'calendar year'. The employer paying the remuneration must not be a resident of the State in which the employment is exercised. Furthermore, should the employer have in that State a permanent establishment (or a fixed base if he performs professional services or other activities of an independent character), the exemption is given only on condition that the remuneration is not borne by a permanent establishment or a fixed base which the employer has in the other State. It should be noted that, under the provisions of Article 17, the exemption does not apply to remuneration of artistes and athletes.

4. Paragraph 3 applies to the remuneration of crews of ships or aircraft operated in international traffic, or of boats engaged in inland waterways transport, a rule which follows up to a certain extent the rule applied to the income from shipping, inland waterways transport and air transport – that is, to tax them in the Contracting State in which the place of effective management of the enterprise concerned is situated. In the Commentary on Article 8, it is indicated that Contracting States may agree to confer the right to tax such income on the State of the enterprise operating the ships, boats or aircraft. The reasons for introducing that possibility in the case of income from shipping, inland waterways and air transport operations are valid also in respect of remuneration of the crew. Accordingly Contracting States are left free to agree on a provision which gives the right to tax such remuneration to the State of the enterprise. Such a provision, as well as that of paragraph 3 of Article 15, assumes that the domestic laws of the State on which the right to tax is conferred allows it to tax the remuneration of a person in the service of the enterprise concerned, irrespective of his residence. It is understood that paragraph 3 of Article 8 is applicable if the place of effective management of a shipping enterprise or of an inland waterways transport enterprise is aboard a ship or a boat. According to the domestic laws of some Member countries, tax is levied on remuneration received by non-resident members of the crew in respect of employment aboard ships only if the ship has the national-

ity of such a State. For that reason conventions concluded between these States provide that the right to tax such remuneration is given to the State of the nationality of the ship. On the other hand many States cannot make use of such a taxation right and the provision could in such cases lead to non-taxation. However, States having that taxation principle in their domestic laws may agree bilaterally to confer the right to tax remuneration in respect of employment aboard ships on the State of the nationality of the ship.

5. It should be noted that no special rule regarding the taxation of income of frontier workers is included as it would be more suitable for the problems created by local conditions to be solved directly between the States concerned.

6. No special provision has been made regarding remuneration derived by visiting professors or students employed with a view to their acquiring practical experience. Many conventions contain rules of some kind or other concerning such cases, the main purpose of which is to facilitate cultural relations by providing for a limited tax exemption. Sometimes, tax exemption is already provided under domestic taxation laws. The absence of specific rules should not be interpreted as constituting an obstacle to the inclusion of such rules in bilateral conventions whenever this is felt desirable.

7. [Omitted]

Commentary on Article 16 concerning the Taxation of Directors' Fees

1. This Article relates to remuneration received by a resident of a Contracting State, whether an individual or a legal person, in the capacity of a member of a board of directors of a company which is a resident of the other Contracting State. Since it might sometimes be difficult to ascertain where the services are performed, the provision treats the services as performed in the State of residence of the company.

2. A member of the board of directors of a company often also has other functions with the company, e.g. as ordinary employee, adviser, consultant, etc. It is clear that the Article does not apply to remuneration paid to such a person on account of such other functions.

3. In some countries organs of companies exist which are similar in function to the board of directors. Contracting States are free to include in bilateral conventions such organs of companies under a provision corresponding to Article 16.

Reservations on the Article:

4. [Omitted]

5. The *United States* reserves its position with regard to this Article. The United States believe that directors' fees should be subject to tax under Article 14.

Commentary on Article 17 concerning the Taxation of Artistes and Athletes

1. Paragraph 1 provides that entertainers and athletes who are residents of a Contracting State may be taxed in the other Contracting State in which their personal activities as such are performed, whether these are of an independent or of a dependent nature. This provision is an exception to the rules in Article 14 and to that in paragraph 2 of Article 15, respectively.

2. This provision makes it possible to avoid the practical difficulties which often arise in taxing entertainers and athletes performing abroad. Moreover, too strict provisions might in certain cases impede cultural exchanges. In order to overcome this disadvantage, the States concerned may, by common agreement, limit the application of paragraph 1 to independent activities by adding its provisions to those of Article 14. In such a case, entertainers and athletes performing for a salary or wages would automatically come within Article 15 and thus be entitled to the exemptions provides for in paragraph 2 of that Article.

3. The provisions of the Article do not apply when the entertainer or athlete is employed by a Government and derives the income from that Government. Such income is to be treated under the provisions of Article 19. Certain conventions contain provisions excluding entertainers and athletes employed in organisations which are subsidised out of public funds from the application of Article 17. The provisions of the Article shall not prevent Contracting States from agreeing bilaterally on particular provisions concerning such entertainers and athletes.

4. The purpose of paragraph 2 is to counteract certain tax avoidance devices in cases where remuneration for the performance of an entertainer or athlete is not paid to the entertainer or athlete himself but to another person, e.g. a socalled artiste-company, in such a way that the income is taxed in the State where the activity is performed neither as personal service income to the entertainer or athlete nor as profits of the enterprise in the absence of a permanent establishment. Paragraph 2 permits the State in which the performance is given to impose a tax on the profits diverted from the income of the entertainer or athlete to the enterprise where for instance the entertainer or athlete has control over or rights to the income thus diverted or has obtained or will obtain some benefit directly or indirectly from that income. It may be, however, that the domestic laws of some States do not enable them to apply such a provision. Such States are free to agree to alternative solutions or to leave paragraph 2 out of their bilateral convention.

5. Where in the cases dealt with in paragraph 2 the exemption method for relieving double taxation is used by the State of residence

of the person receiving the income, that State would be precluded from taxing such income even if the State where the activities were performed could not make use of its right to tax. It is therefore understood that the credit method should be used in such cases. The same result could be achieved by stipulating a subsidiary right to tax for the State of residence of the person receiving the income, if the State where the activities are performed cannot make use of the right conferred on it by paragraph 2. Contracting States are free to choose any of these methods in order to ensure that the income does not escape taxation.

Observation on the Commentary

6. *Canada* and the *United States* are of the opinion that paragraph 2 of the Article applies only to cases mentioned in paragraph 4 above and these countries will propose an amendment to that effect when negotiating conventions with other Member countries.

Reservations on the Article:

7.-8. [Omitted]

9. The *United States* reserves the right to limit paragraph 1 to situations where the entertainer or athlete is present in the other State for a specified period or earns a specified amount.

Commentary on Article 18 concerning the Taxation of Pensions

1. According to this Article, pensions paid in respect of private employment are taxable only in the State of residence of the recipient. The provision also covers widows' and orphans' pensions and other similar payments such as annuities paid in respect of past employment. It also applies to pensions in respect of services rendered to a State or a political subdivision or local authority thereof which are not covered by the provisions of paragraph 2 of Article 19.

2. Some States consider pensions paid out under a public pension scheme which is part of their social security system similar to Government pensions. Such States argue on that basis that the State of source, i.e. the State from which the pension is paid, should have a right to tax such pensions. Many conventions concluded by these States contain provisions to that effect, sometimes including also other payments made under the social security legislation of the State of source. Such payments are for instance sickness benefits, unemployment benefits and benefits on account of industrial injury. Contracting States having that view may agree bilaterally on an additional paragraph to the Article giving the State of source a right to tax payments made under its social

security legislation. A paragraph of that kind could be drafted along the following lines:

'Notwithstanding the provisions of paragraph 1, pensions and other payments made under the social security legislation of a Contracting State may be taxed in that State.'

Where the State of which the recipient of such payments is a resident applies the exemption method the payments will be taxable only in the State of source while States using the credit method may tax the payments and give credit for the tax levied in the State of source. Some States using the credit method as the general method in their conventions may, however, consider that the State of source should have an exclusive right to tax such payments. Such States should then substitute the words 'shall be taxable only' for the words 'may be taxed' in the above draft provision.

3. The treatment under the taxation laws of the OECD Member countries of amounts paid to an employee on the cessation of his employment is highly diversified. Some States regard such a payment as a pension, private or Government as the case may be, paid as a lump sum. In such a case it would be natural to consider the income as falling under Article 18 or 19. In the tax laws of other States such a payment is looked upon as the final remuneration for the work performed. Then it should of course be treated under Article 15 or 19, as the case may be. Others again consider such a payment as a bonus which is not taxable under their income tax laws but perhaps subjected to a gift tax or a similar tax. It has not been possible to reach a common solution on the tax treatment of payments of this kind under the Model Convention. If the question of taxing such payments should arise between Contracting States, the matter therefore has to be solved by recourse to the provisions of Article 25.

Reservations on the Article:

4.-6. [Omitted]

Commentary on Article 19 concerning the Taxation of Remuneration in Respect of Government Service

1. This Article applies to remuneration in respect of government service. Similar provisions in old bilateral conventions were framed in order to conform with the rules of international courtesy and mutual respect between sovereign States. They were therefore rather limited in scope. However, the importance and scope of Article 19 has increased on account of the fact that, consequent on the growth of the public sector in many countries, governmental activities abroad have been considerably extended. According to the original version of paragraph 1 of Article 19 in the 1963 Draft Convention the paying State

had a right to tax payments made for services rendered to that State or political subdivision or local authority thereof. The expression 'may be taxed' was used and this did not connote an exclusive right of taxation.

2. On revision of the Article, paragraph 1 was split into two paragraphs, paragraph 1 concerning remuneration other than a pension and paragraph 2 concerning pensions respectively. Unlike the original provision, sub-paragraph *a.* of paragraphs 1 and 2 are both based on the principle that the paying State shall have an exclusive right to tax the payments. Countries using the credit method as the general method for relieving double taxation in their conventions are thus, as an exception to that method, obliged to exempt from tax such payments to their residents as are dealt with under paragraphs 1 and 2. If both Contracting States apply the exemption method for relieving double taxation, they can continue to use the expression 'may be taxed' instead of 'shall be taxable only'. In relation to such countries the effect will of course be the same irrespective of which of these expressions they use. It is understood that the expression 'shall be taxable only'shall not prevent a Contracting State from taking into account the income exempted under sub-paragraph *a.* of paragraphs 1 and 2 in determining the rate of tax to be imposed on income derived by its residents from other sources. The principle of giving the exclusive taxing right to the paying State is contained in so many of the existing conventions between OECD Member countries that it can be said to be already internationally accepted. It is also in conformity with the conception of international courtesy which is at the basis of the Article and with the provisions of the Vienna Conventions on Diplomatic and Consular Relations. It should, however, be observed that the Article is not intended to restrict the operation of any rules originating from international law in the case of diplomatic missions and consular posts (cf. Article 27) but deals with cases not covered by such rules.

3. The provisions of the Article apply to payments made not only by a State but also by its political subdivisions and local authorities (constituent states, regions, provinces, '*départements*', cantons, districts, '*arrondissements*', '*Kreise*', municipalities, or groups of municipalities, etc.).

4. An exception from the principle of giving exclusive taxing power to the paying State is contained in sub-paragraph *b.* of paragraph 1. It is to be seen against the background that, according to the Vienna Conventions mentioned above, the receiving State is allowed to tax remuneration paid to certain categories of personnel of foreign diplomatic missions and consular posts, who are permanent residents or nationals of that State. Given that pensions paid to retired government officials ought to be treated for tax purposes in the same way as salaries or wages paid to such employees during their active time, an exception like the one in sub-paragraph *b.* of paragraph 1 is incorporated also in sub-paragraph *b.* of paragraph 2 regarding pensions. Since the condition laid down in sub-paragraph *b.* (ii) of paragraph 1 cannot be valid in relation to a pensioner, the only pre-requisite for the receiv-

ing State's power to tax the pension is that the pensioner must be one of its own residents and nationals. It should be noted that the expression 'out of funds created by' in sub-paragraph *a.* of paragraph 2 covers the situation where the pension is not paid directly, by the State, a political subdivision or a local authority but out of separate funds created by them.

5. According to Article 19 of the 1963 Draft Convention, the services rendered to the State, political subdivision or local authority had to be rendered 'in the discharge of functions of a governmental nature'. In the course of the revision of the Article, it was decided to delete that expression. Some OECD Member countries, however, thought that the exclusion would lead to a widening of the scope of the Article. Contracting States who are of that view who feel that such a widening is not desirable may continue to use, and preferably specify, the expression 'in the discharge of functions of a governmental nature' in their bilateral conventions.

6. Paragraphs 1 and 2 do not apply if the services are performed in connection with business carried on by the State, or one of its political subdivisions or local authorities, paying the remuneration. In such cases the ordinary rules apply: Article 15 for wages and salaries, Article 16 for directors' fees and other similar payments and Article 18 for pensions. Article 17 is not mentioned because paragraphs 1 and 2 of Article 19 are to apply to remuneration paid to artistes employed by the State, a political subdivision or a local authority thereof, irrespective of whether such artistes could be said to be rendering services in connection with business carried on by the State, the political subdivision or the local authority. Contracting States, wishing for specific reasons to dispense with paragraph 3 in their bilateral conventions, are free to do so thus bringing in under paragraphs 1 and 2 also services rendered in connection with business. In view of the specific functions carried out by certain public bodies, e.g. State Railways, the Post Office, State-owned theatres etc., Contracting States wanting to keep paragraph 3 may agree in bilateral negotiations to include under the provisions of paragraphs 1 and 2 remuneration paid by such bodies, even if they could be said to be performing business activities.

Reservations on the Article:

7. *Japan* and the *United States* believe that a reference to Article 17 should be added to paragraph 3, so that government-employed artistes may be governed by Article 17 if their services are rendered in connection with a business.

8. The *United States* reserves the right to modify the text to indicate that its application is not limited by Article 1.

Commentary on Article 20 concerning the Taxation of Students

1. The rule established in this Article concerns certain payments received by students or business apprentices for the purpose of their maintenance, education or training. All such payments received from sources outside the State in which the student or business apprentice concerned is staying shall be exempted from tax in that State.

2. In the course of revision of the 1963 Draft Convention it was decided to insert the word 'immediately' in order to make clear that the Article does not cover a person who has once been a resident of a Contracting State but has subsequently moved his residence to a third State before visiting the other Contracting State.

3. [Omitted]

Commentary on Article 21 concerning the Taxation of Other Income

1. This Article provides a general rule relating to income not dealt with in the foregoing Articles of the Convention. The income concerned is not only income of a class not expressly dealt with but also income from sources not expressly mentioned. The scope of the Article is not confined to income arising in a Contracting State; it extends also to income from third States.

Paragraph 1

2. Under this paragraph the exclusive right to tax is given to the State of residence. In cases of conflict between two residences, Article 4 will also allocate the taxation right in respect of third State income.

3. The rule set out in the paragraph applies irrespective of whether the right to tax is in fact exercised by the State of residence, and thus when the income arises in the other Contracting State, that State cannot impose tax even if the income is not taxed in the first-mentioned State. Likewise, when income arises in a third State and the recipient of this income is considered as a resident by both Contracting States under their domestic law, the application of Article 4 will result in the recipient being treated as a resident of one Contracting State only and being liable to comprehensive taxation ('full tax liability') in that State only. In this case, the other Contracting State may not impose tax on the income arising from the third State, even if the recipient is not taxed by the State of which he is considered a resident under Article 4. In order to avoid non-taxation, Contracting States may agree to limit the scope of the Article to income which is taxed in the Contracting State of which the recipient is a resident and may modify the provisions of the paragraph accordingly. In fact, this problem is merely a special

aspect of the general problem dealt with in paragraphs 34 and 35 of the Commentary on Article 23A.

Paragraph 2

4. This paragraph provides for an exception from the provisions of paragraph 1 where the income is associated with the activity of a permanent establishment or fixed base which a resident of a Contracting State has in the other Contracting State. The paragraph includes income from third States. In such a case, a right to tax is given to the Contracting State in which the permanent establishment or the fixed base is situated. Paragraph 2 does not apply to immovable property for which, according to paragraph 4 of Article 6, the State of situs has a primary right to tax (cf. paragraphs 3 and 4 of the Commentary on Article 6). Therefore, immovable property situated in a Contracting State and forming part of the business property of a permanent establishment of an enterprise of that State situated in the other Contracting State shall be taxable only in the first-mentioned State in which the property is situated and of which the recipient of the income is a resident. This is in consistency with the rules laid down in Articles 13 and 22 in respect of immovable property since paragraph 2 of those Articles applies only to movable property of a permanent establishment.

5. The paragraph also covers the case where the beneficiary and the payer of the income are both residents of the same Contracting State, and the income is attributed to a permanent establishment or a fixed base, which the beneficiary of the income has in the other Contracting State. In such a case a right to tax is given to the Contracting State in which the permanent establishment or the fixed base is situated. Where double taxation occurs, the State of residence should give relief under the provisions of Article 23A or 23B. However a problem may arise as regards the taxation of dividends and interest in the State of residence as the State of source: the combination of Articles 7 and 23A prevents that State from levying tax on that income, whereas if it were paid to a resident of the other State, the first State, being the State of source of the dividends or interest, could tax such dividends or interest at the rates provided for in paragraph 2 of Articles 10 and 11. Contracting States which find this position unacceptable may include in their conventions a provision according to which the State of residence would be entitled, as State of source of the dividends or interest, to levy a tax on such income at the rates provided for in paragraph 2 of Articles 10 and 11. The State where the permanent establishment is situated would give a credit for such tax on the lines of the provisions of paragraph 20 of Article 23A or of paragraph 1 of Article 23B; of course, this credit should not be given in cases where the State in which the permanent establishment is situated does not tax the dividends or interest attributed to the permanent establishment, in accordance with its domestic laws.

6. Some States which apply the exemption method (Article 23A) may have reason to suspect that the treatment accorded in paragraph 2 may provide an inducement to an enterprise of a Contracting State

to attach assets such as shares, bonds or patents, to a permanent establishment situated in the other Contracting State in order to obtain more favourable tax treatment there. To counteract such arrangements which they consider would represent abuse, some States might take the view that the transaction is official and, for this reason, would regard the assets as not effectively connected with the permanent establishment. Some other States may strengthen their position by adding in paragraph 2 a condition providing that the paragraph shall not apply to cases where the arrangements were primarily made for the purpose of taking advantage of this provision.

7.-9. [Omitted]

Commentary on Article 22 concerning the Taxation of Capital

1. This Article deals only with taxes on capital, to the exclusion of taxes on estates and inheritances and on gifts and of transfer duties. Taxes on capital to which the Article applies are those referred to in Article 2.

2. Taxes on capital generally constitute complementary taxation of income from capital. Consequently, taxes on a given element of capital can be levied, in principle, only by the State which is entitled to tax the income from this element of capital. However, it is not possible to refer purely and simply to the rules relating to the taxation of such class of income, for not all items of income are subject to taxation exclusively in one State.

3. The Article, therefore, enumerates first property which may be taxed in the State in which they are situated. To this category belong immovable property, referred to in Article 6 which a resident of a Contracting State owns and which is situated in the other Contracting State (paragraph 1), and movable property forming part of the business property of a permanent establishment which an enterprise of a Contracting State has in the other Contracting State, or pertaining to a fixed base which a resident of a Contracting State has in the other Contracting State for the performance of independent personal services (paragraph 2).

4. Ships and aircraft operated in international traffic and boats engaged in inland waterways transport and movable property pertaining to the operation of such ships, boats or aircraft shall be taxable only in the State in which the place of effective management of the enterprise is situated (paragraph 3). This rule corresponds to the provisions of Article 8 and of paragraph 3 of Article 13. It is understood that paragraph 3 of Article 8 is applicable if the place of effective management of a shipping enterprise or of an inland waterways transport enterprise is aboard a ship or boat. Contracting States which would prefer to confer the exclusive taxing right on the State of residence or to use

a combination of the residence criterion and the place of effective management criterion are free in bilateral conventions to substitute for paragraph 3 a provision corresponding to those proposed in paragraphs 2 and 3 of the Commentary on Article 8. Immovable property pertaining to the operation of ships, boats or aircraft may be taxed in the State in which they are situated, in accordance with the rule laid down in paragraph 1.

5. As regards elements of capital other than those listed in paragraph 1 to 3, the Article provides that they are taxable only in the Contracting State of which the person to whom they belong is a resident (paragraph 4).

6. If, when the provisions of paragraph 4 are applied to elements of movable property under usufruct, double taxation subsists because of the disparity between domestic laws, the States concerned may resort to the mutual agreement procedure or settle the question by means of bilateral negotiations.

7. The Article does not provide any rule about the deductions of debts. The laws of OECD Member countries are too different to allow a common solution for such a deduction. The problem of the deduction of debts which could arise when the taxpayer and the creditor are not residents of the same State is dealt with in paragraph 5 of Article

8.-11. [Omitted]

Commentary on Article 24 concerning Non-Discrimination

Paragraph 1

1. This paragraph establishes the principle that for purposes of taxation discrimination on the grounds of nationality is forbidden, and that, subject to reciprocity, the nationals of a Contracting State may not be less favourably treated in the other Contracting State than nationals of the latter State in the same circumstances.

2. It is noteworthy that the principle of non-discrimination, under various descriptions and with a more or less wide scope, was applied in international fiscal relations well before the appearance, at the end of the 19th Century, of the classic type of double taxation conventions. Thus, in a great many agreements of different kinds (consular or establishment conventions, treaties of friendship or commerce, etc.) concluded by States, especially in the 19th Century, in order to extend and strengthen the diplomatic protection of their nationals wherever resident, there are clauses under which each of the two Contracting States undertakes to accord nationals of the other State equality of treatment with its own nationals. The fact that such clauses subsequently found their way into double taxation conventions has in no way affected their original justification and scope. The text of paragraph 1 provides that the application of this paragraph is not restricted by Article 1 to nation-

als solely who are residents of a Contracting State, but on the contrary, extends to all nationals of each Contracting State, whether or not they be residents of one of them. In other words, all nationals of a Contracting State are entitled to invoice the benefit of this provision as against the other Contracting State. This holds good, in particular, for nationals of the Contracting States who are not residents of either of them but of a third State.

3. The expression 'in the same circumstances' refers to taxpayers (individuals, legal persons, partnerships and associations) placed, from the point of view of the application of the ordinary taxation laws and regulations, in substantially similar circumstances both in law and in fact.

4. Consequently if a Contracting State, in giving relief from taxation on account of family responsibilities, distinguishes between its own nationals according to whether they reside in its territory or not, that State cannot be obliged to give nationals of the other State who do not reside in its territory the same treatment as it gives its resident nationals but it undertakes to extend to them the same treatment as is available to its non-resident nationals.

5. Likewise, the provisions of paragraph 1 are not to be construed as obliging a State which accords special taxation privileges to its own public bodies or services as such, to extend the same privileges to the public bodies and services of the other State.

6. Neither are they to be construed as obliging a State which accords special taxation privileges to private institutions not for profit whose activities are performed for purposes of public benefit, which are specific to that State, to extend the same privileges to similar institutions whose activities are not for its benefit.

7. To take the first of these two cases, if a State accords immunity from taxation to its own public bodies and services, this is justified because such bodies and services are integral parts of the State and at no time can their circumstances be comparable to those of the public bodies and services of the other State. Nevertheless, this reservation is not intended to apply to State corporations carrying on gainful undertakings. To the extent that these can be regarded as being on the same footing as private industrial and commercial undertakings, the provisions of paragraph 1 will apply to them.

8. As for the second case, if a State accords taxation privileges to certain private institutions not for profit, this is clearly justified by the very nature of these institutions' activities and by the benefit which that State and its nationals will derive from those activities.

9. Furthermore, paragraph 1 has been deliberately framed in a negative form. By providing that the nationals of a Contracting State may not be subjected in the other Contracting State to any taxation or any requirement connected therewith which is other or more burdensome than the taxation and connected requirements to which nationals of the other Contracting State in the same circumstances are or may be subjected, this paragraph has the same mandatory force as if it enjoined the Contracting States to accord the same treatment to their respective

nationals. But since the principal object of this clause is to forbid discrimination in one State against the nationals of the other, there is nothing to prevent the first State from granting to persons of foreign nationality, for special reasons of its own, or in order to comply with a special stipulation in a double taxation convention, such as, notably, the requirement that profits of permanent establishments are to be taxed on the basis of separate accounts, certain concessions or facilities which are not available to its own nationals. As it is worded, paragraph 1 would not prohibit this.

10. Subject to the foregoing observation, the words '... shall not be subjected ... to any taxation or any requirement connected therewith which is other or more burdensome ...' mean that when a tax is imposed on nationals and foreigners in the same circumstances, it must be in the same form as regards both the basis of charge and the method of assessment, its rate must be the same and, finally, the formalities connected with the taxation (returns, payment, prescribed times, etc.) must not be more onerous for foreigners than for nationals.

Paragraph 2

11. Paragraph 2 merely stipulates that the term 'nationals' applies to all individuals possessing the nationality of a Contracting State. It has not been judged necessary here to introduce into the text of the Article any considerations on the signification of the concept of nationality, any more than it seemed indispensable to make any special comment here on the meaning and application of the word. Obviously, in determining in relation to individuals, what is meant by 'the nationals of a Contracting State', reference must be made to the sense in which the term is usually employed and each State's particular rules on the acquisition or loss of nationality.

12. But paragraph 2 is more specific as to legal persons, partnerships and associations. By declaring that all legal persons, partnerships and associations deriving their status as such from the laws in force in a Contracting State are considered to be nationals for the purposes of paragraph 1, the provision disposes of a difficulty which often arises in determining the nationality of companies. In defining the nationality of companies, certain States have regard less to the law which governs the company than to the origin of the capital with which the company was formed or the nationality of the individuals or legal persons controlling it.

13. Moreover, in view of the legal relationship created between the company and the State under whose law it is constituted, which from certain points of view is closely akin to the relationship of nationality in the case of individuals, it seems justifiable not to deal with legal persons, partnerships and associations in a special provision, but to assimilate them with individuals under the term 'nationals'.

Paragraph 3

14. On 28th September, 1954, a number of States concluded in New York a convention relating to the status of stateless person, under

Article 29 of which stateless persons must be accorded national treatment. The signatories of the Convention include several OECD Member countries.

15. It should, however, be recognised that the provisions of paragraph 3 will, in a bilateral convention, enable national treatment to be extended to stateless persons who, because they are in one of the situations enumerated in paragraph 2 of Article 1 of the above-mentioned Convention of 28th September, 1954, are not covered by that Convention. This is mainly the case, on the one hand, of persons receiving at the time of signature of that Convention, protection or assistance from organs or agencies of the United Nations other than the United Nations High Commissioner for Refugees, and, on the other hand, of persons who are residents of a country and who there enjoy and are subject to the rights and obligations attaching to the possession of that country's nationality.

16. The purpose of paragraph 3 is to limit the scope of the clause concerning equality of treatment with nationals of a Contracting State solely to stateless persons who are residents of that of the other Contracting State.

17. By thus excluding stateless persons who are residents of neither Contracting State, such a clause prevents their being privileged in one State as compared with nationals of the other State.

18. However, if States were to consider it desirable in their bilateral relations, to extend the application of paragraph 3 to all stateless persons, whether residents of a Contracting State or not, so that in all cases they enjoy the most favourable treatment accorded to nationals of the State concerned, in order to do this they would need only to adopt the following text which contains no condition as to residence in a Contracting State:

> 'Notwithstanding the provisions of Article 1, stateless persons shall not be subjected in a Contracting State to any taxation or any requirement connected therewith which is other or more burdensome than the taxation and connected requirements to which nationals of that State in the same circumstances are or may be subjected.'

19. It is possible that in the future certain States will take exception to the provisions of paragraph 3 as being too liberal insofar as they entitle stateless persons who are residents of one State to claim equality of treatment not only in the other State but also in their State of residence and thus benefit in particular in the latter from the provisions of double taxation conventions concluded by it with third States. If such States wished to avoid this latter consequence, they would have to modify paragraph 3 as follows:

> 'Stateless persons who are residents of a Contracting State shall not be subjected in the other Contracting State to any taxation or any requirement connected therewith which is other or more burdensome than the taxation and connected requirements to which nationals of that other State in the same circumstances are or may be subjected.'

20. Finally, it should be understood that the definition of the term 'stateless person' to be used for the purposes of such a clause can only

be that laid down in paragraph 1 of Article 1 of the Convention of 28th September, 1954, which defines a stateless person as 'a person who is not considered as a national by any State under the operation of its law'.

Paragraph 4

21. Strictly speaking, the type of discrimination which this paragraph is designed to end is discrimination based not on nationality but on the actual situs of an enterprise. It therefore affects without distinction, and irrespective of their nationality, all residents of a Contracting State who have a permanent establishment in the other Contracting State.

22. It appears necessary first to make it clear that the wording of the first sentence of paragraph 4 must be interpreted in the sense that it does not constitute discrimination to tax non-resident persons differently, for practical reasons, from resident persons, as long as this does not result in more burdensome taxation for the former than for the latter. In the negative form in which the provision concerned has been framed, it is the result alone which counts, it being permissible to adapt the mode of taxation to the particular circumstances in which the taxation is levied.

23. By the terms of the first sentence of paragraph 4, the taxation of a permanent establishment shall not be less favourably levied in the State concerned than the taxation levied on enterprises of that State carrying on the same activities. The purpose of this provision is to end all discrimination in the treatment of permanent establishments as compared with resident enterprises belonging to the same sector of activities, as regards taxes based on industrial and commercial activities, and especially taxes on business profits.

24. However, the second sentence of paragraph 4 specifies the conditions under which the principle of equal treatment set forth in the first sentence should be applied to individuals who are residents of a Contracting State and have a permanent establishment in the other State. It is designed mainly to ensure that such persons do not obtain greater advantages than residents, through entitlement to personal allowances and reliefs for family responsibilities, both in the State of which they are residents, by the application of its domestic laws, and in the other State by virtue of the principle of equal treatment. Consequently it leaves it open to the State in which the permanent establishment is situated whether or not to give personal allowances and reliefs to the persons concerned in the proportion which the amount of the permanent establishment's profits bears to the world income taxable in the other State.

25. As regards the first sentence, experience has shown that it was difficult to define clearly and completely the substance of the principle of equal treatment and this has led to wide differences of opinion with regard to the many implications of this principle. The main reason for difficulty seems to reside in the actual nature of the permanent establishment, which is not a separate legal entity but only a part of an enterprise that has its head office in another State. The situation of the

permanent establishment is different from that of a domestic enterprise, which constitutes a single entity all of whose activities, with their fiscal implications, can be fully brought within the purview of the State where it has its head office. The implications of the equal treatment clause will be examined below under several aspects of the levying of tax.

A. ASSESSMENT OF TAX

26. With regard to the basis of assessment of tax, the principle of equal treatment normally has the following implications:

a. Permanent establishments must be accorded the same right as resident enterprises to deduct the trading expenses that are, in general, authorised by the taxation law to be deducted from taxable profits in addition to the right to attribute to the permanent establishment a proportion of the overheads of the head office of the enterprise. Such deductions should be allowed without any restrictions other than those also imposed on resident enterprises.

b. Permanent establishments must be accorded the same facilities with regard to depreciation and reserves. They should be entitled to avail themselves without restriction not only of the depreciation facilities which are customarily available to enterprises (straight line depreciation, declining balance depreciation), but also of the special systems that exist in a number of countries ('wholesale' writing down, accelerated depreciation, etc.). As regards reserves, it should be noted that these are sometimes authorised for purposes other than the offsetting – in accordance with commercial accounting principles – of depreciation on assets, expenses or losses which have not yet occurred but which circumstances make likely to occur in the near future. Thus, in certain countries, enterprises are entitled to set aside, out of taxable profit, provisions or 'reserves' for investment. When such a right is enjoyed by all enterprises, or by all enterprises in a given sector of activity, it should normally also be enjoyed, under the same conditions, by non-resident enterprises, or by all enterprises in a given sector of activity, it should in the State concerned, insofar, that is, as the activities to which such provisions or reserves would pertain are taxable in that State.

c. Permanent establishments should also have the option that is available in most countries to resident enterprises of carrying forward or backward a loss brought out at the close of an accounting period within a certain period of time (e.g. 5 years). It is hardly necessary to specify that in the case of permanent establishments it is the loss on their own business activities, as shown in the separate accounts for these activities, which will qualify for such carry-forward.

d. Permanent establishments should further have the same rules applied to resident enterprises, with regard to the taxation of capital gains realised on the alienation of assets, whether during or on the cessation of business.

27. Although the general rules mentioned above rarely give rise to any difficulties with regard to the principle of non-discrimination, the same does not always hold good for the tax incentive measures which most countries, faced with such problems as decentralisation of industry, development of economically backward regions, or the promotion of new activities necessary for the expansion of the economy, have introduced in order to facilitate the solution of these problems by means of tax exemptions, reductions or other tax advantages given to enterprises for investment which is in line with official objectives.

28. As such measures are in furtherance of objectives directly related to the economic activity proper of the State concerned, it is right that the benefit of them should be extended to permanent establishments of enterprises of another State which has a double taxation convention with the first embodying the provisions of Article 24, once they have been accorded the right to engage in industrial or commercial activity in that State, either under its legislation or under an international agreement (treaties of commerce, establishment conventions, etc.) concluded between the two States.

29. It should, however, be noted that although non-resident enterprises are entitled to claim these tax advantages in the State concerned, they must fulfil the same conditions and requirements as resident enterprises. They may, therefore, be denied such advantages if their permanent establishments are unable or refuse to fulfil the special conditions and requirements attached to the granting of them.

30. Finally, it goes without saying that non-resident enterprises are not entitled to tax advantages attaching to activities the exercise of which is strictly reserved, on grounds of national interest, defence, protection of the national economy, etc., to domestic enterprises, since non-resident enterprises are not allowed to engage in such activities.

B. SPECIAL TREATMENT OF DIVIDENDS RECEIVED IN RESPECT OF HOLDINGS OWNED BY PERMANENT ESTABLISHMENTS

31. In many countries special rules exist for the taxation of dividend distributed between companies (parent company-subsidiary treatment, the '*Schachtelprivileg*', the rule '*non bis in idem*'). The question arises whether such treatment should by effect of the provisions of paragraph 4 also be enjoyed by permanent establishments in respect of dividends on holdings forming part of their assets.

32. On this point opinions differ. Some States consider that such special treatment should be accorded to permanent establishments. They take the view that such treatment was enacted in order to avoid double taxation on profits made by a subsidiary and distributed to a parent company. In principle profits tax should be levied once, in the hands of the subsidiary performing the profit-generating activities. The parent company should be exempted from tax on such profits when received from the subsidiary or should, under the indirect credit method, be given relief for the taxation borne by the subsidiary. In cases where shares are held as direct investment by a permanent establishment the

same principle implies that such a permanent establishment receiving dividends from the subsidiary should likewise be granted the special treatment in view of the fact that a profits tax has already been levied in the hands of the subsidiary. On the other hand, it is hardly conceivable on this line of thought to leave it to the State where the head office of the parent company is situated to give relief from double taxation brought about by a second levying of tax in the State of the permanent establishment. The State of the parent company, in which no activities giving rise to the doubly taxed profits have taken place, will normally exempt the profits in question or will levy a profits tax which is not sufficient to bear a double credit (i.e. for the profits tax on the subsidiary as well as for such tax on the permanent establishment). All this assumes that the shares held by the permanent establishment are effectively connected with its activity. Furthermore, an obvious additional condition is that the profits out of which the dividends are distributed should have borne a profits tax.

33. Other States, on the contrary, consider that assimilating permanent establishments to their own enterprises does not entail any obligation to accord such special treatment to the former. They justify their position on various grounds. The purpose of such special treatment is to avoid economic double taxation of dividends and it should be for the recipient company's State of residence and not the permanent establishment's State to bear its cost, because it is more interested in the aim in view. Another reason put forward related to the sharing of tax revenue between States. The loss of tax revenue incurred by a State in applying such special treatment is partly offset by the taxation of the dividends when they are redistributed by the parent company which has enjoyed such treatment (withholding tax on dividends, shareholder's tax). A State which accorded such treatment to permanent establishments would not have the benefit of such a compensation. Another argument made is that when such treatment is made conditional upon redistribution of the dividends its extension to permanent establishments would not be justified, for in such a case the permanent establishment, which is only a part of a company of another State and does not distribute dividends, would be more favourably treated than a resident company. Finally, the States which feel that paragraph 4 does not entail any obligation to extend such treatment to permanent establishments argue that there is a risk that companies of one State might transfer their holdings in companies of another State to their permanent establishments in that other State for the sole purpose of availing themselves of such treatment.

34. The fact remains that there can be very valid reasons for a holding being owned and managed by a permanent establishment rather than by the head office of the enterprise, viz.,

- reasons of necessity arising principally from a legal or regulatory obligation on banks and financial institutions and insurance companies to keep deposited in countries where they operate a certain amount of assets, particularly shares, as security for the performance of their obligations;

- or reasons of expediency, where the holdings are in companies which have business relations with the permanent establishment or whose head offices are situated in the same country as the permanent establishment;
- or simple reasons of practical convenience, in line with the present tendency towards decentralisation of management functions in large enterprises.

35. In view of these divergent attitudes, as well as of the existence of the situations just described, it would be advisable for States, when concluding bilateral conventions, to make clear the interpretation they give to the first sentence of paragraph 4. They can, if they so desire, explain their position, or change it as compared with their previous practice, in a protocol or any other document annexed to the convention.

36. A solution could also be provided in such a document to meet the objection mentioned above that the extension of the treatment of holdings in a State (A) to permanent establishments of companies which are residents of another State (B) results in such companies unduly enjoying privileged treatment as compared with other companies which are residents of the same State and whose head offices own holdings in the capital of companies which are residents of State A, in that whereas the dividends on their holdings can be repatriated by the former companies without bearing withholding tax, such tax is levied on dividends distributed to the latter companies at the rate of 5 or 15 per cent as the case may be. Tax neutrality and the equality of tax burdens as between permanent establishments and subsidiary companies, as advocated by the States concerned, could be ensured by adapting, in the bilateral convention between States A and B, the provisions of paragraphs 2 and 4 of Article 10, so as to enable withholding tax to be levied in State A on dividends paid by companies which are residents of that State to permanent establishments of companies which are residents of State B in the same way as if they are received directly i.e. by the head offices of the latter companies. viz., at the rate of:

- 5 per cent in the case of a holding of at least 25 per cent;
- 15 per cent in all other cases.

37. Should it not be possible, because of the absence of appropriate provisions in the domestic laws of the State concerned to levy a withholding tax there on dividends paid to permanent establishments, the treatment of inter-company dividends could be extended to permanent establishments, as long as its application is limited in such manner that the tax levied by the State of source of the dividends is the same whether the dividends are received by a permanent establishment of a company which is a resident of the other State or are received directly by such a company.

C. STRUCTURE AND RATE OF TAX

38. In countries where enterprises, mainly companies, are charged a tax on their profits which is specific to them, the provisions of para-

graph 4 raise, with regard to the rate applicable in the case of permanent establishments, especially difficult and delicate problems, which here too arise from the fact that the permanent establishment is only a part of a legal entity which is not under the jurisdiction of the State where the permanent establishment is situated.

39. When the taxation of profits made by companies which are residents of a given State is calculated according to a progressive scale of rates, such a scale should, in principle, be applied to permanent establishments situated in that State. If in applying the progressive scale, the permanent establishment's State takes into account the profits of the whole company to which such a permanent establishment belongs, such a rule would not appear to conflict with the equal treatment rule, since resident companies are in fact treated in the same way (cf. paragraphs 55, 56 and 77 of the Commentary on Articles 23A and 23B). States that tax their own companies in this way could therefore define in their bilateral conventions the treatment applicable to permanent establishments.

40. When a system of taxation based on a progressive scale of rates includes a rule that a minimum rate is applicable to permanent establishments, it cannot be claimed a priori that such a rule is incompatible with the equal treatment principle. The profits of the whole enterprise to which the permanent establishment belongs should be taken into account in determining the rate applicable according to the progressive scale. The provisions of the first sentence of paragraph 4 are not observed only if the minimum rate is higher.

41. However, even if the profits of the whole enterprise to which the permanent establishment belongs is taken into account when applying either a progressive scale of rates or a minimum rate, this should not conflict with the principle of the distinct and separate enterprise, according to which the profits of the permanent establishment must be determined under paragraph 2 of Article 7. The minimum amount of the tax levied in the State where the permanent establishment is situated is, therefore, the amount which would be due if it were a distinct and separate enterprise, without reference to the profits of the whole enterprise to which it belongs. The State where the permanent establishment is situated is, therefore, justified in applying the progressive scale applicable to resident enterprises solely to the profits of the permanent establishment, leaving aside the profits of the whole enterprise when the latter are less than those of the permanent establishment. This State may likewise tax the profits of the permanent establishment at a minimum rate, provided that the same rate applies also to resident enterprises, even if taking into account the profits of the whole enterprise to which it belongs would result in a lower amount of tax, or no tax at all.

42. As regards the split-rate system of company tax, it should first be pointed out as being a fact central to the issue here that most OECD Member countries which have adopted this system do not consider themselves bound by the provisions of paragraph 4 to extend it to permanent establishments of non-resident companies. This attitude is

based, in particular, on the view that the split-rate is only one element amongst others (in particular a withholding tax on distributed income) in a system of taxing company profits and dividends which must be considered as a whole and is therefore, both for legal and technical reasons, of domestic application only. The State where the permanent establishment is situated could claim the right not to tax such profits at the reduced rate as, generally, it does not tax the dividends distributed by the company to which the permanent establishment belongs. Moreover, a State which has adopted a split-rate system usually has other economic policy objectives, such as the promotion of the capital market, by encouraging resident companies to distribute dividends. The extension of the reduced rate to the profits of the permanent establishment would not serve such a purpose at all, as the company distributing the dividends is not a resident of the State concerned.

43. This view is, however, disputed. The States in favour of extending the split-rate system to permanent establishments urge that as the essential feature of this system is a special technique of taxing profits which enterprises in a corporate form derive from their activities, and is designed to afford immediate relief from the double taxation levied on the profits distributed, it should be applied to permanent establishments in bilateral conventions against double taxation. It is generally recognised that, by the effects of their provisions, such conventions necessarily result in some integration of the taxation systems of the Contracting States. On this account, it is perfectly conceivable that profits made in a State (A) by a permanent establishment of a company resident in another State (B) should be taxed in State A according to the split-rate system. As a practical rule, the tax could in such case be calculated at the reduced rate (applicable to distributed profits) on that proportion of an establishment's profits which corresponds to the ratio between the profit distributed by the company to which it belongs and the latter's total profit: the remaining profit could be taxed at the higher rate. Of course, the two Contracting States would have to consult together and exchange all information necessary for giving practical effect to this solution. Similar considerations apply to systems where distributions of profits made can be deducted from the taxable income of a company.

44. As regards the imputation system ('*avoir fiscal*' or 'tax credit'), it seems doubtful, at least on a literal interpretation of the provisions of paragraph 4, whether it should be extended to non-resident companies in respect of dividends paid out of profits made by their permanent establishments. In fact, it has identical effects to those of the split-rate system but these effects are not immediate as they occur only at the time of the shareholder's personal taxation. From a purely economic and financial standpoint, however, it is conceivable that such profits should be treated as though they were profits of a distinct company in State A where the permanent establishment of a company which is a resident of State B is situated, and, to the extent that they are distributed, carry the '*avoir fiscal*' or 'tax credit'. But to take the matter further, to avoid all discrimination it is necessary that this

advantage should already have been accorded to shareholders who are residents of State B of companies which are residents of State A. From the practical standpoint, the two States concerned should, of course, agree upon the conditions and procedures for allowing the '*avoir fiscal*' or 'tax credit' to shareholders who are themselves residents of either State, of the companies concerned that are residents of State B.

45. Contracting States which are faced with the problems described above may settle them in bilateral negotiations in the light of their peculiar circumstances.

D. WITHHOLDING TAX ON DIVIDENDS, INTEREST AND ROYALTIES RECEIVED BY A PERMANENT ESTABLISHMENT

46. When permanent establishments receive dividends, interest, or royalties such income, by virtue of paragraph 4 of Articles 10 and 11 and paragraph 3 of Article 12, respectively, comes under the provisions of Article 7 and consequently – subject to the observations made in paragraph 36 above as regards dividends received on holdings of permanent establishment – falls to be included in the taxable profits of such permanent establishments (cf. paragraph 34 of the Commentary on Article 7).

47. According to the respective Commentaries on the above-mentioned provisions of Articles 10, 11 and 12 (cf. respectively paragraphs 30, 22 and 15), these provisions dispense the State of source of the dividends, interest or royalties received by the permanent establishment from applying any limitation provided for in those Articles, which means – and this is the generally accepted interpretation – that they leave completely unaffected the right of the State of source, where the permanent establishment is situated, to apply its withholding tax at the full rate.

48. While this approach does not create any problems with regard to the provisions of paragraph 4 of Article 24 in the case of countries where a withholding tax is levied on all such income, whether the latter be paid to residents (permanent establishments, like resident enterprises, being allowed to set such withholding tax off against the tax on profits due by virtue of Article 7) or to non-residents (subject to the limitations provided for in Articles 10, 11 and 12), the position is different when withholding tax is applied exclusively to income paid to non-residents.

49. In this latter case, in fact, it seems difficult to reconcile the levy of withholding tax with the principle set out in paragraph 4 that for the purpose of taxing the income which is derived from their activity, or which is normally connected with it – as is recognised to be the case with dividends, interest and royalties referred to in paragraph 4 of Articles 10 and 11 and in paragraph 31 of Article 12 – permanent establishments must be treated as resident enterprises and hence in respect of such income be subjected to tax on profits solely.

50. In any case, it is for Contracting States which have this difficulty to settle it in bilateral negotiations in the light of their peculiar circumstances.

E. CREDIT FOR FOREIGN TAX

51. In a related context, when a permanent establishment receives foreign income which is included in its taxable profits, it is right by virtue of the same principle to grant to the permanent establishment credit for foreign tax borne by such income when such credit is granted to resident enterprises under domestic laws.

52. If in a Contracting State (A) in which is situated a permanent establishment of an enterprise of the other Contracting State (B) credit for tax levied in a third State (C) can be allowed only by virtue of a convention, then the more general question arises, as to the extension to permanent establishments of the benefit of conventions concluded with third States, which is examined in paragraph 54 below.

53. It should, however, be pointed out that difficulties may arise as to the amount of the credit to be allowed, if permanent establishments in State A benefit from the convention which State B has concluded with State C. Such amount may be either the amount of tax effectively collected by State C or the amount of tax which State C may collect by virtue either of its convention with State A or its convention with State B. Moreover, the question arises whether such credit is not given twice, i.e. once in State A, where the permanent establishment is situated and again in State B, the State of residence. It is for Contracting States to settle such problems, if necessary, in their bilateral negotiations.

F. EXTENSION TO PERMANENT ESTABLISHMENTS OF THE BENEFIT OF DOUBLE TAXATION CONVENTIONS CONCLUDED WITH THIRD STATES

54. While an enterprise of a State (A) can normally claim, in respect of the permanent establishment which it possesses in another State (B), the benefit of the provisions of the convention between those two States A and B, it nevertheless cannot, should such permanent establishment derive income from a third State (C), invoke the provisions of the convention between States B and C for the benefit of such permanent establishment since it, the enterprise, is in fact resident of neither of those two States (cf. Article 1). This is the consequence of the well-known principle of the relative effect of treaties, which means that they have effect only as between the Contracting States.

55. Nor could such an enterprise invoke for this purpose a most-favoured-nation clause, however general its terms, included in a treaty or agreement concluded between States A and B. In fact, it has always been accepted that such a clause did not apply in the case of double taxation conventions because these are essentially based on the principle of reciprocity. It should, however, be noted that some States have made provision in their double taxation conventions enabling the provi-

sions of the latter to be applied, 'in special cases', to permanent establishments of enterprises of a third State.

Paragraph 5

56. This paragraph is designed to end a particular form of discrimination resulting from the fact that in certain countries the deduction of interest, royalties and other disbursements allowed without restriction when the recipient is resident, is restricted or even prohibited when he is a non-resident. The same situation may also be found in the sphere of capital taxation, as regards debts contracted to a non-resident. It is however open to Contracting States to modify this provision in bilateral conventions to avoid its use for tax avoidance purposes.

Paragraph 6

57. This paragraph forbids a Contracting State to give less favourable treatment to an enterprise, the capital of which is owned or controlled, wholly or partly, directly or indirectly, by one or more residents of the other Contracting State. This provision, and the discrimination which it puts an end to, relates to the taxation only of enterprises and not of the persons owning or controlling their capital. Its object therefore is to ensure equal treatment for taxpayers residing in the same State, and not to subject foreign capital, in the hands of the partners or shareholders, to identical treatment to that applied to domestic capital.

Paragraph 7

58. This paragraph states that the scope of the Article is not restricted by the provisions of Article 2. The Article therefore applies to taxes of every kind and description levied by, or on behalf of, the State, its political subdivisions or local authorities.

59.-66. [Omitted]

Commentary on Article 25 concerning the Mutual Agreement Procedure

I. PRELIMINARY REMARKS

1. This Article institutes a mutual agreement procedure for resolving difficulties arising out of the application of the Convention in the broadest sense of the term.

2. It provides first, in paragraphs 1 and 2, that the competent authorities shall endeavour by mutual agreement to resolve the situation of taxpayers subjected to taxation not in accordance with the provisions of the Convention.

3. It also, in paragraph 3, invites and authorises the competent authorities of the two States to resolve by mutual agreement problems

relating to the interpretation or application of the Convention and, furthermore, to consult together for the elimination of double taxation in cases not provided for in the Convention.

4. Finally, as regards the practical operation of the mutual agreement procedure, the Article, in paragraph 4, merely authorises the competent authorities to communicate with each other directly, without going through diplomatic channels, and, if it seems advisable to them, to have an oral exchange of opinions through a Joint Commission appointed especially for the purpose.

5. Since the Article merely lays down general rules concerning the mutual agreement procedure, the comments now following are intended to clarify the purpose of such rules, and also to amplify them, if necessary, by referring, in particular, to the rules followed at international level in the conduct of mutual agreement procedures or at the internal level in the conduct of the procedures which exist in most OECD Member countries for dealing with disputed claims regarding taxes.

II. COMMENTARY ON THE PROVISIONS OF THE ARTICLE

Paragraphs 1 and 2

6. The rules laid down in paragraphs 1 and 2 provide for the elimination in a particular case of taxation which does not accord with the Convention. As is known, in such cases it is normally open to taxpayers to litigate in the tax court, either immediately or upon the dismissal of their objections by the taxation authorities. When taxation not in accordance with the Convention arises from an incorrect application of the Convention in both States, taxpayers are then obliged to litigate in each State, with all the disadvantages and uncertainties that such a situation entails. So paragraph 1 makes available to taxpayers affected, without depriving them of the ordinary legal remedies available, a procedure which is called the mutual agreement procedure because it is aimed, in its second stage, at resolving the dispute on an amicable basis, i.e. by agreement between competent authorities, the first stage being conducted exclusively in the State of residence (except where the procedure for the application of paragraph 1 of Article 24 is set in motion by the taxpayer in the State of which he is a national) from the presentation of the objection up to the decision taken regarding it by the competent authority on the matter.

7. In any case, the mutual agreement procedure is clearly a special procedure outside the domestic law. It follows that it can be set in motion solely in cases coming within paragraph 1, i.e. cases where tax has been charged, or is going to be charged, in disregard of the provisions of the Convention. So where a charge of tax has been made contrary both to the Convention and the domestic law, this case is amenable to the mutual agreement procedure to the extent only that the Convention is affected, unless a connecting link exists between the rules of the Convention and the rules of the domestic law which have been misapplied.

8. In practice, the procedure applies to cases – by far the most numerous – where the measure in question leads to double taxation which it is the specific purpose of the Convention to avoid. Among the most common cases, mention must be made of the following:
- the questions relating to attribution to a permanent establishment of a proportion of the executive and general administrative expenses incurred by the enterprise, under paragraph 3 of Article 7;
- the taxation in the State of the payer – in case of a special relationship between the payer and the beneficial owner – of the excess part of interest and royalties, under the provisions of Article 9, paragraph 6 of Article 11 or paragraph 4 of Article 12;
- cases where lack of information as to the taxpayer's actual situation has led to misapplication of the Convention, especially in regard to the determination of residence (paragraph 2 of Article 4), the existence of a permanent establishment (Article 5), or the temporary nature of the services performed by an employee (paragraph 2 of Article 15).

9. As regards adjustments to be made correlatively with the reinstatement of profits in the trading results of associated enterprises under the provisions of paragraphs 1 and 2 of Article 9, there is ground for considering that they may properly be dealt with through the mutual agreement procedure when determining their amount gives rise to difficulty.

10. The mutual agreement procedure is also applicable in the absence of any double taxation contrary to the Convention, once the taxation in dispute is in direct contravention of a rule in the Convention. Such is the case when one State taxes a particular class of income in respect of which the Convention gives an exclusive right to tax to the other State even though the latter is unable to exercise it owing to a gap in its domestic laws. Another category of cases concerns persons who, being nationals of one Contracting State but residents of the other State, are subjected in that other State to taxation treatment which is discriminatory under the provisions of paragraph 1 of Article 24.

11. It should be noted that the mutual agreement procedure, unlike the disputed claims procedure under domestic law, can be set in motion by a taxpayer without waiting until the taxation considered by him to be 'not in accordance with the Convention' has been charged against or notified to him. To be able to set the procedure in motion, he must, and it is sufficient if he does, establish that the 'actions for one or both of the Contracting States' will result in such taxation, and that this taxation appears as a risk which is not merely possible but probable. Such actions mean all acts or decisions, whether of a legislative or a regulatory nature, and whether of general or individual application, having as their direct and necessary consequence the charging of tax against the complainant contrary to the provisions of the Convention.

12. To be admissible objections presented under paragraph 1 must first meet a twofold requirement expressly formulated in that paragraph: in principle, they must be presented to the competent authority of the taxpayer's State of residence (except where the procedure for

the application of paragraph 1 of Article 24 is set in motion by the taxpayer in the State of which he is a national), and they must be so presented within three years of the first notification of the action which gives rise to taxation which is not in accordance with the Convention. The Convention does not lay down any special rule as to the form of the objections. The competent authorities may prescribe special procedures which they feel to be appropriate. If no special procedure has been specified, the objections may be presented in the same way as objections regarding taxes are presented to the tax authorities of the State concerned.

13. The requirement laid on the taxpayer to present his case to the competent authority of the State of which he is a resident (except where the procedure for the application of paragraph 1 of Article 24 is set in motion by the taxpayer in the State of which he is a national) is of general application, regardless of whether the taxation objected to has been charged in that or the other State and regardless of whether it has given rise to double taxation or not. If the taxpayer should have transferred his residence to the other Contracting State subsequently to the measure or taxation objected to, he must nevertheless still present his objection to the competent authority of the State of which he was a resident during the year in respect of which such taxation has been or is going to be charged.

14. However, in the case already alluded to where a person who is a national of one State but a resident of the other complains of having been subjected in that other State to an action or taxation which is discriminatory under paragraph 1 of Article 24, it appears more appropriate for obvious reasons to allow him, by way of exception to the general rule set forth above, to present his objection to the competent authority of the Contracting State of which he is a national. Finally, it is to the same competent authority that an objection has to be presented by a person who, while not being a resident of a Contracting State, is a national of a Contracting State, and whose case comes under paragraph 1 of Article 24.

15. On the other hand, Contracting States may, if they consider it preferable, give taxpayers the option of presenting their cases to the competent authority of either State. In such a case, paragraph 1 would have to be modified as follows:

> '1. Where a person considers that the actions of one or both of the Contracting States result or will result for him in taxation not in accordance with the provisions of this Convention, he may, irrespective of the remedies provided by the domestic law of those States, present his case to the competent authority of either Contracting State. The case must be presented within three years from the first notification of the action resulting in taxation not in accordance with the provisions of the Convention.'

16. The time limit of three years set by the second sentence of paragraph 1 for presenting objections is intended to protect administrations against late objections. This time limit must be regarded as a minimum, so that Contracting States are left free to agree in their bilateral con-

ventions upon a longer period in the interests of taxpayers, e.g. on the analogy in particular of the time limits laid down by their respective domestic regulations in regard to tax conventions. Contracting States may omit the second sentence of paragraph 1 if they concur that their respective domestic regulations apply automatically to such objections and are more favourable in their effects to the taxpayers affected, either because they allow a longer time for presenting objections or because they do not set any time limits for such purpose.

17. The provision fixing the starting point of the three-year time limit as the date of the 'first notification of the action resulting in taxation not in accordance with the provisions of the Convention' should be interpreted in the way most favourable to the taxpayer. Thus, even if such taxation should be directly charged in pursuance of an administrative decision or action of general application, the time limit begins to run only from the date of the notification of the individual action giving rise to such taxation, that is to say, under the most favourable interpretation, from the act of taxation itself, as evidenced by a notice of assessment or an official demand or other instrument for the collection or levy of tax. If the tax is levied by deduction at the source, the time limit begins to run from the moment when the income is paid; however, if the taxpayer proves that only at a later date did he know that the deduction had been made, the time limit will begin from that date. Furthermore, where it is the combination of decisions or actions taken in both Contracting States resulting in taxation not in accordance with the Convention, it begins to run only from the first notification of the most recent decision or action.

18. As regards the procedure itself, it is necessary to consider briefly the two distinct stages into which it is divided (cf. paragraph 6 above).

19. In the first stage, which opens with the presentation of the taxpayer's objections, the procedure takes place exclusively at the level of dealings between him and the competent authorities of his State of residence (except where the procedure for the application of paragraph 1 of Article 24 is set in motion by the taxpayer in the State of which he is a national). The provisions of paragraph 1 give the taxpayer concerned the right to apply to the competent authority of the State of which he is a resident, whether or not he has exhausted all the remedies available to him under the domestic law of each of the two States. On the other hand, that competent authority is under an obligation to consider whether the objection is justified and, if it appears to be justified, take action on it in one of the two forms provided for in paragraph 2.

20. If the competent authority duly approached recognises that the complaint is justified and considers that the taxation complained of is due wholly or in part to a measure taken in the taxpayer's State of residence, it must give the complainant satisfaction as speedily as possible by making such adjustments or allowing such reliefs as appear to be justified. In this situation, the issue can be resolved without resort to the mutual agreement procedure. On the other hand, it may be found useful to exchange views and information with the competent authority

of the other Contracting State, in order, for example, to confirm a given interpretation of the Convention.

21. If, however, it appears to that competent authority that the taxation complained of is due wholly or in part to a measure taken in the other State, it will be incumbent on it, indeed it will be its duty – as clearly appears by the terms of paragraph 2 – to set in motion the mutual agreement procedure proper.

22. A taxpayer is entitled to present his case under paragraph 1 to the competent authority of the State of which he is a resident whether or not he may also have made a claim or commenced litigation under the domestic law of that State. If litigation is pending, the competent authority of the State of residence should not wait for the final adjudication, but should say whether it considers the case to be eligible for the mutual agreement procedure. If it so decides, it has to determine whether it is itself able to arrive at a satisfactory solution or whether the case has to be submitted to the competent authority of the other Contracting State.

23. If a claim has been finally adjudicated by a court in the State of residence, a taxpayer may wish even so to present or pursue a claim under the mutual agreement procedure. In some States, the competent authority may be able to arrive at a satisfactory solution which departs from the court decision. In other States, the competent authority is bound by the court decision. It may nevertheless present the case to the competent authority of the other Contracting State and ask the latter to take measures for avoiding double taxation.

24. In its second stage – which opens with the approach to the competent authority of the other State by the competent authority to which the taxpayer has applied – the procedure is henceforward at the level of dealings between States, as if, so to speak, the State to which the complaint was presented had given it its backing. But while this procedure is indisputably a procedure between States, it may, on the other hand, be asked:

- whether, as the title of the Article and the terms employed in the first sentence of paragraph 2 suggest, it is no more than a simple procedure of mutual agreement, or constitutes the implementation of a '*pactum de contrahendo*' laying on the parties a mere duty to negotiate but in no way laying on them a duty to reach agreement;
- or whether on the contrary, it is to be regarded (on the assumption of course that it takes places within the framework of a Joint Commission) as a procedure of a jurisdictional nature laying on the parties a duty to resolve the dispute.

25. Paragraph 2 no doubt entails a duty to negotiate; but as far as reaching mutual agreement through the procedure is concerned, the competent authorities are under a duty merely to use their best endeavours and not to achieve a result. However, Contracting States could agree on a more far-reaching commitment whereby the mutual agreement procedure, and above all the discussions in the Joint Commission, would produce a solution to the dispute. Such a rule could be established either by an amendment to paragraph 2 or by an interpreta-

tion specified in a protocol or an exchange of letters annexed to the convention.

26. In seeking a mutual agreement, the competent authorities must first, of course, determine their position in the light of the rules of their respective taxation laws and of the provisions of the Convention, which are as binding on them as much as they are on the taxpayer. Should the strict application of such rules or provisions preclude any agreement, it may reasonably be held that the competent authorities, as in the case of international arbitration, can, subsidiarily, have regard to considerations of equity in order to give the taxpayer satisfaction.

27. The purpose of the last sentence of paragraph 2 is to enable countries with time limits relating to adjustments of assessments and tax refunds in their domestic law to give effect to an agreement despite such time limits. This provision does not prevent, however, such States as are not, on constitutional or other legal grounds, able to overrule the time limits in the domestic law from inserting in the mutual agreement itself such time limits as are adapted to their internal statute of limitation. In certain extreme cases, a Contracting State may prefer not to enter into a mutual agreement, the implementation of which would require that the internal statute of limitation had to be disregarded. Apart from time limits there may exist other obstacles such as 'final court decisions' to giving effect to an agreement. Contracting States are free to agree on firm provisions for the removal of such obstacles.

28. Finally, the case may arise where a mutual agreement is concluded in relation to a taxpayer who has brought a suit for the same purpose in the competent court of either Contracting State and such suit is still pending. In such a case, there would be no grounds for rejecting a request by a taxpayer that he be allowed to defer acceptance of the solution agreed upon as a result of the mutual agreement procedure until the court had delivered its judgment in the suit still pending. On the other hand, it is necessary to take into account the concern of the competent authority to avoid any divergence or contradiction between the decision of the court and the mutual agreement, with the difficulties or risks of abuse that they could entail. In short, therefore, it seems normal that the implementation of a mutual agreement should be made subject:

- to the acceptance of such mutual agreement by the taxpayer, and
- to the taxpayer's withdrawal of his suit at law concerning the points settled in the mutual agreement.

Paragraph 3

29. The first sentence of this paragraph invites and authorises the competent authorities to resolve, if possible, difficulties of interpretation or application by means of mutual agreement. These are essentially difficulties of a general nature which concern, or which may concern, a category of taxpayers, even if they have arisen in connection with an individual case normally coming under the procedure defined in paragraphs 1 and 2.

30. This provision makes it possible to resolve difficulties arising from the application of the Convention. Such difficulties are not only those of a practical nature, which might arise in connection with the setting up and operation of procedures for the relief from tax deducted from dividends, interest and royalties in the Contracting State in which they arise, but also those which could impair or impede the normal operation of the clauses of the convention as they were conceived by the negotiators, the solution of which does not depend on a prior agreement as to the interpretation of the convention.

31. Under this provision the competent authorities can, in particular:

- where a term has been incompletely or ambiguously defined in the Convention, complete or clarify its definition in order to obviate any difficulty;
- where the laws of a State have been changed without impairing the balance or affecting the substance of the Convention, settle any difficulties that may emerge from the new system of taxation arising out of such changes.

32. Paragraph 3 confers on the 'competent authorities of the Contracting State', i.e. generally the Ministers of Finance or their authorised representatives normally responsible for the administration of the Convention, authority to resolve by mutual agreement any difficulties arising as to the interpretation of the Convention. However, it is important not to lose sight of the fact that, depending on the domestic law of the Contracting States, other authorities (Ministry of Foreign Affairs, courts) have the right to interpret international treaties and agreements as well as the 'competent authority' designated in the Convention, and that this is sometimes the exclusive right of such other authorities.

33. Mutual agreements resolving general difficulties of interpretation or application are binding on administrations as long as the competent authorities do not agree to modify or rescind the mutual agreement.

34. The second sentence of paragraph 3 enables the competent authorities to deal also with such cases of double taxation as do not come within the scope of the provisions of the Convention. Of special interest in this connection is the case of a resident of a third State having permanent establishments in both Contracting States. It is of course desirable that the mutual agreement procedure should result in the effective elimination of the double taxation which can occur in such a situation. An exception must, however, be made for the case of Contracting States whose domestic law prevents the Convention from being complemented on points which are not explicitly or at least implicitly dealt with; in such a case, the Convention could be complemented only by a protocol subject, like the Convention itself, to ratification or approval.

Paragraph 4

35. This paragraph determines how the competent authorities may consult together for the resolution by mutual agreement, either of an individual case coming under the procedure defined in paragraphs 1

and 2 or of general problems relating in particular to the interpretation or application of the Convention, and which are referred to in paragraph 3.

36. It provides first that the competent authorities may communicate with each other directly. It would therefore not be necessary to go through diplomatic channels.

37. Such exchange of opinions will normally take place by letter. However, if the competent authorities deem it useful, in order to reach an agreement more easily, they may also – as provided in the second sentence of paragraph 4 – exchange views orally. They may, however, agree that such exchanges should take place in a commission consisting of representatives of the said authorities.

38. As to this Joint Commission, paragraph 4 leaves it to the competent authorities of the Contracting States to determine the number of members and the rules of procedure of this body.

39. However, while the Contracting States may avoid any formalism in this field, it is nevertheless their duty to give taxpayers whose cases are brought before the Joint Commission under paragraph 2 certain essential guarantees, namely:

- the right to make representations in writing or orally, either in person or through a representative;
- the right to be assisted by counsel.

40. However, disclosure to the taxpayer or his representatives of the papers in the case does not seem to be warranted, in view of the special nature of the procedure.

41. Without infringing upon the freedom of choice enjoyed in principle by the competent authorities in designating their representatives on the Joint Commission, it would be desirable for them to agree to entrust the chairmanship of each Delegation – which might include one or more representatives of the service responsible for the procedure – to a high official or judge chosen primarily on account of his special experience; it is reasonable to believe, in fact, that the participation of such persons would be likely to facilitate reaching an agreement.

III. FINAL OBSERVATIONS

42. On the whole, the mutual agreement procedure has proved satisfactory. The most recent treaty practice shows that Article 25 represents the maximum that Contracting States are prepared to accept. It must, however, be admitted that this provision is not yet entirely satisfactory from the taxpayer's viewpoint. This is because the competent authorities are required only to seek a solution and are not obliged to find one (cf. paragraph 25 above). The conclusion of a mutual agreement depends to a large extent on the powers of compromise which the domestic law allows the competent authorities. Thus, if a convention is interpreted or applied differently in two Contracting States, and if the competent authorities are unable to agree on a joint solution within the framework of a mutual agreement procedure, double taxation is still

possible although contrary to the sense and purpose of a convention aimed at avoiding double taxation.

43. It is difficult to avoid this situation without going outside the framework of the mutual agreement procedure. The first approach to a solution might consist of seeking an advisory opinion: the two Contracting States would agree to ask the opinion of an impartial third party, although the final decision would still rest with the States.

44. The provisions embodied in this Convention, as well as the Commentary related thereto, are the result of close international joint work within the Committee on Fiscal Affairs. A possibility near at hand would be to call upon the Committee on Fiscal Affairs to give an opinion on the correct understanding of the provisions where special difficulties of interpretation arise as to particular points. Such a practice, which would be in line with the mandate and aims of the Committee on Fiscal Affairs, might well make a valuable contribution to arriving at a desirable uniformity in the application of the provisions.

45. It might also be feasible to ask the opinion of certain persons acting as independent arbitrators. In the case of OECD Member countries, the Committee on Fiscal Affairs could, for example, periodically draw up a list of persons from among whom the competent authorities of the two States concerned could choose the third party to be asked to give an advisory opinion.

46.-48. [Omitted]

Commentary on Article 26 concerning the Exchange of Information

I. PRELIMINARY REMARKS

1. There are good grounds for including in a convention for the avoidance of double taxation provisions concerning co-operation between the tax administrations of the two Contracting States. In the first place it appears to be desirable to give administrative assistance for the purpose of ascertaining facts in relation to which the rules of the convention are to be applied. Moreover, in view of the increasing internationalisation of economic relations, the Contracting States have a growing interest in the reciprocal supply of information on the basis of which domestic taxation laws have to be administered, even if there is no question of the application of any particular article of the convention.

2. Therefore the present Article embodies the rules under which information may be exchanged to the widest possible extent, with a view to laying the proper basis for the implementation of the domestic laws of the Contracting States concerning taxes covered by the Convention and for the application of specific provisions of the Convention. The text of the Article makes it clear that the exchange of infor-

mation is not restricted by Article 1, so that the information may include particulars about non-residents.

3. The matter of administrative assistance for the purpose of tax collection is not dealt with in the Article. This matter often forms the subject of a separate agreement, whether bilateral or multilateral, between the Contracting States; alternatively, the provisions on assistance in the field of tax collection may be introduced in the double taxation convention, whenever Contracting States find it preferable.

4. Experience in recent years has shown that the text of the Article in the 1963 Draft Convention left room for differing interpretations. Therefore it was felt desirable to clarify its meaning by a change in the wording of the Article and its Commentary without altering its effects. Apart from a single point of substance (cf. paragraph 13 below) the main purpose of the changes made has been to remove grounds for divergent interpretations.

II. COMMENTARY ON THE PROVISIONS OF THE ARTICLE

Paragraph 1

5. The main rule concerning the exchange of information is contained in the first sentence of the paragraph. The competent authorities of the Contracting States shall exchange such information as is necessary to secure the correct application of the provisions of the Convention or of the domestic laws of the Contracting States concerning taxes covered by the Convention even if, in the latter case, a particular Article of the Convention need not be applied. In order to keep the exchange of information within the framework of the Convention, a limitation to the exchange of information is set so that information should be given only insofar as the national tax in question is covered by the Convention and the taxation under the domestic taxation laws concerned is not contrary to the Convention. An illustration may be cited in this connection: a request for the imposition of a sales tax need not be complied with by the requested State as it is not covered by the Convention.

6. The following examples may clarify the principle dealt with in paragraph 5 above. In all such cases information can be exchanged under paragraph 1.

7. Application of the Convention

a. When applying Article 12, State A where the beneficiary is resident asks State B where the payer is resident, for information concerning the amount of royalty transmitted.

b. Conversely, in order to grant the exemption provided for in Article 12, State B asks State A whether the recipient of the amounts paid is in fact a resident of the last-mentioned State and the beneficial owner of the royalties.

c. Similarly, information may be needed with a view to the proper allocation of taxable profits between associated companies in different States or the adjustment of the profits shown in the accounts of a permanent establishment in one State and in the accounts of the head office in the other State (Article 9, 7, 23A and 23B).

8. Implementation of the domestic laws

a. A company in State A supplies goods to an independent company in State B. State A wishes to know from State B what price the company in State B paid for the goods with a view to a correct application of the provisions of its domestic laws.

b. A company in State A sells goods through a company in State C (possibly a low-tax country) to a company in State B. The companies may or may not be associated. There is no convention between State A and State C, nor between State B and State C. Under the convention between A and B, State A, with a view to ensuring the correct application of the provisions of its domestic laws to the profits made by the company situated in its territory, asks State B what price the company in State B paid for the goods.

c. State A, for the purpose of taxing a company situated in its territory, asks State B, under the convention between A and B, for information about the prices charged by a company in State B, or a group of companies in State B with which the company in State A has no business contacts in order to enable it to check the prices charged by the company in State A by direct comparison (e.g. prices charged by a company or a group of companies in a dominant position). It should be borne in mind that the exchange of information in this case might be a difficult and delicate matter owing in particular to the provisions of sub-paragraph *c.* of paragraph 2 relating to business and other secrets.

9. The rule laid down in paragraph 1 allows information to be exchanged in three different ways:

a. on request, with a special case in mind, it being understood that the regular sources of information available under the internal taxation procedure should be relied upon in the first place before request for information is made to the other State;

b. automatically, for example when information about one or various categories of income having their source in one Contracting State and received in the other Contracting State is transmitted systematically to the other State;

c. spontaneously, for example in the case of a State having acquired, through certain investigations, information which it supposes to be of interest to the other State.

10. The manner in which the exchange of information agreed to in the Convention will finally be effected can be decided upon by the competent authorities of the Contracting States.

11. Reciprocal assistance between tax administrations is feasible only if each administration is assured that the other administration will treat with proper confidence the information which it will receive in the course of their co-operation. At the same time maintenance of such secrecy in the receiving Contracting State is a matter of domestic laws. It is therefore provided in paragraph 1 that information communicated under the provisions of the Convention shall be treated as secret in the

receiving State in the same manner as information obtained under the domestic laws of that State. Sanctions for the violation of such secrecy in that State will be governed by the administrative and penal laws of that State.

12. The information obtained may be disclosed only to persons and authorities involved in the assessment or collection of, the enforcement or prosecution in respect of, or the determination of appeals in relation to, the taxes covered by the Convention. This means that the information may also be communicated to the taxpayer, his proxy or to the witnesses. The information received by a Contracting State may be used by such persons or authorities only for the purposes mentioned in paragraph 1. If the information appears to be of value to the receiving State for other purposes than those referred to, that State may not use the information for such other purposes but it must resort to means specially designed for those purposes (e.g. in case of a non-fiscal crime, to a treaty concerning judicial assistance).

13. As stated above, the information obtained can be communicated to the persons and authorities mentioned but it does not follow from this that it can be disclosed by them in court sessions held in public or in decisions which reveal the name of the taxpayer. The last sentence of the paragraph, however, opens up this possibility. Once information is used in public court proceedings or in court decisions and thus rendered public, it is clear that from that moment such information can be quoted from the court files or decisions for other purposes even as possible evidence. But this does not mean that the persons and authorities mentioned in paragraph 1 are allowed to provide on request additional information received. If either or both of the Contracting States object to the information being made public by courts in this way, or, once the information has been made public in this way, to the information being used for other purposes, because this is not the normal procedure under their domestic laws, they should state this expressly in their convention.

Paragraph 2

14. This paragraph contains certain limitations to the main rule in favour of the requested State. In the first place, the paragraph contains the clarification that a Contracting State is not bound to go beyond its own internal laws and administrative practice in putting information at the disposal of the other Contracting State. However, types of administrative measures authorised for the purpose of the requested State's tax must be utilised, even though invoked solely to provide information to the other Contracting State. Likewise, internal provisions concerning tax secrecy should not be interpreted as constituting an obstacle to the exchange of information under the present Article. As mentioned above, the authorities of the requesting State are obliged to observe secrecy with regard to information received under this Article.

15. Furthermore, the requested State does not need to go so far as to carry out administrative measures that are not permitted under the laws or practice of the requesting State or to supply items of informa-

tion that are not obtainable under the laws or in the normal course of administration of the requesting State. It follows that a Contracting State cannot take advantage of the information system of the other Contracting State if it is wider than its own system.

16. Information is deemed to be obtainable in the normal course of administration if it is in the possession of the tax authorities or can be obtained by them in the normal procedure of tax determination, which may include special investigations or special examination of the business accounts kept by the taxpayer or other persons, provided that the tax authorities would make similar investigations or examination for their own purposes. This means that the requested State has to collect the information the other State needs in the same way as if its own taxation was involved, under the proviso mentioned in paragraph 15 above.

17. The requested State is at liberty to refuse to give information in the cases referred to in the paragraphs above. However if it does give the requested information, it remains within the framework of the agreement on the exchange of information which is laid down in the Convention; consequently it cannot be objected that this State has failed to observe the obligation to secrecy.

18. If the structure of the information systems of two Contracting States is very different, the conditions under sub-paragraphs *a.* and *b.* of paragraph 2 will lead to the result that the Contracting States exchange very little information or perhaps none at all. In such a case, the Contracting States may find it appropriate to broaden the scope of the exchange of information.

19. In addition to the limitations referred to above, sub-paragraph *c.* of paragraph 2 contains a reservation concerning the disclosure of certain secret information. Secrets mentioned in this sub-paragraph should not be taken in too wide a sense. Before invoking this provision, a Contracting State should carefully weigh if the interests of the taxpayer really justify its application. Otherwise it is clear that too wide an interpretation would in many cases render ineffective the exchange of information provided for in the Convention. The observations made in paragraph 17 above apply here as well. The requested State in protecting the interests of its taxpayers is given a certain discretion to refuse the requested information, but if it does supply the information deliberately the taxpayer cannot allege an infraction of the rules of secrecy. It is open to the Contracting States to add further dispensations from the obligation to supply information to the items listed in sub-paragraph *c.*, for example, information protected by provisions on banker's discretion. It has been felt necessary also to prescribe a limitation with regard to information which concerns the vital interests of the State itself. To this end, it is stipulated that Contracting States do not have to supply information the disclosure of which would be contrary to public policy (*ordre public*).

Observations on the Commentary

20.-23. [Omitted]

24. The *United States* believes that this Article should apply to all taxes imposed by a Contracting State, not just taxes covered by the Convention.

Selections from the 1969 Vienna Convention on the law of treaties

concluded in Vienna, 23 May 1969.

SECTION 3. INTERPRETATION OF TREATIES

Article 31. General Rule of Interpretation

1. A treaty shall be interpreted in good faith in accordance with the ordinary meaning to be given to the terms of the treaty in their context and in the light of its object and purpose.

2. The context for the purpose of the interpretation of a treaty shall comprise, in addition to the text, including its preamble and annexes:

a. any agreement relating to the treaty which was made between all the parties in connexion with the conclusion of the treaty;

b. any instrument which was made by one or more parties in connexion with the conclusion of the treaty and accepted by the other parties as an instrument related to the treaty.

3. There shall be taken into account, together with the context:

a. any subsequent agreement between the parties regarding the interpretation of the treaty or the application of its provisions;

b. any subsequent practice in the application of the treaty which establishes the agreement of the parties regarding its interpretation;

c. any relevant rules of international law applicable in the relations between the parties.

4. A special meaning shall be given to a term if it is established that the parties so intended.

Article 32. Supplementary Means of Interpretation

Recourse may be had to supplementary means of interpretation, including the preparatory work of the treaty and the circumstances of its conclusion, in order to confirm the meaning resulting from the application of article 31, or to determine the meaning when the interpretation according to article 31:

a. leaves the meaning ambiguous or obscure; or

b. leads to a result which is manifestly absurd or unreasonable.

Article 33. Interpretation of Treaties authenticated in two or more Languages

1. When a treaty has been authenticated in two or more languages, the text is equally authoritative in each language, unless the treaty provides or the parties agree that, in case of divergence, a particular text shall prevail.

2. A version of a treaty in a language other than one of those in which the text was authenticated shall be considered an authentic text only if the treaty so provides or the parties so agree.

3. The terms of the treaty are presumed to have the same meaning in each authentic text.

4. Except where a particular text prevails in accordance with paragraph 1, when a comparison of the authentic texts discloses a difference of meaning which the application of articles 31 and 32 does not remove, the meaning which best reconciles the texts, having regard to the object and purpose of the treaty, shall be adopted.

Withholding Rate Chart for Interest and Royalties

AUS	**39**	10	10	10	–	10	10	–	10	10	10
10	BEL	**25**	10/0[4]	0[5]/10[4]	–	0	0	10	0	0	10
10	**25**	CAN	**25**	10	15	10/0[4]	10/0[4]	25 / 30	15/0[4] / 32/0	10/0[4]	10
15	15/0[2]	**25**	CHI	**20**	–	6[5]/10[4]	6[5]/10[4]	–	–	7[5]/10[4]	10
10	10/0[1,3]	10/0[1]	**20**	EGYPT	**32**	15	0	32 / 30	–	15	15
–	15/0[1]	15/0[1]	–	**32**	FRA	**33.3**	0	33.3 / 30	0	0	10
10	15	15/0[1,2]	10/0[1,3]	25/0[1]	**45**	GER	**25**	20	0	0	10
10	15	15/0[1,2]	10/0[1]	15 / 20	0	**0**	IND	**30**	–	30 / 21	30 / 20
–	15	15/0[1]	–	32 / 30	45 / 30	15/10[3]/0[1]	**30**	IRE	**32**	0	10
10	15	15 / 32	–	–	0	0	–	**32**	IT	**21**	10
10/0[1]	15	15/0[1]	10/0[1]	25/0[1]	15	0	15/0[1]	10	**30**	JAP	**20**
10	15	10/0[1]	10/0[1]	32 / 20	10/0[1]	10/0[1]	30 / 20	10	10	**20**	
15/0[1]	15/0[1]	15/0[1]	–	–	15/0[1]	15/10[3]/0[1]	15/10[3]/0[1]	–	–	12/0[1]	
–	15	–	–	–	10	0	–	0	10/0[1]	–	
10	10	15/0[1,2]	10/0[1]	–	10/0[2,3]	0	15/10[3]/0[1]	0	15 / 0	10/0[1]	
15/0[1]	15	15	–	–	15/0[1]	15/10[2,3]/1[1]	–	–	15/0[1]	15/0[1]	
–	15	15	–	–	10	10/0[1]	–	–	12/0[1]	10	
10/0[1]	15	15/0[1,2]	10/0[1,2]	32 / 0	0	0	15/10[3]/0[1]	0	15/0[1]	10	
10	10/0[2]	15/0[2]	–	15/0[1]	10	0	–	0	12.5	10/0[1]	
10	15	10	10/0[1]	15/0[1]	10	0	15/10[3]/0[1]	0	10	10	
10	15/0[1,2]	15/0[1,2]	10/0[1]	15/0[1]	0	0	15/10[3]/0[1]	0	15/0[1]	10/0[1]	
–	–	15/0[1]	–	–	10/0[2,3]	5/0[1]		–	0[2,3]	10/0[1]	

INTEREST

www.ingramcontent.com/pod-product-compliance
Lightning Source LLC
Chambersburg PA
CBHW071406230926
51846CB00001B/16
* 9 7 8 9 0 6 5 4 4 5 2 8 5 *